Theological Lexicon of the New Testament

Theological Lexicon of the New Testament

Volume 3

παι–ψευ

Ceslas Spicq, O.P.

Translated and Edited by James D. Ernest

HENDRICKSON
PUBLISHERS

Copyright © 1994 by Hendrickson Publishers, Inc.
P. O. Box 3473
Peabody, Massachusetts 01961–3473
Printed in the United States of America on acid-free paper

ISBN 1–56563–035–1

Translated from: Ceslas Spicq, O.P., *Notes de lexicographie néo-testamentaire*, 3 volumes (Orbis Biblicus et Orientalis 22/1, 2, 3); © 1978, 1982, Editions Universitaires, Fribourg, Switzerland.

Library of Congress Cataloging-in-Publication Data

Spicq, Ceslas, 1901–1993
   [Notes de lexicographie néo-testamentaire.   English]
   Theological lexicon of the New Testament   /   Ceslas Spicq; translated and edited by James D. Ernest.
     p.   cm.
   Includes bibliographical references and index.
   ISBN 1–56563–035–1
   1. Greek language, Biblical—Semantics.   2. Greek language, Biblical—Glossaries, vocabularies, etc.   I. Ernest, James D.   II. Title.
PA875.S613   1994
487′.4—dc20
                                   94–42932
                                      CIP

TABLE OF GREEK WORDS IN VOLUME 3

παιδαγωγός, παιδευτής

paidagōgos, **servant working as a child's guardian and tutor;** *paideutēs,* **teacher, instructor**

These two terms are not synonymous. The first, unknown in the OT, is used twice by St. Paul and in a pejorative sense: "You may have ten thousand *paidagōgoi* in Christ, but at least you do not have many fathers, for in Christ Jesus, through the gospel, I am the one who fathered you."[1] "The law was our *paidagōgos* until Christ" (Gal 3:24). In both cases, the *paidagōgos* is in an inferior position, and in the second case a temporary position; for the law, imposing discipline and punishments on the Israelites, played the role of an overseer or guardian until Christ ushered in the age of liberation.[2]

Etymologically, the *paidagōgos* is one who shows the way to a child, thus one who teaches a child how to behave.[3] Until the age of six or seven, the Greek child was cared for almost exclusively by its mother (cf. Plato, *Prt.* 325 cff.). At that age, it was not allowed to go out alone but was entrusted to a *paidagōgos* who went with it on its walks and took it to school,[4] keeping it away from possible accidents or

---

[1] 1 Cor 4:15; cf. P. Gutierrez, *Paternité spirituelle,* pp. 119ff. M. Saillard, "C'est moi qui, par l'Evangile, vous ai enfantés dans le Christ Jésus (I Cor IV, 15)," in *RSR,* 1968, pp. 5–42.

[2] The law played the role of a jailer. The emphasis is on the absence of freedom (cf. K. Stendahl, "La Loi, surveillant qui conduit au Christ," in *SEÅ,* vol. 18–19, 1955; cf. *RB,* 1956, p. 282); it is in this sense that Cain replied to God that he was not his brother's overseer or guardian (οὐκ εἶναι παιδαγωγὸς καὶ φύλαξ αὐτοῦ, Josephus, *Ant.* 1.56). Cf. παιδαγωγέω τὰς ἐπιθυμίας—control, discipline one's desires (Musonius frag. 7, line 27; frag. 12, line 40; ed. C. E. Lutz, pp. 56, 86).

[3] Cf. E. Schupe, "Paidagogos," in PW, vol. 18, 2375–2385; H. I. Marrou, *Histoire de l'éducation,* pp. 202, 207 = ET, pp. 201, 207; H. M. Gale, *The Use of Analogy in the Letters of Paul,* Philadelphia, 1964, pp. 46ff.

[4] Demosthenes, *C. Euerg.* 47.56. Cf. Plato: "Are you allowed to govern yourself (ἄρχειν σεαυτοῦ) or is this right refused? —How could it be granted? —Then you have someone who governs you? —Yes, the *paidagōgos* whom you see here. —A slave,

---

paidagōgos, S 3807; *TDNT* 5.596–625; *EDNT* 3.2; *NIDNTT* 1.370, 3.775, 778–779; MM 473; L&N 36.5; BAGD 603 ‖ *paideutēs,* S 3810; *TDNT* 5.596–625; *EDNT* 2.3; *NIDNTT* 3.775–778; MM 474; L&N 33.244, 38.5; BAGD 603

dangers,[5] carrying its bags, watching over its outward bearing and behavior, and seeing that it completed its daily program of lessons, games, and various duties (Plutarch, *An virt. doc.* 2; Clement of Alexandria, *Paed.* 1.7.54–55). Usually *paidagōgoi* were slaves, foreigners or invalids incapable of performing other work.[6] Brutal and often drunk (Clement, *Paed.*), they were not sparing with blows, and when the children—in whom they inspired fear—became adolescents, they saw their oversight as a form of tyranny.[7] Such is the classic portrait of the *paidagōgos*.

But in the Hellenistic period, the "accompanying" role of the *paidagōgos* expanded and became nobler; his protection was not exclusively negative. He formed the child's character and morality[8] and even became its private tutor, if not its teacher. The Persian kings chose for their children "the wisest, the most just, the most moderate, the most courageous" (Ps.-Plato, *Alc.* 121 e); some received the title of citizen,[9] and the Egyptian papyri attest that they not only received honoraria[10] but became objects of respect.

---

perhaps? —Of course, our slave. —Strange thing for a free person to obey a slave! And what sort of government does he carry out over you? —He takes me to the house of the schoolmaster" (ἄγων δήπου εἰς διδασκάλου, *Lysis* 208 c; cf. *Resp.* 3.406 a ff.). This tutelage ceases when the youth reaches the age of eighteen, cf. Philo, *To Gaius* 53: "Here is the teacher (διδάσκαλος) of the one who has no more need of learning, the *paidagōgos* of the one who is no longer a child, the admonisher (ὁ νουθετητής) of one who is more sensible than himself"; Epictetus, frag. 97: παῖδας μὲν ὄντας ἡμᾶς οἱ γονεῖς παιδαγωγῷ παρέδοσαν, ἐπιβλέποντι πανταχοῦ πρὸς τὸ μὴ βλάπτεσθαι· ἄνδρας δὲ γενομένους ὁ θεὸς παραδίδωσι τῇ ἐμφύτῳ συνειδήσει φυλάττειν.

[5] Cf. Plutarch, *Lyc.* 17.1: "Old men watch over young men. . . . Far from having only superficial control, they all see themselves as it were as fathers, *paidagōgoi*, and leaders of all the young"; *De aud. poet.* 14; *Quaest. conv.* 3, prol.: "Stripping us of all affected attitudes, shielding us from the surveillance of the rules, like children who get away from their *paidagōgos*"; Dio Chrysostom 72.10.

[6] Josephus, *Life* 429; Ps.-Plutarch, *De lib. ed.* 7; Plutarch, *Mor.* 4 a–b; Plutarch, *Fab.* 5.5; Ps.-Plato, *Alc.* 122 b: "Pericles gave you as a *paidagōgos* one of his slaves who was so old as to be utterly useless."

[7] Plautus, *Bacch.* 422ff. Ps.-Plato, *Ax.* 366 e: the *paidagōgos* is the first of the evils that the child had to undergo at the age of seven; Suetonius, *Nero* 37: "Paetus Thrasea kept the frowning face of a *paidagōgos*." Cf. *SB* 9050, col. IV, 10: ἔγραψα τῷ στρατηγῷ . . . ἵνα μὴ παιδαγωγὸν ἔχω ἄνθρωπον φιλαίτιον (first-second century).

[8] Josephus, *Ant.* 18.212. Hence the title of *Paidagōgos* given to Christ by Clement of Alexandria, who explains: "The *paidagōgos* is an educator . . . his goal is to improve the soul . . . he leads a person into the virtuous life" (*Paed.* 1.1); cf. O. Navarre, "Paedagogus," in *DAGR*, vol. 4, 1, pp. 273ff.

[9] Herodotus 8.75; another example of a citizen-*paidagōgos*, at Athens in the third-second century BC, in J. and L. Robert, "Bulletin épigraphique," in *REG*, 1959, n. 140, who refer to *REA* 1940, p. 303.

[10] *Stud.Pal.* XX, 85 r 11 (p. 76); *P.Tebt.* 112 (p. 473); *PSI* 809, 7: Μακαρίῳ παιδαγωγῷ ὑπὲρ τιμῆς ἱματίου; *SB* 9581, 10.

Funerary monuments even attest to a certain veneration.[11] In the second-third century, a mother, after writing to her son, "see to it that you devote yourself to your *paidagōgos* as it is fitting to do to a teacher," (*melēsatō soi te kai tō paidagōgō sou kathēkonti kathēgētē se paraballein*) concludes: "Greet your highly esteemed *paidagōgos* Eros" (*aspasai ton timiōtaton paidogōgon sou Erōta, P.Oxy.* 930, 18ff.). It is most likely with this nuance of esteem that Paul refers to the tutor-teachers of the Corinthians (1 Cor 4:15), who nevertheless could not be on the same level as the father who conceived his child and retains his full rights as its educator.

Thus the *paidagōgos* comes close to being a teacher-instructor (*paideutēs*), in the first instance because in the Bible the *paidagōgos* is seen as an educator who corrects and punishes,[12] and also because the *paideutēs* is an example and a teacher of life and wisdom more than of knowledge.[13] Finally, like the *paidagōgos* who contributes to the education of the children, the *paideutēs* trains disciples: "you who bear the name of Jew . . . being taught by the law . . . a guide of the blind, a light to those who are in darkness, an educator of the ignorant (*paideutēn aphronōn*), the teacher of infants (*didaskalon nēpiōn*)."[14] But it is still the case that the *paideutēs* proper is a teacher (Sir 37:19), an instructor. In 169 BC, Attalus II of Pergam sent the necessary funds "so that his foundation should remain in perpetuity and the regular compensation of the instructors should be guaranteed."[15]

---

[11] Epitaphs for *paidagōgoi* are numerous; since P. Roussel announced the discovery of one at Constantinople ("Bulletin épigraphique," in *REG*, 1934, p. 241), many others have been discovered at Athens, Bithynia, etc. Cf. J. and L. Robert, "Bulletin épigraphique," in *REG*, 1941, p. 260, n. 139; 1971, p. 431, n. 281. A. Oepke cites *CIL* VI, 1, 2210: "Paidagogo suo καὶ καθηγητῇ item tutori a pupillatu, ob redditam sibi ab eo fidelissime tutelam" (*Der Brief des Paulus an die Galater,* Leipzig, 1937, p. 67).

[12] Hos 5:2—"I am the one who punishes you" (ἐγὼ δὲ παιδευτὴς ὑμῶν, Vulgate *eruditor*); Heb 12:9—"We have our fathers according to the flesh as correctors (εἴχομεν παιδευτὰς) and we incline toward them"; *Pss. Sol.* 8.29—σὺ παιδευτὴς ἡμῶν εἶ.

[13] 4 Macc 5:34—"O law that instructs us, I shall never betray you"; 9:6—Eleazar, "this old man, our master"; Philo, *Good Man Free* 143: "The poets are life-teachers in everything"; Dionysius of Halicarnassus 2.59: παιδευτὴς σοφίας.

[14] Rom 2:20. M. J. Lagrange observes that these two latter expressions are almost synonymous; cf. Plutarch, *Cam.* 10.3.

[15] Dittenberger, *Syl.* 672, 10: οἱ μισθοὶ τοῖς παιδευταῖς εὐτακτέωνται; cf. line 20, 35, 42: "let the instructors be paid each year." In the papyri, παιδευτής appears only once, in the sixth century (*SB* 5941, 2). In the inscriptions, the παιδευτής is associated rather often with the physician (*I.Bulg.* 30, 5; J. and L. Robert, "Bulletin épigraphique," in *REG*, 1938, p. 454, n. 332; 1960, p. 176, n. 261) or the sophist (1955, p. 259, n. 194); cf. 1949, p. 141, n. 167; 1959, p. 183, n. 138 *a*.

πανήγυρις

panēgyris, **festal assembly, sacred festival**

"You have drawn near to Mount Zion and the city of the living God, the heavenly Jerusalem, and myriads of angels in festal assembly" (*panēgyrei*, Heb 12:22). A NT hapax, *panēgyris* (a compound formed from *pan* and *ageirō*) retains the richness of its usual meaning in secular Greek,[1] which must therefore be outlined.

(*a*) The emphasis is first of all on the number and universality of the participants at a meeting (*megalē xynodos*, Thucydides 3.104.4). Usually it is an assembly of all the people of a city or a country, even of people of the same race, hence a public meeting (*P.Oxy.* 41; cf. Theophrastus, *Char.* 6.7), a general or plenary assembly whose members are quite diverse.[2] In

---

[1] Cf. L. Ziehen, "Panēgyris," in PW, vol. 13, 3, pp. 581ff. E. Saglio, on this word, in *DAGR*, vol. 4, 1, p. 313; C. Spicq, "La Panégyrie de Hébr. XII, 22," in *ST*, 1952, pp. 30–38.

[2] "Flaviane Philokrateia has given ten thousand Attic drachmas for anointings with oil, so that with the income from this sum, during the three days of the *panēgyris*, all may have the right to anointings with oil—citizens, foreigners, and slaves" (*I.Bulg.* 2265, 10–17). Josephus, *Ant.* 2.45: "It was the custom for these women to join in the general assembly" (εἰς τὴν πανήγυριν). *Panēgyris* refers to the press of the crowd at the theater (Plato, *Resp.* 10.604 *e*; *P.Oxy.* 2127, 4; *P.Princ.* 61, 15), political meetings (Aeschylus, *Ag.* 845; Dittenberger, *Syl.* 1048, 17), athletic meets (*P.Oxy.* 42, 3; 2476, 12; *SB* 1416, 2 and 16; 5225, 9; 5424, 16), panhellenic fairs which were attended by people from all over (Dittenberger, *Syl.* 298, 19); "Acara, Regium Lepidum, Macri Campi, where each year there is a *panēgyris*" (Strabo 5.1.11; cf. 10.5.4: ἥ τε πανήγυρις ἐμπορικόν τι πρᾶγμα; Pausanias 10.32.9; *P.Fay.* 93, 11; on the annual livestock fairs, cf. Varro, *Rust.* 2, pref. 6). It is because of this diversity of participants that Pythagoras compared life to a *panēgyris* (Diogenes Laertius 8.8. Cicero, *Tusc.* 5.3.9; Epictetus 3.5.10); cf. Wis 15:12—"Life is only a fair (πανηγυρισμός) organized for profit." A. Causse, "La Vision de la nouvelle Jérusalem (Esaïe LX) et la signification sociologique des assemblées de fête et des pèlerinages dans l'Orient sémitique," in *Mélanges syriens offerts à M. R. Dussaud*, Paris, 1939, pp. 739–750.

---

panēgyris, S 3831; *TDNT* 5.722; *EDNT* 3.9; MM 476; L&N 51.4; BAGD 607

the *panēgyris* of Heb 12:22, we may thus see a reference to the density of the heavenly population, a reiteration of *myriades angelōn:* the angels make up a varied multitude that is beyond counting, as is also the case in the demography of the heavenly court in Revelation.

(b) The fundamental meaning of *panēgyris* is "festival": a major gathering of people to celebrate a formal occasion. This is its meaning in its four occurrences in the OT, where *panēgyris* is always associated with *heortē* ("feast"; Hos 2:11; 9:5; Amos 5:21; Ezek 46:11). In fact, this meaning is so predominant that *panēgyris* is normally synonymous with joy: "The usual sorrow is doubled especially on the occasion of feasts for those who cannot celebrate them, for they miss the delight that a large gathering brings."[3] "Full of gratitude for your gifts, those to whom you have dispensed wealth and great favors for their perpetual possession reserve a tithe for you, celebrating each year on the occasion of your festival."[4] Even though these celebrations, which were accompanied by banquets where the wine flowed freely, sometimes degenerated into occasions for license, in themselves they provided rest for the body and joy for the soul;[5] so much so that the word

---

[3] Philo, *Flacc.* 118. At *panēgyreis* one sees "people dressed in white, heads garlanded, beaming, radiating good humor by the gaiety of their countenances . . . attractions, diversions . . . pleasures of all sorts and for all the senses" (*To Gaius* 12; cf. *Cherub.* 92); *Husbandry* 91; Aristophanes, *Pax* 342: "Do not yet allow yourself to celebrate; you are not yet sure of anything. But when we hold her, then rejoice, cry out, laugh; for this will be the time for sailing, living, loving, sleeping, going to *panēgyreis,* feasting, playing the Cottabus, living like Sybarites, singing tra la la"; *P.Oxy.* 2084, 6; *P.Cair.Zen.* 59341 *a* 2 and 11; *SB* 6760, 2ff. The linking of feast and *panēgyris* is constant (*Spec. Laws* 2.176; 3.183; *Moses* 2.159; Xenophon, *Cyr.* 6.1.10; Athenaeus 6.259 *b;* Dittenberger, *Syl.* 867, 52; *Or.* 56, 33 and 69; 90, 49). Alexander celebrates a feast for nine days in honor of Zeus and the Muses (Diodorus Siculus 17.16.4).

[4] Hymn to Isis (*SEG* VIII, 549, 24; with the comments of E. Bernand, *Inscriptions métriques,* p. 645; V. F. Vanderlip, *Four Greek Hymns,* pp. 46ff.). Cf. the *panēgyris* of Pharos, where God is thanked for benefits that are always new (Philo, *Moses* 2.41), or the solemn *panēgyris* in honor of Ptolemy III Euergetes I and Queen Berenice: "Each year there will be a *panēgyris* at state expense, in all sanctuaries in the whole land . . . the day on which the star of Isis rises, which is recognized in the sacred texts as the new year" (Decree of Canopus, in Dittenberger, *Or.* 56, 34–35). Πανηγυρίζω is synonymous with ἑορτάζω, cf. Isa 66:10—"Rejoice, O Jerusalem, and exult in her (πανηγυρίσατε), all you who love her"; Philo, *Moses* 2.211: "Those who were enrolled on the list of citizens . . . had to celebrate a *panēgyris,* spend time celebrating, abstain from work and activities directed toward profit-making . . . ; they had to give themselves some time off and free themselves of all bothersome and tiring cares"; Strabo 11.8.4; 14.1.44; *BGU* 863, 3; *PSI* 374, 15; *P.Oxy.* 705, 35; 2561, 3.

[5] Cf. the nuance of happiness expressed by "the joy of the eyes" (ὀφθαλμῶν πανήγυρις, Aelian, *VH* 3.1). Since participation in sporting festivals entailed a truce between warring parties, the idea of peace is associated with these meetings, cf.

panēgyris was used even for small get-togethers: "You are invited to celebrate the birthday of my son Gennadius (tēn panēgyrin tēs genethliou) by
dining with us on the sixteenth at seven o'clock."[6] Surely this connotation
is at the forefront in Heb 12:22—the society of the angels is a joyful
assembly, the heavenly Jerusalem a place of beatitude. The message for
Christians who are on their way there is that they will find happiness and
exultant joy.[7]

(c) Given the abundant, quasi-technical usage of panēgyris for the
Olympic, Isthmian, Pythian, Nemean, etc., games,[8] we must include a
sports meaning in Heb 12:22. These competitions not only attract the
largest crowds, they also celebrate a victory (cf. Strabo 5.2.7), and here a
reward.[9] In effect, Hebrews defines the Christian life as an athletic trial,
describes the conditions for training and winning, points to the prizes
offered and the crowd of spectators who admire and encourage the athletes

---

Dittenberger, Syl., 483, 7; P.Oxy. 1380, 133; SB 4224 (with the commentary of C. G.
Brandis, in Hermes, 1897, pp. 509–522).

[6] P.Oxy. 1214, 3; likewise PSI 1242, 1 (first century BC); the wedding ceremony is
referred to as a panēgyris by Heliodorus (Aeth. 4.15.3); cf. the new year's festival,
P.Ross.Georg. II, 18, 31 (with commentary, p. 107).

[7] We may refer to Heb 3:11–4:11 (κατάπαυσις, σαββατισμός), emphasizing the
nuances of rest and inviolable peace, to which panēgyris adds the idea of brotherly
harmony. As Philo says concerning the sacred Sabbath: "All the festivals of the year
are in reality daughters of the sacred Sabbath, which is like a mother. . . . In their
ceremonies and in the joy that they stir up, one tastes pleasures unmixed with anxiety
and bitterness, filling both body and soul, the former with the pleasures of life, the
latter with the teachings of philosophy" (Spec. Laws 2.214).

[8] Pindar, Isthm. 4.28: "They did not fail to send their curved chariot to the great
panēgyreis, and they were glad to pay what it cost to send their horses to strive with
all the peoples of Hellas"; Plato, Hp. Mi. 363 c: "It is my custom to go to Elis where I
live, to Olympia, to the panēgyris of the Greeks every time the games take place";
Demosthenes, Corona 91: "Let the Byzantines and Perinthians send delegations to the
Greek panēgyreis, the Isthmian, Nemean, Olympic, and Pythian games"; Aristotle, Rh.
3.3.1406ᵃ22; Strabo 8.3.30; Pausanias 5.4.5; SEG XVI, 55, 8; inscription from Pergamum: πανηγυρικὸν γυμνάσιον (J. and L. Robert, "Bulletin épigraphique," in REG,
1962, p. 135, n. 55; cf. 1956, p. 152, n. 213: κατὰ τὴν Ἡρακλήων ἀγώνων πανήγυριν;
1959, pp. 169–170, n. 66; L. Robert, Monnaies antiques en Troade, Geneva-Paris, 1966,
pp. 18–46); BGU 1704, 9 (cf. Viereck, in Klio, vol. 8, pp. 49ff.); cf. the πανήγυρις
Ἀδριανή at Gaza (RB, 1931, p. 29) and the games of Daphne described by E. A. Parsons,
The Alexandrian Library, Glory of the Hellenic World, London, 1952, pp. 42ff.

[9] Cf. Heb 10:35; 11:6, 26. Isocrates, Paneg. 1: "I am often amazed that the founders
of panēgyreis and the organizers of gymnastic competitions should think physical
advantage to be worthy of such great rewards"; Philo, Alleg. Interp. 2.108: "Work to
be crowned . . . with a noble and glorious crown that no panēgyris among humankind
offers"; Husbandry 91, 117; Dio Cassius 53.1, τὴν πανήγυριν τὴν ἐπὶ τῇ νίκῃ; Manetho
4.74; Critodemus, in CCAG, VIII, 1, pp. 259, 12; 260, 24; P.Oxy. 1416, 16.

of faith (12:1–2). So it is not surprising that the epistle uses a compatible metaphor to evoke the glory and joy that are in store for the victors, namely, the metaphor of the jubilant *polis*, of a *panēgyris* at which the whole assembly of the elect celebrates and sings the praises of the garlanded competitors.

(*d*) All of the Greeks' great national festivals, and especially the Olympic Games, had a religious character.[10] The crowd came together with the priests around a common sanctuary where sacrifice was offered.[11] *Panēgyris* or "sacred festival" is constantly associated with *thysia*.[12] This meaning of liturgical observance is clearly present in Heb 12:22, where the heavenly joy is tinctured by religious seriousness and reverence.[13] On the one hand, the epistle pictures heaven as a place of worship, where the great high priest and *leitourgos* officiates (8:2); on the other hand the myriads of angels are *leitourgika pneumata* (1:14), born agents of divine worship, occupying themselves with praising God and proclaiming God as sovereign

---

[10] Josephus, *War* 5.230: The high priests ascended the altar "only on the Sabbath, the new moon, the celebration of a national festival, or a public observance" (ἡ πανήγυρις πάνδημος); *SB* 8334, 25. Cf. E. N. Gardiner, *Olympia: Its History and Remains*, Oxford, 1925; idem, *Athletics of the Ancient World*, Oxford, 1930, A. J. Festugière, "La Grèce: La Religion," in *Histoire générale des religions*, Paris, 1944, vol. 1, pp. 66ff. M. P. Nilsson, "Festivals," in *OCD*, p. 435; Herodotus 2.59ff.; Strabo 5.2.9; 5.3.5; Dittenberger, *Syl.* 95; 298; 589; 635; 714; 736; 867; *Or.* 305 (a number of these inscriptions have been republished in *LSCGSup*, see the index). *P.Hib.* 27, 76 and 163; *P.Cair.Zen.* 59820, 3.

[11] Isocrates, *Paneg.* 43: "It is right to praise those who established the *panēgyreis*, because, thanks to the practice they left behind, after libations and the abolishing of existing hatreds, we come together, and then, pooling our prayers and sacrifices, we recall how we are related to each other." The liturgical ceremony includes a procession, songs, sacred rites (Dittenberger, *Syl.* 298; Petosiris, in *CCAG* VII, 133, 11). M. P. Nilsson, *Geschichte der griechischen Religion*, vol. 1, p. 778; ET *History of Greek Religion*.

[12] Amos 5:21—θυσίας ἐν ταῖς πανηγύρεσιν; Herodotus 2.62; Strabo 10.5.2; 14.1.20; Pausanias 10.32.14–16; Philo, *Moses* 2.159: "Many sacrifices were of necessity celebrated each day, and especially in the *panēgyreis* and festivals, either of private individuals or publicly on behalf of all"; *Decalogue* 78; *Spec. Laws* 3.183; Nicolaus of Damascus, frag. 62 (ed. C. Müller, vol. 3, p. 396); *SEG* 4.664.19: τὰς θυσίας εἰς τὴν πανήγυριν; *I.Lind.* 419, 6 and 55; *LSCG*, n. 156 B 31; 159, 5–6.

[13] Cf. Philo, *Spec. Laws* 2.160, uniting honor and admiration in the *panēgyris*, θαυμάσαι τε καὶ τιμῆσαι πανηγύρεως ἐκεχειρία. In the cult of Athena: τῆς περὶ τὴν πανήγυριν εὐκοσμίας (*LSAM*, n. 81, 17). Cf. in the ecclesiastical language of the sixth-seventh century, Menos writing to Theodorus to guard his health in order to be able to celebrate the *panēgyris* (feast) of Holy Epiphany for many long years (*P.Oxy.* 1857, 5).

and universal judge: "and let all the angels of God worship him" (*kai proskynēsatōsan autō pantes angeloi theou*, 1:6).

(*e*) There is one last meaning of the pagan *panēgyris* that may have been assumed by the writer of Hebrews. Before it came to refer to the praise of a personage,[14] *panēgyris* (Latin *laudatio*) was used for ceremonial orations written or declaimed by sophists, rhetors, or orators at a great festival before a large audience.[15] This rhetorical meaning shows up in the context of Heb 12:22, where the old and new revelation are contrasted. The ones who heard at Sinai asked that they be spoken to no more, so terrified were they at the manifestations of divine power. The beneficiaries of the new covenant can draw near to Zion and come to the *panēgyris* of the angels, for they are united with the mediator Jesus, whose blood *speaks* better things that that of Abel (verse 24). So they are invited—and this is the point of the image of the heavenly Jerusalem—not to refuse to hear the one who speaks from highest heaven (verse 25). The throne of God is not only an object of worship, an altar to be approached in a liturgical procession (4:16), but is also the source of oracles promulgated on earth, exactly as in Revelation. The *panēgyris* of Hebrews, religious and joyful as it is, is also eloquent. It is no longer the praise of Athens, as uttered by Lysias or Isocrates, but the praise of the glory of God, the expression of his will, the *panēgyris* of the city of the living God, that abides as a perpetual feast.[16]

---

[14] Ἐγκώμιον, cf. L. Robert, *Etudes épigraphiques*, pp. 21ff. F. Durrbach, *Choix*, n. 84, 112. On the praise of a city, cf. L. Robert, "Sur des lettres d'un métropolite de Phrygie," in *Journal des savants*, 1962, pp. 151ff.

[15] Cf. the *Olympic Discourse* of Gorgias, the *Olympic* of Lysias, the *Panegyric* of Isocrates; Aristotle, *Rh.* 3.1408^{b}15; Philo, *Good Man Free* 96; Plutarch, *Tim.* 37.4; Heraclides Ponticus in Iamblichus, *VP* 58–59; P.Oxy. 2084.

[16] "While the other *panēgyreis* meet at long intervals and break up quickly, our city is for those who sustain a perpetual *panēgyris*" (Isocrates, *Paneg.* 46; cf. Thucydides 2.38.1; Ps.-Xenophon, *Ath.* 3.8).

παραγγελία, παραγγέλλω

parangelia, **command, order,** *parangellō,* **to pass the word along, order, prescribe**

→*see also* ἐντολή

According to its etymology, the first meaning of *parangellō* is "announce from one to another," hence, pass the word within the group, give a password, pass along a notice, communicate a message, make known.[1] Thus Claudius Lysias "made known" to Paul's accusers that they should speak against him (Acts 23:30; cf. Josephus, *Ant.* 2.311), and Judas "had his orders passed to those who were with him."[2] In the papyri, in AD 75/76, a borrower is *notified* that he must make good his debt (*P.Yale* 64, 18 and 22); and in the third century, a Roman citizen *informs* Epimachos of the terms of his will.[3]

But even more frequently this verb and the corresponding noun[4] mean "order, prescribe." The subject is God[5] or his Word (*P.Lond.* 1915, 4), Moses

---

[1] Cf. Diodorus Siculus 17.72.4: they urged each other to form a triumphal procession.

[2] 2 Macc 12.5; cf. 2 Chr 36:22—"Cyrus had a proclamation communicated (παρήγγειλε κηρύξαι) throughout his kingdom" (hiphil of the Hebrew *'ābar*); 2 Esdr 1:1. The LXX uses this verb to translate the Hebrew *šāmaʿ*, "call together" (1 Sam 15:4; 23:8; 1 Kgs 15:22; Jer 50:29; 51:27), the hiphil of *ṣāpaq* (1 Sam 10:17), of *zāʿaq* (Judg 4:10), the niphal of *yāʿaṣ*, "consult, take counsel" (1 Kgs 12:6).

[3] *P.Oxy.* 2474, 40; cf. *P.Sorb.* 33, 26: "and indeed Apollonius informed me" (καὶ γὰρ ἐμοὶ παρήγγελλεν Ἀπολλώνιος). In *P.Mich.* 243, 4, the notices or meetings of a club are mentioned; cf. 624, 29; *P.Fouad* 30, 23: "We ask that a copy of this *hypomnēmna* be sent to them by the hand of the bailiff, so that having written *notification* (ἵνα ἔχοντες ἔνγραπτον παραγγελίαν) . . . they may know that they are responsible" (second century); the *publication* of the edict of the prefect Subatianus Aquila was carried out in each town (*P.Yale* 61, 12), like the notification by the *stratēgos* of the inhabitants of different parts of the city (*P.Oxy.* 1187, 30); the Blemmyes notifed the τοποτηρητής (*P.Apoll.* 15, 5); *P.Ryl.* 81, 9; *SB* 7331, 7.

[4] Not in the LXX, cf. παράγγελμα (Hebrew *mišmaʿat*), 1 Sam 22:14.

[5] Philo, *Post. Cain* 29; cf. the divine precepts in Cornutus (*Theol. Graec.* 9), the commands revealed by Zeus (Dittenberger, *Syl.* 985, 2; Philadelphia, first century).

---

parangelia, S 3852; *TDNT* 5.761–765; *EDNT* 3.16–17; *NIDNTT* 1.340–341; MM 480–481; L&N 33.328; BAGD 613 ‖ *parangellō,* S 3853; *TDNT* 5.761–765; *EDNT* 3.16–17; *NIDNTT* 1.340–342; MM 481; L&N 33.327; BAGD 613

or Virtue with their commands (Philo, *Heir* 13; *Prelim. Stud.* 63), the prefect,[6] the *stratēgos* (Onasander, *Strategikos* 25; *P.Oslo* 84, 15; *P.Oxy.* 1411, 16), the *topotērētēs* (*P.Apoll.* 12, 5), an imperial officer (*P.Oxy.* 2268, 5), the *riparius* (*P.Oxy.* 2235, 23), a local VIP (*P.Oxy.* 1831, 6, *meizōn*), the *prostatēs* or president of a club (*P.Mich.* 243, 4; under Tiberius), the gymnastic teacher vis-à-vis athletes (Philo, *Alleg. Interp.* 1.98), above all military commanders: "Holophernes gave the order to his whole army . . . to strike camp . . . and join combat" (Jdt 7:1); Antiochus ordered his troops to parade armed (2 Macc 5:25; cf. 13:10; 1 Macc 5:58).

Consequently, *parangelia* would normally be an injunction, command, order (Philodemus of Gadara, *Rh.* I, pp. 78ff.; *Pap.Lugd.Bat.* VI, 15, 144; *P.Lond.* 1231, 16; vol. 3, p. 109), even a summons (*P.Ness.* III, 29, 3). In this sense the high priest and the Sanhedrin formally forbid the apostles to preach (Acts 4:18; 5:28) and the praetors at Philippi order the jailer to guard their prisoners carefully.[7] But context gives each occurrence of the word a particular nuance that cannot always be specified precisely. When Paniskos writes to his wife Ploutogenia *parēngeila soi exerchomenos hoti mē apelthēs eis tēn oikian sou* (*P.Mich.* 217, 3; third century, republished *SB* 7249), it is possible to translate either "I asked you" or "I ordered you, when I am gone, not to go back to your house." *Parangelia* can take on the mild sense of exhortation or counsel,[8] and it is also known to correspond to the *litis denuntiatio*, the summons to appear in court.[9]

Geminus, *Intro. to Astronomy* 8.7: "The command given by the laws and by the oracles to offer sacrifices in accord with ancestral customs"; Diodorus Siculus 17.4.9; 17.65.4; 17.107.1.

[6] *P.Princ.* 20, 9 and 14; *P.Cair.Isid.* 66, 21. The prefect Valerius Eudaemon in his edict of AD 138: "I bid them refrain from such treachery" (*P.Oxy.* 237, col. VIII, 12). The edict of the prefect Tiberius Julius Alexander says: "I enjoin (παραγγέλλω) them not to do . . . anything unless the prefect has passed on the matter. In addition, I order . . . (κελεύω δὲ καὶ κ.τ.λ.)" (Dittenberger, *Or.* 669, 52; with the commentary of G. Chalon, *T. Julius Alexander.* Κελεύω is often associated with παραγγέλλω in the papyri, cf. *P.Oxy.* 1204, 10; *Stud.Pal.* XX, 283, 7) and in literary Greek (Xenophon, *Hell.* 2.1.4). A. Pelletier, *Josèphe adaptateur,* pp. 277–288.

[7] Acts 16:23–24. The jailer receives the order (παραγγελίαν τοιαύτην λαβών). The authority gives the order: παρ. διδόναι (1 Thess 4:2; *SB* 7835, 12) or παρ. ποιεῖν (Josephus, *Ant.* 16.241; *BGU* 1774, 11).

[8] Commanding goes hand in hand with exhorting (1 Thess 4:11; 2 Thess 3:12; cf. *P.Oxy.* 1840, 4). Plutarch's πολιτικὰ παραγγέλματα (*Praecepta gerendae rei publicae*) are "political advice" (cf. T. Renoirte, *Les "Conseils politiques" de Plutarque,* Louvain, 1951); cf. the collection of ethical principles: Δελφικὰ παραγγέλματα (Dittenberger, *Syl.* 985, 3).

[9] *SB* 4416, 26: παραγγελείαν παραγένωνται εἰς τὸ ἱερώτατον βῆμα; *P.Tebt.* 14, 5; 303. 14; 434 (in 104); *P.Grenf.* I, 40, 6; *P.Oxy.* 484, 18; 2343, 7; *P.Oslo* 2, 19; *P.Mich.* 526, 21; *P.Dura* 20, 19; 21, 10; *P.Michael.* 30, 12; *P.Ness.* 19, 3; *UPZ* 71, 17; Philo, *Flacc.*

In light of these usages, we can see that Jesus gives instructions to the Twelve (Matt 10:5; Mark 6:8) and strongly advises the cleansed leper not to tell anyone about the miracle.[10] But he sharply forbids the apostles to reveal his messianic identity (Luke 9:21—*epitimēsas autois parēngeilen*), and he commands the unclean spirit (8:29), as he orders the Twelve not to leave Jerusalem (Acts 1:4) and to preach to the people (10:42).

St. Paul similarly orders the prophetic spirit of the servant woman (Acts 16:18), but it seems that his *parangeliai* are ethical prescriptions, rules for Christian living (1 Thess 4:2; 2 Thess 3:4, 6; 1 Cor 11:17), with regard to marriage, for example (1 Cor 7:10), or the obligation to work (1 Thess 4:11; 2 Thess 3:10). The verb is imperative,[11] and the commands are repeated;[12] but this is still as much teaching as commanding, giving both doctrine that must be received and rules that must be followed.[13]

In the Pastorals (and the word *pastoral* here means a *mandamus*, like a bishop's letter), St. Paul passes on his instructions to his favorite disciple, who must in turn teach and command:[14] "I asked you to remain faithfully as Ephesus *hina parangeilēs*" (1 Tim 1:3; cf. 6:17). Timothy must act with authority; for him this is a serious obligation: *tērēsai se tēn entolēn* (1 Tim 6:13–14). But if the verb *parangellō* retains all the force of a military command addressed to a soldier (1:18; 2 Tim 2:3), the substantive *parangelia* means rather "mandate, obligation, duty";[15] "This is the mandate that I entrust to you, my child Timothy" (1 Tim 1:18); "The goal of this command is love" (1:5), which is the essence of the gospel and of the whole Christian life.

141; cf. *Chrest.Mitt.*, 1, pp. 36ff.; A. Boyé, *La Denuntiatio introductive d'instance sous le principat*, Bourdeaux, 1922; R. Taubenschlag, *Law of Greco-Roman Egypt*, p. 382.

[10] Luke 5:14 (in Mark 1:44, λέγει); cf. 8:56; Acts 23:22; Josephus, *Ag. Apion* 1.244: recommend hiding the statues; Diodorus Siculus 17.57.6.

[11] 2 Thess 3:4—"You are doing and will continue to do the things that we command." Cf. Acts 15:5, where the Jerusalemites want to compel the converts to observe the law of Moses.

[12] 1 Thess 4:11; 2 Thess 3:10 (παρηγγέλλομεν, imperfect for customary action); cf. *SB* 7404, 38: ἐγώ σοι καὶ πρότερον παρήνγειλα καὶ νῦν παρανγέλλω παραλαμβάνιν τὰ βιβλία.

[13] Cf. 1 Tim 4:11—παράγγελλε ταῦτα καὶ δίδασκε.

[14] The supreme authority transmits orders through intermediaries, cf. Dan 3:4 (LXX): "The herald cried . . . 'You are commanded thus' "; Josephus, *Ant.* 19.31: I charge you to see to it that each one practices his religion seriously; *SB* 6097, 4; cf. D. M. Stanley, "Authority in the Church," in *CBQ*, 1967, pp. 555–573; H. Maehlum, *Die Vollmacht des Timotheus nach den Pastoralbriefen*, Basel, 1969.

[15] The Παραγγελίαι of Hippocrates are not a treatise *De Praeceptis* but *De Officio*: acting as a physician; cf. Plutarch, *Crass.* 15.4: παρ. = candidacy for the consulate; Appian, *BCiv.* 1.21; cf. C. Spicq, *Théologie morale*, vol. 2, p. 579.

παραδειγματίζω

paradeigmatizō, to make an example by punishment or public derision; to disgrace, dishonor

Unknown in the papyri and rare in literary Greek, this verb means to make an example of a malefactor by punishing him;[1] then make an example of by exposing to derision, to public scorn; and finally to disgrace, to dishonor.[2] A NT hapax,[3] *paradeigmatizō* in its four OT occurrences always emphasizes the idea of publicness and has connotations of shame (Jer 13:22, Hebrew *ḥāmam*) and exemplary punishment, as with the hanging of the leaders of Israel (Num 25:4; hiphil of *yāqaʿ*; cited by Philo, his only use of the word, *Dreams* 1.89) or Esther's prayer: "Make an example of the one who took the initiative against us."[4] These usages correspond to our term "to pillory," meaning to expose a guilty party to public scorn.

So we translate Heb 6:6—"The apostates crucify the Son of God on their own account and ridicule him publicly." Their official repudiation of their sworn faith is an insult to Christ, like an insult hurled at him, a sort of repetition of Calvary in caricature, especially of the scenes described by Matt 26:67–68; 27:38–43. The apostate who professes to be one and proves the claim by his actions tramples the Son of God underfoot with the whole world looking on! But in the case in point, it is he who openly manifests his scorn.

---

[1] Polybius 2.60.7: "Aristomachus (tyrant of Argos) had to be led across the Peloponnesus to be made an example through his punishment" (μετὰ τιμωρίας παραδειγματιζόμενον); cf. Menander: "If I catch one of them coming near my window and do not make an example of him (παράδειγμα ποιήσω) for the whole region, you may take me for a man like the rest" (*Dysk.* 484; cf. παράδειγμα φέρω, 863).

[2] Plutarch, *De curios.* 10: Archilochus disgraced himself (ἑαυτὸν παραδειγματίζοντος).

[3] In Matt 1:19 the correct reading is δειγματίσαι, "expose to public disparagement," rather than παραδ. (א, C).

[4] Esth 4:17 q; cf. Ezek 28:17—"I exposed you before kings to make a spectacle of you" (Hebrew *ra'ʾawāh*); cf. *Pss. Sol.* 2.14—"Before the face of the sun their criminal deeds have been revealed" (seems to have been inspired by Num 25:4).

---

paradeigmatizō, S 3856; *TDNT* 2.32; *EDNT* 3.17; *NIDNTT* 2.291, 293; MM 481–482; L&N 25.200; BAGD 614

παραδίδωμι

paradidōmi, to hand over, give back, become ripe, commend (oneself), transmit, deliver, betray

Among the very numerous forms of *didōmi* with a prefix,[1] the compound *paradidōmi* is by far the commonest in the NT; its semantics is interesting, as much because of its orthographic variations, especially in the papyri,[2] as because of its multiple meanings. But given the Koine's taste for expressivity, this compound is often purely synonymous with *didōmi*.[3]

I. — The first meaning is "hand over, give something to someone" (*tini ti*). Thus Jesus "bent his head and gave over [his] spirit" to his father.[4] Human beings are handed over: a slave to his master[5] or a child to its

---

[1] Cf. ἀντι-, "give in exchange"; ἐν-, "give over, abandon"; ἀνα-, ἀπο-, δια-, εἰς-, ἐκ-, κατα-, μετα-, προ-, etc.

[2] Cf. B. G. Mandilaras, *Verb*, n. 92, 219, 308, 374, 385, 393, 394, 412, 540 (1), 681, 728, 741, 742.

[3] Cf. Matt 25:14–15: παρέδωκε . . . ἔδωκεν. Both verbs are used indifferently by the manuscripts A and B (Judg 1:4; Dan 1:2; 2:38; 7:25; etc.); 1 Sam 17:44—Goliath proposes to give David's flesh to the birds of the sky and the beasts of the field; Hos 8:10; Esth 2:13—they gave Esther everything that she wanted to have with her; Philo, *Creation* 139; *Unchang. God* 92; *Flight* 45; *Change of Names* 113; *Post. Cain* 107; *Spec. Laws* 1.21; Josephus, *War* 1.46; 3.33; *Ant.* 7.280, 379; 8.32; *P.Ant.* 92, 9: "Give him the four *solidi*"; *P.Lond.* 1916, 22: "We gave him what we were able to find."

[4] John 19:30—παρέδωκεν τὸ πνεῦμα (cf. Luke 23:46—εἰς χειράς σου παρατίθεμαι τὸ πνεῦμά μου and the variant from the Syriac mentioned by L. Abramowski and A. E. Goodman, "Luke 23:46 ΠΑΡΑΤΙΘΕΜΑΙ in a Rare Syriac Rendering," in *NTS*, vol. 13, 1967, pp. 290–291); *T. Abr.* B 12: Sara παρέδωκε τὴν ψυχήν; Xenophon, *An.* 4.6.1: "Xenophon gave this man to Cheirisophus to serve him as guide."

[5] Deut 23:16; 1 Sam 30:15; Prov 30:10; Bel (Theodotion) 29–30; Jdt 10:15; Esth 2:3—the young women who have been assembled are given over to the care of Hegai, the king's eunuch; 1 Macc 11:40—Trypho went to the Arab Imalkue "to urge him to hand over the child"; 2 Macc 14:31, 33; Judg 11:21—"Yahweh delivered Sihon and all his people into the hands of Israel, who defeated them"; 11:30, 32; 12:3; Philo, *Spec. Laws* 3.120; especially troops (1 Macc 3:34; Josephus, *War* 1.183, 249; *Ant.* 7.233; 12.298; 13.225).

---

paradidōmi, S 3860; *TDNT* 2.169–172; *EDNT* 3.18–20; MM 482–483; L&N 13.142, 21.7, 23.110, 23.200, 33.237, 37.12, 37.111, 57.77; BDF §§187(1), 323(1), 390(3), 402(2); BAGD 614–615

14   παραδίδωμι, *paradidōmi*

mother (Josephus, *Ant.* 1.217), a young woman to her husband (Tob 7:13; *Jos. Asen.* 4.10), but also objects: a scepter (Esth 4:17), a sword (2 Macc 15:15), the helm of a ship to a pilot (Philo, *To Gaius* 149), grain (Josephus, *Life* 73; cf. 69), weapons (*War* 2.450). Raguel "handed over to Tobit Sarah his wife and half his property: slaves, cattle, and money" (Tob 10:10); Judith "handed over to the servant the head of Holophernes" (Jdt 13:9). God hands over Canaan to Israel ("I swore to give the land to your fathers"),[6] a city,[7] a stronghold,[8] the royal palace (Josephus, *War* 1.143). The government is given into the hands of the great (*War* 1.169), the care of the affairs of the land (*Life* 226, *pragmatōn epimeleian*), the administration of Egypt to Joseph (*Ant.* 2.89, *oikonomian;* cf. 6.32), the power (7.30, *archēn;* 7.110, 351; 9.104; 11.321, 334; 14.104; *hēgemonian,* 8.53), the kingdom (7.93, *basileian;* 7.256; 9.280; 10.48, 82; 16.92), the high priesthood to Aaron (4.18; 5.361), the responsibility of offering sacrifices is given to the priests (11.137). In the papyri, things left by the deceased are given over to the heir (*ha kai paredothē, P.Tebt.* 406, 9), bundles of reeds to a friend (*P.Oxy.* 742, 7; second century BC), oil to a factory (*P.Tebt.* 728, 3; second century BC), cats to a third party (*P.Tebt.* 764, 32; *ta Hōrou ktēnē*), a she-ass to its buyer (*P.Corn.* 13, 9), a letter personally delivered (*P.Ant.* 43, verso 1), ankle bracelets (*P.Apoll.* 8, 17), the responsibility for sacred vestments,[9] etc.

II. — The thing given can be simply restitution, a "giving back." Demetrius asks Jonathan to give hostages back to him.[10] This meaning

---

[6] Deut 1:8, 21 (Hebrew *nātan*); Josh 2:24; Tob (Sinaiticus) 14:7—"the land of Abraham will be given to the sons of Israel."

[7] Deut 20:13; Jericho (Josh 6:2, 16); Ai (8:18); Jdt 8:9, 33; Jerusalem (Isa 36:15; 37:10; Jer 21:10; 32:28, 36; 34:2; etc.), Ephron (1 Macc 5:50), Ptolemais (12:45); cf. 15:30; 16:18; Josephus, *War* 5.361, 392, 397, 499; *Ant.* 10.125; 13.180, 190, 202, 388; 14.58.

[8] 1 Macc 12:34; Josephus, *War* 1.167; 2.41, 486; 4.518; 7.209.

[9] *P.Achm.* 8, 17: "Take care to put the cargo up for sale, and if no one offers more, to send them back"; the weavers make and deliver the ordered vestments (*P.Phil.* 10, 18; *P.Cair.Isid.* 54, 8–9; *P.Oxy.* 2230, 12); wine is delivered (*P.Oxy.* 3111, 14), or a boat in good condition (*P.Warr.* 5, 7). Lessees agree, "At the end of the term, we will give over four *arourai* as fallow forage land" (*P.Phil.* 14, 22); "I will give back the olive orchard fertilized and with the picking done" (*P.Phil.* 12, 29; 13, 19); "we have returned 45,700 pounds to the steward of Akanthon" (*P.Cair.Isid.* 13, 22). In a contract for service: ὁμολογῶ παραδόσειν σοι τὸν υἱόν μου . . . ὥστε ὑπηρετεῖν (*BGU* 1647, 3; cf. *P.Oxy.* 2353, 3; 2586, 45); in a marriage contract, Marcellina παραδεδωκέναι ἑαυτὴν ἐκ χηρείας πρὸς γάμου κοινονείαν (*P.Dura* 30, 10). In a metaphorical sense, "Destiny and the Fates delivered me to Hades" (epitaph at Telesion, in E. Bernand, *Inscriptions métriques,* n. 36, 3).

[10] 1 Macc 10:6, 9; Lysander gave back the city to its former citizens (Xenophon, *Hell.* 2.3.7); "I give you back these two men" (*An.* 6.6.34); Antiochus was compelled to return Samosata (Josephus, *War* 1.157, 322).

occurs frequently in the papyri, notably in cases where *paradidōmi* is correlated with *paralambanō* (cf. 1 Cor 11:2, 23; 15:3): "At the end of the lease, I will give back to you (*paradōsō*) goats and sheep in equal numbers, adults of good quality, just as I received from you (*parelabon*)";[11] "After the time I will give back the two *arourai* free of weeds as when I received it";[12] "at the expiration of the lease, I will return the lot to you: two *arourai* just planted in legumes . . . three *arourai* cleared of stubble" (*P.Bour.* 17, 4).

III. — In the parable of the Growing Seed, the farmer finally takes the sickle and harvests when the fruit is ready (*hotan de paradoi ho karpos*, Mark 4:29; cf. Joel 4:13), literally, when it "renders," that is to say, when it is ripe, when the time has come. We may compare Gen 27:20, where Jacob says, "God gave over (Hebrew *qārâh*) the game to me," and Exod 21:13—God provides, brings (Hebrew *'ānâh*) the occasion, permits favorable circumstances.[13]

IV. — *Paradidōmi* also means to give oneself over "to the one who judges justly,"[14] and thence "commend." Paul and Barnabas are commended to the grace of God (Acts 14:26; 15:40), that is, are placed under the Lord's protection, entrusted to his power, as much for their personal safety as for the success of their mission. This meaning is homogeneous with that of the preceding uses of *paradidōmi*—one delivers or abandons oneself into another's hands.[15]

---

[11] *P.Thead.* 8, 25; cf. *P.Alex.* 12, 19 (first-second century); *P.Hamb.* 20, 14. "Order that each one shall receive back his private property" (*P.Oxy.* 3288, 6).

[12] Μετὰ τὸν χρόνον παραδώσω τὰς ἀρούρας καθαρὰς ὡς καὶ παρέλαβον, *BGU* 1018, 24; cf. 1564, 13; 1644, 24; 1645, 18; *P.Mich.* 184, 18 (121 BC); 185, 24 (122 BC); 310, 12 (AD 26–27); 315, 24 (AD 44–45); 558, 20; 563, 18; 587, 31; 633, 25; *P.Mil.Vogl.* 269, 26; 286, 34; *P.Cair.Isid.* 98, 15; 99, 23; 100, 17; 101, 11; *P.Soterichos* 2, 32 (AD 71); *P.Amst.* 41, 80 (first century BC); *P.Vindob.Bosw.* 8, 20; 9 *b* 6; *P.Berl.Zill.* 5; *P.Fam.Tebt.* 45, 11; 47, 25; *P.Mert.* 10, 20; 123, 4; *P.Sorb.* 51, 11 (third century BC): "You took from him the land that he has farmed for many years and gave it to others" (ἑτέροις παραδεδωκέναι). Buildings are also given back: παραδότω τὴν οἰκίαν (*P.Köln* 150, 13; cf. *BGU* 2034, 14; *P.Erl.* 72, 7; *P.Mil.* 55, 18; *P.Mert.* 76, 23; *P.Stras.* 348, 1), for example a bathing establishment (*P.Mich.* 312, 30).

[13] Cf. Herodotus 5.67: the god not permitting (authorizing) what he had planned; 7.18: "act so that with God permitting, nothing may be lacking on your part"; Isocrates, *Phil.* 5.118: give occasion.

[14] 1 Pet 2:23—the innocent person appeals to God, trusting in the purity of his cause. This was not without danger, cf. Str-B (vol. 3, p. 164), who cite (vol. 1, p. 36) the case of Rabbi Eliezer, who is accused of heresy before a Roman judge and tells him, "I stand before the just judge," meaning God; but the magistrate thought he meant himself and thanked the accused (*t. Ḥul.* 2.24). Philo, *Virtues* 171: the law sets the proud before the judgment seat of God alone.

[15] This meaning "abandon" occurs already in Plato (*Euthd.* 285 *c*, ἐμαυτόν), seen clearly in John 19:30 (π. τὸ πνεῦμα); 1 Cor 13:8 (τὸ σῶμα; cf. Josephus, *War* 7.355),

V. — When one parts with a possession (a material or moral good, an opinion, a word, a writing . . .) to give it to others, one "transmits" it. This meaning of *paradidōmi*, particularly frequent in the NT, especially regarding doctrine that is thus made known, is constant in secular Greek: "The ancients transmitted this tradition to us" (Plato, *Phlb.* 16 *c*; Plato, *Ep.* 12.359 *d*); "The various sciences are preserved and transmitted to posterity forever only by means of letters."[16] The epitaph of the perfumer Casios: "rewards and numerous crowns which he was the first to wear and which he passed on to his children" (*SB* 4299, 6); "Andromache passes my letter (*ta grammata*) on to you."[17] Likewise in the LXX: "It is possible for you to observe, not so much according to the ancient histories that have been transmitted to us, as in examining what happens under your feet" (Esth 8:12 *g*); "whatever you deal out (*ho ean paradidōs*), let it be by number and weight" (Sir 42:7). Wis 14:15 has to do with idolatrous religious traditions: a father who had lost his son passed on mysteries and initiations to his subjects (*paredōke tois hypocheiriois mystēria kai teletas*).[18]

Philo uses *paradidōmi* with meanings from "pass on" a calf from the stable to a servant (*Abraham* 108) and the "transmission" of old

---

is traditional (Philo, *Husbandry* 132; *Migr. Abr.* 18; *Moses* 1.3), notably in metaphorical usages: delivered to desolation (2 Chr 30:7), to darkness (*Spec. Laws* 3.6), to oblivion (λήθῃ παραδοθῆναι, *Spec. Laws* 1.28; Josephus, *Ant.* 17.352); cf. "keep silence" (σιγῇ παραδίδοσαν, *Ant.* 17.122; 18.168; 19.48, 132), leave in forgetfulness (σιωπῇ π., *P.Flor.* 309, 5), entrust to memory (Philo, *Worse Attacks Better* 65); throw, deliver to fire (Philo, *Spec. Laws* 1.199, 254; 2.215; Philo, *To Gaius* 356; Josephus, *War* 2.358).

[16] Diodorus Siculus 12.13.2; Demosthenes, *C. Aristocr.* 23.65: "Elsewhere there is no Areopagus—a tribunal concerning which many fine stories are transmitted . . . some certified by our own testimony." History allows an understanding of the character and mores of the hero (πρὸς κατανόησιν ἤθους καὶ τρόπου παραδιδούς, Plutarch, *Nic.* 1.5). "Through these constructions, Herod transmitted his family and friends to immortality without forgetting his own memory" (Josephus, *War* 1.419). "Theudion, having received a poison from Antiphilos, passed it on to Pheroras" (1.592).

[17] *P.Mich.* 213, 8; cf. the documents (τὰ βιβλία) transmitted by their first holder (*P.Fam.Tebt.* 15, 21, 31, 35, etc; 24, 32); τὰ τῆς τάξεως παραδῶσι βιβλία (*PSI* 1361, 5).

[18] Cf. Diodorus Siculus 5.48.4: "Jupiter transmitted to him the rites of the mysteries that were celebrated in Samothrace in ancient times"; Strabo 10.3.7: "The authors of accounts of Cretan and Phrygian traditions (οἱ παραδόντες) and of the sacred rites (ἱερουργίαις) that they involve, which pertain to the celebration of the mysteries (ταῖς μυστικαῖς)"; the aretalogy of Isis (*I.Cumae*, n. 41, 36); *P.Lond.* 46, 335 (vol. 1, p. 75); *Pap.Graec.Mag.* 4, 475: παραδοτὰ μυστήρια; Eusebius, *Praep. Evang.* 2.8.3: τοὺς παραδεδομένους . . . μύθους. On the mystery tradition, cf. A. J. Festugière, *Idéal religieux*, p. 121, n. 4; D. B. Reynders, "Paradosis," in *Recherches de théologie ancienne et médiévale*, 1933, pp. 155–191; J. Dupont, *Gnosis*, Louvain, 1949, pp. 59–62.

fables[19] to the passing down of knowledge, of arts and letters,[20] of cultic ceremony (*To Gaius* 298: *thrēskeia;* cf. 237), and of the sacred books, "passed on for the use of those who are worthy of them" (*Moses* 2.11). Likewise Josephus, who speaks of passing on a password (*Ant.* 19.31, 188) and of history passing on memories for those who want to learn,[21] but especially the transmission of facts recorded in the sacred books (*Ant.* 2.347; 3.89); and of Moses as the one who transmitted the laws.[22]

In the NT, it is the first instance the divine revelation that is passed on: "Everything has been passed on to me by my Father (*panta moi paradothē hypo tou patros mou*), and no one knows the Son but the Father. . . ."[23] What is involved is (1) revelation (*apokalyptō*), (2) the transmission of knowledge (*epiginōskō*) that is (3) total or universal, the sum total of revealed doctrine. According to Luke 1:2, the facts of the gospel have been passed on to us (*kathōs paredosan hēmin*) by "those who were from the beginning eye-witnesses and servants of the word."[24] Believers are those who accept this testimony: "You were obedient from the heart to the rule of doctrine that was passed on to you" (*hypēkousate de ek kardias eis hon paredothēte typon*

---

[19] *Sacr. Abel and Cain* 76; *Plant.* 127; cf. *Decalogue* 55: "the names of the stars have been passed down by the mythographers"; *Change of Names* 95: envy, jealousy, disputes, and rivalries are "passed down" from parents to children.

[20] *Flight* 168–169, 200; *Sacr. Abel and Cain* 64, 78: "The ancient tradition of noble deeds that the historians and the whole tribe of poets have transmitted to the memory of contemporaries and of the generations that followed"; *Moses* 1.23; *Creation* 78: "men have passed on the art that is most necessary and most useful for life"; ibid., 159; *Drunkenness* 198; *Spec. Laws* 4.231.

[21] *Ant.* 1.12, 29, 73; 7.269, 454; 9.208; 15.425; 19.298; *Ag. Apion* 1.15; cf. *War* 6.105: "fame, passing from age to age and always fresh, transmits his immortal memory to posterity." Science and astronomy are transmitted (1.167; *Ag. Apion* 1.181), but also traditional superstitions concerning the deity (*Ag. Apion* 1.211). The Pharisees pass on to the people commandments that are not in the law of Moses (*Ant.* 13.297; 18.12).

[22] *Ant.* 3.280; 4.57, 302, 304; *Ag. Apion* 1.60: "Observing laws and pious practices that have been transmitted to us conformably to these laws, the most necessary work in life"; 2.279: we call time to witness for the virtue of our legislator and the revelation that he transmitted to us from God—time, which puts every undertaking to the test.

[23] Matt 11:27; Luke 10:22 (H. Mertens, *L'Hymne de jubilation chez les Synoptiques,* Gembloux, 1957, pp. 51ff.; *Recueil L. Cerfaux,* vol. 3, pp. 139–169). Jesus reproaches the Pharisees for annulling the word of God in favor of tradition (their school's teaching), "the tradition that you have handed down" (τῇ παραδόσει ὑμῶν ᾗ παρεδώκατε, Mark 7:13).

[24] The αὐτόπται and the ὑπηρέται, bearers of the tradition, *heard* the words with their ears and *saw* the acts of Jesus with their eyes (E. Delebecque, *Evangile de Luc,* on this text), and they transmitted them orally to a new generation of disciples (ἡμῖν).

didachēs).[25] "I praise you that in all things . . . you hold to the traditions as I passed them on to you" (*kathōs paredōka hymin tas paradoseis katechete,* 1 Cor 11:2); the traditions of the universal church, to which every believer must submit, have to do with doctrinal teaching, ethics, and discipline, and even usages and customs (the deportment of women in liturgical assemblies). Regarding traditions of worship and especially articles of faith—for example, the institution of the Eucharist—the apostle takes care not to claim paternity for himself (through personal revelation), and he emphasizes the origin: "I received (*parelabon*) from the Lord (*apo tou Kyriou*) the same thing that I passed on to you (*ho kai paredōka hymin*)."[26] Likewise the most primitive and most essential article of the *credo*, Christ the Redeemer: "I passed on to you in the first place what I myself received (*paredōka hymin en prōtois ho kai parelabon*), that Christ died for our sins . . . and was resurrected."[27] Finally, the whole content of the faith, that is, the whole truth revealed by God, is transmitted to the faithful by an immutable tradition, like a deposit entrusted lest it vary.[28]

---

[25] Rom 6:17. Τύπος means a body of teaching and moral rules conformable to Christ's teaching, a correct presentation of his doctrine. Cf. A. Fridrichsen, "Exegetisches zum Neuen Testament," in *ConNT*, vol. 7, 1942, pp. 6–8 (has in mind a Jewish technical term); J. Kürzinger, "Τύπος διδαχῆς und der Sinn von Rom. VI, 17," in *Bib*, 1958, pp. 156–176; F. W. Beare, "On the Interpretation of Romans VI, 17," in *NTS*, vol. 5, 1959, pp. 206–210; C. H. Dodd, "The Primitive Catechism and the Sayings of Jesus," in *Studies in Memory of T. W. Manson*, Manchester, 1959, pp. 106–118; U. Borse, " 'Abbild der Lehre' (Rom. VI, 17)," in *BZ*, 1968, pp. 95–103; C. Spicq, *Théologie morale*, vol. 2, p. 584, n. 1).

[26] 1 Cor 11:23. The apostle received it from the only authorized source, not by direct transmission (παρά), but through the channel of (apostolic) tradition, with its source or origin (ἀπό) in Jesus. He only delivered it, communicated it, entrusted it to the believers. O. G. Evenson, "The Force of 'Apo' in 1 Cor. XI, 23," in *Lutheran Quarterly*, 1959, pp. 244–246; G. Bornkamm, *Studien zu Antike und Urchristentum*, Munich, 1959, vol. 2, pp. 116ff. J. Jeremias, *Eucharistic Words*, pp. 129–131.

[27] 1 Cor 15:3. Cf. J. Schmitt, "Le 'Milieu' littéraire de la 'tradition' citée dans I Cor. XV, 3b–5," in E. Dhanis, *Resurrexit*, Vatican City, 1974, pp. 169–184.

[28] Jude 3: "I had to write you to exhort you to struggle for the faith delivered once for all to the saints" (τῇ ἅπαξ παραδοθείσῃ τοῖς ἁγίοις πίστει); 2 Pet 2:21—"It would have been better for them not to know (ἐπεγνωκέναι) the way of righteousness than having known it (ἐπιγνοῦσιν) to turn away from the holy commandment that was entrusted to them (ἐκ τῆς παραδοθείσης αὐτοῖς ἁγίας ἐντολῆς)." The baptismal *entolē* is faith in Christ and brotherly love, and also instruction in wisdom (Prov 2:1; Eccl 8:5), God's educative pedagogy (Prov 6:23; 19:6), the expression of his will becoming a moral rule (Ps 19:8; 119:98; Rom 7:12), the doctrine of the Revealer (John 16:48–49), and his sovereign authority (1 Tim 6:14), to which one submits by faith (2 John 6).

Paradidōmi in the NT is also a transmission of power. At the ascension, Jesus proclaims, "All power has been given to me (*edōthē moi pasa exousia*) in heaven and on earth."[29] Again, it is a passing down of property, entrusted with a view to its bearing fruit (Matt 25:14); also of civil and religious laws, institutions and rites which are supposed to be inviolable, and which were passed down by Moses (Acts 6:14, *ta ethē*); and finally the decrees or decisions of the Jerusalem Council, which Paul and Timothy passed along in the cities that they visited so that they would be observed (Acts 16:4, *ta dogmata*).

VI. — The predominant sense of *paradidōmi* (Hebrew *nātan*) in the OT is pejorative; God is almost always the subject, and very often the verb is reinforced with a prepositional phrase: God "is delivering into your hand" your adversaries, enemies, oppressors whom the Lord hands over unconditionally to his people.[30] It is an exceptional case when *paradidōmi* with this meaning has a favorable sense,[31] because one is normally "delivered" into subjection, troubles, evils, suffering, and woe—as when Job is given over to the power of Satan (*paradidōmi soi auton*, Job 2:6; *T. Job* 20.3) or Samson is given over into the hands of the Philistines (Judg 15:12; 16:23–24)—and especially to death;[32] but the links between this "delivering" and

---

[29] Matt 28:18 (cf. Dan 7:14—*kai edothē autō exousia*). In *Corp. Herm.* 1.32: "You are blessed, Father. The one who is your man wants to lend you aid in the work of sanctification, just as you transmitted all your power to him" (καθὼς παρέδωκας αὐτῷ τὴν πᾶσαν ἐξουσίαν). In Luke 4:6, Satan claims that "all power has been given to me" (ἐμοὶ παραδέδοται).

[30] Gen 14:20 (hiphil of Hebrew *nāgar*); Exod 23:31; Lev 26:25; Num 21:2, 34; Deut 1:27; 2:24, 30, 31, 33, 36; 3:2–3; 7:24; 21:10; 23:15; Josh 10:8; Judg 1:4; 4:14, Deborah to Barak: "Arise, for this is the day when the Yahweh has delivered Sisera into your hands"; 8:3; 1 Sam 23:4; 24:5; 2 Kgs 3:18; Ps 27:12; 51:2; 68:10 (they will be delivered into the hands of the sword); 74:19; 78:48; 119:121; Isa 19:4; 34:2; Dan 11:11. To be "delivered" is to be in someone else's power. Holofernes orders his servants to "hand over Achior to the sons of Israel" (Jdt 6:10); "Glorious men were delivered into the hands of others" (Sir 11:6).

[31] Deut 19:12—"The elders of the city shall deliver the murderer into the hands of the blood-avenger"; 1 Macc 15:21—the Roman consul Lucius decided that "pestilent people" will be "handed over to the high priest Simon, so that he may execute justice on them in the king's name."

[32] 1 Sam 11:12—"Deliver these men so that they may be put to death"; 2 Chr 32:11—"deliver to death (εἰς θάνατον) by hunger and thirst"; Jer 26:24; 38:16; Mic 6:14; Ps 118:18—"God has not delivered me to death" (θανάτῳ); 2 Macc 1:17—"May our God be blessed in all things, he who delivered the ungodly to death"; Philo, *Flight* 53: "If one man kills another because God put him in his power"; 65, 93; Josephus, *War* 6.360: a Roman horseman is "delivered to Ardalas to be put to death"; *Ant.* 6.215, Saul's intention is to have David judged and put to death" (παραδοὺς ἀποκτείνῃ); 8.390; 20.200—the Sanhedrin accuses James, the brother of Jesus, who is called

God and justice show that often punishment is involved, which is why he so often "delivered" the chosen people. "The children of Israel did that which was evil in the eyes of Yahweh and Yahweh delivered them into the hands of Midian for seven years";[33] "You have handed us over because of our sins" (Isa 64:6; Sir 4:19); "I hand you over for devastation" (Mic 6:16).

The NT inherits this theology: God gives up his people and lets them give themselves to the worship of stars;[34] he gives idolaters over to impurity and servitude to dishonorable passions,[35] and "he did not spare the angels who sinned, but handed them over to the dark dungeons of Tartarus, where he holds them in reserve for judgment."[36] In the same sense of the word, Paul hands over the incestuous Corinthian man to Satan—who will afflict him with sickness, frustrations, defeats, and ruin—"for the loss of his flesh";[37] or Hymenaeus and Alexander, who had shipwrecked their faith and were consigned to Satan "to learn not to blaspheme any longer."[38] Satan is as it were God's official agent of punishment, carrying out the

---

Christ, of having broken the law and condemns him to stoning; Ag. Apion 2.206: "The law delivers the guilty for stoning"; Life 425: "Vespasian condemned Jonathan to death and handed him over to be killed" (παραδοθεὶς ἀπέθανεν); Philo, Flacc. 96 (βασανισταῖς); Josephus, War 1.655; cf. delivering over to insults (2.246), deliver in chains (1.269; Ant. 5.313: δεδεμένον ἄγειν παρέδοσαν); Philo, Change of Names 173: δεσμωτηρίῳ παραδοῦναι; T. Abr. A 20 (delivered to the grave); Jos. Asen. 4.12 (into slavery).

[33] Judg 6:1; 2:14—"Yahweh's anger was inflamed against Israel, and he delivered them into the hands of marauders who pillaged them"; 13:1; 1 Sam 28:19; 1 Kgs 8:46; 14:16; 2 Kgs 21:14; 2 Chr 6:36; 24:24; 28:5, 9; Isa 65:12; Jer 22:25; Bar 4:6; Ezek 7:21; 11:9; 16:27, 39, etc.; Dan 1:2; Zech 11:6; Sir 23:6—"Do not deliver me to a shameless soul"; Job 16:11—"God delivers me to unrighteous people"; Ps 106:41; Josephus, War 4.370.

[34] Acts 7:42—παρέδωκεν αὐτοὺς λατρεύειν τῇ στρατιᾷ τοῦ οὐρανοῦ (cf. Ezek 20:7, 8, 13; Amos 5:25–27); punishment for worshiping the golden calf.

[35] Rom 1:24 (εἰς ἀκαθαρσίαν), 26 (εἰς πάθη ἀτιμίας), 28 (εἰς ἀδόκιμον νοῦν); Eph 4:19 (ἀσελγείᾳ). Moral disorder is a consequence of and punishment for religious error.

[36] 2 Pet 2:4. The dungeons of Tartarus, a prison, the deepest pit for pure spirits (Philo, Rewards 152); cf. C. Spicq, Épîtres de saint Pierre, on this text.

[37] 1 Cor 5:5. These "temporal" torments have as their end to provoke conversion and assure the salvation of the soul (J. Cambier, "La Chair et l'esprit en 1 Cor. V, 5," in NTS 15, 1969, pp. 221ff.). J. D. M. Derrett, " 'Handing over to Satan': An Explanation of I Cor. V, 1–7," in RIDA, 1979, pp. 11–30). Cf. C. Bruston, "L'Abandon du pécheur à Satan," in RTQR, 1912, pp. 450–458.

[38] 1 Tim 1:20; cf. C. Spicq, Épîtres Pastorales, on this text. T. C. G. Thornton, "Satan—God's Agent for Punishing," in ExpT 83, 1972, pp. 151ff.; J. Dauvillier, Les Temps apostoliques, Paris, 1970, pp. 585ff.

sentences of the heavenly Judge, just as the king handed over the merciless debtor to the torturers.[39]

What is new is that *paradidōmi* is made a technical term for Jesus' passion.[40] This verb is used by the Master in his predictions of his passion ("The Son of Man must be delivered into the hands of men")[41] and by the evangelists;[42] and St. Paul mentions it: "The Lord, on the night that he was handed over (*en tē nykti hē paredideto*) took bread. . . ."[43] The term is to be taken first in its legal and judicial sense,[44] but it conveys moreover a moral or psychological nuance and a theological value. *Paradosis* was also used for treason (*prodosia*). Judas Iscariot is always called *ho paradidous*, "the traitor,"[45] the one who betrays or betrayed Jesus. The verb rather often also connotes this nuance of criminality: desertion to another camp, breach of

---

[39] Matt 18:34—παρέδωκεν αὐτὸν τοῖς βασανισταῖς; cf. Philo, *Spec. Laws* 2.93–94; T. *Abr.* B 10; *SEG* VIII, 246, 8; *BGU* 1847, 26; *P.Ant.* 87, 13–14; C. Spicq, *Dieu et l'homme*, pp. 54ff.; J. D. M. Derrett, *Law in the NT*, pp. 32–47; R. Haase, "Körperliche Strafen in den altorientalischen Rechtssammlungen," in *RIDA*, 1963, pp. 55–75.

[40] W. Popkes, *Christus Traditus: Eine Untersuchung zum Begriff der Dahingabe im Neuen Testament*, Zurich-Stuttgart, 1967; N. Perrin, "The Use of (παρα)διδόναι in Connection with the Passion of Jesus in the New Testament," in *Der Ruf Jesu und die Antwort der Gemeinde* (Festschrift J. Jeremias), Göttingen, 1970, pp. 204–212.

[41] Matt 17:22 (Mark 9:31; Luke 9:44); Matt 20:18–19: "They will hand him over to the Gentiles to mock him" (Mark 10:33; Luke 18:32); Matt 26:2—"The Son of Man must be handed over to be crucified"; 26:45—"will be delivered into the hands of sinners" (Mark 14:41; Luke 24:7).

[42] Matt 27:26—"Pilate had Jesus whipped and handed him over to be crucified" (παρέδωκεν ἵνα σταυρωθῇ, Mark 15:15; John 19:16); Luke 23:25—"he handed Jesus over to their will."

[43] 1 Cor 11:23. The historical fact of the institution of the Eucharist is chronologically determined; this is a mention of the arrest of Jesus and "probably also of his betrayal" by Judas (A. Jaubert, *La Date de la Cène*, Paris, 1957, pp. 93ff.); but "it does not say 'the eve of his death' " (Jaubert, "Le Mercredi où Jésus fut livré," in *NTS*, vol. 14, 1968, pp. 145–164; G. Schille, "Das Leiden des Herrn," in *ZTK*, 1955, p. 181). Cf. *Gos. Pet.* 5: Herod "delivered [Jesus] to the people on the eve of Unleavened Bread, their feast."

[44] Cf. Matt 4:12, John the Baptist had been handed over to Herod Antipas; Mark 1:14; Acts 8:3—Saul dragged off men and women and had them thrown in prison (εἰς φυλακήν); 12:4 (the incarceration of Peter); 21:11 (Paul will be handed over to Gentiles); 28:17.

[45] In the list of the apostles, Matt 10:4—"Judas Iscariot, the same one who betrayed him" (ὁ καὶ παραδοὺς αὐτόν) (Mark 3:19); 26:15—"What will you give me, and I will betray him" (παραδώσω αὐτόν, 26:16, 21, 23, 24, 25, 46, 48); 27:3–4: "I sinned in handing over innocent blood"; Mark 14:10, 11, 18, 21, 42, 44; Luke 22:4, 6, 21, 22, 48; John 6:64, 71; 12:4; 13:2, 11, 21; 18:2, 5, 36; 19:11; 21:20.

sworn faith, betrayal of someone's trust.[46] It is certain that the first Christians saw Christ's crucifixion less as an atrociously painful form of torture than as an ignominy and a result of perfidy.[47] To say that Jesus was handed over, then, means that he was betrayed.

Moreover, *paradidōmi* is also used for people who give themselves in self-sacrifice for God or neighbor, like Shadrach, Meshach, and Abednego, who "delivered their bodies rather than serve and worship any other god than their God."[48] And it was predicted that the Servant of Yahweh would be handed over to death for redemption from sins (Isa 53:6, 12). This religious meaning is inseparable from *paradidōmi* in the death of Jesus: God gave him over (Rom 4:25; 8:32), or he gave himself over (Gal 2:20), offering himself as a sacrifice of acceptable savor (Eph 5:2, *hyper hēmōn*, "for us"). The accent is as much on the love that inspires this offering as on the totality of the gift and its cost: our redemption. Consequently to "deliver oneself" to God or neighbor becomes a major principle of Christian ethics.[49]

---

[46] Josephus, *War* 4.523: "Jacob told Simon that he would betray his country to him, on the basis of the promise that he would always continue to enjoy honors"; 6.387–391: a priest hands over objects from the sacred treasury in order to save his life; *Ant.* 5.131; 6.345. In his edict, Tiberius Julius Alexander denounces certain functionaries who, "on the pretext of state interests, having others' credits ceded to themselves, have had certain persons incarcerated in the *praktoreion* (a prison reserved for debtors to the treasury) and in other prisons" (Dittenberger, *Or.* 669, 15). In the time of the persecutions, people become public accusers or witnesses against members of their own families in order to save their lives: "Brother will hand over brother to death, and a father his children . . ." (Matt 10:21; 24:10; Mark 13:12; Luke 21:16).

[47] Cf. Matt 27:18—"Pilate knew that they were handing him over because of jealousy"; Mark 15:10; Acts 3:13 (Peter to the Jerusalemites): "Jesus, whom you handed over and whom you denied before Pilate," the accursed occupier.

[48] Dan 3:28; Josephus, *Ant.* 2.137: Joseph's brothers offer themselves to be punished in order to save Benjamin; 148, 159; 10.230: Jechonias "voluntarily gave himself up (παραδόντι . . . ἐκουσίως αὐτόν) with his wives and his children in order to save his native city (ὑπὲρ τῆς πατρίδος)"; cf. 9.75; *War* 6.433. Objects are given over or consecrated εἰς λειτουργίαν οἴκου θεοῦ (2 Esdr 7:19); the Levites set apart the whole burnt offerings "to give them to the children of the people" (2 Chr 35:12), and Yahweh "gives over as victims" the cities and peoples of Palestine.

[49] Acts 15:26—Barnabas and Paul, "men who have given over their lives for the Name of our Lord Jesus Christ," do not hesitate to risk death in proclaiming the saving divinity of Jesus; 2 Cor 4:11—"We who continue to live are delivered to death (εἰς θάνατον παραδιδόμεθα) because of Jesus" (διά indicates the reason); Eph 5:25— "Husbands, love your wives, as Christ loved the church and gave himself for it." Love made manifest and effective—which is what *agapē* is—is translated in Christ by a total and definitive act of giving that involves forgetfulness of self and limitless devotion to his church (cf. C. Spicq, *Agapè*, vol. 1, pp. 285–294); thus by virtue of his marriage the husband no longer belongs to himself but is at his wife's service, devoted to her

VII. — *Paradidōmi* often has the judicial meaning "deliver to court or to prison." In 248 BC, Pyrrhus wrote to Zeno: "Know that Etearchos delivered me to the *praktōr* on the tenth of Epeiph" (*P.Mich.* 58, 6; cf. "to the *nomophylax*," *P.Oxy.* 3190, 3); "If you arrest the slave, hand him over to Semphtheus, who will bring him to me" (*P.Hib.* 54, 21; 245 BC); "Send us under good guard the woman who gave you the contraband oil in her possession" (*P.Hib.* 59, 3); "Deliver Pamoun to the police officer whom I have sent."[50] Likewise, the princes of the priests and the elders of the people led and delivered Jesus to Pilate (Matt 27:2; Mark 15:1; cf. John 18:30, 35); the scribes and the chief priests appoint men "to deliver him to the power and authority of the governor" (Luke 20:20; cf. 24:20, *eis krima thanatou*); Paul and certain other prisoners are remanded to the care of a centurion (Acts 27:1); "Pilate gave them the centurion Petronius and some soldiers to guard the tomb" (*Gos. Pet.* 31). The apostles will be handed over before courts (Matt 10:17, 19, *eis synedria*; cf. 24:9; Mark 13:9, 11; Luke 21:12), and every debtor is exhorted to be reconciled with his creditor before the latter delivers him to the judge (*tō kritē*) and the judge to the officer (*tō hypēretē*), lest he be thrown in prison.[51]

---

happiness; "no one lives for himself" (Rom 14:7–8); it is like a religious consecration, according to the model of Christ, who was entirely given over to those who are his.

[50] *P.Cair.Isid.* 129, 2; *P.Berl.Zill.* 8, 23: place in the hands of the police. There is also εἰς φυλακὴν παραδιδότωσαν (*SEG* 9.5.67); παράδος τοῖς φυλακίταις (*BGU* 1912, 3; *P.Lille* 3, 59; *UPZ* 124, 19); παραδώσων ἐν δημοσίῳ τόπῳ (*P.Mert.* 98, 13; *P.Oxy.* 2478, 24; 3204, 20; *P.Brem.* 26, 4; 41, 29).

[51] Matt 5:25; cf. Luke 12:58. J. Vergote, "Le Nouveau Testament et la papyrologie juridique," in *Eos* (Symbolae R. Taubenschlag), 1957, vol. 2, pp. 152ff.

παραθήκη

parathēkē, **deposit**

In the Pastorals, St. Paul three times uses the expression *parathēkēn phylassein*,[1] in a metaphorical sense, in accord with contemporary usage, because not only was money entrusted to the care of a third party,[2] but so

---

[1] 1 Tim 6:20; 2 Tim 1:14 (where the deposit is modified by καλός, i.e., precious or magnificent, because it is God's deposit; cf. similarly Philo, *Worse Attacks Better* 65); at 1:12 it is not entirely clear whether the "depositor" is God or Paul (cf. C. Spicq, *Epîtres Pastorales*, vol. 2, pp. 719ff.). Classical Greek has παρακαταθήκη (cf. Phrynichus, ed. Lobeck, p. 313). The verb παραθεκάζω means "pay a παραθήκη" (G. E. Bean, T. B. Mitford, *Cilicia*, n. 202, 10). The technical term θέμα was used for the deposit of grain in the public granary (*P.Oxy.* 501, 517, 518, 1444; *P.Mert.* 14; *P.Stras.* 127; *P.Lips.* 112–117): ἐν θέματι δημοσίῳ (*BGU* 2126, 12–14); cf. N. Hohlwein, *Termes techniques*, pp. 267ff. M. Lewis, "Notationes legentis," in *BASP*, vol. 13, 1976, pp. 167ff.

[2] *SB* 9291; 10722, 6; *BGU* 2042; *P.Fam.Tebt.* 2; *P.Tebt.* 556 (from AD 33, ed. J. G. Keenan, "Two Papyri from the University of California Collection," in *Proceedings* XIII, pp. 207ff.). Δεπόσιτα were cash deposits made by soldiers who received a bonus, cf. Ign. *Pol.* 6.2. The papyrological attestations are considerable; cf. "St. Paul et la loi des dépôts," in *RB*, 1931, pp. 481–502. For example, cf. *P.Lond.* 298 (vol. 2, p. 206): "The eighth year of Caesar Trajan Hadrian Augustus, the fifth of the month of Gorpiaeus, at Ptolemaïs Euergetis, in the nome of Arsinoïte. Primus Samba, son of Primus, of Persian descent, about fifty-five years old, having a scar on the front of his left leg, declares to Heraclides, son of Treadelphos son of Anoubion, of the deme of Ailanabatis, which is also Althaea, about twenty-five years old, having a scar on his right wrist, that he holds from this latter—he, Primus, the author of the contract— through the bank of Dionysius, which is also Chaeremon, on the street of the Sacred Gate, two thousand silver drachmas, as a surety deposit against all resk and exempt from any charge. As for the two thousand drachmas of the deposit, Primus acknowledges that he must return them to Heraclides whenever Heraclides chooses, without recourse to legal action or judgment or any other delay of any sort or any subterfuges. If he does not turn it over in accord with what is written, he must pay Heraclides double the deposit, in accord with the law of deposits." Cf. R. Taubenschlag, *Law of Greco-Roman Egypt*, vol. 1, pp. 264ff. E. Kiessling, "Über den Rechtsbegriff der

---

parathēkē, S 3866; *TDNT* 8.162–164; *EDNT* 3.22; MM 483–484; L&N 35.48; BAGD 616; ND 2.85

could be a person (*P.Oxy.* 2600, 7; cf. 1 Pet 4:19; *Jos. Asen.* 13.11–12) or a harvest of grain (*P.Oxy.* 3049) or of words, i.e., secrets.[3] According to Philo, the divine gifts entrusted to humans are like deposits that must be guarded carefully,[4] especially in carrying out a public (*Spec. Laws* 4.71) and sacred function: "Not everyone gets to guard the deposit of the divine mysteries" (*Sacr. Abel and Cain* 60, *parakatathēkēn phylaxai*). In this sense the Jews received the oracles of God as a deposit (Rom 3:2).

Ulpian would later define this term contract, the establishment of which required no formality other than the freely expressed consent of the one accepting the deposit: "that which is placed in someone else's custody" ("quod custodiendum alicui datum");[5] the object is deposited for its protection. It remains the property of the depositor;[6] it does not belong to the

---

Parathèkè," in *Proceedings* VIII, pp. 71–77; P. Frezza, "ΠΑΡΑΚΑΤΑΘΗΚΗ," in *Eos* (Symbolae R. Taubenschlag), 1956, vol. 1, pp. 139–172; A. Ehrhardt, "Parakatatheke," in *Zeitschrift der Savigny-Stiftung*, 1958, pp. 32–90; 1959, pp. 480–489; K. Kastner, *Die zivilrechtliche Verwahrung des gr.-ägypt. Obligationenrechts*, Erlangen, 1962; K. Wegenast, *Das Verständnis der Tradition bei Paulus*, Neukirchen, 1962, pp. 144ff. H. A. Rupprecht, *Studien zur Quittung im Recht der graeco-ägyptischen Papyri*, Munich, pp. 51ff. W. Hellebrand, "Parakatheke," in PW, vol. 18, 2, col. 1186–1202. On the irregular deposit (authorization to use money, collection of interest, etc.), cf. W. Litewski, "Le Dépôt irrégulier," in *RIDA*, 1974, pp. 215–262; 1975, pp. 279–315.

[3] Philo, *Prov.* 2.16; *Worse Attacks Better* 65: "Watching (or guarding) is something that is complete, which consists in committing to memory principles of holy things learned by practice. That is what is means to entrust a noble deposit of learning to a faithful guardian." Herodotus 9.45.1; Anaxandrides, in Stobaeus (*Flor.* 41.2; vol. 3, p. 757). Secrets are "word deposits" (Ps.-Isocrates, *Demon.* 22); Ps.-Plutarch, *Cons. ad Apoll.* 28: life is a deposit that must be returned when the gods ask for it. Cf. Isocrates 1.22. In the Hermetic literature, the sacred Book or "Monad" or "Eighth Book of Moses," on the holy Name, holds as a deposit the name of the Lord (*Pap.Graec.Mag.* 13, 742 = vol. 2, p. 121); cf. A. J. Festugière, *Hermès Trismégiste*, vol. 1, pp. 344–345.

[4] *Heir* 104: "Consider that which has been given you to be a loan or a deposit and return it to the one who entrusted and loaned it to you"; 105–106: "Let the one who made the deposit have no reason for criticizing the manner in which you kept it. For the creator of life has entrusted you with the deposit of a soul, of speech, of sensation. . . . Some people immediately divert these deposits to their own profit through selfishness; others on the contrary hold them back in order to make restitution at the most appropriate time."

[5] *Dig.* 16.3.1 proem.; Diodorus Siculus 17.23.5. Aristotle placed it among the συναλλάγματα ἑκουσία (*Eth. Nic.* 5.1131ª4). Someone leaves a deposit with someone else (*I.Thas.* 376, 3–4), a receipt is given: ὁμολογῶ ἔχειν παρὰ σοῦ ἐν παραθήκη κ.τ.λ. (*P.Mich.* IX, 571, 7 = *SB* 9247); *P.Brem.* 51, 9; *P.Hib.* 198, 196; *P.Mert.* 67, 14; *BGU* 1653, 12; *P.IFAO* III, n. 1 (AD 100); restored, *P.Oxy.* 2975.

[6] The law from Ephesus from 85 BC lists types of debt: maritime loans, unsecured loans, deposits in the form of pledged real estate (παραθῆκαι), mortgages, second mortgages, etc. (Dittenberger, *Syl.* 742, 50ff., with the commentary of R. Bogaert,

depository, and the depositary cannot dispose of it. Not only must he guard
it "like something sacred and divine" (Josephus, *Ant.* 4.285), but he must
immediately return it intact when asked, without delay or discussion.[7] This
is the meaning of the constant repeated appearance in the contracts of the
phrase "according to the law of deposits."[8] In addition, Ps.-Plato gave this
definition: *parakatathēkē: doma meta pisteōs* (*Def.* 415 d). Whether a literal or
a metaphorical deposit is intended, the emphasis is always on the good faith
and fidelity of the depositary: "The setting up of a deposit is the most sacred
thing done in social life, because it depends on the good faith of the
depositary."[9] Thus the protection of the gods is invoked,[10] and it was
common to deposit valuables in the temples, which became savings

---

Banques et banquiers, p. 251; H. Kühnert, *Zum Kreditgeschäft in den hellenistischen Papyri
Ägyptens,* Freiburg, 1965; P. Drewes, "Die Bankdiagraphe in den gräko-ägyptischen
Papyri," in *JJP,* 1974, pp. 107, 136ff.).

[7] Almost all the contracts mention the integrity, ἄνευ πάσης ὑπερθέσεως καὶ
εὑρησιλογίας; *P.Alex.* 10, 10 (AD 69–79); *P.Mert.* 67, 17; *Pap.Lugd.Bat.* I, 6, 15–19;
P.Tebt. 386, 22 (12 BC); 556, 13–16; *P.Oxy.* 71, 6 (ἀκίνδυνον καὶ ἀνυπόλογον); 1713, 10;
3049, 14; *BGU* 637, 702, 729, 856; *SB* 11040, etc. Cf. the precision and the fullness of
the attestation, and the restoration of a deposit in the second century, *P.Oxy.* 2975;
cf. N. Lewis, "Notationes legentis," in *BASP,* vol. 11, 1974, pp. 59–59.

[8] Κατὰ τὸν νόμον τῶν παραθηκῶν; *P.Lond.* 943, 9; *P.Ryl.* 662, 15; *P.Oxy.* 1039, 12;
2677, 6; 3134, 9; *P.Athen.* 28, 24 (October 16, 86); *P.Tebt.* 556, 17; *Stud.Pal.* XX, 45, 9;
cf. 2 Macc 3:15. J. Modrzejewski, "La Règle de droit dans l'Egypte ptolémaïque," in
Essays in Honor of C. Bradford Welles (American Studies in Papyrology, vol. 1), New
Haven, 1966, p. 156; W. D. Roth, *Untersuchungen zur Kredit-ΠΑΡΑΘΗΚΗ im römischen
Ägypten,* Marburg, 1970; H. C. Youtie, "P. Michig. inv. 829: ΠΑΡΑΘΗΚΗ," in *ZPE,* vol.
24, 1977, pp. 125–127; *P.Mich.* 671 (gives the bibliography, p. 111).

[9] Philo, *Spec. Laws* 4.30; cf. 4.32: "The person who contests the existence of a
deposit (that has been entrusted to him) should know that he is committing a major
crime in cheating the depositor, in disguising the villainy of his own character with
specious words, in camouflaging his disloyalty with a mask of false loyalty, and finally
in destroying the agreement that he sealed with his own hand, and along with it the
usefulness of oaths; so that he ridicules human and divine law and renegs on two
deposits: that of the friend who entrusted his wealth to him, and that of the eminently
truthful Witness who sees the actions and hears the words of all"; *Unchang. God* 101,
cf. *Plant.* 101; *Cherub.* 14. Hence the scandal of a depositary who takes advantage of
the ignorance of a depositor (illiterate and not having understood the text of the
contract) and refuses to pay back the deposit, as Aurelius Sotas did to Aurelius
Demetrius, who in turn lodged a complaint with the prefect (*P.Oxy.* 71, 10–11). The
association of παραθήκη with πίστις is constant; cf. Epictetus 4.13.13: "You trusted
a faithful man"; Dio Chrysostom 31.65. St. Ambrose, the lawyer, comments on 2 Tim
1:14—"Fides pignori prima debetur" (on Luke 1:12); the historian Conon, in the first
century (in *F.Gr.H.,* vol. 1, p. 204).

[10] Philo, *Spec. Laws* 4.34. Theogenes invokes Thea and Helios against a woman
who stole his savings, which were deposited with her (*I.Delos* 2531); cf. *I.Lind.* 419, 2:
περὶ τὰς παρακαταθήκας τὰς Ἀθάνας (AD 22); Lucian, *Symp.* 22.

banks;[11] such was the case with, among others, the temple at Jerusalem[12] and the Artemision of Ephesus.[13] People often left agreements, documents,[14] and especially wills[15] in these places of safety. The word *parathēkē*, not found in other Pauline letters, fits quite well in 1 and 2 Timothy, which are precisely Paul's last will and testament, instructing his favorite disciple to preserve intact and inviolable the wealth of teaching that he has passed on to him throughout his life.

Sometimes this *parathēkē* has teen taken to mean the pastoral office entrusted to the Ephesian pastor; but in the context of these two epistles, it is much more likely that it refers to the preservation of the "wholesome teaching" (*hygiēs didaskalia*)[16] which must be kept from the degradations or corruptions of heterodoxy. The disciple can draw on supernatural resources for preserving the gospel[17] and the tradition and sheltering them from adulteration, namely, the Holy Spirit who indwells us (2 Tim 1:14) and is supposed to act with particular efficacy in the organs of the ecclesiastical hierarchy.

---

[11] *P.Ross.Georg.* II, 18, 65 and 94; *I.Lind.* II B 43; Dittenberger, *Syl.* 1005, 1015, 1039; cf. ἀμετάθετα δηνάρια (*I.Did.* 331, 7); *LSAM*, p. 38; *LSAMSup*, n. 90, 2; idem, *LSCG*, p. 271; cf. T. R. S. Broughton, "New Evidence on Temple-Estates in Asia Minor," in P. R. Coleman-Norton, *Studies . . . in Honor of A. C. Johnson*, Princeton, 1951, pp. 236–250; H. Vidal, "Le Dépôt 'in Aede,' " in *RHDFE*, 1955, pp. 545–587; C. Préaux, "De la Grèce classique à l'Egypte hellénistique," in *ChrEg*, 1958, pp. 243–255; N. G. Hamilton, "Temple Clearing and Temple Bank," in *JBL*, 1964, pp. 365–370; R. Bogaert, *Les Origines antiques de la banque de dépôt*, Leiden, 1966, N. 97, 130, *passim*.

[12] 2 Macc 3:10–15; 4 Macc 4:3–7; cf. M. Delcor, "Le Trésor de la maison de Yahweh," in *VT*, 1962, pp. 353–377.

[13] Cf. C. Picard, *Ephèse et Claros*, Paris, 1922, pp. 82–90; R. Bogaert, *Banques et banquiers*, pp. 245ff., 263, 331ff.

[14] With respect to the libraries of the Ptolemies, Zosimus writes: "Some of these writings were deposited in each temple, particularly in the Sarapieion" (cited by A. J. Festugière, *Hermès Trismégiste*, vol. 1, p. 268, 10).

[15] Caesar (Suetonius, *Iul.* 83), Augustus (idem, Suetonius, *Aug.* 101; Dio Cassius 56.32), and probably Tiberius and Claudius (Dio Cassius 59.1; 61.1) left their wills at the temple of Vesta. Cf. Ulpian, *Dig.* 43.5.3; 28.4.4; F. Dumont, "Le Testament d'Antoine," in *Mélanges Lévy-Bruhl*, Paris, 1959, pp. 87ff. *RIJG*, vol. 1, p. 113, vol. 2, pp. 69ff.

[16] 1 Tim 1:10; 6:3; Titus 1:9, 13; 2:1, 2, 8; 2 Tim 1:13; 4:3. Cf. S. Cipriani, "La dottrina del depositum," in AnBib 17–18; Rome 1963, vol. 2, pp. 128–140; P. Médebielle, "Dépôt de la foi," in *DBSup*, vol. 2, 374–395.

[17] Cf. 1 Tim 1:11—"The gospel of the glory of the blessed God that has been entrusted to me"; cf. 2 Tim 2:8; 3:10; Col 1:25ff.

παρακοή

parakoē, **disobedience**

→see also εἰσακούω, ἐπακούω, ὑπακούω, ὑπακοή

Unlike the verb *parakouō*, which occurs rather commonly, the substantive *parakoē* is rare. It is unknown in the LXX and in the papyri earlier than the eighth century.[1] The word would hardly be worth discussing except for its theological importance in Rom 5:19. After characterizing Adam's sin (*hē hamartia*, verse 12) as a transgression (*hē parabasis*, verse 14) and a false step (*paraptōma*, verses 15–18; cf. Wis 10:1), St. Paul defines it as disobedience (*parakoē*), the original human transgression, punishable by death:[2] "Just as through the disobedience of one man (*dia tēs parakoēs*) all became sinners, so also through the obedience of one (*dia tēs hypakoēs*) will all be justified."[3] This disobedience of Adam, the antithesis of Christ's obedience,[4] has as its effect the constituting of humankind as a race of sinners. "The notion of original sin is affirmed again, because *kathistēmi*, 'institute, constitute, establish,' indicates more than a juridical assessment."[5]

---

[1] *P.Lond.* IV, 1345, 36; 1393, 52, cited by Moulton-Milligan, remain the only known occurrences; cf. the new and much improved edition of the latter papyrus in *SB* 7241; παρακοή is associated with καταφρόνησις, "scorn."

[2] Cf. A. M. Dubarle, "Le Péché originel dans saint Paul," in *RSPT*, 1956, pp. 213–254; S. Lyonnet, "Le Péché originel et l'exégèse de Rom. V, 12–14," in *RSR*, 1956, pp. 63–84.

[3] Rom 5:19. οἱ πολλοί = πάντες; the multitude means the crowd, the group as a whole; like the "many" at Qumran; cf. CD 14.6; 15.8; R. Marcus, "Mebaqqer and Rabbin in the Manual of Discipline VI, 11–13" in *JBL*, 1956, pp. 298–302; H. Huppenbauer, "רי״ב, רב, רבים in der Sektenregel (1QS)," in *TZ*, 1957, pp. 136–137; J. Jeremias, "πολλοί," in *TDNT*, vol. 6, pp. 536–545.

[4] Ὑπακοή, as at Heb 5:8, is acquiescence (cf. the obedience of the faith, Rom 1:5; to the truth, 1 Pet 1:22). In submitting to divine revelation (1 Pet 1:2, 14), the Gentiles become children of obedience; whereas they were formerly ἐν τῇ ἀγνοίᾳ.

[5] M. J. Lagrange, *Romains*, pp. 111ff.; Cf. F. J. Leenhardt, *Romans*, p. 147–148.

---

parakoē, S 3876; *TDNT* 1.223; *EDNT* 3.29; *NIDNTT* 2.172, 175; MM 485; L&N 36.27; BAGD 618

While *sin* or *transgression* can mean the violation of a law, the failure to observe a commandment, *parakoē* expresses above all a refusal to listen, turning a deaf ear.[6] This etymological nuance is retained in Heb 2:2, where because the *logos* pronounced by the angels was valid (*bebaios*), i.e., authoritative and obligatory, all corruption, whether commission (*parabasis*, Rom 2:23; Gal 2:15) or omission (*parakoē*, the willful and culpable refusal to take the divine word into consideration) was sanctioned by a just penalty.[7]

In 2 Cor 10:6, as in Rom 5:19, *hē parakoē* is contrasted with *hē hypakoē*; the apostle will punish all disobedience—those who do not submit to his oral teachings and precepts—once the obedience or submission of the community is complete, i.e., firm and unanimous.[8]

---

[6] Cf. Jer 11:10; 35:17; Acts 7:57 (συνέσχον τὰ ὦτα); Matt 18:17 (παρακούω); C. Spicq, *Théologie morale*, vol. 2, p. 592ff.

[7] Ἔνδικον μισθαποδοσίαν. This compound, unknown in biblical and secular Greek, emphasizes the direct correlation (confirmed by ἔνδικος) between the sin and the punishment; the retribution is deserved and required (Heb 3:17; 8:9; 10:28; Gal 6:7–8).

[8] J. Héring (*La Second Epître de saint Paul aux Corinthiens*, Neuchâtel-Paris, 1958, p. 79) gives the aorist πληρωθῇ an inchoative sense, taking it to mean "when the time has come to make your submission effective and complete, then there will be *ekdikēsis*, if there is occasion."

παραμυθέομαι, παραμυθία, παραμύθιον

paramytheomai, **to advise, encourage, console, comfort;** *paramythia,* **comfort, encouragement, support;** *paramythion,* **comfort, encouragement**

A compound of the rare denominative verb *mytheomai*, "speak, retell, converse,"[1] and the prefix *para*,[2] the verb *paramytheomai* belongs especially to cultivated Greek.[3] In the Hellenistic period it almost always has affective connotations, with the highly nuanced meanings of "advise, encourage, console, comfort, speak calming words to, appease, soothe."

I. — A number of these occurrences have no particularized meaning,[4] but most are found in a context of trials, difficulties, or sor-

---

[1] Cf. H. Fournier, *Les Verbes "dire,"* pp. 49, 215.

[2] Which allowed the translation *alloquor* (cf. French "allocution") as in the Old Latin (at John 11:31); cf. P. Joüon, "Explication de la nuance méliorative des verbes tels que alloquor, παραμυθέομαι," in *RSR*, 1938, pp. 311–314; Stählin, on this word, in *TDNT*, vol. 5, pp. 816–823.

[3] The references for classical Greek are given by Stählin, loc. cit., and C. Spicq, *Agapè*, vol. 2, pp. 252–265. Alexander sends one of his friends to comfort the wife and mother of Darius (Diodorus Siculus 17.37.3); "They would have for their consolation in their misfortune the similar fate of their companions" (17.69.6). In desperate straits, Demetrius wanted to kill himself. "Nevertheless his friends surrounded him and tried to comfort him" (παραμυθούμενοι, Plutarch, *Demetr.* 49.9).

[4] Cf. Epictetus 4.1.13: "That Caesar is the common master of all should not be a consolation for you (μηδέν σε τοῦτο παραμυθέσθω); you must admit that you are a slave in a large household"; Plutarch, *Quaest. conv.* 1.1.2: "We would have an excellent way of consoling ourselves for our ignorance" (τῆς ἀμαθίας παραμύθιον); 2.1.2: in telling what they have seen, the travelers find "a compensation for their troubles"

---

paramytheomai, S 3888; *TDNT* 5.816–823; *EDNT* 3.32; *NIDNTT* 1.328–329; MM 488; L&N 25.153; BAGD 620 ‖ *paramythia,* S 3889; *TDNT* 5.816–823; *EDNT* 3.32; *NIDNTT* 1.328–329; MM 488; L&N 25.154; BAGD 620 ‖ *paramythion,* S 3890; *TDNT* 5.816–823; *EDNT* 3.32; *NIDNTT* 1.328–329; MM 488; L&N 25.154; BDF §111(4); BAGD 620–621; ND 3.79; 4.14, 166

row.[5] One goes to the troubled person *eis paramythion* (*SB* 10652 B 10; beginning of secondcentury; *I.Lind.* 441, 9: *eis paramythian tou patros*), to console or to comfort.[6] Calm and gentle speech can reassure the heart (*P.Ryl.* 653, 6), dissipate fear (Plutarch, *Alc.* 13.6; *Sert.* 16.2: *epeirato paramytheisthai dia logōn*—"he tried to console with words"), comfort the afflicted (Lucian, *Peregr.* 13). Thus many Jews from Jerusalem "had come to Martha and Mary to console them concerning their brother" (*hina paramythēsōntai autas peri tou adelphou*, John 11:19, 31). We know that consolation, which was practiced among the rabbis as among the Greeks and Romans, was considered a "work of love";[7] but the Johannine use of *paramytheomai* for consolation is in accord with contemporary usage, since this verb and the nouns derived from it apply especially to consolation and comfort concerning a death.[8] It is likely that these visitors

---

(τῶν πόνων παραμυθίαν); *Luc.* 44.3: leisure, calm, the study of letters are the consolation that is most fitting for an old man; *De laude* 2 (539 *e*), *De sera* 13 (557 *f*), *Alex.* 30.10: "Tireos begged him not to take away his greatest consolation in his troubles." Hence the nuance "provide help" (for the saving of the city, *I.Bulg.* XIII, 28, προσπαραμυθούμενος); wealth makes up for the deficiencies of old age (Musonius 17, ed. C. E. Lutz, p. 110, 20; cf. 9, p. 68, 1); *BGU* 1024, col. VIII, 11–21: help from the law for victims, τοῦ βίου παραμυθίαν (fourth-fifth century); cf. R. Taubenschlag, *Opera Minora,* vol. 2, p. 555; *P.Flor.* 332, 19: ἵνα ἔχω παραμύθιον τῆς προελεύσεώς μου (second century); *P.Oxy.* 1298, 2: "To my incomparable master, the consolation of his friends."

[5] Job: "The kings came . . . to visit me and comfort me," *T. Job* 28.2; cf. 34.2, 5; Symmachus ordinarily translates the Hebrew *nāham* with παραμυθέομαι; cf. H. van Dyke Parunak, "A Semantic Survey of *Nāham,*" in *Bib,* 1975, pp. 512–532). Lucian, *Nav.* 14: "I have come to console you in your misfortune"; Plutarch, *Per.* 15.2: console the discouraged; *Amat.* 22: παραμυθία τοῦ πάθους; *De Is. et Os.* 27: Through initiation into his mysteries, Osiris establishes "a lesson in piety and encouragement for men and women who may fall into like adversities"; Dio Chrysostom 30.6; *P.Ross.Georg.* III, 3, 2 and 19 (third century); *IGLAM* 114, 7: τῆς ἐπ᾽ ἐμοὶ λύπης παραμύθιον ἐμ φρεσὶ θέσθε τοῦτον (republished by G. Kaibel, *Epigrammata* 298).

[6] Funerary honors are often presented in the inscriptions as expressions of consolation. At Thessalonica, the city honors the young Claudius Rufrius "for the consolation of his father" (εἰς παραμυθίαν τοῦ πατρός, *IG* X, part II, fasc. 1, n. 173, 15), or wishes to honor and console the father and the grandfather of Baebia Heliodora (τειμῆς καὶ παραμυθίας τῆς περὶ αὐτοὺς χάριν, ibid. 180, 14–16); cf. 207, 13.

[7] 4 Ezra 10:49—"She was mourning her son, and you went to console her"; *MAMA* VIII, 408, 11; 409, 4 and 8; 412, *a* 11, *b* 15, *c* 16; cf. Str-B, "Excursus 23: Die altjüdischen Liebeswerke," vol. 4, pp. 582–607; Ps.-Plutarch, *Cons. ad Apoll.* 2, 6, 7, 9, 32, 37. Seneca, *Marc., Helv., Polyb.,* etc. K. Buresch, *Consolationum a Graecis Romanisque scriptarum historia critica,* Leipzig, 1886; R. Kassel, *Untersuchungen zur griechischen und römischen Konsolationsliteratur,* Munich, 1958.

[8] Xenophon, *Ap.* 26: "I have another consolation, the memory of Palamedes, whose death was like mine"; Philo, *Abraham* 196: "joys that considerably lighten (οὐ

from Jerusalem gave the sisters at Bethany reasons to hope (cf. John 11:22–27); in any case, hope and consolation go together in a large number of texts.[9] Finally, we should note that the term *psēphismata paramythētica* ("decrees of consolation") is used for decrees that are intended both to honor a deceased person and to console the grieving family.[10]

μικρὰ παραμύθια) the sorrow connected with the memory of the child who was sacrificed"; Josephus, *Ant.* 15.61: Herod consoled the grieving women with splendid funerals; 20.94: Helen, deeply grieved by the death of Izates, finds consolation (παραμυθία) in learning that her eldest son will be the heir; *War* 1.627: "Antipater consoled me in the sorrow I felt for the victims"; 3.194: for the inhabitants of Jotapata, "even if they must die, Josephus will be their highest consolation" (παραμυθία); 6.183: "It was a consolation for the dying soldiers to see the sadness of the one in whose service they had given their lives"; 7.392: "the thought of the evils that they would have to endure at the enemy's hand [the Roman army] was a consolation (παραμύθιον) to them [the Jews at Masada] for having to kill them [their wives and children]"; Thucydides 2.44.1: "I offer not so much pity as consolation to the parents (of the dead)"; Dio Chrysostom 27.9. Hence the epitaphs, for example that of the silversmith Canopus: "Here stands this spotless monument, thanks to the care of my wife, a consolation from the one who shared my life" (παραμυθία συνζοίης, E. Bernand, *Inscriptions métriques*, n. 19, 10); of an anonymous deceased nineteen-year-old from the imperial period, who addresses his father: "As consolation, I address this to you" (τοῦτο δέ σοι πέμπω παραμύθιον, ibid. LXXV, 13); of an Egyptian ephebe (πατρὸς καὶ μητρὸς Στρατόλας παραμύθιον εἶναι, G. Kaibel, *Epigrammata* 951, 4); cf. *GVI*, n. 811, 7: οὐδὲν δ' ἐξεύροντο κακοῦ παραμύθιον οἴκτου (Cyprian funerary stele from the first century); 1198, 13; 1499, 2: "Child you were a source of consolation for your parents"; *SB* 4313, 11 (first-second century). According to *T. Abr.* B 13, Death greeted the patriarch, "consolation of travelers in their pilgrimage."

[9] Wis 3:18—"They will have neither hope nor consolation" (παραμύθιον); Philo, *Rewards* 72: Hope is "a consolation implanted in human nature" (συμφυὲς παραμύθιον); *Moses* 1.137: "He was deprived of the hope of consolation"; Thucydides 5.103.1: ἐλπὶς δὲ . . . παραμύθιον οὖσα; Caesar reassures and offers hope to the Romans who expect to endure countless evils (παρεμυθήσατό τε αὐτοὺς καὶ ἐπήλπισεν, Dio Cassius 43, 15, 2). Cf. *P.Oxy.* 939, 26: Demetrius writes to Flavian that he is comforted by his unceasing expectation that he will come.

[10] L. Robert, *Hellenica*, vol. 3, pp. 14–31; vol. 13, pp. 229, 231 (citing numerous examples); M. Guarducci, *Epigrafia greca*, vol. 2, p. 39; cf. *I.Lind.* 441, 9: *IGLAM* 1604, 1633: παραμυθεῖσθαι λυπουμένους περὶ τῆς τῶν φιλτάτων ἀποβολῆς (republished in *MAMA* VIII, 408, 409; cf. vol. 3, 8: λύπης τῶν γονέων παραμύθια; *SEG* VI, 189; *IG* Vol., 2, 517; XII, 7, 239, 394, 399; Dittenberger, *Syl.* 796, 13: παραμυθησομένην τούς τε γονεῖς αὐτοῦ καὶ τὸν πάππον; 866; the most fully developed is 889, 20ff.: παραμυθήσασθαι δὲ τὸν πατέρα αὐτοῦ . . . καὶ τὴν μητέρα αὐτοῦ . . . καὶ τὴν σύνβιον αὐτοῦ . . . καὶ τοὺς γλυκυτάτους ἀδελφοὺς αὐτοῦ . . . καὶ τὰς ἀδελφὰς αὐτοῦ . . . καὶ τοὺς θείους αὐτοῦ Αὐρ. Ζώσιμον καὶ Ἡρακλείδην καὶ τοὺς γένει προσήκοντας γενναίως φέριν τὸ συνβάν (third century).

II. — The meaning "comfort, encourage" is even more widespread than the previous meaning;[11] it is a properly divine activity[12] and in the Bible has a religious meaning. Judas Maccabeus encourages (*paramythoumenos*) his companions: "with the help of the Law and the Prophets, by reminding them of the battles that were already behind them, he filled them with renewed zeal."[13] In St. Paul's language, *paramytheomai* and the related nouns have a technical meaning, *paraklēsis* that teaches, persuades, stimulates. Apostolic "exhortation," at root doctrinal, is the source of courage: "We exhorted you, encouraged you, adjured you to walk worthy of God."[14]

The emphasis is sometimes intellectual: reasoning in order to persuade or advise.[15] Courtiers persuade the authorities to shed innocent blood (Add Esth 16:5); "philosophy reasons with it gently" (*ērema paramytheitai*).[16] This calm, gentle manner of speaking, which reassures and comforts, is a form of *paraklēsis*, especially effective for smoothing out opposition within a community.[17] In any event, the prophet, by virtue of his charism, has a

---

[11] Onosander 36.2: when the general had been defeated, he comforted (παρα-μυθησάμενος) the soldiers who had survived the battle; Xenophon, *Cyn.* 6.25; Philo, *Moses* 2.50: to command without encouraging (ἄνευ παραμυθίας) is the deed of a tyrant addressing not free men but slaves.

[12] Josephus, *Ant.* 6.38: "When the divinity appears to us and comforts us" (παραμυθεῖται); cf. Καλλιόπη παραμυθουμένη (E. Heitsch, *Die griechischen Dichterfragmente*, 2d ed., Göttingen, 1963, n. XXVI, 9); a Greek translation of the Aeneid: "solabar fatis" = παρεμυθούμην μοίραις (*P.Ryl.* 478, 15).

[13] 2 Macc 15:9. "This is not a mere reading from the Holy Scripture, as at 8:23, but an exhortation fed by the Law and the Prophets" (F. M. Abel, *Les Livres des Maccabées*, p. 472). This is what Rom 15:4 calls "the *paraklēsis* of the Scriptures"; cf. Luke 24:31—when Jesus comments on them, the sacred texts cause the heart of the hearers to burn. Cf. the oratorical exercises of the general according to Onasander 1.13: ἡ τοῦ λόγου παρακέλευσις . . . ἡ τοῦ λόγου παρηγορία τὰς ψυχὰς ἀνέρρωσε . . . ὥστε παραμυθεῖσθαι τὰς ἐν στρατοπέδοις συμφοράς.

[14] 1 Thess 2:12—παρακαλοῦντες ὑμᾶς καὶ παραμυθούμενοι καὶ μαρτυρόμενοι. The linking of παρακαλέω and παραμυθέομαι is found again at 2 Macc 15:8-9; 1 Thess 5:14; 1 Cor 14:3; Phil 2:1.

[15] Plutarch, *De Pyth. or.* 29: παραμυθούμενοι . . . καὶ πείθοντες; *De gen.* 20: παραμυθεῖται τοὺς ἀπιστοῦντας; *De tu. san.* 22: μιαρὰ παραμυθία = harmful advice; *De fac.* 17 (an objection's persuasive force); *Praec. ger. rei publ.* 13 (together with διδάσκω); Athenaeus 8.363 *e* 13; 471 *e*; *T. Job* 28.1; 34.2, 5.

[16] Plato, *Phd.* 83 *a*; cf. *Resp.* 5.476 *e*: "Could we not find a way to calm him and persuade him gently, without letting him know that he is not in his right mind?"; Aeschylus, *PV* 1063: "Give reasons that may convince me"; Lucian, *Philops.* 27. Pythagoras introduced music to the soul "in order to charm it" (ἕνεκα καὶ παρα-μυθίας, in Plutarch, *De virt. mor.* 3).

[17] Plato, *Prt.* 346 *b*: "The good cast a veil over them and make themselves praise them; and if they are irritated by some wrong committed by their parents or their country, they calm themselves, they try to be reconciled, they even force themselves

divine power to persuade that contributes to the solid edification of the Christian church: "speaks to humans for their edification, encouragement, and comfort" (*anthrōpois lalei oikodomēn kai paraklēsin kai paramythian*, 1 Cor 14:3).

With respect to Christians who are fearful or timid (*oligopsychoi*), victims of fears, doubts, or scruples, or who lack strength to deal with daily hardships or with persecution, the brethren must encourage them: *paramytheisthe tous oligopsychous* (1 Thess 5:14).

III. — In these words (*paramythion, paramythia, paramytheisthai*), there is more than comfort or encouragement, but a real stimulation, strength for overcoming difficulties.[18] The word is used not only for reassurance (Xenophon, *Hell.* 4.8.1; *paremythounto*), and for encouraging and prodding to action (a letter to Emperor Hadrian: *paramythoumenon kai protreponta*, *P.Fay.* 19, 6); but for supplying a lack (Lucian, *Dom.* 7: *paramytheomai to endeon*), bringing help (cf. *P.Oxy.* 1631, 13: *paramythikē ergasia;* cf. *P.Ryl.* 653, 6: maintaining the irrigation system). Such, it would seem, is the meaning of *paramythion* in Phil 2:1—"If there is any exhortation in Christ, if there is any stimulation to love (*ei ti paramythion agapēs*), if there is any fellowship in the Spirit, if there is any tender mercy and compassion, then complete my joy . . ."[19]

The meaning "sustenance, support" is attested especially for *paramythia*. In 332, three people from Theadelphia complain to the prefect about the number of their fellow-citizens who are evading public service, moving to neighboring nomes and abandoning their own town, "and so we beseech your Mightiness, in our poor and neglected condition, to order the *epistatēs*

---

to love and praise them"; Plutarch, *Them.* 22.5: "ostracism is a means of appeasing jealousy." *Paramythion* is an appeasing (Plato, *Leg.* 4.704 *d;* Plato, *Critias* 115 *b;* Sophocles, *El.* 130; Ps.-Theocritus 23.7; Plutarch, *Brut.* 6); cf. παραμυθία, Plato, *Leg.* 1.625 *b;* Plutarch, *Tim.* 5.3: "He wanted to go and calm him"; Cic. 37.1: Cicero tried to calm Caesar and Pompey.

[18] Thucydides 5.103.1: ἐλπὶς δὲ, κινδύνῳ παραμύθιον οὖσα—hope inspires risk-taking; Aristophanes, *Vesp.* 115: "Through soft words, he persuaded (παραμυθού-μενος) him not to wear the short cloak or go outdoors."

[19] Cf. Bo Reicke, "Unité chrétienne et Diaconie, Philip. II, 1–11," in *Freundesgabe O. Cullmann*, Leiden, 1962, pp. 203–212; C. Spicq, *Théologie morale*, vol. 2, pp. 518ff. *Paramythion* could have the meaning of persuasion or its more traditional sense, consolation-encouragement (J. Gnilka, *Der Philipperbrief*, Freiburg-Basel, 1968, p. 102, translats "Zuspruch," exhortation-consolation), but in its place between παράκλησις and κοινωνία this term should refer to love's power to stir to action (cf. Gal 5:6—πίστις δι᾽ ἀγάπης ἐνεργουμένη). *Agapē* is a subjective genitive, corresponding to Christ and the Holy Spirit (same order in 2 Cor 13:13). It is from this objective source that the Philippians will draw their "resources" for Christian living and brotherly love.

of the peace to hand over our townspeople so that we may through this strengthening (*dia tautēs tēs paramythias*) live in our town and always give thanks to your glorious Fortune."[20] In the Byzantine period, *paramythia* referred to the compensation or surety on a mortgage (*P.Flor.* 382, 65), the security, which was an application of the classical notion of *paramythia*;[21] and the word came to mean "salary, compensation," especially in the bookkeeping formula *hyper paramythias*.[22]

---

[20] *P.Thead.* 17, 17; cf. Wis 19:12—"For their relief, quails came up for them out of the sea"; Plutarch, *Sert.* 10.1: "At at time when the barbarians were in the greatest need of relief."

[21] *P.Grenf.* II, 89, 8; 90, 11; *PSI* 48, 2–5; *P.Michael.* 43, 17; *C.P.Herm.* 64, 4; *P.Oxy.* 1913, 7 (λόγος παραμυθίας); cf. P. M. Meyer's note on *P.Hamb.* 30 (p. 128, n. 1). In monastic Greek, *paramythia* means "refection, collation," cf. A. J. Festugière, *Etudes d'histoire*, p. 187.

[22] *P.Michael.* 43, 15; *P.Princ.* 96, 6–7; *P.Oxy.* 136, 28, 31; 2024, 11; 2038, 14; 2195, 123; *SB* 5285, 35; 10810, 4; *P.Lond.* 1497, 10 (an ἐγγυτικὴ ὁμολογία); 1452, 12 and 32. The editor of this papyrus, H. I. Bell, comments on *paramythia*: "The sense would seem to be something like *softness*, perhaps a (sailor's) gift upon going on duty"; but J. Maspéro observes: "the word is much more precise; quite probably it is an equivalent for the Latin *solatium*, which means an official's 'compensation' or a certain portion of this compensation" (in *REG*, 1912, p. 222; cf. S. Daris, "Frammento di lettera [?] bizantina," in *SPap*, 1963, p. 9). In *P.Berlin* inv. 13916, 4 (fifth century): "I have received . . . for the tax on the *annonae* . . . twenty gold *keratia* and for the *paramythia* one *keration*"; the editor, E. Wipszycka ("Deux quittances d'impôts du Vᵉ et VIᵉ siècle," in *Festschrift zum 150 jährigen Bestehen des Berliner Ägyptischen Museums*, Berlin, 1974, pp. 459ff.), refers to a register of taxes paid by the inhabitants of Aphrodito (*P.Flor.* 297, 243 and 433; sixth century), but neither this papyrus nor *P.Berlin* allows us to specify the nature of the fiscal charge called παραμυθία. E. W. proposes two possible interpretations: (*a*) a supplementary payment (cf. *P.Lond.* V, 1781; *BGU* 1020, where the word refers to a supplementary payment, gifts customarily offered to the owner); (*b*) "a wage, compensation, bonus"; in a receipt, this would be the sum meant for the tax collector.

παραπλήσιον, παραπλησίως

paraplēsion, near, similar to, like; *paraplēsiōs,* similarly, likewise

---

The preposition and the adverb, both unknown in the LXX, are NT hapaxes; and the adverb seems to be attested nowhere in the papyri. Both are formed from *plēsios,* "near, close, neighboring," and etymologically refer to either the closeness of a place[1] or a more or less total resemblance ("almost alike"), at least in classical Greek; but in the Koine the meaning often blurs into "nearly."

Paraplēsion in Phil 2:27 retains the nuance of approximation: Epaphroditus was ill, quite near to or actually on the point of dying; he had a brush with death. In the papyri, it is used to mean "analogous,"[2] for comparing facts, people, or things that are equivalent or "of the same sort";[3] so the meaning is "similar, like," like writing the same things to another cor-

---

[1] Cf. John 4:5—"Sychar was near (πλησίον) the field" Jacob gave to Joseph = *P.Panop.Beatty* 1, 333: "near the theater" (τὸ παραπλήσιον τοῦ θεάτρου); Diodorus Siculus 17.55.5; 17.75.6.

[2] *C.Ord.Ptol.* 53, 15 (taxes); 72 (sanctuary); 240 (artisans of analogous condition); *PSI* 1401, 3; *P.Tebt.* 703, 268; 788, 11; 790, 14; *UPZ* 110, 159: other officials of the same rank; 162, col. III, 22; *BGU* 1768, 12. The shape of the city of Alexandria is very close to that of a *chlamys* (Diodorus Siculus 17.52.3), the system as a whole gave the impression of a city (17.52.5).

[3] Cf. *Ep. Arist.* 63: "other fruits of the same sort"; 127: "through these words and others of the same sort"; 138: "as other idiots say, Egyptians and others like them"; the word is a favorite of Strabo, 11.8.4: "The Sacae launched invasions like those of the Cimmerians and the Treres"; 11.8.7: "The funeral customs and the mores of these peoples are analogous"; 11.10.2: "Margiana is similar to Aria"; 11.11.3; 11.13.9. The Romans suffer reverses when they take on the sea, but they are victorious when they attack men, adversaries of like nature to their own (Polybius 1.37.8); Plutarch, *Ant.* 45.4.

---

paraplēsion, S 3897; *EDNT* 3.33; MM 489; L&N 64.9; BDF §184; BAGD 621 ‖ *paraplēsiōs,* S 3898; *EDNT* 3.33; MM 489; L&N 64.9; BAGD 621; ND 3.79

respondant.[4] The similarity can even amount to identity: "It is and will be the same with Pontus, and this is coming about already."[5] "It is impossible that after the conflagration the world should become like coal" (= "become coal"—Philo, *Etern. World* 90).

The same difficulty of evaluating the degree of similarity appears for *paraplēsiōs* in Heb 2:14, where Christ shares the human conditions after the fashion of his brethren according to flesh and blood. Should we understand this to say "in exactly the same manner" or "in a manner nearly like"—in order to preserve Christ's sinlessness, his human nature not being corrupt[6]— in which case we would say "in his own way,"[7] or perhaps in a vague sense "similarly, likewise," neither including nor excluding some particular difference. This last interpretation is the best attested in the first century: "An equality of the same order is seen in the members of living beings" (Philo, *Heir* 51); "likewise in all the towns" (Josephus, *Life* 187); "the people of Asochis, like those of Japha, gave them a noisy reception" (ibid. 233); "to become a good distance runner, one must have robust shoulders and neck, like an athlete who competes in the pentathlon";[8] "Orpheus made a vow to the gods of Samothrace, just as he did the first time."[9] It would seem that the nuance of Heb 2:14 is that cited by the Greek fathers—"with no difference"[10]—a translation that follows the context. Christ assumed a human nature exactly like that of other mortals, even though its principle of existence was the person of the Word of God—but this is a distinction made by later theology. Nevertheless the choice of the word *paraplēsiōs* seems to hold some nuance—could it be that of the virginal conception?

---

[4] *PSI* 491, 13 (third century BC); cf. Onias' desire to build in Egypt "a temple like the one at Jerusalem" (Josephus, *Ant.* 13.63); "two candelabra like those in the sanctuary" (*War* 6.388); the praetorium is built "after the fashion of a small temple" (3.82).

[5] Polybius 4.40.10; 3.33.17: "we have acted just like those historians who wish to present their lies in a plausible manner."

[6] Cf. Rom 8:3; Phil 2:7; Heb 4:15—"just as we are, yet without sin"; A. Vanhoye, *Exegesis epistulae ad Hebraeos cap. I–II*, Rome, 1968, pp. 194–195.

[7] Cf. Philo, *Abraham* 162: "thought, in its own way, is under the influence of a passion."

[8] Philostratus, *Gym.* 32; cf. 25: "the chest must be as prominent as the hips."

[9] Diodorus Siculus 4.48; cf. Herodotus 3.104: "In the middle of the day, the sun burns Indians and other people equally (or almost equally?)."

[10] Cf. Plutarch, *De curios.* 3: "Just as a chicken on a farm, in spite of the feed put in front of it, will often hide in a corner to scratch around where a grain of barley appears amidst the manure, in the same manner (παραπλησίως) . . . the hidden and secret vices of each household will peck about" (following J. Dumortier's French translation). But Strabo (11.2.2) contrasts the not-well-known origins of the Nile (παραπλησίως) with its course, which is perfectly known (πολὺ τὸ φανερόν); 11.14.12: the sanctuaries of Armenia were destroyed almost as was the temple of Abdera.

παραφέρω

paraphero, to bring, carry off, remove

This verb presents no other difficulty than its multitude of meanings, which can be sorted out only according to context.

I. — The first meaning, "bring," appears in Judg 6:5, where the Midianites bring their tents beyond the borders of their kingdom.[1] The sense is that of carrying something, sometimes in a physical sense, like "waterless

---

[1] Cf. Xenophon, *Cyn.* 5.27: the animal's speed allows it to get out of sight of each object (παραφέρει τὴν ὄψιν) before determining what it is"; Philostratus, *Gym.* 44: "bringing the cooks and the impish kitchen boys"; Josephus, *Ant.* 7.168: Amnon asks his sister to have his meal brought (served) in his room. In a marriage contract, the woman brings (παραφερομένην) her belongings with her (*P.Dura* 30, 12). From this meaning, "cause to appear" (and confront, *P.Oxy.* 1853, 5), "produce" (a copy of a mortgage, *Pap.Lugd.Bat.* VI, 40, 16 = *SB* 7364; cf. G. Rosenberger, *Griechische Verwaltungsurkunden von Tebtynis*, Giessen, 1939, n. 53, 10 and 14), "keep ready" a bath and some food (*P.Amh.* 81, 12; *P.Oxy.* 131, 14). In the papyri, παραφέρω is a technical term in receipts for the *delivery* of wheat (*P.NYU* 7, 12; 9, 1, 10; 11, 1, 5), meat (6, 1), grains (5, 8, 15, 26, 34, 39, 45; 8, 3; 10, 1, 5, 10; 11 *a*, 1; *P.Cair.Isid.* 16, 28, 37, 42; 46, 4; 47, 9, 23, 28, 32), clothing (*P.Oslo* 119, 1 and 9), cattle (*P.Oxy.* 2118, 8). The usual formula for deliveries is παρήνεγκεν—sometimes κατέβαλεν—ὁ δεῖνα ὑπὲρ κ᾽ ἰνδικτίονος κωμητῶν Καρανίδος; sometimes ἔσχαμεν παρά σου (*P.NYU* 5, 1–7, 20–25, 50–55; 11 *a* 162–166; *P.Mich.* 649, 1, 8, 16, 30); receiving clerks attest the receipts: ὑποδίκται κώμης Καρανίδος; for example: "Valerius, son of Antiourios, delivered to the city gate for the third new *indictio*, for the account of the *comites* of Karanis, thirty-two and eleven-twelfths *artabai* of barley . . ." (*P.NYU* 5, 8; cf. the note of the editor, N. Lewis, p. 10); cf. the ostraca of Karanis, in *P.Mich.* VI, 779, 3; 781, 1; 782, 1; 784, 2; 785, 2; 786, 2; VIII, 1008, 1; 1009–1022. Delivery is made to a storeroom (*P.Cair.Isid.* 56, 1; 57, 13) or to the ὁριοδικτία (*P.Mert.* 30, 1); cf. *SB* 7361, 12 (cf. *ZPE*, vol. 15, 1974, p. 149); 9032, 2; 9070, 9, 23, 28; 10729, 1, 11. In guarantee contracts (ἐγγύη), this formula is used: "I will deliver and transport"; τούτους ἢ τοῦτον παραφέρω καὶ παραδώσω ἐν δημοσίῳ τόπῳ (*P.Mert.* 98, 12; cf. *P.Oxy.* 2203, 3; 2238, 15; 2420, 16; 2478, 23–24; *SB* 9512, 15), or in the aorist παρήνεγκα καὶ παρέδωκα (*P.Gen.* 36, 15; *BGU*, 974, 5).

---

paraphero, S 3911; *EDNT* 3.35; MM 491; L&N 15.162, 31.75, 90.97; BAGD 623

clouds carried by the wind,"[2] and sometimes in a mental sense, as when David, pretending to be mad, appears deranged.[3] Compare the English expressions "carried away" and "transports of delight."

II. — The exhortation of Heb 13:9 (*didachais poikilais kai xenais me parapheresthe*) uses the passive in a figurative sense: "to varied and strange doctrines do not let yourself be led"; or "do not be carried off, away from the right path," by these teachings. This epistle often uses compound verbs in *para-* to express a deviation, a turning aside, a marring, a positioning next to the right place: *pararreo* (2:1), *paradeigmatizo* (6:6), *paraiteomai* (12:25), *parapikraino* (3:8, 15–16), *parapipto* (6:6).

III. — The second aorist imperative (*parenenke . . . ap' emou*, Mark 14:36; Luke 22:42; cf. Matt 26:39—*parelthato*) should be translated "remove (or take back) this cup from me."[4]

---

[2] Jude 12 (the passive, ὑπὸ ἀνέμων παραφερόμενα; cf. 2 Pet 2:17—ἐλαυνόμενα = driven along); cf. Plutarch, *Tim.* 28.9: "Many were carried off by the river and . . . drowned"; Marcus Aurelius 4.43: "Hardly is something in sight when it is carried off"; 12.4.5: "If the whirlwind carries you off, let it take your body, your breath, all the rest. It will not take your intelligence." In AD 42, Papaï transported five μετρήται of oil from the oasis of Baharia to Memphis (*P.Fuad I Univ.* 34, 2; cf. *P.Mich.* 493, 14). In the sixth-seventh century, Victor asks George to send someone to transport some VIPs from Thmoinepsobthis (*P.Oxy.* 1853, 6). Cf. Xenophon, *Cyr.* 2.2.4: "The cook made a third round (περιέφερε τὸ τρίτον) for the rest of the distribution (τῆς περιφορᾶς)"; *Ep. Arist.* 316: "just when he was going to borrow (παραφέρειν) some passage from the Scripture, he was stricken with cataracts." A curious metaphorical (?) example from *T. Abr.* B 6: Sarah says to Abraham, "I add (?) and say that (παρεφέρω καὶ λέγω ὅτι) this is one of the three men who were our guests."

[3] 1 Sam 21:14, where the LXX uses παρεφέρετο well to translate the hithpoel of the Hebrew *hālal*, "lose one's reason"; cf. Plutarch, *Tim.* 6.1: "Our judgments . . . are easily shaken up and thrown off (σείονται καὶ παραφέρονται) by the praise or blame of the first person to come along."

[4] F. Field, *Notes on the Translation*, p. 39), translating the active with a passive, translates, "Turn aside, cause (or suffer) to pass by," and cites Plutarch, *Pel.* 9.6: "Phyllidas sought to divert the conversation" (παραφέροντος τὸν λόγον); 10.6: "The first had hardly passed (παραφερομένου) when Fortune raised up a second against them." Moulton-Milligan adds Aratus, *Phaen.* 43: τότε μὲν οὖν παρήνεγκε τὸ ῥηθέν and *P.Eleph.* 11, 5: σὺ δὲ ἕως τοῦ νῦν παρενήνοχας . . . πάνθ' ὑπερθέμενος. But in Mark 14:36; Luke 22:42, the meaning is determined by ἀπ' ἐμοῦ.

παρεισφέρω

pareispherō, to bring in alongside or in addition

This biblical hapax (2 Pet 1:5), "bring in alongside or in addition," rare in classical Greek, is attested in only one papyrus dating from 113 BC: "A certain Thracian from Kerkesephis, whose name I do not know, fraudulently brought oil (*pareisenēnochota elaion*) into the house where Petesuchos lives." It means "bring an amendment" in Demosthenes (*C. Lept.* 20.88) and corresponds to *eispherein psēphisma* in the inscriptions, which means "introduce or propose a decree,"[1] "pay a fine" (*MAMA* VI, 11). This second verb is used for bringing absolute courage into a just war (Onasander 4.2), and the expression *eispherein pasan spoudēn* is used constantly in the sense of putting one's zeal into something, bringing all one's good will to bear.[2]

Everyone agrees that this is clearly the meaning in 2 Pet 1:5, where the compound form corresponds to the Koine's common preference: "So therefore bring all your diligence to bear to add to your faith virtue. . . ." (*kai auto touto de spoudēn pasan pareisenenkantes epichorēgēsate en tē pistei hymōn tēn aretēn*).[3]

---

[1] *I.Magn.* C b 32; cf. LV, 22; *I.Sinur.*, n. 9, 16 (decree for the building of a sanctuary); Dittenberger, *Syl.* 1102, 10.

[2] Josephus, *Ant.* 11.324: Sanballates brought all his zeal to bear on the building of the Samaritan temple; 20.204: the procurator Albinus brought all his efforts to bear to pacify the region and rid it of *sicarii*; Polybius 22.12.12; Diodorus Siculus 1.83; *I.Magn.* 85, 11; a decree from Stratonicea in Caria, at the beginning of the imperial period, in honor of Zeus Panhemerios and Hecate: καλῶς δὲ ἔχι πᾶσαν σπουδὴν ἰσφέρεσθαι ἰς τὴν πρὸς αὐτοὺς εὐσέβειαν (*CIG* II, 2715, *a* 10; cf. J. Chaine, *Les Epîtres catholiques*, Paris, 1939, p. 15); decree of Abdera (Dittenberger, *Syl.* 656, 14; cf. L. Robert, *Opera Minora Selecta*, vol. 1, pp. 320–326; *Syl.* 694, 16).

[3] Compare the honorific decree from the first century BC celebrating Herostratos, "a good man, distinguished by his faithfulness, virtue, justice, piety" (ἄνδρα ἀγαθὸν γενόμενον καὶ διενένκαντα πίστει καὶ ἀρετῇ καὶ δικαιοσύνῃ καὶ εὐσεβείᾳ . . . τὴν πλείστην εἰσενηνεγμένον σπουδήν, Dittenberger, *Or.* 438, 6–9); cf. C. Spicq, *Agapè*, vol. 2, p. 354.

---

pareispherō, S 3923; *EDNT* 3.37; MM 492; L&N 68.64; BAGD 625

παρεπίδημος

parepidēmos, foreigner temporarily in a place, sojourner

→*see also* ξενία, ξενίζω, ξενοδοχέω, ξένος

Among the foreigners, distinguished from the natives in a city in Egypt or Greece were the *katoikountes* (cf. the *paroikoi,* Exod 12:45; Lev 22:10), or residents, who had obtained the right of domicile; and the *parepidēmoi,* or sojourners, foreigners who were only passing through the city, not establishing themselves there;[1] for example, they stayed only long enough to unload cargo or to settle a business matter.[2] Neither category of people has the right to citizenship, but the second are only passing through; their stay is temporary.[3] The verb *parepidēmeō* and the substantive *parepidēmia* occur much more

---

[1] Cf. Plutarch, *Tim.* 38.2: "they led the foreign travelers into his house" (τῶν ξένων τοὺς παρεπιδημοῦντας ἄγοντες εἰς τὴν οἰκίαν); Polybius 30.4.10; Diodorus Siculus 1.83. Cf. P. Jouguet, *Vie municipale,* pp. 55–59, 92–97; N. Hohlwein, *Termes techniques,* pp. 335, 351; *Chrest.Wilck.,* I, 1, 1, pp. 40–55.

[2] For example, peasants passing through Alexandria stay too long and neglect their farm work; "the king forbade sojourning in the city (περεπιδημεῖν) for more than twenty days" (*Ep. Arist.* 110); cf. Dittenberger, *Syl.* 714, 30; *P.Tor.* 8 = *UPZ* 196, 13: τῶν παρεπιδημούντων καὶ κατοικούντων ἐν ταύταις ξένων; J. and L. Robert, "Bulletin épigraphique," in *REG,* 1955, p. 268, n. 216: honors given by τοὶ κατοικεῦντες καὶ γεωργεῦντες καὶ ναυκλαρεῦντες καὶ παρεπιδαμεῦντες ἐν Φύσκῳ. Cf. R. Taubenschlag, *Law of Greco-Roman Egypt,* vol. 2, p. 23; idem, *Opera Minora,* vol. 1, p. 190; vol. 2, pp. 216ff. P. Gautier, *Symbola,* pp. 117ff., 375.

[3] Cf. *SB* 1568, 4: traveling functionaries (cf. Polybius 27.7.3); 9228, 16, βουλόμενος περεπιδημεῖν πρὸς καιρὸν τῇ Σοήνῃ ἐτῶν; *P.Oxy.* 473, 2; *P.Petr.* II, 13, 19: ὅπως τοῦτόν γε τὸν χρόνον παρεπιδημῇς (republished S. Witkowski, *Epistulae Privatae Graecae* 8, 12). Aristophanes of Byzantium (c. 257–180 BC): "A metic is someone from a foreign city who lives in the city, paying a tax according to certain established needs of the city. For a certain number of days, such a person is called a transient foreigner (παρεπίδημος) and is not taxed (ἀτελής); if he exceeds the fixed period, he then becomes a metic and is taxed" (frag. 38; in A. Nauck, *Aristophanis Byzantini Grammatici Alexandrini Fragmenta,* 1848). In Gen 14:13, Abraham is called an *'ibrî,* which is translated περάτης (biblical hapax) by the LXX and commented on thus by St. Jerome: "Hebrew, i.e., transient" (*Epist.* 71.2; 78.33; *Quaest. hebr. in Gen.* 14.13; *in Ezek.* 7.6; *in Jonah* 1.9; *in Jer.* 1.14—"Hebraeus, id ist περάτης et peregrinus transitorque"). Is *Habiru* an ethnic term designating a nomadic, wandering people, to be compared to the *'Ibrîm*

---

parepidēmos, S 3927; *TDNT* 2.64–65; *EDNT* 3.38; *NIDNTT* 1.690; MM 493; L&N 11.77; BAGD 625

commonly than *parepidēmos*, but they always mean a brief sojourn outside one's customary home. For example: foreigners who find themselves temporarily at Priene (*tōn parepidēmountōn xenōn*, *I.Priene*, 111, 139; cf. Dittenberger, *Or.* 268, 9; *SB* 1568, 4, *hoi parepidēmountes en tō Arsinoitē*); praise is given "to the delegates Aristodamos, Aristeus, Antanor, because they sojourned (*parepedamēsan*) and reported in a fashion entirely worthy of the city of Magnesia and the people of Epirus" (*I.Magn.* 32, 40); "Whereas the transients at Philae, *stratēgoi, epistatai* . . . compelled us to pay the costs of their presence. . . ."[4] "The Messenian ephors suffered much on account of the sojourn of Dorimachos."[5]

In the third century BC, Zeno, a native of Caunus, calls himself or is labeled a *parepidēmos* in Egypt.[6] In a will from the same period, a certain Philo leaves to his heirs (his wife and his daughter) a debt of 150 silver drachmas owed him by the Syrian *parepidēmos* Apollonios, also called in Syriac Jonathas.[7] The LXX gives this term a religious meaning, since in prayer the Israelites present themselves as nomads, without hearth or

---

(R. de Vaux, in *RB*, 1956, pp. 261–277, n. 4; 288, n. 2), or a name meaning "refugees, uprooted people," always foreigners in the places where they are so called (*sic*, J. Botéro; cf. G. Cardascia, "Le Statut de l'étranger dans la Mésopotamie ancienne," in *L'Etranger*, Recueils de la société J. Bodin IX, 1; Brussels, 1958, pp. 112ff.)? In any event, the *habiru* and the *'Ibrîm* are both transient and temporary, even if not foreign (H. Cazelles, "Hébreux, Ubru, Habiru," in *Syria*, 1958, pp. 198–217; cf. M. L. Ramlot, in *RevThom*, 1961, p. 435).

[4] Ἐπεὶ οἱ παρεπιδημοῦντες εἰς τὰς Φίλας στρατηγοί (*C.Ord.Ptol.* 52, 22 = *SB* 8396; Dittenberger, *Or.* 139; A. Bernand, *Philae*, I, n. 19); cf. *C.P.Herm.* 6, 13: "I find out about foreigners who come from somewhere else on some occasion to establish themselves here"; *P.Oxy.* 1023, 4; *P.Fouad* 79, 4: "transient in the nome of Oxyrhynchus"; *P.Brem.* 20, 7: Πλουτίωνα παρεπιδημοῦντα οὐχ εὗρον; *BGU* 1762, 5 (first century BC); *P.Oslo* 111, 27 and 88; *SB* 7746, 35; etc. Diodorus Siculus XIX, 61, 1: "Antigonus convened a general assembly composed of soldiers and sojourners" (τῶν τε στρατιωτῶν καὶ τῶν παρεπιδημούντων), French trans. by F. Bizière (*Diodore de Sicile: Bibliothèque historique, Livre XIX*, Paris, 1975, p. 85) who comments (p. 162): "That is to say, those who came with Alexander . . . the translation that seems best to fit the sense of παρεπιδημεῖν, since this verb is used in the inscriptions to refer to transients, especially foreigners sojourning briefly in a city, cf. Dittenberger, *Syl.* n. 640, 5 and 714, 30."

[5] Polybius 4.4.2 (τῇ παρεπιδημίᾳ); a decree of Delphi in honor of Lykinos of Thebes, "who came to sojourn in our city and acted during his stay (παρεπιδαμίαν, *l.* ἐπιδαμίαν, Dittenberger, *Syl.* 738) in a manner worthy of his own people and our city" (*NCIG*, n. X, 20); Dittenberger, *Syl.* 772, 2 (25 BC); 734, 10 (AD 94).

[6] *P.Col.Zen.* 72, 1; *PSI* 389, 3; *P.Mich.* 66, 6, 14, 26; Dittenberger, *Or.* 383, 150; cf. *PSI* 385, 4.

[7] *P.Petr.* III, 7, 15; republished in *C.Pap.Jud.* 126, corrected and commented on by J. Modrzejewski, "Servitude pour dettes ou legs de créance?" in *RechPap*, vol. 2, Paris, 1962, pp. 75–98.

home, whose only security and support is in Yahweh,[8] and also since Abraham says at Hebron "I am a resident alien and a sojourner in your midst";[9] a saying that is evoked at Heb 11:13, where the patriarchs are supposed to have confessed that they were "strangers and exiles on the earth" (*xenoi kai parepidēmoi eisin epi tēs gēs*).

This profession of faith and of hope was influenced by Philo, who said that "every wise soul has received heaven as its country, the earth as a foreign (*xenēn*) land; it considers the corporeal dwelling as someone else's property in which it must sojourn (*parepidēmein*)."[10] When St. Peter addresses "the elect, strangers in the Diaspora" (1 Pet 1:1), he means that the recipients of his letter are not natives and citizens of an earthly country, where they are making only a provisional, relatively brief sojourn; their abode is elsewhere: in heaven (cf. Phil 3:20). This exile is strongly emphasized by repetition: "Dear friends, I urge you as aliens and strangers (*hōs paroikous kai parepidēmous*) to abstain from carnal desires."[11] This is not a chance metaphor but an adequate summary of the supernatural condition of Christians (*hōs* = "as, being"). For them, life is a pilgrimage (Gen 47:9; 2 Cor 5:6–8); they are only "passing through" on earth, so they have the mindset of travelers who do not adopt the thoughts or customs or mores of the country that they traverse;[12] they have a different set of values than the natives that they rub shoulders with. The citizens of heaven keep themselves from all that could sully their holiness (1 Pet 1:13–15).

---

[8] Ps 39:13—"Hear my prayer, for I am a resident alien with you, a sojourner like my forebears" (ὅτι πάροικος ἐγώ εἰμι παρὰ σοὶ καὶ παρεπίδημος); Hebrew *tôšāb*.

[9] Gen 23:4—πάροικος καὶ περεπίδημος ἐγώ εἰμι μεθ' ὑμῶν. P. Dhorme comments: "*gēr wᵉtôšāb*, a foreigner who has been received as a resident in a neighboring country but does not have the rights of a native."

[10] Philo, *Husbandry* 65; cf. *Heir* 267; since the fall, man is a fugitive and an exile (*Cherub.* 1ff.; *Rewards* 16–20; cf. Heb 6:18—οἱ καταφυγόντες; *Pss. Sol.* 17.19). For the vocabulary, cf. *Conf. Tongues* 76ff.: "They have not sojourned as in a foreign land (οὐχ ὡς ἐπὶ ξένης παρῴκησαν). . . . If they had come only for a short stay (παρεπιδημήσαντες), they would have withdrawn again, whereas by establishing themselves solidly, they oblige themselves to stay put indefinitely." For the theology, cf. C. Spicq, *Hébreux*, vol. 1, pp. 83, 123, 269ff.

[11] 1 Pet 2:11; cf. J. B. Souček, "Pilgrims and Sojourners," in *Communio Viatorum*, Prague, 1958, pp. 3–17; H. v. Campenhausen, "S'expatrier 'à cause de la foi,' " in *VSpir*, 459; 1959, pp. 162–181; J. F. Fontecha, "La vida cristiana como pregrinación según la Ep. a los Hebreos," in *Studium Legionense*, Léon, 1961, vol. 2, pp. 251–306; M. Adinolfi, "Temi dell'Esodo nella I Pt," in *Studii Biblici Franciscani*, Jerusalem, 1966, pp. 299–317; idem, "Stato civile de cristiani 'forestieri e pellegrini' (Q Petr. II, 11)," in *Anton*, 1967, pp. 420–434; C. Spicq, *Vie chrétienne*.

[12] Cicero defined the attitude of a foreigner toward the country in which he resides: remaining indifferent to and uncurious about what happens (Cicero, *Off.* 1.34.125).

παρθενία, παρθένος

parthenia, **virginity;** *parthenos*, **unmarried young woman, virgin**

There is no known etymology for *parthenos*,[1] which usually refers to a "young woman" who is not yet married or a "virgin,"[2] as distinct from "woman" (*gynē*): "leaving behind the name of virgin, a young woman is called a woman (or wife)."[3] So this term is usually linked with the idea of

---

[1] P. Chantraine, *Dictionnaire étymologique*, on this word. Cf. G. Delling, "παρθένος," in *TDNT*, vol. 5, pp. 826–837. — The feminine ἡ παρθένη is exceptional, cf. *UPZ* 101, 21 (AD 156).

[2] Homer, *Il.* 22.127: "young man and young woman whisper softly together"; Plato, *Leg.* 794 *c*: "for boys and girls (παρθένοι) above six years, separation of the sexes is enforced"; 8.834 *d*: "little girls or young women" (παῖδας ἢ παρθένους); Aristophanes, *Nub.* 530: "since I was still a girl, I was not permitted to give birth." Marciana, Sirica, Procla, Castar, Asther, and Domna are young women who died at the ages of 15, 18, 19, 14, and 22 years (*CII*, n. 45, 168, 386, 588, 733, 381, 1169); unmarried, without any definite indication as to literal virginity (cf. Plutarch, *Mulier. virt.* 20; *Con. praec.* 2), since παρθένιος means "born of a young woman" (Homer, *Il.* 16.180) who has behaved badly (Pausanias 3.7.7); cf. young married women (Aristophanes, *Eq.* 1302: ὦ παρθένοι = "O young women"; J. Taillardat, *Images d'Aristophane*, n. 647, 767). Cf. A. Brelich, *Paides e parthenoi*, Rome, 1969, vol. 1, pp. 303ff. [In accord with contemporary English usage, "young woman" is used in this English translation where the original French, not only in this article but throughout the work, uses "jeune fille." It seems from the examples given that the term is meant to refer to unmarried females from the teen years into the twenties. It should also be noted that English uses two words ("wife" and "woman") where both French ("femme") and Greek (γυνή) use one. —Tr.]

[3] Sophocles, *Trach.* 148: ἀντὶ παρθένου γυνή; Ps.-Theocritus 27.65: "I came here a virgin, and I return home a woman"; Philo, *Cherub.* 49: "Union for the sake of procreation makes virgins women"; Diodorus Siculus 5.73. Hesiod, *Th.* 514. In *I.Did.* 496 A 5, the gods appear to worshipers of the goddess Demeter Thesmophoros (διὰ παρθένων καὶ γυναικῶν)—whose worship is reserved for women—then to men (literally, to males) and underage children (δ᾽ ἀρρένων καὶ νηπίων). L. Robert

---

parthenia, S 3932; *EDNT* 3.39; *NIDNTT* 1.1072; MM 494; L&N 23.64; BAGD 626–627 ‖ *parthenos*, S 3933; *TDNT* 5.826–837; *EDNT* 3.39; *NIDNTT* 3.1071–1072; MM 494; L&N 15.86, 85.25; BAGD 627; ND 4.222–226

youth (*parthenou koras* = the young virgin),[4] of beauty, and even of nobility.[5] It can then be meant in the strict sense of purity and literal virginity: "My soul is virgin" (*parthenon psychēn echōn*, Euripides, *Hipp.* 1006); "water that flows from a pure spring" (*parthenou pēgēs*, Aeschylus, *Pers.* 613); in the Argolid a fountain was shown in which Juno recovered her virginity each year by bathing (Pausanias 2.38.2–3). In AD 37, the inhabitants of Assos took an oath "by our pure and virgin" (*hagnēn parthenon*) cityguardian goddess.[6] In the classical and Hellenistic periods, not only is this esteem for virginity affirmed—as with Atalanta, who when she "came to the age of puberty wished to remain a virgin"[7]—along with an association between youth and innocent living, but also virginity takes on religious meaning. Virgin goddesses like Artemis,[8] and better, the warrior Athena,[9] are honored. The pagan cults attest to the consecrated virginity

---

(*Hellenica*, vol. 12, Paris, 1960, pp. 544ff.) reckons that the gods appear in different human forms. Cf. P. Lambrechts, "L'Importance de l'enfant dans les religions à mystères," in *Hommage à W. Déonna*, pp. 322–333.

[4] Euripides, *Phoen.* 1730; Aristophanes, *Ran.* 950: "young woman and old woman" (παρθένος χη' γραῦς); Hippocrates, *Genit.* 2.3: "Girls, while they are young, do not menstruate"; *Nat. Puer.* 20.2; Menander, *Dysk.* 4: "Sostratus, smitten with the young woman" (τῆς παρθένου); 34: "the young woman behaves as she was trained"; 290; *Mis.* 306, 465 (*P.Oxy.* 2656).

[5] *Il.* 2.513: "the noble virgin"; Plato, *Hp. Ma.* 287 *e*: "what is noble, in all truth, is a beautiful virgin"; Aristotle, frag. 675 (ed. Rose, 2d ed.): Arete, the beautiful virgin goddess; Menander, *Dysk.* 682: "I let the rope slip three times while looking at the young woman"; 968: "the noble virgin Nike"; Heliodorus, *Aeth.* 4.10.3: "the noble name of virgin"; Philo, *Rewards* 53; *Prelim. Stud.* 124; Josephus, *Ant.* 7.162, 343–344; 11.196–197.

[6] Dittenberger, *Syl.* 797, 21; cf. Dio Cassius 7.8.11: the Vestal Virgins, παρθενεύειν διὰ βίου; "Heracleia died still pure" (ἀγνεύουσαν, *GVI*, n. 1697); Menander, *Sik.*: " 'Your daughter (τὸ θυγάτριον) still lives and in excellent circumstances.' 'Is she still preserved in herself (αὐτὸ τοῦτο)?' 'Yes, she is still a virgin and knows no man (παρθένος γ' ἔτι. ἄπειρος ἀνδρός)' " (A. Blanchard, A. Bataille, "Fragments sur papyrus du ΣΙΚΥΩΝΙΟΣ de Ménandre," in *RechPap*, vol. 3, 1964, pp. 148–149).

[7] Apollodorus, *Bibl.* 2.9.2: παρθένον ἑαυτὴν ἐφύλαττε; cf. 8.2: ὤμοσεν μεῖναι παρθένος. Παρθένοι are young women who sacrifice their lives for their country (σώτειραι); Plutarch, *An seni* 24; Ps.-Plutarch, *Reg. et imp. apoph.* 184, 1; *DKP*, vol. 4, 531. Texts relating to this aspiration to purity in C. Spicq, *Théologie morale*, vol. 2, pp. 818ff.

[8] Artemis remains a virgin: παρθένος ἔμεινεν (Apollodorus, *Bibl.* 1.4.1); her name comes from her integrity (τὸ ἀρτεμές), "because of her love of virginity" (Plato, *Cra.* 406 *b*). Cf. L. Séchan, P. Lévêque, *Les Grandes Divinités de la Grèce*, Paris, 1966, pp. 353ff. K. Warnicke, "Ártemis," in *PW*, vol. 2, 1, col. 1375–1396.

[9] Artemidorus Daldianus, *Onir.* 2.35: "She is bad for courtesans and adulterous women, and also for those who wish to marry, because the goddess is a virgin" (παρθένος γὰρ ἡ θεός); Plutarch, *Demetr.* 26.5.

of their priestesses and their prophetesses, which presupposes that their innocence is valued by the gods, so that their intervention is especially efficacious. The case of the Vestals is only one example,[10] but there are also the Pythia, who drew near to the god "with a virgin soul" (Plutarch, *De Pyth. or.* 22), and many others: "She claims that she will remain a virgin all her life; she is consecrated to the cult of Artemis. . . . She exalts virginity and does not fall far short of divinizing it. She calls it pure, unpolluted, immaculate."[11]

The papyri and especially the inscriptions confirm these meanings: *parthenoi* are "girls."[12] Epitaphs, especially Jewish ones, use the word to point to the youthfulness of the deceased,[13] who had "reached the flower of age" (*CII* 1508), or was of marriageable age.[14] The term takes on a religious coloring in the fourth century BC at Cyrene, where "young women" have to be purified, and are associated with young brides (*nympha*) before the consummation of their marriage, and with women (*gyna*).[15] Cult regulations associate them with children in taking part in cultic ceremonies; they sing hymns in processions.[16] With the decree of Canopus in the

---

[10] "Numa also had watch over the sacred virgins, called Vestals. . . . The pure and incorruptible substance of fire had to be entrusted to pure, spotless beings" (Plutarch, *Num.* 9.9–10; cf. 10.3–4; *Publ.* 8.8; Aulus Gellius, *NA* 1.2). T. Worsfold, *The History of the Vestal Virgins of Rome*, London, 1932; P. Grimal, *Histoire mondiale de la femme*, Paris, 1965, vol. 1, pp. 406ff. On the name *virgo Vestalis*, cf. G. Radke, "Die *dei penates* und *Vesta* in Rom," in *ANRW*, vol. 17, 1, pp. 369ff.

[11] Heliodorus, *Aeth.* 2.33.4–5. Cf. ἱερὰ παρθένος (*P.Mert.* 73, 1). Virgin priestess of Apollo at Epirus (Aelian, *NA* 11.2); of Poseidon, on the island of Calaurea (Pausanias 2.33.2); of Aphrodite, in Sicyonia (Pausanias 2.10.4–5); of Heracles, at Thespiae (Pausanias 9.27.6); of Cybele, at Cyzicus and in Caria; of Anaitis at Ecbatana (Plutarch, *Art.* 27). On the isle of Sein, there were priestesses—*perpetua virginitate sancta*—called Gallizenae (Pomponius Mela 3.48). The ordeal for proof of virginity is located in the cave of Ephesus (Achilles Tatius 6.13ff.). Cf. *IGLS* 2928; E. Fehrle, *Die kultische Keuschheit im Altertum*, Giessen, 1910; J. T. Milik, *Dédicaces faites par des dieux*, Paris, 1972, pp. 374–375.

[12] *P.Ryl.* 125, 28 (AD 28–29); cf. *P.Lond.* 983, 4 (vol. 3, p. 229); *P.Apoll.* 41, 6; *SB* 8545 B 16 a. This is an identity for "girls" who work on a farm (*P.Fay.* 102, 30; *BGU* 894, 6; Philo, *Moses* 1.57). Cf. the proper name Parthenos (*CII* 168 a).

[13] *CII* 45: "Marciana, a young woman of 15 years, rests here"; 106, 168, 320, 381, 385 (at Rome), 588 (at Venice); *IGUR*, n. 927; *SEG* II, 874, 6 (in Libya); *SB* 6167, 2; 6701, 6; 6839; 8366, 2; *CIRB* 130, 4 and 11; 139.

[14] *Stud.Pal.* XX, 15, 6. This "virginity" is temporary, since certain "girls" are married while still young (*P.Amst.* 40, 7).

[15] F. Sokolowski, *LSCGSup*, n. 115 A, 75–76.

[16] A decree relating to the cult of Zeus Sosipolis in 197–196 (*I.Magn.* 98 = Dittenberger, *Syl.* 589; *LSAM*, n. 32, 20), on the occasion of the installation of the statue of Artemis Leukophryene (first half of second century); χοροὺς παρθένων

third century, "sacred virgins" appear at festal assemblies in honor of the gods;[17] in a regulation for the Andanian mysteries, one of the "virgins" is identified as the priestess of Apollo Karneios (*hai parthenoi hai hierai*).[18] This has nothing to do with physical integrity or with virtue; it is a functional title.

The LXX uses *parthenos* (Hebrew *b^etûlâh*) for an adolescent girl who has not been engaged (Exod 22:15–16), "who has not belonged to a man" (Lev 21:3), sometimes emphasizing youthfulness,[19] sometimes physiological virginity: "young virgins who had not had relations with a male" (Judg 21:12). This point is as novel as it is constant ("Here is my daughter, who is a virgin"),[20] but it implies nothing about the virtue or the personal feelings of the one so described: she is a virgin, since she is not married and everyone thinks she is one.[21] This is what confirms the meaning of *partheneia* (Hebrew *b^etûlîm*): physical integrity, the distinctive index of virginity.[22]

αἰδουσῶν ὕμνους εἰς Ἄρτεμιν (*I.Magn.* 100 = Diodorus Siculus 695 = *LSAM*, n. 33, A 29); at Athens, in the cult of Apollo in 129–128: αἱ δὲ παρθένοι φερέτωσαν τὸ ἱερὸν (F. Sokolowski, *LSCGSup*, n. 14, 46). Cf. L. Robert, "Les Inscriptions," in J. des Gagniers, *Laodicée*, pp. 299ff.

[17] Cf. *SB* 8858 = Dittenberger, *Or.* 56, 65: τὰς παρθένους τῶν ἱερέων; 68: ἀναφέρειν τὰς ἱερὰς παρθένους; *P.Mert.* 73, 1: a declaration for "Taophryonis, sacred virgin"; *P.Oxy.* 3177, 2–3: Aurelia Tanentiris declares that her mother was a sacred virgin and that her daughter has become one as well.

[18] *LSCG*, n. 65, 29, 32, 96 = Dittenberger, *Syl.* 736 (92 BC).

[19] Gen 24:14, 16, 43, 55 (Hebrew *na'ar*); 34:3; Deut 22:23—παῖς παρθένος; 22:28; 33:25—νεανίσκος σὺν παρθένῳ; 2 Chr 36:17—Nebuchadnezzar "spared neither young man nor virgin, neither old man nor gray head"; Isa 23:4; Jer 51:22; Lam 1:18; 2:21; Ezek 9:6; Esth 2:17; Job 31:1; Ps 45:11; 78:63; 148:12; Sir 9:5; 1 Macc 1:26—"maidens and youths." With Rebekah ("the young woman was beautiful and was a virgin," Gen 24:16) and in Amos 8:13 ("beautiful virgins") an aesthetic quality is noted: "All young virgins (κοράσια παρθενικὰ) and beautiful to behold" (Esth 2:3). Aseneth: "Eighteen years old, a virgin, gracious, surpassing in beauty all the virgins of the land" (*Jos. Asen.* 1.6; cf. 2.11; 15.8).

[20] Judg 19:24; Lev 21:13–14: the high priest shall marry a woman who is still a virgin (cf. Ezek 44:22); 1 Kgs 1:2—David seeks "a young virgin" (παρθ. νεάνιδα); Lam 5:11—"They have violated the women (γυναῖκας) of Zion, the virgins (παρθένους) of the cities of Judah"; 2 Macc 3:19. Cf. G. J. Wenham, "Betulah, a Girl of Marriageable Age," in *VT*, 1972, pp. 326–348.

[21] Deut 22:19. The virgin daughter of Zion is sometimes Jerusalem (2 Kgs 19:21), sometimes the nation (Isa 37:22; Jer 18:13; 31:4, 21; Lam 1:15; 2:13). Since Israel has had lovers, this metaphor is taken as a title of nobility that erases the past but commits the future.

[22] Deut 22:14, 15, 17, 20: "I took a woman and drew near to her, but I did not find virginity in her"; Judg 11:37–38: Jephthah's daughter, whose womanhood would be wasted. Cf. Antoninus Liberalis, *Met.* 11.1: "With violence Chelidonis was robbed of her virginity"; 13.7; Achilles Tatius 5.21.1: Clitophon "said to be a virgin, if at any rate there is a male virginity" (εἴ τις ἐστι ἐν ἀνδράσι παρθενία); *CIG* IV, 8784 *b*; *Jos.*

Only two texts translate the Hebrew 'almâh as parthenos. The first concerns Rebekah (Gen 24:43); the second speaks of the miraculous sign of salvation given to Ahaz: "The adolescent (hē parthenos) will become pregnant and will bear a son; you shall call his name Immanuel" (Isa 7:14). Matt 1:23 attests its literal messianic meaning.[23] It has been consecrated by the Christian tradition, which refers it to the virgin birth of Jesus.

Philo seems to be the first to have understood parthenia as an actual virtue[24] and gives it its distinguishing traits,[25] always including nobility and beauty.[26] This has to do not only with physical integrity, nor even with simple purity, but with an interior and very spiritual orientation that allows one to enter into relationship with God. God communes "with the nature that is undefiled, pure, in all truth virgin. . . . When God begins to have commerce with the soul, he makes a virgin again of what has become a woman."[27] His model would be the female Therapeutae, contemplatives

Asen. 4.9—"Joseph is a pious man, chaste and virgin" (ἀνὴρ θεοσεβὴς καὶ σώφρων καὶ παρθένος); 8.1; Rev 14:3. — παρθενία (-εία) always translates the Hebrew nᵉûrîm, "youth," whence γυνὴ παρθενίας, "wife of youth," that is, the fiancée when she receives her husband (Jer 3:4; Sir 15:2; 42:10); cf. Prov 5:18; Joel 1:8—"the husband of her youth" (ἐπὶ τὸν ἄνδρα αὐτῆς τὸν παρθενικόν; CII 319—Eirena, the παρθενικὴ σύμβιος of Claudius; cf. 81; H. J. Leon, The Jews of Ancient Rome, Philadelphia, 1960, p. 130). Cf. PSI 41, 5: ἀνδρὶ Παγένει ᾧ συνήφθην ἐκ παρθενίας; SB 11221, 4: ἐκ παρθενείας ἀνδρὶ ἐγαμήθη Πανίσκῳ; P.Lond. 1711, 18; Dittenberger, Syl. 983, 18: ἀπὸ παρθενείας. Cf. Panopolis papyrus 28, 4: ἐκ παρθενείας ἀνδρὶ ἐγαμήθη Πανίσκῳ, in ZPE, vol. 10, 1973, p. 131; reprinted in P.Panop. On the Roman inscriptions a or ab virginitate, cf. M. Humbert, Le Remariage à Rome, Milan, 1972, pp. 64ff., 346ff.

[23] This text has been the object of countless studies (cf. L. Dennefeld, "Le 'Signe' de la prophétie d'Emmanuel," in RSR, 1927, pp. 69–86), notably concerning the meaning of 'almâh, an unmarried young woman. J. Coppens ("La Prophétie de la 'Almah, Isa 7:14–17," in ETL 1952, pp. 648–678). Add J. Massingberd Ford, "The Meaning of 'Virgin,' " in NTS, vol. 12, 1966, pp. 293–299; M. Rehm, "Das Wort 'almah in Isa VII, 14," in BZ, 1964, pp. 89–100.

[24] Cherub. 52: God "spreads like seed the ideas of the immortal and virgin virtues of virginity. . . . You should live as a virgin (παρθενεύεσθαι) in the house of God."

[25] Prelim. Stud. 124: "beauty that is undefiled, without stain, truly virginal" (παρθένιος); Spec. Laws 3.74.

[26] Philo, Husbandry 158: "The intelligent man hopes to marry a virgin of good birth and pure"; Joseph 43; Spec. Laws 1.101. Not only is grace virginal (Change of Names 53; Post. Cain 32; Migr. Abr. 31; Flight 141; Moses 2.7), but also there is "a virgin soul" (παρθένον ψυχήν, Cherub. 51; Migr. Abr. 224; Virtues 37; cf. Euripides, Hipp. 1006); "all the virtues are those of virgins" (Rewards 53; Change of Names 196); there are pure and virgin thoughts (Dreams 2.185; Spec. Laws 2.30), "hands that are pure, and, if one may dare to use a term that entails some imagery, virginal" (Virtues 57) and the "virgin number seven" (Decalogue 102; Spec. Laws 2.56; Rewards 153). Cf. Apollonius Rhodius, Argon. 3.682: αἰδὼς παρθενίη = virginal modesty.

[27] Cherub. 50; Post. Cain 134; Migr. Abr. 225; Quest. Exod. 2.3.

who serve and honor God, for the most part "aged virgins (*gēraiai parthenoi*) who have not observed chastity (*hagneian*) by constraint—like some Greek priestesses—but on their free resolve, from a passionate desire for wisdom: seeking to imbue their lives with it, they have renounced bodily pleasures."[28]

Luke 2:36 is faithful to the language of the LXX when it specifies that the prophetess Anna had lived "with her husband seven years *apo tēs parthenias.*" On the other hand, St. Matthew no longer understands *parthenos* to mean "young woman" (Hebrew *'almâh*) but literally "virgin," since the point is that Joseph is being reassured concerning his fiancée's virtue (Matt 1:23). The meaning of the term in Luke 1:27 is much disputed: Gabriel is sent from God "to a virgin engaged to a man named Joseph . . . the virgin's name was Mary" (*pros parthenon emnēsteumenēn andri . . . to onoma tēs parthenou Mariam*).[29] This text is not to be taken in isolation; it plays an important role in the design of Luke 1–2;[30] the strict meaning "virgin" was retained by the whole tradition, in which the religious meaning has great weight,[31] the ideal of virginity not being unknown among contemporaries (Epictetus 3.22.26–27), notably the Essenes.[32] Not only does Luke write

---

[28] *Contemp. Life* 68; cf. 1QM 7.3–4: "No child, minor, or woman shall come into their camps (of warriors)" at the time of the messianic liberation, because the sons of light, associated with the heavenly host, "consequently find themselves near to God and obliged to lead an angelic life" (G. Vermès, "Quelques traditions de Qumrân," in *Cahiers Sioniens*, vol. 9,. 1955, p. 42), sheltered from any risk of impurity.

[29] E. Delebecque (*Evangile de Luc*) notes: "*Engaged:* the Greek verb (ἐμνηστευμένην) can also mean 'married.' The choice between the two matters little because the Jewish betrothal ceremony gave the fiancé full rights over the fiancée. The word that is set in relief and repeated is 'virgin.' Luke underlines the unprecedented paradox of a woman who is engaged—or married—yet is still a virgin." Perhaps the evangelist was thinking of Lev 21:13–14: the high priest shall marry a woman who is still a virgin.

[30] R. Laurentin, *Structure et théologie de Luc I–II,* Paris, 1957, pp. 176ff. (gives the bibliography, pp. 191ff.). Cf. M. J. Lagrange, "La Conception surnaturelle du Christ d'après saint Luc," in *RB*, 1914, pp. 60–71; 188–208; R. P. Lavaud, "La Virginité dans le Nouveau Testament," in *VSpir*, 1941, pp. 180–190; Sr. Jeanne d'Arc, "La Chasteté et la virginité dans l'Ancien et le Nouveau Testament," in *La Chasteté,* Paris, 1953, pp. 11–36; L. Legrand, *La Virginité dans la Bible,* Paris, 1964.

[31] *Prot. Jas.* 9.1—παρθένον κυρίου; 19.3; *Odes Sol.* 19.6, etc. Cf. G. Graystone, *Virgin of All Virgins: The Interpretation of Luke I, 34,* Rome, 1968; F. Dreyfus, "L'Actualisation de l'Ecriture, III: La Place de la tradition," in *RB*, 1979, pp. 326ff., 337ff. Cf. J. McHugh, *La Mère de Jésus dans le Nouveau Testament,* Paris, 1977, pp. 217–390; J. Winandy, "La Conception virginale dans le Nouveau Testament," in *NRT*, 1978, pp. 706–719; R. E. Brown, K. P. Donfried, J. A. Fitzmyer, J. Reumann, *Mary in the New Testament,* Philadelphia-New York, 1978; B. M. Nolan, *The Royal Son of God,* Fribourg-Göttingen, 1979, pp. 63ff.

[32] A. Guillaumont, "A propos du célibat des Esséniens," in *Hommages à A. Dupont-Sommer,* Paris, 1971, pp. 395–404; cf. J. Blinzler, "Zur Auslegung von Mt. XIX,

parthenos first, before the name of the young woman, but he repeats it and wants to emphasize its weight; it is the title par excellence of the person whom the angel addresses with such great respect, the one whom Christian tradition calls "the Blessed Virgin Mary."

On the other hand, once more, the title of the "parable of the Ten Virgins" (*deka parthenois,* Matt 25:1, 7, 11) is wrong. M. J. Lagrange noted: "The ten virgins are young women, friends of the fiancée, and the fact of their virginity has no bearing on the parable" (on this text). We might even say that the question of their virginity does not arise; here *parthenos* retains its secular and OT sense, "young women"; they are the bride's young companions and friends, and they participate in the joyful procession planned for the marriage ceremony; they surround the bride when she goes to meet her fiancé, who is escorted by young men who are his friends.[33] Five of them are foolish (*mōrai*), scatterbrained, idiots who bring lamps with no oil; and five are sensible (*phronimoi*)—their lamps are filled.

Acts 21:9 is more difficult to interpret. At Caesarea, the evangelist Philip "had four virgin daughters who prophesied" (*thygateres . . . parthenoi prophēteuousai*). The clearest point to be made is that there is a certain connection between virginity and prophecy;[34] but *parthenos* could also be interpreted simply as meaning unmarried young women, thus noting a fact but allowing no conclusion that these *parthenoi* intended never to marry and had a vow of virginity. Otherwise, in pointing out that these young women were virgins, Luke may have intended to point out their singular circumstance: they were really virgins and even had that virtue.

The definite text on virginity in the NT is 1 Cor 7:25–34 ("And concerning virgins," *peri de tōn parthenōn*), which means men as well as women (*Jos. Asen.* 4.9; 8.1); the Lord had given no precept on this matter. The apostle gives his reasoned opinion: virginity is better than marriage for both sexes, first because marriage is inopportune given the dramatic eschatological circumstances, but especially on the spiritual level because the person who is *agamos* has no concern other than the Lord and ways of pleasing him. What is more, the virgin remains holy in both body and

---

12," in ZNW, 1957, pp. 254–270; J. Dupont, *Mariage et divorce dans l'Evangile,* Desclée De Brouwer, 1959, pp. 162ff., 200ff.; C. Daniel, "Esséniens et eunuques (Mt. XIX, 10–12)," in *RevQ,* vol. 23, 1968, pp. 353–390; H. Hübner, "Zölibat in Qumran?" in *NTS,* vol. 17, 1971, pp. 153–167; J. Coppens, "Le Célibat essénien," in M. Delcor, *Qumrân: Sa piété, sa théologie et son milieu,* Paris-Gembloux-Louvain, 1978, pp. 295–305; cf. 379.

[33] Cf. D. Buzy, *Les Paraboles,* Paris, 1932, pp. 475ff.; G. Schwarz ("Zum Vokabular von Matthäus XXV, 1–12," in *NTS,* vol. 27, 1981, pp. 270–276) reckons that *parthenos* must correspond to the Aramaic *šôšbîntâ'* = maid of honor.

[34] "As virgins, they were better suited to carry out their function as prophetesses" (E. Jacquier, on this text), cf. Joel 2:28–29; Acts 2:17; 1 Cor 11:5.

spirit.[35] Virginity means freedom for consecration to the Lord; it means not only bodily purity, but essentially the will of the heart to belong more completely to Christ and to be available for his service.[36] The case of the father who hesitates to let his *hyperakmos* (7:36, about to pass the flower of age) daughter (*parthenos*) marry resembles that of Phokos, who "kept on moving back the time for his daughter's marriage" (Ps.-Plutarch, *Amat. nar.* 4.774 *e*). All things considered, such a father does well if he lets his daughter marry (*kalos poiei*, 7:36), but he does better (*kreisson poiēsei*) if he does not give her in marriage.[37]

Since the OT had portrayed Yahweh as the husband of the nation of Israel, and in Eph 5:22–32 Christ is the husband of the church, St. Paul presents himself as best man in the uniting of the Corinthian community with the Lord, or "as a father gives his daughter to the chosen husband" (E. B. Allo): "I betrothed you to one man (*heni andri*) as a pure virgin (*parthenon hagnēn*) to be presented to Christ."[38] The metaphor refers to all souls that are purified from their sins. The same interpretation has been

---

[35] E. Alzas, "L'Apôtre Paul et le célibat: Etude exégétique sur I Cor. VII, 24," in *RTP*, 1950, pp. 226–232; M. Thurian, *Mariage et célibat*, Neuchâtel-Paris, 1955; J. J. O'Rourke, "Hypotheses Regarding I Corinthians VII, 26–36," in *CBQ*, 1958, pp. 292–298; X. Léon-Dufour, "Mariage et continence selon saint Paul," in *A la rencontre de Dieu: Mémorial A. Gelin*, Le Puy–Lyons–Paris, 1961, pp. 319–329; J. Massingberd Ford, "St Paul, the Philogamist (I Cor. VII in Early Patristic Exegesis)," in *NTS*, vol. 11, 1965, pp. 326–348; C. Spicq, *Théologie morale*, Paris, 1965, vol. 1, pp. 562–566; 816–827; D. Daube, "Pauline Contribution to a Pluralistic Culture," in *Jesus and Man's Hope*, Pittsburgh, 1971, pp. 231ff. J. K. Elliott, "Paul's Teaching on Marriage in I Corinthians," in *NTS*, vol. 19, 1973, pp. 219–225; P. Menoud, "Mariage et célibat selon saint Paul," in *Jésus-Christ et la foi*, Neuchâtel-Paris, 1975, pp. 13–22; T. Matura, "Le Célibat dans le Nouveau Testament d'après l'exégèse récente," in *NRT*, 1975, pp. 481–500, 593–604; R. Penna, "San Paolo (I Cor. VII, 29b–31a) e Diogene il Cinico," in *Bib*, 1977, pp. 237–245.

[36] This status of virginity is absolutely new; but we should note that Paul is careful to explain the superiority of virginity to recent converts from paganism in secular terms: "beauty/nobility," a Greek word connoting honorableness, excellence, and moral good (τοῦτο καλόν, 1 Cor 7:26; καλῶς ποιεῖ, 7:37–38).

[37] 1 Cor 7:36–38. Cf. L. A. Richard, "Sur I Corinthiens (VII, 36–38): Cas de conscience d'un père chrétien ou 'mariage ascétique'?" in *Mémorial J. Chaine*, Lyon, 1950, pp. 309–320; cf. R. Castellino, "I Cor. VII, 36–38 nel diritto orientale," in *Mélanges Tisserant*, vol. 1, pp. 31–42; W. G. Kümmel, "Verlobung und Heirat bei Paulus (I Kor. VII, 36–38)," in *Neutestamentliche Studien für R. Bultmann*, 1974, pp. 275–295.

[38] 2 Cor 11:2 (P. Andriessen, "La Nouvelle Eve, corps de nouvel Adam," in *Aux origines de l'Eglise* [Recherches bibliques 7], Desclée De Brouwer, 1965, pp. 95ff.). Ἁγνός, which literally means "undefiled, pure, consecrated," suggests Philonian "virginity of soul." The emphasis is on "the freshness of a virginal purity" (E. B. Allo). The expression παρθένος ἀγνή is common; cf. Philo, *Rewards* 159; Philo, *Cherub.* 50; *Joseph* 43; 4 Macc 18:7–8; *Jos. Asen.* 15.1, 8; 19.2; *IGUR*, n. 768; *GVI*, n. 1184, 1997.

made with the 144,000 virgins before the Beast and its worshipers:[39] they have been redeemed from the earth; they sing a new song in honor of the Lamb, whom they follow wherever he goes; "these are the ones who have not defiled themselves with women, because they are virgins (*parthenoi gar eisin*) . . . they are immaculate (*amōmoi eisin*)." "Virgins" is to be taken literally, but it is impossible to apply it to all Christians, notably those who are married and could not have been defiled (*emolynthēsan*) by virtue of their marital relations. This must have to do with an elite among the redeemed, a definite category of ascetic Christians, separated from other people, the "firstfruits" taken from the whole of the Christian assembly and consecrated exclusively for the service of God and the Lamb, for whom they constitute a sort of bodyguard.[40] They would have been "defiled" if they had defaulted on their resolve (cf. 1 Tim 5:12—*tēn prōtēn pistin athetēsan*, "they annulled their first commitment"). As things stand, however, they are beyond reproach. We may think of the "eunuchs who make themselves such for the sake of the kingdom of heaven."[41] There is no more energetic way of expressing the will to definitive self-renunciation with regard to sexual satisfactions for the love of God; which is the very definition of Christian virginity.

---

[39] Rev 14:4. These virgins would be all those who have not let themselves be seduced by the great prostitute Babylon (M. E. Boismard, "Notes sur l'Apocalypse," in *RB*, 1952, pp. 161–181). Cf. K. Rückert, "Die Begriffe παρθένος und ἀπαρχή in Apk. XIV, 4–5," in *TQ*, 1886, pp. 391–448; 1887, pp. 105–132; R. Devine, "The Virgin Followers of the Lamb (Apoc. XIV, 4)," in *Scripture*, vol. 16, 1964, pp. 1–5; J. M. Ford, "The Meaning of 'Virgin,' " in *NTS*, vol. 12, 1966, pp. 293–299; C. H. Lindijer, "Die Jungfrauen in der Offenbarung des Johannes XIV, 4," in *Studies in John* (Festgabe J. N. Sevenster), Leiden, 1970, pp. 124–142.

[40] The exegesis of E. B. Allo (on this text), of E. Stauffer, "γαμέω," in *TDNT*, vol. 1, pp. 652–653; C. Spicq, *Théologie morale*, vol. 2, p. 557, n. 2.

[41] Matt 19:12. Cf. Q. Quesnell, " 'Made Themselves Eunuchs for the Kingdom of Heaven,' " in *CBQ*, 1968, pp. 335–358; F. J. Moloney, "Matthew XIX, 3–12 and Celibacy," in *Journal for the Study of the New Testament*, 1979, vol. 2, pp. 42–60.

παρουσία

parousia, presence, arrival, visit, manifestation

Just as the verb *pareimi* has the two meanings "be present" and "become present (arrive)," the substantive *parousia* means sometimes the presence of persons[1] or things;[2] sometimes arrival, coming, visit.[3] In the Hellenistic period, it refers (except in commonplace uses) either to a divine

[1] Jdt 10:18—"the noise of Judith's presence spread throughout the tents"; 2 Macc 15:21—"Maccabeus, considering the presence of these crowds"; 1 Cor 16:17—"I rejoice at the presence of Stephanas, Fortunatus, and Achaicus"; 2 Cor 10:10; Phil 2:12, the contrast ἐν τῇ παρουσίᾳ ἐν τῇ ἀπουσίᾳ. Cf. *P.Oxy.* 903, 15: καὶ ὤμοσεν ἐπὶ παρουσίᾳ τῶν ἐπισκόπων; 3112, 4: "It is necessary for Pasion to be present"; *P.Apoll.* 46, 5; 60, 5; *BGU* 1643, 17; *C.P.Herm.* 45, 2; *P.Mich.* 322, 31, 42 (from AD 46); *P.Gen.* 68, 11, the concluding of a contract ἐπὶ παρουσίᾳ Διδύμου καὶ Παύλου πρεσβυτέρου τῆς αὐτῆς κώμης; *P.Mich.* 427, 31: "without calling for the presence of the contracting parties"; *P.Oxy.* 2134, 26; *P.Ross.Georg.* V, 28, 4; *CPR* I, 19, 7–8; *P.Flor.* 332, 5, μὴ ἐκδεχόμενόν σου τὴν παρουσίαν; *SB* 10311, 3: ἔσχομεν ὑπὲρ παρουσίας κριθῆς (AD 15; cf. 9905, 12; 10200, 26); *P.Petaus* 46, 3; 47, 3. Cf. Nero ordering the Greeks to meet (literally, be present) at Corinth on November 28, AD 67, παρῖναι ἰς Κόρινθον (Dittenberger, *Syl.* 814, 5).

[2] Cf. B. Rigaux, *Saint Paul: Les Epîtres aux Thessaloniciens*, Paris-Gembloux, 1956, pp. 197ff. A. Oepke, "παρουσία," in *TDNT*, vol. 5, pp. 858–871.

[3] 2 Macc 8:12—the approach of the army; 2 Cor 7:6–7: "God gave us relief through the coming of Titus"; Phil 1:26, Paul's return; Josephus, *Life* 90: "having dispatched a courier to let the people of Tiberias know that I was coming"; *War* 4.345: "the Idumeans began to regret that they had come"; *P.Fouad* 87, 35: "I kept the messenger here in my service until the arrival of the noble count"; *P.Lond.* 1913, 8, 12; *P.Petaus* 47, 3. Numerous papyrological references in N. Lewis, *Inventory of Compulsory Services in Ptolemaic and Roman Egypt*, New Haven–Toronto, 1968–1975, under this word. *P.Oxy.* 486, 15: my adversary is absent—my presence is required; 1668, 25: we await your coming; Dittenberger, *Syl.* 730, 15; Iamblichus, *Myst.* 2.8: the coming of the angels; Diodorus Siculus 17.8.14; 17.9.1; 17.10.4; 17.48.2; 18.53.1; 17.77.2; etc.

parousia, S 3952; *TDNT* 5.858–871; *EDNT* 3.43–44; *NIDNTT* 2.887, 898–903, 907, 932–934; MM 497; L&N 25.158, 28.29; BAGD 629–630; ND 4.167–168

manifestation[4]—often very close to *epiphaneia* (1 Tim 6:14; Titus 2:13; 2 Tim 4:1, 8) and *phanerōsis*, and even *apokalypsis*[5]—or the formal visit of a sovereign, his "joyous entry" into a city[6] that honors him as a god (Dittenberger, *Syl.* 814, 36: "the gods always present at his side to protect and preserve him"). Receiving Demetrius Polyorcetes, the Athenians compare him to Demeter because of the similarity of their names and sing "Like the greatest and best loved gods, they now present themselves to our city (*gē polei pareisin*); for this auspicious occasion has brought us Demeter and Demetrius together."[7] The days of the prince's sojourn are considered "holy days" (*hiera hēmera tēs epidēmias tou Autokratoros Traianou Adrianou kaisaros, I.Did.* 254, 10; cf. *P.Tebt.* 116, 57: *en tois [chronois] basileōs parousias*) and sometimes as marking the beginning of a new age. An inscription from Tegea is dated "the sixty-ninth year of the first *parousia* of the god Hadrian in Greece" (in *BCH*, vol. 25, 1901, p. 275). Beginning with the third century BC, there is the *parousia* of a Ptolemy (*P.Petr.* II, 39, *e* 18), then of Ptolemy Philometor and Cleapatra (*UPZ* 42, 18; cf. 109, 12), of Ptolemy II Soter (*P.Tebt.* 48, 13), of Ptolemy Philopator (3 Macc 3:17), of Germanicus (*SB* 3924, 34 = *Chrest.Wilck.*, n. 413), and those of Hadrian.[8]

In line with these usages, the NT uses *Parousia* for the glorious coming of the Lord Jesus at the end of time, his Second Coming.[9] This return of Christ must somehow be filled out with the pomp and magnificence

---

[4]Inscriptions from Epidaurus: τάν τε παρουσίαν τὰν αὐτοῦ παρενεφάνιζε ὁ Ἀσκλαπιός ("Asclepius manifested his coming," third century BC; Dittenberger, *Syl.* 1169, 34). Diodorus Siculus 4.3.3 mentions the triennial *parousia* of Dionysos in the Theban mystery cults; Aelius Aristides, *Orac.* 2.30–32, the *parousia* of Asclepius Soter. According to *Corp. Herm.* 1.22; 1.26 A, divinized souls have their parousia as new gods in their divine sphere.

[5]Cf. C. Spicq, *Agapè*, vol. 3, pp. 15–44.

[6]A. Deissmann, *Light,* pp. 368–373; L. Cerfaux, J. Tondriau, *Culte des souverains,* pp. 422, 448.

[7]Duris of Samos (*Hist.* 22, according to Athenaeus 6.62–63; cf. V. Ehrenberg, "Athenischer Hymnus auf Demetrios Poliorketes," *Antike,* vol. 7, 1931, pp. 279–297; L. Cerfaux, J. Tondriau, *Culte des souverains,* p. 182); cf. Iamblichus, *Myst.* 3.11: "the presence of god shining from on high"; 5.21; Josephus, *Ant.* 3.80, 203: the storm on Sinai signals the presence of God; 9.55; hymns to Isis, intervening to bring help, cf. *SEG* VIII, 548, 34; 550, 28. On the helpful presence of the deities, cf. L. Robert, *Hellenica,* vol. 13, pp. 129–131.

[8]*SB* 9617; cf. B. A. Van Groningen, "Preparatives to Hadrian's Visit to Egypt," in *Studi in onore de Calderini,* Milan, 1956, vol. 2, pp. 253–256; *Chrest.Wilck.*, n. 412.

[9]Matt 24:23, 27; 1 Thess 2:19; 3:13; 4:15; 5:23; 2 Thess 2:1, 8–9; 1 Cor 15:23; Jas 5:7–8; 2 Pet 1:16; 3:4, 12; 1 John 2:28; cf. J. Dupont, *L'Union avec le Christ,* pp. 49ff. A. L. Moore, *The Parousia in the New Testament,* Leiden, 1966; K. H. Schelkle, *Theologie des Neuen Testaments,* Düsseldorf, 1974, pp. 61–78; A. Feuillet, "Parousie," in *DBSup,* vol. 6, pp. 1331–1419.

that characterized royal and imperial "visits." There were great feasts, *panēgyreis*, including speeches of praise, gifts, games, sacrifices, dedications; statutes and buildings were erected, coins and medallions were struck, sentences were commuted,[10] gold crowns were given (Dittenberger, *Or.* 332, 26–39), honors were multiplied. Glory and joy on the part of the people were in response to the prince's active and beneficent presence.[11] All of this pales in comparison to the coming of the Pantokrator, but it explains why the NT uses the term *parousia.*

---

[10] Cf. *SB* 9316; L. Koenen, *Eine ptolemäische Königsurkunde*, Wiesbaden, 1957.

[11] The documents also attest that these festivities were very expensive. For example, this edict of Germanicus in AD 19: "Having learned that in view of my coming (εἰς τὴν ἐμὴν παρουσίαν) there were requisitions of boats and animals, and that dwellings were taken by force for our lodging, and that private citizens were ill-treated . . ." (*Sel.Pap.* II, 211); cf. λόγος παρουσίας τῆς βασιλίσσης εἰς τράπεζα (*sic*) τῆς πόλεως (*O.Wilck.* II, 1481); Dittenberger, *Or.* 139, 9 (= *SB* 8396 = A. Bernand, *Philae*, n. 19); *Syl.* 495, 85; *P.Tebt.* 33; 48, 9: καὶ προσεδρευόντων διά τε νυκτὸς καὶ ἡμέρας μέχρι τοῦ τὸ προκείμενον ἐκπληρῶσαι καὶ τὴν ἐπιγεγραμμένην πρὸς τὴν τοῦ βασιλέως παρουσίαν ἀγοράν; *P.Oxy.* 1764; *O.Bodl.* 254, 972, 1504, 1540; *SB* 6276; 6724; 6992.

παρρησία

---

parrēsia, **freedom of speech, candor, boldness, public speech, categorical affirmation**

This word, a compound of *pan* and *rhēma*, is specifically Greek; there is no corresponding Hebrew word.[1] It belongs to the literary language and is rather rare in the papyri and the inscriptions.

I. — In Greek literature, the first meaning of *parrhēsia* is political: the right to make one's thoughts known, to say what one will.[2] It is a citizen's privilege, the sign of his political liberty, characterizing the democratic regime of the *polis*. The citizen has the right to express his opinions freely in the marketplace.[3]

---

[1] In Lev 26:13, "I made you walk with head held high" (ἤγαγον ὑμᾶς μετὰ παρρησίας), the LXX uses this word to translate the Hebrew *qômmiyyût*, which is a good equivalent but not a translation. To the bibliography on παρρησία given under ἐλπίς (above, vol. 1, p. 490, n. 38), add M. Radin, "Freedom of Speech in Ancient Athens," in *AJP*, vol. 48, 1927, pp. 215–220; E. Peterson, "Zur Bedeutungsgeschichte von παρρησία," in *Reinhold Seeberg Festschrift*, Leipzig, 1929, vol. 1, pp. 283–297; H. Jaeger, "Παρρησία et *fiducia*: Etude spirituelle des mots," in *SP*, vol. 1, Berlin, 1957, pp. 221–239; G. Scarpat, *Parrhesia: Storia del termine e delle sue traduzioni in Latino*, Brescia, 1964; W. C. van Unnik, *Sparsa Collecta*, vol. 1, Leiden 1973, pp. 200ff., vol. 2, pp. 269–305; H. Schlier, "παρρησία," in *TDNT*, vol. 5, pp. 871–886.

[2] Isocrates, *Ad Nic.* 2.28: "Give freedom of speech (δίδου παρρησίαν) to sensible people in order to have counselors for embarrassing matters. Distinguish flatterers from devoted servants"; *De Pace* 8.14; Euripides, *Hipp.* 421: "May the sons whom I have brought into the world have a free man's free speech" (ἐλεύθεροι παρρησίᾳ).

[3] Demosthenes, *3 Philip.* 9.3: "If I tell you several truths frankly, I do not see that you have any reason to be angry about it. You want free speech on every other topic to be the law for everyone in our city"; Plato, *Grg.* 461 *d–e*: "Do I not have the right to talk as much as I please? Athens is the place in Greece where speech is freest"; *Resp.* 8.557 *b*, in a democratic state, "one is free in such a state, freedom (ἐλευθερία) reigns everywhere, with free speech (παρρησία), the ability to say what one pleases"; *Leg.* 3.694 *b*; Aristophanes, *Thesm.* 541: "Making use of the freedom with which all

---

parrēsia, S 3954; *TDNT* 5.871–886; *EDNT* 3.45–47; *NIDNTT* 2.734–737; MM 497; L&N 25.158, 28.29; BDF §§11(1), 198(4), 264(3); BAGD 630–631

This freedom of speech implies the truth of what is said,[4] so that *parrhēsia* means "candor, straightforwardness"; Demosthenes, *1 Philip.* 4.51: "I have laid my thoughts before you without hiding anything, in all candor"; *2 Philip.* 6.31: "I am going to speak to you openly (*meta parrhēsias*); I will not conceal anything"; *4 Philip.* 10.53–54: "If I must speak the whole truth candidly";[5] Philo, *Sacr. Abel and Cain* 12: "Moses said frankly that he did not speak easily"; 35: "I will hide nothing from you but say to you frankly";[6] Diogenes: "I am the liberator of men and the physician of their passions. In short, I want to be the prophet of truth and of candor" (*alētheias kai parrhēsias prophētēs einai boulomai*, Lucian, *Vit. Auct.* 8; cf. *Dial. Mort.* 11.3). Porphyry: "If it is necessary to speak without reticence and with all candor" (*ei gar dei mēden hyposteilamenon meta parrhēsias, Abst.* 1.57.1).

To speak candidly, proclaim the truth, and eschew evasions and lies exposes a person to danger (Josephus, *Ant.* 16.377) and presupposes the overcoming of obstacles; hence the third nuance of *parrhēsia*: "hardiness, courage, audacity, confidence." According to Wis 5:1, "The righteous person stands boldly (*en parrhēsia*) before those who have tormented him";[7] Philo, *Joseph* 73: "I will give opinions that are conducive to the common good, even if they are not of such a nature as to please. . . . I leave flattering words to others. In my speeches I will pursue the salutary and the useful. I will distribute praise, warning, or blame without flaunting foolish and mis-

---

the women here present may speak"; Polybius 2.38.6: "It would not be possible to find a regime and an ideal of equality, of freedom (παρρησίας)—in a word, of democracy—more perfect than with the Achaeans"; 2.42.3; Epictetus 3.22.96; Musonius 9.

[4] Stobaeus, *Ecl.* 4.13 (vol. 3, p. 466, 8): Παρρησίη ἀπὸ γνώμης ἐλευθέρης καὶ ἀληθείην ἀσπαζομένης προέρχεται.

[5] Demosthenes, *C. Aristocr.* 23.204: εἰ δεῖ μετὰ παρρησίας εἰπεῖν τἀληθῆ; *C. Pant.* 37.55: "I am going to tell you candidly"; Plato, *Chrm.* 156 *a*; *PSI* 1335, 11, ἵνα μετὰ παρρησίας εἴπω; Prov 10:10—"The one who criticizes candidly gains peace"; *Ep. Arist.* 125: "friends ready to give useful advice with complete candor"; Josephus, *Ant.* 15.37: Alexander expresses his indignation frankly; *T. Reub.* 4.2; Diodorus Siculus 12.63.2: the ambassadors expressed themselves frankly.

[6] Cf. *Plant.* 8; *Drunkenness* 149; *Conf. Tongues* 165; *Prelim. Stud.* 151; *Good Man Free* 95, 125, 152. In a marriage contract, the spouse commits himself freely and faithfully, with *parrhēsia*, cf. R. Taubenschlag, *Opera Minora*, vol. 1, p. 300.

[7] 4 Macc 10:5—"Terrified by the audacity of these potent words, they cut off his hands and feet" (martyrdom of the third brother); Prov 20:9—"Who would be so bold as to say, 'I am pure of sin'?"; Philo, *Husbandry* 64: one must respond bravely"; *Good Man Free* 150; *parrhēsia* and certitude are linked (Xenophon, *Cyr.* 5.3.8); prediction through astrology: "Their arrogance will disappear and their property will be confiscated" (ἡ παρρησία αὐτῶν ἀναιρεθήσεται, *P.Oxy.* 2554, col. II, 5; third century AD).

placed arrogance, but showing, to the contrary, a sober candor" (*nēphousan parrhēsian*).

This freedom of language, synonymous with candor (Aristotle, *Eth. Nic.* 4.3) is sometimes contrasted with timidity or self-consciousness, sometimes with flattery (Dio Chrysostom 32.26–27). It is practiced between friends who are not afraid to blame each other[8] as well as toward superiors, even tyrants, with whom one must guard one's freedom of speech: "Boldness (*eutolmia*) and freedom of speech (*parrhēsia*) are admirable virtues when they are addressed opportunely to superiors" (Philo, *Heir* 5, who cites Menander's *Paidion*; cf. Stobaeus, *Flor.* 62.19.19; vol. 4, p. 425). Even the servant, if he knows that he has committed no offense, retains this freedom of speech toward his master (*Heir* 6); "Famous people grant the humble free speech" (*Spec. Laws* 4.74); "The man who does not allow anyone in his household to speak freely is a petty tyrant" (*Spec. Laws* 3.138). *Parrhēsia* does not fear the widest publicity; it proclaims its convictions: "Wisdom raises her voice publicly in the streets" (Prov 1:20); "Let those whose actions benefit all use full freedom of expression; let them go out in public and converse with large crowds" (Philo, *Spec. Laws* 1.321; Plutarch, *De exil.* 16).

This *parrhēsia*, which is not confined to speech but includes conduct, does not depend on prejudices and what people will say (Philo, *Flacc.* 4). It is exalted by the philosophers, especially the Cynics, notably Diogenes, who considers it the best thing that can be found in people (*erōtētheis ti kalliston en anthrōpois, ephē parrhēsia*, Diogenes Laertius, 6.2.69; cf. Aelius Aristides 2.401 and the collection of sayings "concerning *parrhēsia*" in Stobaeus, *Flor.* 3.13; vol. 3, pp. 543ff.); "*parrhēsia* is a completely indispensable good" (Philo, *Heir* 14); "The freedom of speech of the good man is so great that he dares not only to speak and cry out, but actually to shout out from real conviction and true emotion" (*Heir* 19). The soul addresses God: "You, master, are my country, my family, my ancestral home; you are my right, my freedom of speech, my abundant wealth" (*Heir* 27); the soul, "because there is something of divine inspiration in it, expresses itself freely" (Philo, *Change of Names* 136); an inscription from Pergamum: "He adorned his life with the noblest freedom of speech" (*kekosmēke ton autou bion tē kallistē*

---

[8] Aristotle, *Eth. Nic.* 9.2.1165ª29: "We must grant friends and brothers the right to say everything to us frankly"; Plato, *Grg.* 487 *a–b*: "To find out if a soul sees well or ill, there must be three qualities: knowledge, goodwill, and candor. . . . An unfortunate timidity inhibits frank speech"; *Lach.* 188 *e*: "I have found Socrates deserving of the most complete freedom of speech." Sir 6:11—"With those of your household, a friend speaks freely"; Philo, *Heir* 21: "*Parrhēsia* is from the same family as friendship: to whom will a person speak frankly if not to a friend? . . . Assurance is the distinctive of a friend." Macro addressed to Gaius "reprimands without dissimulation and in clear terms" (*To Gaius* 41).

parrēsia, Dittenberger, *Or.* 323, 10). But we know of the excesses of Diogenes and his disciples, who think that everything is permitted and breach conventions, the proprieties, and even good sense. *Parrhēsia* degenerates into insolence or impudence toward humans and blasphemy toward the gods.[9] In addition, Philo, who makes a virtue of candor, denounces excess and requires moderation in free speech: this freedom must not be used without respect for neighbor (*Heir* 29; *Dreams* 2.83ff.). Joseph addressed the king "with freedom of speech tempered by modesty" (*parrhēsia syn aidoi*, *Joseph* 107), a candor without impudence (*parrhēsian tēn aneu anaischyntias*, *Joseph* 222); noble souls meet arrogant boasting with candor (Philo, *Good Man Free* 126). The right measure is hard to determine; on the one hand, one must not speak except with a pure conscience (*Spec. Laws* 1.203; Josephus, *Ant.* 2.52, 131) and according to the ties that bind you to your interlocutor;[10] and on the other hand, virtuous *parrhēsia* excludes verbiage with clarity and sobriety.[11] The example of Burrus, "who employed great freedom of speech," is instructive. When Nero asked him a second time about a matter that he had already explained, Burrus replied, "When I have once stated my mind, do not ask me again" (Dio Cassius 62.13). It is this form of *parrhēsia*—categorical affirmation (cf. *parrhēsiazomai*, Philo, *Sacr. Abel and Cain* 66)—that the Lord commanded: "Let your speech be yes [if it is yes], no [if it is no]. Anything in addition comes of evil" (Matt 5:37; cf. Jas 5:12).

II. — In the Gospels, *parrhēsia*, always occurring as an adverbial dative (παρρησίᾳ) or in the locution *en parrhēsia*, is used exclusively (except for John 7:13) regarding Jesus, and almost always with the verbs "say, speak"; it has the quite traditional sense of publicness and clarity. Jesus announces his passion "openly" to his disciples (Mark 8:32); "He said to them clearly (without ambiguity)" (John 11:14); "If you are the Christ, tell us frankly" (John 10:24); "The hour is coming when I will not speak to you in parables,

---

[9] Isocrates, *Bus.* 11.40: it is impious to invent legends and believe in them: "We will not say just anything about the gods" (εἰς τοὺς θεοὺς παρρησίας ὀλιγωρήσομεν); Plato, *Phdr.* 240 *e*: "unruly impudence of language"; *Symp.* 222 *c*: "These words of Alcibiades caused laughter because of their frankness"; Aristotle, *Ath. Pol.* 16.6: Pisistratus' amusement at the farmer's candor. If 1 Macc 4:18 allows seizing the plunder boldly, Sir 25:25 commands, "Allow a wicked wife no freedom of speech"; cf. the leprous Uzziah, no longer having the right to speak freely to whomever he wished (Josephus, *Ant.* 9.226).

[10] Marcus Silanus "had important qualifications for his freedom of speech (to his son-in-law): lofty nobility and relation by marriage" (Philo, *To Gaius* 63).

[11] Contrary to what Plutarch seems to say: "The freedom of speech (ἡ παρρησία) that belongs to a plea for justice gives free rein to pomposity (τὴν μεγαληγορίαν)" (*De laude* 6.541 *d–e*).

but I will speak to you of the father in full clarity" (John 16:25, 29). The nuances of "publicness, freedom," and even "boldness" are clear: "See, he speaks freely and no one says anything to him" (John 7:26; cf. 7:13); they apply not only to his words but also to his attitude and conduct: "No one does things in secret (*en kryptō*) if he wants to become a public figure" (*en parrhēsia*, out in the open, publicly; John 7:4); "Jesus did not show himself in public among the Jews" (John 11:43). This multiplicity of Johannine usages result neither from chance nor from purely literary considerations; it has a theological intention: the divine revelation is clear and is spread as widely as possible (Isa 45:19; 48:16; Prov 1:20). The Word made flesh announces the word of God with full assurance, is fully in control of its spread despite the opposition and schemes of his opponents, and thus announces it boldly, as a light shines in darkness. Summing up his ministry, he testifies to his divine authenticity on the basis of the fact that his testimony has been fulfilled with *parrhēsia:* "I have spoken to the world publicly (παρρησία, openly). I always taught in the synagogue and in the temple, where the Jews meet; I have said nothing in secret (*en kryptō*)" (John 18:20).

This courageous freedom of speech, this liberty of language, is still clearer in the Acts of the Apostles, where it becomes an apostolic virtue, with the emphasis being on the frankness of the preacher and thus on the truth of his message. Peter says, "Let me tell you with full assurance . . ." (Acts 2:29). The members of the Sanhedrin are amazed at the boldness of Peter and John, men with no education and no culture (4:13); the church prays the Lord to grant that his servants may speak his word with boldness, despite threats and hostility (4:29, 31). This is what Paul does at Damascus (9:27–28, *parrhēsiazomenos*), at Pisidian Antioch with Barnabas (13:46), at Iconium (14:3), at Ephesus (19:8), and before King Agrippa in person (26:26); likewise Apollos (18:26). The church spreads, thanks to this free proclamation—full of assurance—of the word of truth. Hence the conclusion of Acts: for two years at Rome, Paul taught "with full freedom and without obstacle" (*meta pasēs parrhēsias akōlytōs*, 28:31). We could cite Plutarch: "You have hearers . . . who ask only to seek and know the truth, banishing any spirit of dispute and polemic, and granting you to say everything with complete freedom" (*syngnōmēs de panti logō kai parrhēsias, De def. or.* 38.431 *d*).

III. — St. Luke's theology is largely dependent upon that of St. Paul. The latter, from his first epistle, saw his preaching as the expression of a freedom of speech guaranteed by the missionary's audacious assurance in the midst of direst danger.[12] Alluding to the events of Acts 16:11–40, he

---

[12] Cf. A. M. Denis, "L'Apôtre Paul, prophète 'messianique' des Gentils," in *ETL,* 1957, pp. 249–259.

writes, "In spite of the sufferings and insults that we had just endured at Philippi, our God gave us the boldness to proclaim the gospel of God to you (*eparrēsiasametha en tō theō hēmōn lalēsai pros hymas*) amid strong opposition" (1 Thess 2:2). The insistence on difficulties, obstacles, and persecutions shows that the point is not simply assurance, but exceptional courage that is not limited to the proclamation of the word but encompasses all of the apostle's conduct. If he has to summon all his human resources, he is especially strengthened by God's help; which explains why he was not vulnerable to fear or shame, but on the contrary was full of pride (cf. 2 Cor 7:4, *kauchēsis;* cf. Heb 3:6, *kauchēma*). He did not give in to the temptation to falsify his message but was resolved to keep putting out the word no matter what it cost: "Nothing will confound me; to the contrary, I will remain fully assured" (Phil 1:20). This is expressed clearly in 2 Cor 3:12— "Having such a hope, we exercise great boldness (*pollē parrēsia chrōmetha*), not like Moses, who used to veil his face," which is glossed by 4:2— "We have set aside all shameful pretense; we do not walk in deception, nor do we distort the word of God. Rather, by the manifestation of the truth we commend ourselves to every human conscience in God's sight." God is the giver of this *parrhēsia*, which does not weaken (Eph 3:12) and grants it in answer to prayer (Eph 6:19). Sometimes it is a matter of the candor that one uses with a friend (Phlm 8) or of the broadest possible publicness: "Having despoiled the principalities and powers, Christ put them on display in public (*en parrhēsia*, conspicuously), leading them in his triumphal procession" (Col 2:15). If deacons who carry out their function well "gain much assurance in the faith that is in Christ Jesus" (1 Tim 3:13), we can understand that this subordinate office can be exercised with the pride of serving, or with frankness in action, a sort of tranquil audacity that allows bold, unswerving expression of convictions, after the fashion of St. Stephen. It allows one to approach one's neighbor without any hesitation, not letting oneself be at all discouraged by criticism, taking initiative freely.

IV. — In the Epistle to the Hebrews, *parrhēsia* has become the virtue of every Christian, linked with hope (Heb 3:6), as at 2 Cor 3:12, and oriented no longer toward people but toward God, as at Job 27:10—the evildoer cannot address God with assurance (*mē echei tina parrhēsian* [Hebrew *šadday*] *enanti autou*); but Joshua addresses the Lord boldly.[13] This is rea-

---

[13] Josephus, *Ant.* 5.38 (Josh 7:7); 2.52—the faithful union of a woman and her husband brings joy, perfect confidence before God and before people (πρὸς τὸν θεὸν παρρησίαν καὶ πρὸς ἀνθρώπους); Job 22:26—"You shall lift up your face toward Eloah" (παρρησιασθήσῃ, hithpael of Hebrew *'ānag*).

soned confidence,[14] a free and easy attitude: purified from sin, Christians can approach the throne of grace in security[15] to receive mercy (Heb 4:16); they are sure to gain entry into the heavenly sanctuary, thanks to the blood of Jesus (10:19). There is no longer any obstacle; this is a right that eliminates hesitation and doubt and justifies boldness. It extends to allowing them to count on a reward: "Do not lose your assurance, which has a great and just reward" (10:35; cf. Dio Chrysostom 34.19—"I fear lest in the end you will abandon your confidence," *dedoika mē teleōs apobalēte tēn parrhēsian*). This certitude of salvation is obviously the product of the theological virtues.

This eschatological *parrhēsia* is that of 1 John: "Abide in him (Christ), so that when he appears we may have assurance (*schōmen parrhēsian*) and may not be confounded by him (*mē aischynthōmen*, dishonored, put to shame; cf. Phil 1:20) at the Parousia" (1 John 2:28). "If our heart does not accuse us, we have assurance toward God" (*parrhēsian echomen pros ton theon*, 3:21); "Love is perfected in this, that we have assurance on the day of judgment" (*hina parrhēsian echōmen*, 4:7). There is no better guarantee of salvation than a soul filled with love.[16] *Agapē* gives audacious confidence in the most fearful of all situations: the day of judgment, when no one is beyond reproach, and condemnations are without appeal. Love excludes worry and apprehension; it reassures. Johannine *parrhēsia*, then, is always a boldness, consisting of freedom and confidence, that allows one to present oneself before a superior without fear, and also before persecutors or any interlocutor who may contradict or accuse. This same filial confidence is expressed in prayer: "See what assurance we have with him: if we ask anything according to his will, he hears us" (5:14).

---

[14] Παρρησία = confidence, *P.Mich.* 502, 9 and 12 (the mutual confidence of two brothers, second century AD). Cf. L. Engels, "*Fiducia* dans la Vulgate: Le Problème de la traduction παρρησία-*fiducia*," in *Graecitas et Latinitas Christianorum Primaeva: Supplementa*, vol. 1, Nijmegen, 1964, pp. 99–141.

[15] Cf. in the sixth century *P.Fouad* 86, 9 and 16: "If the said person finds an audience (εὕρη παρρησίαν) with the most eminent general and consul."

[16] Cf. C. Spicq, *Agapè*, vol. 3, pp. 292ff. P. Althaus, "Liebe und Heilsgewißheit bei Martin Luther: I Joh. IV, 7 a in der Auslegung Luthers," in *Festgabe J. Lortz*, Baden-Baden, 1958, vol. 1, pp. 69–84. We may recall that *parrhēsia* is set in relation with the Holy Spirit (Acts 4:8, 13, 31; cf. 2:4, 29; 18:25–26; 1 John 3:21, 24), who guarantees the truth of the apostles' witness.

πειθαρχέω

peitharcheō, to obey, be persuaded, comply willingly

→*see also* εἰσακούω, ἐπακούω, ὑπακούω, ὑπακοή; πείθω, πείθομαι, πειθός, πεισμονή, πεποίθησις

Normally construed with the dative case, but in Hellenistic Greek sometimes with the genitive,[1] this verb is ordinarily translated "obey," and it is indeed true that in the literature, the papyri, and the inscriptions it often refers to strict obedience: of rulers to God,[2] servants to their masters,[3] princes to their fathers (Josephus, *War* 1.454: *tō patri panta peitharchein*), women to their husbands,[4] private citizens or officials to

---

[1] Cf. E. Nachmanson, "Die Konstruktionen von πειθαρχεῖν in der κοινή," in *Eranos*, 1910, pp. 201–203.

[2] Dan 7:27—"All dominions will be in submission to him and will obey him" (ὑποταγήσονται καὶ πειθαρχήσουσιν αὐτῷ in the LXX, but in Theodotion δουλεύσουσιν καὶ ὑπακούσονται).

[3] Sir 33:29; cf. Menander, *Dysk.* 370: ἕτοιμος πάντα πειθαρχεῖν, "I am ready to obey in everything."

[4] In marriage contracts: δεῖ πειθαρχεῖν γαμετήν γυναῖκα ἀνδρός (*P.Oxy.* 265, 13, first century AD); "Apollonia will live with Philiscos and be obedient to him as wife to husband" (*P.Tebt.* 104, 14; first century BC); πειθαρχοῦσα αὐτῷ ὡς προσήκει (*P.Tebt.* 974, 2; second century BC; Philo, *Creation* 167). In Philo, the verb πειθαρχέω is sometimes used for obedience in the strict sense of the word: of cows to the cowherd (*Dreams* 2.152; *Moses* 2.61), of members of the body (*Spec. Laws* 3.177), of humans to the laws of nature (*Spec. Laws* 1.306), to the commandments of the law (ibid. 1.153; 3.38; 4.150; *Virtues* 94), to kings and rulers (*Abraham* 226; *Spec. Laws* 2.234; 3.163; *To Gaius* 69), to a father's orders (*Drunkenness* 35; *Joseph* 12), to God (*Flight* 99; *Virtues* 63). But the idea is less obedience under compulsion than voluntary submission, acceptance, and docility: "'to hear' is the most precise term for acquiescence, obedience" (*Prelim. Stud.* 68), as with Agrippa following his master's advice (*Flacc.* 26; cf. *Good Man Free* 54), or the great voluntarily submitting to custom (*Change of Names* 104). In this sense, one must "submissively obey the directives of reasonable

---

peitharcheō, S 3980; *TDNT* 6.9–10; *EDNT* 3.62; *NIDNTT* 3.588–589; MM 500; L&N 36.12; BDF §187(6); BAGD 638–639

their superiors,[5] peoples to their conqueror.[6] But on the one hand, there are different nuances with these different instances of submission; and on the other hand the proper verb for obedience in the NT is *hypakouō*, and the peculiar nuance of *peitharcheō*, which is not strictly synonymous with it, must be maintained. When during the storm St. Paul says, "You should have listened to me (*peitharchēsantas moi*) and not left Crete" (Acts 27:21), he does not mean strict submission but voluntary consent. Similarly, when God gives the Holy Spirit "to those who are obedient to him" (*tois peitharchousin autō*, Acts 5:32), this expression means not so much those who remain flawlessly faithful as those who accept his word, submit gladly to his will and his inspiration, and conform to his providential arrangements. This meaning of *peitharcheō*—let oneself be persuaded, willingly comply with a rule—is well attested in literary texts and inscriptions: "It is necessary for the learner to be submissive to the orders of virtue" (*tois parangelmasin aretēs peitharchein*, Philo, *Prelim. Stud.* 63); "to give complete obedience to things that are ordered for the common good" (*peitharchein de pantōs tois hyper tou koinē sympherontos epitattomenois*, *I.Magn.* 114, 8; cf. Dittenberger, *Syl.* 22, 7).

This consent or willingness to fall in with a given arrangement, to adapt to the requirements of an institution, given the nuance of St. Peter's famous principle: *peitharchein dei theō mallon ē anthrōpois* (Acts 5:29), is ordinarily translated "It is necessary to obey God rather than men" (cf. Josephus, *Ag. Apion* 2.293: "What is more just than obeying the laws," *peitharchein tois nomois;* Marcus Aurelius 5.9: "You submit to reason"). But Peter and John had said (Acts 4:19), "Whether it is just before God to listen to you (*akouein*) rather than God, judge for yourselves." Thus it is less a

---

good sense and of education" (ibid. 206), defer to the commands of reason (*Moses* 1.26; *Good Man Free* 47), and above all submit to the requirements of virtue (*Drunkenness* 16; *Prelim. Stud.* 2, 63, 64, 176; *Spec. Laws* 4.95–96; *Moses* 1.329). Being submissive and obedient is the opposite of being stubborn (*Change of Names* 115).

[5] Philo, *Moses* 1.164, 329. Athens in the third century BC, honors the *taxiarchoi* who "under all circumstances never failed to obey the orders of the *stratēgoi*, conforming to the laws" (*SEG* XIV, 17); a century later, the founding regulation of Eumenes II of Pergamum provides that "when the leaders shall have designated the people who are of age to run, if one of them does not wish to obey although he has the strength to do so, he shall be liable to a fine" (*Fouilles de Delphes* III, 3; 238, 17); in the same period, a regulation concerning the functions and duties of the *astynomoi* of Pergamum: "if the private citizens do not obey, the *astynomoi* shall put the works in litigation" (Dittenberger, *Or.* 483, 70 = *SEG* XIII, 521, 82); *P.Panop.Beatty* 1, 211: π. τοῖς κελευσθῖσι; *P.Oxy.* 2476, 12: οἱ ἀγωνοθέται πιθαρχήσουσιν (third century AD).

[6] Polybius 3.4.3: "All recognize the necessity henceforth of obeying the Romans and submitting to their will" (Ῥωμαίων ἀκούειν καὶ τούτοις πειθαρχεῖν ὑπὲρ τῶν παραγγελλομένων).

matter of material obedience than of recognizing authority, of submitting clearly and willingly to this or that hierarchy.

It seems that in Titus 3:1 *peitharcheō* retains the sense of strict, concrete obedience—"Remind them to be in submission to the constituted powers and authorities, to obey, to be ready for every good work"—but the linking of *hypotassomai* and *peitharcheō* enriches the latter verb with the meaning of the former: Christians, in submitting to the authorities, accept their subordinate position, consent to a social and political order, observe the norms of a public institution. Their obedience is not only faithfulness to the laws, but respect and a sort of loyalty toward a power that they are persuaded is legitimate.[7] In this sense of the word, the attitude of the wise person toward Nature will be "a feeling of submission (*peitharchōn*) and goodwill" (Marcus Aurelius 10.14).

---

[7] Cf. King Antiochus III: "If he bids (παρακαλῇ) someone carry out some action regarding his office, let those who belong to the sanctuaries and the others who owe him obedience (καὶ τοὺς ἄλλους οὓς καθήκει πειθαρκεῖν αὐτοῦ) assist him. Certify that we order people to conform (ὑπακούειν) to all that he shall prescribe or order" (*IGLS* 992, 38).

πείθω, πείθομαι, πειθός, πεισμονή, πεποίθησις

peithō, to (try to) persuade; peithomai, to be persuaded; peithos, persuasive; peismonē, persuasion, influence; pepoithēsis, confidence, assurance, boldness

→see also πειθαρχέω

The basic meaning of the verb peithō (conative), peithomai is "persuade, be persuaded,"[1] in whatever fashion: better if by reasoning and entreaty,[2] worse if by money or violence. It runs the whole gamut of nuances, from "convince, accept, believe," to "conform, submit, give in, obey."

All these meaning are found already in Homer, where peithō in the active and transitive sometimes means "persuade": "Priam was not able to persuade the soul of Hector" (Homer, Il. 22.78); "I will persuade him to

---

[1] S. Schulz, Die Wurzel πειθ- (πιθ-), Fribourg, 1952: "The transitive active is perhaps secondary" (P. Chantraine, Dictionnaire étymologique, p. 868); cf. F. M. Abel, Grammaire, 18, n, p; B. Mandilaras, Verb, 209, 802.

[2] Sophocles, OC 520: "Grant it (πείθου), for I myself granted your entreaty." Πειθώ is the goddess Persuasion. "August Persuasion" (Hesiod, Op. 73; Th. 349); "The Athenians accompanied by two great deities, Persuasion and Compulsion" (Πειθώ τε καὶ Ἀναγκαίην, Herodotus 8.11); "to help their mother, behold Desire (Πόθος) and the enchantress Persuasion (Πειθοῖ), who has never been refused" (Aeschylus, Suppl. 1040; cf. Ag. 385); Alcman in Plutarch, De fort. Rom. 4.318 b; Menander, Epit. 338; Philo, Post. Cain 45; Nonnus, Dion. 3.95; O. Guéraud, P. Jouguet, Un Livre d'écolier du IIIᵉ s. av. J.-C., Cairo, 1938, p. 34, line 212; a dedication to Πειθοῖ at Paros (J. and L. Robert, "Bulletin épigraphique," in REG, 1938, p. 450, n. 289), at Cnidos (ibid., 1954, p. 165, n. 228), at Cos (ibid., 1967, p. 522, n. 434).

---

peithō, S 3982; TDNT 6.1–9; EDNT 3.63; NIDNTT 1.588–593; MM 500–501; L&N 25.166, 31.82, 33.301; BDF §§101, 159(1), 187(6), 322, 341, 392(1e), 397(2); BAGD 639 ‖ peithomai, TDNT 6.1–9; EDNT 3.63–64; NIDNTT 1.587–593; L&N 31.46, 36.12, 36.34; BAGD 639–640 ‖ peithos, S 3981; TDNT 6.8–9; EDNT 3.63; NIDNTT 1.588, 592; MM 500; L&N 33.304; BDF §§47(4), 112, 474(4); BAGD 639 ‖ peismonē, S 3988; TDNT 6.9; EDNT 3.67; NIDNTT 1.588, 591–592; MM 502; L&N 33.303; BDF §§ 109(6), 488(1b); BAGD 641 ‖ pepoithēsis, S 4006; TDNT 6.7–8; EDNT 3.70; MM 503; L&N 31.82; BDF § 68; BAGD 643

fight you face to face."[3] Sometimes it is in the middle: "admit, trust"; "without admitting yet (*epeitheto*) that it was indeed his father" (*Od.* 16.192); Athena to Ulysses: "humans place their confidence in weak friends" (20.45); "I am still too young to count on my arm."[4] The perfect expresses persistence in a state of confidence: "The young have confidence in their own strength" (*Il.* 4.325). Hence "hear and believe": *oude me peiseis* = "I will not listen to you" (*Il.* 1.132; 6.360; 9.345); Zeus to Thetis: "so you will believe me" (*pepoithēs*, 1.524); Athena to Ulysses: "Perhaps you will believe me" (*Od.* 13.344); "Thus spoke Athena, and the poor fool believed her" (*peithen, Il.* 4.104). To be convinced and believe is finally to obey: "How can an Achaean readily obey your orders?" (*peithētai, Il.* 1.150; cf. 79); "Son of Atreus, the Argive army will obey your voice above all others."[5]

According to varying contexts, *peithō* can mean to convince others (*Od.* 14.123), to change someone's mind (1.43; cf. Xenophon, *An.* 3.1.26), and notably to appease: "Let us think how to calm him, to convince him with friendly gifts, with soothing words" (*pepithōmen, Il.* 9.112; *Od.* 3.146: he flattered himself that he appeased the goddess). The verb can mean "accept an invitation" (*Od.* 17.177) as well as "submit" (*Il.* 23.645) and "dupe" (*Od.* 2.106), but it also suggests the idea of stimulating, setting in motion: "persuading the storm-winds with the help of the north wind" (*pepithousa thyellas, Il.* 15.26).

In the classical period, the meanings of certitude and belief are well established, especially with the perfect.[6] "I am sure (*pepeismai*) that Protagoras will have no trouble elucidating" the difficulty (Plato, *Prt.* 328 *e*); "I am sure (*pepoitha*) that for him the lightning will come, bringing fire."[7]

---

[3] Homer, *Il.* 22.223; 9.587: "He did not persuade his heart in his chest"; 9.184: "that they may without too much difficulty persuade the proud soul of Aeacides."

[4] *Od.* 16.71 (perfect πέποιθα); 21.132; cf. Pindar, *Pyth.* 10.100: "I put my trust in the kind hospitality of Thorax"; Homer, *Od.* 16.98: "the support that one expected from a brother" (πέποιθε); *Il.* 13.96: "Young warriors of Argos, I have confidence in you"; Aeschylus, *Cho.* 237: "Trust in your valor (πεποιθὼς); you shall recover your father's palace."

[5] *Il.* 23.157; 16.171: rowers must obey their commanders; "Let us obey the black night and prepare our evening meal" (πειθώμεθα, 8.502; 9.65); "I think I know someone who will not obey" (οὐ πείσεσθαι, 1.289). Ulysses: "Do you think that I am of such an age as to remain in the huts, obeying a superior's orders in everything?" (πιθέσθαι, *Od.* 17.21).

[6] Herodotus 9.88: "They were persuaded (ἐπεποίθεσαν) that with money they would pull through"; Sophocles, *Aj.* 769: "I am quite sure (πέποιθα) of winning the glory"; Aeschylus, *Eum.* 826, Athena: "I rely on Zeus" (κἀγὼ πέποιθα Ζηνί).

[7] Aeschylus, *Sept.* 444; Euripides, *Hipp.* 1251: "I will never be able to believe that your son is wicked"; *Andr.* 870: πεισθεὶς λόγοις = trusting the words; Plato, *Ap.* 25 *e:* "You will not get me to believe it, or anyone else in the world"; *Prt.* 338 *a;* Herodotus 1.8, 126; Xenophon, *Oec.* 20.15.

Of course, "persuade, convince" remains the basic meaning.[8] "Sostratus sought to persuade the brother" (Menander, *Dysk.* hyp. 6); "The law defends him against compulsion (*tō biasasthai*); his character defends him against persuasion (*tō peisai*)" (*Dysk.* 254); "you who think of persuading a free young woman to sin" (*Dysk.* 290). So also the meaning "obey." "They thought that the other Milesians would obey" (Herodotus 5.29; cf. 33); "for seven days they obeyed and did as ordered" (6.12); "we should obey him."[9] But our verb is not synonymous with *hypakouō*, first of all because it denotes following advice, giving in to reasons, taking an opinion into account,[10] giving a favorable hearing; one draws inspiration[11] and conforms to it (Xenophon, *An.* 7.3.39), gives one's approval (*An.* 5.6.29) or does as asked (Pindar, *Pyth.* 1.59; Hesiod, *Th.* 474). Finally, having been won over by persuasion (*pepeismenos*, Xenophon, *An.* 7.2.12), one decides,[12] and—

---

[8] Plato, *Resp.* 1.327 c: "Would you be able to convince people who do not want to hear?"; 2.364 b; *Phdr.* 271 c; *Grg.* 453 a: "Rhetoric is a worker of persuasion"; Aeschylus, *Eum.* 724: Apollo persuaded the Parci to make humans immortal; Xenophon, *An.* 7.6.9: "After persuading us, they brought us here with our consent"; *Cyr.* 6.1.34: Araspas asks whether Cyrus "is capable of persuading such a woman"; *Hier.* 1.16, Simonides to Hiero, "a thing of which you could not persuade anyone"; Sophocles, *Phil.* 624: "I will allow myself to be persuaded after I am dead"; Thucydides 3.70.1: they knew how to persuade them to bring over Corcyra to Corinth; 3.75.1: "Nicostratus persuaded the Corcyreans to come to an agreement"; 3.31.1: "These words could not convince Alcibiades" (οὐκ ἔπειθε).

[9] Plato, *Leg.* 4.714 b, πείθεσθαι; *Ap.* 29 d: "I will obey the god rather than you" (πείσομαι δὲ μᾶλλον τῷ θεῷ ἢ ὑμῖν); *Menex.* 248 a: "He will obey the proverb fully"; Sophocles, *Ant.* 67, Ismene: "I intend to obey the powers that be"; *Phil.* 1252: "Even if you use force, I do not intend to obey"; Pindar, *Nem.* 8.10; *Ol.* 13.79; Aeschylus, *Cho.* 297: "One cannot disobey such oracles" (χρησμοῖς πεποιθέναι); Xenophon, *Cyr.* 1.2.8: "Children are taught to obey their officials . . . whom the elders obey blindly." Diodorus Siculus 4.31.5: "Hercules, forced to obey the oracle."

[10] Herodotus 6.100: "The Athenians followed (πείθονται) the advice of Aeschines"; 7.144: "On the advice of the god (τῷ θεῷ πειθομένους), the Athenians resolved to stand up to the barbarian"; Aeschylus, *PV* 1014: "If my reasons cannot convince you" (πεισθῇς λόγοις); 1063: "Give opinions that can convince me"; *Cho.* 781: "I will go and I will follow your advice" (πείσομαι λόγοις); Sophocles, *OC* 1442, Antigone to Polynices: "Give in to me (ἐμοὶ πιθοῦ)—do not urge me to do what must not be done (μὴ πεῖθ' ἃ μὴ δεῖ)"; Xenophon, *Hell.* 6.5.16: people urge (ἔπειθον) Agesilaus to attack separately. Menander, *Dysk.* 712: "None of you can make me change my mind about it" (μεταπεῖσαι).

[11] Thucydides 2.2.4: "Rather than listening to those who had called them in (οὐκ ἐπείθοντο) . . . they decided . . ."; 6.33.1: "Not only do they not listen (οὐ πείθουσιν), but one is thought to be mad"; Menander, *Dysk.* 38: "The young woman inspired in us (πέπεικεν) a certain kind regard for herself."

[12] Herodotus 1.163: "The Phocaeans did not let themselves be persuaded" (οὐκ ἔπειθε); 8.134: Mys convinced a man of Lebadeia whom he paid to go down into the

this is the second point—it is a voluntary commitment to action, like a stimulus to participate in an undertaking.

Given the importance of personal conviction in the person from whom one wishes to obtain something, we can understand that Aristotle should have posed the question, "Must one obey one's father in everything?" (Eth. Nic. 9.2.1164[b]22–23). He replies that one need not grant one's father everything any more than one sacrifices everything to Zeus.[13] Musonius also asks himself whether to obey in everything (panta peithesthai, frag. 16) and answers that one cannot submit to unjust or shameful commands: "He is obedient who listens to the voice of obligation and follows it assiduously." One must obey Zeus, whose law ordains that people should be virtuous; so one must discern whether paternal orders are good, honest, and beneficent.

In the inscriptions, the meaning "persuade" is predominant from the fourth centuryBC on. The constitutive decree of the second Athenian confederation (377 BC) prescribes: "The people shall immediately appoint three delegates who shall go to Thebes to persuade (peisousi) the Thebans to act for the best."[14] But there is also the meaning "accord, consent" in the lease of a garden by the coreligionists (orgeōnes) of the physician Hero: "if a cordial understanding (peithei) comes about with Charops and the

---

cave of Trophonius (μισθῷ πείσας); Lysias 21.10: "giving him the price, I hired Phantias as pilot"; Plato, Euthd. 272 c, Socrates to Crito: "I had already persuaded (πέπεικα) others to become my fellow disciples, and I will try to persuade even more to follow me here"; Euripides, Med. 982: "The veil's charm and heavenly beauty will persuade her to put it on"; Sophocles, Phil. 901; Xenophon, An. 1.3.19: "Either he must persuade us to follow or we must convince him to send us back on friendly terms"; 5.1.14; Polybius 4.64.2.

[13] P.Hercul. 176. In this same papyrus, a letter of Epicurus to an orphaned child says, "It is good for you to obey your grandfather and grandmother in everything (πάντα πείθῃ). . . . They all love you because you obey them in everything (ὅτι τούτοις πείθῃ πάντα," lines 10 and 14; republished by G. Milligan, Selections from the Greek Papyri, Cambridge, 1927, p. 6). Cf. P.Ryl. 77, 34: πειθόμενος τῇ ἐμαυτοῦ πατρίδι.

[14] J. Pouilloux, Choix, n. 27, 74. Cf. 33, 4, regarding the sale of citizenship in the third century: since the administrative assembly of the city has to vote according to the reasons explained for the admission of new citizens, it is provided that these will "enter into the patrē (a tribe of the Thasians) that they persuade." At Daphne, "We have appointed him high priest of these sanctuaries, being persuaded (πεπεισμένοι) that their administration will be seen to in a full and satisfactory fashion" (Dittenberger, Or. 244, 29 = IGLS, n. 992). In the hymn to Isis from the first century BC: "You persuade the Nile, which rolls gold along, and you bring it back to the Egyptian soil each season" (E. Bernand, Inscriptions métriques, n. 175, col. II, 17 = SB 8139, 17). The epitaph of the euergetēs ("benefactor") Apollonius in the second century BC: "believe me" (E. Bernand, Inscriptions métriques 6, 22 = SEG VII, 768 = SB 8230).

orgeōnes."[15] Then there is "convince" in the honorific decree of Istrus for Agathocles around 200 BC: "He convinced (*epeise*) the barbarians to do our city no harm"; "For six hundred *chrysoi*, he convinced Zoltes and the Thracians not to invade the territory"; "He convinced King Rhemaxus to give us five hundred horsemen for our defense."[16] Finally, there is "drag along, lead": "as far as possible, without letting himself be dragged along by the one who has just breached (the texts written on the stele)."[17]

The papyri add hardly any new shades of meaning,[18] but the frequency of the occurrences confirms the classical meanings while nuancing them, notably in Zeno's correspondence: *pepeismai* = "I am persuaded."[19] To be persuaded is to be convinced and have confidence:[20] *pithontos soi* = having

---

[15] *NCIG*, n. 27, 22 (fourth century BC). In the dedication of the Moschion to Osiris: σαφῶς ἐρεῖς πεισθεὶς ἐμοὶ θ[――] (E. Bernand, *Inscriptions métriques*, n. 108, 40 = *SB* 8026), we may interpret "surely you will say with me," i.e., in accord with my voice.

[16] *NCIG*, n. VI, 19, 31, 50, 55.

[17] Dittenberger, *Syl.* 142, 24: a pact between Athens and Chios (fourth century BC).

[18] Moulton-Milligan notes the parallels of *peithō* as a conative present, "Apply persuasion," "seek to persuade," as in Acts 26:28, the corresponding aorist ἔπεισα in *P.Tor.* 1, col. VIII, 36 = *UPZ* 162; *BGU* 164, 26; *P.Oxy.* 294, 22. For the second perfect πέποιθα with the dative, *BGU* 1141, 17 (cf. 2 Cor 10:7; Phil 1:14; Phlm 21); the intransitive is construed with the genitive in *PSI* 538, 7. As for the middle or passive "I am persuaded," we may cite *P.Petr.* II, 11 (1), 4 (S. Witkowski, *Epistulae Privatae Graecae* 3 = G. Milligan, *Selections from the Greek Papyri*, Cambridge, 1927, n. 3), a letter of Polycrates to his father: "If you come, I am sure (πέπεισμαι) that I will easily be able to introduce you to the king"; *BGU* 1118, 40; *P.Oxy.* 268, 7: "the sum that they have each agreed to accept" (AD 58); 1293, 13; *P.Ryl.* 176, 3; *P.Fay.* 133, 12.

[19] *SB* 9220 *a* 7; *b* recto 6; *P.Mich.* 29, 9: "If you examine the matter, you will be persuaded that we are useful to you"; cf. *P.Tebt.* 762, 4: "I am persuaded that, if God wills, he will be secure" (third century BC); *P.Mil.Vogl.* 24, 22: ἐγὼ πεπεισμένος μου τῇ διανοίᾳ (second century AD); *P.Oxy.* 2190, 23: He persuaded (ἔπειθεν) the sons of Apollonius to go to Didyma (first century); *P.Mich.* 502, 14: πείσῃς τὴν μητέραν = persuade our mother; *P.Hib.* 204, 6: "I will persuade my employers"; *P.Genova* 11, 3 (= *SB* 10730); 23, 2; *UPZ* 218, col. I, 17: "with effort, I have now convinced him"; *P.Princ.* 68, 8: γράφε μοι πεπεισμένος ὅτι . . . ; *P.Lond.* 1916, 27: "Write me so that we may have certitude"; *P.Tebt.* 768, 16; *SB* 10803, 7.

[20] *PSI* 1309, col. II, 7; 1413, 8; *P.Yale* 41, 10: "Apollonius will explain to you and convince you"; *P.Oxy.* 2980, 8: "You have no need to be persuaded of this"; 3106, 9; *P.Hamb.* 87, 16; *C.P.Herm.* 8, 14; 9, 22; *P.Mert.* 12, 9, a letter to a physician, in AD 58: "I have confidence that (πείθομαι ὅτι) I can retain a certain degree of serenity and be able . . ."; *P.Lond.* 1929, 10; *P.Mich.* 87, 6 (letter to Zeno): ἐπὶ σοὶ πεποιθώς = having confidence in your support; 485, 11: "Urge Valerius to write to Pius, having confidence (πειθόμενον) in my good faith"; *SB* 9450, 8.

confidence in you (*SB* 7354, 5; cf. line 8: "look, do not trust," *blepe, mē pisthēs*), rely on (*P.Fouad* 26, 41) and believe (*SB* 4630, 6), and finally being in accord (*P.Oxy.* 2562, 11: *episthēmen pros heautous*), "agree, give one's consent." This is how the verb is often used in contracts where one subscribes to what is written or to what has been read: "with this agreement, with whom they also consent after reading it" (*tē homologia tautē, hois kai ex anagnōseōs pepismenoi eisin, P.Mich.* 322 *a* 37; a division of property in AD 46; cf. lines 39, 43–47); "because I consent to it as it stands" (*dia to pepeisthai me kathōs prokitai*).[21] Not only does one attest to one's good faith ("confidently without any guile," *pepeismenōs pantos dolou chōris, BGU* 2203, 13; "willing and in agreement, without force or deception," *hekōn kai pepeismenos aneu bias kai apatēs, P.Köln* 157, 11); but this freely given consent is elaborated upon ("willing and in agreement, out of a self-chosen decision," *SB* 8988, 49; 9586, 9; 9763, 25; "we think it good and we agree," *eudokoumen kai peithometha*),[22] with full knowledge of the facts ("we know and agree," *oidamen kai pepismetha, P.Oxy.* 1868, 2). The meaning thus confirmed is a guarantee ("I will confirm and I agree to everything as it is set down," *bebaiōsō kai pithomai pasi hōs prokeitai, PSI* 1239, 23). Hence the meaning to obey, submit, be ready to carry out a certain decision or conform to given instructions.[23] In *Apokrimata* 56 (p. 7), we may translate the imperative *peithou* either "obey" or "execute" (cf. 12; *SB* 9526, 12 and 56).

For their part, the prefects or *epistratēgoi* use the euphemism *pepeismai* to express (in the repression of an abuse) their confidence in their subjects' obedience to their decrees. For example, Tiberius Julius Alexander: "I am persuaded that in the future no one will any longer recruit farmers or tenants by force."[24]

---

[21] *P.Mich.* 351, 31 (AD 44); 659, 291: πίθωμαι πᾶσι ὡς πρόκειται; line 300; *PSI* 11246, 5: ἐν πᾶσι πέπεισμαι; *SB* 8986, 27; 6266, 9: ὁμολογοῦμεν ... καὶ πεπεισμένοι; 6704, 9; 7033, 77; 7668, 3; 11042, 24 (= *P.Col.* VII, 188); 12215, 4; *P.Ross.Georg.* III, 33, 8; *BGU* 1865, 2; 2168, 21; 2185, 18; *P.Lips.* 28, 28.

[22] *PSI* 1239, 21; *P.Mich.* 659, 287 and 296; *SB* 9763, 54, 56; 9889, 6; 10784, 11; *P.Oslo* 129, 8.

[23] Ἐπιτρόπῳ, πεισθεὶς τοῖς γραφῖσι, *P.Panop.Beatty* 1, 85; 2, 86: τοῖς προσταχθεῖσιν πεισθείς; *P.Alex.* 25, 26: ἐν τούτῳ ἑαυτοὺς πείσωμεν; *P.Fam.Tebt.* 19, 9: ὅπως πείθονται τοῖς κεκριμένοις (= *SB* 9252, 9; cf. 9225, 6). It seems that πείθομαι means to be ready to stand as a candidate, to take on an office (in the second-third century), cf. *P.Oxy.* 1252, verso col. II, 28; *Stud.Pal.* XX, 58, col. I, 10; *P.Ryl.* 77, 34; *P.Ross.Georg.* II, 40, 16, 17, 19.

[24] *BGU* 1563, 37 (= Dittenberger, *Or.* 669 = *SB* 8444); *P.Brem.* 2, 10; *P.Oxy.* 3025, 12; cf. *P.Oxy.Hels.* 47 *b* 21: "I am sure that you will do everything on your own."

With the LXX, the verb *peithō* takes on an entirely different tone. The meaning "persuade" is rare and late,[25] and "believe" is exceptional: "I believe (*pepeismai*) all that the prophet Jeremiah says."[26] Rather, this verb almost always corresponds to the Hebrew *bāṭaḥ* or one of its derivatives and thus expresses confidence (Deut 28:52; Judg 9:26; 18:10, 27). But one can put one's trust either in false supports or in the true God:[27] "What is the meaning of this confidence in which you trust?"[28] The faith of Israel is to put its trust in Yahweh,[29] which means relying on him (2 Chr 14:10, niphal of the Hebrew *šā'an*; 16:7–8; Isa 10:20; 17:7) or taking shelter under his wings.[30] To have this confidence is to feel secure; also, the Hebrew *lābeṭaḥ*, Greek *pepoithōs*, means that one dwells, lives, or walks in security;[31] that is, one rests in quiet tranquility.[32]

The Letter of Aristeas asks, "What is the end of eloquence?" and answers, "to persuade the adversary (*to peisai ton antilegonta*) . . . persuasion comes about by the power of God."[33] Philo often gives the verb the meaning "persuade"[34] or "be convinced," for example, of the existence of the Most

---

[25] Jdt 12:11; Wis 16:8; 2 Macc 7:26; 9:27: letter from King Antiochus: "I am persuaded (πέπεισμαι) that my son will follow my intentions scrupulously"; 4 Macc 2:6; 9:18; 16:24; cf. win someone to one's cause (4:45; 11:14) with money (10:20); convince him (4:34; 4 Macc 8:12).

[26] Tob 14:4; cf. assurance (πεποιθώς), Prov 14:16; Jdt 2:5—"You shall take men who are sure of their strength"; 4 Macc 5:16; "obey" (6:4; 8:17, 26; 10:13; 12:4–5; 15:10; 18:1).

[27] Isa 30:3; 31:1; 42:17; Jer 7:14; 48:7, 13; 49:11; Bar 3:17; 1 Macc 10:71, 77; 2 Macc 10:34; 12:14; Jdt 7:10; Zeph 3:2; Job 31:24; Prov 28:25; 29:25; Wis 13:7; 14:29; 16:24; Sir 32:24.

[28] 2 Kgs 18:19–22; 2 Chr 32:10, 15; Isa 30:12; 36:4–9; 50:10; 59:4; Jer 7:4, 8; 9:3; 46:25; 49:4; Ezek 33:13; Job 6:20; 39:11; Ps 49:6; 135:18; 146:3; Prov 11:28; 2 Macc 8:18.

[29] 2 Kgs 19:20; Isa 12:2; 33:2; 37:10; Jer 17:7; 39:18; Sus 35; Ps 25:2; 125:1; Prov 3:5; 16:20; 21:22; Wis 3:9; 2 Macc 7:40; 15:7.

[30] Ruth 2:12 (πεποιθέναι, Hebrew *ḥāsâh*); 2 Sam 22:3 (cf. Isa 8:17, piel of the Hebrew *qāwâh*); Ps 2:12; 11:1; 57:1; 118:8; cf. Isa 22:24; hang (Hebrew *tālâh*).

[31] Lev 25:18–19; Deut 33:12, 28; Judg 8:11; 1 Sam 12:11; Amos 6:1; Jer 12:5; 23:6; 32:37; Job 11:18; Prov 10:9; Sir 4:15.

[32] Isa 14:7 (Hebrew *šāqaṭ*); 30:15; 32:17–19; 47:8; 58:14; Jer 28:15; 48:11; 1 Macc 9:58.

[33] *Ep. Arist.* 266; cf. 252: "How can one be free of error? By doing everything with deliberation and reflection, without allowing oneself to be imposed upon (πειθόμενος, convince or seduce, bend) by unfavorable talk"; 5: "I am convinced (πέπεισμαι) that you will willingly learn what I want to recount"; one puts one's confidence in might (147–148, 193).

[34] *Alleg. Interp.* 3.80: "royal intelligence imposes less than it persuades"; *Post. Cain* 55; *Prelim. Stud.* 107; *Dreams* 1.77; *Joseph* 189, 269; *Moses* 1.85; 2.257; *Spec. Laws* 1.79; *Good Man Free* 96.

High God,[35] but he is far from being the writer who uses it most often in the sense "obey": *Cherub.* 9: "to obey virtue is fine"; *Alleg. Interp.* 1.95: "the man obeyed God's counsels" (*Abraham* 252, 256); *Drunkenness* 33: "submit as a child does to its parents"; *Dreams* 2.24, 108: "a servant, I learned to obey them as masters."[36]

In the whole literature, it is the writings of Josephus that use this word most abundantly (nearly five hundred occurrences), obviously in rather varied meanings. "Persuade" and "convince" are predominant,[37] but with multiple nuances, because if no one consents and surrenders easily (*War* 1.32, 144, 254; *Life* 149; *Ag. Apion* 2.117, 153), others refuse their consent[38] and ingenious ways must be devised to gain it (*Ant.* 4.251; 7.172; *Ag. Apion* 2.200–201), being confident of success: "I will persuade Caesar" (*War* 2.201) and bringing proofs (*Ant.* 8.48). It is with words, speeches, and arguments that one succeeds in convincing.[39] Sometimes it is a matter of mere opinion,[40] sometimes advice,[41] or requests (*Ant.* 20.121, 135, 142, 145, 161), even attempts to entice (*War* 1.274; *Ant.* 2.41, 50) or finally incite to

---

[35] *Sacr. Abel and Cain* 60; *Worse Attacks Better* 131; *Husbandry* 56; *Decalogue* 87; *Virtues* 120; *Good Man Free* 95; *To Gaius* 3, 37, 198, 233, 240. Cf. *Husbandry* 63: "those who are convinced (οἱ πεπεισμένοι) that they can master unreasonable forces"; *Spec. Laws* 1.45; *Flacc.* 174; "decide" (*Joseph* 225); "trust in, put one's confidence in" (*Spec. Laws* 2.197; 1.62; 4.1, 174; *Abraham* 232).

[36] Philo, *Unchang. God* 50: reflection is like "an incorruptible judge who obeys the suggestions of right reason"; 183; *Husbandry* 40; *Sobr.* 33: "obeying the suggestions of right reason"; *Conf. Tongues* 59; *Abraham* 85: "the good man obeys an oracle"; 88, 192; *Spec. Laws* 2.230: "an army in submission to its leader's orders."

[37] Josephus, *War* 1.76, 365, 483; 2.340; 4.218, 230, 518; 5.528; 7.253, 410; *Ant.* 1.113, 276; 7.261; 8.308, 350; 10.9, 161; 12.164, 292, 300, 341; 20.97, 167; *Ag. Apion* 2.169. In the perfect passive, πέπεισμαι, "I am certain," *War* 5.544; *Ant.* 5.90; 6.291, 317; 8.108, 11.3, 176, 315; 12.150; 13.246, 294; 14.308; 15.265; 16.304. The Essenes "were convinced that not one woman keeps faith with just one man" (*War* 2.121, πεπεισμένοι; cf. 1.107, 622, 643; *Ant.* 1.9); "these men who are now certain of holding on to victory" (2.437).

[38] *Ant.* 6.259; 10.115; *Life* 19: "I did not convince them"; 73; so one tries to change their minds, to win them over to our ideas (17, 56, 123, 193) and ends up persuading them (60, 77, 87, 103); they accept (63), but sometimes at a great cost (*War* 1.655; 4.104). *Peithō* is sometimes synonymous with "believe": "to be convinced that God extends his watch and his authority over all and everywhere" (*Ag. Apion* 2.294), cf. *Ant.* 6.237: refusing to believe; 10.35; 16.79; *War* 1.482.

[39] *War* 1.613; 2.405; 3.201, 315, 345, 389; 4.185, 237, 321, 353, 504, 507, 639; 6.375, 502; 7.426; *Ant.* 1.167; 2.113, 271; 7.213; 8.245; 9.134; 13.79, 115, 217; 14.168, 184; 15.126; 16.108; 17.87; 18.3; 20.42; *Life* 113: "my arguments persuaded the crowd"; 308: "These words convinced them."

[40] *War* 1.215: "Herod let himself be persuaded by these opinions"; 1.224; 6.134, 287; 7.415, 423; cf. *Life* 417: "Titus Caesar invited me (ἔπειθέν με) a number of times to take what I wanted for myself from the ruins of my country."

action (*Life* 190) and hence "convince";[42] from there, one may urge, charge, or order.[43]

The shades of variation with the meanings "accept" or "submit" are just as varied: one may be influenced (*Ant.* 5.243, 269, 315), respond to an invitation (5.168), give in to opinions or requests,[44] consent,[45] give one's accord (*Ant.* 5.172; 20.32; *Life* 151), follow advice that is given.[46] Often, however, it is obedience in the strict sense and submission that is intended: the young must obey their elders (*Ant.* 3.47); one obeys God, the law and lawmakers (1.41, 190; 2.287; 5.152; 6.131, 136; *Ag. Apion* 2.162), the words of prophets (*Ant.* 9.51, 59, 267; 10.105), priests (*Ag. Apion* 2.194), officials (*Ant.* 14.232), justice (17.316), an edict (19.314), orders.[47]

Finally, *peithō* has the meaning "put one's confidence in, trust" (*War* 5.369; 6.348) promises, wealth or arms, numbers, persons.[48] One is "proud (*pepoithōs*) of one's tall and handsome figure" (*War* 2.57) or the influence of one's father-in-law (1.447); but above all one must count on God's help.[49] The NT, especially St. Paul, retained all this richness of meaning.

When transitive (in the present, the imperfect, and the aorist), conative *peithō* means "want or try to persuade." At Caesarea, King Agrippa says to Paul, "You want to persuade me to become a Christian."[50] Defining his ministry, the apostle declares, "Knowing (*eidotes*) what the fear of the Lord

---

[41] *War* 1.114: Aristobulus "advised his mother to spare the lives" of threatened persons, 124, 360; *Ant.* 1.278; 6.208: "David, persuaded by this excellent advice"; 7.214, 235, 10.51; 11.197; *Ag. Apion* 1.100.

[42] *War* 1.61: "Hyrcanus convinced Antiochus with three hundred talents to lift the siege," 126, 290, 575, 603, 642; *Ant.* 2.139; 8.5; 9.143, 200, 232; 11.223; 12.387; 14.164; 17.55, 63; 18.42, 329; 20.70, 163, 236; *Life* 29, 42, 55, 65, 132, 271, 273, 391. Thus members of garrisons are "persuaded" (*War* 1.175, 187, 190, 248; 2.590; 3.357).

[43] *Ant.* 1.74, 109, 216; 2.291; 5.151, 321; 7.15, 17; 18.82; 20.62, 69, 120, 216, 220; *Life* 185.

[44] *War* 1.135, 267, 506, 538; 2.238; 5.128; *Ant.* 2.30; 18.268.

[45] *War* 1.159, 318; *Ant.* 5.282; 12.237; 16.322; 18.48; 20.78, 178.

[46] *War* 1.391, 434, 576; *Ant.* 6.249; 8.277; 9.148; 11.146; 12.283; 14.14. That is why πείθω is sometimes completely synonymous with "appease": "Antipater appeased Murcus" (*War* 1.224, 227; *Ant.* 1.201); to persuade a crowd it to appease it (*Life* 388, cf. 140); "being agreeable to these orders, the soldiers remained calm" (*War* 2.621; *Ant.* 7.127).

[47] *Ant.* 11.218; 14.52, 88, 409; 18.89, 159; *Ag. Apion* 2.226: "obedience to the laws is a proof of virtue."

[48] *War* 1.55, 202, 373, 374; 2.21, 41, 209, 361, 364, 378, 583; 3.463; 4.10; 6.24, 330, 372; *Ant.* 11.114; 13.298, 17.119; *Life* 116, 373.

[49] *War* 2.394; 3.484; *Ant.* 7.122; 8.256; 18.266.

[50] Acts 26:28 (present indicative, με πείθεις). The king adds ἐν ὀλίγῳ, which commentators explain with χρόνῳ ("in a short time") or πόνῳ ("with little effort"),

is, we try to persuade people";[51] but in the language of St. Luke, the verb has a technical meaning: "try to convince"[52] an audience to act, to adopt a certain way of life, to "persevere in God's grace."[53] At Ephesus, the silversmith Demetrius noted that in almost all of Asia, the apostle had convinced and won over (*peisas*) a considerable crowd everywhere he preached (Acts 19:26). With regard to individuals, where the giving of opinions and advice is concerned, persuasion brings appeasement. The princes of the priests say to the guards at Jesus' tomb: "If the matter reaches the ears of the procurator, we ourselves will appease him."[54] Thanks to love shown in action, "we know that we are of the truth, and before him we will set our hearts at rest (*peisomen*),"[55] we will convince it even while it is making accusations against us.

In the perfect and the pluperfect (with *epi, eis, en* plus the dative), *peithō* has the meaning, so common in the LXX and in Philo, of "have confidence,

---

or λόγῳ ("with few words"), or even "at little cost"; it would be best to interpret "almost, yet a little" (cf. Josephus, *Life* 151).

[51] 2 Cor 5:11 (present indicative, πείθομεν). Paul is faithful in his ministry to the mission he received from God, the Lord to whom he belongs and whom he reveres. One can also understand from the context that he wants to conciliate minds and defend himself against suspicion, and so make people favorably disposed, win themselves over to him. Cf. Gal 1:10—"Is it the favor of humans that I want to win (πείθω) or that of God?" Cf. A. Feuillet, " 'Chercher à persuader Dieu' (Gal I, 10 a)," in *NovT*, 1970, pp. 350–360.

[52] At Corinth, Paul "tried to convince (conative imperfect ἔπειθεν) Jews and Greeks" (Acts 18:4) that Jesus is the Christ; at Ephesus, he argues and tries to convince the Jews concerning the kingdom of God (διαλεγόμενος καὶ πείθων, present participle, Acts 19:8), as every orator does with his audience (cf. Josephus). At Rome, Paul, giving testimony to the kingdom of God, tried to convince his hearers (πείθων) regarding Jesus by a demonstration relying on the Law and the Prophets (Acts 28:23).

[53] Acts 13:43 (imperfect ἔπειθον). It is not necessary for a crowd to be persuaded or convinced to mobilize; it can be convinced by any means or pressure whatsoever: "the princes of the priests and the elders convinced the crowds (ἔπεισεν, aorist indicative) to ask for Barabbas' freedom and Jesus' death" (Matt 27:20). At Lystra, the Jews of Antioch and Iconium convince the crowd (aorist participle, πείσαντες) and stone Paul (Acts 14:19). Tyrians and Sidonians request, win over to their view, and convince (πείσαντες) Blastus, Agrippa's chamberlain, to support their request to the king (Acts 12:20).

[54] Matt 28:14, ἡμεῖς πείσομεν (future indicative). On tomb violations and fraudulent transfers of corpses, cf. J. Schmitt, "Nazareth, (Inscription dite de)," in *DBSup*, vol. 6, col. 356.

[55] 1 John 3:19 (Homer, *Il.* 9.112; Xenophon, *An.* 3.1.26). On the debate that takes place in the conscience, cf. Philo, *Quest. Gen.* 4.26; on the accusation of the heart, Prov 18:17; Augustine, *Perf. Just.* 28. Cf. A. Champdor, *Le Livre des morts*, Paris, 1963, p. 84.

trust."[56] In the parable about the expulsion of demons, the stronger one takes away from the vanquished the panoply in which he had placed his confidence.[57] It is assurance, like that of those who are sure that they are righteous (*tous pepoithotas hoti*, perfect participle) and scorn others (Luke 18:9), whereas they ought to place their confidence in God and God's mercy.[58] This confidence, then, is certitude: "I give thanks, being sure of this (*pepoithōs auto touto*): the one who has begun this excellent work in you will carry it through to completion on the day of Christ Jesus" (Phil 1:6); "To remain in the flesh is more necessary for your sake. In this certitude I know that I am going to remain with you all" (1:25; cf. 2:24). If the apostle's confidence is so strong, it is because it is founded on the Lord,[59] but he also uses the perfect *pepoitha* as the papyri do, where a superior (diplomatically or pedagogically) expresses his conviction or desire that those subject to him will be obedient: "I am persuaded in the Lord that you will not think otherwise."[60] The nuances of the middle and passive voices are varied; sometimes falling into line with an opinion,[61] following a suggestion,[62] expressing a more or less strongly held opinion;[63] some-

---

[56] Matt 27:43—"He trusted in God" (perfect indicative, πέποιθεν ἐπί) is a quotation of Ps 22:9. Heb 2:13—"I will put my trust in him" (πεποιθὼς ἔσομαι ἐπ' αὐτῷ) is a quotation of Isa 8:17.

[57] Luke 11:22 (pluperfect, ἐφ' ᾗ ἐπεποίθει); cf. Ps 48:7; Prov 11:28. S. Légasse, "L''homme fort' de Luc XI, 21–22," in *NovT*, 1962, pp. 5–9.

[58] Rom 2:19—the Jew is confident that he is a guide of the blind (perfect πέποιθας), whereas God and his law are light, and not the person himself (σεαυτόν); 2 Cor 1:9—"We have carried our death sentence in ourselves, so that we may not remain confident in ourselves (perfect participle, μὴ πεποιθότες), but in God who raises the dead"; 10:7—"if someone is persuaded that he is Christ's" (with connotations of presumption); Phil 3:3—"We are the circumcision . . . . we place no confidence in the flesh."

[59] 2 Thess 3:4—"We have placed our confidence in the Lord regarding you" (perfect indicative, πεποίθαμεν); cf. Phil 1:14.

[60] Gal 5:10; cf. 2 Cor 2:3—"I had this confidence in all of you (πεποιθὼς, perfect participle), that my joy is your joy," because the solidarity of brotherly love requires sharing the same feelings: rejoicing with those who rejoice. Phlm 21: "I write with full confidence in your obedience."

[61] Acts 5:39, Gamaliel: if the work comes from God, it cannot be defeated; 27:21, in the storm, the centurion pays more attention to the opinions of the pilot and the shipowner than to Paul's words.

[62] Acts 23:21—Paul's nephew denounces the plot against Paul to the tribune: "Do not believe them" (μὴ πεισθῇς, aorist passive subjunctive), do not trust them.

[63] Acts 26:26—"I do not believe (οὐ πείθομαι, present middle indicative) that he (King Agrippa) knows nothing of these matters"; 2 Tim 1:5—"I am persuaded that the faith of your grandmother Lois and your mother Eunice is also in you"; Heb 13:18—"we believe that we have a clear conscience."

times, in fact usually, expressing an absolute conviction, faith in the literal sense: the brothers of the wicked rich man would not be persuaded even if they saw a dead person resurrected;[64] the people were convinced that John the Baptist was a prophet (20:6—*pepeismenos estin*, perfect passive participle). After St. Paul's sermons at Thessalonica and at Rome, Luke notes that some were persuaded (= believed) and others did not believe.[65] Here again the apostle uses the perfect to express pedagogical optimism that is respectful and stimulating for his superiors: "I am persuaded (*pepeismai*) regarding you, brothers, that you are yourselves full of goodwill, having all knowledge, capable of admonishing each other."[66] But when he speaks of his conviction in his faith, Paul's certitude is as complete as it is well-founded: "I am sure (*pepeismai*) that neither death nor life . . . will be able to separate us from the love of God."[67]

Finally, the meaning "obey" is evident in Heb 13:17—"obey your leaders and be in submission" (present middle imperative, *peithesthe tois hēgoumenois hymōn*)—and in Jas 3:3—"We put bits in horses' mouths so that they will obey us." One obeys the truth (Gal 5:7) or unrighteousness (Rom 2:8); that is to say, one conforms to certain moral principles, submits to and remains faithful to their requirements, just as one joins with, is won over by certain persons (Acts 4:36–37, *epeithonto*, imperfect middle).

Peithos. — This adjective, corresponding to the classical *pithanos*, "persuasive," is not only a biblical hapax, but is not attested elsewhere in Greek: "My speech and my preaching (have) not (consisted) of persuasive words of wisdom, but in demonstration of Spirit and of power."[68] We must

---

[64] Luke 16:31. C. F. Evans, "Uncomfortable Words," in *ExpT* 81, 1970, pp. 228–231.

[65] Acts 17:4; 28:24; cf. 21:14—during the farewells at Caesarea, Paul says that he is ready to be imprisoned and to die for Jesus; "as he would not be persuaded (μὴ πειθομένου, present middle participle), we remained quiet (ἡσυχάσαμεν)."

[66] Rom 15:14—the apostle includes all the Roman Christians without noting a single exception; Heb 6:9—"Even though we speak like this, dear friends, we are persuaded (πεπείσμεθα) that you are in a better situation, favorable for your salvation."

[67] Rom 8:38—confidence based on the faithfulness of God's love and on experience gained in daily trials; 2 Tim 1:12—"I am sure (πέπεισμαι) that the one in whom I have placed my trust has the power to keep my deposit until that Day"; Paul is sure of his Lord and Savior; he affirms his full and complete conviction that the Almighty will without fail accomplish his promises; Rom 14:4—"I know and I am absolutely certain in the Lord (οἶδα καὶ πέπεισμαι) that there is nothing impure in you," a total conviction because it rests on the teaching of Jesus, who rejected the distinction between clean and unclean foods.

[68] 1 Cor 2:4—οὐκ ἐν πειθοῖς σοφίας λόγοις, ἀλλ' ἐν ἀποδείξει πνεύματος καὶ δυνάμεως. Such is the text in ℵ, B, D, E, F. Vulg. "in persuasibilibus sapientiae verbis"; Origen, *Cels.* 6.2 (cf. *RB*, 1957, p. 478); but the variants are numerous (cf. H. Lietzmann,

interpret this as meaning that faith is based not on the philosophy, rhetoric, logic, or wisdom of preachers who are able to entice minds, but on the public and incontestable (apodictic) testimony of the Hebrew, who manifests himself (*pneumatos*, genitive of cause) in the assurance and the power inspired in preacher and hearers alike. It is the contrast between human discourse, demonstrative reason on the one hand, and on the other omnipotent outpourings or exhibitions of the Holy Spirit reaching the heart.

Peismonē. — This noun does not appear in Greek before the biblical hapax in Gal 5:8. Before saying, "I am persuaded (*pepoitha*) regarding you . . ." (5:10) and after having asked, "Who has hindered you from obeying (*peithesthai*) the truth?" the apostle goes on, "This *peismonē* is not from the one who calls you." We can take the noun in a passive sense as referring to a new conviction of the Galatians, of which they have recently been persuaded; but more likely it has the active sense of a suggestion that cannot come from God, referring to the Judaizing preachers who must have inclined the Galatians to abandon Paul's gospel. Thus *peismonē* would have a pejorative meaning: a bad influence. This can still be detected in Ignatius of Antioch: "Christianity is not a work of persuasion but a work of power" (Ign. *Rom.* 3.3; quoted in the sixth century, *P.Lond.* 1674, 36).

Pepoithēsis. — A late coinage from the perfect *pepoitha*, and unknown in the papyri, this substantive is a hapax in the LXX: "What is the meaning of this confidence (Hebrew *biṭṭāḥôn;* cf. Isa 36:4; Eccl 9:4) in which you trust" (2 Kgs 18:19); and in Philo: "Counting on the virtues of their ancestors" (Philo, *Virtues* 226); but Josephus uses it six times in the sense of assurance or boldness (regarding a quarrel, *Ant.* 11.299); of confidence in

---

An die Korinther I–II², Tübingen, 1923, p. 11). The oldest manuscript, 𝔓⁴⁶, omits λόγοις (P. Benoit, "Le Codex paulinien Chester Beatty," in *RB*, 1937, p. 73); g 18 (Tischendorf) Sah. Arm. Ambrosiaster read the dative of the noun πειθώ: "in the persuasion (ἐν πειθοῖ) of the speech of human wisdom"; this reading preferred by J. Huby, in *Science religieuse: Travaux et recherches*, Paris, 1944, pp. 245–247; J. Héring, *La Première Epître de saint Paul aux Corinthiens*, Neuchâtel-Paris, 1949 ET The First Epistle of Saint Paul to the Corinthians, trans. A. W. Heathcote and P. J. Allcock, London, 1962, p. 15; and G. Zuntz, *The Text of the Epistles*, London, 1953, pp. 23ff., who thinks that there never was an adjective πειθός; and yet it is never explained by the Fathers of the church, who thus seem to suppose that its meaning is well known to their audiences. For the rest, there is no difference of meaning between the two readings. Cf. Josephus, *Ag. Apion* 2.223: Plato "surpassed all the other philosophers by the power of his talent and his persuasive eloquence"; 2.116. The substantive πειθώ means the faculty or talent of persuasion (Aeschylus, *PV* 172; Plato, *Leg.* 4.722 *b*), speech more fit for persuasion, eloquence (Euripides, *IA* 104; Aristophanes, *Nub.* 1398), the temptation that one has in mind (Aeschylus, *Ag.* 385, βιᾶται δ' ἁ τάλαινα πειθώ), obedience (Xenophon, *Cyr.* 2.3.19; 3.3.8); contrasted with constraint (Josephus, *War* 2.8, 562; cf. *Ant.* 17.209).

oneself (19.317), in one's strength (1.73), in arms or money (3.45); it can be inspired by someone else's attitude (5.74) or by God (*apo tou theou*, 10.16). One depends or relies on a *dynamis*. St. Paul is the only NT author to use this term (four times in 2 Cor, out of a total of six)—which is very close to *parrhēsia*. Usually it refers to his own personal confidence.

(*a*) Confidence in people. The apostle, henceforth certain of the Corinthians' respect for him and the good welcome that they will give him, decided in this assurance (*tautē tē pepoithēsei*) to go to see them (2 Cor 1:15). In the meanwhile, he sends a brother to them to gather the collection; and this brother is all the more zealous because he has great confidence in them (*pepoithēsei pollē tē eis hymas*), confidence gained either on his own visits to Corinth or from Titus's accounts (2 Cor 8:22). One can also depend on human advantages, Israelite privileges: a Hebrew, son of a Hebrew, Paul would have reason to put his confidence in the flesh (Phil 3:4—*kaiper egō echōn pepoithēsin kai in sarki*).

(*b*) One can also depend on God: Jesus Christ, "in whom we have boldness and access with confidence through faith in him" (*en hō echomen tēn parrhēsian kai prosagōgēn en pepoithēsei dia tēs pisteōs autou*, Eph 3:12). Assurance and confidence bring access to God; they come from faith in the power and love of God, which make it possible to draw near to him. One is sure of being welcomed.

(*c*) This assurance is a personal feeling produced in the heart by Christ: "We have such assurance (*pepoithēsin toiautēn echomen*) through Christ before God" (2 Cor 3:4). Paul's confidence in the efficacy of his ministry is not an illusion, not vainglory, not presumption; it is based solidly on the certitude that a tree is recognized by its fruits. What is more, this certitude is produced in him by Christ in person. Much more than that, it is true and authentic in God's presence, which means that it is valid and in line with God's own judgment. Hence the apostolic authority and even boldness which Paul does not hesitate to put into play against his detractors (2 Cor 10:2).

πεῖρα, πειράζω, πειρασμός, ἀπείραστος

peira, attempt, trial, testing, experience, proof; peirazō, to try, tempt; peirasmos, temptation, trial, testing; apeirastos, inexperienced, not susceptible to temptation

In classical Greek, peira means "attempt, trial, experience" and sometimes "a putting to the test";[1] and these meanings are retained in the Koine. Zeno knows from experience whether or not the potter Pettukamis is capable (P.Cair.Zen. 59500, 1; cf. P.Princ. 169, 3); Ammonius asks his brother, "Try to do this for me."[2] But the meaning "proof" is asserted: "He found a man to supply the proof" (Menander, Dysk. 722); "You have given me sufficient proof of your character" (Dysk. 770); Moschion "gave proof of a gifted mind";[3] hence an athletic "trial."[4] The LXX uses this word to trans-

---

[1] Sophocles, El. 470: "the adventure that I am going to try may cost me dearly someday"; cf. P. Chantraine, Dictionnaire étymologique, on this word, who also points out the meaning "an attempt to seduce a woman," and the compounds ἐμπειρία, "experience"; ἐμπειρικός, "experienced"; ἐμπειράομαι, "make trial of"; cf. ἄπειρος, "without experience, inexpert" (Heb 5:13; Pap.Lugd.Bat. XX, suppl. C 7), ἀπείραστος, "having no experience" (Demosthenes, Corona 18.249); cf. below.

[2] P.Oxy. 3057, 18 (first-second century); cf. 1415, 29; PSI 377, 10; BGU 1027, 11: οἵου ὀλέθρου πῖρας ἐποιεῖτε . . . ἡ πῖρα πραγμάτων ἐπειδείξει; Dittenberger, Syl. 1239, 18: πᾶσι τοῖς κακοῖς πεῖραν δώσει.

[3] SB 8026, 10 (ἔδωκε πεῖραν = SEG VIII, 464; E. Bernand, Inscriptions métriques, n. 108, 10); P.Princ. 119, 57 (= SB 10989; A. E. Hanson, "Memorandum and Speech of an Advocate," in ZPE, vol. 8, 1971, pp. 15–27).

[4] Preliminary trial (J. and L. Robert, "Bulletin épigraphique," in REG, 1968, p. 439, n. 147); Philostratus, Gym. 11: "wrestling supplies a double proof, of what it knows and what it can do."

---

peira, S 3984; TDNT 6.23–36; EDNT 3.64; NIDNTT 3.798–799; MM 501; L&N 68.58; BAGD 640 ‖ peirazō, S 3985; TDNT 6.23–36; EDNT 3.64–7; NIDNTT 3.798–799, 801–802, 808–810; MM 501; L&N 12.36, 27.31, 27.46, 68.58, 88.308; BDF §§101, 171(2), 310(1), 392(1a); BAGD 640 ‖ peirasmos, S 3986; TDNT 6.23–36; EDNT 3.64–67; NIDNTT 3.798–800, 802; MM 501; L&N 27.46, 88.308; BAGD 640–641 ‖ apeirastos, S 551; TDNT 6.23–26; EDNT 1.119; NIDNTT 3.798–799, 802, 809; MM 56; L&N 88.309; BAGD 83

late the Hebrew *massâh* (Deut 33:8), and elsewhere uses it for an experience;[5] likewise Philo: "Every day we have experience of it" (*Worse Attacks
Better* 131); "I have had the experience for a long time";[6] but it is emphasized that these experimentations are sources or means of knowledge.[7]
Philo does not use *peirasmos*, nor does Josephus, who gives preference to
peira meaning "proof,"[8] "test" (*Ant.* 20.28), "trial" and "test"[9] or "attempt,"[10] but also "means, occasion, expedient."[11]

The expression *peiran lambanō*, "to make an attempt, to experiment,"
is traditional.[12] Deut 28:56 uses it for the woman "who will not venture to
put the sole of her foot on the ground" (piel of the Hebrew *nāsâh*); Heb

---

[5] Wis 18:20—πεῖρα θανάτου (cf. 2:24; S. Lyonnet, "Le Sense de πειράζειν in Sap.
II, 24 et la doctrine du péché originel," in *Bib*, 1958, pp. 27–36); 18:25, the experience
of divine wrath; 2 Macc 8:9—the general Gorgias was accustomed to the things of
war, he had experience of them; cf. 4 Macc 8:1—"the tyrant, conquered in his first
attempt. . . ."

[6] Philo, *Abraham* 251; *Spec. Laws* 1.106: "the woman who has had the experience
of another marriage" (= *Virtues* 114); *Spec. Laws* 2.103; cf. the meaning "proof" (*Joseph*
37; *Moses* 1.306), "trial" (*Good Man Free* 103), "undertaking" (*Flacc.* 43, 53); "means,
combination" (*Virtues* 34). Πεῖρα is close to δοκιμασία (*Flight* 149; *Spec. Laws* 4.153;
cf. Josephus, *War* 2.161; Plutarch, *Mor.* 15.230 *a* ; Ps 95:9; 2 Cor 13:5; Heb 3:9; Jas
1:2–3; 1 Pet 1:6–7).

[7] Philo, *Abraham* 209; *To Gaius* 216: "He knew not only by hearsay, but by
experience"; 255: "before long you will know from experience."

[8] The Essene candidate must offer proof of his temperance (*War* 2.138; *Ant.*
5.184); give proof of one's aptitude (*Ant.* 1.300); the proof that Elijah is a true prophet
(9.23), proof of courage (12.339), of loyalty (15.193; 16.48; *Life* 160), of strength (*Ant.*
3.19; 13.152).

[9] *War* 5.516: "they tested the points of their swords"; 7.51, 81, 193; *Ant.* 2.293;
3.11; 5.107, 110: trial of facts; 8.166: convinced by experience, not by mere hearsay;
8.168, 219, 300; 15.316; 18.303.

[10] *Ant.* 3.315; 5.40; 10.142; *Life* 219; *Ag. Apion* 2.183; attempted rape, 2.215; *Ant.*
2.55. The only religious meaning is "tempt God" (*Ant.* 4.107).

[11] *War* 2.200: the Jews did not give in before any of these means, 355; 3.218; *Ant.*
2.161; 5.325; 10.192; 14.473. Cf. verify a usage, experiment with a medicine (Dioscorides, *Mat. Med.*, pref. 15), controlled observation, scientific experimentation
(Philodemus of Gadara, *Inf.* 7.34, 37; 15.20; 16.36).

[12] F. Field, *Notes on the Translation*, pp. 232f., quotes Diodorus Siculus 12.24; 13.52;
15.48; Plutarch, *Pomp.* 73.1: "Pompey experienced defeat and flight"; Chariton, *Chaer.*
8.4.5: "Do not try to give him a mother-in-law"; Pausanias, 2.33.3; Achilles Tatius
6.20.3; Aesop, *Fab.* (ed. de Fur.). We may add Plato, *Grg.* 448 *a*; Xenophon, *Cyr.* 6.1.54:
"he tried to have them pulled" (ἐλάμβανε τοῦ ἀγωγίου πεῖραν); Philo, *Abraham* 251;
Spec. Laws 1.106; *Good Man Free* 103; Josephus, *War* 2.340, 581: "I will put your military
discipline to the test before combat"; *Ant.* 2.60; 4.1, 191; 8.217; *Life* 125; Polybius 2.36.9:
"tempt fortune"; *SEG* VIII, 574, 21; *UPZ* 110, 129: "If you do not want to experience
sanctions"; *P.Oxy.* 1681, 10; 2704, 14; *P.Cair.Zen.* 59495, 4; *P.Tebt.* 712, 14; *SB* 7452, 21.

11:29, 36 for the Egyptians who tried to cross the Red Sea, and for martyrs who experienced derision and floggings.

In preference to the denominative *peiraomai*, the Koine uses *peirazō*,[13] which is rare in secular Greek, but to which biblical language gives an altogether singular density,[14] with the basic meaning "trial"[15] and always translating the piel of the Hebrew *nāsâh*. Its secular meanings are rather rare,[16] but always it is a question of trial and exploration. Hence the religious and moral meaning, "temptation," which is a trial of virtue by means of affliction or adversity, or even by Satan's inter-

---

[13] Πειράζω means "put to the test"; hence "try to make, seek to seduce" (a woman), in a favorable or an unfavorable sense: "mistreat, attack." Cf. the Latin *periculum*, "danger, peril," and *peritus*, "experienced." Cf. Homer, *Od.* 9.281, Polyphemes to Ulysses: "He wanted to try me"; Plato, *Prt.* 342 *a:* "I want to try to expose you . . ."; Epictetus 1.9.29: "to test me, Rufus was accustomed to speak to me"; Plutarch, *Cleom.* 7.4: "troubled at the thought that they wanted to test him because they suspected him"; Polybius 2.6.9: try to get revenge; Dionysius of Halicarnassus, *Comp.* 6.7.1: "Now I will try to speak (πειράσομαι λέγειν), to the extent that I understand." In a monologue of Hercules, it has to do with an athletic trial (*P.Oxy.* 2454, 20); cf. *P.Yale* 32, 9: let him try to pour the olives without crushing them (257 BC); *P.Oxy.* 2410, 10: he tried to get rid of two *arourai* of our royal land; 2982, 12: "I will try to get there quickly"; *P.Oxy.Hels.* 49, 3: "try to send the letters as quickly as possible"; *PSI* 927, 25; *P.Alex.* 28, 23; *P.Lond.* 1917, 12: "captivated, I remained in the kitchen garden."

[14] It is worth noting that Philo uses this verb only four times, always in OT quotations (*Alleg. Interp.* 3.162, 167; *Prelim. Stud.* 163; *Dreams* 1.195). Its use is also rare with Josephus, but more personal: "Under the pretext of serving the law, these men were attempting something more profound" (*War* 1.654); "this wonder had already been experienced (noted) when the city was taken" (5.411); "have experience of widowhood" (*Ant.* 6.210); ὁ πειρασθείς = the one who experienced such an outrage (sodomy), *Ag. Apion* 2.215.

[15] Cf. A. Sommer, *Der Begriff der Versuchung im Alten Testament und Judentum*, Breslau, 1935; J. H. Korn, Πειρασμός: *Die Versuchung des Gläubigen in der griechischen Bibel*, Stuttgart, 1937; M. E. Andrews, "Peirasmos: A Study in Form-Criticism," in *ATR*, 1942, pp. 229–244; C. Spicq, *Théologie morale*, vol. 1, pp. 222–266; H. B. Oikonomos, Πειρασμοὶ ἐν τῇ Παλαιᾷ Διαθήκῃ, Athens, 1965.

[16] Judg 6:39—Gideon wants to repeat the "trial of the fleece"; 1 Sam 17:39—David tries to walk in armor, "because he had never tried it"; 1 Kgs 10:1, the Queen of Sheba comes to see Solomon "to test him with riddles" (1 Chr 9:1); Sir 13:11—the powerful man learns and puts you to the test with his long speeches; Dan 1:12, 14: "prove your servants for ten days"; 1 Macc 12:10—"We tried to send someone to renew our brotherhood." The author of 2 Macc tries to sum up the five books of Jason of Cyrene (2:23); Macron tries to administer the affairs of the Jews peacefully (10:12), Lysias tries to cooperate for their good (11:19). Cf. 4 Macc 9:7—"Try then, tyrant" to compel us; 12:3, he seeks to persuade the youngest of the Maccabees; 15:16—their mother is tried by cruel suffering.

vention.[17] In the faith of Israel, God is always its author; it is a basic element of his pedagogy: *per molestias eruditio.* The two most significant instances are those of Abraham, whom God tested by asking him to sacrifice Isaac (Gen 22:1), and of the wandering of the chosen people in the wilderness (Exod 15:25). These trials are a sounding or a test that allows Yahweh to assess the quality of his servants; this purpose is mentioned endlessly.[18] But the "temptation" reveals not only what is hidden, demonstrates not only the sincerity and the moral resources of the believer, but is also for the believer a means to perfection, because he has to suffer in order to remain faithful to his resolves and his decision for God; he emerges from the trial purified and more convinced than ever to serve his Lord, whose sovereignty over him he thus confesses to be total.[19] This is why Jdt 8:25 paradoxically urges giving thanks to "the Lord our God, who puts us to the test like our fathers"; and this is why David, who is so religious, asks, "Search me, Yahweh, test me, examine my heart and my mind" (Ps 26:2), because he knows that those whom "God has put to the test, he has found worthy of himself" (Wis 3:5). The wisdom writings insist on the benefits of this painful pedagogy by attributing it to the divine wisdom: "Wisdom tries her sons by her precepts" (Sir 4:17) and takes them on difficult paths. Her disciples are called to experience for themselves what is good or bad for their souls (Sir 37:27; 39:4). If they have thought they could find happiness in the joys of this world, they recognize that these pleasures are empty (Eccl 2:1), and that is the confession of their wisdom (7:23; cf. Wis 2:17; 19:5). Finally, on the psychological level, "The one who has not been tried knows little."[20]

---

[17] Job 1:9ff. Cf. J. Lévêque, *Job et son Dieu,* Paris, 1970, vol. 1, pp. 179ff. A. M. Durable, "La Tentation diaboloque dans le livre de la Sagesse II, 24," in *Mélanges Tisserant,* pp. 187–195.

[18] Exod 16:4—"I test the people *to find out* if they will walk according to my law or not"; Deut 8:2—"*to know* what you have in your heart, if you will keep his commandments or not"; 13:3—"*to know* if you love Yahweh your God with all your heart and with all your soul"; Judg 2:22—"*to know* whether or not they will keep Yahweh's ways, walking according to them, as their fathers kept them"; 3:4; 2 Chr 32:31.

[19] Exod 20:20—"Fear not, for it is in order to test you that Elohim has come, and so that the fear of him may be before your face so that you will not sin any more"; Dan 12:10—"Many will be purified, made spotless, and proved [by fire]. The impious will continue to act with impiety"; Wis 11:9.

[20] Sir 34:10. The Vulgate of 34:11 is more absolute: "Qui tentatus non est, qualis sit? He knows nothing; he does not know himself. He does not know his weakness or his great need of God's help; he has not gained the power to triumph in life's difficulties" (Job 7:1ff.). The Christian tradition takes up the axiom: stagnant water becomes foul and miry, but the waters of a river are more beautiful, clear, transparent, and the stones are what makes the brook sing; or again: just as the stars shine in the

People are thought to "tempt God"[21] when they seek to obtain signs or proofs of his goodness or power, or when they make untimely demands; they irritate God because of their lack of faith and undue demands, which amount to a kind of defiance, which is monstrous on the part of a creature.

The substantive *peirasmos* did not appear in secular Greek before the first century,[22] but it remained unknown in the papyri. The LXX gave it the meaning "temptation":[23] "They called the place Massah (*Peirasmos*) because there they tempted God" (Exod 17:7; cf. Deut 6:16; 9:22; 29:2; Ps 95:8), and it is repeated that "in temptation Abraham was found faithful" (Sir 44:20; 1 Macc 2:52), because "To the one who fears the Lord no evil will come; but if he is in trial, he will again be delivered" (Sir 33:1). The whole moral life of the wise person depends on his clear-headedness and victory in testing: "The furnace proves the potter's vases. The testing of a person is in his reasoning" (Sir 27:5), which discerns the just and the unjust, the good and the evil, and makes good choices that are in accord with God's will. Hence the universal maxim: "Child, if you wish to serve the Lord, prepare your soul for testing" (*eis peirasmon*, 2:1).

NT theology and language inherit these conceptions of *peirasmos*,[24] but the major "temptation" was that of Christ, which is reported by the

---

night and hide from us in the daytime, so true virtue cannot be seen at all in prosperity but shines forth splendidly in adversity.—This is what the Greeks meant by the formula πάθει μάθος (adversity makes wise, suffering brings understanding) taken up in Heb 5:8, cf. Herodotus 1.207; Aeschylus, *Ag.* 177, the comic poet Sotades (J. U. Powell, *Collectanea Alexandrina*, Oxford, 1925, p. 244, n. 23 = J. M. Edmonds, *Attic Comedy*, vol. 2, p. 556), Memnon (*F.Gr.H.*, p. 356, 13). Philo, *Moses* 2.55, 280; *Migr. Abr.* 34; *Prelim. Stud.* 162; *Heir* 73; *Flight* 138; *Dreams* 2.107; cf. J. Coste, "Notion grecque et notion biblique de la 'souffrance éducatrice' (A propos d'Hébr. V, 8)," in *RSR*, 1955, pp. 481–523; H. Dörrie, *Leid und Erfahrung: Die Wort- und Sinn-Verbindung* παθεῖν-μαθεῖν *im griechischen Denken*, Mainz, 1956; K. Clinton, "The 'Hymn to Zeus' ΠΑΘΕΙ ΜΑΘΟΣ and the End of the Parodos of Agamemnon," in *Tradition*, 1979, pp. 1–19.

[21] Num 14:22—"These people who have tempted me ten times and who have not heard my voice"; Jdt 8:12; Ps 78:41, 56; 95:9; 106:14; Wis 1:2; Sir 18:23; cf. Isa 7:12.

[22] Dioscorides, *Mat. Med.* preface: τοὺς ἐπὶ τῶν παθῶν πειρασμούς. Philaenis, Περὶ ἀφροδισίων, in *P.Oxy.* 2891, frag. 1, col. 2: Περὶ πειρασμῶν (a seducer's attempts), cf. K. Tsantsanoglou, "The Memoirs of a Lady from Samos," in *ZPE*, vol. 12, 1973, pp. 183–195.

[23] In the sense of a difficult trial, Deut 4:34; 7:19. Sir 6:7 recommends not having too much confidence in a new friend; the guarantee of a trial is needed (cf. 27:7). Eccl 3:10; 4:8; 5:2, 13; 8:16 use πειρασμός to translate the Hebrew 'inyān, "occupation, task, event."

[24] In the secular sense, St. Paul, a new convert, makes many attempts to join the disciples at Jerusalem, who doubt his sincerity (Acts 9:26; imperfect tense for continued action, ἐπείραζεν); the missionaries "tried to enter Bithynia" (16:7); the Jews, "having taken Paul in the temple, tried to kill him" (26:1—imperfect middle

three Synoptics[25] and which puts down "temptation" as an essential element in the life of disciples, like a wandering in the wilderness. The Devil submitted the Savior to an "examination" to find out about his identity, and he especially tempted him to substitute a political and earthly messianism for redemption by the cross, and finally to "tempt God" by performing wonders having no other point than to signal the vainglory of their author. Christ emerged victorious from these *peirasmoi* by quoting Scripture, that is, by conforming strictly to the will of God. In the course of his ministry, he underwent many other trials or temptations, all the difficulties of his existence, the traps set by his enemies, the reproofs of the religious leaders—which affected him deeply[26]—and he says to the Twelve, "You are the ones who have stayed with me in my trials" (Luke 22:28—*en tois peirasmois*). The trials of the agony at Gethsemane,[27] when he still had the chance to escape death and the tortures of Calvary, were certainly the most painful.

ἐπειρῶντο = repeated attempts); the meaning "painful trials" in 20:19. — Both of the great OT testings are reprised: Abraham (Heb 11:17; cf. Gen 22:1; Philo, *Abraham* 167–207; Josephus, *Ant.* 1.222–236; cf. T. Reik, *The Temptation*, New York, 1961) and the generation of the wilderness (Heb 3:8–9; cf. Ps 95:7–11); but we have to eliminate ἐπειράσθησαν at Heb 11:37, which is a dittographic corruption of ἐπρίσθησαν (C. Spicq, *Hébreux*, vol. 1, p. 429; G. Zuntz, *The Text of the Epistles*, p. 47; R. V. G. Tasker, "The Text of the 'Corpus Paulinum,' " in *NTS*, vol. 1, 1955, p. 184). — Finally, the "temptation of God" by Israel in the wilderness is recalled at 1 Cor 10:19; this is what Ananias and Sapphira did to see whether the Holy Spirit would illuminate Peter concerning their fraud (Acts 5:9); this is what the apostles and presbyters at Jerusalem would have been doing if they had not seen in the conversion of Cornelius a sufficiently clear sign of the divine will and had called for a more obvious miracle (Acts 15:10).

[25] Matt 4:1; Mark 1:13; Luke 4:2. The bibliography is considerable, cf. P. Ketter, *Die Versuchung Jesu nach dem Berichte der Synoptiker*, Münster, 1918; P. Samain, "L'Accusation de magie contre le Christ dans les Evangiles," in *ETL*, 1938, pp. 484–490; R. Schnackenburg, "Der Sinn der Versuchung Jesu bei den Synoptikern," in *TQ*, 1952, pp. 297–326; A. Feuillet, "Le Récit lucanien de la Tentation (Lc. IV, 1–13)," in *Bib*, 1959, pp. 613–621; Feuillet, "L'Episode de la Tentation d'après l'Evangile selon saint Marc (I, 12–13)," in *EstBib*, 1960, pp. 49–73; M. Steiner, *La Tentation de Jésus dans l'interprétation patristique de saint Justin à Origène*, Paris, 1962; H. Riesenfeld, "Le Caractère messianique de la Tentation au désert," in *La Venue du Messie* (Recherches bibliques, vol. 6), Bruges, 1962, pp. 51–63; and especially J. Dupont, *Les Tentations de Jésus au désert*, Bruges, 1968 (gives the complete bibliography).

[26] Matt 16:33; Mark 8:33 (Peter's wanting to turn Jesus away from the cross); Matt 12:38; 16:1; Mark 8:11; Luke 11:16 (the Pharisees ask for a sign); Matt 19:3; Mark 10:2 (the question about divorce, intended to test him); Matt 22:18; Mark 12:15 (tribute to Caesar); Matt 22:35 (the greatest commandment); Matt 27:40 ("Come down from the cross!"). Cf. *Gos. Truth* 19.18–30: "The wise [who are so] in their heart came testing (πειράζειν) the Master, but he confounded them, showing that they were empty."

[27] Jesus' soul was troubled (τετάρακται, John 12:27) in this conflict (agony)

The Epistle to the Hebrews gives them a major place in its Christology: the experience of suffering that Jesus underwent because of the likeness of his human nature to ours first taught him compassion for our weaknesses,[28] then gave him the power to "come to the aid of those who are being tried (or tempted),"[29] like a conqueror coming to the aid to those who are still embroiled in battle.

God is the one who tests, and the Christian, aware of his weakness, asks the favor of exemption from this examination: "Lead us not into temptation" (mē eisenenkēs hēmas eis peirasmon).[30] Eispherō (here in the aorist subjunctive) means "lead, transport, bring, introduce," and followed by eis, "cause to enter into" the peirasmos, which is not an incitation to evil, a wicked solicitation—which is what "temptation" suggests in modern English—but a difficult or painful trial. This test permits an assessment of the strength, the faithfulness, the love of the believer (which is a good thing), but it is dangerous, and that explains the humble request to be excused from it.

---

between the horror of an undeserved death and submission to the Father's will; Heb 5:7-8. Cf T. Boman, "Der Gebetskampf Jesu," in NTS, vol. 10, 1964, pp. 266–267; E. Best, The Temptation and the Passion, Cambridge, 1965; A. Feuillet, L'Agonie de Gethsémani, Paris, 1977.

[28] Heb 4:5. Christ, having sensitivities like our own, has the same reactions that we have in the face of pain and death; so he feels our troubles, participates in them, suffers with us (συμπαθεῖν). Cf. K. Bornhäuser, "Die Versuchungen Jesu nach dem Hebräerbrief," in Theologische Studien M. Kähler dargebracht, Leipzig, 1905, pp. 69–86; C. Spicq, Hébreux, vol. 1, pp. 94ff. B. Gerhardsson, The Testing of God's Son, Lund, 1966; P. Pokorný, "The Temptation Stories and their Intention," in NTS, vol. 20, 1974, pp. 115–127.

[29] Heb 2:18. Since compassion was indispensable for the high priest of the new covenant, the Son of God had to take on human nature in order to acquire it, because participation in the same sufferings makes companions in misfortune compassionate and devoted. In addition, Christ henceforth lends his aid to humans. He is their βοηθός (Latin adjutor). Boētheia is a word used especially for medical care. A decree of Cos honors the physician Xenotimos, who "always brought help to those who needed it" (Dittenberger, Syl. 943, 12; third century BC; cf. IG, XI, 4, 633 and 693); Diodorus Siculus 14.71: "the help (or care, βοήθεια) of physicians became ineffective because of the seriousness of the illness. . . ." The βοήθημα is the "remedy"; cf. N. van Brock, Vocabulaire médical, Paris, 1961, pp. 244ff. — According to Luke 10:18; 11:21–22, Jesus is the "strong man" who expels Satan from sinful men whom he had possessed. The expulsions of minor demons were signs of the devil's defeat.

[30] Matt 6:13. A formula without OT parallel (cf. David: "Test me, try me," Ps 139, 23), but with equivalents in Rabbinic Judaism (cf. Str-B, vol. 1, p. 422). The best commentaries are those of J. Carmignac, "Fais que nous n'entrions pas dans la tentation," in RB, 1965, pp. 218–226; Recherches sur le "Notre Père," Paris, 1969, pp. 236–304; cf. T. van Bavel, "Inferas–Inducas: A propos de Mtth. VI, 13 dans les œuvres de saint Augustin," in Revue Bénédictine, 1959, pp. 348–351.

Pagans, Jews, and sinners often used the excuse that some deity had forced them to do evil,[31] but Sir 15:11–15 protests that God can not urge evil, and Philo says that God is only the cause of good (*Decalogue* 176). Jas 1:13–14 takes up this teaching: "Let no one when he is tempted say, 'I am being tempted by God.' For God cannot be touched by temptations to evil[32] and neither does he tempt anyone. In reality, each one is tempted when drawn away and enticed by his own covetousness." The immediate cause of the temptation is internal: *epithymia*, that evil and imperious desire that each person has, which draws the heard and sets a snare[33]—which takes account of the warfare described by St. Paul (Rom 7:14–24).

In this latter text, *peirazō* is clearly pejorative, as it is also in all the instances where the temptation is attributed to the devil. Just as Jesus was tempted by the devil—for no wicked inclination could come from his immaculate human nature (Matt 4:1)—it is Satan who intervenes to snatch away the word from human hearts in order to keep them from being saved (Luke 8:12). Christian spouses are not to deprive each other "lest Satan

---

[31] Homer, *Il.* 19.86–87; *Od.* 1.32, 34; Euripides, *Or.* 285; *Phoen.* 1612ff.; Plautus, *Aul.* 4.10.7; Prov 19:3; Philo, *Alleg. Interp.* 2.19; *Decalogue* 176; *Flight* 15; *Worse Attacks Better* 32, 122; Josephus, *War* 2.164.

[32] Ὁ γὰρ θεὸς ἀπείραστός ἐστιν κακῶν could be interpreted three ways: (1) God cannot be tempted to evil; (2) God has no experience of evils; (3) God cannot be tested by wicked humans (P. H. Davids, "The Meaning of ἀπείραστος in James 1:13," in *NTS*, vol. 24, 1978, pp. 386–392). The verbal adjective ἀπείραστος (biblical hapax), capable of bearing many nuances (the manuscripts write also ἀπείρατος, cf. Josephus, *War* 3.307: escape a calamity; 5.364: it was not a new experience for them; 7.262: the Sicarii did not fail to implement any plan that aimed at the ruining of their victims). It is used especially in Christian literature: *Const. App.* 2.8.2: ἀνὴρ ἀδόκιμος ἀπείραστος; *Acts John* 57, the presbyter to the apostle John, "To tempt you would be to tempt someone who cannot be tempted"; 90; Ps.-Ignatius, *Ad Philip.* 11: "how to tempt the untemptable?" (other references in J. B. Mayor, *The Epistle of St. James*, 3d ed., London, 1910, pp. 51–53). In Jas 1:13, ἀπείραστος is taken in an active sense, *intentor malorum*, by the versions (Vulgate Sah. Boh. Ethiop.): God does not push anyone into sin; but for one thing, this interpretation makes the following proposition a tautology (πειράζει δὲ αὐτὸς οὐδένα), and for another, this adversative δέ supposes precisely another meaning in the preceding proposition. In addition, almost all moderns adopt the passive sense (cf. ἀνήκεστος = uncurable; ἀβίωτος = intolerable; ἀματάβλητος = unchangeable) and understand it to mean that God cannot be tempted by any evil; "untemptable" means that he has no experience of evil and no evil can seduce him.

[33] Cf. K. G. Kuhn, "Πειρασμός, ἁμαρτία, σάρξ im N.T. und die damit zusammen-hängenden Vorstellungen," in *ZTK*, 1952, pp. 200–222. The equivalent of the rabbinic "evil inclination" (*yēṣer harāʿ*). Cf. J. Bonsirven, *Judaïsme palestinien*, vol. 2, pp. 18ff. W. D. Davies, *Paul and Rabbinic Judaism*, 2d ed., London, 1955, pp. 20–35; R. E. Murphy, "Yéser in the Qumran Literature," in *Bib*, 1958, pp. 334–344; J. Cantinat, *Les Epîtres de saint Jacques et de saint Jude*, Paris, 1973, on this verse.

tempt you because of your trouble in remaining continent" (1 Cor 7:5); he
can even ruin the fruits of the apostolic ministry (1 Thess 3:5). The source
of the tribulations of the faithful sifts them, hoping that they will fail.[34]
His sinister interventions are so universal and unrelenting that Jesus calls
him *ho peirazōn*, "the Tempter."[35]

All of NT pastoral theology emphasizes, after the fashion of the OT,
the preponderant role of *peirasmos* in the life of believers. It occurs in
various periods with greater or lesser intensity (*en kairō peirasmou*, Luke
8:13) and in varied forms, the most pronounced form being "tribulation,"
painful and dangerous personal or social conditions that put everyone's
faithfulness to the test: "Dear friends, do not consider the fiery trial you are
suffering something strange."[36] In fact, this *peirasmos* is providential, is a
test of Christian authenticity, for the participants in Christ's sufferings
(1 Pet 4:13); it is a purification, like that of metal in a furnace.[37] This
marvelous fruitfulness makes it possible to understand that for a believer
under the new covenant the most dangerous and painful *peirasmos* can be
a source of joy and even gladness. Jesus had commanded believers to bear

---

[34] Rev 2:10, to the church at Smyrna: "Do not fear what you are about to suffer.
See, the devil is at hand to throw some of you in prison, so that you will be tempted"
(ἵνα πειρασθῆτε). St. Augustine explains: "Deus tentat, ut doceat; diabolus tentat, ut
decipiat" ("God tempts in order to teach; the devil tempts in order to ensnare," *Serm.*
2.3; 57.9; 71.10; *En. in Ps.* 55.2, 9, 11).

[35] Matt 4:3 (Luke 4:13), repeated in 1 Thess 3:5 (cf. 1 Chr 21:1; Zech 3:1–2). At
Qumran, an analogous attribution of temptation to Belial: "He acts in their heart"
(1QH 6.21–22); "shares in the manifestation of their wicked nature" (7.3–4); CD
4.13–18 (the three snares of Belial), 5.18–19: "Belial stirred up Jannes and his brother
in his malignity, when Israel was saved for the first time"; 4QFlor, frag. 1–2, 1.8–9
(*T. Benj.* 6.7 = 7.2; for *Jub.* 17.16, it is Mastema who tempts Abraham). Cf. E. Fascher,
Jesus und Satan, Halle, 1949; H. A. Kelly, "The Devil in the Desert," in *CBQ*, 1964, pp.
190–220.

[36] 1 Pet 4:12. Christians are scandalized at being unpopular and ostracized; but
the Lord predicted that they would be handed over before tribunals, hated, and beaten
(Mark 3:9–13; John 15:18–20; 16:33). The image of the furnace suggests anguish and
dire danger. — According to Gal 4:14, St. Paul's malady, his "thorn in the flesh," was
a "trial" for the faith of the Galatians: how could God's envoy be so infirm and so
unprovided for? How to resist the temptation to scorn or disdain him? To the contrary,
the apostle says, the believers received the apostle "as an angel from God!"

[37] Cf. Ps 17:3; 66:10; Prov 27:21 (C. Spicq, "La Persécution, loi de la vie chrétienne," in *Hommage aux Catholiques suisses*, Fribourg, 1954, pp. 87–99; B. Dehand-
schutter, "La Persécution des Chrétiens dans les Actes des Apôtres," in J. Kremer, *Les
Actes des Apôtres*, Gembloux-Louvain, 1979, pp. 541–546). Tertullian quotes a *logion
agraphon*: "Neminem intemptatum regna coelestia consecuturum" ("No one can get
into the kingdom of heaven without passing through temptation," *Bapt.* 20); cf. J.
Jeremias, *Unknown Sayings*, trans. R. H. Fuller, London, 1957, pp. 56–59.

fruit by persevering;[38] Jas 1:2 explains, "Always reckon it as joy, brethren, to be exposed to trials of all sorts (*peirasmois poikilois*), knowing that the trial of your faith produces patience."[39] "Happy is the person who endures trial, for after being proved he will receive the crown of life that [God] has promised to those who love him" (Jas 1:12). This is the blessedness of hope. 1 Pet 1:6 goes one better: "This is what fills you with joy, even while at present you are afflicted—since it is necessary for a little while—by various trials."[40]

On the other hand, there is a danger of succumbing when a Christian has committed an offense (*en tini paraptōmati*) and someone who is "spiritual" attempts to restore him; the latter must act with gentleness (*en pneumati praytētos*), "for you also are capable of being tempted" (Gal 6:1). No one is indefectible.[41] This propensity to sin is particularly frequent with those who want to get rich (*hoi boulomenoi ploutein*); "they fall into temptation (*empiptousin eis peirasmon*) and snares and many foolish and harmful desires that plunge people into ruin and perdition."[42] So missionaries who are false apostles are to be tested, like the Nicolaitans who disturb the community at Ephesus; as a result of this discernment they are recognized as liars.[43] Finally, Christians must also "test" them-

---

[38] Luke 8:15. Cf. *Recueil L. Cerfaux*, 1962, vol. 3, pp. 111–122.

[39] Cf. J. Marty, *Epître de Jacques*, p. 28; *2 Apoc. Bar.* 52.6—"Enjoy yourselves in the sufferings that you now endure."

[40] Joy dominates in all forms of trials and temptations (cf. W. Nauck, "Freude im Leiden," in *ZNW*, 1955, pp. 66–80), because these are considered providential and therefore beneficent. The Christian accepts them as coming from God himself—whatever secondary causes there may be—"it is necessary" (Mark 13:7; E. Fascher, "Theologische Beobachtungen zu δεῖ," in *Neutestamentliche Studien für R. Bultmann*, Berlin, 1954, pp. 228–254); cf. "the blessed passion."

[41] Rom 5:12—πάντες ἥμαρτον. Cf. H. Clavier, "Tentation et anamartésie dans le N.T.," in *RHPR*, 1967, pp. 150–161.

[42] 1 Tim 6:9. Cupidity has grim consequences; this is a traditional theme (Sir 31:5—"the one who loves money will not be justified"; 8:2; 14:3ff.; 21:4; Prov 15:27; 23:4; 28:20; Matt 6:24; Mark 4:19; Luke 12:13ff.; Jas 5:1). St. Paul distinguishes riches (1 Tim 6:17ff.) and those who want to get rich (Sir 27:1—ὁ ζητῶν πληθῦναι; Juvenal, *Sat.* 14.176: "dives qui fieri vult"; *Anth. Pal.* 11.2: ἤθελον ἂν πλουτεῖν). These inevitably find occasion of sin in their path, and they fall (ἐμπίπτειν, iterative present): injustices, lies, exactions, frauds, swindles, thefts of all kinds, which are like so many baited snares that the greedy cannot resist; once caught, they cannot get free. Cf. Plutarch, *De cupid. divit.* (a sickness of the soul, a passion that is never satisfied); *Crass.* 1.4–5; 2.1; 3.1; 6.6; 14.5; Lucian, *Nav.* 27; at Qumran, 1QH 4.12; 3.26; CD 4.15–19. H. Kosmala, "The Three Nets of Belial," in *ASTI*, Leiden, 1965, pp. 1–113.

[43] Rev 2:2. The apostles have ceaselessly warned the faithful against false apostles who seek to abuse them (Matt 24:1, 11, 24; 1 Cor 6:9; 15:33; Gal 6:7) and exhort them to exercise spiritual judgment (Acts 20:29; 1 Thess 5:21; 2 Cor 11:13–15; Eph 4:14;

selves; the *peirasmos* that makes one turn in upon oneself is an examination of conscience.[44]

Although *peirasmos* is painful and dangerous, God matches it to our strength, so that no one can ever say that it is insurmountable: "No temptation has come upon you that is not of human proportions, but God is faithful, who will not let you be tempted beyond your strength, but with this temptation will also produce this outcome (*ekbasin*, result) that you may bear it."[45] Jesus had taught that prayer is the secret of victory: "Watch and pray, that you may not come into temptation" (Matt 26:41 = Mark 14:38 = Luke 22:40, 46; cf. 1 Pet 5:8ff.). He himself had prayed for Peter, that he should not fail (Luke 22:32). It is the faith of the church that "the Lord knows how to deliver the godly from testing" (2 Pet 2:9), that is, those who seek divine help. To the church at Philadelphia, which imitated Christ's patience, Christ prophesied: "Because you have kept the word of my patience, I also will keep you in the hour of temptation that is ready to come upon the whole inhabited world to test those who dwell upon the earth."[46] We may add with 2 Pet 5:7–8 that faith makes it possible to resist the devil's most violent assaults.

---

1 John 3:7; 4:1—"Do not believe every spirit, but test the spirits to discern whether they are of God"); at Qumran, preachers of lies, "teachers of Ephraim," 4QpNah 2.8 (A. M. Denis, *Les Thèmes de connaissance dans le Document de Damas*, Louvain, 1967, p. 106). Cf. C. Spicq, *Théologie morale*, vol. 1, pp. 278ff. E. Cothenet, "Les Prophètes chrétiens," in M. Didier, *L'Evangile selon Matthieu*, Gembloux, 1972, pp. 299ff.; W. C. van Unnik, *Sparsa Collecta*, vol. 1, pp. 402–409; F. L. Hossfeld, I. Meyer, *Prophet gegen Prophet*, Fribourg, 1973; D. Hill, "False Prophets and Charismatics," in *Bib*, 1976, pp. 327–348; M. Krämer, "Hütet euch vor den falschen Propheten," *Bib*, 1976, pp. 349–377.

[44] 2 Cor 13:5—"Test yourselves (πειράζετε) [to see] whether you are in the faith; prove yourselves (δοκιμάζετε)." Cf. G. Therrien, *Le Discernement dans les Ecrits pauliniens*, Paris, 1973, pp. 46ff., 113.

[45] 1 Cor 10:13. Cf. the opening of the *Orestes* of Euripides, quoted by Cicero: "There is no word so formidable, no bad fate, no evil that has come from the wrath of the heavenly beings, that human nature is not capable of bearing it" (*Tusc.* 4.9.63). Cf. the prayer of the Essene psalm (11QPs^a 155.11 = 5ApocSyrPs 3.11): "Do not put me through a trial that is too difficult for me" (M. Philonenko, "L'Origine essénienne des cinq psaumes syriaques de David," in *Sem*, vol. 9, 1959, p. 42).

[46] Rev 3:10. We can hardly be precise about whether this has to do with the persecutions of the first-second century or those of an Antichrist, a *Nero redivivus* in the course of history, or finally the troubles preceding the Parousia (cf. S. Brown, "The 'Hour of Trial,' Rev. II, 10," in *JBL*, 1966, pp. 308–311). What is certain is that the Lord will keep his own from falling; their victory is secured in advance (John 16:33).

περιαιρέω

periaireō, to remove (from around)
→*see also* ἐξαιρέω

Common in the LXX, where it most often translates the hiphil of the Hebrew *sûr*, "take away, remove," this verb means literally "remove from around," i.e., take off something that one is wearing, especially a garment[1] or a veil (Gen 38:19), like Moses when he spoke with God.[2] Next comes the meaning "to detach," for example the anchors from a ship;[3] and finally "remove" means "move away, cause to disappear,"[4] as when hope of being saved from the storm fades to the point of disappearing altogether (imperfect passive, *periēraito*, Acts 27:20).

---

[1] Gen 38:14; Deut 21:13; Jdt 10:3; Jonah 3:6; UPZ 122, 13 (with violence = despoil, snatch). One removes a ring from one's finger (Gen 41:42; Esth 3:10; Josephus, *Ant.* 19.185), an adornment or jewelry (Exod 32:2–3, 24; 33:6); *Pss. Sol.* 2.22, a cloak (Philo, *Dreams* 1.100); a woman "with bare head, stripped of the symbol of modesty" (*Spec. Laws* 3.56); Moses "took off his body, which enveloped him like a shell" (*Virtues* 76; cf. 111; trim one's nails); "when the rest had been suppressed" (*Rewards* 172).

[2] Exod 34:34; a text used at 2 Cor 3:16; cf. J. Goettsberger, "Die Hülle des Moses nach Ex. XXXIV und II. Kor. III," in *BZ*, 1924, pp. 1–17.

[3] Acts 27:40 (cf. R. Ricard, "Les Navigations de saint Paul: La Tempête de quatorze jours en Méditerranée," in *Etudes*, 1927, pp. 458ff.); cf. "cut off": "Cyrus removed archery from the military exercises" (Xenophon, *Cyr.* 2.1.21); in peace offerings, one removes the fat, the lobe of the liver with the kidneys (Lev 3:4, 9–10, 15; 4:8–9, 31, 35; 7:4). On administrative, financial, or judicial lists, one strikes the names of the deceased (*P.Tebt.* 300, 11; *Stud.Pal.* XX, 36, 8), or former owners (*P.Oslo* 105, 8; *SB* 6800, 7; 7360, 11; 10249, 12; from AD 59); a figure is crossed out (*P.Cair.Zen.* 59147, 3).

[4] To remove foreign gods or mediums is to get them out of Israel (Josh 24:14, 23; 1 Sam 7:3, 4; 28:3; 2 Chr 32:12; 33:15; 34:33; Jer 4:1); cf. Prov 27:22—"his folly will not depart"; Bar 4:34—"I will take away the joy of his numerous population"; Josephus, *War* 1.179: "Crassus carried off two thousand gold talents" from the temple at Jerusalem; *Ant.* 20.212: "Herod plundered the Holy Land's artistic treasures to decorate Berytus." Cf. *P.Cair.Zen.* 59659, 7: thieves stole two asses belonging to Zeno.

---

periaireō, S 4014; *EDNT* 3.73; MM 504; L&N 13.38, 15.204, 54.24, 68.43; BAGD 645

The sole theological usage of *periaireō* in the NT is in Heb 10:11, where the priests of the old covenant busy themselves with the offering of daily sacrifices, which, however, "can never take away sins." The verb, like *aphaireō* (10:4) expresses first of all the idea of removing something that one has in oneself,[5] the extraction of which is thought to be difficult (cf. Thucydides 1.108.3: rase fortifications). The idea is not that of a diverting or of an ordinary relinquishing but of a complete suppression. This nuance of abolition is well attested: the husband abrogates or annuls his wife's vows (Num 30:13, 14, 16; hiphil of *pārar*); the royal quality of the house of Saul is abolished;[6] a dispute that is settled is said to be abolished (*P.Got.* 13, 11); the *stratēgoi* take away from the tax collectors any pretext or occasion for extortion (*P.Panop.Beatty* 2, 237; cf. *Pap.Lugd.Bat.* I, 21, 23). In the religious sphere, God totally removes sins (1 Chr 21:8), removes injustices (Zeph 3:15), takes away infirmities (Deut 7:15) and death.[7] But sin is so deeply embedded in humans that the OT economy was powerless to root it out.[8] Only the sacrifice of Jesus Christ succeeded in removing it.

---

[5] Eli says to Hannah, "Rid yourself of your wine" (1 Sam 1:14); cf. Ps 119:43—"Do not remove the word of truth from my mouth" (hiphil of the Hebrew *nāṣal*); cf. Exod 8:4, 7: "Take away the frogs from me and my people."

[6] 2 Sam 3:10 (hiphil of *'ābar*); Zech 10:11; cf. 2 Macc 4:38.

[7] Exod 10:17; cf. Num 17:20 (hiphil of *šākak*, cause to cease); Ps 119:22: "Remove insults and scorn far from me" (Hebrew *gālal*); Jer 4:4—"Get rid of the hardness of your heart"; Prov 4:24; Philo: remove, cut off sin or impurity (*Plant.* 99, 103, 109; *Alleg. Interp.* 2.63; 3.21, 127); Marcus Aurelius 12.2.2: "If you grow used to doing likewise, you will deliver yourself from the thousand things that trouble you."

[8] With regard to a scheming monk in the sixth century: "I pray your fatherly Holiness . . . to be zealous in rooting out impiety from our monasteries" (*P.Fouad* 86, 18); *T. Job* 43.4—"Our sins are taken away, our iniquity is buried."

περικάθαρμα, περίψημα

---

perikatharma, peripsēma, **wash-water, offscouring, filth; ransom**

---

1 Cor 4:13—"We have become as the filth of the earth, the refuse of all, up to the present" (*hōs perikatharmata tou kosmou egenēthēmen, pantōn peripsēma heōs arti*). These two terms, which are quite vulgar and very close in meaning (cf. Hesychius, *peripsēma: perikatamagma*), are used for the wash-water and scrapings from dirty dishes, which is thrown out after washing or purification,[1] thus any kind of uncleanness or filth.[2] Finally, they are terms of abuse and base insult when applied to humans.[3] No doubt this nuance of lowliness is to be retained in 1 Cor 4:13. It is even probable that the apostle was treated as "filth" by the people in the course of some disturbance at Ephesus, Corinth, or elsewhere.

---

[1] Ammonius, p. 143: καθάρματα τὰ μετὰ τὸ καθαρθῆναι ἀπορριπτούμενα; cf. Moulton-Milligan, on the word περικάθαρμα (intensive of κάθαρμα; cf. Hauck, on this word, in *TDNT,* vol. 3, pp. 430–431).

[2] Julius Pollux, *Onom.* 5.163: τῶν ἐν ταῖς τριόδοις καθαρμάτων ἐκβλητότερος, κοπρίων ἐκβλητότερος; synonyms: βδέλυγμα, σκύβαλα, κοπρός-κοπρία (cf. L. Robert, *Hellenica,* vol. 1, pp. 73–74; idem, *Documents de l'Asie mineure,* pp. 72–73).

[3] Demosthenes, *C. Mid.* 103: "The despicable Euctenon, that scum"; *Corona* 128: "What have you done, you slime, with virtue—you and yours"; Aristophanes, *Plut.* 454; Apollonius Rhodius: "Callimachus, the outcast (τὸ κάθαρμα), the butt, the hardhead" (*Anth. Pal.* 11.275); Philo, *Moses* 1.30; *Virtues* 174: "He considers the others as refuse, as nothing" (καθάρματα, τὸ μηδέν); Josephus, *War* 4.241: "The scum and offscouring of the whole country, these wretches . . . invaded the holy city"; Epictetus 3.22.78: "Priam sired fifty no-goods" (περικαθάρματα); Lucian, *Hermot.* 81, ἀνδράποδα καὶ καθάρματα (cf. H. D. Betz, *Lukian von Samosata und das Neue Testament,* p. 67; numerous references in Wettstein). But περίψημα is also used as a formula for unworthiness and humility, as in this epitaph from Carthage, where a widow has incribed concerning her husband: εὐψύχει, Κύριέ μου Μάξιμε, ἐγώ σου περίψημα τῆς καλῆς ψυχῆς (*CIL* VIII, 1, 12924); cf. *Barn.* 4.9; 6.5.

---

perikatharma, S 4027; *TDNT* 3.430–431; *EDNT* 3.74; *NIDNTT* 1.479–480, 3.102; MM 506; L&N 49.53; BAGD 647 ‖ *peripsēma, TDNT* 6.84–93; *EDNT* 3.80; *NIDNTT* 1.479–480; MM 510; L&N 79.53; BAGD 653

In Prov 21:18 (*perikatharma*, translating the Hebrew *kōper*) and Tob 5:19 (*peripsēma*), the two nouns have the sense of ransom.[4] The second noun has a religious meaning in Dionysius of Alexandria: Christians "after caring for their brother (who had the plague) died themselves, having transferred to themselves the death of others . . . departing as the offscouring of their brothers" (*apiontes autōn peripsēma*, in Eusebius, *Hist. Eccl.* 7.22.7). The purifying agent, in effect, is thought to absorb the impurity of the purified object (cf. *P.Tebt.* 550: *perikath*[?] and thus cleanse it; and since St. Paul adds a complement to each term ("of the world" . . . "of all"), his words recall the formula *peripsēma hēmōn genou* ("become our offscouring") pronounced at Athens, according to Photius (*Lex.*, p. 425, 3) and the *Suda*, when criminals were thrown into the sea as expiatory victims for warding off public calamity.[5] On the sixth and seventh of the month Thargelion, the city was purified (*polin kathairein*) by the cathartic ritual of the *pharmakoi*, which could be compared to the scapegoat of Lev 26:21–22: Two men who were driven through the city were supposed to take on its impurities. Then they were chased from the city to get rid of the uncleanness with which they were laden. Thanks to these "human cures,"[6] the evil

---

[4] This meaning of περίψημα—the price of liberation from a fault—is confirmed by Hesychius, who gives as equivalents ἀντίλυτρα, ἀντίψυχα; by *P.Mich.* 473, 18 (beginning of the second century): "Since you caused me to lose 1,200 drachmas, consider that amount a ransom (reparation) for my son" (ὡς ἔβλαψές με χιλίας διακοσίας δραχμάς, περίψημά μου τοῦ υἱοῦ ἀπέλθωσιν, meaning so that the son of Tabatheus, who was guilty of killing Menas, might escape criminal prosecution); cf. J. Modrzejewski, "Quelques remarques à propos de l'homicide et la rançon dans le droit d'Egypte romaine," in *Iura*, 1957, pp. 93–101). Less clear is the letter of Didumaris to Paniskos: ὅτι ἐσώθητε μετὰ τῶν τέκνων ὑμῶν καὶ περίψημα ὑμῶν τὰ παρελ. οτα (*P.Petaus* 29, 5), which the editors translate, "Ich habe mich sehr gefreut zu hören, daß ihr mit euren Kindern gerettet seid und die vergangenen Ereignisse euch zum Heil gerieten (?)" ("I was very pleased to hear that you, together with your children, have been rescued and the things that happened have turned to your salvation"). They adopt the restoration παρελ. οτα = παρελθόντα and comment "Mit περίψημα in der Bedeutung 'Sühnopfer, Sündenbock' ergibt das als Sinn 'Das, was geschehen ist, hat euch rein, frei gemacht.' Faßt man περίψημα als 'verachtenswerten Gegenstand, Diener' usw., könnte man etwa 'ihr seid Herr der Situation' interpretieren. Beides ist nicht recht befriedigend." ("With περίψημα understood to mean 'atonement, scapegoat,' the meaning is 'what happened has cleansed you, freed you.' If we understand περίψημα as referring to something to be scorned, a slave, and so on, then we could almost translate, 'You are master of the situation.' Neither is fully satisfactory.") Cf. περικάθαρμα, *P.Oxy.* 2331, 10.

[5] Cf. Ign. *Eph.* 8.1: περίψημα ὑμῶν = "I am your expiatory victim"; 18.1: "my spirit is the victim of the cross."

[6] These φαρμακοί are attested at Ephesus, from the sixth century BC (Hipponax, frags. 4 and 37; ed. Bergk; cf. O. Masson, "Sur un papyrus contenant des fragments

is abolished. We cannot exclude from 1 Cor 4:13 this sense of sacrifice through which the guilt-bearer expiates and purifies those who offer him. Thus the meaning would be that St. Paul, scorned and rejected by people, sacrifices himself for them (2 Cor 4:10ff.; 6:9; Phil 2:17); he is willing to become an expiatory victim, and by so doing he assimilates his apostolic function to that of the crucified Redeemer, Christ (Gal 6:17; Col 1:24–25).

---

d'Hipponax: P. Oxy. 2176," in *REG*, 1949, pp. 302, 311ff.), at Athens (the *Thargēlioi*), Abdera (Ovid, *Ib.* 465–469), Apollonia (Dittenberger, *Syl.* 707), Cyprus (Strabo 14.8.3), Marseille (Servius, on *Aen.* 3.57; cf. PW, vol. 14, col. 2143), etc. Cf. L. Moulinier, *Le Pur et l'impur dans la pensée des Grecs*, Paris, 1952, pp. 95–100; E. des Places, *La Religion grecque*, Paris, 1969, pp. 92ff. Stählin, "περίψημα," in *TDNT*, vol. 6, pp. 84–93.

περιλείπομαι

---

perileipomai, to remain (after someone or something has been removed)

This passive verb refers to the result of a subtraction, that which remains. According to 2 Macc 1:31, after the liquid was poured on the wood and the sacrifice was consumed by fire, "Nehemiah ordered them to pour the remaining liquid on the large stones";[1] in 8:14, it refers to the Israelites' remaining property after the high priests have taken what they want.[2] It is used for ships that succeed in making it through (Polybius 1.37.2), fields that remain uncultivated (*UPZ* 110, 168), a remaining portion (*BGU* 1132, 12; from 13 BC), animals reserved for sacrifice (*PSI* 409, 12).

But this verb is also used for human survivors (*P.Giss.* 82, 23: *pros to hēmas tous eti perileipomenous*), "the remnant of Israel and of Judah" (2 Chr 34:21), old men who would have seen Solomon's temple in its original glory (Hag 2:3), the survivors of a batallion received by Agesilaus (Plutarch, *Ages.* 22.8). It is in this sense that 1 Thess 4:15, 17 contrasts the dead (literally, "those who have fallen asleep," *tous koimēthentas*), and "we who are (still) alive, those left" (*hēmeis hoi zōntes, hoi perileipomenoi*). The present passive participle *perileipomenoi* was current with this meaning in the first century: "Those of the priests who survive (*hoi perileipomenoi tōn hiereōn*) reconstitute the genealogies, extracts from the archives" (Josephus, *Ag. Apion* 1.35); "Every time one of the brothers was led away, those who remained (*hoi perileipomenoi*) said, 'Do not dishonor us, brother' " (4 Macc 13:18); at the martyrdom of the seventh brother, the tyrant thought that the mother, "already having lost so many sons . . . would urge the one who remained to obey and save himself" (12:6; cf. Herodian, *Hist.* 2.1.7).

---

[1] Τὸ περιλειπόμενον ὕδωρ. C. Mugler comments on περιλείπειν, leave as a remainder: "a verbal expression indicating that a subtraction involving two geometric elements, lines, areas, or volumes leaves a remainder" (*Terminologie géométrique*, p. 343).

[2] Τὰ περιλελειμμένα. Cf. *PSI* 571, 14: "I have nothing left"; Dittenberger, *Syl.* 852, 46: ἔτι πλείστη περιελείπετο ὕλη. —πειρλειπῇ in *SB* 8979, 12 is a false reading; cf. H. C. Youtie, *Scriptiunculae*, vol. 2, pp. 956ff.

---

perileipomai, S 4035; *EDNT* 3.74; *NIDNTT* 3.247; MM 506; L&N 85.66; BAGD 648

περιπίπτω

peripiptō, to fall around or beside, turn over, to befall, to happen upon
→see also ἐμπίπτω; πίπτω

The primary sense of this word ("fall around, beside; turn over") and the secondary sense ("collide," Plutarch, *Them.* 15.4) are both found in 2 Macc 9:7, where after Antiochus has suddenly tipped out of his chariot "all the limbs of his body were tortured because of the violence of his fall" (*dyscherei ptōmati peripesonta*).[1]

Things that happen to us are said to "befall" us (Epictetus 3.2.1; *SB* 8858, 15; 10654, 6; *C.Ord.Ptol.* 83, 30), or else we "fall into" them (2 Macc 6:13; Josephus, *Ant.* 20.48); and when we meet people unexpectedly we "fall upon" them (Josephus, *War* 3.499; *P.Oxy.* 1639, 20). Usually the circumstance is unpredictable or unforeseen. This element of chance, whether lucky or unlucky, is expressed by the phrase *peripiptein periptōmati*. Thus it was Ruth's luck to happen upon a parcel of land belonging to Boaz (Ruth 2:3), and the messenger bringing news of Saul's death happened to be on Mount Gilboa (2 Sam 1:6; cf. *BGU* 1881, 8). The circumstantial character of the situation, event, or meeting is seen partly from the use of the verb predominantly with *ean* (*T. Dan* 4.5; *P.Mert.* 43, 5), *ei* (*PSI* 1265, 11; *P.Tebt.* 704, 20), *mēpote* (*UPZ* 108, 34; 144, 33); cf. Menander, *Dysk.* 244: "If something should happen to her, the blame will touch me as well."

All these examples are of untoward events or sad situations: to be suddenly stricken with a punishment (2 Macc 6:13; cf. Josephus, *Ant.* 20.48); touched by misery and need (*PSI* 767, 42; *SB* 9401, 7), danger (Josephus, *Life* 83), captivity and servitude (*Ant.* 8.229; *T. Jos.* 10.3), serpents and

---

[1] Diodorus Siculus 17.12.5: "The Theban horsemen fell down on their own weapons."

---

peripiptō, S 4045; *TDNT* 6.173; *EDNT* 3.76; *NIDNTT* 1.608; MM 507; L&N 15.85, 37.11, 90.71; BDF § 202; BAGD 649

scorpions (Philo, *Alleg. Interp.* 2.84, 86), shipwreck (*T. Abr.* A 19), all sorts
of misfortunes (Josephus, *War* 7.219) and evils (2 Macc 10.4; Marcus Aurelius 2.11; Dittenberger, *Syl.* 495, 58), notably sickness,[2] all "that a person
tries to avoid" (Epictetus 3.2.1; cf. Philo, *Spec. Laws* 1.224). It is with these
connotations in mind that we read of the misadventure of the man who
was traveling from Jerusalem to Jericho when "he suddenly fell into the
hands of brigands" (*lēstais periepesen*).[3] Cf. the Pythagorean Hipparchus:
"for this reason being about to fall into the hands of either brigands or a
tyrant" (*ē lēstais dia touto mellontes peripiptein ē tyrannō*, in Stobaeus, *Flor.*
108.81; vol. 4, p. 982; cf. Diogenes Laertius 4.50: *pleōn . . . lēstais periepese*;
Artemidorus Daldianus, *Onir.* 3.65). In a context that is just as catastrophic,
the ship taking Paul to Rome washes up on the island of Malta where it
strikes "a place between two seas."[4]

Jas 1:2 uses the verb in a figurative and pejorative sense—as do Prov
11:5 (*peripiptei adikia*), *P.Tebt.* 278, 32 (*thymou peripesite*, beginning of the
first century), and Philo (*Unchang. God* 73)—with respect to the various
temptations to which Christians may be exposed (*hotan peirasmois peripesēte
poikilois*). There is no reason to limit these temptations to trials that come
from without, but the choice of this verb—rather than *eispherō* (Matt 6:19),

---

[2] 2 Macc 9:21; Josephus, *Ant.* 10.25; *Ag. Apion* 1.305, 313. Περιπίπτω is part of
the medical vocabulary, cf. Hippocrates, Dioscorides, Galen (in W. K. Hobart, *Medical
Language*, pp. 129ff.). In the course of a civil war at Gortyn in the third century BC,
the physician Hermias of Cos "saved a good number of citizens smitten by wounds
and by evils that were not benign diseases" (decree of Cnossos; Dittenberger, *Syl.* 528,
10). In the fourth century AD, the public physician Aurelius Eulogius, after examining
the body of the εἰρήναρχος of Teis, sends his medical certificate to the λογιστής of
Oxyrhynchus: "lifeless corpse, no trace of wound or contusion, succumbed to an
acute illness" (ὀξείῳ νοσήματι περιπεσών, *P.Rein.* 92, 12).

[3] Luke 10:30; cf. F. Field, *Notes on the Translation*, p. 61.

[4] Acts 27:41, περιπεσόντες δὲ εἰς τόπον διθάλασσον (the Vulgate transliterates,
"in locum dithalassum"). It is not possible to identify this τόπος with certainty.
Διθάλασσος (*bimaris*, Horace) was a term for Corinth, which is built on the isthmus
that separated the Aegean Sea from the Ionian Sea; its two ports (Cenchraea and
Lechaion) open onto these "two seas" respectively. Strabo explains that "the Euxine
Sea is a sort of double sea" where two promontories (to the east and the west) narrow
the intermediary channel and form two large basins (2.5.22); he judges that "it is not
likely that the Atlantic Ocean is divided into two seas (διθάλαττον) separated by
isthmuses narrow enough to block a complete circuit" (1.1.8). At Malta, some have
suggested a channel separating Malta and the isle of Salmonetta, where there is a
promontory jutting out that is battered by waves on two sides. More likely, reference
is made to a sand bank, a shoal where the water breaks. Dio Chrysostom, *Or.* 5.9 is
cited: Syrta is famous because of its shoals (βραχέα καὶ διθάλασσα) and its long sand
banks (καὶ ταινίαι μακραί); cf. J. Renié, *Actes des Apôtres*, Paris, 1949, p. 344; E.
Haenchen, *Acts*, pp. 708ff.

eiserchomai (26:41; Mark 14:38; Luke 22:40, 46), *lambanō* (1 Cor 10:13), *empiptō* (1 Tim 6:9), *hypomenō* (Jas 1:12)—emphasizes that they are unexpected, unlooked for;[5] they are abrupt encounters, and one bumps into them as into obstacles. On the other hand, the encounter brings grief and regret; it tends to disturb the Christian's peace. One is disoriented by this "putting to the test" of one's faithfulness. Cf. 1 Pet 1:6—"suffering grief in various trials" (*lypēthentes en poikilois peirasmois*). This is why St. James urges the opposite response—"count it a complete joy"—because it is the occasion for a greater good.

---

[5] Cf. Josephus, *Ant.* 4.293: καὶ μὴ τότε ἃ δεῖ ποιεῖν ἐπιζητοῦντες ἀπαρασκεύαστοι τοῖς καιροῖς περιπέσητε.

περιποιέομαι, περιποίησις

peripoieomai, **to preserve, reserve, keep for oneself, acquire; to bring about, to effect for oneself;** *peripoiēsis*, **an acquiring or preserving**

In the middle voice, the verb *peripoieō* means "preserve, reserve, keep for oneself." "The one who seeks to preserve his life (*tēn psychēn autou peripoiēsasthai*) will lose it (*apolesei autēn*), and the one who loses it will save it (*zōogonēsei autēn*)" (Luke 17:33). This meaning of "saving a life" occurs repeatedly in secular Greek[1] as well as in the LXX,[2] where it often contrasts with *apothnēskō* (Ezek 13:19; cf. Ps 79:11) and *apollyō* ("the profit that they had gained is lost," Jer 31:36; cf. Prov 6:32; Heb 10:39).

The meaning "acquire for oneself" predominates, whether with respect to goods (Gen 31:18; 36:6; Hebrew *rākaš*), a reputation (1 Macc 6:44, with the reflexive pronoun, which is pleonastic: *peripoēsai heautō onoma aiōnion;* cf. Xenophon, *An.* 5.6.17; *Ep. Arist.* 121; *P.Ryl.* 712, 4; *PSI* 1075, 7), power (Thucydides 1.9.2), the crown (Josephus, *Ant.* 14.386), the goodwill of another (Polybius 3.6.13), a friend.[3] Thus God has acquired a people (Isa

---

[1] Xenophon, *Cyr.* 4.4.10, Cyrus says to the Assyrian prisoners: "Today by obeying me you save your lives" (τὰς ψυχὰς περιποιήσασθε); meaning to economize (Xenophon, *Oec.* 2.10; 11.10); cf. to spare (Isa 31:5; Hebrew *pāsaḥ*), to keep (1 Sam 25:39, Hebrew *ḥāśak;* 2 Sam 12:3; Jdt 11:9; Job 27:17).

[2] Ezek 13:18—"The lives of my people are ensnared, and they save their (own) lives" (καὶ ψυχὰς περιεποιοῦντο, piel of the Hebrew *ḥāyâh*); 2 Macc 3:35, Heliodorus offers a thanksgiving sacrifice to God, who has preserved his life (τῷ τὸ ζῆν περιποιήσαντι). Usually περιποιεῖν, "leave," has no object and means "leave alive" (Gen 12:12; Exod 1:16; 22:17; Num 22:33; Josh 6:17; 9:20; Judg 21:11; 1 Sam 15:3, 9, 15; 1 Kgs 18:5). Cf. 2 Chr 14:12—"So many Ethiopians fell that not one of them was left alive," ὥστε μὴ εἶναι ἐν αὐτοῖς περιποίησιν (Hebrew *miḥyâh*, literally surviving).

[3] Menander, *Dysk.* 815: "You want to make a friend (βούλει περιποιήσασθαί τινα φίλον). Try—and good luck."

---

peripoieomai, S 4046; *EDNT* 3.76; *NIDNTT* 2.838–839; MM 507; L&N 21.24; BAGD 650 ‖ *peripoiēsis*, S 4047; *EDNT* 3.76; *NIDNTT* 2.838–839; MM 508; L&N 57.62, 90.74; BAGD 650

43:21), the church.[4] He has become its acquirer and owner;[5] he has exclusive rights to the redeemed; they are his personal property, the people whom he has acquired (*laos eis peripoiēsin*, 1 Pet 2:9; cf. Exod 19:5). The emphasis is on the original acquisition and the strictly guarded ownership of the "holy nation," over which God retains permanent mastery (cf. Sir Prologue 11), but there is an affective value; the *s^egulâh* (Hebrew) is a treasure that one possesses as one's own.[6]

Peripoieomai also means "to bring about, to effect for oneself," as when deacons "who serve well gain a good standing for themselves."[7] The meaning can be close to the active "procure" (cf. Prov 22:9; 2 Macc 15:21), common in the inscriptions for "supply resources" for a people or a city. A decree from Samos in the third century BC, in honor of Boulagoras: "He procured many advantages and much profit for the city through his judgments" (*SEG* I, 366, 22); a century later, a decree of the Athenian *klērouchoi* for Euboulos of Marathon: "through his sustained efforts, he often secured the interests of the Athenians of Delos" (*I.Delos* I, 1498, 16); a decree of Hanisa in Cappadocia in favor of Apollonius, "bringing his zeal and ardor to bear, through a legal proceeding he procured for the people the inheritance (claimed by others)."[8]

---

[4] Eph 1:14—εἰς ἀπολύτρωσιν τῆς περιποιήσεως (*Inbesitznahme*, H. Schlier, *Der Brief an die Epheser,* Düsseldorf, 1957, p. 71; "The down payment on our inheritance, in consideration of the redemption that will be its acquisition"; N. Hugedé, *Éphésiens*, p. 44, who gives *peripoiēsis* an active sense: "the fact of possessing." M. Barth, *Ephesians*, vol. 1, p. 97, distinguishes between the act of saving or preserving life, acquiring a piece of property, the state of ownership; cf. 1 Pet 2:9); Acts 20:28—τὴν ἐκκλησίαν τοῦ θεοῦ, ἥν περιεποιήσατο. For the textual criticism of this verse, cf. E. Jacquier, *Actes*, pp. 615. For the theology, cf. J. Dupont, *Discours de Milet*, pp. 168ff.

[5] The most common meaning of περιποιέω in the papyri is "acquire, obtain"; cf. *P.Oxy.* 2349, 38: τῷ περιποιηθησομένῳ (AD 70); *P.Brem.* 22, 4; *P.Lond.* 1915, 26; *P.Mich.* 87, 7; the sheep that I have bought for you (third century BC); *SB* 7246, 11; 8444, 63—"they often got nothing more."

[6] On the *s^egulâh*, cf. Deut 7:6; 14:2; 1 Chr 29:3; Mal 3:17 (F. Dreyfus, "Le thème de l'héritage dans l'Ancien Testament," in *RSPT*, 1958, pp. 15ff., 27, 38; H. Wildberger, *Jahwes Eigentumsvolk*, Zurich, 1960); cf. *P.Oxy.* 1892, 34 (sixth century).

[7] 1 Tim 3:13. Βαθμός is a degree or rank. To the references given by C. Spicq, *Epîtres Pastorales*, vol. 1, p. 416ff., add for this idea *P.Tebt.* 703, 276: "If you are irreproachable in your conduct, you will be considered worthy of advancement" (third century BC); inscriptions from Sardis and Side: κόμες πρώτου βαθμοῦ = "comes primi ordinis" (cf. J. and L. Robert, "Bulletin épigraphique," in *REG*, 1968, p. 518, n. 478).

[8] C. Michel, *Recueil*, n. 546, 18 (commented on by L. Robert, *Noms indigènes*, pp. 457ff.); cf. Dittenberger, *Syl.* 495, 135: οὐκ ὀλίγα χρήματα περιεποίησε τῇ πόλει (decree of Olbia for Protogenes); decree of Araxa in Lycia for Orthagoras: "He served all the interests of the city" (in J. Pouilloux, *Choix*, n. IV, 68). In the papyri: "I will secure two loads for you" (ἵνα σοι ἐν Μεμνονείοις περιποιήσω ἀγώγια δύο, *SB*

The substantive *peripoiēsis*, a technical term in business language, rare in the LXX and the papyri,[9] is used three times in the NT in an eschatological sense, and in a formula that appears to be stereotyped: Christians are predestined *eis peripoiēsin sōtērias*, i.e., for the possessing of salvation,[10] or *eis peripoiēsin doxēs* (for the possessing of glory, 2 Thess 2:14). In Heb 10:39—"We are not people for shrinking back and being destroyed (*eis apōleian*), but people of faith for the possessing of life (*eis peripoiēsin psychēs*; the *nomen actionis* for the act of possessing)." The saving of the soul, as opposed to perdition, is the definition of the spiritual salvation of a person, called *sōtēria psychōn* in 1 Pet 1:9.[11]

6096, 4 = *O.Bodl.* 1999); bring about a marriage (ibid. 8003, 4); *P.Oxy.* 2148, 17 (in AD 27); fulfill one's military service (*UPZ* 14, 12).

[9] 2 Chr 14:12; Mal 3:17 (Hebrew s^egulâh); Hag 2:9—"In this place, I will give . . . peace of soul for the obtaining (of salvation) to whoever contributes to the building of this temple" (added to the Hebrew). In the three occurrences in the papyri, two mean property: *P.Tebt.* 317, 26, κατὰ τὸ τῆς περιποιήσεως δίκαιον (second century AD); *SB* 10537, 34: καὶ περιποίησιν ἀποδείξαντες ἐμοῦ (third century); cf. *P.Rein.* 52, 2: "You have already been instructed in writing to give an accounting for the preserving (or acquiring, or keeping?) and shipping of the grain" (third-fourth century); *T. Zeb.* 2.8—ἵνα γένηται περιποίησις τῷ Ἰωσήφ.

[10] 1 Thess 5:9 (cf. B. Rigaux, *Thessaloniciens*, pp. 570ff.); Ps.-Plato, *Def.* 415 c: Σωτηρία· περιποίησις ἀβλαβής ("salvation: the act of preserving safe and sound"); Isa 31:5—περιποιήσεται καὶ σώσει; 1 Macc 6:44—σῶσαι τὸν λαὸν αὐτοῦ καὶ περιποιῆσαι.

[11] That toward which faith is directed, its goal, is the salvation of the soul (cf. Jas 1:21), which will only be completed in the future (Jas 5:21). Cf. *Enoch* 48.8: "In the day of their trouble and their affliction, they will not save their souls"; *Book of Mysteries*: "They do not know what will happen to them, nor how to save their souls from the mystery to come" (1Q27 1.4); texts cited by G. Dautzenberg, "Σωτηρία ψυχῶν (I Petr. I, 9)," in *BZ*, 1964, pp. 269–276; idem, *Sein Leben bewahren*, Munich, 1966; cf. *P.Tebt.* 56, 11: σῶσαι ψυχὰς πολλάς (with respect to a famine; second century BC). In secular Greek, περιποιέω often means to save a city or a country (Thucydides 2.25.2; Josephus, *War* 1.180); in Philo, it usually means "procure for oneself, secure" wealth (*Conf. Tongues* 112; *Flacc.* 130), glory and liberty (*Good Man Free* 94, 138), joy (*Prelim. Stud.* 161), stability (*Heir* 125; *Good Man Free* 96), but above all "appropriate, acquire, enter into possession of" virtue (*Rewards* 27, 31, 51; *Dreams* 1.162; *Spec. Laws* 1.149; *Cherub.* 12, 13; *Worse Attacks Better* 64, 120), which allows a person to secure a perfect existence (Philo, *Husbandry* 157; *Drunkenness* 58; *Flacc.* 138; *Flight* 17); resting in God and the contemplative life especially gain peace and joy (*Flight* 174, 176); God himself supplies the victory (*Moses* 1.216) and the Powers that give quality to that which is without quality (*Spec. Laws* 1.47). It is God who grants that we may procure the Beautiful (*Alleg. Interp.* 3.136) and "enter into possession of that which was not ours before" (*Unchang. God* 86).

περιφρονέω

periphroneō, to be reflective, circumspect; to scorn, despise
→*see also* καταφρονέω

This biblical hapax has positive and pejorative meanings. The positive sense is "to be reflective, circumspect."[1] The pejorative sense is "to scorn, despise," which is the meaning in Titus 2:15—"Let no one despise you" (*mēdeis sou periphroneitō*). So it seems that this verb is synonymous with *kataphroneō*, since Paul wrote to Timothy "Let no one despise your youth" (*mēdeis . . . kataphroneitō*, 1 Tim 4:12). There is nevertheless a shade of difference; the latter verb means "turn up one's nose at, have no respect for, take no account of, pay no heed to."[2] Again and again in the papyri of *P.Enteux.* complainants consider that this or that official pays no attention to them (44, 4; 68, 11) because they are orphans (9, 6), or aged (25, 8; 26, 9; 48, 7), or foreign (29, 11), or widowed (13, 6). In the case of Timothy, at the head of the church at Ephesus, his youth was a handicap because it inclined the believers to despise or simply ignore his authority.

Titus, on the other hand, had an energetic temperament. He gave firm instruction and corrected sinners. He ran the risk of running afoul of the weak points and the temper of the Cretans, who might stand up to him or at least react disdainfully. Thus the inhabitants of Corcyra, priding themselves on their superiority, treated the Corinthians disdainfully (*periphronountes*, Thucydides 1.25.4), and Pericles "out of a presumptuous con-

---

[1] Cf. περίφρων, describing Artemidora in her epitaph (E. Bernand, *Inscriptions métriques*, n. 58, 3), but 4 Macc 8:28—the Maccabean brothers "were disdainful of passion"; cf. Plutarch, *Cam.* 6.3: "starting from such weak and despised origins."

[2] The slave of two masters holds to one and pays no attention to the other (Matt 6:24); taking no account of little children (Matt 18:10), of the infinite goodness of God (Rom 2:4; cf. 2 Cor 11:22); Christian slaves show inadequate respect for their Christian owners (1 Tim 6:2).

---

periphroneō, S 4065; *TDNT* 3.633; *EDNT* 3.80; *NIDNTT* 1.461–462; MM 510; L&N 76.25; BAGD 653

fidence, for the pleasure of winning and to show off his strength, faced the Lacedaemonians."[3] Thus there is an element of insolence in *periphronēsis*, as in the case of children who rebel against their parents' authority and fail to show them the respect (*tēn timēn*) that is due them.[4]

Nevertheless, *periphroneō* and *kataphroneō* are often synonymous. Audacious and arrogant false teachers "despise authority" (*kataphronountas*, 2 Pet 2:10); this is rejection and rebellion. For their part, Eleazar and the Maccabeus brother despise pain (4 Macc 6:9; 14:1, *periphroneō*); cf. Christ, who despised the shame of the cross (*kataphroneō*, Heb 12:2), and in the papyri of the seventh-eighth century, where more than mere negligence or abstention is involved: "I had to abandon my humble occupation."[5]

---

[3] Plutarch, *Per.* 31.1 (περιφρονῆσαι); cf. *Thes.* 1.5: "when the fable boldly flaunts (αὐθαδῶς περιφρονῇ) credibility and is completely out of line with verisimilitude."

[4] Ὅσοι δ᾽ ἂν τῶν νέων περιφρονῶσι τοὺς γονεῖς, Josephus, *Ant.* 4.260 (cf. Deut 21:18); cf. 5.200—"their troubles were due to their contempt for the laws."

[5] *P.Apoll.* 27, 5: καὶ ἠναγκάσθην περιφρονῆσαι τοῦ ἐλαχίστου μου πράγματος; cf. *P.Ross.Georg.* III, 51, 22; *SB* 4774, 9.

πίπτω

piptō, to fall, fail

→*see also* ἐμπίπτω; περιπίπτω

In the Bible, sparrows and grain fall to the earth.[1] When the subject is a human, sometimes the word refers to a fall,[2] sometimes to the act of throwing oneself on someone's neck.[3] Usually one falls on one's face to venerate someone;[4] directed toward God, this prostration is an act of adoration. Metaphorically, those who fall, as opposed to those who remain standing, are those who fail, sinners,[5] with a connotation of degeneration: "Remember whence you have fallen" (Rev 2:5; cf. Luke 10:18).

[1] Matt 10:29; 13:4–5; Mark 4:4–8; Luke 8:5–14; John 12:24; cf. the mountains (Hos 10:8; Luke 23:30); hail (Exod 9:19), the sun (Rev 7:16), a hair (1 Sam 14:45; 1 Kgs 1:52), a cloak (2 Kgs 2:14), a sword (2 Sam 20:8; 2 Kgs 6:6); someone falls from the roof (Deut 22:8); an animal falls into a clay pot (Lev 11:33). Cf. Josephus, *Ant.* 4.275; 19.87; Strabo 2.5.8; Archimedes, *Spir.* 15.14—"one of the lines falls at the end of the spiral"; Eusebius, *Praep. Evang.* 1.9.21: "the period falls before the Trojan War."

[2] Mark 9:20; into fire or water (Matt 17:15), into a pit (15:14; cf. Menander, *Dysk.* 628: "He was going down when he slipped and fell"—καὶ πέπτωκεν—to the bottom of a well), in the desert (Num 14:32; Heb 3:17); cf. *Gos. Pet.* 18: because of the deep darkness at Golgotha, "many went about with lamps, thinking that it was night, and they fell" (ἐπέσαντο [*sic*]).

[3] Tob 11:9, 13. One throws oneself onto one's bed (1 Macc 6:8; *Jos. Asen.* 9.1); one falls into a trap (Tob 14:10; Ps 35:8; 141:10; Sir 28:26; Amos 3:5), into misfortune (2 Macc 10:4; cf. Iamblichus, *Myst.* 2.10 = 93.8: τῷ κακῷ περιπίπτειν, fall into evil), under the blow of trouble or judgment (2 Macc 3:6; Jas 5:12; *BGU* 1761, 14; 1812, 7), into disobedience (Heb 4:11).

[4] Gen 17:3 (Hebrew *nāpal*); Num 14:5; 16:4; Matt 2:11; 4:9; 17:6; 18:26, 29; 26:39; Mark 5:22; Luke 5:12; 8:41; 17:16; John 11:32; Acts 10:25; 1 Cor 14:25; Rev 1:17; 11:16; 19:10; 22:28. πίπτειν εἰς, ἐπί, πρός, παρά, ἔμπροσθεν; cf. Josephus, *War* 1.621; *Ant.* 3.310.

[5] Rom 11:22; 14:4; 1 Cor 10:12 (cf. H. A. Brongers, "Darum, wer fest zu stehen meint, der sehe zu, daß er nicht falle, I Kor. X, 12," in *Symbolae Biblicae et Meso-*

piptō, S 4098; *TDNT* 6.161–166; *EDNT* 3.90–91; *NIDNTT* 1.608, 610–611; MM 514; L&N 13.59, 13.97, 13.122, 15.118, 15.119, 17.22, 20.60, 23.105, 24.40, 24.93, 30.107, 56.32, 68.49, 75.7, 87.56, 90.71; BDF §§77, 80, 81(3); BAGD 659–660

But there are different sorts of falls. If the *paidotribēs* teaches the ephebes "how to overcome enemies without falling on the ground" (*SEG* XX, 662, 10), it is nevertheless possible to stumble and fall but rise again (Rom 11:11—"Did they stumble so as to fall?"—*mē eptaisan hina pesōsin*), which is the situation of the just and of the Jews, and which gives grounds for hope.[6]

The interpretation of 1 Cor 13:8 is more delicate: *hē agapē oudepote piptei*,[7] which has sometimes been understood to mean "Love never falls (from its rank)" (E. B. Allo) or "never loses its prerogatives."[8] The apostle contrasts *agapē* with the passing charisms that will disappear (*katargeomai*) and cease (*pauomai*), bringing together the present (the present indicative, *piptei*) and the future (*oudepote*, "never at any time") and making *ou . . . piptō* synonymous with *menō* ("abide").[9] Clearly excellence is implied,[10] and the context shows that staying power is involved. But is the point that love is long-lived or that it is permanent? In the latter case, the text would mean

---

potamicae Fr. M. Th. De Liagre Böhl Dedicatae, Leiden, 1973, pp. 56–70); this meaning is constant in Philo, *Abraham* 269; *Change of Names* 54–56; 154–156; *Alleg. Interp.* 2.100ff., cf. *Husbandry* 94, 122; *Pss. Sol.* 1.5; Josephus, *Ant.* 18.280; 19.294.

[6] The turn of phrase is tradition: "They stumble and fall" (Ps 27:2); "if he falls he is not floored" (37:24); "seven times the just person falls and rises again" (Prov 24:16; cf. 25:26); "if I fall I rise again" (Mic 7:8); "many will stumble, and they will fall and be broken" (Isa 8:15); "she falls to rise no more" (24:20; cf. 28:13); "Does one fall and not rise again?" (Jer 8:4; cf. 6:15; 46:6, 12). A guard forces one of the Maccabeus brothers to get up again every time he falls (4 Macc 6:7–8; cf. 2.14). "The just person has stumbled . . . and fallen" (*Pss. Sol.* 3.5); "those who take a slippery path stumble and fall" (Philo, *Abraham* 269). Cf. Stobaeus, *Ecl.* 7.63 (vol. 3, p. 329, 12): βάλλομεν, οὐ πίπτουσι.

[7] Certainly we must read πίπτει with ℵ, A, B, C, Clement of Alexandria (*Quis dives*), K. Aland–M. Black; against ἐκπίπτει, read by D, G, K, L, Tertullian.

[8] J. Héring (*La Première Epître de saint Paul aux Corinthiens*, Neuchâtel-Paris, 1949, p. 120 ET = pp. 141–142); cf. M. F. Lacan, "La Charité jamais ne succombe" ("Les Trois qui demeurent, I Cor. XIII, 13," in *RSR*, 1958, p. 325). On this verse, cf. W. Michaelis, "ἡ ἀγάπη οὐδέποτε πίπτει," in *Paulus—Hellas—Oikumene*, Athens, 1951, pp. 135–140.

[9] 1 Cor 13:13; cf. W. Michaelis, "πίπτω," in *TDNT*, vol. 6, p. 165; H. Conzelmann, *First Corinthians*, p. 255; C. Spicq, *Agapè*, vol. 2, pp. 93ff.; idem, *Théologie morale*, vol. 2, p. 499. F. Dreyfus, "Maintenant la foi, l'espérance et la charité demeurent toutes les trois (1 Cor 13:13)," in *AnBib* 17–18, 1961, pp. 403–412.

[10] Cf. the fallen house of David (Acts 15:16; Amos 9:11); "she is fallen, Babylon the Great" (Rev 14:8; 18:2; Isa 21:9); Rev 17:10 (Hos 7:7; Amos 9:11); Sir 1:30—"Do not rise lest you fall"; cf. 2:7; 13:21; 19:1. None of Yahweh's words fall to the earth (1 Sam 3:19; 2 Kgs 10:10) or fail to have an effect (Josh 23:14). Philo, *Rewards* 6: "Whole lives founder, and once ruined are difficult to restore"; Philostratus (*Gym.* 43): the athletes proved not to be inferior in these sorts of combat (οὐδὲ ἐκεῖ πίπτοντες) but worthy of the prize for valor and trophies.

that love holds fast, does not yield, does not let itself be defeated;[11] consequently it does not cease to act and to inspire virtuous activity. But on the ne hand, it must grow cold in the last days (Matt 24:12); and on the other hand *piptō* is predominantly used in the sense of "succumb, fall dead, perish"[12] or—when the subject is a house, a wall, a city—"collapse, be annihilated."[13] While this meaning does not necessarily exclude the one discussed before, the text would mean that love is never abolished, never ceases to exist, even in heaven.[14] It is indestructible, *en aphtharsia* (Eph 6:24), whereas faith and hope are limited with respect to time.

[11] In this sense, cf. Exod 23:5—the ass gives out under its burden; Deut 22:4; Jdt 7:22—"women and young men, exhausted by thirst, fell in the streets of the city and in the roads leading to the gates and had no more energy"; Dan 10:9—"I fell exhausted"; Luke 16:17—"It is easier for heaven and earth to pass away than for one word of the law to fall (disappear)." Cf. Plutarch, *Per.* 8.5: "When I leveled him in battle, he maintains that he did not fall."

[12] Exod 19:21; 32:28; Lev 26:7-8; Num 14:3; Judg 5:27; Job 14:10; 1 Macc 5:12; 6:42; 9:1, 18; 10:50; 11:74; etc. Josephus, *Ag. Apion* 2.212; *Life* 24; *War* 1.102, 172; *I.Thas.* 332, 11; *SEG* XX, 661, 11: "Vanquished, he fell like a tree in a squall" (epitaph of a *paidotribēs*, second-third century); *Jos. Asen.* 16.16: "The bees fell to the earth dead"; *P.Oxy.* 475, 25: "He fell and killed himself." Philo, *Etern. World* 128: to fall, breathing one's last; cf. Xenophon, *Cyn.* 9.20: "the deer fall, winded"; *Anth. Pal.* 6.48: "Evening star, how have you disappeared?" (πῶς ἔπεσες).

[13] Josh 6:20; Judg 16:30; Ezek 13:11, 14; 38:20; Sir 49:13; 1 Macc 12:37; Matt 7:25, 27: οἰκία οὐκ ἔπεσεν; Heb 11:30; Rev 11:13; 16:19; Josephus, *War* 3.254; *Ag. Apion* 1.192; *Ant.* 15.122; 16.18.

[14] The papyri are no help. They use πέπτωκεν for what has been "paid," recorded in a bank. *P.Mich.* 235, 3: "Paid at the bank of the *nomarchia*" (AD 41); *P.Tebt.* 279, 1 (third century BC); 350, 3 (AD 70); 580; *P.Hamb.* 169, 3; 182, 16; *P.Oslo* 140, 9: πέπτωκεν εἰς ἀναγραφὴν διὰ Πτολεμαίου (a *paramonē* contract, second century BC); *SB* 9297, 1 (the recording of a marriage contract; 86 BC), cf. 6942; 8965, 3; 8966, 3; 8967, 1; *P.Stras.* 336, *a* 15; *b* 16; cf. *P.Mich.* 32, 13: Since I arrived, nothing has been paid; πίπτειν = pay a tax (*P.Hib.* 66, 2; cf. a decree of the Acarnanian league, *IG* IX, I², 5), use revenues (Dittenberger, *Syl.* 976, 87; 1116, 8; *I.Lind.* 419, 28, 37, 48. *C.Ord.Ptol.* 47, 18 = *P.Tebt.* 6, 29).

πιστικός

pistikos, **trustworthy, authentic**

This adjective, used to describe the costly nard that Mary of Bethany poured over Jesus (Mark 14:3, Vulgate *spicatus;* John 12:3, Vulgate *pisticus*), does not occur in the LXX. It is most likely derived from *pistos*, "worthy of confidence, faithful,"[1] and it is usually used to describe humans[2] as "trustworthy persons," especially with respect to the handling of money (*P.Apoll.* 83, 9; 87, 1 and 9; 97, col. II, 20). Since this meaning cannot apply to the perfume in the Gospel account, other explanations have been sought.[3]

---

[1] Plato, *Grg.* 455 *a:* a believable opinion; Artemidorus Daldianus, *Onir.* 2.32: γυνὴ πιστικὸς καὶ οἰκουρός. The reading πιστικῶς in Plutarch, *Pel.* 8.2 is erroneous (read πιστῶς).

[2] *P.Ryl.* 692, 20: οἶδα γὰρ ἐγὼ τὸ ἀσφαλές σου καὶ γοργὸν καὶ πιστικόν (third century); *SB* 9608, 3: ἀπέστιλα εἰς τὴν πόλιν διὰ πιστικοῦ ἀνθρώπου; 7241, 26 (= *P.Lond.* 1393); *P.Got.* 29, 5: ἐκέλευσεν ὁ πιστικός, ἵνα ἀπολύσουσιν ὅλα τὰ γαιδάρια (sixth-seventh century). At Daphne: "Here lies Callopios . . . having a most faithful soul" (ἔχων πιστικωτάτην ψυχήν, *IGLS,* 1030, 2). —In *P.Cair.Isid.* 11, 39, 41, 43–46; 40, 2; 48, 2, 4; 49, 2–5, πιστίκιον is the winnowed spelt (Latin *spelta munda*) that the *sitologoi* hand over to the ἀποδέκται πιστικίου; cf. J. Bingen, "L'Edit du Maximum et les papyrus," in *Proceedings* XI, p. 373.

[3] A derivative of πίνω, hence "liquid," or of πιέζω, hence "distilled," a corruption of τῆς στακτῆς (a name for myrrh in small quantities, a very fragrant perfume, according to Polybius 26.10); cf. P. L. Couchoud, "Notes de critique verbale sur St. Marc et St. Matthieu," in *JTS,* 1933, p. 128; cf. J. E. Bruns, "A Note on John XII, 3," in *CBQ,* 1966, pp. 219–222), a scribal error for σπικάτον (Wettstein, cf. the Vulgate in Mark, "nardi spicati"). Galen 12.604 *k* is cited: τὰ πολυτελῆ μυράτων πλουσίων γυναικῶν ἅ καλοῦσιν αὐταὶ σπίκατα. Referring to the Sinaitic Syriac reading ܦܣܛܩܐ, this would be nard with pistachio (M. Black, *Aramaic Approach,* pp. 223–225) or Indian picita, the name of the plant being *Nardostachus jatamansi* (R. Köbert, "Nardos Pistike—Kostnarde," in *Bib,* 1948, pp. 279–281); C. K. Barrett, *St. John,* p. 343; cf. Pliny, *HN* 12.42–46; μαρδόσταχυς, in E. M. Husselman, "Lists," in *P.Coll.Youtie* II, p. 560.

---

pistikos, S 4101; *EDNT* 3.91; MM 514; L&N 79.97; BDF §113(2); BAGD 662

But *pistikos* is in fact used to describe things, in particular oil,[4] and there is nothing wrong with the translation "a perfume of true nard."[5] This is how Theophylact understood the text: "it means either a species of nard that is called '*pistikē*' or else genuine nard" (*pistikēn de nardo noei, ētoi eidos nardou, houtō legomenon pistikē, ē tēn adolon nardon,* on Mark, *PG,* vol. 123, 645 *b*). These perfumes were quite expensive and were often counterfeited.[6] "Nard is counterfeited with pseudonard. . . . Pure (*sincerum*) nard is distinguished by its lightness, its reddish-brown color, the sweetness of its fragrance, its pleasant flavor" (Pliny, *HN* 12.26.12; cf. 13.1.16: "so many ways of counterfeiting"). Thus the perfume of Mary of Bethany was extremely expensive pure, "authentic"[7] nard.

---

[4] In a record of a payment of oil (λόγος ἐλαίου), *P.Got.* 18, 2: ὑπὲρ πιστικοῦ τὼν αὐτοῦ διαφόρων ἐλαίου (seventh century); a service contract, *P.Mil.* 48, 5 (= *SB* 9011): πιστικῶν ἀποπληρῶσαι δίχα τῆς χρίας τοῦ μυροπολίου; cf. the mosaic of *pistikon* in the antechamber to the baptistry at Antioch (*IGLS* 778, 2). Eusebius, *Dem. Evang.* 9.8.9: τοῦ πιστικοῦ τῆς καινῆς διαθήκης κράματος.

[5] "Un parfum de nard vrai," the translation of P. Joüon, *L'Evangile de Notre-Seigneur Jésus-Christ,* Paris, 1930, pp. 260, 534.

[6] Cf. E. Nestle, "Die unverfälschte köstliche Narde," in *ZNW,* 1902, pp. 169–171.

[7] The translation of M. J. Lagrange, *Marc,* p. 367; *Jean,* p. 321. Cf. R. Schnackenburg, *John,* vol. 2, pp. 367, 522.

πίστις

pistis, faith, confidence, fidelity, guarantee, loyalty

→*see also* ὑπόστασις

No secular text can offer a parallel to NT or OT "faith,"[1] but *pistis*, which derives from *peithomai* ("be persuaded, have confidence, obey"), connotes persuasion, conviction, and commitment, and always implies confidence, which is expressed in human relationships as fidelity, trust, assurance, oath, proof, guarantee.[2] Only this richness of meaning can

---

[1] Obviously, the Christian papyri retain this theological meaning, *C.P.Herm.* 9, 20: ἐν πίστει ἔχε; *P.Lond.* 1915, 15: "those who are weak in the faith" (quoting Rom 14:1); 1919, 19. On πίστις in the papyri, cf. Gerhard-Gradenwitz, "ΩΝΗ ΕΝ ΠΙΣΤΕΙ," in *Philologus*, vol. 63, 1904, pp. 499–563; D. Schäfer, "Zu dem ptolemäischen ΠΙΣΤΕΙΣ," *Philologus*, vol. 88, 1933, pp. 296–301; W. Schmitz, Ἡ Πίστις *in den Papyri*, Cologne, 1964; A. J. Festugière, *Etudes d'histoire*, pp. 136ff. Διὰ τῆς σῆς πίστεως can be translated "responsibility," cf. *P.Vindob.Tandem*, n. 4, 25.

[2] Cf. Demosthenes, *C. Lept.* 20.164: "Our city will show loyalty (πιστή), justice (δικαία), and fidelity (ἀψευδής) in all its obligations. . . . (Otherwise) it will be accused of disloyalty (ἄπιστος), envy, dishonesty"; Demosthenes, *C. Zenoth.* 32.16: "If you gave him the funds on his word (εἰς πίστιν ἔδωκας), then why did you take security (τὰ βέβαι᾽ ἐποιοῦ) before the crime? If you did not trust him (εἰ δ᾽ ἀπιστῶν ἐτύγχανες) . . ."; Herodotus 9.92: the Samians take an oath to support the Greeks, πίστιν τε καὶ ὅρκια ἐποιεῦντο; 9.106: the Samians and other islanders swear to remain faithful to the alliance, πίστι τε καταλαβόντες καὶ ὁρκίοισι ἐμμενέειν τε καὶ μὴ ἀπο-στήσεσθαι; Xenophon, *Hell.* 1.3.4: πίστεις πεποιημένος, "having made an agree-ment"; Thucydides 4.86.2–3: "I offer quite substantial guarantees (πίστεις διδούς) . . . ; they may have the greatest confidence"; 5.45: "Alcibiades persuaded the Lace-daemonians by a solemn assurance" (πείθει πίστιν αὐτοῖς δούς); Menander, *Dysk.* 308: πίστιν ἐπιθεὶς διατελεῖν στέργων, "solemnly undertaking to love her always." Cf. E. Fraenkel, "Zur Geschichte des Wortes fides," in *RhMus*, vol. 71, 1916, pp. 187–199; R. Heinze, "Fides," in *Hermes*, vol. 64, 1929, pp. 140–166; L. Lombardi, *Dalla "Fides" alla "Bona Fides,"* Milan, 1961; A. Piganiol, "Venire in Fidem," in *RIDA*, vol. 5, 1950, pp. 339–347; W. Waldstein, "Entscheidungsgrundlagen der klassischen römischen Juristen," in *ANRW*, vol. 15, 1976, pp. 68ff.

---

pistis, S 4102; *TDNT* 6.174–228; *EDNT* 3.91–97; *NIDNTT* 1.593–595, 597–606, 3.1211–1213; MM 515; L&N 31.43, 31.85, 31.88, 31.102, 31.104, 33.289; BDF §§163, 206(2), 233(2), 400(2); BAGD 662–664; ND 2.94

account for the faith (*pistei, kata pistin, dia pisteōs*) that inspired the conduct of the great Israelite ancestors of Hebrews 11.[3]

The usage of *pistis* in the papyri is usually legal, and its predominant meaning is "guarantee, security." Pursuant to a loan granted him by Zeno, Philo reckons that his creditor is claiming more than his due. The judges ask for a statement of credits and debts that both parties agree is correct, and they decide—with respect to the contested sums—that the adversaries must exchange guarantees (*pisteis*) in the Serapeum of Parmeniscos.[4] In 108 BC, 150 *artabai* of borrowed grain are guaranteed by a mortgage on the cultivated lands owned by the borrowers; these ask the *epistatēs* of Akoris to require written guarantees from their lender.[5] *Pisti Didymou*

---

[3] Heb 11 shows the influence of Philo's kind of faith: confidence in God's word, reliance on the divine guarantee, steadfast hope in what must come to pass, confident obedience, essential moral force (cf. C. Spicq, *Hébreux*, vol. 1, pp. 76ff. A. Beckaert, *De Praemiis et Poenis*, Paris, 1961, pp. 21ff. E. Starobinski-Safran, *De Fuga*, Paris, 1970, p. 214, n. 2). Faith, "the proof of invisible realities" (Heb 11:1), can be compared to Philonian ἔλεγχος—"conviction" (*Flight* 118, 131, 203), argument, exhibit, means of proof (*Joseph* 107; *Virtues* 34, 46, 55; cf. V. Nikiprowetzki, "La Doctrine de l'elenchos chez Philon," in *Philon d'Alexandrie*, Colloques du CNRS, Paris, 1967, pp. 255ff.)—but can also mean any sort of testimony (tablets, hearsay, a witness; cf. *LTGR*, p. 101), and derives in the first instance from Aristotle's definition of rhetoric: "Among the modes of persuasion (τῶν δὲ πίστεων), some are extrinsic to the art of persuasion (e.g., testimony, confessions, documents), others technical (e.g., the character of the orator, putting the audience in a certain frame of mind, and the proof provided by the speech itself)" (Aristotle, *Rh.* 1.2.1355ᵇ35).

[4] *P.Cair.Zen.* 59355, 102 and 127 (cf. A. Würstle, "Untersuchungen zu Cair. Zén. III, 59355," in *JJP*, vol. 5, 1951, pp. 9–103); *P.Ryl.* 28, 187: πους ἀριστερὸς ἐὰν ἄλληται, σημαίνι αὐτὸν ἐπὶ λόγῳ καὶ πίστι πλανηθῆναι; J. Pouilloux, *Choix*, n. 27, 30: "to those who have concluded the treaty with Athens and its allies . . . the people shall give guarantees." This *pistis* is sometimes a formal obligation, an oath (ibid. 35, 24 and 34), which is a means of proof.

[5] *P.Rein.* 18, 10 and 31; cf. *BGU* 1639, 16; 1662, 16; 1810, 3: δέδονθ' ὑμῖν πίστεις ἀπὸ ὑποκειμένης; *P.Tebt.* 14, 10; 41, 22: "the guarantees that we have obtained from Lysanias, cousin to the king and *stratēgos*" (second century BC); *P.Oxy.* 94, 18; 486, 7; 506, 15; 1644, 20; *P.Mich.* 188, 18; 189, 21; 605, 16 and 24; *P.Ant.* 42, 5; *P.Oslo* 40, 33: "You have a guarantee for all that I cannot show a written receipt for"; *P.Harr.* 85, 13: "I will pay monthly interest with a guarantee on myself" (second century AD); *SB* 7636, 4: ἔχετε τὰς πίστεις, ἐφ' ᾧ παραγενόμενοι ἐργασθήσεσθε ἐν τῇ κώμῃ (first century BC). The document embodying a pledge is itself a *pistis* (*UPZ* 119, 31; 124, 30; cf. *P.Oxy.* 2110, 38: ἡ πίστις τῶν ὑπομνημάτων; *P.Lips.* 41, 6: κατὰ τὴν πίστιν τοῦ γραμματείου; *Chrest.Mitt.*33, 6); and the term refers to a safe-conduct, *P.Tebt.* 741, 10–13: "Let safe-conducts be given to the persons mentioned so that they may apply themselves to the mission that they have undertaken until I arrive on site and examine their assertions with the requisite care" (second century BC); 895, 38, 117; *P.Yale* 60, 15: "all the safe-conducts that I have granted hitherto shall be invalid" (ἀκύρων οὐσῶν καὶ ὧν ἐὰν ἐπενέγκω πίστεων); *BGU* 1811, 8; 1812, 4: "(the farmers) who have

means "with Didymos's guarantee" (*P.Warr.* 5, 15) or "Didymos stood surety" (*P.Princ.* 26, 5). *Pistis* must be given this meaning of "guarantee" in Acts 17:31—God has given a "guarantee" through a man that he will resurrect the dead; and that is the meaning of *hypostasis* in Heb 11:1— "Faith is the guarantee of things hoped for,"[6] well translated in the Peshitta by *pyso*. The substantive *hypostasis*, literally "that which is placed beneath," hence "support, base, foundation," has already been used (Heb 1:3) in its philosophical meaning, "substance" as opposed to accidents, "reality" as opposed to appearances. Hence its psychological and moral meaning: "that which is at the bottom of one's soul, firmness, confidence, courage"; but in the papyri, it also refers to a right of possession, the entirety of an inheritance (*P.Oxy.* 138, 26; 488, 17; 1274, 15; *P.Harr.* 90, 2), its guarantee (*P.Eleph.* 15, 3), or better, the collection of documents stored in the archives as surety and constituting the evidence for a property right (*P.Oxy.* 237, col. IV, 39; VIII, 26, 34, 42; *UPZ* 222). Thus faith is the true title attesting to one's ownership of the heavenly property that one hopes for, and thus the guarantee that one will obtain them in the future.[7]

Faith is also "plighted faith," respect for a commitment, the carrying out of obligations (*P.Mert.* 32, 2), as with the young widows who "have rejected their first faith."[8] This *pistis*, which encompasses good faith,

---

obtained safe-conducts from us shall not be arrested until they have finished the harvest" (49/48 BC); 1156: "until they are entirely cleared, let them not be allowed to answer us with safe-conducts, to take refuge at a sacred altar or in a place of asylum . . . to benefit from any protection' " (cf. F. von Woess, *Das Asylwesen Ägyptens in der Ptolemäerzeit und die spätere Entwicklung*, Munich, 1923, pp. 184–192); *P.Berlin* inv. 11837: "Nicholas to Pnepheros, Necthanoubis, and their father Petesouchos. Here are safe-conducts, on the condition that you work in person in your town, and no one will arrest you. . . . But you should not have left in this way without reason. Who could have forced you to go? Or what wrong did you suffer?" (cited by C. Préaux, *Economie royale*, p. 544). Thus *pisteis* are letters of protection for a given person (someone pursued by creditors or sought by officials) allowing him to keep at his work or take on the responsibilities of his post.

[6] Ἔστιν δὲ πίστις ἐλπιζομένων ὑπόστασις. Cf. C. Spicq, *Hébreux*, vol. 2, p. 337; H. Dörrie, "Zu Hebr XI, 1," in *ZNW*, 1955, pp. 196–202.

[7] Faith in Hebrews already contains the germ of its final τελείωσις, because "it is impossible for God to lie" (Heb 6:18); not only does it persuade us of the existence of invisible realities, it confers a right to possess them; thus it is the guarantee of a hope that cannot be thwarted. We may note the frequent connection between faith and inheritance, Acts 26:18; Rom 4:16; Gal 3:14; Heb 6:12; 1 Tim 3:13: "deacons have great assurance in (the guarantee of) faith, which is (based) on Jesus Christ." Cf. Philo, *Abraham* 268: πίστις κλῆρος εὐδαιμονίας, "faith, the heritage of happiness."

[8] Τὴν πρώτην πίστιν ἠθέτησαν, 1 Tim 5:12. Moulton-Milligan cite *Corpus Inscriptionum Atticarum*, App., ὑποκατέχετε ὑμεῖς αὐτὴν ταῖς ἐσχάταις τιμωρίαις ὅτι πρώτη ἠθέτησεν τὴν πίστιν πρὸς Φήλικα τὸν ἑαυτῆς ἄνδρα. We may compare Rev

loyalty, and fidelity, is described as "ingens vinculum fidei" ("the great bond of faith," Livy 8.28) and is the basis of all contracts.[9] This is probably the sense of 2 Tim 4:7—"I have kept the faith."[10] This refers not to the conservation of the (theological) faith, but to fidelity (cf. Josephus, *War* 6.345: *pisteis etērēsa* = "I kept my word"; *Ant.* 15.134), and more exactly to the fidelity shown by those who serve a superior, such as mercenaries, royal and imperial officials, those who have a duty:[11]

2:13—οὐκ ἠρνήσω τὴν πίστιν μου; but ἀθέτεω here has its legal meaning, annulling an obligation or agreement (Gal 3:15; Heb 10:28; cf. 2 Macc 13:25; 14:28), an oath (1 Macc 6:22). ἀθετέω πίστιν = "fidem irritam facere" (Polybius 8.36.5; 22.16.1; 23.8.7). The Essenes were persuaded that no woman kept faith with one man, τηρεῖν τὴν πρὸς ἕνα πίστιν (Josephus, *War* 2.121). To revoke an agreement (1 Macc 15:27) is perjury and treason against God (Isa 1:2; Jer 3:20; 5:11). "Numa was the first to raise a temple to Πίστις. . . . He made swearing by Faith the most important oath for the Romans, and it is still used today" (Plutarch, *Num.* 16.1; cf. Dionysius of Halicarnassus 2.75). *I.Thas.* 174, 7. At Delos, in 98–97, nine people, apparently slaves, dedicate a statue of Good Faith (Πίστις) to the gods, *I.Delos*, 1761; Dittenberger, *Syl.* 727, 19; P. Bruneau, *Recherches sur les cultes de Délos*, Paris, 1970, p. 617. Plighted faith is like divinized Fides, an expression of confidence based on the religion of good faith and fidelity.

[9] Cicero, *Off.* 1.23; Polybius 7.12, Aratus to Philip V of Macedonia: "See whether it is not better to take your soldiers away and leave no other garrison than respect for your obligations"; 10.37.3; cf. J. Imber, "*Fides et nexum*," in *Studi in onore V. Arangio-Ruiz*, Naples, 1953, vol. 1, pp. 339–363; P. Boyancé, "Fides et le serment," in M. Renard, *Hommages à A. Grenier*, Brussels, 1962, vol. 1, pp. 329–341; idem, "Les Romains peuple de la fides," in *BAGB*, 1964, pp. 419–435; J. Vogt, "De fide servorum," in *Mélanges A. Piganiol*, Paris, 1966, vol. 3, pp. 1499–1514; S. Calderone, Πίστις-*Fides*, Messina, 1964.

[10] Τὴν πίστιν τετήρηκα. Cf. J. M. T. Barton, "Bonum certamen certavi . . . fidem servavi," in *Bib*, 1959, pp. 878–884. Moulton-Milligan and A. Deissmann (*Light*, p. 309) cite an inscription from the theater of Ephesus, where Marcus Aurelius Agathopus thanks Artemis ὅτι τὴν πίστιν ἐτήρησα, and Dittenberger, *Or.* 339, 47: προχειρισαμένου τοὺς τὴν πίστιν εὐσεβῶς τε καὶ δικαίως τηρήσοντας (*GIBM*, Part III, n. 587 b 5). The formula τὴν πίστιν τηρεῖν is well attested in the epigraphy of Asia Minor in the sense of faithfulness to a commitment.

[11] Πίστις refers to the powers that derive from the possession of the king's confidence (L. Robert, *Hellenica*, vol. 11–12, 1960, pp. 105–106, cites Polybius 5.41.2; 6.35.8; 16.22.2; C. B. Welles, *Royal Correspondence*, n. 44, 1; 66, 11; 67, 13). Cf. the epitaph of the mercenary Diazelmis: "I gave the princes of Egypt my zeal and my fidelity" (E. Bernand, *Inscriptions métriques*, n. 10, 8 = *SEG* VIII, 497); the epitaph of the officer Apollonius: γλυκερὰν τηρῶν ἅμα πίστιν, "I was a devoted man, I respected sweet fidelity" (ibid. 5, 13); another: χρηστός, εὐγενής, ἁπλοῦς, φιλοβασιλεύς, ἀνδρεῖος, ἐμ πίστει μέγας (in C. Austin, *Comicorum Graecorum Fragmenta*, n. 300, col. I, 3); a physician of Heraclea: ζῶντα καλῶς καὶ ἐπιεικῶς καὶ φιλανθρώπως . . . πίστει καὶ σωφροσύνῃ καὶ δικαιοσύνῃ (*MAMA* VI, 114 B 9); "It is necessary to choose an overseer who in all fidelity and to the profit of the most sacred treasury will carry

Paul testifies to his painstaking faithfulness to his duty as apostle in the service of Jesus Christ.[12]

Pistis, then, implies complete loyalty (1 Tim 1:5, *pisteōs anypokritou; P.Abinn.* 59, 17: "I, Plas, will restore to you completely, in all loyalty"; *P.Mert.* 90, 12: *pisteōs kai epieikias charin*). Heb 10:22 links fullness of faith and a true heart (*alēthinos*), in other words, sincerity and fidelity, just as the papyri link *pistis* and *alētheia; P.Oxy.* 70, 4: "every valid written contract has *pistis* and *alētheia*" (*pasa kyria engraphos synallagē pistin kai alētheian echei*); *P.Flor.* 32 *b* 14: "I swear . . . that I have made the copy truly and faithfully" (*exomnymi . . . ex alētheias kai pisteōs tēn apographēn pepoiēsthai*); *P.Stras.* 152, 14: "that I have made the copy truly and faithfully" (*ex alētheias kai peisteōs tēn apographēn pepoiēsthai*); BGU 1151, 17. Cf. 1 Thess 2:13; 1 Tim 2:7; Titus 1:1. The *pistos anēr* is a man worthy of confidence (1 Tim 1:12), loyal citizen, faithful friend, someone who is trusted: "if you find someone who is completely trustworthy among those who are with you" (*ean tina heurēs kata parontas echonta peistēn pollēn, P.Fay.* 122, 22); "being well-disposed and showing complete fidelity toward me" (*eunoousē moi kai pasan pistin moi endeiknymenē, P.Oxy.* 494, 9); "thanks to his kindness, his faithfulness, and his family ties" (*eunoia kai pisti kai tē tou genous oikeotēti, P.Tebt.* 326, 10); BGU 326, col. I, 15; *P.Lips.* 28, 31: "to watch over . . . with noble fidelity" (*phylaxai . . . meta kalēs pisteōs,* an act of adoption). Testators often appeal to the fidelity of their executors or their heirs in carrying out their final wishes (*P.Oxy.* 1901, 48; 2474, 6, 22; *P.Stras.* 277, 7); but numerous

---

out the oversight of the ships" (*P.Panop.Beatty* 1, 50; cf. 169, 181, 186; *P.Oxy.* 727, 21). A Jewish epitaph for a certain Samuel links faithfulness and thankfulness: γνῶναι δύνασαι πόσση πίστις ἠδὲ χάρις (*CII* 1451).

[12] Cf. *P.Stras.* 40, 18: "all my faithfulness toward his person"; *PSI* 1265, 4. We may compare the *Gnomon of the Idios Logos* 18 (= *BGU* 1210): "Inheritances left in trust (τὰς κατὰ πίστιν γεινομένας κληρομονίας) by Greeks for Romans or by Romans for Greeks are confiscated by the decision of the divine Vespasian. Those who declared the trust, however (οἱ μέντοι τὰς πίστεις ἐξωμολογησάμενοι), received half of the inheritance." The testator places on the putative heir, a trustee, the obligation to restore the inheritance to a third party who could not legally be named as heir; cf. *BGU* 326, 15; *P.Oxy.* 907, 7; 2348, 7; *SB* 7630, 11. M. Taylor, "The Function of ΠΙΣΤΟΣ ΧΡΙΣΤΟΥ in Galatians," in *JBL,* vol. 85, 1966, pp. 58–76. C. Panagopoulos (*Vocabulaire,* pp. 225ff.) mentions that good faith is especially emphasized in financial operations, justice, and general administration. At Odessos, an *agoranomos* fulfilled his functions πιστῶς (*I.Bulg.* 230 bis) and an upright official faithfully pleaded the cause of his fellow citizens (ibid. 63 bis). At Olbia, it is the virtue of a *stratēgos* (B. Latyschev, *Inscriptiones Antiquae,* vol. 1, n. 42, 13). According to Plutarch, fidelity is a prerequisite for a glorious public career; for example, in pleading against a powerful adversary for a weaker party (*Praec. ger. rei publ.* 805 B). One of the qualities of the man of politics is to know how to "find trustworthy and talented people" (ibid. 812 C).

complainants who had thought that their adversaries would show fidelity toward them declare that they have been deceived (*P.Cair.Isid.* 74, 11; *P.Mert.* 91, 12; *P.Oxy.* 71, col. II, 11). Normally a complainant expresses confidence in the judge (*P.Stras.* 296 r 16). *Pistis eunoias* is confidence inspired by the beneficence of the statesman (Plutarch, *Praec. ger. rei publ.* 28.821 b; *Ti. Gracch.* 33.7); cf. *pistin echein:* "have confidence in" (idem, Plutarch, *Mor.* 1101 c) or, more frequently, "merit or have the confidence of" (ibid. 91 a; 146 b; 699 d; 984 f; *Praec. ger. rei publ.* 14.809 f; 15.812 f;31.822 f). In Luke 17:5, *prosthes hēmin pistin,* the only instance in the Third Gospel where *pistis* is not preceded by the definite article, we must translate "Have faith in us."[13]

It is often impossible to distinguish between practical fidelity and good faith.[14] For example: "knowing the faithfulness (sincerity) of my goodwill" (*epi tosouton pistin eunoias mathousa, P.Mil.Vogl.* 73, 11); "trusting in my good faith and my assurance" (*peithomenon tē emē pistei kai dexia, P.Mich.* 485, 12). In a stipulation of a contract (a deposit, a divorce, etc.),[15] the signatory sometimes completes this common formula to emphasize his fidelity: "In good faith the buyer has asked and in good faith the seller has confessed" (*pistei epērōtēsen ho ēgorakōs kai pistei hōmologēsen . . . ho peprakōs, P.Dura* 26, 28; 31, 32); "making good and urging in his own good faith, Hermeias Hephaistas" (*bebeiountos kai tē idia pistei keleuontos Hermeiou Hēphaista, BGU* 887, 4; *SB* 9219, 4, 24; *PSI* 1254, 8); "speak as an ambassador and a person worthy of trust" (*hōs presbytēs kai pisteōs axios eipe, P.Lips.* 32, 2); "from Deios, who professes his good faith" (*para tou Deiou exomologoumenou tēn pistin, P.Mil.Vogl.* 25, col. III, 32; *P.Flor.* 86, 11). This good faith and goodwill are often called *kalē pistis* (*P.Tebt.* 418, 15; *P.Oxy.* 2187, 29; *P.Cair.Isid.* 94, 11;

---

[13] E. Delebecque, *Etudes grecques,* p. 103.

[14] In the power of attorney issued by Thaesis to her husband to allow him to collect funds due to her, "she gives her consent to all actions taken by her husband Ptollion conformably to the power of attorney, provided that he restores all to Thaesis by virtue of the good faith obligations that are incumbent upon him" (τῆς πίστεως περὶ αὐτὸν οὔσης, *P.Fouad* 35, 11; cf. *BGU,* 1662, 16; *P.Oxy.* 506, 15). The person acting as proxy has obligations of loyalty to the principal; he must satisfy his obligations; he has a personal responsibility (τῇ ἰδίᾳ πίστει πράττει, *BGU* 388, col. II, 13; cf. *P.Fam.Tebt.* 27, 16; *P.Oxy.* 1634, 13; *SB* 8987, 9). We might compare ὑπακοὴ πίστεως (Acts 6:7; Rom 1:5; 16:26) and ἀξίως ἀνεστρέφησαν αὐτῶν τε καὶ τὰς ἐνχειρισθείσας αὐτοῖς πίστεως (Dittenberger, *Syl.* 932, 7). In a decree of Delphi in 125 BC, Athens has taught the Greeks that "the greatest good for humans consists in relations of mutual good faith" (G. Daux, *Delphes au IIe et au Ie siècle,* Paris, 1936, p. 369). Cf. *P.Mich.* inv. 257, 18: πίστι ἐπερώτησεν . . . πίστι ὡμολόγησεν (published by F. T. Gignac, in *BASP,* vol. 13, 1976, p. 95).

[15] On good faith in contracts (ἡ πίστις τῶν συναλλαγμάτων), cf. *PSI* 76, 3; J. G. Keenan, "The Case of Flavia Christodote," in *ZPE,* vol. 29, 1978, p. 193.

BGU 1574, 18; *SB* 7523, 2; 7996, 7; 9174, 11; 9193, 7), but fidelity also enters in: "We will pay faithfully" (*meta kalēs pisteōs, P.Oxy.* 913, 14; 3089, 16). This same idea is expressed by *hē agathē pistis* (*P.Oxy.* 140, 16; *BGU* 314, 19; *P.Mil.* 48, 13 = *SB* 9011). This honesty of intent and action is often highlighted with the words *hygiēs-hygiainō* ([be] sound, healthy), cf. *P.Oxy.* 1031, 18; 2120, 8: "carrying through soundly and with all fidelity" (*hygiōs kai meta pasēs pisteōs diapraxamenos*); *SB* 8029, 13: "with sound fidelity, not negligently" (*meth' hygious tēs pisteōs akataphronētōs*); *Pap.Lugd.Bat.* XI, n. 2, col. I, 10: carrying out a public service "soundly and faithfully, flawlessly" (*hygiōs kai pistōs amemptōs*); *P.Hamb.* 19, 17; *PSI* 86, 13; *Stud.Pal.* XX, 34; *P.Flor.* 2, 10, 45, 143; *P.Stras.* 177, 20; 532, 9–10. We may compare soundness in the faith (*hina hygiainōsin en tē pistei,* Titus 1:13; cf. 2:2).

In the NT, *pistis* is often linked with *agapē* (1 Tim 1:14; 2:15; 4:12; 6:11; 2 Tim 2:22; Phlm 5) and once with *phileō* (Titus 3:15). In the first case, the ideas are specifically religious, but Greek and Roman ears were accustomed to hearing *fides* and *amicitia* together.[16] Thus the inhabitants of Oxyrhynchus showed their goodwill, faithfulness, and friendship toward the Romans (*hē pros Rhōmaious eunoia te kai pistis kai philia hēn enedeixanto, P.Oxy.* 705, 32 = *C.Pap.Jud.* 450), just as the Alexandrian Jews commend their request to Claudius on the basis of their fidelity and friendship (*dia tēn pros Rhōmaious pistin kai philian,* Josephus, *Ant.* 19.289; cf. Polybius 2.11.5; 2.12.2; 20.9.12; 20.10.2).

---

[16] Dittenberger, *Syl.* 675, 20; *Or.* 557, 16; cf. M. Lemosse, *Le Régime des relations internationales dans le haut Empire romain,* Paris, 1967, pp. 70, 77. Plutarch, *Cleom.* 21.5: "fill the city with friends and faithful and sure allies" (φίλων καὶ συμμάχων πιστῶν καὶ βεβαίων); Plutarch, *Ti. Gracch.* 12.6: a faithful servant; *C. Gracch.* 16.6: his most faithful friends; etc.

πλεονεξία

pleonexia, **consuming ambition, greed**

This substantive, which etymologically (*pleon-echō*) means "have more, want more," can be used in a favorable sense for gain or profit;[1] but in practice it means either "consuming ambition" (Xenophon, *Hell.* 3.5.15; *Cyn.* 18.10; Diodorus Siculus 19.1.3) that aims at supremacy and is linked with arrogance (Philo, *Moses* 1.56; *T. Jud.* 21.8—"exalted [*hypsoumenoi*] in *pleonexia*" ; cf. *T. Naph.* 3.1; *T. Gad* 2.4; 5.1; *T. Asher* 5.1; *T. Benj.* 5.1; Musonius, frag. 3; ed C. E. Lutz, p. 40, line 28) and is thus a social vice, since equality rules out superiority (Philo, *Spec. Laws* 4.54—*to ison pleonexias allotrion*; cf. *Change of Names* 103; *Contemp. Life* 70); or more often "greed" for wealth, covetousness gone amuck, various forms of *epithymia* (Josephus, *Ant.* 17.253; Musonius, frag. 17, p. 108, line 13), the desire to have what is forbidden, more than one's due[2]—for example, in a sharing out (Philo, *Moses* 1.324). Not only is *pleonexia* insatiable (Sir 14:9) and excessive (Philo, *Rewards* 121), it is also aggressive and does not hesitate to wrong a neighbor or gain his property through extortion. Thus it is synonymous with hardness and rapacity (Josephus, *War* 7.256), reducing a human to the level of the wild beasts, which were "born to live through violence" (*apo bias kai*

---

[1] Judg 5:19—"They did not take a monetary profit"; Epictetus 2.10.9: "to acquire goodness of soul for the price of a head of lettuce, perhaps, or of a chair; what profit?" (ὅση ἡ πλεονεξία); cf. Philo, *Post. Cain* 162: "all that the body seeks to amass" (πλεονεκτεῖν); Xenophon, *Cyr.* 1.6.28, in a fight against wild animals, "you tried always to be in a better position than them (μετὰ πλεονεξίας) to fight them." In scientific jargon, πλεονάζω means "to have a surplus," cf. Geminus, *Intro. to Astronomy* 8.40, 44, 45, 49, 58, 59; 13.24: one quantity, duration, or number exceeds another.

[2] Hab 2:9—"Woe to the one who gains a dishonest profit (Hebrew *beṣaʿ*) for his house"; Jer 22:17; Ps 119:36; Xenophon, *Cyr.* 1.6.29; Thucydides 2.84, 1; Diodorus Siculus 17.70.5: "The Macedonians in their plundering were excessively greedy."

---

pleonexia, S 4124; *TDNT* 6.266–274; *EDNT* 3.102–103; *NIDNTT* 1.137–139, 2.845–846; MM 518; L&N 25.22, 88.144; BAGD 667

pleonexias, Musonius, frag. 14; p. 92, line 22; Dio Chrysostom 38.31). It is a vice of rulers and officials.[3] It should be compared on the one hand to the disinterestedness of St. Paul, who was never moved by flattery or greed;[4] and on the other hand to the greed of the false teachers, who not only approach their ministry like business persons with an eye on the bottom line but even derive dishonest gain by exploiting those who are taken in by false exegesis, myths, and syrupy speech.[5]

The parable of the Foolish Rich Man, who values life in terms of material wealth, is a commentary on the warning "Guard against all *pleonexia*" (Luke 12:15; cf. Musonius 4, p. 48, line 9; frag. 6, p. 52, line 18; frag. 8, p. 62, line 17; Dio Chrysostom 13.32; 17.22), which is included in the sin lists of Mark 7:22 and Rom 1:29 (cf. Philo, *Sacr. Abel and Cain* 32), presented in the former as one of twelve evil things that come out of a man's heart and defile him, in the second as the fruit of a perverted mind.[6] In Mark, greed is associated especially with carnal disorders, as in Eph 4:19;

---

[3] Ezek 22:27—"The leaders are like wolves . . . shedding blood, killing people to extract a profit"; Wis 10:11; Philo, *Decalogue* 155: "oligarchy and mob rule, those pernicious systems, give rise to anarchy and usurpation"; cf. Philo, *Spec. Laws* 2.43: αἱ πλεονεξίαι καὶ ἀντεπιθέσεις; Josephus, *Ant.* 6.86; Plutarch, *Pomp.* 39.6: "Those who had to deal with him found him quite willing to put up with their greed and harshness"; *Ages.* 20.6: "He presented as evidence their mediocrity or greed in the performance of their duties"; Thucydides 3.82.8: "The cause of all these evils was the seeking of power out of greed and ambition"; cf. 1.40.1: "they are full of violence and greed" (βίαι καὶ πλεονέκται); *UPZ* 110, 68 and 136; *P.Panop.Beatty* 2, 135, 240; *P.Princ.* 20, 11: παραγγέλλω οὖν αὐτοῖς παύσασθαι τῆς τοιαύτης πλεονεξίας (= *SB* 8072). Cf. R. C. Trench, *Synonyms*, pp. 81–84; C. Spicq, *Théologie morale*, vol. 1, p. 186; S. Lyonnet, L. Sabourin, *Sin, Redemption, and Sacrifice*, pp. 50ff.

[4] 1 Thess 2:5. St. Paul sends the brethren to Corinth to organize the collection, so that it may be the expression of true generosity, not an act of plundering or extortion (καὶ μὴ ὡς πλεονεξίαν, 2 Cor 9:5); cf. E. Klaar, "Πλεονεξία, -έκτης, -εκτεῖν" in *TZ*, 1954, pp. 395–397.

[5] 2 Pet 2:3 (ἐμπορεύεσθαι); 2:14; cf. "insidious greed" (Philo, *Good Man Free* 79); *T. Moses* 7.6—"Devouring the substance of the poor and claiming to do so in the name of justice" (E. M. Laperrousaz, "Le Plus Ancien Témoin de l'existence du Testament de Moïse," in *Sem*, vol. 19, 1970, p. 64). *P.Oxy.* 1828, 4: ὁ ψεύστης καὶ ὁ πλεονέκτης is from *Herm. Sim.* 6.5.5 (cf. S. G. Mercati, "Passo del Pastore di Erma riconosciuto nel Pap. Oxy. 1828," in *Bib*, 1925, pp. 336–338).

[6] Cf. Eph 4:19—"dulled moral sensibility"; Philo, *Spec. Laws* 4.5: "greed, a baneful passion and difficult to cure"; *Moses* 2.186—"our enemy and the source of our misery," healed by the Therapeutai (*Contemp. Life* 2; cf. *Good Man Free* 78). In medicine, *pleonexia* is a state of excess that disrupts the balance of the humors and has harmful effects on the health (as does ἔνδεια, in the opposite direction, cf. Plato, *Tim.* 82 a); cf. Philistion of Locri (W. H. S. Jones, *The Medical Writings of Anonymus Londinensis*, Cambridge, 1947, xx, 35–36); Hippocrates, *Aff.* I, c. 20; Hippocrates, *Vict.* c. 71 and 77; *Loc. Hom.* c. 9; J. Jouanna, *Hippocrate: La Nature de l'homme*, Berlin, 1975, p. 256.

5:3; Col 3:5; Philo, *Spec. Laws* 1.173 (cf. 1 Cor 5:10–11); in Romans, it is linked mainly with injustice and wickedness.[7]

The secular literature denounces greed as a very great vice: "Greed is a very great evil for humans; for those who wish to have their neighbors' goods often fail and are vanquished."[8] St. Paul portrays it as the object of God's wrath (Col 3:5) and excludes the greedy from a share in the kingdom of God (1 Cor 6:10; Eph 5:5), and 2 Pet 2:3, 14 calls them "accursed."

---

[7] Cf. the linking of πλεονεξία and ἀδικία (*Ep. Arist.* 277; Philo, *Rewards* 15; *Contemp. Life* 70; *Sacr. Abel and Cain* 32; Josephus, *Ant.* 6.86; Strabo 7.4.6; *PSI* 446, 9; Musonius, frag. 20, p. 126, line 18) or κακία (Philo, *Spec. Laws* 1.278; 2.52; *Contemp. Life* 2) and opposition to justice (*Good Man Free* 159; Josephus, *Ant.* 3.67). Usurpation is often associated with pillaging and banditry (cf. ἅρπαξ, 1 Cor 5:10–11; 6:10), *T. Dan* 5.7—the sons of Judah ἔσονται ἐν πλεονεξίᾳ ἁρπάζοντες; Philo, *Husbandry* 83; *P.Abinn.* 50, 3 (= *SB* 9690). It is not surprising that in petitions and lawsuits the greed and injustice of the adversary are denounced; *P.Tebt.* 735, 8; *P.Fay.* 124, 24; *PSI* 1052, 4; *P.Cair.Isid.* 62, 5 (= *SB* 9167; cf. 10564, 16). Cf. A. Vögtle, *Tugend- und Lasterkataloge*; S. Wibbing, *Die Tugend- und Lasterkataloge im N. T.*, Berlin, 1959.

[8] Πλεονεξία μέγιστον ἀνθρώποις κακόν· οἱ γὰρ θέλοντες προσλαβεῖν τὰ τῶν πέλας ἀποτυγχάνουσι πολλάκις νικώμενοι—Menander, in Stobaeus, *Flor.* 10.3 (vol. 3, p. 408). Plutarch, the greed of the rich and of the Macedonians (*Cleom.* 3.1; 16.1) links this vice with debauchery, soft living, and luxury (Plutarch, *Agis* 3.1; 10.5), injustice (*Ti. Gracch.* 9.2; cf. *C. Gracch.* 20.8). It motivates the lowest sort of compromises (*Agis* 5.4: πλεονεξίας ἕνεκα; cf. *Ti. Gracch.* 9.3). Cf. the description of insatiability (ἀπληστία) in Galen (*Anim. Pass.* 1.38) and of φιλαργυρία in 1 Tim 6:10, with similar attestations in C. Spicq, *Epîtres Pastorales*, vol. 1, p. 564; add to this *Sib. Or.* 2.115; 3.235; *Anth. Pal.* 9.394, and especially Plutarch, *De cupid. divit.* (*Mor.* 523 c ff.).

πληροφορέω, πληροφορία

plērophoreō, **to convince fully, accomplish fully, fully discharge (a debt or obligation);** *plērophoria,* **fullness, richness**

The noun, unknown in the LXX, is attested in the papyri by only one text that is so badly mutilated that it is not possible to determine in what sense it is used.[1] In three of the four NT occurrences, it means "fullness": fullness of understanding (of the mystery of God),[2] of hope (meaning its definitive realization; Heb 6:11—*pros tēn plērophorian tēs elpidos achri telous*), of faith (meaning absolute certitude, without doubt or hesitation; Heb 10:22—*en plērophoria pisteōs;* cf. *1 Clem.* 14.1: *tis peplērophorēmenos agapēs*). In 1 Thess 1:5, St. Paul declares that he has preached the gospel not only in words, but "with power (*en dynamei*) and in the Holy Spirit and with much *plērophoria.*" Given the absence of the preposition *en* before *plērophoria,* we could translate "complete assurance," but if St. Paul had meant that, he would have written *en pasē parrēsia* (Phil 1:20; cf. 2 Cor 3:12; 7:4; 1 Tim 3:13; *meta pasēs parrēsias,* Acts 28:31); and at any rate it would be odd for the apostle to emphasize his personal conviction. So it is better to translate "with power, with the Holy Spirit and every kind of richness."[3]

---

[1] *P.Giss.* 87, 25 (cf. A. Deissmann, *Light,* pp. 86–87). Hesychius says πληροφορία· βεβαιότης = certitude.

[2] Col 2:2—εἰς πᾶν πλοῦτος τῆς πληροφορίας τῆς συνέσεως; we could take it to mean "with full conviction," but with "wealth" the sense is rather quantitative, and the redundancy—or pleonasm—functions as a superlative; cf. N. Hugedé, *Colossiens,* p. 102.

[3] "En puissance, en Esprit Saint et abondance de toute sorte," trans. B. Rigaux, *Thessaloniciens,* pp. 77ff.

---

plērophoreō, S 4135; *TDNT* 6.309–310; *EDNT* 3.107–108; *NIDNTT* 1.733, 735, 737; MM 519; L&N 13.106, 33.199, 68.32; BDF §119(1); BAGD 670 ‖ *plērophoria,* S 4136; *TDNT* 6.310–311; *EDNT* 3.107–108; *NIDNTT* 1.733. 735; MM 519–520; L&N 31.45; BAGD 670

The verb *plērophoreō* plainly has the meaning of full and complete conviction[4] in the case of Abraham, who is convinced (*plērophorētheis*, aorist participle) that God has the power to make good on his promise (Rom 4:21); in the case of Christians who are unsure about what practical stance to take but who are to act only with a conviction that is thought out, mature, justified in their conscience (Rom 14:5—"let each one be fully convinced in his own mind," *hekastos en tō idiō noi plērophoreisthō*, present passive imperative); in the words of Epaphras, who prays for the Colossians "that you may stand perfect, fully assured in all the will of God."[5] This perfect passive participle *peplērophorēmenoi* can also be translated "accomplished, well established," but the important thing is that it is practically synonymous with *teleioi*, "perfect, complete," and that it has to do with being confirmed, strengthened, stabilized; which is close to the sole use of *plērophoreomai* in the OT, "the heart of the sons of men is filled (*eplērophorēthē en autois*) with [the desire] to do evil."[6]

But in 2 Tim 4:5 ("Do the work of an evangelist, completely fulfill your ministry"—*tēn diakonian sou plērophorēson*) and 4:17 ("The Lord helped me and strengthened me so that through me the proclamation

---

[4] A meaning well attested by *1 Clem.* 42.3: "So they received instructions and, full of certitude (καὶ πληροφορηθέντες) by the resurrection of our Lord Jesus Christ, . . . they went out to announce the good news." Ign. *Magn.* 8.2: "The prophets were inspired by grace, so that the unbelievers might be fully persuaded that there is only one God" (εἰς τὸ πληροφορηθῆναι τοὺς ἀπειθοῦντας); Hegesippus: πολλῶν πληροφορηθέντων, "many were completely convinced" (in Eusebius, *Hist. Eccl.* 2.23.14); *Martyrdom of Pionius* 4.17: "the judgment of the world is imminent; we are completely convinced of it for many reasons" (κρίσις γὰρ τῷ κόσμῳ ἐπίκειται, περὶ ἧς πεπληροφορήμεθα διὰ πολλῶν, in H. Musurillo, *Christian Martyrs*, p. 140, 26).

[5] Col 4:12—ἵνα σταθῆτε τέλειοι καὶ πεπληροφορημένοι ἐν παντὶ θελήματι τοῦ θεοῦ. Cf. the epitaph from a sarcophagus of Ravenna (cf. F. Cumont, *Symbolisme funéraire*, p. 299), which should be read thus: "χαῖρε καλλιφενής," εἴποι σοι, "πληροφοροῦ ψυχή"—"May she (the goddess Isis) say to you, 'Hail, O shining one; be fully assured, O soul' " (A. J. Festugière, "Initiée par l'époux," in *Monuments Piot*, Paris, 1963, pp. 135–146). The husband assures his wife that through her initiation she can be sure that Isis will know her and welcome her.

[6] Eccl 8:11 (Hebrew *mālā'*). Cf. *T. Gad* 2.4—ἐπληροφορήθημεν τῆς ἀναιρέσεως αὐτοῦ, "we were resolved (literally, completely full of the intention) to kill him." With this emotional flavor, cf. this letter from the sixth century: ἐπειδὴ πεπληροφόρημαι, ὅτι φιλεῖτε ἐμὲ ὁλοψύχως καὶ ἐγὼ καταρ [. . .] ἀγαπῶ ὑμᾶς (*SB* 7655, 6; cf. line 20: ἐπειδὴ χρεωστῶ ὑμάς πληροφορῆσαι, πίστευσον); or this magical papyrus from the third century: "let her give me complete satisfaction, let her love me, let her cherish me" (πληροφοροῦσα, ἀγαπῶσα, στέργουσα ἐμέ, *P.Lond.* 121, 910, vol. 1, p. 113; republished *Pap.Graec.Mag.* 7, 910); cf. in the sixth-seventh century: καὶ πληροφορήσῃ ὁ θεὸς τὴν ὑμετέραν λαμπρότητα (*P.Erl.* 120, 5); ὅτι πληροφορεῖ αὐτὸν ὁ θεός (*P.Berl.Zill.* 14, 6).

might be carried out"—*to kērygma plērophorēthē*—"and all the Gentiles might hear"), the verb clearly means "accomplish perfectly," "carry out the best one can." This meaning is found in the papyri with respect to carrying out a promise or an agreement: "Insofar as on each occasion I give you written confirmation with respect to the matters in this document, I will not be guilty of neglect" (*hoti hoson hekastote dia grammatōn se plērophorō peri tōn ontōn en tois enthade grammasin, egō ouk esomai aitios ameleias, PSI* 1335, 27; third century; cf. 1345; sixth-seventh century); "having been fully satisfied by the power that was exhibited" (*plēro-phorētheis malista ek tēs dynameos tēs emphaneistheisēs, SB* 8988, 38; eighth century). Sometimes the papyri give this verb the sense of completing a piece of business, of finishing with a subject.[7] This usage confirms the nuance of 2 Tim 4:17—the apostle is aware that he is crowning or putting the final touches on his calling as a *kēryx* (1:11) by finishing off his ministry with this last proclamation at Rome. But in the papyri the commonest use of *plērophoreō* is "pay off a debt," meaning either a financial or a moral obligation[8]—which emphasizes the force of the command in 2 Tim 4:5, "Fulfill your ministry completely." This *diakonia* is a sacred assignment from God (Acts 12:25; Col 4:17; cf. 2 Cor 4:1; 5:18; 1 Tim 1:12). It is an obligation that cannot be shirked, a function that must be carried out perfectly and to the last.

Hence the narration *peri tōn peplērophorēmenōn en hēmin pragmatōn* (Luke 1:1) must be translated as in the versions (Old Latin, Vulgate, Palestinian Syriac, Sahidic and Bohairic Coptic), "an account of the deeds accomplished among us,"[9] despite the fact that the Peshitta and Eusebius

---

[7] *P.Amh.* 66, 42 (second century AD): the *stratēgos* invites the complainant to produce witnesses ἵνα δὲ καὶ νῦν πληροφορήσω, "so that I may make an end of the matter"; cf. *BGU* 747, col. I, 11).

[8] *P.Oxy.* 509, 10 (second century): πεπληροφορημένος τοῖς ὀφειλομένοις μοι = I have received full satisfaction from my debtors; *BGU* 665, col. II, 2 (first century); *P.Lond.* 1164, *g* 11 (vol. 3, p. 163); *P.Fouad* 26, 43 (a complaint to the prefect, second century): "although he received the full interest at the rate of one *statēr*"; *PSI* 737, 14 (second-third century): τοὺς ἐφετείους φόρους πληροφορεῖσθαι; 1411, 6: πε-πληροφορηκέναι ἀποδοῦσαν πάντα τὰ αὐτῇ ἐπιβάλλοντα. According to S. Eitrem (*Symbolae Osloenses,* vol. 10, 1932, p. 153, n. 63; cf. *Berichtigungsliste,* vol. 3, p. 179, n. 6944), the edict of Hadrian from 136 should be completed as follows: λέγει· [καίπερ πληροφορηθεὶς] ἀντ[ὶ τοῦ] ἐπ[ι]δεέστερ[ον] ἀναβῆναι (*P.Osl.* 78, 4–5); *P.Apoll.* 28, 13; 63, 9; 91, 13: "He has paid us that *kēnsistikos* of which we informed him" (payment receipt from the eighth century).

[9] Cf. M. J. Lagrange, "Le Sens de Luc I, 1 d'après les papyrus," in *Bulletin d'ancienne littérature et d'archéologie chrétienne,* vol. 2, 1912, pp. 96–100; H. Pernot, *Les Deux Premier Chapitres de Matthieu et de Luc,* Paris, 1948, pp. 124ff.; H. Schürmann, *Lukasevangelium,* vol. 1, p. 5. E. Delebecque, who sees in πληροφορέω the twofold idea

took this perfect passive participle to mean total conviction.[10] The decisive events of salvation were brought to completion, perfected by Christ. There is perhaps a reference to the perfect fulfilling of the Scriptures,[11] the fullness of the accomplishment, and also completion.

---

of a complete fulfillment and a fulfillment of authentic acts, translates: "an account relative to the acts perfected (French "parachevés") among us" and comments: "Luke uses a verb that is more expressive and richer in substance than the verbs close in meaning in the rest of his Gospel: πληρόω and its compounds . . . τελέω and the words of that family. . . . The verb πληροφορέω does quite well for expressing the 'perfecting' of acts that are out of the ordinary while at the same time guaranteeing their authenticity" (Evangile de Luc, p. 2; idem, Etudes grecques, p. 3).

[10] Eusebius, Hist. Eccl. 3.24.15: "the account of things that he himself knew with complete certitude" (ὧν αὐτὸς πεπληροφόρητο λόγων).

[11] Cf. πληρόω, Luke 4:21; 9:31; 24:44; Acts 1:16; 3:18; 13:27; and πληροφορέω, Rom 4:21. Cf. E. Trocmé, Le "Livre des Actes" et l'histoire, Paris, 1957, p. 46.

πολιτεία, πολίτευμα, πολιτεύομαι, πολίτης

---

politeia, constitution, system of government, (right of) citizenship; *politeuma*, (place of) citizenship, act of administration, association, resident community of foreign nationals; *politeuomai*, to live (as a citizen); *politēs*, citizen

---

The "urban" or "civic" metaphors for the Christian life in the NT, and especially in St. Paul, are quite coherent. Heaven is like a city (*polis*); Christ is its sovereign (*Kyrios*), and it has its own laws and constitution (*politeia*), namely, the gospel. Christians are its citizens (*politai*; cf. this Christian letter from the fourth century: "for we believe that your citizenship is in heaven"—*pisteuomen gar tēn politian sou en ouranō, SB* 2265, 5) and are not treated as foreigners or sojourners there; they have the rights of citizenship (*politeuma*) and are fellow-citizens of the saints (*sympolitai*). Such a citizenship carries with it rights and privileges but also obligations and responsibilities. Each one is then required to "live as a citizen" (*politeuomai*), i.e., according to the laws and the spirit of this city, conformably to its statutes.

I. — The heavenly Jerusalem is the "city of the living God,"[1] the perfect and eternal city,[2] where the elect will be gathered together and to which

---

[1] Πόλει θεοῦ ζῶντος, Heb 12:22; cf. 11:10, 16; 13:14; Gal 4:26; Phil 3:20; Rev 3:12; cf. R. Knopf, "Die Himmelsstadt," in *Neutestamentliche Studien: Festschrift G. Heinrici*, Leipzig, 1914, pp. 213–219; K. L. Schmidt, *Die Polis in Kirche und Welt*, Basel, 1939; W. Bieder, *Ekklesia und Polis im Neuen Testament und in der alten Kirche*, Zurich, 1941; V. Ehrenberg, *The Greek State*, Andover, 1974; bibliography in O. Böcher, "Die heilige Stadt im Völkerkrieg," in *Josephus-Studien* (dedicated to O. Michel), Göttingen, 1974, pp. 55–76.

[2] On the Greek *polis*, cf. Fustel de Coulanges, *La Cité antique*, 28th ed., Paris, 1924, p. 151; G. Glotz, *La Cité grecque*, 2d ed., Paris, 1953; C. B. Welles, "The Greek City," in *Studi in onore di A. Calderini*, Milan, 1956, pp. 81–99; A. Aymard, "Les Etrangers dans les cités grecques," in *L'Etranger* (Recueils de la société J. Bodin, IX, 1), Brussels, 1958, pp. 124ff. —On its government, cf. H. Francotte, *Mélanges de droit public grec*, 2d ed.,

---

politeia, S 4174; *TDNT* 6.516–535; *EDNT* 3.130; *NIDNTT* 2.801–804; MM 525; L&N 11.67, 11.70; BAGD 686 ‖ *politeuma*, S 4175; *TDNT* 6.516–535; *EDNT* 3.130; *NIDNTT* 2.801–805; MM 525–526; L&N 11.71; BAGD 686 ‖ *politeuomai*, S 4176; *TDNT* 6.516–535; *EDNT* 3.130; *NIDNTT* 2.801–804; MM 526; L&N 41.34; BAGD 686 ‖ *politēs*, S 4177; *TDNT* 6.516–535; *EDNT* 3.130; *NIDNTT* 2.801–804; MM 526; L&N 11.68; BAGD 686

they are constantly drawing nearer (*proselēlythate*, Heb 12:22) during their pilgrimage on this earth. In other words, the city is first of all seen as a dwelling place, the center for a group or a populace.[3] The citizen (*politēs*) is one who—living in community with his compatriots[4]—is a legal subject and participates in the political life of the city (cf. Plutarch, *Cim.* 17.3). St. Paul was more than a little proud of his home city: "a citizen of Tarsus in Cilicia, no obscure city" (Acts 21:39); to which we may compare this third-century Roman inscription: "Tarsus, the first and greatest and most noble metropolis."[5]

II. — The defining characteristic of a *politēs* is possessing *politeia*, the right of citizenship.[6] Rome and the Greek cities used to grant this honor[7] to their benefactors, to particularly deserving persons, veterans and military leaders, politicians, men of letters, officials, physicians whose merits

---

Rome, 1964, pp. 225ff. D. Nörr, *Imperium und Polis in der hohen Prinzipatszeit,* Munich, 1966.

[3] "The city" stands for its inhabitants, Matt 12:25; Luke 4:43; Acts 14:21; 16:20; cf. πᾶσα ἡ πόλις, Matt 8:34; 21:10; Mark 1:33; Acts 13:44; 21:30; Strathmann, "πόλις," in *TDNT,* vol. 6, p. 522–523. In the biblical vocabulary, "city" (Hebrew *'ir, qiryâh*) can mean a mere town (cf. Sychar, John 4:5; Nazareth, Matt 2:23), a built-up area of any size.

[4] Οἱ δὲ πολῖται κοινωνοὶ τῆς μιᾶς πόλεως, Aristotle, *Pol.* 2.1–2.1261ᵃ; cf. 1.1.1252ᵃ1 and 8; 3.6.1278ᵇ19 (cf. M. Defourny, *Aristote: Etudes sur la "Politique,"* Paris, 1932; A. E. R. Boak, "Politai as Landholders at Karanis," in *JEA,* 1954, pp. 11–14); cf. C. C. Richardson, "The Meaning of πολιτευταί in Justin, I Apol. 65, 1," in *HTR,* 1936, pp. 89–91. In the Bible, the πολίτης is the neighbor or companion (Hebrew *ra'*, Jer 29:23; 31:34; Prov 11:9, 12; 24:43), the compatriot or kinsman (Gen 23:11; Zech 13:7; 2 Macc 5:6, 8, 23; Luke 19:14; Heb 8:11 = Vulgate *proximum; T. Job* 29.1; cf. *IGLS* 4015, 7: τὸν ἑαυτῶν πολίτην), the inhabitant (Luke 15:15) or citizen in the strict sense of the word (2 Macc 4:5, 20; 9:19; 14:8; 15:30). Israelite citizenship depended on blood ties and was established by genealogical lists, cf. J. Jeremias, *Jerusalem,* pp. 275ff., 284ff., 297ff. On the semantics of πολίτης, cf. G. Redard, *Noms grecs en* -ΤΗΣ, -ΤΙΣ, pp. 20–31.

[5] Τάρσος ἡ πρώτη καὶ μεγίστη καὶ καλλίστη μητρόπολις, *IGLAM,* n. 1480 = Dittenberger, *Or.* 578 = *IGUR,* n. 80. Other glorious titles of Tarsus in Ruge, "Τάρσος," in *PWSup* IV, A 2, col. 2424ff.

[6] Josephus, *Ant.* 19.281: "The Jews of Alexandria possessed ἴσην πολιτείαν with the other inhabitants"; *Ag. Apion* 2.39: "The people of our race who live at Antioch are called Antiochenes, because they were given citizenship (τὴν πολιτείαν) by the city's founder, Seleucus" (cf. the excellent commentary of M. Stern, *Greek and Latin Authors on Jews and Judaism,* Jerusalem, 1974, vol. 1, pp. 398–402). 4 Macc 3:20— Seleucus IV Philopator recognized the Jews' citizenship (τὴν πολιτείαν αὐτῶν ἀποδέχεσθαι); Diodorus Siculus 19.2.8: "Timaeon of Corinth gave Syracusan citizenship to all who desired it."

[7] Τιμή; cf. *SEG* IX, 40, 58; Dio Cassius 41.24.1: "Caesar granted honors to many . . . he gave all the inhabitants of Cadix Roman citizenship. . . . He granted them this privilege. . . ."

they wished to honor or reward or whose services they wanted to gain.[8] Thus citizenship was a title of nobility (*eugeneia*) that placed its beneficiary in the ranks of the aristocracy.[9] But this "decoration" could also be bought, not only in Greek cities that by this means bolstered their impoverished treasuries[10] but also at Rome (at first only with difficulty—the price varied between 200 and 1,000 drachmas). Antony was generous in this respect (Cicero, *Phil.* 5.4.11); Claudius gave citizenship without restraint[11] and it became a veritable commodity, like merchandise with fluctuating prices.[12] In fact, the number of *cives*, one million in 70/69 BC, increased by a factor of four by 28 BC, of five by AD 14, nearly six by AD 47;[13] and the prestige of the title was correspondingly diminished.

---

[8] In 46, Caesar awarded citizenship to any freeborn foreigner who would come to Rome to practice medicine or teach the liberal arts, hoping thus to establish them in the city (Suetonius, *Iul.* 42). In 40, Octavian granted citizenship to a *nauarchos* from Rhosos in Syria, "whereas Seleucus . . . campaigned with us . . . he often suffered and took great risks for us, never shrinking from enduring ills; he manifested his attachment and loyalty to the republic; he linked his own fortune with our preservation; he made all sacrifices for the Roman Republic; in our presence as in our absence he rendered service. . . . In recompense, he has received immunity and citizenship" (*IGLS* 718, 12–18, 91). The first important "Westerner" to receive Athenian citizenship was T. Trebellius Rufus of Toulouse, an *eques*, who was high priest in Gaul; he received a priestly appointment at Rome and was willing to be an archon and even a citizen at Athens under Domitian. The second person was the emperor Hadrian (cf. J. H. Olivier, "The Athens of Hadrian," in *Les Empereurs romains d'Espagne*, Paris, 1965, p. 125); cf. H. Francotte, *Mélanges de droit public grec*, p. 306; A. Aymard, "Les Etrangers dans les cités grecques," pp. 131ff. J. and L. Robert, "Bulletin épigraphique," in *REG*, 1964, p. 237, n. 533.

[9] Cf. the *honestas, dignitas, honor* that Antoninus Pius accorded Tymandenos in giving him citizenship (*MAMA* IV, 236). Cf. Dittenberger, *Syl.* 796; C. B. Welles, *Royal Correspondence*, n. 45 (commentary by M. Holleaux, *Etudes d'épigraphie*, vol. 3, pp. 199–254); G. Humbert, "Civitas," in *DAGR*, vol. 1, 1217–1220.

[10] Musicians, athletes, lower-ranking officers, and sophists paid dearly (μεγάλοις τιμήμασιν, Nicolaus of Damascus, ed. Müller, p. 354) to become citizens of Athens or Rhodes (L. Robert, *Hellenica*, vol. 1, pp. 37–42; idem, *Opera Minora Selecta*, vol. 1, pp. 617ff. J. Pouilloux, *Choix*, n. 33; R. Bogaert, *Banques et banquiers*, pp. 247, 358). Augustus forbade Athens to sell citizenship to anyone (Dio Cassius 54.7); Hadrian restored the right to do so; L. Robert, *Hellenica*, vol. 1, pp. 39–42.

[11] Dio Cassius 60.17: "sometimes individually, sometimes en masse." Cf. the two great Alexandrian bankers, Tiberius Claudius Demetrius and Tiberius Claudius Isidorus, who were Roman citizens in the year 50 (*P.Oxy.* 2471, 3).

[12] By giving jars of wine to imperial freedmen, anyone could become a Roman citizen (G. Boulvert, *Les Esclaves et les affranchis impériaux sous le haut-empire romain*, Aix-en-Provence, 1964, vol. 1, p. 363).

[13] Cf. *Res Gest. Divi Aug.* 8.1; Tacitus, *Ann.* 11.25. Whereas Roman citizenship was highly prized in Egypt in the first century, it no longer was in the second century (cf. I. Biezunska-Malawist, "L'Extension du droit de cité romaine en Egypte," in *Proceedings*

This information greatly enhances our understanding of the clash between the chiliarch Claudius Lysias, who boasted that he had purchased citizenship at a high cost (*egō pollou kephalaiou tēn politeian tautēn ektēsamēn*) and Paul, who answered "But it was mine by birth" (Acts 22:28–29). Inheriting the title greatly increased its value.[14] Apart from the honor involved, citizenship conferred many practical advantages.[15] Especially with respect to legal proceedings, the *civis* was free to choose his court in his own country and to be judged according to its laws or to appear before Roman magistrates.[16] St. Paul used this right to appeal to the

---

IX, pp. 277–285). By his edict of 212/213, Caracalla granted Roman citizenship to all inhabitants of the Roman world (*Dig.* 1.5.17; *P.Giss.* 40, 1).

[14] Cf. in AD 92, this legionary declaring under oath "se civem Romanum esse" (V. Arangio-Ruiz, "Minima de Negotiis," in *Studi in onore di U. E. Paoli*, Florence, 1956, pp. 2ff.). Paul obtained his citizenship in the best possible way, by legal filiation (R. Monier, G. Cardascia, J. Imbert, *Histoire des institutions et des faits sociaux*, Paris, 1956, pp. 415ff.), but we have no idea when or under what circumstances his ancestors gained this right (cf. J. Schwartz, "A propos du statut personnel de l'apôtre Paul," in *RHPR*, 1957, pp. 91–96; P. Miguens, "Pablo prisoniero," in *Studii Biblici Franciscani*, vol. 8, 1958, pp. 74ff. W. Seston, "Tertullien et les origines de la citoyenneté romaine de S. Paul," in *Freundesgabe O. Cullmann*, Leiden, 1962, pp. 305–312, who suggests that Paul's mother was Roman). The *cognomen* "Paulus" would not be a reference to a Roman patron; it would have been chosen because it sounds like "Saul" (Acts 13:9; cf. A. N. Sherwin-White, *Roman Society*, pp. 151ff.).

[15] Equality before the law, immunity, exemption from customs taxes and tribute, from public levies and burdensome duties. Inheritance rights and property rights were greatly enhanced (cf. *PSI* 1183, first century AD). Hence the praise of Aelius Aristides: "Of all the things that can be said in praise of the Romans, one thing is by far most worthy of attention: the magnanimity they have demonstrated in the matter of citizenship and even their very way of thinking of this right. Indeed, the world has never seen the like" (*Orat. Rom.* 59); cf. E. Volterra, "Manomissione e cittadinanza," in *Studi in onore di U. E. Paoli*, pp. 695–715). Nevertheless, the Greek cities were even more generous, granting along with *politeia* inviolability of person and property (ἀσυλία, ἀσφάλεια), exemption from the taxes and levies payable by foreigners (ἀτέλεια), the right to acquire real property (ἔγκτησις), and προξενία, which made the foreigner a guest who received help and assistance from the city (*I.Bulg.* 41, 13; 42, 1–2; 307, 6–8; 309, 4–6; 312, 8–9; *I.Thas.* 179, 6; *I.Car.* 166, 30; *P.Lond.* 1912, 55, etc.). The *Sicyonios* was "a story of citizenship" (A. Blanchard, A. Bataille, "Fragments sur papyrus du ΣΙΚΥΩΝΙΟΣ de Ménandre," in *RechPap*, vol. 3, 1964, p. 111; cf. pp. 130–131, 135).

[16] Cf. the privileges granted to Seleucus of Rhosos in 36–34, P. Roussel, "Un Syrien au service de Rome et d'Octave," in *Syria*, 1934, pp. 33–74; J. Lesquier, *L'Armée romaine en Egypte*, Cairo, 1918, pp. 312ff., 333. H. Braunert, "Griechische und römische Komponenenten im Stadtrecht von Antinoopolis," in *JJP*, 1962, pp. 73–88; A. Stenico, "Civiltá romana e civiltá meroitica nella Bassa Nubia," in *Atti del convegno di studi su la Lombardia e l'Oriente*, Milan, 1963, pp. 276–300.

supreme jurisdiction of the emperor,[17] just as he referred to the *lex Valeria* (c. 300 BC) and the *lex Porcia* (c. 198 BC) that prohibited the scourging of Roman citizens.[18]

Politeia also refers to the organization or system of government of the state, its constitution, its ancestral institutions,[19] and finally "the common-wealth of free men," the life of the citizen within his city, his political activity, all the forms of interaction with the life of the state.[20] Hence pagans—outsiders, "cut off from the commonwealth of Israel and foreign-ers to the covenants" (*apēllotriōmenoi tēs politeias tou Israel kai xenoi tōn diathēkōn*, Eph 2:12)—were not only incapable of being incorporated in the Israelite theocracy, but they were as alien as they could be to the covenants, "without Christ," having no hope of salvation (Acts 26:6–7), without God's providence and help. Only citizens benefited from the protection of the *polis* and its worship.[21] But through baptism, the Gentiles became *sympolitai tōn*

---

[17] Acts 25:11–12. Cf. A. H. M. Jones, "I Appeal unto Caesar," in *Studies Presented to D. M. Robinson*, St. Louis, 1953, vol. 2, pp. 918–920.

[18] Acts 16:37–38; cf. Cicero, *Verr.* 2.5.170: "If a Roman citizen is bound, it is an infraction; if he is struck, it is a crime; if he is killed, it is almost a parricide." A. N. Sherwin-White, *The Roman Citizenship*, Oxford, 1939; F. de Visscher, "Le Droit de cité romaine," in *Acta Congressus Madvigiani*, Copenhagen, 1958, vol. 1, pp. 281–291). The context in Acts shows that *politeia* is a "virtual" privilege that the possessor can make actual at will, cf. J. and L. Robert, "Bulletin épigraphique," in *REG*, 1958, p. 180, n. 16).

[19] 2 Macc 4:11; 8:17; 13:14; 4 Macc 8:7; 17:9; Aristotle, *Ath. Pol.; Pol.* 2.6.1265ª15; Philo, *Abraham* 242: "democracy is the best form of government"; *Decalogue* 155; Josephus, *Ant.* 13.245; Strabo 4.1.12: "The Cavari adopted the political system of the Romans"; *P.Oxy.* 1119, 21; cf. K. von Fritz, *The Theory of Mixed Constitution in Antiquity*, New York, 1954; A. Aalders, *Die Theorie der gemischten Verfassung im Altertum*, Amsterdam, 1968. *Politeia und Republica* (Palingenesia IV), Wiesbaden, 1969.

[20] Philo, *Spec. Laws* 3.3; Dittenberger, *Syl.* 496, 173 (cf. C. Mossé, *Les Institutions grecques*, Paris, 1967, pp. 12, 196, 204, 208; M. A. H. El-Abbadi, "The Alexandrian Citizenship," in *JEA*, 1962, pp. 106–123; E. Pólay, "Der status civitatis," in *JJP*, vol. 16–17, 1971, pp. 71–83). Strathmann ("πόλις," in *TDNT*, vol. 6, p. 519) cites the meanings distinguished by Plutarch, *De unius in rep. dom.* 2: (*a*) μετάληψις τῶν ἐν πόλει δικαίων (the rights of citizenship; cf. *Gnomon of the Idios Logos* 47; *P.Oxy.* 65, 4); (*b*) βίος ἀνδρὸς πολιτικοῦ καὶ τὰ κοινὰ πράττοντος (the life of a man who participates in public affairs); cf. *Hermes Trismegistus*, frag. 23.54: "the savage conduct of men"); (*c*) μία πρᾶξις εὔστοχος εἰς τὰ κοινά (a public enactment or a govern-mental measure); (*d*) τάξις καὶ κατάστασις πόλεως διοικοῦσα τὰς πράξεις (the constitution of a state, form of government). We must add municipal territory as an administrative unit (*I.Bulg.* 2235, 125; *SEG* XII, 349: ἡ βουλὴ καὶ ἡ πόλις καὶ ἡ πολιτεία, with the commentary of F. Papazoglou, "Une signification tardive du mot ΠΟΛΙΤΕΙΑ," in *REG*, 1959, pp. 100–105; cf. *regio* in the sense of "city territory," *IGLS* 2550, 8; with the commentary of the editors, V, p. 238).

[21] Cf. R. Taubenschlag, *Law of Greco-Roman Egypt*, vol. 2, pp. 18ff. C. Spicq, *Théologie morale*, vol. 1, pp. 422ff. E. A. Judge, *The Social Pattern of Christian Groups in*

hagiōn, "fellow citizens with the saints and members of the family of God";[22] their names are written in the rolls of the heavenly Jerusalem (Luke 10:20), and they possess full rights of citizenship and the attendant privileges, in particular equality with the "natives," i.e., the Jews (cf. Eph 2:14–16) or the angels, those great elder denizens of the celestial city (Heb 12:23), and even brotherhood with them, since they are henceforth members of the same family (*oikeioi*, Gal 6:10; 1 Tim 5:8). They are no longer outsiders (*allotrioi*).

III. —*Politeuma*, which is sometimes synonymous with *politeia* (Dittenberger, *Syl.* 543, 6), appears in the fourth century BC[23] and can refer to an act of administration, government, legislation (Josephus, *Ant.* 1.5; 11.157; *Ag. Apion* 2.145), the party in power (cf. the constitution of Carthage, Polybius 3.8.2), but more formally an association (*SB* 8929, 18: "for the provisions of the association"—*epi tōn tou politeumatos euōchiōn*); 9812, 3–6: an association of soldiers in Alexandria (*politeuma tōn en Alēxandreia pheromenōn stratiōtōn* = *SEG* XX, 499), or a community, a civic body, a political

---

the First Century, London, 1960, pp. 18–29. Around AD 15, the Ionians ask Marcus Agrippa to exclude, if not to force, the Jews from citizenship: "if they wish to be considered like their compatriots (συγγενεῖς), they must worship the same gods" (Josephus, *Ant.* 12.125–126; cf. Acts 19:34).

[22] Eph 2:19. In Josephus, *Ant.* 19.175, *sympolitai* comprise a group larger than family and friends. The inscriptions and the papyri mention the affection and benevolence of which they were the object: "Having heard of the benevolence that you show toward all your fellow citizens" (*P.Col.Zen.* 11, 2); "Salus Antonis Priskos my fellow citizen" (*SB* 9017; XXIII, 7); "our compatriots join us in presenting this petition" (*P.Oxy.* 1119, 19). An honorific decree is voted for Theodorus, συνπολιτευομένων εὐεργεσίας ἕνεκεν (*SB* 9977, 5 = *SEG* XIII, 579, = Dittenberger, *Or.* 145; cf. 143, 6; *Syl.* 504, 6). The verb συμπολιτεύομαι = live as a fellow citizen (Josephus, *Ant.* 19.306); "Do you not think that your fellow citizens (οἱ συμπολιτευόμενοι) will pursue you?" (Epictetus 3.22.99); οἱ διάδοχοι καὶ εἰσαγγελεῖς καὶ οἱ ἐπισυνηγμένοι ἐν Βοιωτοὶ καὶ οἱ συμπολιτευόμενοι, ὧν τὰ ὀνόματα ἐν τῇ στήλη ἀναγέγραπται (*SB* 6664, 12; second century BC); ξένοι Ἀπολλωνιᾶται καὶ οἱ συνπολιτευόμενοι κτίσται, ὧν τὰ ὀνόματα ὑπόκεινται (ibid. 8066, 3; first century BC). In 7–4 BC, at Attaleia in Pamphylia, ὁ δῆμος καὶ οἱ συνπολειτευόμενοι Ῥωμαῖοι honor M. Plautius Silvanus (*SEG* VI, 646). The συμπολιτεία is a confederation or community composed of citizens and incorporated members; it unites two or more cities, Strabo 14.636; *IGLAM* 394, 1290; cf. J. Pouilloux, *Choix* IV, 57–62 (honorific decree for Orthagoras of Araxa, second century BC), especially L. Robert, *Villes d'Asie Mineure*, pp. 54–64; H. Volkmann, "Sympoliteia," in *DKP*, vol. 5, col. 447–449.

[23] Isocrates, *Areop.* 7.78; Plato, *Leg.* 12.945 *d*; diagramma of Ptolemy I Soter: πολίτευμα δ' ἔστω οἱ μύριοι (*SEG* IX, 1 = *SB* 10075, 5–6; bibliography in C. Spicq, *Théologie morale*, vol. 1, p. 426, n. 6); cf. W. Ruppel, "Politeuma," in *Philologus*, 1927, pp. 268–312, 433–454 (clarification by M. Launey, *Armées hellénistiques*, vol. 2, pp. 1064–1085); summary by Strathmann, *TDNT*, vol. 6, p. 519–520.

entity.[24] Tōn Ioppitōn politeuma is the citizenry of Joppa (2 Macc 12:7). The women of Panamara are invited as a group to the feasts of Hera and are distinguished as such from the men.[25] In the strict sense of the word, a politeuma is an organization of citizens from the same place, with the same rights (isonomoi) in the midst of a foreign state.[26] We have particularly full information for the Jewish communities at Berenice in Cyrenaica,[27] at Antioch (Josephus, Ant. 12.28–33; War 7.44ff.), and especially at Alexandria,[28] colonies of immigrants living in the midst of a populace of a different race, but having a religious character, professing the worship of the true God.[29]

So we see how St. Paul could write "For our part, we are citizens of heaven,"[30] especially since the "community" at Philippi, largely made up

---

[24] Strabo 3.4.8. Decree of Hanisa in Cappadocia: "Apollonius is without fail an excellent man vis-à-vis our community" (first century BC, C. Michel, Recueil, 546, 7; with the commentary of L. Robert, Noms indigènes, pp. 476ff., who cites numerous epigraphic texts). ISE, n. 87, 20).

[25] Τὸ πολείτευμα τῶν γυναικῶν (W. Ruppel, "Politeuma," pp. 449–452); cf. Philo, Husbandry 81, the best women, "enrolled in the community of virtue (τῷ τῆς ἀρετῆς ἐγγεγραμμέναι πολιτεύματι) under Miriam's leadership."

[26] Cf. the Idumeans at Memphis (Dittenberger, Or. 737, 2), the Phrygians domiciled in 3 BC in a city of Egypt (ibid. 658, 3), Caunians at Sidon (ibid. 592, 1; cf. L. Perdrizet, "Le πολίτευμα des Cauniens à Sidon," in RArch, 1899, pp. 42–48), the Cretans in the Arsinoite nome (P.Tebt. 32, 17; second century BC), the Lycians at Alexandria (SB 6025, 4; 8757), the Boeotians from the Xoite nome (ibid. 6664, 9), the Cilicians from the Fayum (ibid. 7270, 5). On the known politeumata cf. J. Modrzejewski, "La Règle de droit dans l'Egypte ptolémaïque," in Essays in Honor of C. B. Welles, New Haven, 1966, pp. 145ff. R. Taubenschlag, Opera Minora, vol. 1, pp. 573ff.

[27] In 8–6 BC, its politeuma honors Decimius Valerius Dionysius (CIG 5362, 25–26; cf. J. and G. Roux, "Un décret du politeuma des Juifs de Bérénikè en Cyrénaïque," in REG, 1949, pp. 281–296). In AD 25, it honors Marcus Tittius (R. Cagnat, IG, Paris, 1911, vol. 1, 1024; E. Gabba, Iscrizioni greche e latine per lo studio della Bibbia, Turin, 1958, n. 19; M. Engers, "πολίτευμα," in Mnemosyne, 1936, pp. 154–161; cf. Josephus, Ant. 14.115).

[28] Ep. Arist. 310: "The elders of the group of translators and the delegates of the politeuma (of Alexandrian Jews) as well as the leaders of the people made this declaration . . ." (cf. the exegesis of V. A. Tcherikover, Corpus Papyrorum Judaicarum, p. 9; cf. pp. 6, 32); Josephus, Ant. 12.108; 19.281; Ag. Apion 2.32ff.; War 2.487; Philo, Flacc. 74–80; To Gaius 194 (cf. J. Schwartz, "L'Egypte de Philon," in Philon d'Alexandrie, Paris, 1967, pp. 38ff.); PSI 1160, 5 = SB 7448; P.Tebt. 700, 38 = C.Ord.Ptol. 50; cf. H. I. Bell, Jews and Christians in Egypt, pp. 10–21.

[29] Cf. SB 6664, 9: ἱερεὺς τοῦ πολιτεύματος; 7875, 3: ἱερατεύσας τοῦ πολιτεύματος τῶν Φρυγῶν.

[30] Phil 3:20—ἡμῶν τὸ πολίτευμα ἐν οὐρανοῖς ὑπάρχει (cf. A. Rolla, "La cittadinanza greco-romana e la cittadinanze celeste de Filippesi III, 20," in AnBib 18, Rome, 1963, pp. 75–80; J. Lévie, "Le Chrétien, citoyen du ciel," ibid., pp. 81–88). The

of Antony's veterans, and then Augustus's (Strabo 8.331; Appian, *BCiv.* 5.3.11 and 13; Dio Cassius 51.4.6) enjoyed the municipal rights of the *jus italicum*. Not depending on a governor but reporting directly to the imperial capital, represented by a proconsular praetor, its inhabitants were proud of their "country" and their autonomy.[31] The Pauline *politeuma* of Philippians, then, is not so much a reference to their citizenship, nor even their status as a "colony"; it should be understood in terms of their metropolis or capital city, which lists its members among its citizens.[32] It is a community of foreign nationals (foreigners to paganism) with a threefold meaning: (*a*) local (the *politēs* has ties to a place, a city)—our *politeuma* is in heaven; (*b*) political—like every analagous *civitas*, conferring liberty and equality on all its members, full rights; (*c*) constitutional and legal— exclusive dependency on the supreme authority of the *Kyrios*, Jesus.[33]

IV. — Such a status brings with it a certain spirit and a certain way of life corresponding to the *polis* that one is a part of and the *politeuma* that one is under.[34] The Israelites had a particularly vivid awareness of their place in their people's tradition and law, of what they called *politeuesthai*, "living as a citizen";[35] which leads to personal behavior that is conformed

---

Vulgate translated "conversatio nostra"; cf. H. Hoppenbrouwers, "Conversatio," in *Graecitas et Latinitas Christianorum*, Supplementa I (Mélanges C. Mohrmann), Nijmegen, 1964, pp. 51ff.

[31] P. Collart, *Philippes, ville de Macédoine*, Paris, 1937, pp. 223ff. P. Lemerle, *Philippes et la Macédoine orientale*, Paris, 1945, pp. 13ff. Military *politeumata* occur frequently— *SEG* XX, 499, 3: τὸ πολίτευμα τῶν ἐν Ἀλεξανδρίᾳ . . . στρατιωτῶν = *SB* 9812; G. Humbert, "Colonia," in *DAGR*, vol. 1, p. 1311ff. E. Kornemann, in *PW*, vol. 4, 7, 511–588.

[32] Cf. E. Stauffer, *Die Theologie des Neuen Testaments*, Gütersloh, 1948, p. 275 ET = *New Testament Theology*, trans. John Marsh, New York, 1956.

[33] Cf. Philo, *Joseph* 69: "I am free . . . I mean to be enrolled on the greatest and noblest civil register, that of this universe" (πολιτεύματι τοῦδε τοῦ κόσμου); *Conf. Tongues* 78, the wise are like resident aliens (παροικοῦντες), "they consider their true country to be the heavenly place where they enjoy all their rights (πατρίδα μὲν τὸν οὐράνιον χῶρον ἐν ᾧ πολιτεύονται); the earthly expanse where they dwell is foreign soil"; cf. *Contemp. Life* 90: the Therapeutai are citizens of heaven.

[34] Lycurgus did not permit the Spartans to leave their country freely and travel elsewhere, where they would risk picking up foreign habits, imitating the ways of ill-formed peoples and accepting principles of government (πολιτευμάτων) different from his own" (Plutarch, *Lyc.* 27.6). In 20/19: τὸ πολίτευμα τῶν Ἀλεξανδρείων ἀκέραιον ὑπάρχον ἄθρεπτοι καὶ ἀνάγωγοι γεγονότες ἄνθρωποι μολύνωσι (*C.Pap. Jud.* 150, 5–6 = *SB* 7448); *P.Oxy.* 2266, 18. J. A. O. Larsen, "Lycia and Greek Federal Citizenship," in *Symbolae Osloenses*, vol. 33, 1957, pp. 5–26.

[35] Esth 8:12—"The Jews govern themselves according to very just laws" (δικαιοτάτοις δὲ πολιτευομένους νόμοις); they live according to the laws of God (1 Macc 6:11) and conform themselves to their ancestral customs (11:25). Cf. 3 Macc 3:4—σεβόμενοι δὲ τὸν θεὸν καὶ τῷ τούτου νόμῳ πολιτευόμενοι. To align one's life

to the common law, a nuance of public life. In this sense, St. Paul proclaims before the Sanhedrin: "I have lived before God with a clear conscience,"[36] observing the laws of the divine *politeia*. According to Xenophon (*Cyr.* 1.1.1), this verb means subscribe to a rule, submit to a discipline (*Ep. Arist.* 31; Dittenberger, *Syl.* 618, 12; the oath of Itanos: "I will live . . . according to the laws"—*politeosomai . . . kata tous nomous, I.Cret.* 4.8.28 = *Syl.* 526); it becomes synonymous with *peripateō, anastrephō, poreuomai, diexagō, prassō*, but is always opposed to *idiōteuō*, "to live as a private individual."[37] It is with civic connotation that the apostle instructs Christians, "Live as a citizen worthy of the gospel of Christ,"[38] conforming as such to the laws of the celestial city. To live out one's citizenship is to conduct oneself according to the demands of the *politeia*, which means first of all being willing to take on a public function, to consider oneself in all of one's actions as a member of a social body,[39] and accordingly to say nothing and do nothing

---

with the law is to live according to the law or under the law (τῷ νόμῳ πολιτεύεσθαι, 4 Macc 2:8, 23; 4:23; 5:16). Moses taught "the people entrusted to his government" (τοὺς κατ᾽ αὐτὸν πολιτευομένους, Philo, *Rewards* 4). The Jews define themselves as a people living in accord with the laws contained in their books (*Ep. Arist.* 31). Josephus, at the age of nineteen, began to live in accord with the principles of the sect of the Pharisees (ἠρξάμην πολιτεύεσθαι τῇ Φαρισαίων αἱρέσει κατακολουθῶν, *Life* 12; cf. 262; *Ant.* 12.38), like Tiberius Polycharmus who "lived according to all the commands of Judaism" (ὃς πολειτευσάμενος πᾶσαν πολειτείαν κατὰ τὸν Ἰουδαϊσμόν, *CII* 694, 6).

[36] Acts 23:1, πεπολίτευμαι τῷ θεῷ. Cf. in 164, ἐγὼ γὰρ πιστεύσας σοί τε καὶ τοῖς θεοῖς πρὸς οὓς ὁσίως καὶ δικαίως πολιτευσάμενος ἐμαυτὸν ἀμεμψιμοίρητον παρέσχημαι (*UPZ* 144, 14 = *P.Paris* 63); cf. the κόρη κόσμου, "the blessed life with the gods" (in Stobaeus 1.49.44; vol. 1, p. 395, 22).

[37] Philo, *Migr. Abr.* 159: ὁ πολιτευόμενος τρόπος = political mores; *Good Man Free* 76. A decree of Samos in the third century BC in favor of some judges who came from Myndos: "being desirous that the citizens who were at odds, once reconciled, should live in harmony" (ἐν ὁμονοίᾳ πολιτεύεσθαι, *SEG* I, 363, 17); "May it please the council and the people that the Samians should be Athenian citizens, participating in public affairs (πολιτευομένους) as they see fit" (J. Pouilloux, *Choix*, n. 23, 13; cf. 27, 20). In *P.Hib.* 63, 11: πολιτευσόμεθα ἀλλήλοις = have good relations. The price of an *artabē* of grain shall be conformed to that in effect at the market of Alexandria (κατὰ τὴν πολιτευομένην τιμὴν ἐν τῇ ἀγορᾷ Ἀλεξανδρείας, *Pap.Lugd.Bat.* XI, 14, 7).

[38] Phil 1:27, πολιτεύεσθε (cf. R. R. Brewer, "The Meaning of *politeuesthe* in Philippians I, 27," in *JBL*, 1954, pp. 76–83; K. Bornhäuser, *Jesus Imperator Mundi*, Gütersloh, 1938); Pol. *Phil.* 5.1–2, ἐὰν πολιτευσώμεθα ἀξίως αὐτοῦ συμβασιλεύσομεν αὐτῷ; *1 Clem.* 6.1: "An immense multitude of the elect have come to join these people who have lived in holiness" (ὁσίως πολιτευσαμένους); 21.1; 51.2; 54.4: ταῦτα οἱ πολιτευόμενοι τὴν ἀμεταμέλητον πολιτείαν τοῦ θεοῦ.

[39] Πολιτεύεσθαι πρός τινα means "behave properly, carry out one's obligations toward someone"; cf. Diodorus Siculus 19.23.1: "Peucestes did what he had to"; 19.46.2: "Pytho conducted himself properly toward the whole army"; 19.79.7; 19.90.5.

that is not appropriate for a citizen of heaven (cf. *UPZ* 110, 78 = *P.Paris* 63). But it is also a call to honor, to preserve one's country's spirit or mindset— *noblesse oblige*—and this nuance of praise is in literary terms in agreement with the usage of the inscriptions[40] and the papyri: "the rest of the citizens who choose to act more nobly."[41]

From the fourth century, the papyri use πολιτευόμενος to mean a functionary (*P.Fuad I Univ.* 16, 1), a venerable member of the municipal council (*P.Mil.* 45, 3; 64, 2; republished in *SB* 9515; 9503; *P.Oxy.* 2418, 8; 2718; *P.Mert.* 43. 2; *P.Lips.* 37, 2; *P.Lond.* 233, 4 = vol. 2, p. 273; *Pap.Lugd.Bat.* XI, 11, 4), a *curialis* (*P.Sorb.* 63, 1; *P.Oxy.* 1921, 2; *P.Mich.* 613, 2; 624, 3, 11; *P.Stras.* 272, 4; *Pap.Lugd.Bat.* XII, 10, 2; *C.P.Herm.* 52, 2; 53, 3; *P.Iand.* 40, 10; *P.Apoll.* 75, 4; *SB* 7425, 7; 8699, 12; 8988, 31; 9461, 20; N. Lewis, "Four Cornell Papyri," in *RechPap*, 1964, vol. 3, p. 33, 5).

[40] B. Latyschev, *Inscriptiones Antiquae*, n. 420, 11: καλῶς πολειτευσάμενον; 425, 13: πολειτευσάμενον ἐν πᾶσιν ἀγνῶς; 691, 7; κάλλιστον πολίτευμα ἐπολιτεύσατο (*IG* IV², 81, 9; cf. J. and L. Robert, "Bulletin épigraphique," in *REG*, 1941, p. 247, n. 58); τοῖς εὐσεβέστατα καὶ κάλλιστα πολειτευομένοις καὶ παρὰ θεῶν τις χάρις καὶ παρὰ τῶν εὐεργετηθέντων ἐπακολουθεῖ (Dittenberger, *Syl.* 708, 25); ἐνδόξως πολειτευσάμενον (F. K. Dörner, *Bericht über eine Reise in Bithynien*, Vienna, 1952, n. 10, 25); ἄριστα πολειτευόμενον (*I.Olymp.* 441; 442; 447; 449); δικαίως πολειτευσάμενον (ibid. 468). "Let all of the Acarnanians appear without fail to celebrate with piety the worship of the gods, and even towards the peoples who are related or are friends, a noble politics, worthy of their ancestors" (J. Pouilloux, *Choix*, n. 29, 59); a dedication from Thespia in the first century BC, to Athanias, "who carried out his political activity with great success and glory" (πολιτευσάμενον ἄριστα καὶ ἐνδοξότατα, ibid. 44, 9). In the Byzantine period, πολιτευόμενος often means "habitual, customary" (*P.Giss.* 105, 7–8; *P.Genova* 37, 5, where the editors make reference to Justinian, *Edict.* 11, pr. e 1; Justinian, *Nov.* 83, 8, 2; 52 pr.).

[41] Οἱ ἄλλοι πολῖται οἱ αἱρούμενοι βέλτιον πολιτεύεσθαι, *SB* 8852, 15; cf. *P.Col.Zen.* 11, 5. In a list of groups of tax collections, διὰ τῶν πολιτευομένων refer to a classification of taxpayers (*P.Apoll.* 75, 4). The adjective αἰδέσιμος, which is sometimes used with them, is equivalent to our "Reverend."

πολυτελής

polytelēs, expensive, rare, luxurious, precious

In its various usages, this adjective means "oppressively expensive" or "rare and luxurious," even "sumptuous" (*SB* 10498, 6), in any event requiring a major outlay;[1] and hence "precious,"[2] like certain perfumes (Mark 14:3) or wines of a great vintage (Wis 2:7). It is the usual adjective for valuable stones, either as construction materials[3] or as what we would call precious stones;[4] and for rich clothing,[5] sometimes with a pejorative

---

[1] Thucydides 7.27: keeping the thirteen hundred light troops "seemed too expensive." The inscription of Rosetta mentions expensive work for the embellishing of the temple (ἔργα πολυτελῆ; Dittenberger, *Or.* 90, 33; cf. *SEG* VIII, 784, 1). The inscriptions mention large expenditures by the *agoranomoi*: "Having been *agoranomos* at great expense (ἀγορανομήσαντά τε πολυτελῶς) and having provided for the heating of two heatable porticos" (L. Robert, "Les Inscriptions," in J. des Gagniers, *Laodicée*, pp. 265, 267; cf. G. E. Bean, T. B. Mitford, *Cilicia* 7, n. 21, 23; 152, 7); *MAMA* VIII, 408, 7: ἀγορανομίαις πολυτέλεσιν; IV, 152, 5: ἀγορανομήσαντα πολυτελῶς. This generosity was seen especially in banquets: μετὰ πάσης δαπάνης πολυτελοῦς (Dittenberger, *Syl.* 783, 41; first century BC; *Or.* 525, 5); πεποιημένον ἑστιάσεις καὶ ἐπιδόσεις ἐκ τῶν ἰδίων πολυτελεῖς (*MAMA* VIII, 484, 18–19; cf. 471, 8–9; Xenophon, *Hier.* 1.20: costly feasts), and the adverb is synonymous with πλουσίως (*I.Sard.* 55, 8 = *SEG* IV, 636) or πολυδαπάνως (*MAMA* VI, 372, 6; Dittenberger, *Syl.* 799, 14–15; Strabo 5.1.7; Diodorus Siculus 1.52.2; 17.70.5; 17.91.6; other references in L. Robert, ibid., in J. des Gagniers, *Laodicée*, p. 267). Cf. the θυσίας πολυτελεῖς offered by Antiochus I of Commagene (*IGLS* I, 1444).

[2] *P.Mil.Vogl.* 74, 4: πολυτελὲς ὕδωρ (second century). Cf. precious goods or property (Prov 1:13, κτῆσις, Hebrew *yāqār*); costly materials used by the artisan (Philo, *Heir* 158; Josephus, *Ag. Apion* 2.191; Philostratus, *Gym.* 42).

[3] Isa 28:16; 1 Chr 29:2; inscription of Rosetta (Dittenberger, *Or.* 90, 34; cf. 132, 8); *SB* 8881, 8; what Herodian calls λίθοις τιμίοις.

[4] Jdt 10:21; Esth 5:1; Job 31:24; Sir 45:11; 50:9; Dan 11:38; Josephus, *Ant.* 12.40; Plutarch, *De cohib. ira* 13; Callixenes (in Athenaeus 6.202 *d*), Lucian, *Im.* 11; *Ep. Arist.* 66, 79, 80, 114; *Jos. Asen.* 2.7; 3.10; 18.5; *T. Job* 28.5; 32.5. In Prov 3:15; 8:11; 31:10, the LXX translates the Hebrew *penîîm*, "pearls," or *penînîm*, "coral," as "precious stones." On luxurious buildings, cf. Diodorus Siculus 17.52.3–4; 17.71.3; on luxurious presents and weapons, ibid. 17.76.8; 17.100.4.

[5] Xenophon, *An.* 1.5.8: luxurious tunics; Philo, *Sacr. Abel and Cain* 21: pleasure is "dressed in sumptuous clothings"; Josephus, *War* 1.605: during his stay at Rome,

---

polytelēs, S 4185; *EDNT* 3.133; MM 527; L&N 65.3; BAGD 690

nuance.[6] Thus St. Paul asks Christian women to come to church correctly attired "not with braided hair, gold, pearls, or costly clothing."[7] This is not a ban on elegance or a certain sort of style, but on flashy luxury or a provocative appearance that not only could stir up envy or lust[8] but also is altogether out of place when a sinful creature presents herself before God and comes to implore his mercy. Taking up the wisdom theme that places spiritual beauty high above all the joys of the world,[9] St. Peter also instructs Christians to adorn themselves with virtues rather than with jewels and cloaks. "This is precious before God" (*ho estin enōpion tou theou polyteles*, 1 Pet 3:4) does not mean that a gentle and quiet *pneuma* is very costly, since its value is not monetary; but as with the "seven mountains of precious stones" of *Enoch* 18.6, which hold stones that are medicinal and beautiful (colored, etc.), we are to understand that the feminine virtues are very useful in God's sight, for he regards and values them highly.

Antipater "bought expensive clothing"; Plutarch, *Apoph. lac.* 7; *Mulier. virt.* 23: a young Gaul condemned to death by Mithridates "was wearing a rich and costly garment (καλὴν ἐσθῆτα καὶ πολυτελῆ) when he was arrested"; *Agis* 18.8; Diodorus Siculus 17.70.3; *PSI* 418, 19: "if you think that this coat (τὸ τριβώνιον) is too expensive"; 616, 25 (rug or blanket). Thieves tried to grab these magnificent garments, αἰσθῆτι πολυτειμοτάτη (*P.Oxy.* 1121, 20; cf. C. Spicq, "Pèlerine et vêtements," in *Mélanges Tisserant*, vol. 1, pp. 400ff.).

[6] Philo, *Dreams* 2.53: "Who then is the skilled artisan who makes these robes of ruinous purple?"; Josephus, *Ant.* 15.91: "Nothing was good enough for this extravagant (πολυτελεῖ) woman, who was enslaved to her greed." Cf. the prodigalities of Demetrius (Plutarch, *Demetr.* 19.4).

[7] 1 Tim 2:9. Luxury in women's clothing is also condemned by Musonius, οὐ τὴν πολυτελῆ καὶ περιττήν (frag. 19; ed. C. E. Lutz, p. 120, 19).

[8] Lucian, *Vit. Auct.* 12: "Listen, everyone! Here is a luxury item that calls for a rich buyer: a life full of sweetness, a life of super-happiness"; cf. Diogenes Laertius 2.75: οὐδὲν κωλύει καὶ πολυτελῶς καὶ καλῶς ζῆν.

[9] Prov 3:14–15; Wis 7:9–11; 1 Pet 1:7.

πόνος

ponos, tiring labor, hard work, fatigue, suffering, pain

The first attested meaning of *ponos* is "tiring labor, hard work," after which one rests,[1] and then "the product of labor,"[2] a meaning that is particularly common in the LXX: "A people whom you do not know will eat the fruit of your labor."[3] In various contexts, *ponos* refers to the work of one's hands (Josephus, *Ant.* 19.113), physical efforts (*sōmatikōn ponōn*, Dittenberger, *Syl.* 708, 11), spiritual efforts (*ponoi psychēs*),[4] brief suffering

---

[1] Homer, *Il.* 1.467; 10.164; *Od.* 11.54; cf. the Christian inscription at Thasos, n. 370, 14, 16: "What endless pain (πόνος ἄπιρος) the death of a small child would have brought if Christ had not given its parents respite (ἀνάπαυμα)"; Menander, *Dysk.* 830: rather than "life in luxury at another's expense, I prefer to get it by my work"; Philo, *Creation* 167: "Man knew labors (πόνους), difficulties, and sweat in order to procure the necessities"; *Alleg. Interp.* 3.38, 251; Philo, *Moses* 1.37; exhausting work (*Alleg. Interp.* 1.84; Philo, *Sacr. Abel and Cain* 23; *Conf. Tongues* 92; *Spec. Laws* 1.125); labor, the enemy of ease (*Sacr. Abel and Cain* 35), "without break or respite" (39); Josephus, *War* 3.74, 253; 4.373; *Ant.* 1.238; 3.254; 5.134. Synesius, *Hymn.* 1.495: ἄμπαυμα πόνων; Wis 5:1; 15:4; *P.Oxy.* 2704, 2: "Nothing can be expected from our farming and the labors expended on it" (καὶ τῶν ἐπ' αὐτῇ πόνων). A monument at Agrios: "leading a simple life, in all sorts of labors, far from wealth and malicious envy" (E. Bernand, *Inscriptions métriques*, n. 114, col. IV, 12).

[2] Pindar, *Pyth.* 6.54: "the ornamented work of the bees"; Euripides, *Phoen.* 30: "the fruit of my travail" (τὸν ἐμὸν ὠδίνων πόνον); Xenophon, *An.* 7.6.9: "he gathered the fruit of our toils" (τοὺς ἡμετέρους πόνους ἔχει).

[3] Deut 28:33 (Hebrew *yeḡîaʿ*); Ps 78:46; 105:44; 109:11—"the fruit of his labor"; 128:2; Prov 3:9; 5:10; Wis 3:15; 8:7; 10:10; Sir 14:15; 28:15; Jer 20:5; Ezek 23:29; cf. Philo, *Moses* 1.53: profit from another's labor; Philo, *Husbandry* 155; Josephus, *War* 2.598; *Ant.* 18.266; 20.265.

[4] J. and L. Robert, "Bulletin épigraphique," in *REG*, 1952, p. 199, n. 188; cf. ἡδὺν πόνον (*GVI*, n. 1185, 3); Philo, *Husbandry* 91; *Prelim. Stud.* 166; *Alleg. Interp.* 3.38. Musonius asks what is the best means of livelihood for a philosopher (frag. 11) and replies: work in the fields, where the φιλόπονοι make bodily efforts (πονεῖν), but κατὰ φύσιν. This is the life of a free man who earns his own living by his work; farming leaves leisure to the soul to reflect and become wiser, which is what every philosopher wants to do, and it does not diminish his dignity.

---

ponos, S 4192; *EDNT* 3.135; *NIDNTT* 1.262; MM 528; L&N 24.77, 42.49; BAGD 691

(2 Macc 7:36), like the pain of childbirth (Isa 66:7), and other toils that are constantly renewed.[5] Sometimes it is only a matter of fatigue produced by effort,[6] which is linked to exercise (Philo, *Alleg. Interp.* 3.135: *askēsei kai ponō; Migr. Abr.* 31); sometimes pain (*Moses*1.284: *ponos ē mochthos*), all that is "bitter and unpleasant" (*Post. Cain* 156) and opposed to pleasure (4 Macc 1, 4, 9, 20). The range extends from simple care (Philo, *Heir* 48) and simple difficulties (Wis 9:16; Sir 29:4), like those of a voyage (*P.Ryl.* 624, 4: *tous tēs hodou ponous*), but accompanied by dangers[7] and hence by moments of crisis ("I am in difficulty summer and winter," *P.Col.* IV, 2, n. 66, 17) to evil of the most diverse sorts,[8] what we call "trials,"[9] misfortune (Isa 59:4), calamity (Obad 13, Hebrew *'êd*), sufferings that overwhelm the heart (Sir 3:27; Isa 53:11; 65:14; Jer 6:7; Bar 2:25); hence the pairing *kopos kai ponos*, trouble and woe.[10]

Effort, labor, and care vary with the circumstances, first of all in education: "the disciplinarian approach to education gives much trouble" (Plato, *Soph.* 230 a); "the effort of education" (*paideias ponon*, Philo, *Migr. Abr.* 223; *Spec. Laws* 2.240; *PSI* 875, 24); then in the assimilation of "sciences

---

[5] Sophocles, *Trach.* 30; *SEG* VII, 527, 13: ἀναδεχόμενος πόνον ἐκ νυκτὸς καὶ μεθ' ἡμέραν; A. Bernand, *El-Kanaïs*, n. 8, 2: "Many times I was tested by intensified troubles" (cf. E. Bernand, *Inscriptions métriques* 164 2). Simonides has Danae, holding her little son Perseus in her arms, say, "My child, great is my pain" (D. L. Page, *Poetae Melici Graeci*, Oxford, 1962, frag. 543, 7). Dionysius of Halicarnassus, *Comp.* 6.26.18: "It depends entirely on those who consent to take the trouble and put themselves out that these precepts should be serious and efficacious, or insignificant and useless."

[6] Philo, *Sacr. Abel and Cain* 114; *Alleg. Interp.* 3.135: "the shoulder is the symbol of effort and fatigue"; *Worse Attacks Better* 9; *Migr. Abr.* 221; *Change of Names* 193; Wis 10:9—"Wisdom delivers those who have served her from fatigue."

[7] Josephus, *War* 4.89; *Ant.* 17.271; *BGU* 1747, 22: οὐδὲ πόνον οὐδὲ κίνδυνον (64–63 BC) = *SB* 7410; M. Holleaux, *Etudes d'épigraphie*, vol. 1, p. 95; J. and L. Robert, "Bulletin épigraphique," in *REG*, 1946–47, p. 348, n. 183; Josephus, *Ant.* 1.283; 16.94; 19.317.

[8] Menander, *Dysk.* 179: "harshness, that is the ill that he suffers from"; Exod 2:11—"the burdens (Hebrew *sᵉbālôt*) that weigh upon the Hebrews"; Num 23:21 (Hebrew *'āmāl*); Jer 4:14; Ps 7:16; *SB* 6584, 6 (πόνου parallel to κακοῦ).

[9] Pindar, *Nem.* 10.147: "Among mortals there are few faithful companions in trials (ἐν πόνῳ), few who want to share our labors (καμάτου μεταλαμβάνειν)"; Plato, *Phd.* 247 b: "There [in the vault of heaven] the soul faces trial, there the supreme struggle (ἀγών)"; Wis 19:16—terrible trials; a Christian epitaph of Makaria: "She has heavenly crowns as recompense for her trials" (μισθόν πόνων, *SB* 5719, 6; E. Bernand, *Inscriptions métriques*, n. 60).

[10] Ps 10:7, 14; 90:10; Jer 20:18; cf. Gen 41:41—"God made me forget all my trouble"; Job 3:10; 5:6; Prov 21:7. In the third century, a Roman citizen bequeaths his *arourai* to his steward Epimachus "in gratitude for the trouble he went to" for the sake of the prosperity of my affairs (*P.Oxy.* 2474, 37).

that cost much effort to learn."[11] In the practice of a trade, the laborer "uses four times as much time and trouble preparing grain."[12] In hunting, "the fawn pursued with effort (syn ponō) will be caught by the dogs" (Xenophon, Cyn. 9.6); "one exhausts the animal with fatigue" (ponō, ibid. 9.20; cf. Josephus, Ant. 2.2, 334). In war, "It is for their country that they toil and fight with enemies."[13] In athletics, "those who go to work at gymnastic exercises" (Plato, Leg. 1.646 c); young people are "more exhausted by their efforts (ponois) than this type of exercise (en agōnia) entails."[14] Finally, and especially, in the medical vocabulary: "With patients who have long fevers, there come . . . many pains in the joints" (ta arthra ponoi, Hippocrates, Aph. 4.44; cf. 45; Plato, Phdr. 244 b); with the Athenian fever, "the illness descended upon the chest" (Thucydides 2.49.3);

---

[11] Plato, Resp. 7.526 c; Philo, Dreams 1.6: "The approach to knowledge costs much toil and trouble"; 1.120; Spec. Laws 1.32; To Gaius 246; Josephus, War 1.16 (great efforts of the historian); Ant. 1.2, 9; 12.14; 19.321; P.Grenf. 1.1, 18: "it is a painful subject"; SB 8422, 3: the deciphering of an acrostic poem, the effort of interpretation is a simple, trouble-free labor; cf. P.Hal. XII, 7: ἵνα μὴ πόνος; which is contrasted with πλήρη πόνων (BGU 1024, col. VII, 29), μετὰ μεγάλου πόνου (SB 10529, B 7; Josephus, War 5.36; Ant. 7.138); cf. Philo, Husbandry 103. The opposite of effort (πόνος) is negligence (ἀπονία, Philo, Heir 212) or slackness (Josephus, Ant. 2.201). Cf. the vision of Maximus: "My nature invited me to cultivate the mystique of labor" (μύστην πόνων), i.e., to write a poem (SEG VIII, 814; E. Bernand, Inscriptions métriques, 168, 5; A. J. Festugière, Hermès Trismégiste, vol. 1, pp. 47–49).

[12] Plato, Resp. 2.369 e; Josephus, Ant. 17.347. Cf. the ponoi of a governor (J. and L. Robert, "Bulletin épigraphique," in REG, 1961, n. 220, n. 536).

[13] Homer, Il. 17.158; cf. 6.77; 17.718; 21.524–25; Pindar, Isthm. 6.79: "Ajax, in the labors of Ares an extraordinary hero among all the warriors"; Hesiod, Th. 881 (war of the gods and the Titans); Ps.-Hesiod, Sc. 305: "the horsemen took great pains"; Aeschylus, Ag. 330: the exhausting wanderings of night fighting; Pers. 327; Xenophon, Lac. 4.7: "bear military labors" (στρατιωτικοὺς πόνους ὑποφέρειν). Philo, Moses 1.322; μνῆμα πόνων Ἄρεως (J. and L. Robert, "Bulletin épigraphique," in REG, 1952, p. 140, n. 43); Josephus, Ant. 5.130; 13.398; 18.7; 19.299.

[14] Philostratus, Gym. 29; cf. 30: respiration is labored during exercises (ἐν τοῖς πόνοις), 45, 48; Philo, Dreams 1.168: "athletic training preparatory to the efforts required by competition in the arena"; Joseph 223; Spec. Laws 2.98, 99; Rewards 27, 36; Prelim. Stud. 164; Plutarch, De prof. in virt. 4 (76 F): πόνος καὶ ἄσκησις. "The child braved the hard labor of the pancratium" (L. Moretti, Iscrizioni agonistiche greche, Rome, 1953, n. 55, 3; cf. n. 47; I.Lind. 699, b 8); the ponoi are the athletic trials themselves (GVI, n. 763, 5; Anth. Pal. 9.588.6), the ἀγών and the γυμνασία of the martyr (4 Macc 11:20). Commenting on the epitaph of a pancratist from Phrygian Dorylaeum (GVI, n. 253, 5), L. Robert (Hellenica, vol. 11–12, Paris, 1960, pp. 342–349) strongly emphasized this agonistic meaning of ponos. Cf. the herald positions reserved for former athletes, μόνους τοὺς ἐν ἀσκήσει καὶ πόνοις γεγενημένους ἀγωνιστάς (PSI 1422, 29).

those who have just been circumcised are in pain (Gen 34:25, Hebrew *kā'ēḇ*); the trouble of insomnia.[15]

Antisthenes is the first to give *ponos* its technical moral meaning and consider it a good thing.[16] The Stoics classify it as "indifferent" (Diogenes Laertius 7.102; cf. 7.166). Musonius poses the question: "The proposition that *ponos* is not an evil does not seem plausible to me; the contrary proposition, that *ponos* is an evil, seems more plausible, because every evil is to be avoided" (frag. 1); but he concludes that *ponos* is not an evil, and he reports the question posed by a young Spartan to the philosopher Cleanthes, "Is *ponos* a good thing?" (cf. Diogenes Laertius 7.172). He was "so well trained in virtue that he believed that *ponos* was closer to the nature of good than to that of evil." This is also Philo's opinion: "*ponos*, enemy of ease," without which nothing noble is possible among mortals (*Sacr. Abel and Cain* 35–41; 42–45), is rewarded by God (Philo, *Alleg. Interp.* 1.80), especially effort toward goodness and virtue (*Sacr. Abel and Cain* 120; *Worse Attacks Better* 27). So he adds a great deal to the pagan ethic that exhorted disdaining *ponos* (Musonius, frag. 7).

Philo is the one who introduced *ponos* into the ethical vocabulary. He is the only one to praise effort or toil at length—*philoponia*[17]—to the point that he contrasts the virtuous with those who no nothing of effort (*Worse Attacks Better* 34: *ponon ouk eidotes*). Indeed, *ponos* is linked with zeal in the service of God (*Sacr. Abel and Cain* 37): "All good things come from toil and increase with it" (ibid. 40, 41, 113, 115, 120). Nevertheless, it is not effort pure and simple that deserves praise, but effort carried through with art (*Worse Attacks Better* 17: *ho ponos . . . ho meta technēs*) and with the goal of

---

[15] Sir 31:20; cf. 37:30 (discomfort); Isa 1:5; 53:4; Jer 14:18; 2 Macc 9:18; 1 Kgs 8:37 (Hebrew *maḥªlâh*, sickness); *P.Oxy.* 234, col. II, 24 (against earache); *SB* 10762, 3, an amulet ἀπὸ πάσης νόσου καὶ πόνου κεφαλῆς (cf. *Jos. Asen.* 10.8—"I have a bad headache and am resting on my bed"); 11226, 3, a question to an oracle: εἰ ἐξοῦ μοι γέγονεν ὁ πόνος καὶ θεραπείαν μοι διδοῖς; cf. 8026, 29 (stele at Moschion): "that the balm for my woes be revealed to you"; E. Bernand, *Inscriptions métriques*, 167, 10 (hymn to Mandoulis): "that I may rejoin my family and my servants, in my country, without sickness and without painful fatigue" (χαλεποῖο πόνοιο); 170, 10 (a *proskynēma*): "May Herod return and regain his country, without sickness and painful fatigue" (χαλεποῖο πόνοιο). Aristophanes, *Ran.* 829: "what caused so much pain for the lungs" (πολὺν πόνον).

[16] Diogenes Laertius 6.2. Cf. D. Dudley, *A History of Cynicism*, London, 1937, p. 13).

[17] Philo, *Prelim. Stud.* 166; *Post. Cain* 157. *Philoponia*, joined with exercise (*askēsis*), is particularly the virtue of the courageous athlete who spares himself no trouble; but it is also used for officials and judges who are zealous in their responsibilities, and for the *grammateus* who watches over his students, cf. C. Panagopoulos, *Vocabulaire*, pp. 222ff.

virtue.[18] God "changes the bitterness of effort to sweetness" (*Post. Cain* 154); he does not let effort go unrewarded for those who struggle (ibid. 78, *tois askētais*). So one must persevere in "continuous, tireless *ponos*."[19]

So when St. Paul writes of Epaphras that "he does not cease to struggle for you (*pantote agōnizomenos*) in his prayers" (Col 4:12) and that he "exerts great efforts" (*echei polyn ponon*, 4:13) for the Christians of Colossae, Laodicea, and Hierapolis,[20] he is not only using a traditional athletic metaphor but also suggesting that this servant of Christ embodies a costly state of mind and activity, concerns and cares, efforts and fatigue, physical and spiritual suffering; that he is engaged in a taxing labor that requires overcoming a thousand difficulties. We would say "takes great pains, goes to a great deal of trouble."

The three occurrences of *ponos* in Revelation have the meaning "suffering" or "calamity": at the punishment of the kingdom of the Beast, the godless "gnawed their tongues in agony" (*ek tou ponou*).[21] The medical metaphor is used with regard to blasphemers: "because of their pains and their wounds" (*ek tōn ponōn autōn kai ek tōn helkōn autōn*, Rev 16:11). Finally, in the age to come there will be no (*ouk estai eti*) death, no mourning, no crying, no *ponos* (21:4), that is, no labor, fatigue, suffering, misfortune;[22] it is the end of all trials, the abolition of sin's punishments.

---

[18] *Drunkenness* 21, 94; *Sobr.* 38, 65; *Migr. Abr.* 144, 167; *Prelim. Stud.* 108: "rugged struggles for the good"; 162: "the feast of the soul is effort that has reached its goal"; *Post. Cain* 95: "the Beautiful is a perfect good, *ponos* an imperfect advantage"; *Change of Names* 170: "effort goes along with the useful, ease (ῥαστώνη) with the harmful"; *Moses* 1.154; 2.183–184; *Good Man Free* 69; *Spec. Laws* 4.124. These thoughts derive from the Pythagorean doctrine of the Υ, where the hard toil of the route to the summit will be followed by rest. F. Cumont (*Lux Perpetua*, pp. 263–279) compares *Vers d'or* 66, Pythagorean: "after healing your soul you will save it from these toils" (ψυχὴν δὲ πόνων ἀπὸ τῶνδε σαώσεις, p. 404), and the tomb inscription of a disciple of Pythagoras who taught the obligation to work as the first rule of life (τὸν πόνον; F. Cumont, *Symbolisme funéraire*, p. 422). Pagan mysteries insisted on it: "salvation comes from struggle" (ἐκ πόνων σωτηρία, Firmicus Maternus, *Err. prof. rel.* 22.1); ἀγαθὸν οἱ πόνοι, αἱ δὲ ἡδοναὶ ἐκ παντὸς τρόπου κακόν (Iamblichus, *VP* 85).

[19] *Flight* 41; *Spec. Laws* 2.260; *Worse Attacks Better* 27; *Migr. Abr.* 220; *Change of Names* 86; cf. Sir 11:21; Menander, *Dysk.* 862: "everything is gained through perseverance in effort."

[20] *SB* 9484, 13: ὁ πόνος γὰρ αὐτῶν ἐπὶ τούτων ἄλλων (letter from the second century).

[21] Rev 16:10; i.e., in order not to cry out and acknowledge their bankruptcy, not to expose their fears, or not to express their pain, their failed ambitions, their wounded pride, their ruined prosperity (E. B. Allo).

[22] Synesius, *Hymn.* 1.419–420; 436–437 links πόνους and μερίμνας, ὀδύνας. Cf. the epigram dedicated to Apollonius of Tyana, son of Ouranos (of Heaven), ὅπως θνητῶν ἐξελάσιε πόνους, published by R. Merkelbach, *ZPE*, vol. 41, 1981, p. 270.

πορθέω

---

portheō, to sack, ravage, ruin, lay waste

This verb, unknown in the LXX, is current from Homer to the Koine with the meaning "sack, ravage, ruin" a city, "lay waste" a territory.[1] The word implies physical or moral violence against persons.[2] Its three NT occurrences pertain to the persecution of the church by St. Paul before his conversion, so that in Acts 9:21 (*ho porthēsas . . . tous epikaloumenous to onoma touto*) several French translators make this verb synonymous with *diōkō* (1 Cor 15:9; Phil 3:6): "Is this not the one who persecuted (or hunted down) those who call upon this name at Jerusalem?"[3]

---

[1] Homer, *Il.* 4.308; *Od.* 14.264; Herodotus 1.84; 3.58; Aeschylus, *Sept.* 583: "destroy the city of his fathers, the gods of his race, by sending a foreign army against them"; Pindar, *Nem.* 4.26: "Telamon ruined Troy"; Isocrates, *Evag.* 9.62: "Evagoras ravaged Phoenicia"; Philo, *Conf. Tongues* 47; *Flacc.* 54; *Moses* 1.69; Josephus, *Ant.* 10.135, the sacking of Jerusalem in 586 (cf. *3 Apoc. Bar.* 1.1—πορθῆσαι τὴν πόλιν); *War* 4.534, Simon of Gerasa "ravaged the towns and cities" (synonymous with λυμαίνεσθαι; cf. Acts 8:3); 4 Macc 4:23, Antiochus "plundered their city"; around 200 BC, a decree of Istros honoring Agathocles mentions that the Thracians are besieging Bizona and laying waste its territory (τήν τε χώραν πορθούντων, *NCIG*, n. VI, 26); in the sixth century AD, the inscription of King Silko in Nubia: ἐπόρθησα τὰς χώρας αὐτῶν (Dittenberger, *Or.* 201, 17 = *SB* 8536, 17).

[2] Euripides, *Phoen.* 565: "You will see many captive virgins suffer the brutal violence of their enemies" (βίᾳ πορθουμένας); Philo, *Flacc.* 54: "As at the capture of a city, Flaccus allowed those who wanted to do so to pillage the Jews" (πορθεῖν ᾽Ιουδαίους); 4 Macc 11:4—"What have we done that you should torture us so?"; *BGU* 588, 2: πορθοῦντες ὑμᾶς (first century AD); *P.Lond.* 1677, 26, 36, 52 (sixth century).

[3] Persecuted or pursued. The *Bible de Jérusalem* translates *s'acharnait*, "dogged, went at fiercely and relentlessly," which gives the right idea (cf. *NJB*, "did such damage"), but the verb never has exactly this sense in known Greek; still less *malmenait*, "handled roughly" (E. Osty, J. Trinquet; cf. the English *mauled*). Better to say *maltraitait*, "mistreated" (Loisy).

---

portheō, S 4199; *EDNT* 3.137; MM 529; L&N 20.374; BAGD 693

In Gal 1:13—"You have heard of my doings when I was in Judaism: I persecuted the church of God beyond measure and ravaged it" (*hoti kath' hyperbolēn ediōkon tēn ekklēsian tou theou kai eporthoun* [G: *epolemoun*] *autēn*). *Eporthoun* should be taken as a conative imperfect, "I would have liked to annihilate it."[4] The imperfect *eporthei* in Gal 1:23 is the same: the Christians of Judea said, "The one who once persecuted us (*ho diōkōn pote*) today preaches the faith that he then wanted to destroy (*hēn pote eporthei*)."[5] Here *pistis* has its objective sense, "doctrine,"[6] which matches the singular "church of God," referring not to a particular community but to the whole primitive church.[7]

---

[4] Cf. A. Oepke, *Der Brief des Paulus an die Galater*, Leipzig, 1937, p. 22: "und sie am liebsten vernichtet hätte"; F. Mussner, *Der Galaterbrief*, Freiburg-Basel, 1974, p. 78: "und sie zu ruinieren suchte."

[5] A. Oepke, *Der Brief des Paulus an die Galater*, p. 28, "den er einst verstörte."

[6] Rightly refusing a weakened meaning for πορθέω and contrasting this verb with οἰκοδομέω, P. H. Menoud takes it to mean that before his conversion St. Paul attacked the faith of the believers rather than their persons; there was no blood on his hands. Paul undermined the faith of the church by trying to demonstrate from the Scriptures that the crucified one could not be the Messiah ("Le Sens du verbe ΠΟΡΘΕΙΝ, Gal. I, 13, 23; Act. IX, 21," in *Apophoreta: Festschrift E. Haenchen*, Berlin, 1964, pp. 178–186; reprinted in P. Menoud, *Jésus-Christ et la foi*, Neuchâtel-Paris, 1975, pp. 40–47). Philo often uses πορθέω metaphorically: to sow devastation in the spirit (*Plant.* 159) or in the heart (*Good Man Free* 38); the passions lay waste the whole life of those who feed them (*Decalogue* 49; *To Gaius* 114).

[7] Cf. L. Cerfaux, *La Théologie de l'Eglise suivant saint Paul*, 2d ed., Paris, 1965, p. 164, n. 1.

ποταπός

potapos, of what origin, from what country; of what sort, of what kind

Potapos, the only form of this word found in the Greek Bible, is the Hellenistic variation of *podapos*,[1] formed by popular assimilation to *pote*.[2] The basic meaning is "of what origin, from what country?" This meaning remains common in the Koine, in the literary language[3] as well as in the inscriptions, for example in this Jewish epitaph from the first century: "Ask Samuel, son of Doras, who he is, whence he comes."[4] This sense is perhaps not absent from Matt 8:27, where, after the miracle of the calming of the storm, the people ask, "*Potapos estin houtos*, that even the wind and the sea obey him?" This could be just a synonym for the interrogative *tis*, "Who then is this?" (cf. the parallels at Mark 4:41; Luke 8:25), but we cannnot rule out the nuance "What is his origin? Where does he come from?" Similarly, when the Virgin Mary is surprised by the very unusual greeting addressed to her by an invisible being: *dielogizeto potapos eiē ho aspasmos houtos* (Luke 1:29; D reads *podapos an*). Certainly she is trying to understand the meaning of the angel's words (*epi tō logō*), but she is probably also trying to place the angel.[5] In any event, this is the interpretation taken in

---

[1] Cf. Phrynichus (ed. Lobeck, p. 45). Ποδαπός is still used in literary Greek, by Menander, *Mis.* (*P.Oxy.* 2657, 31); Josephus, *Ant.* 7.32; Lucian, *Vit. Auct.* 3: Ποδαπὸς εἶ σύ, " 'What country are you from?' 'From Samos.' "

[2] Cf. J. H. Moulton, W. F. Howard, N. Turner, *A Grammar of New Testament Greek*, vol. 1, p. 95; vol. 2, pp. 112, 375; vol. 3, p. 48.

[3] Menander, loc. cit., ποδαπὸς εἶ, ξένε; Erotian, writing about the "sacred disease" (epilepsy), so called because it could be sent by the gods, says that it could also have a natural origin, ποταπῷ χρῆται τύπῳ ὁ νοσῶν (frag. 33, *De Morbo Sacro*, p. 108); *P.Oxy.* 413, 155: ποταπὰ περιπατεῖς.

[4] Ἐρώτησον τίς, ποταπός—*CII* 1451, 8 = *C.Pap.Jud.* 1451 = *SB* 7904. This is a variant of the formula τίς, πόθεν, found often in epigrams (*MAMA* I, 176, 1-2; *I.Olymp.* 225, 8; *Anth. Pal.* 9.648). Numerous examples in L. Robert, *Hellenica*, vol. 2, p. 97; vol. 4, p. 47.

[5] E. Delebecque (*Evangile de Luc*, p. 6) translates quite accurately, "She pondered from what country this sign of respect came" (Fr. "Elle calculait de quel pays provenait

---

potapos, S 4217; EDNT 3.141; MM 530; L&N 58.30; BAGD 694–695

Prot. Jas. 11.1—"She looked around her, to the right and to the left, (to see) where the voice was coming from" (*pothen hautē hē phōnē*).

All the other NT occurrences mean "of what sort, what kind," synonymous with *poios*[6] but with an intensive nuance, pointing to a distinctive category:[7] "If this man were a prophet, he would know who and of what sort this woman is (*tis kai potapē hē gynē*) who is touching him and that she is a sinner" (Luke 7:39). The nuance is admiration in Mark 13:1—"What stones, what a building!"; 2 Pet 3:11—"Seeing that everything is to be dissolved in this way, what sort of people should you not be (*potapous dei hyparchein*) through the holiness of your conduct." "What sort of persons" expresses originality and greatness, the distinctive nature of these great beings. It is almost an exclamation, as at 1 John 3:1—"Behold what manner of (extraordinary) love the Father has given us (*potapēn agapēn dedōken hēmin*) that we should be called children of God; such we are." Here *potapos* seems to combine three meanings: *qualis, quantus, unde.*[8] The kind of love, *agapē*, that we are given is an exceptional, prodigiously generous love, coming from heaven; its nature is divine.

---

cette marque de respect-là") and comments: "there is no reason not to give to the recent form ποταπός the meaning of the classical ποδαπός; cf. 7:39."

[6] Cf. the reading of D in Acts 20:18—"You know how (ποταπῶς, read πῶς) I conducted myself."

[7] Sus 54: "under what tree and in what place in the garden did you see them?"; Philo, *To Gaius* 370: "Terrified as we were, still asking ourselves what would be decided, what the finding would be, of what sort the verdict would be" (ποταπὴ γένοιτ' ἡ κρίσις); *Alleg. Interp.* 1.91: "what intelligence is and of what sort"; Josephus, *Ant.* 6.39: after enduring all sorts of evils; 6.345: what sort of person = of what worth; 8.72: what sort of outcome, victory or defeat, would result from this battle; *War* 2.32; 1.390: "that the question will be what sort of friend I was (ποταπὸς φίλος) and not whose friend"; *Ag. Apion* 1.255: Amenophis had learned from another king what the nature of the gods was (ποταποί τινές εἰσι); *Apoc. Pet.* 4: ποταποί εἰσι τὴν μορφήν = so that we might see what their form was; Hymn of Isidorus to Isis: what is the name of this One? (*SB* 8141, 29 = *SEG* 8.551); Ptolemy, *Flor.* 3.8: ποταπός τις εἴη; *Acts Paul Thec.* 2: Titus had described Paul's appearance to Onesiphorus; Lucian, *Par.* 22: ποταπὸς δὲ οὗτος ὁ φίλος, ὅστις οὐ βέβρωκεν οὐδὲ πέποικε μεθ' ἡμῶν. In the second century, *P.Mich.* 492, 21: "If you know that the town secretary put me down for a *leitourgia*, let me know what sort of *leitourgia* he assigned me to"; *SB* 9636, 10, a veteran seeking lodging, mentions the neighbors, ποταποὺς κωμίτας ἔχωμεν; in the third century, "Write to tell me what sort (of purple) you want me to bring" (*P.Oxy.* 1678, 16).

[8] Of what sort, how great, from where. The nuance "from where" is vital with St. John, who describes each being according to its origin: ἐπίγειος-ἐπουράνιος (John 3:12); ἐκ τοῦ οὐρανοῦ-ἐκ τῆς γῆς (3:31); ἐκ τῶν κάτω-ἐκ τῶν ἄνω (8:23); ἐκ τούτου τοῦ κόσμου-οὐκ ἐκ τοῦ κόσμου (8:23; 15:18; 17:14–15; 1 John 2:16; 4:5–6; 5:4); ἐκ τοῦ διαβόλου-ἐκ τοῦ θεοῦ (1 John 3:8–9), etc.

ποτίζω

potizō, **to cause or give to drink, water, irrigate**

The first meaning of this verb, "cause to drink, give to someone to drink,"[1] is used first of all for people. Lot's daughters decide, "Let us cause our father to drink wine" (Gen 19:32–35; hiphil of Hebrew *šāqâh*); Hagar "gave the boy to drink";[2] a physician "gave the patient pure wine to drink" (Hippocrates, *Aph.* 7.46) and occasionally administered his potion badly.[3] When Jesus was crucified, a soldier took a sponge, soaked it with vinegar, fastened it to a reed, and "gave him to drink" (*epotizen auton*, Matt 27:48; Mark 15:36), thus fulfilling the prophecy of Ps 69:21. Animals are watered: "On the Sabbath day, does not everyone water his ox or ass?"[4] *Potizō*, finally, is used for the water that waters and moistens the surface of the ground (Gen 2:6; 13:10), a garden (2:10; Deut 11:10), a vineyard (Isa 27:3), trees (Eccl 2:6; Sir 24:31), plants.[5]

---

[1] In principle with a double accusative, τί τινά = something to someone (Gen 24:17), but cf. *Tabula of Cebes* 5.2, a Neopythagorean writing from the first century: τοὺς εἰσπορευομένους εἰς τὸν βίον ποτίζει τῇ ἑαυτῆς δυνάμει (dative of the thing, accusative of the person); the opposite at 14.

[2] Gen 21:19; Rebekah caused Jacob to drink (24:18, 45); Exod 32:20; Num 5:24, 26; 20:8; 1 Sam 30:11; Judg 4:19.

[3] Aristotle, *Ph.* 2.8; 199ª; cf. Philostratus, *Gym.* 14. For "cause to drink" Rufus of Ephesus used πίνω or ἐπιπίνω (*Ren. Ves.*, ed. Daremberg pp. 12, 3; 33, 6) or προποτίζω (p. 26, 6); "give to drink" (διδόναι πίνειν, pp. 8, 6; 28, 6).

[4] Luke 13:15—ἀναγαγὼν ποτίζει; Gen 24:14—"I will also water the camels," flocks (29:2, 3, 7), sheep (29:8, 10; Exod 2:16, 17, 19), all the beasts of the field (Ps 104:11). The charioteer waters the horses (Plato, *Phdr.* 247 *e*); "I am that Daphnis . . . who brought heifers and bulls here to drink" (Theocritus 1.121); Diodorus Siculus 19.94.9: the Nabateans lead their flocks to these reservoirs and water them three days in a row; Dittenberger, *Or.* 483, 169.

[5] Philo, *Post. Cain* 125ff.; *Unchang. God* 37; Xenophon, *Symp.* 2.25: "When the deity waters the plants too much, they cannot stand up or let the wind blow through"; *Anth. Pal.* 1.100: "The Nile, with its floods, knows how to water the earth."

---

potizō, S 4222; TDNT 6.159–160; EDNT 3.142; NIDNTT 2.274–275; MM 531; L&N 23.35, 43.9; BDF §§155(7), 159(1); BAGD 695

In the papyri, the verb is constantly used in the sense of "irrigate";[6] and in the third century BC (*P.Cair.Zen.* 59155, 3; *P.Tebt.* 787, 26; *P.Haun.* 9, 3); "water the ground immediately by hand" (*eutheōs potison tēn gēn apo cheros, SB* 6733, 3; cf. *P.Stras.* 193, 5); Psentaes writes Zeno, "I irrigated (*soi epotisa*) half of the thousand *arourai* for you" (*P.Lond.* 2061, 3); "the water in the canal has not risen more than a cubit, so the ground has not been irrigated" (*potizesthai, Pap.Lugd.Bat.* XX, A, p. 266; *P.Wisc.* 77, 37).[7]

By making God the subject of this verb, the LXX gives it a religious value: "I will give water in the desert and streams in the steppe to water my people, my chosen" (Isa 43:20); "God waters the sons of Adam with the torrent of his delights" (Ps 36:8); "floods of abundance" (78:15). Wisdom gives her disciple "the water of wisdom" to drink.[8] Hence the catechetical commands[9] that are taken over by the NT: "Whoever shall give one of these little ones even a glass of cold water to drink (*hos ean potisē*) because he is a disciple, truly I tell you, that one shall not lose his reward" (Matt 10:42; Mark 9:41). In the parable of the Last Judgment: "I was thirsty and you did not give me anything to drink" (Matt 25:35, 37, 42)!

St. Paul uses the verb metaphorically: "I have given you milk to drink (*gala hymas epotisa*), not solid food" (1 Cor 3:2); the image of the milk diet

---

[6] Numerous references given in Moulton-Milligan, notably *P.Oxy.* 938, 5: since the oxen were in very poor condition and could not work, "as a result, the ground was not irrigated" (τῆς γῆς διὰ τοῦτο μὴ ποτιζομένης); S. Witkowski, *Epistulae Privatae Graecae* 18, 7, letter regarding a vineyard: ὀχιτεύομεν καὶ ποτίζομεν = we have made canals and irrigated. Cf. Philo, *Conf. Tongues* 38: the farmer puts his feet on the steps of the treadmill used for drawing water "when he wants to water his field" (ὅταν ἐθελήσῃ ποτίσαι τὰς ἀρούρας).

[7] Likewise in AD 29–30: διόρυκος δι' οὗ ποτίζετε ὁ κλῆρος, *P.Mich.* 256, 4; cf. 263, 10; 267, 6; 272, 4; 273, 4; 327, 38; *P.Mert.* 11, 10, 13, 31 (AD 39–40); 27, 13; 79, 10; *P.Fam.Tebt.* 3, 14: διῶρυξ δι' ἧς ποτίζεται ἡ ἄρουρα (first century AD); 23, 10; BGU 1645, 11; *P.Oslo* 155, 3–4; *P.Amst.* 88, 4, 9; *P.Laur.* 11 A, 16–21; 14 A, 10; *P.Col.* VII, n. 172, 11, 13; *Pap.Lugd.Bat.* XIX, 10, 14; *SB* 7379, 37; 7599, 31; 8546, 16; Dittenberger, *Or.* 200, 16.

[8] Wis 15:3; Jer 35:2—"You shall give them wine to drink." Philo, *Alleg. Interp.* 2.86–87: "He himself watered the souls that are friends of God and quenched their thirst from a well that he himself brought forth out of his own wisdom." Often this "watering" is pejorative: God pours out a "wine of dizziness" (Ps 60:4), a "spirit of stupor" (Isa 29:10), poisoned waters (Jer 8:14; 23:15), a "wine of rage" (25:15; cf. Rev 14:8); "I will water the earth with your rotting (corpse)" (Ezek 32:6; to Pharaoh); "You will make them drink tears in abundance" (Ps 80:6).

[9] Hab 2:15—"Woe to him who gives his neighbor a poisoned cup to drink until they are drunk so that he can behold their nudity"; Job 22:7: "You did not give drink to the thirsty"; Prov 25:21—"If your enemy thirsts, give drink to him," quoted at Rom 12:20—ἐὰν διψᾷ, πότιζε αὐτόν; Sir 29:25—"You shall give to eat and to drink without receiving thanks."

reserved for babies was current as a way of referring to elementary teaching, as opposed to the deeper doctrine fed on by the "spirituals."[10] "I planted, Apollos watered (epotisen), but God gave the increase. Now neither is the one who plants anything, nor the one who waters (ho potizōn), but the one who gives the increase, namely, God. The one who plants and the one who waters (ho potizōn) are but one . . . but each one will receive his own wage in proportion to his own labor."[11] The one who waters only works from the outside, but his kopos—which is tiring and useful—merits a reward, because he contributes to the fruitfulness of the planting.

The most important text from the theological point of view is the one where the apostle compares the church to the human organism, its unity and the solidarity of its members:[12] "We have all been watered by one Spirit" (pantes hen Pneuma epotisthēmen, 1 Cor 12:13). This aorist passive refers to baptism (cf. ebaptisthēmen), which infuses new life and new power.[13] Compare the image of drinking in John 7:37–39: "If anyone thirsts, let him come to me and drink . . . rivers of living water will flow from within him (Isa 48:21). He said this concerning the Spirit that those who believed in him were going to receive" (John 4:13–14). The filling of the Holy Spirit causes effects comparable to those of drunkenness (cf. Acts 2:13—"they are full of new wine"), but it is poured out from heaven: "The gifts of God, brought by the blowing (epipneusthenta) of the highest graces" (Philo, Prelim. Stud. 38). From there on, the apostle's thought was inspired not

---

[10] 1 Cor 3:1; cf. Heb 5:12–14; 1 Pet 2:2; Philo, Husbandry 9; Epictetus 2.16.39; 3.24.9.

[11] 1 Cor 3:6–8. Cf. W. Pesch, "Der Sonderlohn für die Verkündiger des Evangeliums (I Kor. XIII, 8, 14f und Parallelen)," in J. Blinzler, Neutestamentliche Aufsätze: Festschrift J. Schmid, Regensburg, 1963, pp. 199–206; M. A. Chevallier, Esprit de Dieu, paroles d'hommes, Neuchâtel, 1966, pp. 35ff. S. Fugita, "The Metaphor of Plant in Jewish Literature of the Intertestamental Period," in JSJ, vol. 7, 1976, pp. 30–45.

[12] Cf. J. Havet, "Christ collectif or Christ individuel en I Cor. XII, 12?" in ETL, 1947, pp. 499–520.

[13] Cf. J. Héring, La Première Epître de saint Paul aux Corinthiens, pp. 112f. ET = pp. 129–130. C. Senft, La Première Epître de saint Paul aux Corinthiens, Neuchâtel-Paris, 1979, p. 161; G. J. Cuming, "ἐποτίσθημεν (I Corinthiens XII, 13)," in NTS, vol. 27, 1981, pp. 283–285 (translates "nous avons été arrosés, de l'eau a été versée sur nous" [we have been watered, water has been poured on us]). Following Clement of Alexandria (PG 74.889 b), a certain number of exegetes connect this spiritual drink to the Eucharist (E. Käsemann, Leib und Leib Christi, Tübingen, 1939, p. 176; L. Cerfaux, La Théologie de l'Eglise suivant saint Paul, Paris, 1965, p. 219; A. Feuillet, Le Christ sagesse de Dieu, pp. 101ff.). Others, relying wrongly on St. John Chrysostom (Hom. on 1 Cor 30.2; PG 61.251), think of confirmation (F. Prat, La Théologie de saint Paul, 6th ed., Paris, 1923, vol. 2, p. 316; J. Huby, St. Paul: Première Epître aux Corinthiens, Paris, 1946, p. 289).

only by the OT, where God gives water to his own, but by the current of thought flowing from Philo, who had often underlined this teaching: "Melchizedek brings wine instead of water, and he gives it to souls to drink unmixed so that they may find themselves possessed by a divine drunkenness that is more sober than sobriety itself."[14] Those who are still at the preliminary stage of instruction, "thirsty as they are for knowledge, settle near the sciences that can quench their thirst and water their souls" (*potizein tas psychas autōn*, *Flight* 187); "This well is the divine wisdom, from which drink . . . all souls that are enamored of contemplation, that are possessed by a love of perfection" (*Flight* 195); "The divine word goes forth like a wellspring of wisdom, after the fashion of a river, to water and irrigate the Olympian and celestial sprouts and plants of souls that are enamored of virtue, as if they were in Paradise" (*Dreams* 2.242).

So the choice of *potizō* in 1 Cor 12:13 suggests first of all fullness and abundance. (The corresponding French word, *abreuver*, often has this nuance of "fill"—hence the magnificence of God's gift, which floods even the mountains [Ps 104:13]—or "inundate," cover with waters that overflow or come flooding in.) There are also nuances of excellence,[15] of fervor (cf. drinking in someone's words) and gladness (Philo, cf. the fruit of the Holy Spirit, Gal 5:22); of fruitfulness (cf. John 6:53–54), because dry lands are watered so that they will be productive; and finally of immanence, impregnation, and assimilation, because if one drinks to quench one's thirst, the thirst is not satisfied until the liquid is swallowed, absorbed.

---

[14] Philo, *Alleg. Interp.* 3.82; 1.84; Philo, *Post. Cain* 126–158. The Alexandrian returns often to this *sobria ebrietas: Creation* 71; *Drunkenness* 146: filled with graces, the soul is joyful, carried away with enthusiasm; 152: "the soul that is filled with the pure wine of sobriety is no longer in its whole being anything other than a libation, a libation offered to God"; *Flight* 21, 166: the wise person "found wisdom at hand, descended from heaven in the rain. He inhaled it in pure form, took pleasure in it, and remained drunk with sober drunkenness"; *Good Man Free* 13; *Moses* 1.187; *Contemp. Life* 89. Texts commented on by H. Lewy, *Sobria Ebrietas*, Giessen, 1929.

[15] The wife in Cant shows her love: "I gave you perfumed wine to drink, the nectar of my pomegranates" (Cant 8:2); cf. Jer 16:7—"drink the cup of consolation."

πραγματεία, πραγματεύομαι

pragmateia, (civic or cultic) business; *pragmateuomai,* to tend to business, manage profitably

In the LXX, the noun and the verb are both used almost exclusively for royal and cultic matters.[1] *Pragmateia* retains the meaning of public business in the edict of Tiberius Julius Alexander, who, with respect to the farming of taxes (*telōneia*) and term leases (*misthōsis ousiakē*) acknowledges: "some harm to *ta pragmata* has resulted from the fact that many people without experience in such an activity (*toiautēs pragmateias*) have been compelled to undertake it" and orders: "It is fitting that those who are capable should carry out these activities (*pragmateuesthai*) of their own free will and with zeal."[2] But the broad meaning "occupation" (*UPZ* 9, 13;

---

[1] For building the house of Yahweh; 1 Kgs 9:1; 10:22 (Hebrew *ḥāšāq*, attach, link); 1 Chr 28:21; Dan 6:4; 8:27. The only exception, 2 Macc 2:31, where πραγματεία refers to the narration of events by the historian, as in Polybius 1.1.4; 1.3.1; Josephus, *Ant.* 1.5: ἐγκεχείρισμαι πραγματείαν; 14.218: οἱ ἀναγινώσκοντες τὴν πραγματείαν = the readers of this history; cf. Aristotle, *Ph.* 2.7.30.198ᵃ. In his *Géminos: Introduction aux phénomènes* (Paris, 1975, p. 203), G. Aujac establishes two meanings of this noun in the mathematician: "(1) a subject of studies (5.13), the manner in which a certain point is handled (8.55); (2) a treatise covering a certain question (5.24)." For the verb, cf. 6.9; 16.32.

[2] Dittenberger, *Or.* 669, 12–13 = *BGU* 1563 = *SB* 8444 (AD 68); cf. public function (*P.Oxy.* 3025, 9; letter of the *epistratēgos*, July 17, 118); *SB* 8393, 33 (letter of Diocletian to the inhabitants of Elephantine). But a commercial or personal matter: περὶ πραγματείας, ἧς καὶ ὡμολογήκεις μοι (ibid. 6713, 16; third century BC; cf. 9050, col. VI, 5; *P.Oxy.* 806, from 20 BC). Nevertheless, a πραγματευτής is not necessarily a merchant (*P.Lips.* 64, 30; *P.Oxy.* 1880, 5), but is often a steward, a "businessman" (*P.Oxy.* 3041, 7; 3048, 15, 18; *IGLS* 1098; *MAMA* VIII, 182, 9; 385), cf. L. Robert, *Hellenica*, vol. 10, p. 83; vol. 11–12; p. 291; *Etudes anatoliennes*, pp. 241, 263, 310. In the papyri, πραγματεῖαι sometimes means "functionaries" (*UPZ* 20, 42, 53; 110, 25–26; *P.Tebt.* 5, 143, 161 = *C.Ord.Ptol.* 53). Commenting on the title πραγματευτής given to Aurelius Lucius in *BGU* 2126, col. II, 1, J. D. Thomas distinguishes three possible meanings: landowner (*P.Brem.* 74; *P.Oxy.* 512, 1257, 2130, 2271, 2421, 2668; *P.Michael.* 23), an auxiliary official in the collecting of taxes (*P.Tebt.* 307, 357, 360, 580, 605, 607;

---

pragmateia, S 4230; *TDNT* 6.640–641; *EDNT* 3.144; *NIDNTT* 3.1155, 1158; MM 532; BAGD 697 ‖ *pragmateuomai,* S 4231; *TDNT* 6.641–642; *EDNT* 3.144; *NIDNTT* 3.1155, 1158; MM 532; L&N 57.197; BAGD 697

P.Mich. 174, 8; second century AD) is the definition in 2 Tim 2:4, which observes that no soldier involves himself in the affairs of this life (*empleketai tais tou biou pragmateiais*), conformably to the language of Philo, who uses *pragmateiai* for "the occupations that we live by."[3] In other worlds, the soldier on a campaign is engaged full-time, is on duty from morning to night and no longer occupies himself with working for his living. No other job demands such exclusive dedication to duty as that of the soldier.

The verb *pragmateuomai* can have the commonplace meanings "strive" (Plutarch, *Them.* 19.4; Josephus, *Ant.* 12.180), "give oneself over to one's pursuits" (Xenophon, *Cyr.* 2.4.26; Philo, *Flacc.* 57; *P.Oxy.* 2106, 16), "be busy about a matter" to bring it to completion (Philo, *Dreams* 1.53; *P.Tebt.* 812, 9). In the papyri, its most common meaning is "carry out a function."[4] When it is a private matter, the *pragmateuomenos* is a businessman or agent;[5] when it is public business, the participle describes the official (*P.Oxy.* 34, 2; *P.Hamb.* 168, *a* 12), especially in the royal administration[6] and specifically the tax collector;[7] all those who see to the king's business.

P.Oxy. 825, 2567; *P.Mert.* 15; *P.Princ.* 131; *P.Ross.Georg.* V, 61), a subordinate agent to the *procurator* of the tax department (*P.Oxy.* 2265; *P.Ross.Georg.* II, 26; *P.Panop.Beatty* 1, 210; "A Document Relating to the Estate of Claudia Isidora Reconsidered," in *JJP,* 1974, p. 241).

[3] Philo, *Moses* 2.211; "the activities that concern the earning and pursuing of the means of living" (2.219; cf. *Spec. Laws* 2.65); cf. *BGU* 1747, 20 (64 BC). Cf. the *epitropos* of the Thebaid, accusing before the *strategoi* the soldiers and sailors who were conducting business in the ports and the neighboring towns (*P.Panop.Beatty* 2, 102, πραγματευόμενοι); and Epictetus 3.24.36; Dio Chrysostom 3.66.

[4] *Gnomon of the Idios Logos* 70: "People who occupy a public office do not have the right to buy or to lend at interest in the places where they carry our their function" (ἐν οἷς πραγματεύονται τόποις).

[5] *P.Dura* 13 a, 9 (acting in a real estate purchase); *P.Mil.* 71, 16, 25 = *SB* 9264 (transformation of an ἄγραφος γάμος into an ἔγγραφος γάμος); 9090, 3; *Stud.Pal.* XX, 50, 23; *P.Stras.* 284, 23; Plutarch, *Sull.* 17.2: "Quintus Titius, a well-known businessman." In 4 BC, "an oath taken by the inhabitants of Paphlagonia and the Romans conducting business among them" (Dittenberger, *Or.* 532, 6 = F. Cumont, *Studia Pontica,* 66, who refers to many analogous formulas cited by Kornemann, *De Civibus Romanis in Prov. Consistentibus,* 1891, pp. 102ff.); cf. the oath from Assos: ἔδοχεν τῇ βουλῇ καὶ τοῖς πραγματευομένοις παρ' ἡμῖν Ῥωμαίοις καὶ τῷ δήμῳ τῶν Ἀσσίων (Dittenberger, *Syl.* 797, 10; AD 37).

[6] *P.Grenf.* II, 37, 4; *P.Hib.* 198, 141 and 149 (= *C.Ord.Ptol.* 11, 1 and 9); *P.Tebt.* 840, 1; 904, 3 (*C.Ord.Ptol.* 47, 5; cf. 62, 5); *UPZ* 106, 5; cf. 172, 2; *P.Mich.* 232, 1 and 22 (= *SB* 7568; cf. 9316, col. II, 15 = *C.Ord.Ptol.* 34); *SB* 9629, 6 and 9; *P.Rev.* col. XX, 15; *PSI* 1310, 27).

[7] *P.Tebt.* 350, 5 (AD 70); *P.Col.Zen.* 120, 12 = *C.Ord.Ptol.* 28, tax returns should be addressed to the tax farmer; *P.Hib.* 66, 2; *P.Mich.* 60, 2; *SB* 6275, 14: εἰς ἀνάλωμα τῷ πραγματευομένῳ (= *C.Ord.Ptol.* 25; cf. 17, 11; 18, 10 - *P.Rev.,* col. 36, 11; 37, 11); *P.Sorb.* 21, 7 and 17: director of the wool farms; cf. *O.Wilck.* I, 303.

Given on the one hand this title of nobility and financial specialization, and on the other hand the religious or cultic use of the verb in the LXX, we can see what an appropriate word this is in the parable of the ten minas: the nobleman gives ten minas to his servants, telling them, "Turn them to good account until I return" (*pragmateusasthe en hō erchomai*, Luke 19:13), i.e., put them to work earning returns in business or in the bank while I am away. The *douloi* here are not slaves, but free men, more specifically officials in the service of the claimant to the throne who must demonstrate their competence and faithfulness by drawing a profit from what they have received. The emphasis is on this exploiting, this turning to good account;[8] for this reason J. Dauvillier compared the parable to a provision in Sumero-Akkadian law,[9] namely 99 in the Code of Hammurabi: the contract "for selling, buying, and investing for profit."[10] *Ussâp*, from the verb *apasu*, "increase," is the distinctive element of the contract, referring to the profits to be made by the traveling agent who, in the course of his journeys will sell, then buy, then sell again and finally buy again; his enterprising spirit and his business acumen will allow him to realize considerable profits. So *pragmateuomai* means not "do business" but administrate, manage profitably the capital at your disposal.

---

[8] Cf. Luke 19:16—προσηργάσατο = yielded; verse 18: ἐποίησεν = produced; Matt 25:16—ἠργάσατο = bore fruit; ἐκέρδησεν = profited.

[9] J. Dauvillier, "La Parabole des mines ou des talents et le 99 du code de Hammurabi," in *Mélanges J. Magnol*, Paris, 1948, pp. 153–165. On the diffusion of Mesopotamian law in the first century, cf. J. Modrzejewski, "Note sur le P. Strasb. 237," in *Eos* (Symbolae R. Taubenschlag) 1957, vol. 3, pp. 149ff. R. Taubenschlag, *Opera Minora*, vol. 2, pp. 505–526.

[10] "If a businessman has given money to an agent to sell and buy and invest abroad, the traveling agent shall invest for profit the money that has been . . . to him [——]." Cf. οἱ πραγματευόμενοι Ῥωμαῖοι, Roman merchants, as a group, enjoying their own rights in the Greek world, in *I.Assos*, n. XIII, 1; XIV, 2; XIX, 1; XX, 1; XXI, 1; XXVI, 10; XXVII, 16.

πράκτωρ, σπεκουλάτωρ

praktōr, court officer; *spekoulatōr,* attending soldier or bodyguard available for special assignments

---

"The judge will hand you over to the agent, and the agent will throw you in prison."[1] The debtor here is one who would be wise to reach an amicable settlement with his creditor, because if the creditor files suit, the debtor will certainly be sent to prison for his debts. The carrying out of the judge's sentence is entrusted to the *praktōr,*[2] which is sometimes translated "police soldier" sometimes "court officer." Well-attested in Greece in the classical period,[3] this official is charged with collecting monetary fines at

---

[1] Luke 12:58—ὁ κριτής σε παραδώσει τῷ πράκτορι, καὶ ὁ πράκτωρ σε βαλεῖ εἰς φυλακήν. Cf. the inscription of the *astynomoi* at Pergamum: "The *astynomoi* shall conduct a hearing and pass sentence as seems right to them; if, even then, some (private persons) do not obey them, the *stratēgoi* shall impose the legal fine on them and entrust its collection to the *praktōr*" (παραδότωσαν τῷ πράκτορι πράσσειν, Dittenberger, *Or.* 483, 7); *P.Hal.* I, 126: μηδὲ ὁ πράκτωρ μηδὲ οἱ ὑπηρέται παραλαμβανέτωσαν τούτους. The link between ἀντίδικος and πράκτωρ, already seen in Demosthenes, *C. Theocr.* 58.20, is also found in *P.Oxy.* 533, 11, 23 (second-third century).

[2] Πράκτωρ is used only here in the NT, and only once in the OT, where it translates the Hebrew participle *nōgśîm,* "those who use force, compel, demand, treat roughly"; Isa 3:12—"O my people, your oppressors (πράκτορες) glean you."

[3] Andocides, *Myst.* 77, 79; Demosthenes, *C. Macart.* 43.71; *C. Theocr.* 58.20. 48 (cf. J. and L. Robert, "Bulletin épigraphique," in *REG,* 1942, p. 355, n. 144; 1958, p. 300, n. 396). In the inventory of the treasury of Athena at Imbros (published by *NCIG,* n. XXI, 4, 14), the three πράκτορες, who made up a commission, were financial controllers. They established the inventory of the property belonging to the sanctuary and did the appraisals. Similarly, the association of the μύσται of the god Mandros set up a commission of πράκτορες to gather the funds for the purchase of a chair for this association (*I.Cumae,* 37, 15 and 49). In Aeschylus, *Eum.* 319, the Erinyes appear as πράκτορες αἵματος to make the criminal pay his blood-debt; the *praktōr* is a

---

praktōr, S 4233; *TDNT* 6.642; *EDNT* 3.145; *NIDNTT* 3.1157; MM 533; L&N 37.92; BAGD 697 ‖ *spekoulatōr,* S 4688; *EDNT* 3.263; MM 582; L&N 20.70, 33.196; BDF §§5(1*b*), 109(8); BAGD 761

the demand of the magistrate who imposes them. A good parallel would be our bailiff, then our tax collector.[4] The office is copiously attested in the papyri from the Ptolemaic and Roman periods.[5]

Praktores appear very frequently in the papyri from the third century AD as agents of courts of justice, either as tax collectors and receivers or as executors of private debts.[6] In the former case: "Chrysippos, *praktōr*, asks that Asclepiades, son of Dorion, be forced to pay the (tax) money" (*P.Lille* 28, 13); in the latter, the complainant asks the *stratēgos* to make the *praktōr* intervene to recover what a certain Peithias owes him (*P.Magd.* 41, 5). Similarly, two tax collectors demand payment from Phileas for a debt of four silver drachmas (*P.Fay.* 14, 1; cf. *BGU* 530, 36). As a fiscal agent recovering debts owed the state, the *praktōr* is described as *praktōr tōn basilikōn* (*prosodōn; UPZ* 153, 12, 24; 154, 11; 155, 12; *SB* 1178 *a* 12; 3937, 12; *P.Petr.* III, 26, 14–15). As a collector of private debts, he is called *praktōr tōn idiōtikōn*,[7] but if *xenoi* (resident aliens) are involved, he is called *praktōr tōn xenikōn*. Thus in a royal ordinance of the second century BC relating to taxes on transactions: "On slaves sold by the executors of private debts (*xenikōn praktores*), the buyers shall pay 19 drachmas per 100, in addition to the action fee of 1 percent" (*P.Col.* 480, 15). Having been assaulted and struck by Peithias, a complainant—who cannot file a lawsuit—asks the king to write the *stratēgos* to send the *xenikos praktōr* to "make Peithias pay the price of his violence and give it to me" (*P.Enteux.* 74, 17; cf. *P.Flor.* 55, 26; *P.Oxy.* 1203, 11; *BGU* 1325, 40; 1826, 47; 1827, 24; *PSI* 1105, 8; *P.Fam.Tebt.* 29, 15, 41; *P.Tebt.* 5, 221). These agents are stationed in particular towns (*P.Lund* IV, 1, 10; *P.Corn.* 16, 20; *O.Mich.* 126, 2; *P.Hamb.* 80, 1; 81, 1, 8; 82, 4; 83, 5; cf. *P.Ryl.* 659, 7), at Memphis (*UPZ* 118, 1, 15, 24), at Oxyrhynchus (*PSI* 1328, 5, 19, 61), at Bacchias (*SB* 11106, 3–4); thus it is easy for them to draw up papers; otherwise, they move (*P.Mich.* 505, 8; *P.Cair.Zen.* 59499, 46: *ho praktōr elthen pōlōn auten; P.Tebt.* 21, 3–5; 35, 8; *SB* 7244, 37; 7376, 20).

---

watchful avenger (*Suppl.* 647; Aeschylus, *Ag.* 111). For the evolution of this institution according to the inscriptions, cf. H. Schaefer, "Πράκτωρ," in PW, vol. 22, 2, col. 2538–2548.

[4] In an act of donation from AD 87, the witness Pausanias is presented as εἰσαγωγεὺς καὶ πράκτωρ καὶ τῶν σωματοφυλάκων, i.e., bailiff, tax collector, member of the bodyguard (*P.Dura* 18, 10, 32; 19, 19).

[5] Cf. S. Plodzień, "The Origin and Competence of the ΠΡΑΚΤΩΡ ΞΕΝΙΚΩΝ," in *JJP*, vol. 5, 1951, pp. 217–227; J. Vergote, "Le Nouveau Testament et la papyrologie juridique," in *Eos* (Symbolae R. Taubenschlag), 1957, vol. 2, p. 153.

[6] *P.Hal.* I, 47, 54, 116, 119; *P.Cair.Zen.* 59136, 6; 59367, 9; 59460, 6, 12; 50490, 46, 53; *P.Col.* 480, 15; *P.Hamb.* 168 *a* 19; *P.Hib.* 30, 18,; 814, 2, 40. Cf. R. Taubenschlag, *Law of Greco-Roman Egypt*, pp. 401ff., 410, 416.

[7] *P.Col.Zen.* 54, 48; *P.Mich.Zen.* 71, 1; *P.Hib.* 34, 7; *SB* 7446, 1; 7450, 50.

When the *praktōr* collects taxes in kind, he is *praktōr sitikōn;*[8] for taxes payable in money, he is *praktōr argyrikōn.*[9] But these taxes or imposts are almost beyond numbering.[10] Thus there are *praktores dēmosiōn* (*P.Ryl.* 141, 6), *laographias* (*BGU* 1892, 75; *P.Mich.* 582, 16; *P.Alex.* 16, 2, 11; *P.Ryl.* 595, 1 and 189; from AD 57; *P.Col.* I, recto, 1 *a-b; SB* 1026, 15; cf. W. L. Westermann, C. W. Keyes, *Tax Lists and Transportation Receipts from Theadelphia,* New York, 1932, pp. 3ff. *O.Oslo* 8, 3; 10, 3), *politikōn* (*PSI* 776, 2; *P.Oxy.* 1419, 2), *hierōn* (*P.Eleph.* 17, 5; 25, 2); *metropolitikōn* (*P.Oxy.* 1538, 18), *stephanikōn* (*aurum coronarium; BGU* 62; 362, 542; 548; *P.Lond.* 474, 477; *PSI* 733, 5 and 38; *P.Stras.* 199, 2; *SB* 10293, 16; *P.Oxy.* 1441, 1), *balaneiou* (*BGU* 362; *P.Rein.* 130; *SB* 10424, 1, from July 2, AD 65), *annōnas oxou* (*P.Mich.* 390, 4), *ousiakōn* (for the lands attached to estates, *P.Mich.* 599, 1), *gerdiakou* (the tax on weavers),[11] *elaiou* (*P.Tebt.* 119, 54), *geōmetrias* (*P.Rein.* 134, 3; *O.Wilb.* 35–39), *chōmatikou* (tax on dikes, *P.Sorb.* 65, 1), *naubiou* (*P.Fam.Tebt.* 35, 4; *P.Oxf.* 9, 5), etc.

Obvoiusly one official could not carry out all these tasks;[12] so there were not only associates who together with him formed a board in a given locality—*hoi metochoi praktores*[13]—but also numerous subordinates:

---

[8] *BGU* 414; 425, 457, 515; 2063; 12; *SB* 11025, 15; *P.Oxy.* 1196; 2235, 19: "No tax has ever been paid to the *praktores* for this land"; *O.Mich.* 25, 2: Αὐρήλιος Ὧρος καὶ Κοπρίων πράκτορες σιτικῶν κώμης Φιλαδελφίας; cf. *O.Aberd.* (ed. G. Turner) n. 22, 3; 31, 1; *O.Brüss.Berl.* (ed. P. Viereck), n. 8, 5; 65, 1.

[9] *BGU* 15; 25; 41; 42; 1891, 467; *PSI* 1236, 6; *P.Mil.Vogl.* 183, 4; 237, 5; *P.Oslo* 29, 2; 116, 2; *P.Sorb.* 66, 1: "Apollonides and Antonios, cash tax collectors of Notos" give a receipt for the payment of taxes in cash; *P.Stras.* 188, 2; 195, 3; *P.Fam.Tebt.* 39, 11; *P.Corn.* 16, 3; 42, 3; *SB* 11259; 11245; *P.Wisc.* 42, 3 (cf. 38, 1: λόγος πρακτορείας; *C.P.Herm.* 22, 1; H. C. Youtie, *Scriptiunculae,* vol. 1, p. 407, n. 29); *O.Ont.Mus.* II, 100–126, 130, 149, 202, 214; cf. n. 224: ἀχυροπράκτορες.

[10] Cf. the tax rolls from Karanis; *P.Mich.* IV, 224, 6332, 6333, 6343, 6388, 6402, 6417; S. L. Wallace, *Taxation in Egypt,* Princeton, 1938 (index, p. 506); *O.Bodl.* III (index, pp. 197–199).

[11] *P.Mich.* 598, 2; from AD 49. In 91, the death certificate for a weaver-slave is addressed not to the βασιλικὸς γραμματεύς (*P.Mert.* 9; *BGU* 2021, 2087; *P.Phil.* 6; *P.Petaus* 4–9), nor to the γραμματεῖς μητροπόλεως (*P.Mich.* 579; *P.Oxy.* 2564, 2761; *P.Stras.* 528, 530; *P.Mert.* 84), nor to the κωμογραμματεύς (*P.Stras.* 200, 306, 312, 522; *P.Mich.* 538; *P.Phil.* 7; *BGU* 2331; *P.Petaus* 3), but to the πράκτορες χειρωναξίου γερδίων (*P.Oxy.* 2957, 1); this is because the deceased is a taxpayer, cf. W. Brashear, "P. Sorb. inv. 2358 and the New Statistics on Death Certificates," in *BASP,* vol. 14, 1977, p. 8.

[12] In AD 185, to help the πράκτορες ἀργυρικῶν, who did not have the personnel to collect all the numerous taxes, the *stratēgos* of the Arsinoite nome appoints four assistants to this *leitourgia* (*P.Mich.* 536).

[13] *O.Mich.* 7, 5; *P.Oslo* 116, 2; *P.Princ.* 125, 4; 130; 18; *P.Fam.Tebt.* 39, 3; *P.Fouad* 66, 4; *P.Alex.* 16, 2, 11; 124 (p. 28), 464 (p. 29); *P.Corn.* 16, 3; 42, 3; *P.Hamb.* 81, 1, 8; 82, 4; 83, 5; cf. *P.Mich.* 647, 4: οἱ κοινωνοὶ πράκτωρες. In the second century, at Tebtunis,

cheiristai (*SB* 9203, 4; 9237, 1, 9, 25; *BGU* 345), *grammateis* (secretary, scribe, or clerk; *P.Sorb.* 65, 2; *P.Kroll* 2, 12), *boēthoi* (*O.Mich.* 6, 4: Hermogenes *boēthos tōn praktorōn*) and especially the *hypēretai*, who are by far the most commonly mentioned. These are often portrayed as assistants or adjuncts of the *praktōr* with the power to represent him and act in his name,[14] hence having the same powers. In Matt 5:25, a parallel text to Luke 12:58, the judge hands over the recalcitrant debtor to a "beadle" or bailiff who has him incarcerated: *ho kritēs tō hypēretē* (cf. *UPZ* 118, 18, *tou kritēriou hypēretēs*). But the very term *hypēretēs* indicates that this is an underling, a subordinate officer.[15] Furthermore, the *hypēretēs* is almost anonymous, whereas the *praktōr* is almost always named,[16] because he is the titled officer. Finally, it is always mentioned that the action is done *dia praktorōn* (*P.Erl.* 48, 31; *P.Lond.* 2016, 9; *P.Brem.* 43 r 20, 29; *P.Bon.* 33, 4; *SB* 7196 r, col. VI, 13; v col. IV, 16; 8972, 2, 5, 8) or *meta praktorsi* (*P.Erl.* 105, 86) and that the debtors address and pay only them,[17] whereas these expressions are never used with *hypēreteis*. In short, *hypēreteis* act on the orders of their superiors: *hypēretēs ho para tou praktoros* (*P.Hamb.* 168, *a* 19; third century BC).

Obviously, these tax collectors were not always tenderhearted folk, and sometimes they abused the modest circumstances (*metriotēs*) of those subject to them (*P.Ryl.* 659, 7); the latter are rightly or wrongly "disturbed" by their investigations and lodge complaints (*P.Lond.* 2008, 7; third century BC; cf. *P.Cair.Zen.* 59460). Abuses are inevitable (*PSI* 1160, 8). Sometimes it even happened that with the connivance of his secretary or the town secretary the *praktōr* tried to rip off a taxpayer (*Pap.Lugd.Bat.* XIII, 22, 7,

the μέτοχοι πράκτορσι collected the φόρος ἐδαφῶν on a tract of land (*P.Mil.Vogl.* 283, 2 and 7).

[14] *P.Hal.* I, 147: ὁ πράκτωρ ἢ ὁ ὑπηρέτης (a complaint against the depositions of false witnesses); lines 54, 116: ὁ πράκτωρ ἢ ὁ ὑπηρέτης πραξάτω καθάπερ ἐγ δίκης ἐκ τῶν ὑπαρχόντων; line 119 (a complaint against assaults).

[15] *Ep. Arist.* 111. In *P.Mich.* 505, 4–6, where the ὑπηρετής and the πράκτωρ intervene, the former is only a bank clerk who gives a sum of money to the latter: δεδωκέναι τῷ πράκτορι ὡς ἵνα σοι μεταβάληται. But αὐτοὺς τοὺς πράκτορας μετὰ καὶ τοῦ ὑπηρέτου (*SB* 7529, 15).

[16] *P.Mil.Vogl.* 183 *a* 11: Τρύφων πράκτωρ; 237, 5: Ἥρωονος πράκτωρ ἀργυρικῶν; *BGU* 1851, 5: Ζωίλῳ πράκτορι; *P.Cair.Zen.* 59367, 9: Κράτωνα τὸν πράκτορα; *P.Rein.* 130, 6: Petemenophis the collector (AD 35); 134, 1: Chesmois, cash tax collector; 136, 1: Asclas and Soter; 137, 1; *P.Ryl.* 595, 1: Nemesionos (AD 57); *UPZ* 153, 12, 14: Onomarchos; etc.

[17] *P.Oxy.* 2140, 7; *P.Mich.* 383, 3, 17, 21; *P.Princ.* 70, 11: ἔδωκας τοῖς πράκτορσιν λόγον (cf. H. C. Youtie, *Scriptiunculae*, vol. 2, pp. 891, 894); *P.Petr.* 13, 17, 6: παραγέγραμμαι τῷ πράκτορι ὡς ὀφείλων πρὸς τὰ ἀμπελικά; *P.Fam.Tebt.* 26, 3, 9; *BGU* 530, 36 (first century AD). Cf. the receipts from πράκτορες: *BGU* 1891, 2, 467; 2028, 3, 7; 2067, 6; 2103, 4; 2288, 3; 2289, 5; 2290, 6; *P.Fay.* 35; 42; 47; 51; 53–55, etc.

10, 16; *P.Mert.* 8, 19). But normally these court officers had the responsibility of carrying out judicial sentences;[18] their functioning was strictly limited. For example, an ordinance of Ptolemy Euergetes II in 121–118 BC: "The collectors of private debts (*tous tōn xenikōn praktoras*) shall not arrest the royal farmers or their subordinate workers, nor the other subjects who according to earlier ordinances cannot be enslaved, under any pretext" (*P.Tebt.* 5, 222; cf. *P.Rein.* 18, 39–42). Already in the third century BC, *P.Hal.* I, 126 forbids the *praktōr* and his assistants from arresting members of the privileged classes (royal emissaries, etc.): *mēde ho praktōr mēde hoi hypēretai paralambanetōsan toutous*. During the time of Claudius or Nero, someone declares "he never gave an armed guard to a tax collector" (*oudeni dedōken tois praktōrois machairōphoron, P.Mich.* 577, 7).

Nevertheless, as we can see from Luke 12:58, it was indeed the *praktōr* to whom the magistrate gave the arrest warrant (cf. *P.Oslo* 20, 3; *P.Tebt.* 34) so as to put the debtor in prison (*desmōtērion*).[19] It is surprising that imprisonment for debts was contemplated at this time, since an ordinance of Ptolemy VI Philometor or Ptolemy V Epiphanes (163 or 186 BC) had forbidden the practice, though only in Egypt:[20] "None of the *stratēgoi, epistatai, epimeletai,* tax collectors, . . . or other officials who manage the affairs of the king, the cities, and the temples shall arrest anyone for a private debt or offense or out of personal animosity" (*SB* 9316, col. II, 12). But was this execution of a writ against the person of the debtor ever actually suppressed? Not only do we see the practice eventually accepted by borrowers in the first century BC (*P.Oxy.* 1639, 16–17; *P.Yale* 60, 12–13; from the year 6–5) and actually carried out in AD 23 (*P.Oxy.* 259), but in 68, the edict of the prefect of Egypt, Tiberius Julius Alexander, has to intervene once again because of the imprisonment of debtors and reserve the *praktoreion* for debtors to the state alone: "As certain ones, under the pretext of serving the interests of the state, have had outstanding debts payable to others transferred to themselves and have imprisoned certain people in the *praktoreian* and in other prisons (*kai eis allas phylakas*), which I have heard were closed precisely in order that the recovery of debts should

---

[18] *P.Lips.* 120; *P.Oxy.* 712; *BGU* 970; 1038; *UPZ* 118; *P.Tebt.* 707; *P.Mert.* 59. Cf. R. Sugranyes de Franch, *Etudes sur le droit palestinien à l'époque évangélique,* Fribourg, 1926, pp. 51ff.

[19] *BGU* 1138, 12, 14 (twelfth year of Augustus); cf. *P.Mich.* 383, 8 (from AD 106–109). The πρακτόρειον was originally the place where the πράκτωρ worked, before it became a prison; cf. at Mylasa ἐμβάλλεσθαι εἰς τὸ πρακτόρειον (Dittenberger, *Or.* 515, 32). At Theadelphia, in AD 3–4, the πράκτωρ is accompanied by a guard, τὸν φυλακείτην (*P.Mert.* 8, 19).

[20] Cf. C. Préaux, *Economie royale,* pp. 537–543. The Rosetta Stone (Dittenberger, *Or.* XC, 13–14).

be carried out against property, not persons. . . . I order that in no case shall free men be incarcerated in any prison whatsoever (*eis phylakēn hēntinoun*), unless they are criminals, nor in the *praktoreion*, except for debtors to the imperial treasury."[21] These liberal measures must have been unknown in first-century Palestine.[22]

The *spekoulatōr* occasionally appears together with the *telōnēs* and the *praktōr* in accounts from the second century AD (*P.Cair.Goodsp.* 30, col. VII, 31; cf. real estate registries from the fourth century, *P.Flor.* 71, 652, 763, 811). This official also carried out the functions of the tax collector in the fourth century, as in this sworn declaration: "To Valerius . . . apion, *spekoulatōr* and gold and silver tax collector" (*spekoulatori apaitētē chrysou kai asēmou*, *P.Cair.Isid.* 127, 1; *P.Mich.* 644, 13). Hence the complaints about harrassing investigations in connection with the *embolē tou sitou* (*P.Oslo* 88, 20; *P.Oxy.* 1223, 21) and even outright accusations (*CPR* V, 2, n. 12, 4). This person is in effect an official with wide-ranging responsibilities (*P.Ross.Georg.* V, 61, 61 A verso 2ff.; cf. I, 17, 22; *P.Oxy.* 3079, 6) and rather high in rank, since one is seen, still in the fourth century, addressing to the chief of police of Taampemou an order to immediately provide an ass and a guard to the sentinal he has sent to him (*P.Oxy.* 1193, 1). This appears to be a superior officer: "I handed you over to my lord Halladius, but also to my master Hesychius the *spekoulatōr*" (*parathemēn de se kai tō kyriō mou Helladiō, alla kai tō despotē mou Hēsychiō tō spekoulatori*, *P.Oslo* 59, 9). He is associated with the *eparchos* (*P.Oxy.* 1223, 21), with the *dēmosioi iatroi* (*P.Harr.* 133), and with the *frumentarii*.[23] He may have a certain amount of wealth,[24] or at least freedom of action. In the fifth century, the *spekoulatōr* Gennadios invites "his lord Makarios" to dinner to celebrate the birth of his son (*P.Oxy.* 1214, 1). His dignity is apparent in the Lebanese inscription dedicated to the health and victory of the reigning sovereigns by "Severa . . . wife of Theodoros, former *spekoulatōr*" (*apo spekoulatoros*, *IGLS* 2980; cf. *P.Mich.* 469, 24; *P.Laur.* 42, 4).

---

[21] Dittenberger, *Or.* 669, 15–18 = *SB* 8444. G. Chalon, *T. Julius Alexander*, pp. 115ff.

[22] Cf. the parable of the Unforgiving Servant (Matt 18:23–35), who "cast his debtor in prison (ἔβαλεν αὐτὸν εἰς φυλακήν) until he should pay what he owed" (verse 30); but the Master hands him over to the torturers (παρέδωκεν αὐτὸν τοῖς βασανισταῖς). Cf. C. Spicq, *Dieu et l'homme*, pp. 54–61; J. Modrzejewski, "Servitude pour dettes ou legs de créance (Note sur CP Jud. 126)," in *RechPap*, vol. 2, Paris, 1962, pp. 75–98.

[23] *P.Mich.* 472, 16; *CIL* VI, 3358; cf. Fiebiger, "Frumentarii," in *PW*, vol. 7, col. 123; F. Lammert, "Speculatores," ibid., series II, vol. 3 A 2, col. 1583–1586.

[24] Cf. *P.Cair.Isid.* 32, 9: grain receipt from the third century, in the name of Ptolemaeus and Thaisarion, son of Penerates the *spekoulatōr*; *P.Erl.* 105, 34 (fourth-century accounts).

Such are the features of this personage, unknown in the LXX, that can be drawn from the papyri, all rather late. None of this matches the name of the office (Hellenized from the Latin *speculator*) or the picture in Mark 6:27 of a low-ranking underling: "The king (Herod), immediately sent a guard (*spekoulatora*). . . . He went and decapitated him (John) in the prison, brought the head on a platter, and gave it to the young woman." Etymologically, a *speculator* is one who looks (from afar), observes,[25] then a scout, spy, explorer;[26] finally, one who brings news, a messenger, courier.[27] Since these men are always near the prince, waiting for his mail to be ready, they become bodyguards (Tacitus, *Hist.* 2.11; Suetonius, *Claud.* 35) and are called upon to perform quite varied services. In the imperial army, the *speculatores* perform different functions than in the pretorian guard (*CIL* III, 1650); they are attached to the headquarters staff of the provincial governor,[28] under the orders of an *optio* (*CIL* 14137[1]) with the rank of *principalis.* In a given legion (*CIL* VI, 3358: "speculator exercitus Britannici") they constituted a "schola speculatorum" (ibid. III, 3524).

As underlings who were available for all sorts of assignments, *spekoulatōres* could carry out an execution. M. J. Lagrange[29] compares Mark 6:27 to the Hebrew *rāṣîm*, runner-bodyguards who sometimes served as executioners; thus "the king (Saul) said to the runners who were with him, 'Turn around and put to death the priests of Yahweh' " (1 Sam 22:17; cf. 2 Kgs 10:25). This meaning of *speculator* is current in the first century in Latin authors: "The centurion in charge of the execution ordered the guard to sheathe his sword (*condere gladium speculatorem jubet*) and led the prisoner back" (Seneca, *Ira* 1.18.4); "During the civil war, a master who was on the list of the proscribed was hidden by his slave, who put the rings of the condemned man on his fingers and his clothing on his back. He presented himself thus to the police (*speculatoribus occurrit*), saying that he

---

[25] Pliny, *HN* 11.8.8; Cicero, *Nat. D.* 2.140; Livy 31.24.

[26] Caesar, *BGall.* 1.47.6; 2.11.2; 5.49.8; Livy 28.2. Cf. Ps.-Aristotle, *Mund.* 6.398 *a:* "slaves of the king, couriers and spies (ἡμεροδρόμοι τε καὶ σκοποί), messengers, and men who watch for signals."

[27] *CIL* 5.271; *Bell. Afr.* 31.4: "in praetorio dedens per speculatores et nuntios imperabat"; Tacitus, *Hist.* 2.73; Suetonius, *Calig.* 44; Livy 40.7. On these imperial couriers cf. "Essai sur le cursus publicus sous le haut-empire romain," in *Mémoires . . . Académie des Inscriptions et Belles-Lettres,* vol. 14, 1940, pp. 327–336.

[28] *BGU* 2332, 6 (deed of sale in the fourth century): Aurelius Hol receives from Flavius Adelphos, *spekoulatōr* of the prefect's *officium* in the province of Augustamnica (σπεκουλάτωρι τάξεως ἡγεμονίας Αὐγουσταμνικῆς), an advance payment of 12,000 talents of silver for wine. It seems that these *spekoulatōrs* functioned as quartermasters.

[29] *Evangile selon saint Marc,* p. 162.

asked nothing more than that they should carry out their orders and stretched out his neck to them" (Seneca, *Ben.* 3.25). So also in the acts of the martyrs. At the moment of his execution, St. Paul prayed in Hebrew, and while he was praying, "as the *spekoulatōr* relieved him of his head, milk spurted into the soldier's garments" (*hōs de apetinaxen autou ho spekoulatōr tēn kephalēn, gala epytisen eis tous chitōnas tou stratiōtou, Mart. Paul* 5; ed. Lipsius, p. 115, 17). In the *Acts of Appian,* the *spekoulatōr* could be a *speculator Augusti,* i.e., a member of the imperial bodyguards, chosen from the pretorian cohort.[30]

So we must classify the *spekoulatōr* of Mark 6:27, a biblical hapax, as one of the Latinisms of the Second Gospel.[31]

---

[30] H. A. Musurillo, *Pagan Martyrs,* p. 213.

[31] Like κεντυρίων (Mark 15:39, 44, 45), λεγιών (5:9, 15), δηνάριον (6:37; 12:15; 14:5), κοδράντης (12:42), ξέστης (7:4), etc.

πραϋπάθεια, πραΰς, πραΰτης

praypatheia, moderation, mildness, leniency; *prays*, moderate, mild, lenient; *praytēs*, moderation, mildness, leniency

These terms, which have no etymology, are used relatively little in the inscriptions and are exceptional in the papyri; they belong to the literary language, where they have a rather curious semantic evolution. To be sure, their meaning has to do with mildness, but that definition is rather loose.[1]

Praos, a word that is not found in Homer, appears for the first time in Herodotus, but it is the verb *praynō* that is originally most used. In Ps.-Homer, *H. Hermes* 1.417, Apollo, who is angry, lets himself be calmed by the lyre;[2] in Hesiod, patient mules are tamed (Hesiod, *Op.* 797; *Th.* 254).

---

[1] The major study on the question is that of J. de Romilly, *La Douceur dans la pensée grecque*, Paris, 1970, who gives a comparative analysis of *philanthrōpia*, *sōphrosynē*, *syngnōmē*, *epieikēs*, *ēpios*, and observes at the outset that in the subjective sense, "mild" (or gentle or sweet, French *doux*) is the opposite of "bitter" (Fr. *amer*) and is synonymous with "pleasant" (Fr. *agréable*; the sweetness of living, of seeing the light); as a human attitude it is the opposite of violence, harshness, and cruelty. In the sphere of ethics, "mildness means kindness of manners, benevolence shown toward others. . . . Toward the unfortunate, it becomes close to generosity and goodness; toward the guilty it becomes leniency and understanding; toward the unknown, people in general, it becomes humaneness and almost charity! In political life, likewise, it can be tolerance, or again, clemency, depending on whether one is dealing with citizens, or with subjects, or with conquered people. At the root of these various meanings, there is nevertheless a single disposition to accept others as those who are wished well" (p. 1).

[2] Ps.-Homer, *H. Ares* 10 (actually an Orphic hymn of the fourth-fifth century AD): "From on high shed your mild brightness on our lives." An inscription from Lebadaea in the third century honors the mildness of Artemis (*IG* VII, 3101). Hymn to Isis (first-third century): Ἐγὼ πραΰνω καὶ κυμαίνω θάλασσαν (*I.Cumae*, n. 41, 43).

---

praypatheia, TDNT 5.939; EDNT 3.146; MM 534; L&N 88.59; BAGD 698 ‖ *prays*, S 4239; TDNT 6.645–651; EDNT 3.146–147; NIDNTT 2.256–264; MM 534; L&N 88.60; BDF §§26, 47(4); BAGD 698–699 ‖ *praytēs*, S 4240; TDNT 6.645–651; EDNT 3.146–147; NIDNTT 2.256–259; MM 534; L&N 88.59; BDF §§26, 47(4); BAGD 699; ND 4.170

Xerxes seeks to calm his team (Aeschylus, *Pers.* 190; cf. Xenophon, *Eq.* 9.10: calm a horse); Darius counsels Atossa to calm their son with gentle words.[3] In medicine, *praynō* expresses the diminution of evil: "the fever lessened."[4]

In the classical period, *praotēs*, a calm and soothing disposition, is contrasted with rage and savagery (Plato, *Symp.* 197 *d*). It implies moderation (Aristotle, *Eth. Nic.* 1125 *b*), which permits reconciliation (Chilon, in Stobaeus 4.7.24; vol. 4, p. 255). Solon makes it a precept: "Be mild toward your own" (*pros isthi*, Stobaeus 3.1.72; vol. 3, p. 115). Hero is a beneficent sovereign who is "full of mildness toward the citizens" (Pindar, *Pyth.* 3.71); and for the first time the kindnesses of this quality are specified: Jason, exuding affable words with a mild voice, set forth the bases of a conciliating debate (*Pyth.* 4.136). The *praotēs* of the Spartan general Brasidas gained everyone's sympathy.[5]

In the orators, *praotēs* becomes a leniency and an indulgence—which is not without naivete—that is characteristic of the natural goodness of the Athenians.[6] Andocides, for example, owes his impunity to the Athenians and their lack of leisure (Lysias, *C. Andoc.* 34); "The leniency of your character, Athenians, gives great help to the guilty" (Demosthenes, *C. Mid.* 184; cf. *Embassy* 104; *C. Timocr.* 51); "Will their impudent and criminal acts find leniency with you?"[7] This forbearance, which implies mutual aid

---

[3] Aeschylus, *Pers.* 837; cf. Herodotus 2.121 δ: he pretended to calm down; 2.181: "unless the anger of Amasis was softened."

[4] Hippocrates, *Epid.* 7.118; Aretaeus, *SD* 1, 2, 3, for those who suffer with migraines, "darkness lessens their pain" (cf. N. van Brock, *Vocabulaire médical*, p. 211). Cf. Prov 18:14—"A man's spirit sustains him (πραΰνει; pilpel of the Hebrew *kûl*) when he is ill." The adjective *praos* is used in this sense by Plato: children ask a physician to care for them as gently as possible (*Lg.* 4.720 *a*). Philo (*Sacr. Abel and Cain* 121) compares the wise person's stance toward the wicked to that of a physician who "softens" a patient's pain; *Unchang. God* 65. The epitaph of Cosmas, a Cretan veterinarian, presents himself as ὡς ἀληθῶς πρᾷος καὶ ἡσύχιος ἀνήρ (*I.Cret.* II, p. 100, n. 8).

[5] Thucydides 4.108.3; cf. Aristophanes, *Pax* 934: "Let them be mild-spirited (ἤπιοι). So we shall be lambs for each other, and with our allies more accommodating (πραότεροι)"; 998: "a sweetening leniency," substituting for violence, can unite the Greeks. Euripides, *Bacch.* 436, compares Dionysus to a dangerous animal who shows himself to be tame (*praos*).

[6] Isocrates, *Antid.* 20: the Athenians, "the most merciful and mildest of all men," 300.

[7] Demosthenes, *C. Timocr.* 170; cf. 218: "To be indulgent toward such individuals . . . would be to habituate and instruct in crime the vast majority among you"; Aristotle, *Ath. Pol.* 22.4: "the habitual *praytēs*" of the Athenians permitted the supporters of the tyrants to stay when the tyrants themselves were ostracized; Polybius 1.72.2–3: the Carthaginians do not name as governors those who act toward

between associates,[8] is the mark and the virtue of a political regime: "In a democracy, there is more mildness (than in an oligarchy)";[9] laws are rigorously established, but "in punishment there is more leniency than the laws ordain."[10] Also, *praotēs* is synonymous with "moderation";[11] it makes rulers more accommodating and humane.[12] "I want to urge you . . . to try mildness and humaneness. . . . Harshness (*chalepotēs*) is painful for those who practice it and those who suffer it; *praotēs* is well esteemed with humans and all other living beings" (Isocrates, *Phil.* 116); it "mellows" all relations (Isocrates, *Paneg.* 47; cf. 102; Xenophon, *Cyr.* 2.1.29) between citizens (Plato, *Resp.* 2.375 c) even while it remains implacable toward enemies (*Tim.* 18 a). Thus *praotēs* spreads throughout the land (Isocrates, *Evag.* 49, 67; *Hel.* 37) and even adversaries are won over (Xenophon, *Ages.* 1.1.20). In AD 41, Emperor Claudius asks the Alexandrians to live with the Jews in mutual kindness: "If both sides will abstain from these things and live with mildness and philanthropy toward each other" (*ean toutōn apostantes amphoteroi meta praotētos kai philanthrōpeias tēs pros allēlous zēn ethelēsēte, P.Lond.* 1912, 101).

Since *praotēs* is opposed to roughness and severity, corrects violence and the excesses of tyranny, and moves judges and the powerful to clemency, it became a constant epithet for the emperor, kings, and high officials. Agrippa considered it to be a trait of royalty more than a virtue (Josephus, *Ant.* 19.334). Plato attributed it to the kings of Atlantis (*Critias* 120 e);

---

their citizens "with mildness and humaneness"; much different is the *praotēs* of the Romans (3.98–99; 28.3.2).

[8] H. Bolkestein, *Wohltätigkeit und Armenpflege im vorchristlichen Altertum*, Utrecht, 1939, pp. 108–109.

[9] Demosthenes, *C. Andr.* 51; cf. *C. Timocr.* 163; Isocrates, *Areop.* 67: "No one could praise the leniency of those people more than that of the democracy"; 20; *Panath.* 56: "These facts establish how much more moderate and mild we have shown ourselves in the practice of political affairs"; *Nic.* 2.8; 3.16–17, 32; *Antid.* 70: "the mildest of all regimes"; Plato (*Resp.* 8.558 a) notes that in a democracy certain convicted criminals freely circulate in public, as if no one cared about them or saw them.

[10] Isaeus, in Stobaeus 4.7.25; vol. 4, p. 255; cf. Plato, *Leg.* 9.867 b: for murders committed in anger but without premeditation, milder penalties must be inflicted (τιμωρίαι πραότεραι).

[11] Isocrates, *Panath.* 56: "We have shown ourselves much more moderate and mild (μετριώτερον καὶ πραότερον) in the practice of political affairs"; 121; *Antid.* 125, Timothy treated the cities taken by force with greater mildness and faithfulness than any other allied city showed; *Ep. 7 ad Tim.* 5 and 12.

[12] Demosthenes, *Chers.* 33: "You political men ought to have accustomed yourselves to being πράους καὶ φιλανθρώπους"; Aristophanes, *Pax* 936: "we shall be lambs for each other, and more accommodating with our allies."

Agesilaus was indulgent toward private offenses and very mild toward his friends (Xenophon, *Ages.* 11.6.10; cf. 2). At Syracuse, Hiero II "settled the situation with such moderation (*praos*) and generosity that the Syracusans . . . made him their general" (Polybius 1.8.4). Ptolemy VI Philometor, more than anyone else, was mild and good (Polybius 39.7.3; with Philip V, this meekness was a mere facade, 10.26.1). Demetrius had "a certain *praotēs* that drew all hearts toward him" (Diodorus Siculus 19.81.4; cf. 11.67.3). According to Philodemus of Gadara, the *praotēs* of the good king, who does not take vengeance for plots, wins sympathy.[13]

With Plato and Aristotle the contours of *praotēs* come into focus. The former sees it as a quality of the good person (*Leg.* 5.731 *d*); the latter makes it a virtue, contrasting it with wrath and vengeance; the *praos* is inclined to forgive (*Eth. Nic.* 4.11.1125^{b}ff.; *Rh.* 2.3.1380$^{a;}$ Ps.-Aristotle, *Mag. Mor.* 2.7.1108^{a}6). *Praotēs* is without hatred and spitefulness (Plato, *Resp.* 6.500 *a*) and moderates the punishment of offenses (*Leg.* 9.863 *d*). But—and this is a notable innovation—the *praos* keeps his serenity in all the misfortunes that come his way, bearing them calmly and patiently: the wise man, if he happens to lose a son, a brother, wealth, "bears it as mildly as possible."[14] In a privileged fashion, the teacher learns *praotēs*

---

[13] *Hom.* 7.12–16. One cannot fail to attribute *praotēs* to Pompey (Plutarch, *Pomp.* 33.2), Alexander (*Alex.* 58.7–8), Agis (*Agis* 21.5), Aristides (*Arist.* 23.1), Cimon (*Cimon* 6.2), Flamininus (*Flam.* 6.2), Lycurgus (*Lyc.* 28.13), Timoleon (*Tim.* 3.4; 37.6), Brutus (*Brut.* 30.6), Caesar and Augustus (Dio Cassius 43.20; 53.6; cf. Josephus, *War* 6.383: Titus, διὰ πρᾳότητα, welcomed fugitives; *Ant.* 17.212; Archelaus) and other notables. At Amorgos, a man is praised for his *kosmiētēs* and *praotēs* (*IG* XII, 7, 240), like Anicetus in Phrygia (*MAMA* I, 237), Lucius Antonius at Aphrodisias (*MAMA* VIII, 524, 7). At Pergamum, Aelius Isidorus is ὁ πρᾷος ἰδίαι, mild in his private life (*IGRom.* IV, 504); at Megara, a young man who is "mild (*praos*) and kindhearted [is] beloved by all" (*IG* VII, 115–117; Kaibel, 462). In the sixth century AD, Theodorus is "mild, naturally generous, accommodating" (*Anth. Pal.* VII, 606 = *GVI*, n. 485); cf. C. Panagopoulos, *Vocabulaire*, pp. 216–222. L. Robert (*Hellenica*, vol. 4, Paris, 1948, p. 16; vol. 11–12, p. 551; pp. 223ff.) mentions Praos as a proper name at Athens in the fourth century, and also several personal names formed on this root (*IG* II², 1928, 20; VII, 600).

[14] Plato, *Resp.* 3.387 *e*; cf. Plato, *Lysis* 211 *e*; *Menex.* 249 *c*; *Crito* 43 *b*: Socrates has always had an even temper in his past life, but "never so much as in this present misfortune (imprisonment) . . . with such calmness, such mildness (ῥαδίως . . . πράως) you endure it." Cf. Xenophon, *An.* 1.5.14: "He spoke tranquilly (πράως) of what he had suffered"; Epictetus 3.10.6: bear events with patience; 2.22.36; 4.7.12; Josephus, *Ant.* 5.167; 7.117; Plutarch, *Dem.* 22.3, after a bereavement, "to bear such losses with mildness and serenity"; *Per.* 34.1, "bore unpopularity and hatred calmly and in silence"; 39.1; *Cat. Mai.* 24.10, who "bore the death of his eldest son with calm and philosophy"; *De adul. et am.* 57 *e*; *De cohib. ira* 13.462 *a*: Nero endured the loss of the ship with more moderation; *De frat. amor.* 11.484 *b*: when Athenodorus had suffered great prejudice, he showed neither indignation nor regret, but bore his brother's folly

by remaining patient in the face of the errors and objections of his interlocutors: "Only put more mildness into your teaching so as not to force me to abandon it."[15]

Menander shows how Cnemon, who is awkward and surly (chalepos, dyskolos), became accommodating; his praotēs is the victory of goodwill.[16] But in Plutarch "praotēs has the place of honor" to an exceptional degree, as J. de Romilly puts it.[17] He praises it in almost all his heroes and states that "deliberateness and mildness are the essential qualities of the states-man and are passed on to him by reason and education" (Cor. 15.4). Nicocles had said, "Temperament alone does not make sovereigns severe or mild. . . . Have less confidence in my mildness than in your virtue" (Isocrates, Nic. 3.55), and Epictetus 3.20.9 emphasizes that the trainer exercises the athlete's patience, calmness, and mildness (to anektikon, to aorgēton, to praon). Likewise animals are taught to remain calm and docile,[18] barbarians are "tamed" when they are made milder (exeprayne, Plutarch, De Alex. fort. 330 a), and honest people learn to maintain their serenity: "the person who is accustomed to apply himself to affairs with flexibility and moderation is very mild and agreeable in his dealings with other people" (eukolōtatos . . . kai praotatos, De tranq. anim. 7.468 e; cf. De frat. amor. 17.488 b). This implies submission to reason (De cohib. ira 1.453 b–c), mod-eration of the passions (praotēs pathōn, De prof. in virt. 83 e; cf. 78 b; 80 b–c), and self-mastery (Fab. 17.7). But then this balance between insensitivity and cruelty (De virt. mor. 445 a) is a virtue that is put between courage and

---

with indulgence and serenity; De aud. poet. 35 d; reading and listening to works of poetry teaches us to bear our own misfortunes with mildness.

[15] Plato, Grg. 489 d; cf. Euthd. 302 c: "speak better and do not prepare your lessons so roughly" (μὴ χαλεπῶς); Resp. 1.345 a; Meno 75 d; Phdr. 268 e; Philostratus, VS 2.17. The teacher must impose his authority with meekness, even if he is contradicted (P.Mich. 219, 8; third century AD); Plutarch, Pomp. 60.8, who "endures this untimely scoffing with mildness." In discussions and debates one learns to listen with calm and benevolence before formulating criticisms (De audiendo 40 b). Marcus Aurelius 11.18 urges that the most violent person should be admonished with meekness.

[16] Menander, Dysk., hyp. 12; 779; cf. P.Oxy. 2329, 24 (C. Austin, Comicorum Graecorum Fragmenta, n. 256). Irritated, one calms down (Josephus, Ag. Apion 1.267). Antigonus in his old age took things ēpiōs and praōs (Ps.-Plutarch, Reg. et imp. apoph. 182 a). "How charming is a father who is mild and young at heart" (ὡς ἡδὺ πρᾷος καὶ νεάζων τῷ τρόπῳ πατήρ, Menander, frag. 749, p. 211; ed. Kock).

[17] Cf. H. Martin, "The Concept of praotēs in Plutarch's Lives," in GRBS, vol. 3, 1960, pp. 64–73.

[18] Isocrates, Antid. 211: by certain methods horses, dogs, and most animals, even lions (213), are given "more mildness"; mildness engendered in the most ferocious animals inspires admiration (214). Cf. Sent. Sextus 545: παιδευτικὸς θέλων εἶναι ἄσκει πραΰτητα.

justice (ibid. 2.441 *b*), and even a divine virtue,[19] superior to purely intellectual qualities.[20]

The *praos* has a mild look (Plutarch, *De cohib. ira* 6.456 *a*), a smiling countenance (4.455 *a–b*), a soft voice (Xenophon, *Symp.* 1.10), a tranquil demeanor (*praotēs poreias, Per.* 5.1; *Fab.* 17.7); is accommodating and affable (*Arist.* 23.1), courteous (*Alex.* 58.8), charming and gracious (*Ages.* 20.7; *Aem.* 3.6), but also quiet and reserved (*De frat. amor.* 16.487 *c*), and at the same time easygoing and welcoming toward all (*Praec. ger. rei publ.* 32.823 *f*). His character is conciliatory.[21] He does not like quarrels (*Lyc.* 25.4) and remains patient as Socrates was toward a shrewish wife and stupid children (*Cat. Mai.* 20.3). In the event of a misunderstanding, he is not slow to be reconciled (*De frat. amor.* 18.489 *c*). His simple and affable ways (*Conv. sept. sap.* 3.148 *d*) may captivate opponents (*De frat. amor.* 16.487 *c*; cf. *Luc.* 29.6; *Pomp.* 33.2); this is the triumph of *praotēs*, because "the characteristic of mildness, pardon, and reconciliation, is to lift up, save, spare, fortify" (*De cohib. ira* 10.458 *c*).

Philo had already emphasized most of these traits, but meekness was not really part of his theological vocabulary (he preferred *hēmerotēs*). The virtue of *praotēs* is put in action with peace and calmness (Philo, *Moses* 1.328, 2.279; *hēsychē te kai praōs, Creation* 81) and moderation that come easier with age, when the passions are more tamed (103, *epieikeia kai praotēs*; cf. Dio Cassius 55.12). Thus it presupposes self-mastery (*Sacr. Abel and Cain* 27) and translates into a friendly look and a soft voice (*Moses* 1.331; *Abraham* 153). Philo emphasizes tranquility, affability, and a sort of mellowness;[22] the virtue is not to be impassible to or thrown into convulsions by

---

[19] *De sera* 5.551 *c:* "mildness and longsuffering are divine aspects of virtue"; cf. *Lyc.* 28.13: "I judge Lycurgus's character according to his meekness and his justice in all the rest. I see even the divinity itself add its testimony in his favor." For Themistius, *praotēs* can make the king godlike (Themistius, *Or.* 19.226 *d;* 229 *a–b*).

[20] *De def. or.* 1.395 *a;* this *praytēs* is "a mildness full of good grace . . . that does not show sourness or harsness at retorts." While in the NT *praytēs* is a permanent and indispensable virtue for Christians, in Plutarch's biographies it is often a purely occasional trait. Thus the *prays* Artaxerxes (*Art.* 1.1; 2.1; 4.4) was nevertheless merciless toward Mithridates and had his own son Itarios put to death.

[21] Without asperity. Cf. *De cohib. ira* 453 *b:* the farmer makes the land smooth and fertile, soft and workable, just as mildness disposes a person to good deeds; cf. Xenophon, *Oec.* 19.17: farming is a humane and kindly art, i.e., one that easily divulges its secrets; Pindar, *Ol.* 13.85: the bit that makes Pegasus docile. — The opposites of πραΰτης are ἀγριότης (Plato, *Symp.* 197 *d*), βίαιος (*Leg.* 1.645 *a*), ὀργιλότης (Aristotle, *Eth. Nic.* 4.11.1125[b]26), ἀποτομία (Ps.-Plutarch, *De lib. ed.* 187), ὑβριστής (Dio Chrysostom, *Or.* 3.40), especially χαλεπότης (Plato, *Resp.* 1.354 *a;* 2.375 *c;* 6.472 *f;* 493 *b;* *Leg.* 9.867 *b;* Aristotle, *HA* 9.1).

[22] Cf. *Creation* 34: "the evening quietly (πράως) welcomes the burden of darkness"; *Alleg. Interp.* 1.42: "the gentle wind (πνοή) is like a breeze and a peaceable and

misfortune, but to moderate one's feelings, to "lighten the weight of events in quietness and calm" (*hēsychē kai praōs, Abraham* 257). The fat from the breast of the sacrificial victims, which is reserved for the priests, symbolizes "gentle mildness" (*Spec. Laws* 1.145). Masters are gentle with servants (*Decalogue* 167). Prudence "takes care to remain in kindness, mildness, and affability" (*tēn eumenē kai praeian kai hileōn, Alleg. Interp.* 1.66). This discretion was that shown by Macro in reprimanding Gaius quietly and mildly (*hēsychē kai praōs*), bending over to speak in his ear so that no one else would hear (Philo, *To Gaius* 43). We might also say that this is God's discretion.[23]

In light of the secular parallels, it is not surprising that the OT attributed *praytēs* to Moses[24] (Num 12:3; Sir 45:4; cf. Josephus, *Ant.* 3.97, 316) to David (Ps 132:1), to Artaxerxes (Esth 5:1 *e*), to the high priest Onias (2 Macc 15:12), and to the Messiah.[25] It *is* surprising, however, to see the LXX uses *prays* and *praytēs* exclusively to translate the Hebrew words *'ānāw, 'ānî, ʿanāwāh, 'ānāh*, always expressing humility and abasement;[26] *prays* is even synonymous with *tapeinos* (Isa 26:6; cf. Sir 10:14) to the point that unlike *chrēstotēs, praytēs* is never attributed to God. This new meaning appears in the first occurrence of the term, regarding Moses, who was "very *prays* (Hebrew *'ānāw*), the most *prays* man on earth" (Num 12:3). This can hardly have to do with "non-violence"—since the mediator of the covenant, in resisting Pharaoh's oppression, had killed an Egyptian (Exod 2:12)—rather,

---

mild exhalation (ἠρεμαία καὶ πραεῖα)"; *Migr. Abr.* 101: like dew from heaven, God made "the rain of celestial intelligence fall upon us without violent inundation but tranquilly, mildly (ἠρέμα καὶ πράως), like a beneficent dew." We could say of the Philonian *praos* that he is "all sweetness," according to the designations of fruit trees in *P.Cair.Zen.* 59033, 12: σύκινα Χῖα, ἐρινεά, Λύδια, πραέα, φοινίκεα, ὀλονθοφόρα.

[23] *Worse Attacks Better* 117: "The wellspring of divine wisdom flows more calmly and peaceably" (ἠρεμαιοτέρῳ καὶ πρᾳοτέρῳ); 146: "God in his goodness will correct our offenses with mildness and indulgence" (ἐπιεικῶς τε καὶ πρᾳοτέρῳ); *Pap. Graec.Mag.* 4, 1046: "To me, O Lord, show yourself to be ἱλαρός, εὐμενής, πραΰς, ἀμήνιτος." In a fifth-century speech, οὐκ ἐπιεικής οὐ πρᾶος, οὐκ εἰδὼς ἐρυθριᾶν (published by K. Treu, in *Proceedings* XV, vol. 2, p. 14).

[24] Beginning with the third century BC the spellings πραΰς, πραΰτης substituted for πρᾶος, πρᾳότης (cf. E. Mayser, *Grammatik*, vol. I, 1, p. 121; BDF §§26 and 47), but there is still πρᾶος in 2 Macc 15:12 (cf. the genitive πραέως, 1 Pet 3:4) and πρᾳότης (Esth 3:13).

[25] Zech 9:9. According to *T. Abr.* A 1.1, the patriarch lived the 995 years of his life in quietness (ἡσυχία), gentleness (πραΰτης) and righteousness.

[26] Cf. C. Spicq, "Bénignité, mansuétude, douceur, clémence," in *RB*, 1947, pp. 321–329; P. van den Berghe, " 'Ani et 'Anaw dans les Psaumes," in R. de Langhe, *Le Psautier*, Louvain, 1962, pp. 273–295. According to J. Dupont, *Béatitudes*, pp. 25–29, the first meaning of the Hebrew *'ānāw* would be "bent, abased, bowed down, prostrated," hence the humble and modest person.

it means a religious quality involving radical submission to God and modesty in dealings with other people. As it happens, Moses shows "clemency" by praying for his sister Miriam when she is stricken with leprosy after plotting against him. It is worth noting that apart from Dan 4:19 (a soft voice), the OT never uses *prays* with a secular meaning. The *praeis* are the "humble of the earth" (Job 24:4), the abased, the poor, exploited by the wicked, to whom they have to give in. Therefore they are blessed by God (Zeph 3:12), who teaches them (Ps 25:9; cf. Matt 11:25), saves them (Ps 76:9; 147:6; 149:4), relieves them on the day of misfortune (Ps 94:13, *praynō*), and finally "toppling the thrones of princes makes the *praeis* sit in their stead" (Sir 10:14; cf. Luke 1:51–53). These "humble possess the land" (Ps 37:11) and rejoice to hear Yahweh's praise (Ps 34:2). These, then, are religious people, whose outstanding model will be the Messiah-King, who appears not proudly on a noble war-horse but "humble, mounted on an ass," to enter his capital (Zech 9:9; cf. Matt 21:5).

OT *praytēs* is perfect submission to the divine will (Ps 132:1), and the Lord loves the combination of faithfulness and meekness (Sir 1:27; 45:4) that characterizes his people. In contrast to prideful exaltation, these folk always remain modest (Sir 10:28); if a poor person accosts them, they reply gently (Sir 4:8); if a woman expresses herself with modesty, her husband is no common mortal (Sir 36:23)! This absence of any immoderation characterized Onias, "of modest bearing and gentle manner (*praon de ton tropon*), distinguished in his speech and gifted from childhood with all the practices of virtue" (2 Macc 15:12). A person who conducts himself in that manner is loved by all people who are accepted by God (Sir 3:17). This is no longer a matter of self-mastery or of reining in one's anger, but of a heart disposition and comportment characterized by restraint and modesty. It is the distinctive mark of souls that belong to God and "fear" him, have a sense of his transcendence and of their own poverty. Having been tested, they have acquired an approachable manner, measured speech, reserved attitudes. Their *praytēs* is not so much mildness as indulgence (French *mansuétude*). The Latin word *mansuetudo* derives from *mansuesco*, literally, "accustom to the hand," hence "tame"; so *mansuetudo*, "taming,"[27] came to mean serene receptiveness, as opposed to impetuosity or insolence, hostility or gruffness. It is in a way the docile and respectful attitude of a servant toward his master, always ready to submit.

If the NT heightens and focuses these essential meanings, it does not change them by making *praytēs* a major Christian virtue. It is notable that

---

[27] Cf. A. Ernout, A. Meillet, *Dictionnaire étymologique de la langue latine*, Paris, 1932.

this noun is unknown in the Gospels and the adjective *prays* is found only in Matt (and at 1 Pet 3:4), but with remarkable significance: "Blessed are the *praeis*, because they shall inherit the earth."[28] This is a resumption of Ps 37:11, where *praeis* translates the Hebrew *ʿnāwîm*. So it means the poor, the small, the persecuted, and better—as the Syrians understood—the "humble" in the moral sense. It is not the sociological condition that is exalted, but religious submission and confidence in God, which translates into patience and mildness.[29] The stable happiness of peace and security that is promised them is "possession of the land," not occupation of the land (of promise), the land of Israel in the political sense; still less "all the land," the whole world,[30] but entrance into the kingdom of God here below and ultimately in heaven. The "inheritance" here is blessedness for the destitute who have looked to God for everything.

Totally submissive toward God and meek toward people, Jesus presented himself as "meek and lowly of heart" (*prays kai tapeinos tē kardia*) and on these grounds invites people to receive his teaching (Matt 11:29). Thus he reveals his innermost soul, but he also takes up a tradition that is constant from Pindar and Isocrates and that attributes *praytēs* to teachers. Far from being despotic, the Master must be patient and discreet toward his students lest he discourage or offend them; in his condescension he puts himself on their level and answers their problems, being at their service. At the entrance of the Messiah-King into his capital on Palm Sunday, Matt 21:5 quotes Zech 9:9—"Your king comes to you, humble (*prays*, Hebrew *ʿānî*), mounted on the foal of an ass,"[31] the mount of the poor, and not on a horse, the warrior's noble mount.

---

[28] Μακάριοι οἱ πραεῖς, ὅτι αὐτοὶ κληρονομήσουσι τὴν γῆν, Matt 5:4. This is the second beatitude, which takes up the first ("Blessed are the poor"); cf. J. Dupont, *Béatitudes*, vol. 1, pp. 251ff.

[29] J. Dupont, *Béatitudes*, vol. 3, pp. 486–545.

[30] In this correlation between "merit" and "reward" in the beatitude, we must not nevertheless exclude a note of psychological attraction and seductiveness that the whole literary tradition attributes to *praytēs*: meekness wins hearts, and its silent triumph, which knows no borders, may be universal.

[31] Albertus Magnus saw the meaning well: "When everyone sees the Lord carried gently (by the colt of the ass), let people be built up to faith, and let them be ashamed not to be mildly disposed toward him to whom even a beast of little intelligence and hitherto unbroken was tame" ("Cum videntibus omnibus Dominum mansuete portari [a pullo asinae], homines ad fidem aedifacarentur, et verecundarentur non mansuescere ad eum, ad quem animal parvi sensus, et adhuc indomitum mansuescebat," *In Lucam* 19.30; ed. Borgnet, vol. 23, p. 582; ibid. 19.35, p. 586). Cf. R. Bartnicki, "Das Zitat von Zach. IX, 9–10 und die Tiere im Bericht von Matthäus über den Einzug Jesu in Jerusalem (Mt. XXI, 1–11)," in *NovT*, 1976, pp. 161–166.

Using a bold metaphor, 1 Pet 3:4, addressing Christians, appeals to "the secret person, the one of the heart, in the incorruptibility of a meek and calm spirit."[32] These women are to accept the dependency they are in vis-à-vis their husbands, whom they hope to convert to the faith (cf. the beatitude of the meek, Matt 5:4), with the help of the meekness that disarms opponents (2 Tim 2:25), according to Israel's experience (Ps 149:4–5). Aware of their weakness, docile, and submissive, these Christian women are "poor" folk who know no bitter zeal. They are often mistreated, even insulted, but they remain peaceful (Titus 3:2) and disposed to forgive (2 Cor 10:1; Gal 6:1). Like the Messiah, they neither dispute nor cry out (Matt 11:29; 12:19). Thus they imitate the Suffering Servant and obtain the victory of good over evil.

As for *praytēs* (eleven times in the epistles), it is first of all the characteristic of the apostle. "What do you want? Shall I come to you with a rod, or with love and in a spirit of meekness?" (*ē en agapē pneumati te praytētos*)[33] is almost a quotation of Job 37:13, where God's will is realized either by the rod (Hebrew *šēbeṭ*) or by lovingkindness (*ḥeseḏ*) linked with justice; but St. Paul links *praytēs* and *agapē*. If the *rhabdos* (rod), used for punishment, symbolizes Israelite and Greek education,[34] the apostle's love is that of a father, without violence, all gentleness and serenity; it persuades rather than rails. Moreover, it is not the man who commands; St. Paul exhorts "by the meekness and gentleness of Christ" (*dia tēs praytētos kai epieikeias tou Christou*),[35] setting these opposite submission, because *praytēs* disarms opponents.

This meekness is poured out into the hearts of all Christians by the Holy Spirit,[36] and it is what maintains unity and harmony between all

---

[32] Τοῦ πραέως καὶ ἡσυχίου πνεύματος; Musonius asks the philosopher to endure adversity peaceably: πράως δὲ καὶ ἡσύχως οἴσει τὸ συμβάν (frag. 10, ed. C. E. Lutz, p. 78, 10).

[33] 1 Cor 4:21; cf. D. Daube, "Paul a Hellenistic Schoolmaster?" in R. Loewe, *Studies in Rationalism, Judaism and Universalism, in Memory of L. Roth*, New York, 1966, pp. 67–71.

[34] Cf. Philo, *Prelim. Stud.* 94; *Change of Names* 135 (cf. M. Alexander, *De Congressu Eruditionis Gratia*, Paris, 1967, p. 168, n. 2). The rod is used for the correction of delinquents (1QS 11.1; Thucydides 5.50; cf. *LSAM*, n. 9, 29; *LSCG*, n. 83, 24). Keepers of flocks are called "rod-bearers" (*P.Oxy.* 1626, 9; *P.Panop.Beatty* 2, 241, 274).

[35] 2 Cor 10:1 (cf. Matt 11:29). R. Leivestad, "The Meekness and Gentleness of Christ," in *NTS*, vol. 12, 1966, p. 159.

[36] Gal 5:23. After "love, joy, peace, patience" in the list of the fruit of the Spirit, come "faithfulness, meekness, temperance." Jas 1:21 urges receiving "with humility (ἐν πραΰτητε δέξασθε) the word implanted (in you), which can save your souls." Here *praytēs* is not only fervent acceptance and submission but the initiative to hear the word of God and the assent of the heart to what it says (cf. Ps 132:1; 76:9).

members of the community: "I urge you . . . to lead a life worthy of the calling that you have received, in all humility, meekness, and patience; bear with one another with love"[37] without grumbling. "You, God's chosen ones, put on compassion, kindness, humility, meekness, patience; bear with one another and forgive one another, if anyone has a complaint against another."[38] So if one member of the community "is taken in a fault, you who are spiritual must restore him in a spirit of meekness, taking care for yourselves, for you yourselves are also capable of being tempted."[39]

The *praytēs* of believers cannot be confined to relations with other Christians; it has to extend to all people. "Remind the faithful not to slander anyone, not to be quarrelsome, but conciliatory (*epieikeis*), showing constant humility toward all people."[40] This receptiveness toward one's neighbor, this affability, this kindness in relations, which are manifestations of love (*agapē*), must be plain for all to see: "Who among you is wise and understanding? Let him show it by good conduct, by acts marked with the humility that belongs to wisdom" (*en praytēti sophias*, Jas 3:13). This then is a characteristic of Christian comportment, a touchstone of a person who possesses *agapē*; such a person cannot be other than *prays*.

This virtue, which is required in teachers (Matt 11:29) and educators (2 Cor 10:1; Gal 6:1) because it is persuasive (Matt 5:4), is especially necessary in dealings with the undisciplined or refractory: "A servant of the Lord must be not combative but affable (*ēpios*) toward all . . . instructing opponents with humility" (2 Tim 2:25). After all, such people may be acting in good faith, so their objections must be accepted with patience, without annoyance. Through meekness, which unites humility and clemency (cf. Dio Cassius 48.3; 55.12, 17), one can remain calm and bring back the errant and the guilty. The aim is to save souls, not to triumph over a conquest. This is the same attitude that 1 Pet 3:15 commands for all believers: "always ready to give an answer to anyone

---

[37] Eph 4:2; cf. M. Barth, *Ephesians*, vol. 2, pp. 454–459.

[38] Col 3:12. Humility, self-effacement, is an antidote to self-love; *praytēs*, which is completely gentle, avoids clashes; patience reins in irritation and assures the maintenance of peace.

[39] Gal 6:1. Meekness is a classical quality of the "corrector," but here the motive is new: awareness of one's own potential for failure in similar circumstance to those in which the offender fell. This honest and humble approach leaves no room for arrogance or harshness; cf. royal souls, some of whom are arrogant, others humble, τὰς δὲ ὑπερηφάνους, τὰς δε πραείας (*Hermes Trismegistus*, frag. 26.8).

[40] Titus 3:2; same linking of πραΰτης and ἐπιείκεια, *MAMA* VII, 524, 7.

who asks the reason for the hope that is in you, always with humility and respect."[41]

Praypathia (a biblical hapax), which seems to be synonymous with *praytēs*,[42] is commended by St. Paul to Timothy: "Man of God . . . pursue righteousness, piety, faith, love, constancy, meekness" (1 Tim 6:11), all indispensable virtues for the pastor who will be serene, accessible to all, not given to violent reaction, fomenting peace.

---

[41] Ἀλλὰ πραΰτητος καὶ φόβου; these two latter words must constitute a hendiadys: deferential meekness. As for the ἀλλά, it must be understood as explained by J. Carmignac ("L'Importance de la place d'une négation . . . [Philippiens II, 6]," in *NTS*, vol. 18, 1972, p. 156): "after an affirmative proposition, ἀλλά means not 'but,' but 'however, moreover, notwithstanding, nevertheless.' This meaning, which is already clearly attested in Homer, for example in the Iliad 1.116 and Odyssey 1.6, is altogether classical in Greek. Cf. F. M. Abel, *Grammaire*, p. 346, n. 78 n." This self-control in the heat of argument is commended by Plutarch, *De sera* 5; *De Pyth. or.* 1.

[42] Cf. Philo, *Abraham* 213: Abraham usually gave in to quarrelsome and unruly people "because of mildness of temperament of their master"; πραϋπαθής: good-natured (*Spec. Laws* 4.93), accommodating (*To Gaius* 335); πραοπαθεῖν: to be meek (*Flight* 6).

πρεσβεία, πρεσβεύω

presbeia, **embassy, delegation;** presbeuō, **to act as ambassador**

A presbeutēs can be an emissary, a messenger, an envoy (2 Chr 32:31; 1 Macc 13:21; 14:21, 22, 40; 15:17), like a presbys,[1] hence a mere spokesman;[2] but normally, in the Hellenistic period, this was an ambassador in the full sense of the word, sent by the Greek cities to each other and to the kings.[3]

---

[1] Num 21:20; 22:5; Deut 2:26; Isa 39:1; 57:9; 68:9; an ambassador to peace talks, 1 Macc 9:70; 10:51.

[2] An ambassador is sent with letters that specify the object of his mission (Josephus, Ant. 12.225, 227). Cf. Philo, Giants 16; Abraham 115; Plant. 14 (angels, cf. Heir 205; Julius Pollux, Onom. 8.137: ὁ δὲ πρεσβευτὴς εἴη ἂν καὶ ἄγγελος διάκονος). A letter of Augustus: "the presbeis whom you sent to me in Gaul" (P.Oxy. 3020, frag. 1, col. I, 4; col. II, 2); Jos. Asen. 7.4: the Egyptians sent Joseph their messengers with gold, silver, and precious gifts. A θεωρός was "a special ambassador with a sacred mission to a foreign land" (G. Daux, in REG, 1967, p. 294). SEG II, 257; XVIII, 235; 288; XIX, 381; ISE, n. 91; M. Holleaux, Etudes d'épigraphie, pp. 433–448.

[3] In the second century BC, a decree of Phalanna for the judges from Metropolis: "Thaumandros and Antisthenes were sent by our city on an embassy to the city of Metropolis to ask for a court to regulate trials and the rendering of accounts. . . . The citizens of Metropolis honored our ambassadors with appropriate honors" (NCIG, n. 12, 3, 10); a decree of Miletus (second century) in honor of Eirenias; "sent as an ambassador, he was zealous in his interview (with King Eumenes)" (ibid. VII, 9); "So that the Thasians may know of the piety of Hestiaios toward the gods, his zeal for our people, and the gratitude of this city, let an ambassador be appointed to take this decree to them" (I.Thas. 169, 27; cf. 170, 28; 174, A 3); P.Corn. 11, 1: "To Aurelius Apollonius, presbytēs of the most famous city of the Alexandrians"; P.Dura 38, 11: "To Flavius Antiochus, the emperor's presbytēs"; SB 7263, 5; 7944, 2; Josephus, War 7.58. Presbyteis are constantly the recipients of honorific decrees, I.Delos 1621, 1699, 1855; I.Car. 166, 4, 8, 12, 19: "After ambassadors were sent regarding the interests of the city of Ktesicles . . . he thought to obtain what we were asking for"; SEG I, 151; VI, 555;

---

presbeia, S 4242; EDNT 3.147–148; NIDNTT 1.192–193, 197; MM 534; L&N 37.87; BAGD 699 ‖ presbeuō, S 4243; TDNT 6.681–683; EDNT 3.147–148; NIDNTT 1.192–194, 197; MM 534; L&N 38.88; BAGD 699

The role of these emissaries could vary—according to *P.Col.Zen.* 60, 5, there was a "treaty on embassies." Sometimes they were tools in political intrigue, as when some fellow citizens of a claimant to the throne "sent an embassy after him (*apesteilan presbeian*) to say, 'We do not want this man to reign over us' ";[4] sometimes they defended financial interests, as at Samos in the third century BC, where "the citizens called for an embassy to be sent to Antiochus to recover their property and Boulagoras was designated ambassador . . . and performed with absolute zeal and devotion" (*SEG* I, 366, 9). Usually they establish or strengthen good relations between cities[5] and above all negotiated treaties of alliance and friendship (1 Macc 4:11; cf. 8:17; 15:17). It is in this sense that, finding himself in an inferior

---

XVIII, 216; XX, 28, 730; *SB* 8300, 3 (first century AD); *MAMA* VI, 103; considerable documentation in E. Olshausen, *Prosopographie der hellenistischen Königsgesandten,* Louvain, 1974.

[4] Luke 19:14; cf. Philo, *To Gaius* 239: "As suppliants we ask for time to choose ambassadors and send them with a petition to the master (the emperor)"; the letter of Claudius to the Alexandrians: "as if you lived in two cities that you should send two embassies" (*P.Lond.* 1912, 91); *PSI* 1160, 11 (= *SB* 7448); 1434, 5; decree for Orthagoras of Araxa, "sent on an embassy (ἀποσταλεὶς πρεσβευτής) by the people to each of the cities . . . he did not fail to carry out his mission (τὰς πρεσβείας) in a fashion worthy of our people . . . then, sent on a mission to the ambassadors of Rome who were with Appius, and again on a mission to the Roman ambassadors who were with Poplius, he carried out his two missions in a manner worthy of our people and of the confederation, and he served all the interests of the city; he accomplished, moreover, many other missions, without asking for traveling expenses" (J. Pouilloux, *Choix,* n. IV, 5ff.). A decree from Apollonia from the second century BC honors Pamphilos, who had carried out numerous embassies: "When the ten legates came from Rome (τῶν δέκα πρεσβευτῶν ἀπὸ Ῥώμης) to set affairs in order with Cnaeus, the proconsul, at Apamea, Pamphilos went to them and conducted himself in an excellent and effective manner on behalf of his country . . . with all zeal and ardor he put each matter in order (the territorial standing of the front part of Asia Minor in the wake of the defeat of Antiochus III)." Next he was sent to Rhodes, where "he and his fellow ambassadors (μετὰ τῶν συμπρεσβευτῶν) fought against the natives who were our adversaries. . . . Having carried out numerous other embassies for the common good (ἄλλας τε πλείονας πρεσβείας πρεσβεύσας ὑπὲρ τῶν κοινῶν) and having behaved properly in all of them and having dealt correctly with matters, he continued to supply numerous advantages to the city" (*I.Car.* 167, 1ff., 9ff., 15ff.); L. Robert, *Etudes anatoliennes,* p. 322. In the Byzantine period, πρεσβεία means intercession, supplication (*P.Ness.* 52, 1; *SB* 7428, 17).

[5] A decree of Argos in the fourth-third century in honor of the Rhodians: "Argos sent an embassy to Rhodes . . . now they have sent an embassy to Philias . . . to give notice that Rhodes has never flagged in its devotion to Argos and that it will continue to pursue the same policy in the future" (*NCIG,* n. VIII, 9, 12); cf. Dittenberger, *Syl.* 412, 6; "the marvelous embassy" of Abraham's servant, who chose Rebekah as wife for his son" (Philo, *Prelim. Stud.* 11).

position, a king under attack "sends an embassy (*presbeian aposteilas*) to sue for peace."[6] Examples are common. Deut 20:10–12 prescribes: "When you draw near to a city to do battle with it, you shall invite it to come to terms . . . if it does not make peace with you, if it goes to war against you, you shall besiege it," which Josephus paraphrases, "When you are about to go to war, send an embassy and heralds to those who are willingly hostile" (*mellontas de polemein presbeian kai kērykas pempein para tous hekousiōs polemious, Ant.* 4.296). "Trypho knew that Simon was on the verge of joining battle with him; he sent him messengers (*presbeis*)" to ask for the money that he claimed Jonathan owed (1 Macc 13:14). Around 200 BC, "when the Thracian, commanded by Zoltes, appeared with an army of consequence in Scythia, marching against the Greek cities that had submitted to Rhemaxos, Agathocles was elected ambassador. He crossed enemy territory, passing through a good number of tribes, not shrinking from danger, and he persuaded the barbarians not only to do our city no harm but also to track down and return all the livestock that had previously been carried off by the pirates."[7]

As for the verb *presbeuō*, it is used only twice in the Bible, by St. Paul, who uses it for an ambassador of Christ: "On Christ's behalf, then, we are ambassadors (*hyper Christou oun presbeuomen*), given that God is urging through us (*di' hēmōn*). We ask on behalf of Christ, be reconciled to God" (2 Cor 5:20); "Pray for me that I will be given an open mouth to announce boldly the mystery of the gospel, of which I am ambassador in chains" (*presbeuō en halysei,* Eph 6:20). The apostle gives himself a title of nobility, for a legate is a noteworthy personage,[8] at the top of the military hierarchy,

---

[6] Luke 14:32, ἐρωτᾷ τὰ πρὸς εἰρήνην is a Hebraism that normally expresses greetings: Judg 18:15; 1 Sam 10:4; 17:22; 25:5; 30:21; 2 Sam 8:10—ἐρωτῆσαι αὐτὸν τὰ εἰς εἰρήνην; *T. Jud.* 9.7—αἰτοῦσιν ἡμῖν τὰ πρὸς εἰρήνην; Josephus, *Ant.* 12.405: τὰ πρὸς τὴν μάχην = ready for battle; cf. Ps.-Plutarch, *Cons. ad Apoll.* 14: τὰ πρὸς τὸν θάνατον = death is to be expected. J. M. Creed, *The Gospel According to St. Luke,* London, 1953, p. 195.

[7] A decree from Istros in honor of Agathocles, in *NCIG,* n. VI, 17; cf. lines 28, 33: "once again chosen as ambassador to Thrace and to Zoltes the chief of the Thracians, he extended the pacts and agreements previously concluded with them"; line 49, 54; *I.Kour.* 87 (with the observations of R. S. Bagnall, T. Drew-Bear, in *ChrEg,* 1974, pp. 188ff.). Cf. Dio Chrysostom 1.27.

[8] Cf. the letter of Cn. Cornelius Dolabella, proconsul of Macedonia, "to the council and people of Thasos. Your ambassadors . . . , worthy men and our friends, sent by a worthy people, our friend and ally, were presented before me . . ." (*I.Thas.* 175, 2). Cf. the honorific decree for a Tabenian in the first century AD who "was ambassador to peoples, to (Roman) leaders who came through (Asia) as consuls, and to *dynasteis*" (L. Robert, *Etudes anatoliennes,* p. 325; cf. Dittenberger, *Syl.* 374, 37); honorific decree of the province of Asia for Quintus Pomponius Flaccus, "who carried out the office

and *presbeuōn* and *presbeutēs* are technical terms for imperial legates in the Greek Orient.[9] For example, in the second century AD, when Emperor Claudius acknowledges receipt of the "gold crown" that a gymnastic club sent him on the occasion of his victorious campaign in Britain, his letter ends thus: "The ambassadors were (*hoi presbeuontes ēsan*) Tib. Cl. Hermas, Tib. Cl. Cyras, Dion son of Miccalos, an Antiochene" (*P.Lond.* 1178, 14; vol. 3, p. 216). A decree at Thespiae for young volunteer soldiers mentions the names of two delegates to the imperial authorities: "Envoys from the city (*hoi presbeuontes*): Eirenaios, Bentios. Eirenaios fulfilled this mission for the third time as a volunteer."[10]

That the apostle indeed means *presbeuō* in the full sense of the word is proven by the very way in which he describes his mission: (*a*) *hyper Christou*, on behalf of Christ (cf. *I.Priene* 108, 164: "he served as ambassador on behalf of the township"—*epresbeusen hyper tou dēmou*, 129 BC; Dittenberger, *Syl.* 591, 5; 656, 15; 805, 7: "having often served as ambassador on behalf of his country"—*presbeusanta pollakis hyper tēs patridos*); hence, not in the Lord's place, but in his service; (*b*) the justification of this mission: "seeing that God exhorts through us."[11] The sovereign speaks through his ambassador (*di' hēmōn*; cf. 1 Macc 10:51; Eph 6:19, *en anoixei tou stomatos mou*); the credit given the ambassador's words corresonds with the authority of the sovereign. Paul is not the one who matters—he does not act in his own name, and his message does not originate with himself—he represents

---

of night *stratēgos* with all legality and went on an embassy to Rome at his own expense" (L. Robert, "Les Inscriptions," in J. des Gagniers, *Laodicée*, p. 265, 11); the questions asked of an oracle: "will I be ambassador (εἰ πρεσβεύσω)? will I be senator?" (*P.Oxy.* 1477, 16). An ambassador is thus much more highly esteemed than a κῆρυξ (1 Tim 2:7; 2 Tim 1:11; Epictetus 3.21.13). Hence the sociable reception that Alexander, for example, gave to embassies (Diodorus Siculus 17.2.2; 17.4.9; 17.113.4).

[9] Meaning cited by A. Deissmann, *Light*, p. 374, who makes reference to the examples furnished by D. Magie, *De Romanorum Juris Publici Sacrique Vocabulis Sollemnibus in Graecum Sermonem Conversis*, Leipzig, 1905, pp. 89ff. Today we may refer to the examples and classification (ambassador, legate of the *hēgemōn*, the proconsul, the emperor) of H. J. Mason, *Greek Terms*, pp. 147, 153.

[10] *NCIG*, n. XV, 25, 27. The disinterestedness of ambassadors is often mentioned in the inscriptions; cf. *MAMA* VI, 3, at Laodicea: "Terentius Longinus . . . after twice serving without pay on embassies to Lucius Aelius Caesar in Pannonia and to the great emperor Titus Aelius Hadrianus Antoninus Augustus Pius at Rome." Their devotion is similarly emphasized, as in the decree of the Athenian cleruchies for Euboulos of Marathon: "sent on several embassies, he often, through sustained effort, secured the interests of the Athenians of Delos" (*I.Delos* 1498, 14).

[11] Ὡς, followed by an explanatory participle, is epexegetic; it means not "as if" but "inasmuch as"; cf. T. Muraoka, "The Use of ΩΣ in the Greek Bible," in *NovT*, 1964, pp. 60ff.

Christ, and when he speaks, his words are to be taken as coming from God;[12] (*c*) the goal of the apostolic embassy is to offer reconciliation with God, and Paul begs his hearers to accept this offer.[13] Ambassadors (*hoi presbeuontes*) inform (1 Macc 14:21; *I.Delos* 175, 2) in the same terms with which they have been instructed (1 Macc 10:51).

---

[12] Cf. P. E. Hughes, *Paul's Second Epistle to the Corinthians*, 4th ed., Grand Rapids, 1973, pp. 209ff.

[13] J. Dupont, *La Réconciliation dans la théologie de saint Paul*, Bruges-Paris, 1953; J. F. Collange, *Enigmes de la deuxième Epître de Paul aux Corinthiens*, Cambridge, 1972, pp. 266–274. In the fourth century BC, "the city of Argos sent an embassy to Polyperchon to beg him to free the people of Pallantion (who were taken prisoner) when the land of Pallantion was conquered by Menemachos, and Polyperchon freed the people and granted this favor to Argos" (*SEG* XI, 1094, 18). A century later, the inhabitants of Gortyn sent an embassy to Cnossos to ask for a physician (Dittenberger, *Syl.* 528, 2).

προβάλλω

proballō, to bring or put forward, present; to bud

At Ephesus, the Jews in the midst of the mob "pushed Alexander to the fore" (proballontōn auton, Acts 19:33). This meaning—"bring forth, present"—recurs constantly in the papyri and the inscriptions.[1] "I had the misfortune of being nominated by the citizens as grain commissioner, although I was not of age to take on this leitourgia . . . I was put forward by certain persons who were acting out of jealousy" (P.Mich. 23, 3; third century BC); "You were wrong to nominate us for the office of ktēnarchos" (SB 10202); "Having been officially presented by the inhabitants of the town for the above-mentioned jobs."[2]

In the LXX, the physical meaning "bring out, cast forward" is seen when the third Maccabee brother "stuck out his tongue as soon as they asked" (to cut it off, 2 Macc 7:10); when twenty youths throw themselves against the wall,[3] when Razis "tore out his own entrails, took them with

---

[1] Moulton-Milligan cite P.Ryl. 77, 43: ἐμάθομεν τὸν Ἀχιλλέα προβαλόμενον ἑαυτὸν εἰς ἐξηγητείαν (644, 6, 10 is too mutilated to yield a meaning); P.Oxy. 1424, 5; Dittenberger, Syl. 1104, 29: ἡ σύνοδος . . . ὁμοθυμαδὸν προεβάλετο τοὺς εἰσοίσοντας αὐτοῖς τὰς καθηκούσας τιμάς; 797, 23: φίλους τε κρινεῖν, οὕς ἂν αὐτὸς προαιρῆται, καὶ ἐχθρούς, οὕς ἂν αὐτὸς προβάληται.

[2] C.P.Herm. 21, 13; cf. Stud.Pal. XX, 54, 6: τοῖς προβαλομένοις τὸν ἡμέτερον υἱόν . . . εἰς κοσμητείαν τῆς αὐτῆς πόλεως (= Chrest.Wilck., n. 402); SB 5231, 9 (first century); 7696, 45: εἰς τὴν πρυτανίαν ταύτην; line 61: εἰς κοσμητείας; Fouilles de Delphes III, 3; 239, 16: "Let the archons appoint those whom the majority shall nominate" (second century BC). In Prov 22:21—"those who put you forward" are "those who sent you" (Hebrew šālaḥ). Often it is a question of "putting forward" an excuse; cf. Thucydides 1.27.4; 2.87.3; P.Panop.Beatty 1, 87, 154, 157; SB 8987, 36.

[3] 2 Macc 10:35; cf. Xenophon, An. 1.2.17: Cyrus "order the whole column to present arms and advance"; 6.5.16: "advance upon the enemy with shields in front"; Polybius 1.18.3; 1.48.10; 2.5.5; 3.72.9; 3.113.6 = deploy, place in advance.

---

proballō, S 4261; EDNT 3.152; MM 537; L&N 23.195; BAGD 702

both hands, and threw them at the mob."[4] But in Judg 14:12, 13, 16, Samson sets forth a riddle.[5]

None of these texts is analogous to the use of *proballō* in the parable of the Fig Tree, Luke 21:30. Where Mark 13:28 and Matt 24:32 have "when the leaves have come out" (*ekphyē*), Luke reads "when they have put forth."[6] Clearly this verb has a very wide range of meaning, and only the context can provide specificity.[7] Here we must translate "when they are already budding." The agricultural parallels from the first century have been cited. With respect to plants that flower and give off fragrances, Dioscorides, *Mat. Med.* 2.205: "in the summer it produces a milky-white flower" (*therous de galaktinon anthos proballei*); 4.50: "in the autumn the leaves produce a smell" (*proballei de kata to phthinopōron ta phylla tragou osmēn*); Josephus, *Ant.* 4.226: "if the plants produce fruit before the fourth year" (*an karpon probalē ta phyta*); Epictetus 1.15.7: "Nothing great is produced suddenly, since it is not so even with the grape and the fig. If you said to me now, 'I want a fig,' I would answer that it takes time. Let the flowers appear first, then the fruit (*eita probalē ton karpon*), and finally let it ripen." Since this meaning is not attested in the papyri, we must conclude that it belongs to literary Greek, where its usage attests to a traditional rhetorical topos.

---

[4] 2 Macc 14:46; cf. Plutarch, *Per.* 28.2: "He had their bodies thrown out with no burial"; Prov 26:18—"throwing words to men" (Hebrew *yārâh*).

[5] Hebrew *ḥûd*. Cf. the use of προβάλλω for texts that set forth geometrical problems to be solved (C. Mugler, *Terminologie géométrique*, p. 356); Hippocrates, *Acut.* 8.1: "As a rule, physicians do not even raise such questions; and perhaps even if they were raised, they would not be answered"; Galen, *Anim. Pass.* 2.57: set forth as a problem.

[6] Ὅταν προβάλωσιν ἤδη. E. Delebecque (*Evangile de Luc*) translates: "Tous les arbres, dès qu'ils poussent leurs pointes."

[7] In optics, προβάλλω refers to the changing field of vision as projected in front of the body by the eyes, "la projection du flux visuel suivant l'orientation des yeux, en avant du corps" (C. Mugler, *Terminologie optique*, p. 321). In obstetrics, babies that stick an arm or leg out (Hippocrates, *Mul.* 1.69; other references in W. K. Hobart, *Medical Language*, pp. 75, 140ff.). In sports, for the boxer who is on guard, in a defensive posture (LSJSup, p. 125). Without a technical meaning: "keep before the eyes" (*Ep. Arist.* 212); in the Byzantine period: a party to a contract who did not know how to write and could not sign drew a cross with his own hand (προβαλόντος τῇ αὐτοῦ χειρί †, *P.Mich.* 607, 35). Philo, for whom this is a favorite verb, uses it in the pejorative moral sense of rebuffing or rejecting vice (*Abraham* 22, 104, 137, 210), those who dishonor virtue (*Moses* 2.9; *Spec. Laws* 2.60; *Virtues* 136, 200), with a nuance of aversion (*Post. Cain* 134; *Moses* 1.45–46).

προβιβάζω

probibazō, to instigate

It is difficult to pin down the meaning of this NT hapax.[1] When Herodias asks for the head of John the Baptist, Matt 14:8 specifies *probibastheisa hypo tēs mētros autēs*. This is usually taken to mean "urged on by her mother";[2] but the two occurrences in the LXX mean inculcate, instill in the mind (Exod 35:4, hiphil of the Hebrew *yārâh*; Deut 6:7, piel of the Hebrew *šānan*), and this is the meaning retained by F. Field.[3] Even though it is attested by only a single Byzantine papyrus (*P.Lond.* 1708, 262), it will do here, with the idea being "upon her mother's instigation." Support comes from Musonius, replying to the objection "Is it not unreasonable for a man who is capable of influencing the young to study philosophy (*probibazein neous eis philosophian*) to work the earth or busy himself with manual labor?" (ed. C. E. Lutz, frag. 11, p. 82, 23).

---

[1] Certainly we must reject the reading προεβίβασαν in D², Ψ, P, Chrysostom at Acts 19:33 and retain συνεβίβασαν, "they indoctrinated" (𝔓⁷⁴, ℵ, A, B, E, cf. 1 Cor 2:16), cf. E. Haenchen, *Acts*, p. 574.

[2] Προβιβάζω = cause to advance; cf. Dio Cassius 58.23: "Tiberius promised to elevate (literally, push) Caius to other duties"; *P.Mur.* 116, 15 (= *SB* 10305; remarriage contract, AD 124), προβιβάσεται δὲ Ἐλεαῖος Σίμωνος τὴν αὐτὴν γαμικήν κο[ινωνίαν]: if Eleaios, son of Simon, promotes the marital society; *P.Sarap.* 88, 4, letter to Heliodorus at Anoubion: τὸ πένθος μοι ἑκάστης ἡμέρας προβιβάζω, "my pain increases (or is prolonged) every day, because none of those who should have carried letters to you has left"; *P.Petaus* 27, 24: προβιβάζω αὐτά = I urge them along.

[3] F. Field, *Notes on the Translation*, p. 11, who does not retain the connotation of temporal priority expressed by the Vulgate's *praemonita*, "instructed ahead of time"; but this is explained by Mark 6:24—"She went out and asked her mother, 'What shall I ask for?' " This nuance—"instruct"—is the resolute choice of A. H. McNeile, *The Gospel According to St. Matthew*, London, 1952, p. 210.

---

probibazō, S 4264; *EDNT* 3.153; MM 538; L&N 33.299; BAGD 703

προθυμία, πρόθυμος, προθύμως

prothymia, **eagerness;** *prothymos,* **willing, eager;** *prothymōs,* **eagerly**

These terms present no difficulty for interpreters. With some exceptions,[1] they indicate a positive disposition, goodwill; the Koine usually uses them in the heightened sense of eagerness and ardor.[2] This is the nuance when Eleazar declares: "I will prove worthy of my age, leaving to the young a noble example by dying well, willingly and generously, for the venerable and holy laws."[3]

---

[1] Thucydides 3.82.8: in power struggles, passionate ardor (τὸ πρόθυμον) arises from greed and ambition; 8.68.1: "Peisander was openly the most ardent enemy of democracy"; Philo, *Virtues* 205: "he hastened to choose lying, meanness, and vice"; Josephus, *War* 2.624: they are eager to denounce their fellow citizens.

[2] In literary texts, these terms are used especially for passionate ardor (Plutarch, *De virt. mor.* 8) or for ardor in combat: "the Athenians showed themselves full of ardor in battle" (*Phoc.* 14.7; Plutarch, *Cat. Min.* 8.2; cf. Polybius 5.4.7; 5.64.7; 5.85.8); 2 Macc 11:7—"All together, they advanced with ardor" (προθύμως); 15:9—Judas Maccabeus encouraged those who were with him and "made them even more ardent" (προθυμοτέρους); 4 Macc 16:16, the mother of the Maccabees says to her children: "Contend ardently for the law of our fathers" (ἐναγωνίσασθε προθύμως ὑπὲρ τοῦ πατρῴου νόμου); Hab 1:8—the Chaldeans are like vultures who are eager (Hebrew *ḥûš*) to devour; Philo, *Moses* 1.260: ἀγωνισταὶ πρόθυμοι; 1.315: "the reserve troops were not inferior in ardor to those who were fighting"; *Decalogue* 146; *Spec. Laws* 4.111; Josephus, *Ant.* 15.124; 18.374; Xenophon, *Cyr.* 1.6.13: "the means of inspiring ardor in an army"; 1.4.22: "the others, more ardent to pursue"; Polybius 1.20.15: a vessel charges headlong. Diodorus Siculus 17.9.1, 3: "Each one was full of ardor for fighting"; 17.19.6; 17.21.6; 17.30.1; 19.24. 1; 19.54.6; 19.61.4; 19.83.4: "the battle was tough owing to the ardor of the two sides."

[3] 2 Macc 6:28—εἰς τὸ προθύμως καὶ γενναίως. This meaning—"spontaneously, willingly"—occurs frequently: Solomon uses for worship "every willing person with skill" (πᾶς πρόθυμος ἐν σοφίᾳ, 1 Chr 28:21, Hebrew *nādîb*); 2 Macc 4:14—"the priests no longer show any ardor for the service of the altar"; *Ep. Arist.* 94: "a group eager to arise without being ordered to serve"; a decree from Thespiae in the second century AD: "the names of the young soldiers who volunteered for the expedition (τῶν προθύμως ἐκπεμφθέντων νέων ἐπὶ τὴν στρατείαν) . . . May it please the magistrates, the council, and the people that distributions and honors reserved for councillors be granted henceforth to the young soldiers who volunteered for the expedition (τοῖς προθύμοις πρὸς τὴν ἔξοδον)" (*NCIG*, n. XV, 3, 17); "that those who are able should

---

prothymia, S 4288; *TDNT* 6.697–700; *EDNT* 3.156; MM 540; L&N 25.68; BDF §400(2); BAGD 706 ‖ *prothymos,* S 4289; *TDNT* 6.694–697; *EDNT* 3.156; MM 540; L&N 25.69; BAGD 706 ‖ *prothymōs,* S 4290; *EDNT* 3.156; MM 540; L&N 25.69; BAGD 706

Rather frequently one of these terms is used for the eager welcome in store for certain persons (Tob 7:8; Josephus, *Life* 142: foreigners welcomed at Tarichaea; *T. Job* 11.1), for a teaching,[4] for events (Philo, *Abraham* 246), for petitions: "Whereas King Attalus . . . gave an eager welcome to our requests (*epakousas prothymōs ta axioumena*) and sent the city 18,000 silver drachmas for the teaching of the children."[5] In various contexts, the nuance ranges from simple goodwill to cordiality to devotion to zeal;[6] but almost always there is an element of fervor,[7] even enthusiasm (Diodorus Siculus 19.91.5), and in any event generosity—at least in biblical Greek.

---

carry out these activities willingly, with zeal" (Dittenberger, *Or.* 669, 13); receive a reward eagerly (Polybius 5.37.2).

[4] Acts 17:11—the Jews of Beroea received the word with great eagerness; 4 Macc 1:1—ὅπως προσέχητε προθύμως τῇ φιλοσοφίᾳ; Philostratus, *Gym.* 53: "Fearful souls are the quickest to learn what to avoid"; Philo, *Change of Names* 270: "the disciple, without being compelled, shows what he has learned with eagerness"; *Spec. Laws* 1.49; Xenophon, *Cyr.* 1.3.7; *SB* 6262, 15: σπούδασον οὖν τάχιον ἐλθεῖν πρὸς ἐμέ, ἵνα με διδάξῃ ὡς πρόθυμός ἐστίν; *I.Magn.* 97, 74: δέχεται μετὰ πάσης προθυμίας.

[5] J. Pouilloux, *Choix*, n. XIII, 6; cf. Xenophon, *Hell.* 1.1.34: "the Athenians were well-disposed to grant what Thrasyllos had come to ask"; Aglaos of Cos "eagerly devoted himself to all of the requests of the Cretans, trying to be a source of good things for all who petitioned him" (*I.Delos* 1517, 24). Letter of Eumemes II to a city in Caria: "You will in the future find us quite eager to grant, as much as we are able, what is advantageous to your people" (C. B. Welles, *Royal Correspondence*, n. XLIX, 9). Theodorus and Amynander, kings of Athamania, write to Theos: "having listened willingly (προθύμως), we grant your petition" (ibid., n. XXXV, 6); *P.Col.Zen.* 3, 12; 115, h 6; Philo, *Contemp. Life* 71: "their zeal and eagerness are always ready to outstrip requests"; Diodorus Siculus 17.64.4: "The inhabitants gave a warm welcome to Alexander and his army"; 17.91.8; 19.86.5; Plutarch, *Ti. Gracch.* 17.7; *Dem.* 27.7: "all the citizens welcomed him enthusiastically"; *Cic.* 11.2; 26.1: "Cicero received Crassus eagerly"; *Phoc.* 15.2, etc.

[6] Cf. together with εὔνοια; the oath of allegiance of mercenaries to King Eumenes I: παρέξομαι δὲ καὶ τὴν ἄλλην χρείαν εὐνόως καὶ ἀπροφασίστως μετὰ πάσης προθυμίας εἰς δύναμιν εἶναι τὴν ἐμήν (*I.Perg.* 13, 30); letter of Antiochus I to Meleager, governor of the satrapy of the Hellespont in 275 BC: διὰ τὸ φίλον ὄντα ἡμέτερον παρεσχῆσθαι ἡμῖν τὰς καθ᾽ αὐτὸν χρείας μετὰ πάσης εὐνοίας καὶ προθυμίας, "Because of our friendship he provided services to us on his own with goodwill and eagerness" (C. B. Welles, *Royal Correspondence*, n. XI, 14); from the same person to the same recipient: ὁρῶντες οὖν αὐτὸν εὔνουν ὄντα καὶ πρόθυμον εἰς τὰ ἡμέτερα πράγματα (ibid., n. XII, 11 = Dittenberger, *Or.* 221, 61); a decree for judges from Samos: "Whereas the people of Myndos show full goodwill and devotion for reconciliation with our fellow citizens" (πᾶσαν εὔνοιαν καὶ προθυμίαν παρεχόμενοι, *SEG* I, 363, 10); *T. Job* 11.6; M. C. Sahin, "Five New Inscriptions from Halicarnassus," in *ZPE*, 1976, p. 19; *SEG* II, 258, 20, 28.

[7] Cf. together with σπουδή and ἐκτενής; Philo, *Migr. Abr.* 218: follow the path of wisdom μετὰ σπουδῆς καὶ προθυμίας; *Contemp. Life* 71; *Spec. Laws* 1.144; *Sacr. Abel and Cain* 59; letter of Antiochus II to the city of Erythrea: "they asked with such fervor

182 προθυμία, *prothymia*, etc.

In Sir 45:23, Phineas "by the goodness of his generous soul (*en agathotēti prothymias psychēs autou*) obtained pardon for Israel," and in 2 Chr 29:31: "All those who were generous of heart (*pas prothymos tē kardia*) brought whole burnt offerings."[8] It is in this sense that the Lord contrasts the weak flesh with the *pneuma prothymon* (Mark 14:38; Matt 26:41); this ardor or eagerness of spirit is that of the apostles, who were resolved to remain faithful to Christ through whatever dangers might come; but in the presence of these dangers, the fragility of their "flesh" (*sarx*) became evident.[9]

The four occurrences of *prothymia* in 2 Cor 8:11, 12, 19; 9:2 all have to do with the spontaneity, quickness,[10] and generosity of heart evidenced in the Corinthians' willingness to contribute to the collection for the saints at Jerusalem,[11] a benevolent deed, but he urges them to trans-

---

and urgency (μετὰ πάσης σπουδῆς καὶ προθυμίας) that we should be friendly toward you" (C. B. Welles, *Royal Correspondence*, n. XV, 11 = Dittenberger, *Or.* 223); *P.Paris* 63, 149 (= *UPZ* 110; 164 BC); *BGU* 1768, 7; *P.Fouad* 77, 24–25; honorific decree for Boulagoras, who "followed Antiochus as far as Sardis, displaying absolute devotion" (ἐκτενῆ καὶ πρόθυμον ἑαυτὸν παρεχόμενος, *SEG* I, 366, 21; cf. XIII, 458, 14; Dittenberger, *Syl.* 442, 9; 620, 8; 1107, 15; 579, 6 = L. Robert, *Opera Minora Selecta*, 1969, p. 505); honorific decree of the Dionysiac artists: προθύμως καὶ ἐκτενῶς ἑαυτὸν συνεπιδιδοὺς εἰς τὸ συναύξεσθαι τὸ τεχνίτευμα (Dittenberger, *Or.* LI, 10); Dionysodoros "showed zeal and eagerness for the interests of the people" (ἐκτενῆ καὶ πρόθυμον ἑαυτὸν εἰς τὰ τοῦ δήμου παρασκευάζει πράγματα, *I.Thas.*, n. 171, 14); "I have a strong desire to be of service to everyone" (ibid. 186, 10; cf. *I.Did.* 375, 8).

[8] Hebrew *nādîb*; cf. 2 Chr 29:34: the Levites were more eager or more fit (προθύμως = Hebrew *yišrê lēbāb*, literally "upright of heart") than the priests to sanctify themselves. On zeal for *leitourgia*, cf. *UPZ* 50, 35.

[9] When St. Paul declares to the Romans that he will bring them the gospel τὸ πρόθυμον (Rom 1:15), we may translate "gladly," meaning with goodwill, well-disposed: Xenophon, *Hell.* 6.5.43; Josephus, *Ant.* 12.133; Diodorus Siculus 17.4.3; 17.10.2; 17.59.3; 17.96.2: "gladly, willingly"; Plutarch, *Cic.* 4.6; 9.7; Plutarch, *Cat. Min.* 46.7: οὐ προθύμως = unwillingly; *Ant.* 43.6, "eager"; 45.2, "ardent." *I.Priene* III, 7, the Megabyzus (chief priest of Artemis) at Ephesus contributed with full goodwill to the completion of the sanctuary of Athena, περὶ τοῦ ναοῦ τῆς ['Αθηνᾶν] τὴν συντέλεσιν πᾶσαν προθυμίαν ποιησάμενος), but it is preferable to retain a nuance of fervor, if only to avoid banality. *P.Mich.* 57, 1: οἶμαι μέν σε οὐκ ἀγνοεῖν τὴν ἡμετέραν φιλοτιμίαν καὶ προθυμίαν εἰς σέ—"I do not think that you are unaware of our zeal and ardor to serve you," 248 BC; *P.Apoll.* 42, 13: "I will come to bring my greetings with the greatest diligence" (μετὰ προθυμίας πολλῆς, eighth century AD); even a nuance of impatience is not rare in the papyri: προθύμως θελήσοντι ἐξωνήσασθαι αὐτά (*P.Oxy.* 2411, 36; cf. 1864, 11).

[10] Promptness is a distinctive of Philonian *prothymia*, marked by spontaneity (αὐτοκέλευστος πρ., *Moses* 2.137; *Spec. Laws* 1.144; *Change of Names* 270) as well as quickness (*Spec. Laws* 2.83).

[11] P. Joüon ("Notes de lexicographie hébraïque," in *Bib*, 1935, pp. 422–430), observing that the Hebrew verb *nādab* is always used for a generous impulse, an

late this basic good intention (*hē prothymia tou thelein*) into action. In fact, all the texts insist that *prothymia* is active, puts intentions into effect (cf. *P.Oxy.* 2190, 6: "I did something worthy of the good intention"— *axion ti tēs prothymias epraxa;* first century AD); it must be deployed, demonstrated. In the fifth century AD, an Athenian decree honors the Samians "for their good conduct and their eagerness to do as much good as possible";[12] "carrying out the appointment with all eagerness" (*meta pasas prothymias tan apodexim poioumena,* Dittenberger, *Syl.* 532, 6; third century BC; *I.Bulg.* 659, 21; 2264, 7); a decree from the same period honors three ambassadors sent to Zalmodegicos, king of the Getae, because they "demonstrated limitless zeal (*pasan prothymian paraschomenoi*) and brought back more than sixty hostages" (*SEG* XVIII, 288, 9). It is not so much a matter of spontaneity (*Ep. Arist.* 226), or even ardor and zeal (ibid. 20; Josephus, *Ant.* 4.42), but of practical submission, loyal obedience to orders. Lysimachos acknowledges: "the people obeyed willingly";[13] likewise Attalus at Amlada, granting freedom to the hostages: "Since I have seen that you were sorry for your former offenses and that you submitted willingly to the orders of our government";[14] a *dioikētēs* writes to a subordinate: "It does not seem impossible if you devote yourselves wholeheartedly to the matters."[15] In AD 68, the prefect

---

inspiration to liberality, takes 2 Cor 9:2 (προθυμίαν ἡμῶν) as corresponding to the Hebrew substantive nᵉḏāḇâh, an offering and generous gift from man to God; he translates "générosité." At Qumran, however, the (nᵉḏaḇîm) are those who have volunteered to keep the divine commandments or volunteers for his faithfulness (1QS 1.7, 11); "Here is the rule for all the men of the community who have freely committed themselves (nᵉḏaḇîm) to turn from evil and hold fast to all that he has commanded" (5.1).

[12] Ὅτι εἰσὶν ἄνδρες ἀγαθοὶ καὶ πρόθυμοι ποιεῖν ὅ τι δύνανται ἀγαθόν (J. Pouilloux, *Choix,* n. XXIII, 9).

[13] Ὁ δῆμος . . . ὑπήκουσεν προθύμως (C. B. Welles, *Royal Correspondence* VI, 12 = Dittenberger, *Or.* 12 = *I.Priene* 15); cf. *P.Princ.* 68, 9 (second century); *Spec. Laws* 2.83: "to anticipate orders willingly and zealously"; Plutarch, *Cleom.* 33.6; 27.6; *Cic.* 29.1; *Ant.* 70.2: "Timon kissed Alcibiades tenderly" (κατεφίλει προθύμως).

[14] C. B. Welles, *Royal Correspondence,* n. 54, 11; cf. ibid. 58, 9, a letter of Attalus to Attis, priest of the temple of Cybele at Pessinus: "I have seen your zeal for our business" (πρόθυμον ὄντα πρὸς τὰ ἡμέτερα πράγματα).

[15] Δοκεῖ δὲ οὐκ ἀδύνατον εἶναι ὑμῶν προθύμως ἑαυτοὺς εἰς τὰ πράγματα ἐπιδιδόντων; *P.Tebt.* 703, 120 (third century BC); *UPZ* 110, 159–160; *P.Panop.Beatty* 2, 47: τὴν ἑαυτοῦ προθυμίαν ἐνδίξασθαι, "Let him show his own zeal"; *PSI* 1261, 16: ταῦτα προθύμως καὶ εἰς ἐμὴν τιμὴν ποιήσεις; *SB* 7259, 46 (= Dittenberger, *Or.* 740), ὅπως πολλοὶ μᾶλλον προθυμότερον τὰ νομιζόμενα ἐπιτελῶσι; 9415, col. XX, 6: ἵνα πάλιν προθυμότερον ποιήσουσιν.

Tiberius Julius Alexander prescribes: "I want the people to be zealous in farming."[16]

If we keep in mind that most of these occurrences are found in honorific decrees, and that a certain number of them have religious meanings,[17] we must conclude that Hellenistic *prothymia* is not only a widely used term, but a noble word that honors its possessor and is especially well-suited for functionaries, for public officials.[18] We should place 1 Pet 5:2 in this context: "Shepherd the flock of God that is among you not out of compulsion (*anankastōs*) but willingly (*hekousiōs*), not for shameful gain but out of devotion (*prothymōs*)." *Prothymia* here is spontaneous, disinterested, not "calculating," as with Athenodoros of Rhodes, who "gave very devoted help to the grain commissioners, advancing money to them interest-free,"[19] or people who "lend willingly and eagerly, with no intention of receiving anything back other than the capital" (Philo, *Virtues* 83). *Prothymia* describes not only the way one acts,[20] but the spirit that inspires the action. It is the quality of a prince (*Spec. Laws* 4.170) and a benefactor.[21]

---

[16] Dittenberger, *Or.* 669, 57 (προθύμως γεωργεῖν); cf. *SB* 7361, 9: βουλόμενοι ὡς καὶ ἀεὶ προθυμότατα συντελῖν τὰ ἀνήκοντα τῇ γῇ ἔργα; *PSI* 621, 7: πᾶν γὰρ τὸ δυνατὸν καὶ προθύμως καὶ ἀόκνως ποιήσομεν.

[17] Cf. the LXX; Josephus, *Ant.* 4.213, thanks to the phylacteries, everyone will be able to see God's favor toward the Jews (τὸ περὶ αὐτοὺς πρόθυμον τοῦ θεοῦ); *P.Panop.Beatty* 2, 49: "so that the zeal of you all for the divine command may be clearly known"; *P.Ant.* 95, 13: "so that, with God's help, I may be able to take care of business"; *SB* 8929, 9 (= Dittenberger, *Or.* 737): εὐσεβῶς τε διακείμενος πρὸς τὸ θεῖον προθύμως πεπόηται (second century BC).

[18] Moses the shepherd: "no task deterred him; he was always at work and ready for his responsibilities" (αὐτοκελεύστῳ προθυμίᾳ εἰς δέον, Philo, *Moses* 1.63); cf. the decree of Istros for Agathocles, around 200 BC: "full of devotion (πρόθυμον ἑαυτὸν παρεχόμενος) in the offices that he held, in public service and in councils, he never failed to speak and act for the best on every occasion, in the interest of the people" (*NCIG*, n. 6, 5; cf. 5, 9: "demonstrating limitless zeal"); *I.Bulg.* 41, 5: *SEG* XVIII, 245, 14, 20; XIX, 468, 27; etc.

[19] A decree of the people of Histiaea (Dittenberger, *Syl.* 493, 10: προθύμως καὶ ἀργύριον ἄτοκον κτλ.). The adverb is often used for the execution of financial obligations, cf. *P.Cair.Isid.* 1, 13 = *SB* 7622; cf. 7246, 7.

[20] Philo, *Moses* 1.52: the young women "went wholeheartedly (προθύμως) about the task of filling the drinking troughs"; 1.333: "Full of ardor and joy, these men put their loved ones and their flocks in safety."

[21] In 306 BC the honorific decree for Malousios of Gargara is motivated by τὴν ἄλλην προθυμίαν ἐμ πᾶσιν τοῖς καιροῖς παρεχόμενος (Dittenberger, *Syl.* 330, 7 = *I.Ilium*, n. 1), τἆλλα δὲ προθύμως ὑπηρετεῖ (line 28), ὁ Γαργαρεὺς ἐπιμεμέληται προθύμως (line 60); cf. ibid. n. 32, 10; 33, 38, 60; 40, 5; etc. Diodorus Siculus 19.81.4: "a certain mildness (πρᾳότης) drew all hearts toward him, δι' ἧς εἰς προθυμίαν ἐξεκαλεῖτο πάντας." Prothymos is a proper name, *PSI* 524, 4; *P.Mil.* inv. 69, 55 (ed. S. Daris, "Elenco di spece cultuali," in *P.Coll.Youtie* I, p. 108.)

προκοπή, προκόπτω

prokopē, **progress;** *prokoptō,* **to progress, advance**

The substantive is unknown in classical Greek[1] and the verb in the LXX. Both mean literally a move forward, an extension, and are used most often in the figurative sense of progress, growth, advancement.[2]

The meaning is often neutral ("Night has advanced; day is near"),[3] sometimes pejorative (heretics will constantly get worse—*prokopsousin epi to cheiron*[4]—in the direction of impiety, 2 Tim 2:16); but usually it has to do with improvement and success. Philip, prefect of Jerusalem, learns that Judas Maccabeus was progressing little by little (*kata mikron eis prokopēn erchomenon*) and that his successes were becoming more and more frequent.[5] This is the most common meaning of *prokoptō* in the epistolary

[1] The work of L. Edelstein (*The Idea of Progress in Classical Antiquity,* Baltimore, 1967) studies the idea, not the word.

[2] The substantive is often synonymous with αὔξησις (Polybius 3.4.2: the growth and progress of the Roman power) and βελτίωσις (Philo, *Etern. World* 43: people are used to knowing growth, progress, improvement, or their opposites; *Abraham* 26). The first meaning of προκόπτω is transitive, "draw out, lengthen a metal plaque by hammering it"; hence "prepare, open a road" (Thucydides 4.60.2); in an intransitive sense: "advance along a route" (Josephus, *Ant.* 2.134, 340; 3.42; Thucydides 7.56.3).

[3] Rom 13:12, ἡ νὺξ προέκοψεν (K H. Schelkle, "Biblische und patristische Eschatologie nach Rom. XIII, 11–13," in *Sacra Pagina,* Paris-Gembloux, 1959, vol. 2, pp. 357–372); cf. Josephus, *War* 4.298, τῆς νυκτὸς προκοπτούσης = at the moment when night is coming on; *Pap.Lugd.Bat.* I, 17, 6, τοῦ χρόνου προκόψαντος = time having passed by; *P.Stras.* 180, 11.

[4] 2 Tim 3:9, 13; cf. the progress of sedition, Josephus, *Ant.* 4.59: τῆς ἐπὶ τὸ χεῖρον προκοπῆς; *T. Jud.* 21.8, προκόψουσιν ἐπὶ κακῷ; Polybius 5.16.9; cf. Xenophon, *Hell.* 7.1.6: advance not at all, not arrive at the goal.

[5] 2 Macc 8:8; cf. Polybius 2.12.7: τῆς ἐπὶ τὸ βέλτιον ἤρξαντο προκοπῆς = the Romans began to get back on their feet; Josephus, *Ant.* 18.340: their qualities carried

prokopē, S 4297; *TDNT* 6.703–719; *EDNT* 3.157–158; *NIDNTT* 2.128, 130–131; MM 542; L&N 13.57; BAGD 707 ‖ *prokoptō,* S 4298; *TDNT* 6.703–719; *EDNT* 3.157–158; *NIDNTT* 2.128, 130; MM 542; L&N 13.57, 42.18, 59.64, 67.118; BDF §308; BAGD 707–708; ND 2.95, 4.36

papyri, where the writer expresses the hope that his correspondent will be well and will prosper: *errōsthai se euchomai kai prokoptein;*[6] and it is in this sense of continual and effective advancement in knowledge and in morals that we read Gal 1:14—"Progressing in Judaism more than most of those of my age in my nation, surpassing them in zeal for the traditions of my ancestors."[7]

Such progress becomes generally known and draws more and more esteem from those who know about it.[8] Likewise, the arrest and trial of Paul turned out "rather for the advancement of the gospel, for throughout the praetorium and everywhere else, my chains have become well-known in Christ, and most of the brethren, encouraged in the Lord . . . are proclaiming the word with increased boldness."[9] In Phil 1:25, the apostle's presence should contribute to Christians' progress and joy in the faith.[10] This moral and religious meaning is ever clearer in 1 Tim 4:15—"Let your progress be manifest to all."[11] Thanks to his training (verses 7–8),

---

the Parthians to a high level of power (προὔκοψαν ἐπὶ μέγα δυνάμεως); Diodorus Siculus 14.98; 17.69.4: "those who could make progress in some sort of industry"; Philo, *Sacr. Abel and Cain* 113: "Try to achieve progress and improvement (προκοπὴν καὶ βελτίωσιν), for it is progress that makes toil bearable."

[6] *P.Stras.* 140, 15 = *P.Sarap.* 100 = *SB* 8022; cf. *P.Mich.* 209, 4: πρὸ μὲν πάντων εὔχομέ σαι ὑγειένειν καὶ προκόπτειν, "above all, I pray for your health and success"; *P.Hamb.* 104, ἐρρῶσθαί σε εὔχομαι διὰ βίου καὶ προκόπτοντα τὰ μεγάλα; *P.Ryl.* 233, 16: εὔχομαι σε τὸν Κύριον ἰδεῖν ἐν μείζοσι προκοπαῖς, ἐν ἁδραῖς εὐημερίαις; *P.Brem.* 15, 34: ποιεῖν σε τὰς ἁδροτάτας προκοπάς; *P.Oxy.* 122, 15; *P.Gen.* 74, 3; *PSI* 1437, 8; *P.Tebt.* 276, 39: the alignment of certain planets will favor prosperity from birth, ἀπὸ νεότητος τὰς προκοπὰς ἀποτελοῦσιν; *proskynēma* of Maximus: "Grant me, O Lord, great success in the army. . . . I will pour out to you libations for this success" (*SEG* XXIV, 1224, 4, 7). Progress in the accomplishment of tasks, κατὰ προκοπὴν τῶν ἔργων (*P.Oxy.* 1631, 20; *P.Mert.* 24, 10).

[7] Προέκοπτον ἐν τῷ Ἰουδαϊσμῷ ὑπὲρ πολλοὺς συνηλικιώτας ἐν τῷ γένει μου; A. Deissmann (*Light,* p. 179) compares *BGU* 423, 17, where Apion, a soldier in the Romano-Egyptian fleet of the second century, writes to his father: "Thou hast taught me well and I therefore hope to advance quickly, if the gods will."

[8] *Ep. Arist.* 242: "This conduct will advance us in their esteem"; Josephus, *Ant.* 20.205: καθ' ἑκάστην ἡμέραν ἐπὶ μέγα προὔκοπτε δόξης, "each day the high priest Ananias advanced greatly in reputation." *T. Gad* 4.5—τῶν εὐπραγούντων ἐν προκοπῇ ἀκούων καὶ ὁρῶν; B. Latyschev (*Inscriptiones Antiquae,* n. 79, 6), μέχρι τὰς τῶν Σεβαστῶν γνώσεως προκόψαντος.

[9] Phil 1:12, εἰς προκοπὴν τοῦ εὐαγγελίου (cf. the reporting of victory and military progress in *P.Giss.* 27, 7: εὐαγγελίζοντι τὰ τῆς νείκην αὐτοῦ καὶ προκοπῆς). Thus there is progress and victory for the *kerygma.*

[10] Εἰς τὴν ὑμῶν προκοπὴν καὶ χαρὰν τῆς πίστεως.

[11] 1 Tim 4:15: ἵνα σου ἡ προκοπὴ φανερὰ ᾖ πᾶσιν. The emphasis is on the visibility of this progress and the perception of it by witnesses, as when an athlete's physique improves day by day and stirs admiration; this will help strengthen Timothy's

Timothy will no longer be seen as an inexperienced novice; he will progress continually.

Scholars traditionally mention that *prokopē* is a technical term in Stoic philosophy,[12] and it is indeed true that this term is used for a person's moral and spiritual evolution. According to Chrysippus, the sage is a person who is progressing (*prokoptōn*) from folly to wisdom, from vice to virtue.[13] But if the Stoa contributed greatly to the spread of this term in the first century and used it for moral values (*hē prokopē pros aretēn,* Epictetus 1.4.3ff.), this usage cannot be said to have influenced the NT writers, at least not directly, because the idea of *prokopē* was so generally current without reference to origin or technical signification. Thus Philo—who was knowledgeable about contemporary philosophy—defines moral progress as "that which is incomplete and strives for completion,"[14] and distinguishes two or three classes of people: the perfect person (*ton teleion*) and the one who is progressing morally (*ton prokoptonta*) have a strong and ardent desire for the good and already share in the divine fixity and stability (*Dreams* 2.234–237); "for the wicked (*tōn phaulōn*), God is Lord and Master; for those who are progressing and improving (*tōn en prokopais kai beltiōsesi*) he is God; but for the best and most perfect (*tōn d' aristōn kai teleiotatōn*), he is Lord and God" (*Change of Names* 19). If the capability for improvement and perfection (*Post. Cain* 78) never disappears (*Husbandry* 166; cf. Cleanthes, in Stobaeus,

---

authority in the eyes of the Ephesian Christians; cf. φανερός, Acts 4:16; *I.Priene* VIII, 42: ὅπως δ' ἂν ᾖ φανερὰ πᾶσιν; *I.Bulg.* 659, 21; *P.Tebt.* 333, 12.

[12] A. Bonhöffer, *Epiktek,* p. 128; E. V. Arnold, *Roman Stoicism,* 1911, p. 325 (who sees Pompey as a type of the *proficiens*); G. Stählin, "Fortschritt und Wachstum," in *Festgabe J. Lortz,* Baden-Baden, 1958, vol. 2, pp. 13–25; idem, in *TDNT,* vol. 6, pp. 703–719; O. Luschnat, "Das Problem des ethischen Fortschritts in der alten Stoa," in *Philologus,* 1958, pp. 178–214; G. T. Montague, *Growth in Christ,* Kirkwood-Fribourg, 1961, pp. 165ff.

[13] Cf. Chrysippus, frag. 45, 217, 530, 532 (ed. *SVF,* vol. 3, 104, 18; 51, 37, 142, 17, 33); Bion (in Diogenes Laertius 4.50); Posidonius (ibid. 7.91: "The proof of the reality of virtue is that people like Socrates, Diogenes, and Antisthenes have progressed toward it"; cf. 127); Epictetus 1.4: περὶ προκοπῆς; idem, *Ench.* 48; Seneca, *Ep.* 71.36: "magna pars est profectus velle proficere"; cf. G. Verbecke, "Augustin et le Stoïcisme," in *Recherches Augustiniennes,* Paris, 1958, pp. 69ff.

[14] Philo, *Alleg. Interp.* 3.249: προκοπή . . . ἀτελὲς ἐφιέμενον τοῦ τέλους; *Drunkenness* 82: Jacob was going to exchange his progress for perfection; Plutarch, *Quaest. conv.* 2.3.2: "progress is the middle ground between natural dispositions and perfection"; *De comm. not.* 10: "With respect to moral progress people resemble not the blind but the near-sighted, not those who have drowned, but those who are swimming and are near the port." Cf. W. Völker, *Fortschritt und Vollendung bei Philo von Alexandrien,* Leipzig, 1938.

vol. 2, p. 65, 10), "all progress depends on God" (*Alleg. Interp.* 2.93; cf. *P.Lund* II, 1, 4 = *SB* 8088).

Epictetus sensibly observes: "It is ridiculous to imagine that one can progress in things that one knows nothing about" (2.17.4). Moreover, it is commonplace to keep track of progress in scientific knowledge,[15] in moral education, and in the assimilation of wisdom. Ben Sirach says, "Progress came to me through wisdom."[16] Philo repeats that study and instruction make for progress toward perfection,[17] and Josephus notes that wisdom produced progress in Daniel, Mishael, and Abednego (*sophias en prokopē genomenous*, *Ant.* 10.189). It is in this sense that "Jesus grew in wisdom and in stature with God and with men."[18] We may cite this eulogy for a young citizen of Istropolis: "he laid a foundation for himself, progressing in stature and advancing toward godliness" (*hypestēsato tē te hēlikia prokoptōn kai proagomenos eis to theosebein*, Dittenberger, *Syl.* 708, 18; first century BC). And we might add this epitaph from Aphrodisia: "children who departed in the midst of progress."[19]

---

[15] Philo, *Flight* 213: "You who were progressing and deepening your knowledge of the cycle of preliminary instruction"; Josephus, *Life* 8: "My great progress in studies earned me a reputation for memory and superior intelligence"; Plutarch, *De prof. in virt.* 10: νέῳ ... ἀνδρὶ γευσαμένῳ προκοπῆς ἀληθοῦς ἐν φιλοσοφίᾳ; Marcus Aurelius 1.17.8: "I did not advance very far in rhetoric, poetry, and other studies"; Diodorus Siculus 16.6: "Dio had made great progress in the study of philosophy"; Lucian, *Hermot.* 63; προύκοπτον ἐν τοῖς μαθήμασι; cf. G. Pire, *Stoïcisme et pédagogie de Zénon à Marc-Aurèle*, Liege-Paris, 1958, p. 65.

[16] Sir 51:17: προκοπὴ ἐγένετό μοι ἐν αὐτῇ (cf. σοφία, verse 17 *b*; παιδεία, verse 16). The Hebrew is different: "for me its yoke was an honor." Cf. Plutarch, *De prof. in virt.* 7: ἀληθὴς προκοπή.

[17] Philo, *Sacr. Abel and Cain*; cf. *Flight* 172: "the teacher is capable of effecting progress in us, but only God ... can effect supreme perfection in us"; cf. *Husbandry* 166; *P.Iand.* 3, 5: ταχέως μὲν περὶ παιδείαν προκόπτει. Around the turn of the millennium, a decree from Delphi (*Fouilles de Delphes* III, 4, 59) honors the rhetor Artemidorus who "manifested (toward the Delphians) the same zeal as toward his own country and his fellow citizens; by working together with the foremost and best citizens for progress in education and letters (εἰς προκοπὴν παιδίας καὶ λόγων), he procured worthy people for Delphi also" (L. Robert, *Noms indigènes*, p. 491).

[18] Luke 2:52—προέκοπτεν τῇ σοφίᾳ καὶ ἡλικίᾳ καὶ χάριτι; J. E. Renié, "Et Jesus proficiebat sapientia et aetate et gratia apud Deum et homines," in *Studia Anselmiana* 27–28 (Miscellanea A. Miller), Rome, 1951, pp. 340–350; H. Riedlinger, *Geschichtlichkeit und Vollendung des Wissens Christi*, Freiburg-Basel, 1966, pp. 48–54; H. Temple, "Christ's Holy Youth According to Lk II, 52," in *CBQ*, 1941, pp. 243–250.

[19] E. Bernand, *Inscriptions métriques*, n. XXXV, 12, ἥν λίπον ἐν προκοπαῖς.

προπετής

propetēs, recklessly hasty, impulsive (with overtones of injustice)

Certainty is impossible in translating the two NT occurrences of this adjective. At the riot at Ephesus, the clerk asks his fellow citizens to do nothing *propetes* (*mēden propetes prassein*, Acts 19:36), and according to 2 Tim 3:4, people in the last days will be *prodotai, propeteis*. Literally, the term means "fallen forward," hence "inclined toward."[1] Figuratively, it expresses lack of control or quickness, in either a favorable or a pejorative sense;[2] in the latter case, it means reckless precipitousness.[3]

The adjective, unknown in the papyri, is used in the LXX only by the Wisdom writers for prattlers who talk without thinking, but the fact that they are abominated and promised ruin indicates that this is one of the gravest sins of speech; moreover, *propetēs* does not exactly match the original Hebrew.[4]

---

[1] Hippocrates, *Prog.* 3: "the tendency to sink in the bed and slide toward the feet"; *Art.* 1: "the top of the humerus naturally inclines in this direction"; Xenophon, *Hell.* 2.3.15: Critias stooped (προπετὴς ἦν) to having many people executed"; 2.3.30: "He is the one who was most inclined to transform the democracy."

[2] Aristotle, *HA* 9.1.5.608^b: "the females have more liveliness"; Isocrates, *Demon.* 1.15: "Abstain from immoderate laughter (γέλωτα προπετῆ) and presumptuous talk"; Aeschines, *In Tim.* 1.191: "unbridled sensual pleasure (αἱ προπετεῖς τοῦ σώματος), passions that are never assuaged, these are the things that inhabit the haunts of brigands"; Josephus, *Ant.* 5.106 = without reason or motive; Diodorus Siculus 15.29.

[3] Cf. the account for the allotment for a "five-day" work detail, from the third century AD: τοὺς λόγους τῶν πενθημερῶν μὴ προπετῶς γράφῃς, ἕως ἂν ἔλθῃς εἰς τὸ λογιστήριον τοῦ στρατηγοῦ (*SB* 9925, 3; to be added to P. J. Sijpesteijn, *Penthemeros Certificates in Greco-Roman Egypt*, Leiden, 1964).

[4] Sir 9:18—"The person who speaks recklessly is hated for his volubility"; Prov 10:14—"The mouth of the foolish (Hebrew *ewîl*) is a disaster in the offing"; 13:3: "the one who opens his mouth (Hebrew *pāśaq*) to ruin." Roman soldiers "catch those who speak thoughtlessly" (προπετεῖς), i.e., who speak ill of Caesar without thinking about who they are talking to (Epictetus 4.13.5) or without dreaming of the consequences,

---

190 προπετής, *propetēs*

With respect to action, the *proteteis* are those who are impulsive, who get carried away[5]—like a bolting horse (cf. *proalēs*, Sir 30:8)—who cannot reason soundly and who make themselves known by their violence, people who wreck everything, who take wild chances. The Greeks grouped them with the reckless and the bold: *hoi thraseis propeteis* (Aristotle, *Eth. Nic.* 3.10.1116[a]7); "giving free rein to your recklessness and boldness" (*tē sautou propeteia kai thrasytēti*, Demosthenes, *C. Andr.* 22.63); "the Romans showed more boldness and daring" (*tharraleōteron kai propetesteron*, Polybius 3.102.11; contrasted with the prudence and circumspection of their adversaries); "quick to rush at everyone" (Xenophon, *Cyr.* 1.4.4, contrasted with *aidous*); "Cleitos, a bold and reckless young man" (*thrasys te kai propetēs neanias*, Josephus, *Life* 170); "Herod had enough self-control not to do something rash (*tou mē propetes ti poiēsai*) under the influence of passion."[6] At the beginning of the third century, a tax collector complains that his methods are criticized as unjust and violent (*prepetōs epi tauta*, *P.Oxy.* 3028, 7).

In light of these usages, we should understand the *propeteis* in 2 Tim 3:4 to be frenzied and unjust; and the Ephesian rioters are warned against not "reckless precipitousness" but uncontrolled or ill-considered aggression.

like Cyrus asking "impulsively (προπετῶς), like a child who no longer fears anything" (Xenophon, *Cyr.* 1.3.8); cf. dangerous procedures (πρὸς τὸ προπετῶς τι πράττειν, Demosthenes, *C. Leoch.* 44.58).

[5] Hotheaded, Philo, *Spec. Laws* 3.175; *Dreams* 2.182 (vehement); *Unchang. God* 163.

[6] Josephus, *Ant.* 15.82. Cf. the προπέτεια of Uzzah (2 Sam 6:7). In Demosthenes, *C. Arist.* 23.130, *propeteia* corresponds to anger; both are opposed to moderation (μετριωτέρα); *P.Tebt.* 268, 47: ἡ σὴ προπέτεια (fragment of a classical work, third century AD; cf. *P.Cair.Masp.* 97, col. II, 42; sixth century). An ostracon from the same period links indifference and rashness, προπετεία [δ'] ἀνεπιστρεψία, εἰκαιότης, ἕτεραι τοιαῦται [μυρίαι], in C. Austin (*Comicorum Graecorum Fragmenta*, n. 318), who cites a mutilated fragment of Menander, where προπετῶς ἐπι[. . . seems to have the sense of attacking (n. 257, 100; cf. J. M. Edmonds, *Attic Comedy*, vol. 3 A, p. 344).

προσκαρτερέω, προσκαρτέρησις

proskartereō, to be firm, endure, persevere, remain faithful to a person or a task; *proskarterēsis*, constancy, diligence, perseverance, persistence

---

Given the Koine's love for compound forms and its tendency to reinforce the expressivity of words, we might think that *proskartereō* would hardly differ from plain *kartereō*—"be firm and courageous, endure,"[1] even "persevere" (2 Macc 7:17), which is the meaning of *proskartereō* in Tob 5:8 (in א). When Moses commands the explorers of Canaan, "Be courageous" (Num 13:20), the LXX uses *proskarterēsantes* to translate the hiphil of the Hebrew ḥāzaq.

Nevertheless, the usage of *proskartereō* (usually with the dative) shows new connotations, whether of remaining faithfully attached to a person or of applying oneself exclusively to a certain thing, devoting oneself to it tirelessly. In the first case, Simon the sorceror, after being baptized, stuck close to Philip (*ēn proskarterōn tō Philippō*, Acts 8:13); the centurion Cornelius calls one of the soldiers who is in his service.[2] We may compare Mark 3:9, where Jesus asks his disciples "that a boat be kept ready for him" (*hina ploiarion proskarterē autō*), i.e., at his disposal, so that he may use it when he wants.

---

[1] Heb 11:27; cf. Job 2:9; Sir 2:2; Philo, *Husbandry* 152; Epictetus 1.26.12; *T. Job* 4.10.

[2] Acts 10:7—τῶν προσκαρτερούντων αὐτῷ; cf. *P.Lond.* 196, 3 (vol. 2, p. 153), προσκαρτερεῖν τῷ Νεοκύδει; *P.Brem.* 48, 17: προσκαρτερεῖν αὐτῇ (AD 118); *P.Giss.* 79, col. II, 9: "Epaphroditus has hitherto been guilty of no negligence but is devoted to us and to all your affairs" (ἀλλὰ προσκαρτερεῖ ἡμῖν καὶ πᾶσι τοῖς πράγμασί σου—AD 117); *P.Oxy.* 530, 9: "I have long been devoted to the affairs of Pausirion." Horus is attached (προσκαρτερήσαντι) to the baths for a salary of one drachma per day (P. J. Sijpesteijn, *The Family of the Tiberii Julii Theones*, Amsterdam, 1976, n. XV, 4).

---

proskartereō, S 4342; *TDNT* 3.618–619; *EDNT* 3.172; *NIDNTT* 2.767–768; MM 548; L&N 34.2, 35.28, 68.68; BDF §202; BAGD 715 ‖ *proskarterēsis*, S 4343; *TDNT* 3.619–620; *EDNT* 3.172; *NIDNTT* 2.767–768; MM 548; L&N 68.68; BAGD 715

According to Rom 13:6, the tax officials constantly apply themselves to their task (*eis auto touto proskarterountes*). This diligence is already clear in Daniel, where the two elders frequent the house of Joakim (*houtoi prosekarteroun en tē oikia Iōakim*, Sus 6, Theodotion) and is not rare in the papyri:[3] "The little one greets you; she is diligent in her studies" (*aspazetai se hē meikra kai proskarterei tois mathēmasi*, *P.Brem.* 63, 24). It is always a matter of persevering, not letting up,[4] as is seen in the technical use of the verb in the legal vocabulary: the defendant and the complainant are at the disposition of the court until the final settlement of the suit, as in this summons from 104/5: "Let them keep themselves at the disposition of the court of the same governor until my claim against them is satisfied."[5] Thus

---

[3] In AD 104, the command of the prefect Gaius Vibius Maximus for the census provides "that they devote themselves diligently to their farming" (τῇ προσηκούσῃ αὐτοῖς γεωργίαι προσκαρτερήσωσιν, *P.Lond.* 904, 27; vol. 3, p. 125); cf. the request of two brothers selected as farm workers on the royal estate (δημόσιοι γεωργοί) that one of them be released "so that we may be able to devote ourselves also to our own farming" (ἵνα δυνηθῶμεν καὶ τῇ ἑαυτῶν γεωργίᾳ προσκαρτερεῖν, *P.Amh.* 65, 3; republished in *SB* 9050, col. III, 3 and A. Kränzlein, "Die Papyri Vind. inv. 2582 a, 25824 b und Amh 65," in *JJP,* vol. 6, 1952, pp. 195–237); the edict of the prefect Q. Aemilius Saturninus, ἵνα διὰ τὴν σὴν τύχην δυνηθῶμεν προσκαρτερεῖν τῷ ἔργῳ (*P.Lund* IV, 1, 20; republished in *SB* 9340; second century); προσκαρτερῶν τῇ στρατηγίᾳ ἀδιαλίπτως εἰς τὸ ἐν μηδενὶ μεμφθῆναι (*P.Oxy.* 82, 4; third century); ephebic inscription in honor of a *kosmētēs* (καὶ τοῦ διατηρηθῆναι τὴν εὐφημίαν αὐτοῖς προσκαρτερῶν ἐπιμελῶς καὶ προσεδρεύων, Dittenberger, *Syl.* 717, 84); Polybius 1.59.12: ἐπιμελείᾳ προσκαρτερῶν.

[4] *P.Brem.* 16, 15: "It is enough that Hierakion perseveres and to me . . ." (ἀρκετὸς γάρ ἐστιν Ἱερακίων προσκαρτερῶν καὶ ἐμοὶ . . .); inscription of Antiochus I of Commagene at Nimrud Dagh, Arsameia, and Selik (*IGLS,* n. 1, 130, 168; 47, col. III, 17; IV, 2–3; 51, 14 = Dittenberger, *Or.* 383).

[5] Προσκαρτερήσωσι τῷ τοῦ αὐτοῦ ἡγεμόνος βήματι ἄχρι οὗ ἐκβιβασθῇ ἃ ἔχω πρὸς αὐτούς, *P.Oxy.* 2852, 33; cf. 261, 12: Demetria pleads physical weakness as an excuse for being absent, οὐ δυναμένη προσκαρτερῆσαι τῷ κριτηρίῳ διὰ γυναικείαν ἀσθένειαν (AD 55); 260, 14: προσκαρτερήσειν μέχρι οὗ ἃ ἔχωμεν πρὸς ἑαυτοὺς ἐγβιβασθῇ (AD 59); 2597, 8; *P.Hamb.* 4, 7: προσκαρτερήσειν τῷ ἱερωτάτῳ τοῦ κρατίστου ἡγεμόνος . . . βήματι (AD 87); *P.Oslo* 19, 4; *PSI* 806, 17 (cf. 1265, 8; E. Wipszycka, in *JJP,* vol. 16–17, 1971, p. 228); *P.Ross.Georg.* II, 27, 6; *P.Stras.* 196, 16; *P.Mich.* 533, 7: Heracleides swears to the prefect in 137 that he will be present at the tribunal until the sentence is handed down (προσκαρτερήσειν τῷ βήματι μέχρι οὗ διευθύνω ἃ πρός με ἔχει Ἡρακλείδης); *P.Fouad* 22, col. II, 13, a lawsuit between members of the same family, AD 125: Isidora takes an oath to appear at Alexandria to settle her dispute with Deios, "and I will remain at the disposal of his excellence the *archidikastēs* until I have completed by business with Deios" (καὶ προσκαρτερήσειν τῷ κρατίστῳ ἀρχιδικαστῇ ἄχρι ἂν ἐκβιβάσω ἃ ἔχω πρὸς τὸν Δεῖον); *BGU* 628, 9; *P.Mert.* 91, 4, a petition to the *stratēgos*: the complainant asks that his adversaries be notified of his complaint so that they may be informed and may present themselves before the tribunal until the difference between them is

proskerterēsis has a connotation of waiting without lapse,[6] but with a nuance of stubbornness, like that of the tribe of Ephraim besieging Bethel (Josephus, *Ant.* 5.130), and finally the verb refers to the exertion of great efforts, especially in military language: "Epaminondas bade his soldiers hold fast" (Xenophon, *Hell.* 7.5.14); "the soldiers, by persevering (or "with great effort," *proskarterēsantes*) dislodged four stone blocks" (Josephus, *War* 6.27); "the others pursued the operations with all their might" (Polybius 1.55.4; cf. Achilles Tatius 1.10.7: "if she remains obstinate, do not use force," *kan men proskarterē, epischēs tēn bian*).

These components should be kept in mind when we look at the five NT texts that remark on or call for perseverance in prayer. The idea is constant diligence, effort that never lets up, confident waiting for results; and several times these characteristics are emphasized by the periphrastic construction of the participle with the imperfect of the verb to be, showing continuity and suggesting perseverance that does not falter or fail: "these were all persevering with one accord in prayer" (*houtoi pantes ēsan proskarterountes homothymadon tē proseuchē*).[7] When the apostles refuse to wait on tables so that they may devote themselves to prayer and the ministry of the word (Acts 6:4), their dedication has connotations of exclusivity. The application of the verb *proskartereō* to prayer, a usage without parallel in secular Greek and in the LXX, is original to the NT authors; its frequency points as much to an actual state of affairs in the primitive church as to an apostolic demand. It is regrettable that the theological treatises on prayer did not explore the richness of the meaning of this expression, because it is the apostolic translation of the Master's precept "that they ought always to pray . . . and never lose heart" (*to dein pantote proseuchesthai . . . kai mē enkakein*, Luke 18:1; cf. 1 Thess 5:17).

The substantive *proskarterēsis*, "constancy, diligence, persistence" (Philodemus of Gadara, *Rh.* 1.11), unknown in the papyri, is a biblical hapax describing Christian prayer; it should be understood as having the same richness of meaning as the corresponding verb: "Live a life of prayer and supplication; pray always, in the Spirit. Keep at it with tireless perseverance (*eis auto agrypnountes en pasē proskarterēsei*), with intercessions for

---

settled (ἵν᾽ εἰδῶσιν καὶ προσκαρτερήσωσιν τῷ σῷ δικαστηρίῳ ἄχρις ἂν τὰ μετοξὺ ἡμῶν πέρατος τύχῃ).

[6] *P.Oxy.* 1764, 4: "For a number of days we have been waiting for Phileas the butcher" (πολλαὶ ἡμέραι προσκαρτεροῦμεν Φιλέῳ τῷ μοσχομαγείρῳ); *P.Ross.Georg.* II, 31, 11: "For a long while I waited for Hermaiscos to pay the seven staters; finally he gave me twenty-four drachmas"; *P.Mil.Vogl.* 189, 7; *PSI* 598, 7: προσκαρτέρησον οὖν ἕως ἂν Ἐτέαρχος παραγένηται.

[7] Acts 1:14; 2:42 (cf. P. H. Menoud, *La Vie de l'église naissante*, Neuchâtel-Paris, 1952, pp. 23–24; J. A. Fitzmyer, *Semitic Background*, pp. 271–303); 2:46; 6:4; Rom 12:12.

all the saints" (Eph 6:18). The word is found again in Jewish acts of emancipation at Panticapaeum in AD 80 in a rather enigmatic formula: *chōris is tēn proseuchēn thōpeias te kai proskartereseōs;*[8] also *chōris tou proskarterein tē proseuchē epitropeuousēs tēs synagōgēs tōn Ioudaiōn kai theon sebōn.*[9] We translate: the slave shall be free "except [for his obligation] to attend the prayer service regularly"; the Jewish synagogue is the best example of a place for prayer to God.

---

[8] B. Latyschev, *Inscriptiones Antiquae,* vol. 2, n. 52, 53, 364. *RIJG* (vol. 2, p. 299) translates "aller librement . . . excepté dans la maison de prière consacrée au culte et à la persévérance" ("go freely . . . except in the house of prayer, which is consecrated to worship and perseverance"). J. B. Frey (*CII* 683, 14; 684, 21; 691, 20): total liberty for the freed slave "except with respect to prayer, to which he will owe devotion and diligence"; προσκαρτέρησις is attested in an inscription from Andros in the sense of devoting oneself to a profession (W. Peek, "Griechische Inschriften," in *Ath. Mitt.* 1934, p. 69).

[9] *CIRB,* n. 71, 6–7; Republished by B. Lifshitz, "Notes d'épigraphie grecque," in *RB,* 1969, p. 95; cf. M. Hengel, "Proseuche und synagoge," in *Tradition und Glaube* (Festgabe K. G. Kuhn), Göttingen, 1971, p. 174; ἡ προσκαρτερία (*I.Priene* 109, 101; from 120 BC).

προσλαμβάνομαι

proslambanomai, to take in addition, seize, conquer, take with oneself, aid, assist, take in, add, receive

---

This compound of *lambanō*, "take, receive, possess," can keep the same meaning; for example, Heracles says to his son, "Take me here to lift me up" (Sophocles, *Trach.* 1024; cf. Aristophanes, *Lys.* 202). But at *Ach.* 1215 ("Take [*labesthe*] my leg, take it again [*proslabesth'*], my friends"), Aristophanes retains the significance of *pros-* ("additionally"; Polybius 3.70.2; cf. Euripides, *Med.* 885; *Hipp.* 1011) added to the simple verb: "take in addition." Thus one takes a food with one's bread (Xenophon, *Mem.* 3.14.4; cf. *Symp.* 4.8) or "adds" dishonor to misfortune (Thucydides 5.111.3; *Tht.* 207 *c*; *Phdr.* 272 *a*). Hence the meanings "add,[1] adjoin, bring along": "Cyrus took with him a large number of horsemen and peltasts" (bearers of light shields, Xenophon, *Cyr.* 1.4.16); "If I had joined him to you as an ally" (*An.* 7.6.27; Sophocles, *OC* 378); then "come to the aid of": Dio undertook a campaign against Dionysius and "with the help of the people (*proslabōn ton dēmon*) expelled him" (Aristotle, *Pol.* 5.10.32); and finally "take, conquer" cities or lands (Xenophon, *Hell.* 4.4.1). — In the middle voice, *proslambanomai* retains this latter meaning (Polybius 1.37.5), and likewise "take with oneself" (volunteers, Chariton, *Chaer.* 8.2.14); but above all it means "take part in an enterprise, come to the aid of, assist": "It was right that you should lend me your help" (Plato, *Leg.* 10.897 *d*); "Clearchus put his own hand to the work . . . men who had passed the age of thirty also took part."[2]

---

[1] *Ep. Arist.* 2 quotes an iambic trimeter: προσμανθάνειν ἀεί τι καὶ προσλαμβάνειν ("Always to learn and enrich oneself").

[2] Xenophon, *An.* 2.3.11–12; cf. Aristophanes, *Pax* 9: "help me, in the name of the gods"; Chariton, *Chaer.* 8.2.13: "I will not let you have regrets, with the help of the gods."

---

proslambanomai, S 4355; *TDNT* 4.15; *EDNT* 3.175; *NIDNTT* 3.747–748, 750; MM 549–550; L&N 15.127, 15.167, 15.180, 18.2, 34.53; BDF §169(2); BAGD 717

In the LXX, two occurrences have the meaning "add, adjoin,"[3] one means "receive, accept" (those banished from Jerusalem, 2 Macc 10:15), and the other five have theological meanings. God is the subject of the verb, but in each case the underlying Hebrew is different: God decides to take Isr as his people (1 Sam 12:22; *'āśâh* with the double nuance of acquiring and instituting); "From on high he stretched forth his hand, he grasped me, he drew me out of the great waters" (Ps 18:16, Hebrew *māšâh*); "If my father and mother were to abandon me, Yahweh would take me in" (Ps 27:10, Hebrew *'āsap*); "Happy is the one whom you choose and take for yourself to abide with you in your court" (Ps 65:4, Hebrew *qārab*, bring near, present); "You will guide me with your counsel, and then afterward you will receive me in your glory" (Ps 73:24, Hebrew *lāqaḥ*, "seize, take, conquer, carry off"). This usage in the Psalms shows that *proslambanō* is an element in Isr's religious language and could not fail to have an influence on NT usage.

With Philo, the meaning "add" is predominant. An illness of the soul is added to bodily illness (*Unchang. God* 66; *Migr. Abr.* 55), sorrow to sorrow (*Moses* 2.225), new joys to past happiness (*Virtues* 67); if there are too few people in the household, one takes a neighbor in addition to eat the lamb (*Heir* 193); tax collectors add to their brutality the immunity that is assured by their masters' directives.[4] The nuances "to take for oneself" (Philo, *Sacr. Abel and Cain* 119), "acquire" (*Decalogue* 136; *Good Man Free* 12, 159) and "take to oneself" (*Plant.* 64) are well attested; but we may emphasize "to master" (*Conf. Tongues* 110, the passions) and "seize" (*To Gaius* 347). In Josephus, "add" is less frequent,[5] but "adjoin" (in the sense of taking on associates) and "receive help" recur endlessly;[6] which attests the common

---

[3] Wis 17:10—"wickedness always adds to the difficulties"; 2 Macc 8:1—Judas Maccabeus and his companions, recruiting partisans in the villages, join themselves to those who stand firm in Judaism.

[4] *Spec. Laws* 2.93; cf. 3.101; *Decalogue* 25; *Joseph* 7; *Moses* 1.68: "the bush found still more splendor"; 133; *Virtues* 100: "Moses added something greater"; *To Gaius* 114, passion "receives the simultaneous help of vanity and ambition"; *Alleg. Interp.* 2.23: "the vegetative power augmented by imagination"; cf. fetuses that stay longer in their mothers' wombs (1.9).

[5] *War* 1.35: "Bacchides with his natural cruelty exaggerated the godless orders of the prince"; 1.446: "Their hatred was doubled by frank speech"; 1.483; *Ant.* 1.306: "She added to this woman's fame"; 4.296: add profit; 15.160: a new prestige; 19.351: he received in addition Judea, Samaria, and Caesarea. Hence "amass" (3.56). Cf. "increase one's experience" (Thucydides 6.18.6); add new acquaintances to one's collection (Isocrates, *Demon.* 1.18); "adding what we need to our assets" (Andocides, *De Pace* 3.23).

[6] *War* 1.329: "Herod attached auxiliaries"; 2.67: "Varus attached an additional 1500 armed men to his forces"; 2.425, 427, 588; 4.138; *Ant.* 5.120: "having received

social nuance of this verb in the first century. The meaning "take by force" is not absent: "the rebels sought to take the upper city in addition to the places that they already occupied" (*War* 2.424).

In the papyri, it is often a question of "receiving" what is due,[7] but also of "adjoining" persons as witnesses (*P.Mert.* V, 32: "bringing with me the same Panas," *proslabonta syn emoi ton auton Panan*), associates (*P.Dura* 13 *a* 10, *metochous proslabesai*), partners (*P.Oxy.* 3092, 4: *proslambanesthai autous koinōnous; P.Amh.* 100, 4: *proselabeto ton Kornēlion koinōnon*), or collaborators (*P.Fay.* 12, 10: *proslabomenos synergon Ammōnion*), who provide their services (*UPZ* 19, 25, *diakonein hēmin*) and their help (*P.Oxy.* 71, col. II, 9: *eis boētheian*). In 157 BC a new meaning appeared, "to enlist" in an army. A *prostagma* of Ptolemy VI Philometor and Cleopatra II says, "To Demetrius. Enlist (*proslabesthai*) Apollonius the Macedonian in the company of Dexilaos" (*P.Lond.* 23, 21; vol. 1, p. 38 = *UPZ* 14, 14; cf. 208, 3; 214, 1). Similarly, in the same period, an honorific decree for Orthagoras of Araxa: "Our people were quite zealous toward them (the people of Orloanda) to obtain their liberty and their integration (*proslēphthōsin*) into the confederation of the Lycian people. . . . By his action he contributed to their integration (*eis to proslēphthēnai autous*) into the community of Lycians."[8] This reception into a community is not merely official but also implies emotional ties (*UPZ* 144, 11: *proseilēpsai philon*), as in the marriage contract in *P.Mur.* 115, 5, from the second century AD: the husband "has agreed and concluded to reconcile anew and take back the same Salome . . . as his legitimate wife."[9]

Simeon's help"; 6.108; 14.84, 452; 18.4; 19.60; *Life* 39: "they were obliged to take on the Galileans as allies"; *War* 1.561: "Alexander's son could in addition rely on his father-in-law"; 1.567, 568: "the wife of Pheroras allied with her mother, her sister, and the mother of Antipas"; 4.616: Vespasian wrote to Tiberius Alexander "that he would gladly take him as a collaborator and helper"; *Ant.* 3.64: "Aaron, to whom Raguel was joined"; 5.63; *Ag. Apion* 1.241: "Osarsiph associated some of the other priests with himself."

[7] *P.Lond.* 2004, 30 (third century BC); *P.Cair.Zen.* 59355, 144 (= *SB* 6771; cf. 6727, 5; 9150, 7; 10308, 4); *P.Mich.* 67, 25; 84, 16. In 50 BC, a *prostagma* of Cleopatra VII and Ptolemy XII says, "Whoever reports violators of these dispositions to the *stratēgos* of the nome will obtain . . . if he is a slave, in addition to his freedom, the sixth part (of the fortune of the guilty party)" (*BGU* 1730 = *SB* 7419; *C.Ord.Ptol.* 73, 15; cf. 50, 31 = *P.Tebt.* 700, 51).

[8] J. Pouilloux, *Choix*, n. IV, 56 and 61. Cf. Plutarch, *Pel.* 27, 3: "Pelopidas recruited mercenaries on the spot"; decree of Canopus: priests προσλαμβανομένων ἐκ τῆς πέμπτης φυλῆς τῶν Εὐεργετῶν θεῶν ἄλλων πέντε (Dittenberger, *Or.* 56, 31). In the meaning "fix, attach," cf. Aristotle, *Part. An.* 2.9.654b and 27; 3.7.670a14; *HA* 1.17a22.

[9] Republished *SB* 10305 (cf. Xenophon, *Lac.* 1.9); cf. *P.Tebt.* 61 *a* s: τῶν προσληφθέντων εἰς τὴν κατοικίαν; *P.Petaus* 28, 14: ἐπὶ δὲ ὕβριν προσέλαβα. In a very

In the NT, the verb *proslambanō* is used only in the middle voice. The first text is difficult. When Jesus has announced his passion, Peter *proslabomenos auton* "began to rebuke him, saying, 'God forbid, Master, it shall not be' " (Matt 16:22; Mark 8:32). How should this be translated? A. Schlatter cites Josephus, *Ant*. 18.4 as a parallel: Judas the Gaulanite "assured himself of the help of Saddok, a Pharisee" (*Saddōkon Pharisaion proslabomenos*).[10] St. Matthew, however, comments on *proslabomenos* with "began to rebuke him," and it is difficult to see how the aorist participle here could mean "come to the aid of, help" Jesus. Other moderns see here a synonym of *paralambanō*, "take along with oneself," so that Peter "drew him aside" or "apart"; but this meaning is not attested. Why not refer instead to the numerous occurrences of this verb in the sense of "take by force, seize, master" and see here an illusion to the impetuosity of the apostle, who adds and opposes a claim against Christ's affirmation, wanting to cause him to change his mind. This would account for the quite brusque character of Christ's response: "Get behind me, adversary; you are setting up a stumbling-block" (*skandalon*, Matt 16:23), an obstacle on the way of the cross.

On the other hand, the five occurrences in Acts are completely traditional. At Thessalonica, "jealous Jews took as allies (*proslabomenoi*) some wicked men" (Acts 17:5); at Ephesus, Priscilla and Aquila, after hearing Apollos, "took him with them (*proselabonta auton*) and explained the way of God to him more precisely" (18:26). At the end of the storm, St. Paul says to his companions, "Today is the fortieth day that you have been in suspense and fasting and have taken nothing *more* to eat" (*mēthen proslabomenoi*). When the apostle himself started to eat, "all were encouraged and also took food" (*autoi proselabonto trophēs*, 27:36). At Malta, "the barbarians showed us uncommon humaneness (*ou tēn tychousan philanthrōpian*) . . . receiving (*proselabonto*) us all, because of the rain and cold that had come on" (28:2). Note well this link between kind and beneficent humaneness and reception. Nothing has less of a juridical flavor than help given to shipwreck victims. Here, the heart receives and helps the neighbor. In this same way *proslambanomai* became with Paul a Christian virtue.

In four occurrences, the apostle Paul uses the present or aorist middle imperative (*proslambanesthe, proslabou*) three times. "Receive the one who is weak in the faith."[11] This is not about taking aside a brother whose

---

mutilated Christian inscription from Baalbek, it seems that baptismal illumination is in view: προσλαμβάνων φῶς (*IGLS* 2834, 4).

[10] A. Schlatter, *Der Evangelist Matthäus*, p. 516.

[11] Rom 14:1. These "weak" ones, who appear suddenly in the vegetarian controversy, are ascetics who abstain from certain foods, or scrupulous folk—or better, converts—whose consciences have not been sufficiently enlightened by the new faith.

conduct is not in harmony with ours. The verb indicates that we must take him with us and introduce him warmly into our fellowship. This is more than a manifestation of brotherly love; it is a primitive requirement of the Christian religion, formulated thus: "The one who eats must not scorn the one who does not eat, and the one who does not eat must not judge the one who eats, because God has received him" (*ho theos gar auton proselabeto*, Rom 14:3). He has chosen him as his own, taking him from the world to make him a believer and bring him into his church. How can this divinely established brotherhood be refused? The new exhortation is "Receive then one another, just as Christ has received you, for the glory of God" (Rom 15:7). The two propositions correspond precisely: *dio proslambanesthe allēlous* on the one hand and *kathōs kai ho Christos proselabeto hymas* on the other. Christ's welcome of all of his own without distinction with a view to the perfect unity of the community is the model for each Christian's welcoming of all his fellow-Christians, and at the same time is an individual precept. This is an evocation of the hospitality which was the first mani-festation of brotherly *agapē* in the primitive church[12] and which must of course be present at the outset in every community.[13]

Cf. J. Dupont, "Appel aux faibles et aux forts dans la communauté romaine (Rom. XIV, 1–XV, 13)," in AnBib 17, Rome, 1963, vol. 1, pp. 357–366.

[12] Rom 12:13—"pursue hospitality"; 1 Tim 3:2—the bishop must be hospitable; 1 Pet 4:9, all Christians must be φιλόξενοι; Heb 13:2; 3 John: the thoughtfulness and generosity of Gaius in receiving traveling Christians not known to him personally (C. Spicq, *Agapè*, vol. 3, pp. 311–312) are praised by St. John in the manner of an "honorific decree" analogous the one that the Lycian confederation, the council and people of Myra, of Patara, and of Telmessos sent in AD 43 to the Roman Junia Theodora, who was staying in Corinth, and whose hospitality was so remarkable (*SEG* XVIII, 143, 25ff., 48, 75ff.); her beneficiaries testify for her (lines 9, 16, 32, 61). Cf. the honorific decree of Athens in 347/6: "Let the envoys Sotis and Theodosius be praised for their good offices on behalf of travelers from Athens to the Bosporus" (Dittenberger, *Syl.* 206, 49ff.). At Chersonese, a benefactor of the city is praised for having practiced personal hospitality toward the people of the city in time of famine (ἰδιόξενοι, B. Latyschev, *Inscriptiones Antiquae*, III, n. 68, 25); cf. Cimon, the most hospitable of the Greeks, who had a large meal prepared every day for a large number of people (Plutarch, *Cim.* 10.4); all the poor were admitted (10.1). He surpassed the ancient hospitality and kindness of the Athenians (φιλοξενίαν καὶ φιλανθρωπίαν, 10.6). Here pagan hospitality is not at issue, but the brotherly love commanded by the Master (Matt 25:35, 38, 43–44; J. Winandy, "La Scène du Jugement dernier [Mt. XXV, 31–46]," in *ScEccl*, 1966, pp. 169–186; P. Miquel, "Hospitalité," in *Dict.spir.*, vol. 7, 808ff.). Whoever "receives" a brother receives Christ in person (Matt 10:40–42; C. Spicq, *Théologie morale*, vol. 2, pp. 809–815). This welcome was so universal and so generous that abuses occurred; *Did.* 11.3–6 reacts against these.

[13] W. Barclay (*NT Wordbook*, pp. 107–109) interprets the apostle's exhortations in terms of the LXX, where God "receives" his people (1 Sam 12:22; Ps 27:10; 65:4) and

In a concrete case, St. Paul tells Philemon to observe this principle towards Onesimus, a runaway slave who would normally have been punished. "If you have any regard for the bonds that unite us, receive him as if he were myself" (*proslabou auton hōs eme*, Phlm 17). According to the previously cited texts, he is not only being asked to receive this guilty person into his house, nor simply to pardon him, but even to treat him with complete respect, generosity, and attentiveness. As a parallel we may cite *BGU* 1141, 37, from 34 BC: "Twice I received him into my house" (*dis proselabomēn auton eis oikon par' eme*). We may add a Latin letter of recommendation addressed to a military tribune in the second century, in which Aurelius Archelaus commends to him his friend Theon: "I ask you, my lord, to look upon him as if he were myself, for he is such a man as should be loved by you."[14]

---

in terms of the Greek meaning of *proslambanomai*: "take someone as an associate, aide, partner" and concludes that to "receive" a believer in the church is to treat him is an ally, an auxiliary, an assistant who brings his help to the life of the community; a stable and beneficent active member of the family, by no means a stranger. According to the papyri, we can see such a person as a soldier enrolled in an army. He has been enlisted in the Christian militia in order to be of effective service there, which he can do only in union with his fellow soldiers. The verb *proslambanomai* meant all of this to Jesus' disciples.

[14] "Peto domine ut eum ante oculos habeas tanquam me est enim tales omo ut ametur a te," *P.Oxy.* 32, 6–10 = R. Cavenaile, *Corpus Papyrorum Latinarum*, Wiesbaden, 1958, n. 249.

προτρέπομαι

protrepomai, to urge forward, stir up, exhort

Protrepō, "urge forward," is used above all in the transitive and with a figurative meaning, "stir up, exhort."[1] Nevertheless, the aorist middle participle, which is a NT hapax at Acts 18:27, is not without difficulty: from Ephesus, since Apollos "wanted to pass over to Achaea, the brethren exhorted (him) and wrote to the disciples to receive him." This translation follows Chrysostom in supposing that *auton* should be understood between *protrepsamenoi* and *hoi adelphoi*, which is contrary to the usage in the papyri and the inscriptions.[2] And why exhort Apollos, since he himself has the desire to go to Corinth (*boulomenou de autou dielthein*)? We could translate, "the brethren encouraged him," but that is not exactly what the verb means.[3] According to Codex Bezae and the Harclean Syriac, it was Corin-

---

[1] 2 Macc 11:7—"Maccabeus exhorted the others to risk themselves along with him to help their brothers"; 4 Macc 12:7—"When his mother had exhorted (the seventh brother) in Hebrew"; 15:12—"the mother exhorted her children, together and individually, to die for the sake of piety"; 16:13—"she exhorted them, supplicating them to die for the sake of piety" (προετρέπετο ἱκετεύουσα); Xenophon, *Cyr.* 2.2.14: "it is by making them weep that the law urges citizens toward justice"; Thucydides 8.63.3: Peisander's delegation urged the noteworthy leaders to establish an oligarchy.

[2] *P.Ryl.* 77, 48: "we urged him to assume the office of *kosmētēs*" (ἡμῶν δὲ προτρεπομένων αὐτὸν ἀναδέξασθαι τὴν κοσμητείαν); decree from the second century BC in honor of Eirenias, who "thanks to his own personal authority, stirred up King Eumenes to give the city 160,000 *medimnoi* of wheat for the building of a gymnasium" (προτρεψάμενος αὐτὸν δοῦναι τῇ πόλει δωρεάν, *NCIG*, n. VIII, 6).

[3] Nevertheless, urging or incitement is oftened tempered and leaves room for the free initiative of the person urged; cf. *P.Panop.Beatty* 2, 128: "it would be well, if through a public announcement, προτρέψασθαί σε τοὺς βουλομένους πλέον προσκομίζειν ὄφελος τῷ ταμείῳ"; *P.Oxf.* 12, 6: "since you engage me to join with you . . ." (contract for association in the second century); Dittenberger, *Or.* 339, 90: ἵνα . . . ζηλωταὶ μὲν τῶν καλλίστων γίνωνται, προτρέπωνται δὲ πρὸς ἀρετήν; cf. Xenophon, *Mem.* 1.4.1; Josephus, *Ant.* 7.262: προτρεψαμένου τοῦ Ἀμασᾶ—at the suggestion of Amasa, all the Israelites did likewise."

---

protrepomai, S 4389; *EDNT* 3.182; MM 554; L&N 33.300; BAGD 722

thians at Ephesus who, having heard Apollos, asked him to come to their country (*parekaloun dielthein . . . eis tēn patrida autōn*); Apollos did not take the initiative for this apostolic mission. We can remove the difficulty by referring *protrepsamenoi* not to Apollos but to the Corinthians, who were urged to write a letter of recommendation (cf. Rom 16:1; 2 Cor 3:1ff.; Col 4:10): having exhorted, the brothers wrote, or they wrote exhorting, or the brothers exhorted by means of a letter.[4]

The papyri offer numerous parallels to this invitation to make a voyage: "Theon, my brother, salutes you and urges you (*protrepetai se*) to come to see us at Bacchias" (*P.Mich.* 496, 19); "urge brother Castor, if he is going to come" (*protrepsai Kastora, ean mellē elthein, embalesthai tous hēmeterous, SB* 7349, 6); "we urged him to come with us to survey the flood plains" (*proetrepsamen exelthein ham' hēmein epi ton horismon tōn nēsōn,* ibid. 10649, 5); "I urged the father of one of them to come with us to you" (*proetrepsa men oun ton patera tou henos autōn katelthein met' autōn pros se,* ibid. 9415, col. XVIII, 12); "when the envoy encouraged him and urged him to go to Egypt" (*tou presbeutou protrepsamenou kai parormēsantos eis Aigypton elthein,* Josephus, *Ant.* 12.166). The urging is a function of affection or admiration,[5] as with *Pap.Lugd.Bat.* XVII, 16, *b* 15—"for my friend urged me strongly"[6]—and *SB* 7517, 6, where the subject of the verb is "benevolence": "Your benevolence impels those who have been wronged to come to you fearlessly" (*hē sē eumeneia protrepetai tous adikēthentas aphobōs soi proseinai*).

The invitation is often very pressing, like the strong urging to serve in a *leitourgia*,[7] to make payments or pay taxes (*P.Ryl.* 617, 12; *P.Ross.Georg.* III, 9, 10), to meet one's obligations,[8] to carry out tasks (*SB* 9102, 17), and

---

[4] Cf. M. Zerwick, *Biblical Greek*, §262.

[5] Cf. Wis 14:18—"The ambition of the craftsman impelled even those who did not know the king to intensify their worship" (ἡ τοῦ τεχνίτου προετρέψατο φιλοτιμία).

[6] Πολλὰ γάρ με προετρέψατο ὁ φίλος. Republished in *SB* 10286 (second-third century). This nuance of affection often appears in letters; *P.Mich.* 496, 5: ἤδη προτρέπομαι ἐπιστέλλειν ἡμῖν περὶ τῆς ὑγείας σου, "I urge you to write me immediately concerning your health" (second century); *SB* 9533, 4: ἀσπάζομαι καὶ προτρέπομαί σε τὸ αὐτὸ ποιεῖν ὑπὸ χεῖρα (second century); 7335, 6: προτρέπομαι σε γράψαι μοι ἥδιστα ποιήσοντι; *P.Brem.* 21, 9, καὶ σὲ δὲ προτρέπομαι ἐπιτρέπειν μοι περὶ ὧν βούλει ὅς (sic) ἥδιστα ποιήσοντι.

[7] *P.Oxy.* 2569, 14; *P.Cair.Isid.* 81, 9 = *SB* 7676. One is urged by the *stratēgos* and the people to such an undertaking (*UPZ* 110, 165; second century BC); cf. Josephus, *Ant.* 5.171: οὔτε προτρεπομένων οὔτε κωλυόντων.

[8] *P.Mich.* 485, 10: "I pray you, brother, to act once again on my behalf and urge Valerius to write to Peios, having confidence in my good faith"; *P.Oxy.* 1252, verso 32.

especially to take on a responsibility.[9] The verb occurs commonly in honorific decrees mentioning that an athlete was "stirred up" to take part in a competition[10] or an official was urged to accept his office.[11] It is possible that this noble sense of the word motivated the selection of this verb in Acts 18:27 to make the arrival of Apollos at Corinth somewhat official.

---

[9] *Pap.Lugd.Bat.* VI, 15, 3: cf. the honorific inscription of an association for its president: αὐτοί τε ἅπαντες προτρεψάμενοι τοὺς δοκοῦντας ἐν ἑαυτοῖς εὐθέτους εἶναι τῆς ἀρχιερωσύνης (*SB* 8267, 11; from 5 BC). An *agōnothetēs*, at his own expense, puts up a statue of a victorious athlete: ἐτείμησε Αὐρ. Μεννέας β´ θέμεως ἀγωνοθέτης Αὐρ. Ἀλέξανδρον Τιειου προτρεψαμένης τῆς πόλεως ἐνδόξως ἀγωνισάμενον πυθικῶν πανκράτιον (*MAMA* IV, 132).

[10] Inscription at Aphrodisias for Aurelius Achilles, ὅτι προτρεψαμένης αὐτὸν ὡς πατρίδος τῆς πόλεως εἰς τὸ τελεώτατον τῶν ἀγωνισμάτων. This athlete took the Olympic victory from Ephesus; that city had urged him to participate in its games, as if it were his own country (ed. L. Robert, *Opera Minora Selecta*, vol. 1, p. 620, who gives numerous other references, p. 165); cf. Dittenberger, *Syl.* 1073, 37, ἐπὶ πλεῖστον ἀγωνίζεσθαι προτρεπόμενος.

[11] Honorific decree from 107 BC for the praetor Diophantos, ἐπὶ τὰ κάλλιστα καὶ ἐνδοξότατα τὸν βασιλέα προτρεπόμενος (Dittenberger, *Syl.* 709, 5); cf. the decree of Lebedos for a judge from Samos, προτρέπωνται δὲ καὶ οἱ λοιποὶ εἰς τὰ παρακαλούμενα προθύμους ἑαυτοὺς ἐπιδιδόναι (L. Robert, *Hellenica*, vol. 11–12, p. 205, 19).

204 πρόφασις, *prophasis*

πρόφασις

prophasis, **a reason proffered, pretext, excuse**

Derived from *prophainō*, unknown in the OT (cf. 2 Macc 3:26), *prophasis* is used five times in the NT, always in a pejorative sense; four of the occurrences are datives of manner and circumstance, used adverbially.[1] Its first meaning is "a reason that is proffered" without any psychological or moral connotation,[2] but it is most commonly used to mean "pretext," a motive set forth deceitfully,[3] as with the sailors who "let down the boat to

---

[1] Πρόφασει; cf. F. M. Abel, *Grammaire*, § 45 q; K. Deichgräber, "Πρόφασις," in *Quellen und Studien zur Geschichte der Naturwissenschaften und der Medizin*, vol. 3, 1932, pp. 209–225.

[2] *SB* 8987, 38: εἰς τὴν τούτων πρόφασίν τε καὶ αἰτίαν. T. *Job* 8.5; Xenophon, *Cyr.* 3.1.27, Tigranes to Cyrus: "the offenses that we have committed probably give you reason to mistrust us"; Josephus, *Ant.* 13.427; *War* 2.348; *P.Lips.* 64, 8: διὰ τὴν πρόφασιν ταύτην = for this reason; *P.Oxy.* 1880, 12: ἕνεκεν τῆς προφάσεως; 1897, 5; 2110, 15, 34, 37; 2420, 16; 2478, 23; *P.Erl.* 105, 7, 9; 109, 7; 132; *P.Ant.* 44, 6: διὰ τῶν ἐνπιπτουσῶν προφάσεων = for the reasons mentioned; *P.Mert.* 98, 12; *C.P.Herm.* 2, 7: προφάσεις ἀπαραίτητοι, compelling reasons kept me from joining you; *P.Mich.* 486, 12: πρόφασις παρολκῆς, reason for a delay; Dittenberger, *Syl.* 888, 137: διὰ γὰρ τὰς προειρημένας ταύτας προφάσεις. F. Robert, ("Prophasis," in *REG*, 1976, pp. 317–342) demonstrates that πρόφασις in the medical vocabulary means first of all "first manifestation, initial period, precursor phenomenon, preparatory phase," then "observable, visible cause," finally "cause" in general, synonymous with αἰτία. Similarly in Thucydides: ἀληθεστάτη πρόφασις = the truest cause (1.23.6), with the nuance of intention, explanation (6.6.1).

[3] "The high officials and satraps sought a grievance against Daniel, but they could find no motive or fault, because he was faithful. These men said, 'Since we can find no grievance against Daniel, let us find something against him in the law of his God' " (Dan 6:5–6; Theodotion); cf. Demosthenes, *C. Olymp.* 48.39: "In all that he says, there is nothing but imaginary suspicions, false excuses, and bits of trickery" (προφάσεις ἄδικοι καὶ πονηρίαι); ibid. 48.42; 48.50; Menander, *Dysk.* 135: "He is quite pleased to have found a pretext"; 322: "I do not want to send you back on an empty pretext" (οὐ πρόφασιν εἰπὼν βούλομ' ἀποπέμψαι κενήν); Josephus, *War* 1.654:

---

prophasis, S 4392; EDNT 3.182; MM 555; L&N 33.437, 88.230; BAGD 722

the sea on the pretext (*prophasei*) that they had to distance the anchors from the bow" (Acts 27:30); the sailors wanted to flee, and they used a false pretext, but St. Paul saw their true intent.

Prophasis often takes on this nuance of lying and pretense: one acts on a hidden motive under the cover of one that is perceptible or respectable.[4] This fallacious character appears in Mark 12:40; Luke 20:47, denouncing the scribes who make a show of praying at length.[5] This hypocrisy, rejected by St. Paul,[6] is that of certain preachers denounced in Phil 1:18 whose intentions are not pure; they preach the gospel out of "envy and strife" (*dia*

"These men, under the pretext of serving the law, were in reality serving a deeper design; thus they had to be punished for impiety"; 5.424; *Ant.* 15.185: in entrusting Mariamne and her mother Alexandra to the keeping of the Ituraean Soemus, Herod finds an occasion or a pretext to honor him; *War* 4.394: "They feared that their initial opposition would give him a pretext to act against them"; *Ag. Apion* 1.72: "After I have produced the evidence supplied by these peoples, I shall also mention those Greek historians who have spoken of the Jews, in order to deprive those who are jealous of us this last pretext for controversy against us"; Thucydides 5.53: "The same summer, war broke out between Epidaurus and Argos, the pretext being the sacrificial offering to Pythian Apollo that the Epidaurians were supposed to send for their pasture land, which they did not send"; *SB* 8444, 15 (= Dittenberger, *Or.* 669): "As some, under the pretext of the interests of the state, having the debts of others ceded to themselves, have had certain people incarcerated," line 17, 37; *P.Mich.* 581, 14: "on the pretext that I was guilty of theft" (second century); 529, 50; 530, 25; 624, 12; *P.Oxy.* 903, 35; 2235, 13; 2407, 49; *Pap.Lugd.Bat.* VI, 37, 13. The rebels gave Cleomenes a pretext for complaining (Plutarch, *Cleom.* 3.6; cf. *Ant.* 12.1; 42.1; 53.2).

[4] Hos 10:4—λαλῶν ῥήματα προφάσεις ψευδεῖς, "uttering words to disguise lies"; Josephus, *Life* 79: ἐν προφάσει φιλίας, "under the cover of friendship"; 282: "on the pretext of an urgent call"; *SB* 9801, 14: "Everything indicates clearly that they sold the tomb ἀκαταχρημάτιστον under the guise of a lease (προφάσει μισθώσεως) . . . consequently, they will have to restore it" (first century, cf. F. De Visscher, *Le Droit des tombeaux romains*, Milan, 1963, pp. 197–224); *SB* 10044, 14.

[5] Προφάσει μακρὰ προσευχόμενοι; a sentence repeated in Matt 23:14 (sometimes placed after verse 12), but absent from the Vulgate and rejected by the critics.

[6] 1 Thess 2:5—"We have never had recourse to flattery . . . nor disguised greed" (προφάσει πλεονεξίας, as translated by B. Rigaux, *Thessaloniciens*). The Vulgate took this to mean "occasion"; a well-attested meaning of πρόφασις; Cleomenes asks Nicagoras of Messene what occasion brings him to Egypt (Plutarch, *Cleom.* 25.2); *P.Fay.* 20, 11: "on the occasion of my succession to the empire"; *BGU* 1024, col. VI, 21: "Finding the occasion, Zephyrios said"; *P.Mich.* 503, 22: εἰ πρόφασιν ἔχεις ἐλθεῖν εἰς Ἀλεξάνδριαν, "if you have occasion to come to Alexandria"; *SB* 6751, 8; ἵνα τὴν πρόφασις τῶν ναυπηγῶν λύσωμεν (third century BC); 8003, 6: ὡς ἔτυχεν περὶ ταύτης τῆς προφάσεως (Christian letter, fourth century); 9557, 18: καὶ προφάσεις καὶ ἀναβολὰς καὶ ἀναδόσις ποιησάμενος (cf. M. Hombert, "Bulletin épigraphique," in *REG*, 1966, pp. 183–184); 10463, 1, 3: τῇ προφάσει δι' ἧς γράφω . . . ἡ δὲ πρόφασις αὐτή ἐστιν . . . ; 10567, 43; *P.Gron.* 19, A 15: μὴ προπάσις (*sic*) σχῇς; *P.Oxy.* 2416, 15; *P.Ross.Georg.* IV, 3, 17; 11, 6.

phthonon kai erin), then "out of selfish ambition" (*ex eritheias*), and finally "not from pure motives" (*ouch hagnōs*) and on a pretext (*prophasei*). This ministry is incited by jealousy, the purpose being to make the apostle's chains heavier,[7] that is, to supplant him and undermine his authority. Other Christians "preach Christ out of goodwill, acting in love" (verses 15–16). The apostle concludes, "What does it matter? In one way or another, under pretext or in truth (*eite prophasei eite alētheia*), Christ is preached, and in that I rejoice." This dichotomy between true and false motives is classical: *prophaseis anti tōn alēthōn pseudeis.*[8]

Prophasis finally has the sense of excuse—valid or not[9]—notably that of ignorance: *agnoias prophasin hypoteimēsamenos* (*P.Oxy.* 1119, 11). In this meaning, John 15:22—"If I had not come and spoken to them, they would have no sin, but now they have not excuse for their sin"[10] of willful blindness.

---

[7] Cf. Philo, *Moses* 1.247: "Those who are pained by a neighbor's success find satisfaction in seeing ills befall him"; Heraclitus, *All.* 6.3: "Malevolent envy (ὁ φθόνος) always seeks to sully and denigrate"; Josephus, *Ag. Apion* 1.122–123; Dionysius of Halicarnassus, *Pomp.* 3: "The Lacedaemonians gave in to jealousy and fear" (φθόνῳ προφάσεις); *P.Thead.* 14, 34: "They accuse us out of jealousy"; *P.Ryl.* 144, 21; *P.Oxy.* 237, col. VI, 21; 533, 14, ἵνα μὴ ἔχωμεν στομάχους μηδὲ φθόνον; cf. C. Spicq, *Agapè*, vol. 2, pp. 244–252.

[8] Demosthenes, *Corona* 225; falsifying the true motives for dealings (τὴν μὲν ἀληθῆ πρόφασιν τῶν πραγμάτων, ibid. 156); cf. the truest motive, τῇ ἀληθεστάτῃ προφάσει (Thucydides 6.6.1); ordinarily, "the truest reason is also the least avowed" (τὴν μὲν γὰρ ἀληθεστάτην πρόφασιν, ἀφανεστάτην δὲ λόγῳ, ibid. 1.23.6); the "pretext" is contrasted with the "true reason" or the underlying intention (διάνοια, ibid. 6.76.2); "the Athenians . . . march against us with considerable forces on the pretext (πρόφασιν) of helping the Segestans and reestablishing the Leontinians; in reality (ἀληθὲς) the motive was to possess Sicily and especially our city" (ibid. 6.33.2); *P.Tebt.* 27, 82, οὔτε γὰρ βίαν οὔθ᾽ ἑτέραν ἡνδηποτοῦν πρόφασιν προσδεξόμεθα.

[9] Prov 18:1, προφάσεις ζητεῖ; Plutarch, *Rom.* 35.1: "As for the faults that they commit, no plausible excuse is found for them" (ἐνδεᾶ προφάσεως); *P.Michael.* 17, 2: "they will have an excuse"; *P.Tebt.* 702, 17; *Pap.Lugd.Bat.* VI, 24, 93: "no excuse for the lateness" (second century); *SB* 7404, 52; 8024, 10, ἔνδοξεν δὲ ἐκ τινος προφάσεως πονηροῦ δαίμονος (act of divorce, fourth century); *Stud.Pal.* XX, 86, 22; *P.Mich.* 486, 12; *T. Job* 11.11—"of all that I have entrusted to you in the interest of the indigent (προφάσει πενήτων) I shall take nothing from you."

[10] Νῦν δὲ πρόφασιν οὐκ ἔχουσιν περὶ τῆς ἁμαρτίας αὐτῶν; cf. Josephus, *Life* 167: "they were lacking in loyalty to me, with no excuse" (ἄνευ προφάσεως). In the medical vocabulary, *prophasis* has the technical meaning "cause"; sometimes it refers to the phenomenon that precedes the sickness or is its point of departure; sometimes the apparent or triggering cause; sometimes the active cause, in which case it is synonymous with αἴτιον, cf. J. Jouanna, *Hippocrate: La Nature de l'homme*, Berlin, 1975, pp. 291ff.

προχειρίζομαι

procheirizomai, **to choose ahead of time, establish, designate, appoint, destine**

In secular Greek, this verb in the middle voice and with a personal object in the accusative means "choose ahead of time, establish, designate, destine."[1] In the LXX, it is used especially for people chosen beforehand for a certain mission;[2] and, with the exception of Dan 3:22,[3] it is a noble term, because those entrusted with a mission have been elected or appointed on account of their competence and integrity. They are trustworthy envoys, qualified representatives of God, or the king, or of some other high authority.[4]

---

[1] The verb προχειρίζω is common in Galen, cf. W. K. Hobart, *Medical Language*, pp. 202–203.

[2] Ἀποστέλλω or ἐξαποστέλλω; cf. Exod 4:13 (the intermediary through whom God transmits his message, Hebrew *šālaḥ*); 2 Macc 3:7 (the king, having chosen Heliodorus, his prime minister, sent him); 8:9 (Ptolemy, having designated Nicanor, son of Patroclus, of the rank of the first friends, sent him without delay); 14:12 (Demetrius, having chosen Nicanor, sent him; cf. Josh 3:12; Polybius 3.40.2: "the Romans resolved to send"—πέμπειν); Diodorus Siculus 12.27.1.

[3] In Dan 3:22 (LXX) it is talking about men who have "prepared" or delivered those condemned to the furnace and who were were themselves burned by the flames.

[4] Plutarch, *Caes.* 58.8; Plutarch, *Galba* 8.3; Polybius 1.11.3: "they chose one of the two consuls as the commander"; 2.43.1: "the cities electing in turn a secretary general and two generals"; in the second century BC, Pamphilos is the object of an honorific decree of Apollonia for having put the public finances in order, "the citizens chosen each year (τῶν προχειριζομένων ἀνδρῶν) directing each matter in accord with the decree such that there was no further loss" (*I.Car.* 167, 22); cf. *P.Cair.Zen.* 59042, 3; Dittenberger, *Or.* 339, 46: προχειρισαμένου τοὺς τὴν πίστιν εὐσεβῶς τε καὶ δικαίως τηρήσοντας; cf. line 50. In the first century AD: the members of the association of Zeus Most High choose as their president Petesouchos, who is worthy of this position and the *koinon* (πρῶτον μὲν προχειρισάμενοι ἐπ᾽ ἑαυτῶν ἡγούμενον Πετεσοῦχον Τεεφβέννιος, ἄνδρα λόγιον, τοῦ τόπου καὶ τῶν ἀνδρῶν ἄξιον, *SB* 7835, 5 = *P.Lond.*

---

procheirizomai, S 4400; *TDNT* 6.862–864; *EDNT* 3.186; *NIDNTT* 1.475–476; MM 556; L&N 30.89; BAGD 724

It is in this quasi-technical sense that Acts uses this verb—unknown in Philo and Josephus—regarding either Christ ("that God may send to you Jesus, the one predestined to be Messiah")[5] or Paul ("the God of our fathers chose you in advance [proecheirisato se] to know his will," Acts 22:14; "I have appeared to you to establish you as a minister and witness of the things that you have seen [procheirisasthai se] . . . ; the Gentiles to whom I am sending you [apostellō]," 26:16). An official appointing or delegating is always referred to. In the inscriptions and the papyri, the verb figures in the vocabulary of administration, referring to functionaries or persons officially chosen to carry out a certain function: Boulagoras, in the third century BC, was "chosen by the people several times (procheiristheis te pleionakis hypo tou dēmou) as their representative in public litigation" (SEG I, 366, 20); in the second century, the chief of police of a town makes his report regarding "one of the guards of Tebtunis who was appointed by Ptolemaeus, the district archiphylaktēs" (tōn ek Tebtyneōs phylakitōn procheiristhentōn hypo Ptolemaiou, P.Tebt. 731, 3); in the first century, in a rental contract, it means that Demetrius must make payments to the broker or to the treasurer of the association, who will be appointed.[6]

2710; cf. C. Roberts, T. Skeat, A. D. Nock, "The Guild of Zeus Hypsistos," in HTR, 1936, p. 40, 44); in AD 43, the members of an association voted unanimously to elect one of their members, an excellent person (προχειρίσαι τινὰ αὐτῶν ἄνδρα ἀγαθώτατον), Cronion, son of Herodes, to be superintendent for one year (P.Mich. 244, 4); likewise, in 47, the salt merchants unanimously elect Apunchis, an excellent man, as inspector and collector of public taxes (ibid. 245, 4 = SB 8030). In the second century BC, it is mentioned that the persons appointed are competent to draw up contracts in accord with the law of the land: ἵνα ἐπιτήδειοι προχειρισεῶσιν καὶ συγκριθῶσι γράφειν τὰ συναλλάγματα ταῦτα (P.Ryl. 572, 30) or πρεσβείαν . . . αὕτη προχειρίζηται τοὺς ἐπιτηδείους (PSI 1160, 12, first century AD).

[5] Acts 3:20, καὶ ἀποστείλῃ τὸν προκεχειρισμένον ὑμῖν χριστόν, Ἰησοῦν, which can also be translated, "Jesus, who has been constituted as Christ for you"; several miniscules read προκεκηρυγμένον, "who was preached ahead of time"; Vulgate "qui praedicatus est."

[6] P.Ryl. 586, 8: τῷ προχειρισθησομένῳ τοῦ κοινοῦ; cf. line 14, 23; Dittenberger, Syl. 601, 5; 873, 14: διὰ τὸν ἄρχοντα . . . ὃν προεχειρίσασθε; PSI 1236, 2: "to Flavius, Marion, Discoros, and Apion, προχειρισθεῖσι ὑπὸ Κλαυδίου . . . ἐπιστρατήγου"; P.Lond. 376, 5 (vol. 2, p. 77); P.Oxy. 2117, 2: "To their very dear friend . . . of the city of Oxyrhynchus, appointed by (προχιρισθέντι ὑπὸ) his excellency Claudius the epistratēgos"; 2118, 5; Pap.Lugd.Bat. VI, 18, 4: "Maron . . . keeper of the archives at Hericlides, also called Valerius, was appointed by Apollonides, stratēgos of the district of Polemon" (προχειρισθέντι ὑπὸ Ἀπολλωνίδου στρατηγοῦ) to be inspector of the Oxyrhynchite nome" (117–118); P.Princ. 127, 2: "To Zoilus, Trypho, and their associates, appointed to receive and transmit this statement" (προχειρισθεῖσι πρὸς παράλημψιν καὶ κατακομιδὴν βιβλίων πεμπομένων εἰς Ἀλεξάνδρειαν, 159/160); P.Mil.Vogl. 254, 7: "the following have been designated for the banquet, and today

The perfect passive participle *prokecheirismenon* (Acts 3:20) is a stylistic element in formulas for registration. In AD 48, a contract was "recorded by [. . .], adjunct to Theon, the delegate of the association of *agoranomoi*."[7] In 53, in a sworn agreement, six elders, farmers of the province of Oxyrhynchus, "swear to the officially constituted inspectors of sowing for the nome."[8] From the same year we have the identical declaration of five elders, farmers from the village of Ares (*P.Fouad* 19, 6). Sometimes it is the inspectors of sowing that are designated (*P.Oxy.* 2185, 5; in 92); sometimes tax collectors (*hoi prokechirismenoi praktores*, *P.Fay.* 14, 1; from 124 BC); sometimes the geometer who draws up a certificate of measurement;[9] sometimes a friend who designates his delegate: "For Castor . . . I Trypho, his fellow ephebe, whom he has appointed."[10]

---

they have received this nomination" (προεχειρίσθησαν ἐπὶ τῆς ἑστίας, καὶ σήμερον ἐπεστάλησαν οἱ ὑπογεγραμμένοι, with the names following); *P.Ryl.* 572, 63: τὰ ὀνόματα τῶν προξειρισθησομένων κατὰ τὸν νόμον ὑπόταξον; *BGU* 1821, 14 (51/50 BC); *P.Berl.Zill.* 2, 22; *SB* 6794, 3; 7173, 9.

[7] *P.Fouad* 35, 16: σὺν Θέωνι τῷ προκεχειρισμένῳ ὑπὸ τῶν μετόχων ἀγορανόμων κεχρημάτισθαι; *P.Oxy.* 320, 25, in AD 59 (cf. M. V. Biscottini, "L'Archivio di Tryphon tessitore de Oxyrhynchos," in *Aeg*, 1966, p. 266).

[8] *P.Fouad* 18, 11: τοῖς προκεχειρισμένοις τὴν τοῦ νομοῦ κατασποράν; cf. *P.Rein.* 94, 13, a similar declaration under oath of two delegates of the "*hierotektones* of the temple of Thoeris, of Isis, of Sarapis, and of the very great *theoi paredroi*, designated by their fellow *hierotektones*" (serving in a collegial association, προκεχειρισμένων ὑπὸ τῶν συνϊεροτεκτόνων); *BGU* 1198, 2: παρὰ Σωτηρίχου τοῦ Νούχιος ἱερέως προκεχιρισμένου δὲ καὶ ὑπὸ τῶν συνιερέων Ἀρυώτου.

[9] *UPZ* 117, col. I, 10: Ἔγραψεν Ἀσκληπιάδης ὁ προκεχειρισμένος πρὸς τῇ γεωμετρίᾳ ὑπὸ Σαραπίωνος; repeated col. II, 4–5 (second century BC); cf. 126, 7.

[10] *SB* 8403, 7 = Dittenberger, *Or.* 188, 7: Τρύφων ὁ συνέφηβος καὶ προκεχιρισμένος ὑπ' αὐτοῦ (July 5, 89); cf. *P.Corn.* 16, 21: Ἑρμαίῳ προκεχιρισμένῳ παρὰ Πλουτίωνος; *P.Oxf.* 8, 1 (in 104/105, with the note of the editor, E. P. Wegener). In Polybius 3.40.14, the nuance of authority is clear: "the Romans sent to his aid armies that had been destined for Scipio" (τὰ τῷ προκεχιρισμένα στρατόπεδα; cf. προχειροτονεῖν, Acts 10:41).

πρωτότοκος

prōtotokos, **firstborn**

Only five occurrences of this term can be cited from the papyri, and all of them are from the fourth century. One is in a certificate of adoption (*huion gnēsion kai prōtotokon*, *P.Lips.* 28, 15); the others are in magical papyri, with respect to animals (*P.Oslo* 1, 312: "taking the umbilical cord of a firstborn ram"; *Pap.Graec.Mag.* 4, 1092, 1101, 3150). It is rare in the inscriptions,[1] and the literary texts that attest it are Jewish- or Christian-inspired.[2]

So this is in effect a biblical term, used 130 times in the LXX,[3] usually in the proper literal of the word, firstfruits of a (human or animal) mother's womb. There are religious connotations, because the firstborn is consecrated to Yahweh;[4] a qualitative connotation, because it is the "firstborn

---

[1] At Myconos, around 200 BC, in a religious calendar, for a pregnant sow that is giving birth for the first time: ὗν ἐνκύμονα πρωτοτόκον (Dittenberger, *Syl.* 1024, 16). A. Deissmann (*Light*, pp. 91–92) mentions two epitaphs, one from Trachonitis, where a pagan priest owes his office to his birthright, ἱερεὺς γάρ εἰμι πρωτοτόκων ἐκ τελετῶν; the other is Roman: a firstborn who died at the age of two years (πρωτότοκον, διετές) is called son of the sun (ἡλιόπαις) because he was born on a Sunday.

[2] Philo, *Spec. Laws* 1.138–139: the firstborn males; Josephus, *Ant.* 1.54; 2.313; 4.71; 5.31 (contrasting τοῦ πρώτου παιδός to τὸν νεώτατον τῶν παίδων); 1QH 3.8: "Like a woman in travail with her firstborn child . . ."; *Sib. Or.* 3.627: firstborn lambs and goats that are sacrificed; *Jos. Asen.* 1.11: "the firstborn son of Pharaoh," cf. 4.15; 23.1; 25.4; 29.9; *Anth. Pal.* 8.34: "It is not a vain sacrifice . . . of the firstborn that Nonna has offered to God"; 9.213: two children, the elder and the younger.

[3] It translates the Hebrew *bᵉkôr/bᵉkirâh*, except in Gen 25:25 (*ri'šôn*); Exod 34:20 (*peṭer*); cf. H. Cazelles, "Premiers-nés dans l'Ancien Testament," in *DBSup*, vol. 8, 482–491.

[4] Exod 13:2, 15; 22:19; Lev 27:26; Num 3:13; 8:17; Deut 15:19; Neh 10:37; cf. S. Daniel, *Philon: De Specialibus Legibus*, Paris, 1975, pp. 222–223.

---

prōtotokos, S 4416; *TDNT* 6.871–881; *EDNT* 3.189–191; *NIDNTT* 1.667–669; MM 557; L&N 10.43, 13.79, 87.47; BDF §120(1); BAGD 726–727

of the father's vigor" (Gen 49:3; Num 1:20; Ps 78:51), it is the best or the most excellent (Ezek 44:30; cf. Philo, *Prelim. Stud.* 98); an affective connotation, because it is the best-loved;[5] an honorific connotation, since the firstborn, through the birthright, shares in the the father's authority and is given much property.[6]

All of these nuances appear in figurative uses of the term, for example, when God says to Moses, "Israel is my firstborn" (Exod 4:22), and Luke probably had them in mind when he wrote concerning Mary, "She gave birth to her firstborn" (*eteken ton huion autēs ton prōtotokon*, Luke 2:7). He chose this word because of these connotations, and perhaps also to signal that this Davidic firstborn might be a claimant to messiahship.[7] There is some surface ambiguity, because "firstborn" can be a reference to later offspring;[8] but on the one hand, the title *prōtotokos* was given immediately after birth (Exod 13:2; 34:19; Philo, *Cherub.* 54); and on the other hand, the literature[9] and the inscriptions attest that a "firstborn" can be an only child. At Leontopolis in Lower Egypt, the epitaph of a Jewish woman of Arsinoe in 5 BC mentions that she died bringing her firstborn into the world; obviously this child could have had no younger brothers: "Fate, through my labor pains with my firstborn child, brought me to the end of my life."[10]

Apart from Heb 11:28 (cf. Ps 78:51), the other occurrences of *prōtotokos* in the NT are figurative, all expressive of honor, dignity, or pre-

---

[5] 2 Sam 13:21—"David loved Amnon as his firstborn son"; 1 Chr 3:1; cf. Josh 6:26; 1 Kgs 16:34; Jer 31:9; Mic 6:7; Zech 12:10; *Pss. Sol.* 13.8; Heliodorus, *Aeth.* 4.8.6: "a mother whose beloved son has cost her many pains" (ὁ μοῦ πρωτοτόκος καὶ πολύθρηνος γενομένη).

[6] 2 Kgs 3:27—"The king of Moab took his eldest son, the one who was to reign in his place"; 1 Chr 5:1–2; 2 Chr 21:3—"He had given the reign to Joram, because he was the eldest"; Ps 89:28—"I will make him the highest firstborn of the kings of the earth, and my favor will rest on him forever, and my covenant will be faithful to him"; Philo, *Sacr. Abel and Cain* 118, 119, 126.

[7] Cf. H. Schürmann, *Lukasevangelium*, p. 104.

[8] M. J. Lagrange (*Luc*), cites Lucian, *Demon.* 29: εἰ μὲν πρῶτος οὐ μόνος, εἰ δὲ μόνος οὐ πρῶτος; cf. A. Feuillet, "Premier-nés dans le Nouveau Testament," in *DBSup*, vol. 8, 491–512. On the "brothers" or cousins of Jesus, cf. J. McHugh, *The Mother of Jesus in the New Testament*, London, 1975, pp. 200–254, 451–452.

[9] *Pss. Sol.* 18.4—"Your correction comes upon us as upon a firstborn, only son" (ὡς υἱὸν πρωτότοκον, μονογενῆ); 4 Ezra 6:58—"We, your people, whom you have honored and whom you have called firstborn and unique, dear and well-beloved."

[10] Ὠδεῖνι δὲ Μοῖρα πρωτοτόκου με τέκνου πρὸς τέλος ἦγε βίου, *CII* 1510, 6 = *C.Pap.Jud.*, vol. 3, n. 1510 = *SEG* I, 570, = *SB* 6647 = *GVI*, n. 643; cf. J. B. Frey, "La signification du terme πρωτότοκος d'après une inscription juive," in *Bib*, 1930, pp. 373–390.

eminence,[11] especially with respect to Christ, the "firstborn of all creation" (prōtotokos pasēs ktiseōs, Col 1:15), who has a primacy of excellence in the order of creation[12] that could be described as cosmic. He is also the firstborn with respect to the dead (prōtotokos ek tōn nekrōn, Col 1:18) and thus has primacy in the order of resurrection, not simply because he was the first to come forth from the grave, but because he came forth as the all-powerful sovereign, the prince of a new humanity (Rev 1:5, ho archōn); finally, Christ is honored with a primacy in the eschatological order, because in glory he will be "firstborn among many brethren" (prōtotokos en pollois adelphois, Rom 8:29); as the first one resurrected, he will be the source of all other glorifications,[13] and "his brothers" will worship him in love.

A single NT text refers to creatures as firstborn in a figurative sense: Heb 12:23, "the assembly of the firstborn" (ekklēsia prōtotokōn), which exegetes take to mean either the patriarchs, or Christians who have already died, or the first converts and martyrs, or all the members of the church militant, or the angels in heaven. In all cases, prōtotokos is a title of honor, suggesting the privileges discussed above.[14]

---

[11] In this sense of the word, Joseph is called "the firstborn of God" (Jos. Asen. 21.3). Cf. A. Durand, "Le Christ Premier-Né," in RSR, 1910, pp. 56–66; E. A. Cerny, "Firstborn of Every Creature (Col I, 15)," Baltimore, 1938; T. W. Buckley, The Phrase 'Firstborn of Every Creature' (Col I, 15) in the Light of Its Jewish and Hellenistic Background, Rome, 1961, H. J. Gabathuler, Jesus Christus, Haupt der Kirche—Haupt der Welt: Der Christushymnus Kolosser I, 15–20, Zurich-Stuttgart, 1965; A. Feuillet, Christologie paulinienne et tradition biblique, Paris, 1973, pp. 48, 170, 230.

[12] Heb 1:6—"When he brought forth his firstborn into the universe, he said, 'Let all the angels of God worship him' "; cf. A. Vanhoye, "L'οἰκουμένη dans l'Epître aux Hébreux," in Bib, 1964, pp. 248–253; W. Michaelis, "Die biblische Vorstellung von Christus als dem Erstgeborenen," in ZST, 1954, pp. 137–157; idem, in TDNT, vol. 6, pp. 871–881.

[13] Cf. B. Rey, "Créés dans le Christ Jésus: La Création nouvelle selon S. Paul," Paris, 1966, pp. 177ff.

[14] Cf. Sir 36:11—"Have pity, O Lord, on the people called by your name, and on Israel whom you have made like a firstborn" (πτωρογόνῳ, which a corrector of Sinaiticus read as πρωτοτόκῳ); L. R. Helyer, "The Prototokos Title in Hebrews," in Studia Biblica et Theologica, vol. 6, 1976, pp. 3–28.

πύργος

pyrgos, **tower, watchtower, fortress, palace, house, apartment**

This term refers to quite diverse structures, from a simple house in a town or a roof apartment[1] to a palace, like that at Malatha in Idumea, to which Agrippa retired (Josephus, *Ant.* 18.147), or the luxurious dwelling of Aseneth (*Jos. Asen.* 2.1–2; 14.5), a watchtower, a defensive tower jutting out over the walls,[2] especially one that dominates a city gate. There are also "towers set up before a port to break the threatening waves and guarantee a safe refuge for those who enter" (4 Macc 13:6), not to mention the "wooden towers" that were strapped onto elephants (1 Macc 6:37; cf. the *pyrgomachountes* who do battle in these towers, Polybius 5.84.2) or the towers with ladders that attackers threw against fortifications in order to be on the same level as the defenders (Philo, *Spec. Laws* 4.229; Josephus, *War* 5.292; Polybius 5.99.5: towers spaced at intervals of one hundred feet and provided with guard-doors). Metaphorically, a tower, because of its height and strength, can suggest the elaboration of a coherent and bold

---

[1] Herodotus 2.95: the Egyptians climb up to sleep in towers, where the mosquitos cannot reach them; Xenophon, *An.* 4.4.2: in Armenia, "most dwellings had towers"; *P.Giss.* 67, 16: "a bedroom on the tower" (time of Trajan and Hadrian). Cf. Judg 9:46–47: "all the leading people of the Tower of Shechem assembled"; 9:49, 51, 52; *m. B. Bat.* 1.1; *b. B. Bat.* 5b; *1 Enoch* 89.50—"A large, high tower was built on the house (Jerusalem) for the Lord of the sheep"; cf. 89.56; *Pap.Lugd.Bat.* XIII, 14, 19, in his will *per aes et libram* a veteran leaves a third of his tower (τρίτον μέρος πύργου μου), i.e., his house, to two slaves (second century AD). Pliny the Younger describes his property in the Laurentine: "There is also another tower. In this tower, one chamber overlooks the sunrise and the sunset; below that, there is a vast storeroom and stockroom; on the ground floor there is a dining room . . . that overlooks the garden" (Pliny, *Ep. ad Gallum* 2.17.13); cf. P. Grimal, *Les Jardins romains*, Paris, 1943, pl. X fig. 1; E. Rizzo, *Pittura ellenistico-romana*, Milan, 1929, pl. 157 *a*.

[2] Neh 3:25–26; Ps 121:7—πυργόβαρις. The northern face of the establishment at Qumran was dominated by a massive two-story tower, partly jutting out, built in the first century BC, which gives the present ruins the appearance of a fort.

---

pyrgos, S 4444; *TDNT* 6.953–956; *EDNT* 3.300; MM 560; L&N 7.23; BAGD 730

intellectual system ("the tower of atheism")[3] or, because of its very elaborate perfection, aesthetic splendor.[4]

The most famous tower in the Bible and in all of human history is the tower of Babel, "whose top is in the heavens" (Gen 11:4, 5, 8), a ziggurat, amply commented on by Philo, who saw it as the "sign of an extraordinary madness."[5] But the tower most often referred to in the OT is the walled fortress;[6] these massive towers make it possible to get at attackers from the side and catch them in crossfire. They are usually for the defense of a port or a city. Sometimes *pyrgos* refers to a donjon (Isa 30:25; *T. Jud.* 5.5), sometimes the whole fortified city (Judg 8:9; Philo, *Conf. Tongues* 128, 130), sometimes to small forts scattered through the countryside (1 Macc 16:10; 2 Macc 10:36). The towers of the wall around Jerusalem were especially numerous and famous,[7] and they had

---

[3] Philo, *Conf. Tongues* 196; cf. 113, 115: "our madmen symbolically build the arguments for their vice, as if they were building a tower"; 133; the nuance is pejorative (ibid. 83, *Dreams* 2.284: building unwholesome doctrines to the height of a tower; *T. Levi* 2.3) and can indicate unreasonable exaltation, cf. Aristophanes, *Pax* 749; *Ran.* 1004; J. Taillardat, *Images d'Aristophane*, n. 750.

[4] Such are the comparisons of Cant 4:4—"Your neck is like the tower of David, built for a trophy"; 7:4—"like an ivory tower"; 8:10—"my breasts were like towers," meaning both developed and guarded. Cf. Tob 13:17—"Jerusalem will be rebuilt . . . its towers and walls made of pure gold."

[5] Philo, *Conf. Tongues* 5; cf. 1, 107, 134, 142, 155, 158; *Post. Cain* 53; *Sib. Or.* 11.10, 11.12. Cf. H. Gressmann, *The Tower of Babel*, New York, 1929; A. Busink, *De Toren van Babel*, Groningen, 1938; idem, *De Babylonische Tempeltoren*, Leiden, 1949; L. H. Vincent, "De la tour de Babel au temple," in *RB*, 1946, pp. 403–440; A. Parrot, *La Tour de Babel*, Paris, 1953.

[6] 2 Chr 14:6—"Let us surround these cities with a wall, with towers, gates, and locks"; 37:5—"Hezekiah rebuilt the whole crumbling wall and raised towers upon it"; Jdt 7:32; Isa 2:15; Ezek 26:4, 9; 1 Macc 5:5, 65—"Judas burned the towers of the wall of Hebron"; 13:33; 2 Macc 10:18, 20, 22. Diodorus Siculus mentions that the Thebans had a declaration read from atop a high tower (17.9.5) and that Alexander shook the towers and the "curtains" (τὰ μεσοπύργια) with a battering ram (17.25.5), knocking them down to the foundations (17.25.5), or building a wooden tower one hundred cubits high, full of catapults (17.26.6; 17.45.2) with combat stations (17.45.5). He even built towers on ships, allowing him to put up flying bridges and to reach enemy walls (17.32.7–8; cf. 17.71.4; 17.87.5).

[7] 2 Chr 26:9—"Uzziah build towers at Jerusalem, at the Corner Gate, at the Valley Gate, and at the Angle, and he fortified them"; 1 Macc 1:33—"They rebuilt the City of David with a large, very strong wall and strong towers"; 4:60; Ps 48:13—"Count the towers of Zion; consider her ramparts." Josephus, *War* 5.156: "The walls were dominated by towers that were twenty cubits broad and twenty cubits high; they were square and solid like the wall itself. In their joining and their beauty, the stones did not fall short of those of the temple. Above the imposing mass of the towers . . . were magnificent chambers, and above these, upper chambers and cisterns for collecting

names.[8] Thus according to Luke 13:4, the "Tower of Siloam" fell on eighteen people, killing them. It can perhaps be identified with the first foundations found of a tower built along the canal of Siloam.[9] In any event, we may compare Josephus, *War* 5.292: Titus ordered the building of three towers fifty feet tall to be erected on each embankment, so that the defenders of the ramparts might thus be put to flight. In the middle of the night, one of these accidentally fell. Josephus relates the melee that followed and the panic that spread, even though no one died.

Another sort of *pyrgos* is the watchtower in the countryside (2 Chr 26:10, 15; 27:4; cf. Judg 7:5), where a sentinel was posted (2 Kgs 9:17; 17:9; 18:8) to watch for marauders, jackals, and the occasional fox that attacked fruits, crops, or flocks (watchmen are remunerated, cf. *P.Oxy.* 2024, 8 and 22: "for the tower guards, seven *artabai*," *tōn phyllattōn tōn pyrgōn art.* ζ'; 2197, 131). Such a tower is often conical and stands about three meters high. They could be used for storing provisions (1 Chr 27:25). In Isa 5:2, the tower is presented as the complement of a fence or hedge around a vineyard; this wording is taken up in the parable of the Vineyard and the Tenants (Matt 21:33; Mark 12:1).[10]

But there is also the man who wants to build a tower and must first sit down and "count the cost" (Luke 14:28). This is not an inexpensive vine-

---

the rainwater. . . . The third wall had ninety of these towers. The middle was had forty towers, the old was had sixty. . . . The tower Psephinus, near which Titus camped, was seventy cubits high . . . and was octagonal in form."

[8] The Tower of Hananel (Neh 3:1; Jer 31:38; Zech 14:10); "You, tower of the flock (Hebrew *migdal-'ēder,* cf. Gen 35:21), Ophel, daughter of Zion" (Mic 4:8); the Tower of the Ovens (Neh 3:11; 12:38). Cf. at Caesarea the Tower of Strato (*P.Cair.Zen.* 59004, 2); in Spain the Turris Hannibalis (Pliny, *HN* 2.71, 73) and the Turris Augusti (Mela 3.18), etc.

[9] Attackers seize towers by tearing them down (Judg 8:17), by burning (1 Macc 5:65), by opening breaches in them (13:43), or by forcing the door (2 Macc 14:41; *P.Tebt.* 47, 16; second century BC). A tower is rebuilt from its foundations (*SB* 1598, 5).

[10] Cf. Str-B, vol. 1, pp. 868ff. M. Hubaut, *La Parabole des Vignerons homicides,* Paris, 1976, pp. 21ff. *Stud.Pal.* XX, 218, 16; *Pap.Lugd.Bat.* XIII, 14, 19; *P.Cair.Masp.* I, 67097: a contract to sell a farm, including a field with vines and date palms, a wine-press or cistern, a well, a tower, and a μονή; III, 67313. In *P.Fam.Tebt.* 23, 7–8, a certain Didymus sells part of his field and a fourth of his πυργομαγδώλ, his guard-tower, in the vicinity of Tebtunis. The *magdolon* (line 8) is the building where the watchman alerts the villagers who are busy in the fields to the presence of a marauder. These guard towers could be the property of a community that assesses a tax to pay the guards, the μαγδωφύλακες (cf. E. Kiessling, "Magdophylax," in PW, vol. 14, 1, p. 300). In Africa, localities are called *Turris* for the defensive works that guarantee the protection of the region; cf. S. Lancel, *Actes de la conférence de Carthage en 411,* Paris, 1972, vol. 1, p. 137; vol. 2, p. 712, 33; 846, 35; 849, 3 = Turris Alba; 894, 184, = Turris Blanda; *CIL* VIII, 8209; 22774.

yard tower built with dry stone, but a grandiose palace. One recalls that Herod was above all a great builder of towers. Notably, he built Hippicus, a square tower thirty cubits high; "above, a reservoir held rainwater, and above this was a two-story dwelling, twenty-five cubits high . . . the total height was eighty cubits" (Josephus, *War* 5.163–166). The height of the tower called Phasael was ninety cubits (ibid. 5.169). The tower called Mariamme was only fifty-five cubits high,[11] but its apartments were more luxurious and ornate than those of the other towers.[12]

These texts show that *pyrgos* is a quite variable form in ancient architecture, not only because it may be square or cylindrical, but because it may be a defensive tower, a watchtower, or a dwelling (either a simple house or one part of an important residence)[13]—in the papyri, usually the main building of a farm.[14] In the papyri, *pyrgos* appears in contracts for rentals,

---

[11] Josephus, *War* 5.171. Cf. 2 Macc 13.5—"At Berea there was a tower fifty cubits high"; Jdt 1:3—Arphaxad "built towers a hundred cubits high at the gate of the city" (Ecbatana); 1:14. In a dream, the sleeper finds himself in Alexandria atop a high tower (με εἶναι ἐπάνω πύργου μεγάλου, *UPZ* 78, 29; second century BC; cf. 146, 27). The πυργίον of *P.Tebt.* 780, 11 is only ten cubits high (= twenty feet). Cf. the two-story tower (πύργος δίστεγος), which seems to be the most common variety (*P.Oxy.* 243, 15; cf. π. διώρυφος, *SB* 9556, III, 9). But four- or five-story buildings in the form of a tower were not rare; cf. R. Martin, *L'Urbanisme dans la Grèce antique*, Paris, 1956, pp. 232ff.

[12] On friezes and architectural fittings, cf. R. Martin, *L'Urbanisme dans la Grèce antique*, pp. 202ff.

[13] *P.Oxy.* 243, 15, 17, 38; 248, 29, from AD 80: a rural estate (ἔπαυλις) includes two courtyards, a tower, a dovecote, and commons (πύργος καὶ περιστερεὼν καὶ αὐλαὶ καὶ ἕτερα χρηστήρια). The importance of a dwelling can be summed up in the number of its towers: ἐν τοῖς πύργοις (*BGU* 740, 5); cf. οἰκία διπυργία (*P.Gen.* 44, 12; *BGU* 2339, 9; *P.Hamb.* 14, 9; *CPR* I, 28, 10; *P.Lond.* 348, 12; vol. 2, p. 215; 1179, 32, 60; vol. 2, pp. 145–146; *P.Oxy.* 247, 23: τρίτον μέρος οἰκίας διπυργίας, ἐν ᾗ κατὰ μέσον αἴθριον, from AD 90. *PSI* 1112, 21; 1159, 20; *P.Ross.Georg.* II, 18, 360); cf. the purchase of the second story of the third *pyrgos* (*P.Stras.* 110; third century BC), τετραπυργία, Plutarch, *Eum.* 8.9: Eumenes gives his men the farms and homes in the country (τὰς κατὰ τὴν χώραν ἐπαύλεις καὶ τετραπυργίας; Polybius 31.26.11; Strabo 17.838.)

[14] F. Preisigke ("Die Begriffe πύργος und στέγη bei der Hausanlage," in *Hermes*, 1919, pp. 423–432) sees *pyrgos* only as "commons," the farm buildings that shelter the workshops and the threshing floors (cf. *P.Mil.Vogl.* 251, 15; *BGU* 2033, 12; *P.Lond.* 371, 3, vol. 2, p. 244: πύργος ἐν ᾧ βαφεῖον καὶ ἕτερα χρηστηρία: a dyer's workshop on the ground floor), whether or not these buildings were in the form of a tower. It is true that the vast majority of papyrological documents refer to farms (*P.Mich.* 226, 21: θησαυρὸν ἐνεργὸν ἐν ᾧ πύργος, from AD 37) and country houses: περὶ τοῦ παλαιοῦ πύργου τῆς οἰκίας (*P.Mich.* 212, 17; from the second century. 666, 8: μονῆς καὶ πύργου καὶ ἐπαύλεως; *ZPE*, vol. 13, 1974, n. 7–8; *P.Vindob.Tandem*, n. XXVIII, 10). But on the one hand the texts do not say if the tower is incorporated in the building (nevertheless, the *pyrgos* of *BGU* 1273, 15 is at the corner of two streets; cf. the corner

sales, mortgages, and marriage, in cadastres, even in complaints to the stratēgos or a police chief.[15] But while in the Bible *tower* often has religious value, referring to the strength and certainty of divine protection, it has only a secular meaning in the papyri.

In the inscriptions—which often mention or commemorate the building of a tower, whether as a military edifice,[16] a rural estate,[17] or an urban monument[18]—we note that the Olythian *proxenos* Heracleodoros dedicated

---

tower, πύργος ἐπιγώνιος, V. Martin, "Relevé topographique des immeubles d'une métropole: P. Gen. inv. 108," in *RechPap*, vol. 2, 1962, p. 51 = *q* II, 5–6; cf. p. 40 = A II, 32; again in *SB* 9902); on the other hand, sometimes the tower is distinct from the "outbuildings" (*P.Lond.* 216, 10, vol. 2, p. 186; *BGU* 650, 8: πύργος καὶ ἕτερα; *SB* 10696, 4: τὸν πύργον καὶ τὰ συνκύροντα), sometimes it is said to be inhabited (*P.Tebt.* 47; *BGU* 1273, 12), sometimes it is mentioned separately from the μονή, the small building where the farm workers live (σὺν λάκκο ὁλοκλήρο καὶ μονῆς καὶ πύργο, *P.Michael.* 60, 4; cf. 40, 66; 42 A 17; B 11; 46, 10; *P.Lond.* 1695, 8). Furthermore, on the basis of iconographic monuments (frescos, mosaics, etc.), P. Grimal ("Les Maisons à tour hellénistiques et romaines," in *Mélanges d'archéologie et d'histoire*, Paris, 1939, pp. 28–59) and Maria Nowicka (*La Maison privée dans l'Egypte ptolémaïque*, Warsaw, 1969, pp. 131ff; idem, "A propos des tours-πύργοι dans les papyrus grecs," in *Archeologia* [Warsaw], vol. 21, 1970, pp. 53–61) have shown that the tower constituted a well-defined architectural type for both dwellings and working buildings.

[15] *P.Tebt.* 779, 13: "By night he built a wall against our tower" (175 BC); *P.Ryl.* 138, 20 (AD 34): under the cover of darkness, a certain Orsenouphis broke into an estate belonging to the imperial family and stole from the tower five rakes, five hay sickles, fifteen measures of wool, and two hundred drachmas of silver.

[16] J. and L. Robert, "Bulletin épigraphique," in *REG*, 1944, p. 217, n. 130 *a*; 1955, p. 277, n. 250; ὁ βοῦργος = small stronghold (M. Schwabe, "The βοῦργος Inscription from Caesarea Palaestinae," in *J. N. Epstein Jubilee Volume*, Jerusalem, 1950, pp. 273–283; B. Lifshitz, "Inscriptions grecques de Césarée en Palestine," in *RB* 1961, p. 123, n. 16). Some say that the Latin *burgus* = *turris* was borrowed from the Greek πύργος (cf. M. Labrousse, "Les Burgarii et le cursus publicus," in *Mélanges d'archéologie et d'histoire*, Paris, 1939, pp. 151–167; S. Appelbaum, "Economic Life in Palestine," in S. Safrai, M. Stern, *The Jewish People in the First Century*, Assen-Amsterdam, 1976, vol. 2, p. 644, n. 4; συντηρεία βουργαρίων, Dittenberger, *Syl.* 880, 54); but the origin is probably Germanic (*burg*), and the Latin *burgus* also entered into Hebrew, cf. L. Robert, *Noms indigènes*, p. 14.

[17] J. and L. Robert, "Bulletin épigraphique," in *REG*, 1950, p. 183, n. 173; *IGLAM*, n. 425, 8: καὶ ἄλλον οἶκον πρὸς τῷ πύργῳ. A rural estate is described, with its farm (αὐλή), dwellings (οἰκίαι), and tower (πύργος), cf. *I.Sinur.*, p. 86, n. 51, 11.

[18] *I.Bulg.*, n. 12, 3 ([μονο]πύργον); 57, 8: τὴν σχοινίαν τὴν μεταξὺ τῶν δύο πύργων οἰκοδομήσας καὶ στεγάσας (first century), 1730; *MAMA* VI, 2: dedication for a monumental gate of the city of Laodicea: τοὺς πύργους καὶ τὸ τρίπυλον; *IGLS*, 1610: "This tower (traveler's quarters) was built in the year 837, in the month of Panemos"; 2507: "Under the very venerable and very holy . . . bishop, this tower was built"; cf. *I.Did.*, p. 53 *b*: τῆς οἰκοδομίας τοῦ πύργου (?); *P.Oxy.* 2624, frag. 28 *e*: οὐ πόλισμα, οὐ πύργος, οὐ δόμος ἐύκτιτος (?).

"the tower and the hall and the statue to all the gods" (*theois pasin ton pyrgon kai tēn exedran kai ton andrianta, I.Thas.* 376, 2). But the Christian inscriptions follow the biblical tradition of using *tower* not only as a safe refuge but as a sign of his protection and a pledge of his watchful care: "Lord, keep this tower and those who dwell in it" (*IGLS* 328); God through his providence has righted "a tower bent by time and the shaking of the earth" (ibid. 785, 4); "the construction of the tower (of the wall) is, with the help of God, the work of the Macedonian quarter" (ibid. 2828, at Baalbeck; cf. 478, 1). Hence the name "Tower of the Lord"[19] and its religious meaning: "Christ Jesus, be for us a Protector-God, a house of refuge, and a mighty tower in the presence of the enemy" (ibid. 1811; cf. 1814); "In the name of the Father and of the Son and of the Holy Spirit, by the intercession of St. Mary, Mother of God and Virgin forever, and of the glorious archangels and chief apostles, this tower was built" (ibid. 1913).

---

[19] *IGLS* 2628; cf. 1630: "To protect his country with wisdom, John, abundant in good counsel and spending money unstintingly, presents this tower to his friends as a refuge, through the zeal of Paul the deacon"; 1726: "I Thomas, apostolic visitor by the grace of God, having made a vow and a request to God for the expiation of my sins, for the glory of his name, have raised this tower"; 1768: "the tower was raised, with God, for the salvation and health of the brethren and the servants." A. J. Festugière, *Etudes d'histoire,* pp. 212–223. Cf. *3 Apoc. Bar.* 2.7—τὸν πύργον τῆς θεο-μαχίας; 3.6; Ps.-Philo, *Bib. Antiq.* 32.15: "The knowledge of the Lord is there, which builds a tower in you" (*turrificat,* πυργοποιεῖ); 32.1: Israel is the tower built by God, as he drew Eve from Adam and Adam from the earth; *SB* 11240, 7: ἑτοίμος ἔχω οἰκοδομῆσαι νέον πύργον. We note that in the Latin inscriptions, from the first century, *burgus* (originally meaning "a tower") was the transliteration for πύργος; then βοῦργος came to refer to a "small stronghold" (Procopius, *Aed.* 4.6.36; cf. 4.6.21). Cf. B. Lifshitz, "Césarée de Palestine," in *ANRW, Prinzipat,* vol. 8, pp. 512ff.

ῥᾳδιουργία

rhadiourgia, ability, unconcern, unscrupulousness, scheming

At Cyprus, St. Paul denounces the *magus* Elymas as being "full of all guile and all *rhadiourgia*."[1] This term, which appears only in the Koine (literary and popular), is a biblical hapax and could be translated "scheming." But its meaning is very broad. First, it means facility at doing something: "We did not speak to those who were too young concerning the things of love, lest with facility added to the violence of their passions they should give themselves over to it without hestitation" (Xenophon, *Cyr.* 1.6.34); thence easiness, unconcern, indolence,[2] then lack of conscience, unscrupulousness: "There are two ways of being struck. One corresponds to the case of the slave whose misdeeds have deserved the blows of the free man—who, having acted unconscionably (*dia rhadiourgian*), is stretched out on the wheel; the other is that of any inanimate object whatsoever."[3]

The most common meaning is "deception, trickery." In a case of fraud, Cato files suit.[4] This dishonesty appears most often in financial matters:

---

[1] Πλήρης παντὸς δόλου καὶ πάσης ῥᾳδιουργίας, Acts 13:10; cf. C. K. Barrett, "Light on the Holy Spirit from Simon Magus (Act. VIII, 4–25)," in J. Kremer, *Les Actes des Apôtres*, Gembloux-Louvain, 1979, p. 289.

[2] Xenophon, *Cyr.* 7.5.74: "If we were to adopt an easy existence (ῥᾳδιουργίαν) and the enjoyment of a lax life (ἡδυπάθειαν), we would soon disgust ourselves"; Xenophon, *Mem.* 2.1.20 = softness; Polybius 12.9.5: "The laws and customs of the Locrians of Italy do not correspond at all to the laxity of slaves (οὐ τῇ τῶν οἰκετῶν ῥᾳδιουργίᾳ) but to a colony of free men."

[3] Philo, *Cherub.* 80; cf. the adjective ῥᾳδιουργός, the unscrupulous man (*Worse Attacks Better* 165; *Conf. Tongues* 152), contrasted with πιστός (*SB* 7241, 15–16). The verb ῥᾳδιουργέω, "alter, distort": "It is not easy to give credence to most of the historians of Alexander. They play with the facts" (Strabo 11.6.4); Plutarch, *Mor.* 2.829 d.

[4] Ῥᾳδιουργίας προὔθηκε κρίσιν, Plutarch, *Cat. Min.* 16; cf. Philo, *Post. Cain* 43: "a life of intrigue, of unscrupulous mischief, of trickery, mingled with passions and full of vices." The *Suda* defines rhadiourgos: πλαστογράφος καὶ ὁ κακοῦργος ἁπλῶς. Rhadiourgoi are swindlers (Philo, *Dreams* 2.148; cf. *Sacr. Abel and Cain* 32).

---

rhadiourgia, S 4468; TDNT 6.972–973; EDNT 3.207; MM 562; L&N 88.301; BAGD 733

"The association of criminals and thieves (*rhadiourgoi kai kleptai*) usually founders in this fashion: through the lack of reciprocal justice and in a general way mutual breach of trust" (Polybius 4.29.4). This meaning, "swindling," is almost the only meaning attested in the papyri. In 216 BC, a woman complains that her coat has been stolen and asks the *stratēgos* for punishment of the theft (*peri de tēs rhadiourgias, P.Magd.* 35, 11; republished *P.Enteux.* 30). In 114, Marres, priest of Soknebtunis, is angry at the falsification of a figure in his contract. The *synallagmatographos* had written down a rent of thirty-six *artabai* instead of thirty. This was a swindle (*to para touto rhadiourgēmenas*); "I have been treated in a flagrantly unjust manner" (*ēdikēmenos kath' hyperbolēn, P.Tebt.* 42, 16). A defenseless (*aboēthēton*) woman asks the *oikonomos* that she not be defrauded of the guarantee of her dowry "because of the *rhadiourgia* of the accused"(*dia tou enkaloumenou rhadiourgian, P.Tebt.* 776, 31; cf. *BGU* 226, 14). In the second century AD, the prefect of Egypt stipulates that in order to contest a debt a person will have to declare that the contract is a fake or that fraudulent or deceptive means were used.[5]

In Acts 13:10, it is not a question of money or even of some particular action, but a character trait, a dominant vice. Elymas is called a "son of the devil," who is the father of lies (John 8:44). The association with *dolos*, "ruse, trick, fraud," invites us to translate, "full of all trickery and mischief."[6]

---

[5] *P.Oxy.* 237, col. VIII, 15: εἴτε πλαστῶν γραμμάτων ἢ ῥᾳδιουργίας ἢ περιγραφῆς ἐνκαλεῖν, cf. *UPZ* 162, col. VI, 3; *P.Stras.* 40, 30 (sixth century). The jurisdiction of the prefect of Egypt around 133–137 extends περὶ πλαστογραφίας καὶ ῥᾳδιουργίας (*SB* 10929, 10).

[6] Eusebius denounces the "deceitful temptations" of the demon, πρὸς τὰς τοῦ δηλωθέντος κακοτέχνους ῥᾳδιουργίας.

ῥίπτω

rhiptō, **to throw, throw away, get rid of, lay out, scatter**

This verb is used in the NT with the same meanings as in classical Greek and the LXX (Hebrew *šālak*).

(*a*) "To throw." For example, throwing a ship's rigging and anchors into the sea.[1] It is better to be thrown into the sea—i.e., to die a cruel death—than to be a cause of stumbling.[2]

(*b*) "To throw away, rid oneself of."[3] The object may be things like money (Ezek 7:19), as when Judas, before going to hang himself, throws the

---

[1] Acts 27:19—τὴν σκευὴν τοῦ πλοίου ἔριψαν (better attested than ἐρίψαμεν, H, L, P, Harclean, Peshitta, Bohairic; the vague σκεῦος would be the usual term for a ship's armament, cf. J. Vars, *L'Art nautique dans l'antiquité*, Paris, 1887, p. 61); Acts 27:29. Cf. cast into the sea, Xenophon, *Cyn.* 9.20; Achilles Tatius 2.11.5; 3.2.9: "the pilot ordered the cargo to be thrown [into the sea]" = *T. Job* 18.7; Exod 15:1, 4, 21; Neh 9:11; Exod 1:22 (in the Nile); Jer 51:63 (in the Euphrates); 2 Kgs 2:21 (in the water); 2 Kgs 2:21 (in the water); 2 Chr 30:14 (in the Kidron); Philo, *Alleg. Interp.* 2.102; *Drunkenness* 111; *Husbandry* 82; *Moses* 2.249; cf. *Good Man Free* 115; same meaning as ἀπορίπτω (Acts 27:32).

[2] Luke 17:2; cf. Plutarch, *Rom.* 18.1: "the Tarpeian Rock, from which criminals were thrown"; Xenophon, *Cyr.* 3.1.25: "they anticipate death by throwing themselves into the void"; Menander, *Dysk.* 583: "Nothing is left for you but to throw yourself into the abyss"; Josephus, *War* 1.150: "They threw themselves over the precipices in large numbers"; Judg 9:53—"A woman threw a millstone onto the head of Abimelech and fractured his skull"; 11:21–22; *P.Fouad* 29, 9: "one of them cast a stone, and my son . . . sustained a head injury"; *P.Lips.* 40, col. I, 17; *T. Zeb.* 2.7—μὴ ἀποκτείνωμεν αὐτὸν ἀλλὰ ῥίψωμεν αὐτὸν εἰς ἕνα τῶν ξηρῶν λάκκων τούτων; cast into the fire (Exod 32:24; Jer 36:23; Ezek 5:4; 4 Macc 12:20; 17:1). A stone devoted to Isis bears this dedication: "Thrown by his horses (ῥιφθεὶς ἐξ ἵππων) from his carriage, Isidorus, for being saved, as an act of thanksgiving for his feet, has dedicated the image of his foot to the blessed (Isis)" (*SEG* XX, 501 = *SB* 10161; L. Robert, *Hellenica*, vol. 10, p. 281).

[3] Ῥίπτω is the technical verb for throwing away one's weapons; Plato, *Leg.* 12.944 *b*; Xenophon, *Cyr.* 4.2.33; Josephus, *War* 2.625; 1 Macc 5:43; 7:44; 11:51; *BGU* 1024, col. III, 16; one sheds one's clothing (2 Kgs 7:15); *P.Tebt.* 48, 23: "throwing away his ἱμάτιον, he took flight"; *P.Fouad* 85, 13: "she promised either to bring him to an

---

rhiptō, S 4496; *TDNT* 6.991–993; *EDNT* 3.212–213; MM 564; L&N 15.217, 16.10, 85.37; BDF §§ 13, 68, 101, 308; BAGD 736

pieces of silver in the temple (Matt 27:5); or persons, as with the demon who "having thrown the possessed person down in their midst came out of him, doing him no harm."[4] The nuance of abandonment and rejection is 14:9—"You have cast me behind your back"; Neh 9:26—"They have cast your law behind themselves"; Joel 1:7; Philo, *Flacc.* 37: cast off.

(c) "Unload, unburden oneself." When this is done at the feet of someone of high station, there are connotations of veneration and confidence: the crowds cast their sick at Jesus' feet (Matt 15:30), as Judah threw himself at Joseph's feet to appease his anger (Josephus, *Ant.* 2.159), or as an old man threw himself to the ground and knelt before Dionysius (*P.Oxy.* 1089, 31; cf. *T. Job* 39.9). With respect to things, *rhiptō* means "to leave" (on the spot, *P.Ryl.* 125, 25: "they left the box in my house empty"—*eripsan en tē oikia mou tēn pyxida kenēn*) or "to replace," for example, the lead weight on the opening of the ephah (Zech 5:8; cf. Judg 8:25).

(d) The LXX often uses the verb for throwing corpses into a field or into a tomb,[5] especially the perfect passive participle *errimmenos* (Hebrew *nāpal*),[6] which would be the equivalent of our "recumbent" or "laid out" (French *gisant*), as in Josephus, *Ant.* 6.362: "laid out on the ground" (*epi gēs errimmenous*). The participle can also refer to beggars sleeping on the hard ground (Epictetus 3.26.6) and more generally to objects placed, arranged,[7] or even scattered here and there (*Enoch* 21.3–4; *BGU* 1857, 9). This pejorative connotation is present in Matt 9:36—Jesus "took pity on them because they were weary and lying on the ground (*hoti ēsan eskylmenoi kai errimmenoi*), like sheep without a shepherd." They were not only exhausted but also abandoned, without resources, scattered and dispersed;[8] only a pastor could gather them together and assure their survival.

---

agreement or to have the case thrown out before the magistrate"; one rids oneself of all care (*C.P.Herm.* 10, 9; same meaning as ἐπιρίπτω, 1 Pet 5:7; cf. Luke 19:35); cf. Josephus, *Ant.* 16.248.

[4] Luke 4:35. Hagar, expecting her child to die, threw him under a bush (Gen 21:15); Joseph's brothers threw him into a cistern (Gen 37:20); 2 Sam 18:17; Jer 38:6; Dan 6:8, 13, 17, 24 (the lions' den).

[5] 2 Kgs 9:25–26; 13:21; Tob 1:17; 2:3; Isa 14:19; Jer 22:19; 26:23; 41:9; 50:30; Ezek 19:12.

[6] Judg 4:22; 15:15; 1 Kgs 13:24–25, 28; Jer 14:16; 36:30; Ep Jer 71; Ps 88:6; Jdt 6:13; 14:15; 1 Macc 11:4; Josephus, *Ant.* 6.191: the Philistines see Goliath lying on the ground, ἰδόντες ἐρριμμένον; Philo, *Dreams* 2.269; *Joseph* 25; leave unburied.

[7] Josephus, *Ant.* 3.7; *P.Lips.* 40, col. II, 20; *PSI* 404, 8: ἔστι δὲ ὑπαίθριον τὸ στιππύον ἐρριμμένον ἐν τοῖς Παταικίωνος (third century BC); *P.Cair.Zen.* 59467, 5; *P.Oxy.* 1915, 17; cf. Epictetus 1.23.10; *T. Abr.* A 5: "God placed the thought of Abraham's death in the heart of Isaac" = B 4.

[8] 2 Macc 3:29—"This man lay silent, without hope, with no one to help"; Josephus, *War* 4.324: the priests "were nude, exposed to sight (ἐρριμμένοι γυμνοί),

(e) It is more difficult to interpret Acts 22:23—in the temple court, the Jews, exasperated at Paul, "cried out, cast (their) cloaks (*kai rhiptountōn ta himatia*) and threw dust in the air."[9] This is reminiscent of Job's three friends, who "raised their voices and wept; each tore his cloak (*rhēxantes hekastos tēn heautou stolēn*) and poured dust on his head."[10] But *rhiptō* does not mean "to rend, tear" (*diarhēssō*); it would be better to translate "tear off, pull off" (Isa 33:12) remembering that the motive is anger or indignation, as when Moses threw down the tables of the law and broke them (Exod 32:19; Deut 9:17). As Plato says, "What a statement you have just made! In setting it forth, you should expect to see a great number of people, and people not to be taken lightly, hurriedly cast off their garments (*hoion rhipsantas ta himatia*) and strip, take up whatever weapons are ready to hand, and rush at you with all their might."[11]

This is a theatrical gesture,[12] one customarily used by lawyers;[13] it has with good reason been compared to the Roman *jactatio togarum*.[14] But we

---

to be devoured by dogs and wild beasts"; *P.Paris* 19, col. II, 3: καλῶς οὖμ ποιήσεις ἐπιτροφήν μου ποιησάμενος, ἔρρειμαι γὰρ κακῶς διακείμενος ἀπ' ἐκείνου (third century BC). Cf. Philo, *To Gaius* 326: cast off into the darkness.

[9] Interpreters have suggested that the Jews "tore" their garments as a sign of mourning (but this is not the right verb for that), or that they "took them off" to prepare to stone Paul (which is not credible, given that they were in the sacred precincts). On the gesture of throwing one's cloak (Luke 19:35), cf. the note of E. Delebecque, *Evangile de Luc*, p. 121.

[10] Job 2:12 = *T. Job* 28.3; cf. Josephus, *War* 2.322: "the high priests could be seen covering their heads with dust, tearing their vestments, exposing their chests" (γυμνοὺς δὲ τὰ στέρνα τῶν ἐσθήτων διερρηγμένων); 4.324; cf. E. Haenchen, *Acts*, p. 633, n. 1; Plutarch, *Cic.* 37.2: pulled in both directions (ῥιπταθείς).

[11] Plato, *Resp.* 5.474 *a*; cited by H. J. Cadbury (Excursus, "Dust and Garments," in F. J. F. Jackson, K. Lake, *The Beginnings of Christianity*, London, 1933, vol. 5, pp. 269–277; H. J. Cadbury, *The Book of Acts in History*, London, 1955, pp. 38, 54), who sees these gestures as intended to ward off the curse that Paul's attitude was expected to provoke.

[12] Heliodorus, *Aeth.* 6.8.3: Charicleia "was taken by fits of rage and despair, furiously undid her hair, tore her clothing (θοἱμάτιον περιρρηξαμένη)" which she calls "the pantomime of our pain"; Plutarch, *De superst.* 3: Jewish women, ῥίψεις ἐπὶ πρόσωπον; cf. *T. Abr.* A 11: Adam, seeing the multitudes going to perdition, "grabbed his hair and his beard and threw himself at the foot of the throne, groaning and weeping."

[13] In the *Acts of Isidorus* (Recension B = *P.Lond.* inv. 2785, 37 = H. Musurillo, *Pagan Martyrs*, p. 22 = idem, *Acta Alexandrinorum*, Leipzig, 1961, p. 15) the lawyer makes a gesture with his hand and throws his cloak: ὁ ῥήτωρ τῇ δεξιᾷ . . . τὸ ἱμάτιον ἔρριψεν; cf. Dio Chrysostom 1.114; Gregory of Nazianzus, *Or. Bas.* 15, PG, vol. 36, 516: "they cry, they throw dust in the sky (οὐρανῷ πέμπουσι κόνιν), they beat the air."

[14] Ovid, *Am.* 3.7.74: "Revocate, Quirites, et date jactatis undique signa togis."

do not know exactly what the gesture was. In any event, *rhiptō* should mean "agitate" rather than "throw,"[15] which is confirmed by the medical vocabulary, in which *rhiptō* is used for convulsions[16] and by the examples cited by F. Field,[17] following Wettstein.

---

[15] Cf. Wis 18:18—"thrown down half dead, one here, one there"; Xenophon, *Cyn.* 9.20: the deer throw themselves into the sea or a body of water "with disorderly leaps."

[16] W. K. Hobart, *Medical Language*, p. 2.

[17] F. Field, *Notes on the Translation*, p. 136; cf. Aristaenetus, *Ep.* 1.26 (admiration for a dancer): ὁ δὲ δῆμος ἀνέστηκέ τε ὀρθὸς ἀπὸ θεύματος . . . καὶ τῷ χεῖρε κινεῖ καὶ τὴν ἐσθῆτα σοβεῖ; Lucian, *Salt.* 83 (hamming up the role of Ajax μαινόμενος): ἀλλὰ τό γε θέατρον ἅπαν συνεμεμήνει τῷ Αἴαντι, καὶ ἐπήδων, καὶ ἐβόων, καὶ τὰς ἐσθῆτας ἀπερρίπτουν. Cf. the texts of Anacreon, Melanippides, Timotheus, and the *adespota*, cited by D. L. Page, *Poetae Melici Graeci*, Oxford, 1962, n. 382 *b*; 501, 8; 758; 791, 165; 939, 19; 1037, 14; idem, *Supplementum Lyricis Graecis*, Oxford, 1974, n. 477, 11.

ῥυπαρία, ῥυπαρός, ῥύπος

rhyparia, dirtiness, filth; *rhyparos*, dirty, filthy; *rhypos*, dirtiness, filth

The nouns mean "dirtiness, filth" (Plutarch, *De vit. pud.* 2: nurses scrub the dirt from small children; *Phoc.* 18.4: "a poor old man, dressed in a dirty cloak"; Plutarch, *De sera* 26) and the adjective "dirty." They are used for impure metals (Dioscorides 5.74; cf. 1.56), for base and trivial remarks: "In describing the sublime, one must not stoop to dirty and disgusting details" (*eis ta rhypara kai exybrismena*, Ps.-Longinus, *Subl.* 43.5; *T. Jud.* 14.3, *en dialogismois rhyparois*). In the papyri, *rhyparos* refers to grain that has not been winnowed or purified,[1] and especially to debased coinage.[2]

In the Bible, the term "dirty clothes" (as opposed to festal clothes) appears in Zech 3:3-4 and again in Jas 2:2, contrasting the man with luxurious clothing and the poor man in a worn and dirty garment, just as when Pharaoh orders "that the prisoner be given splendid clothing instead of the filthy garment that he has."[3] Stains or dirt are washed

---

[1] *P.Fay.* 16, 10 (first century BC); *P.Tebt.* 1057, 5; *P.Ryl.* 715, 3 and 8; *C.P.Herm.* 77, 3; *P.Oxy.* 1906, 1; 1910, 17; 1947, 2; *P.NYU* 11, 200; cf. *P.Athen.* 50, verso 4 and 14, ῥυπαροῦ μετρηταί; *O.Bodl.* 397, ὑπὸ δώματος ῥυπαροῦ. In *P.Oxy.* 234, col. II, 18, ῥυπῶδες = discolored. Cf. ῥυπαρῶς, [to act] in a dirty way (Epictetus 2.9.4).

[2] *P.Tebt.* 238, 6: twelve devalued silver drachmas (AD 23); *P.Fay.* 52, *a* 3; *P.Ryl.* 194, 3; *Pap.Lugd.Bat.* VI, 39, 4; *P.Mich.* 224 (3045); 225 (526); 372, col. II, 9; *P.Rein.* 134–137; *BGU* 1613 B, col. II, 20 (AD 69/70); 1898, 166; *P.Mert.* 64, 5, 9 (with the editors' note, p. 47); etc. Cf. V. B. Schuman, in *Aeg*, vol. 32, 1952, p. 249; idem, "The Income of the Office of the ΠΡΑΚΤΟΡΕΣ ΑΡΓΥΡΙΚΩΝ of Karanis," in *BASP*, vol. 12, 1975, pp. 34ff. Cf. the bath tax in *P.Cair.Mich.* 359 (*P.Cair.Mich.*, pp. 25ff., 33).

[3] Philo, *Joseph* 105: καὶ ἀντὶ ῥυπώσης λαμπτὰν ἐσθῆτα ἀντιδόντες; *Apoc. Pet.* 21, 30: ἄνδρες ῥάκη ῥυπαρὰ ἐνδεδύμενοι (in lieu of punishment); Josephus, *Ant.* 7.267 : Memphibostos, ῥυπαράν τε τὴν ἐσθῆτα περικείμενος; *Sib. Or.* 5.188; Dio Cas-

---

rhyparia, S 4507; *EDNT* 3.215; *NIDNTT* 1.479; MM 565; L&N 88.256; BAGD 738 ‖ **rhyparos**, S 4508; *EDNT* 3.215; *NIDNTT* 1.479; MM 565; L&N 79.52, 88.257; BAGD 738 ‖ **rhypos**, S 4509; *EDNT* 3.215; *NIDNTT* 1.479; MM 565; L&N 79.55; BDF §51(2); BAGD 738 away; 1 Pet 3:21 points out that the purpose of baptism is not to get rid of bodily dirt.[4]

In classical Greek, moral stains are filth,[5] and it is not surprising that Jas 1:21 gives *rhyparia* this figurative meaning of a stain that one washes away in order to be clean (*katharos*, John 13:10); similarly Teles and Plutarch use this term for sordid greed.[6] The transition from the literal to the moral meaning of *rhypos* was clear in the LXX ("Who will draw the pure from the unclean? No one")[7] and common in literary texts: "Making your soul pure (*katharēn psychēn*) and washing away that which soils it";[8] "These meditations (on the stars) purify stains here below" (Marcus Aurelius 7.47).

---

sius 65.20: "Vitellius put on a sorry-looking tunic, dirty and torn"; Artemidorus Daldianus, *Onir.* 2.3; *BGU* 1564, 10: ἐφ᾿ ᾧ ποιήσουσι τὸν ἱματισμὸν ἔκ τε καλῆς καὶ λευκοτάτης ἐρεᾶς χωρὶς παντὸς ῥύπου (second century); *P.Giss.* 76, 3: τρίγωνας ῥυπαρὰς β᾿ καὶ στολὴν ὁμοίως λευκήν; a law of Gambreion regarding mourning apparel, ἔχειν φαιὰν ἐσθῆτα, μὴ κατερρυπωμένην (Dittenberger, *Syl.* 1219, 6; third century BC). Job 9:31 links refuse (ῥύπος) and clothing.

[4] 1 Pet 3:21—οὐ σαρκὸς ἀπόθεσις ῥύπου. The nouns ῥυπαρία and ῥύπος refer to something that is sticky and greasy, like suint (Hippocrates, *Fract.* 21) or earwax; idem, *Liqu.* 4.2; Clement of Alexandria, *Paed.* 2.10.87; *Pap.Graec.Mag.* 36, 332: μῖξον δὲ καὶ ταῖς κριθαῖς καὶ ῥύπον ἀπὸ ὠτίου μούλας = *P.Oslo* 1, 332.

[5] Cf. L. Moulinier, *Le Pur et l'impur dans la pensée des Grecs*, pp. 25, 38, 60.

[6] Teles speaks of people not using their wealth, οὐ χρωμένους δὲ τούτοις δι᾿ ἀνελευθερίαν καὶ ῥυπαρίαν (in Stobaeus, *Flor.* 97.31); Plutarch, *Mor.* 2.60 d: οἰκονομικὸς χωρὶς ῥυπαρίας = Pertinax was thrifty without being sordid (text inserted by some manuscripts in Dio Cassius 76.5). Cf. Julius Pollux, *Onom.* 3.116: μικροψυχία, ἀνελευθερία, μικροπρέπεια, καὶ ὡς Κριτίας, ῥυπαρία. The legend of St. Pelagia, p. 6, 30, concerning baptismal purification, is cited: ἀφῆκεν ἐν τῷ ὕδατι πᾶσαν αὐτῆς τὴν ῥυπαρίαν.

[7] Job 14:4—τίς γὰρ καθαρὸς ἔσται ἀπὸ ῥύπου (Hebrew *ṭāmē'*), cited by Philo, *Change of Names* 48; cf. Job 11:15; Isa 4:4—"when the Lord has washed the filth (Hebrew *ṣō'âh*) from the daughters of Zion and rinsed the blood from the midst of Jerusalem." It is clear from Plutarch that ῥυπαρία is very pejorative: "We see no animal other than the pig taking so much pleasure in the mire and in the unclean and filthy places" (τόποις ῥυπαροῖς καὶ ἀκαθάρτοις, *Quaest. conv.* 4.5.3).

[8] Lucian, *Vit. Auct.* 3: τὸν ἐπ᾿ αὐτῇ ῥύπον ἐκκλύσας; cf. Philo, *Unchang. God* 7: "If we make an effort to be grateful . . . we will purify ourselves of our faults and wash away the stains that taint our lives" (ἐκνιψάμενοι τὰ καταρρυπαίνοντα τὸν βίον); Rev 22:11.

σανίς

sanis, plank, board

From its first occurrences, sanis, "plank, board," was used for a leaf of a wooden door.[1] Thus the epitaph of Lysandros, dead at Karanis at age twenty, says, "During the night, my companions did not make the cedar doors resound";[2] and thus the brothers who want to preserve their sister's virginity propose barricading or blockading her: "If she is a door, we will set up planks of cedar against her."[3] This wood can be of all sorts, from that which is carried by camels,[4] the lid of a trunk (kibōton) in which the priest Jehoiada bored a hole (2 Kgs 12:9), and writing tablets,[5] to the cedar floors in the rooms for eating and resting in the royal palace (Josephus, Ant. 8.134; SEG XXII, 114, 17, en sanidi leleukōmenē—1st century AD).

---

[1] Homer, Od. 2.344; Il. 9.583: Oineus "shook the well-joined planks of the door"; 12.121: "He did not find the leaves of the gate closed, nor the long door-bar"; 12.453, 461: "the door groaned . . . the planks were smashed."

[2] Κεδροπαγεῖς σανίδας, SEG I, 567, 6 = SB 6706 = GVI, n. 1680 (who dates the inscription to the third-second century BC).

[3] Cant 8:9, Hebrew lûaḥ, which is "said of objects with a smooth surface: a stone table (Exod 24:12ff.), metal panels (1 Kgs 7:36), wooden planks (Exod 27:8; 38:7; Ezek 27:5). . . . [Here] the word is used for planks used inside a door to bar its leaves. They are of cedar, a precious wood . . . strong and incorruptible" (A. Robert, R. Tournay, Le Cantique des Cantiques, Paris, 1963, p. 311).

[4] SB 9075, 8; cf. P.Col.Zen. 5, 57: "at Libanos, prices of woods"; Plutarch, Per. 28.2: Pericles had the soldiers of the Samian navy, already half-dead, tied to planks and finished off with clubs.

[5] Dio Cassius 42.32: Antonius "broke the tablets on which these two laws were written"; Dittenberger, Syl. 975, 30: ἀναγράψαντες εἰς τὴν σανίδα; 1011, 15.

---

sanis, S 4548; EDNT 3.228; MM 568; L&N 7.79; BAGD 742

Sanis is especially used for ships, whether for the sides (Ezek 27:5; Anth. Pal. 9.415.6), the gangway (Euripides, Hel. 1556; Polybius 1.22.5), the planks, like those that saved the shipwreck victims in Acts 27:44,[6] or the "floor" of a floating bridge burned by pirates (Philo, To Gaius 129).

---

[6] Ἐπὶ σανίσιν; "the substantive σανίς could refer to the sides, which would mean that the hull of the ship was broken up, but most likely it refers to the boards used to secure the cargo in the hold and keep it from sliding when the ship rolled and pitched" (J. Renié, Actes des Apôtres, Paris, 1949, p. 344); cf. P.Flor. 69, 21 and 24: ἐξηλοῦσι σανίδες [πλ]ατείας ἑτέρου τοίχου τοῦ προκειμένου πλοίου (fragment of an account from the third century BC); P.Cair.Zen. 59755, 12 (list of a ship's furnishings), where the editor proposes the reading ἐστρωμένον, διὰ νηὸς σανίς, following P.Lond. 1164, h 7 (vol. 3, p. 164; third century AD).

σαργάνη, σπυρίς

sarganē, spyris, **basket**

These two substantives, unknown in the LXX,[1] seem almost synonymous, since St. Paul, in his escape from Damascus, was let down the wall *en sarganē* according to 2 Cor 11:33 (omitted by F, G) and *en spyridi* in Acts 9:25.[2]

Some have wanted to see *sarganē* as a fish basket,[3] while it is actually a woven wicker basket with varied uses: "*Peltai* (small shields) are hidden in large straw and wool baskets (*en angesin*), . . . smaller weapons in baskets full of raisins and figs (*en sarganais*), and daggers in amphoras of grain, dried figs, and olives" (Aeneas Tacticus 29.6). In the papyri, it is a container for grain or wine,[4] or more precisely, a unit of measure,[5] the weight of a shipment, valued at 150 pounds in *P.Cair.Isid.* 10, 4ff.; 13, 50; 16, 22; 17, 2ff.;

[1] Hebrew has four terms for "basket": *sal,* for bread loaves and cakes (Gen 40:16; Lev 8:2; Num 6:15) or meat (Judg 6:19); *dûd,* for fruit (Jer 24:1–2, figs); *ṭene',* for provisions (Deut 26:2, 4; 28:5, 17); *kᵉlûb,* literally, "woven," used for fruit (Amos 8:1–2) but also for a bird cage (Jer 5:27).

[2] On the parallelism of these two texts, cf. C. K. Barrett, *New Testament Essays,* London, 1972, pp. 95ff. This mode of transport, used for an escape in Josh 2:15; 1 Sam 19:12, is also the way one can be hoisted up to the monastery of St. Catherine at Sinai.

[3] Probably by making it a derivative of σαργῖνος (Aristotle, *HA* 9.2.610ᵇ, classes σαργῖνοι among fish that live in schools, between smelt [ἀθερίναι] and needle-shaped fish) or of σαργός, the sargus, another species of fish (ibid. 5.11.542ᵇ).

[4] *P.Flor.* 269, 7: τὰς οἰνηγὰς σαργάνας; *P.Cair.Masp.* 67010, 19: μεμεσωμένας σ[αργάναι]ς σιτίνου τε καὶ ξηροῦ χόρτου (*Berichtigungsliste,* vol. 3, p. 34); *P.Flor.* 175, 32: ἔχουσι σαργένας (or σαργάνας) οἰνηγάς (M. David, p. 58); *P.Lond.* 1770, 20: ἀχύρου σιτίνου σαργάνας (M. David, pp. 99, 271); *P.Cair.Goodsp.* 30, col. 23, 13 (second century).

[5] *O.Mich.* 779, 5; 780, 5; 783, 3; 788, 1–2; *O.Bodl.* q., 17; *P.Oxf.* 16, 15: "Each year I will give you a *sarganē* of combustible straw"; *P.Oxy.* 2272, 21; 2154, 23: "Send me at least one *sarganē* of small straw"; *SB* 1970; 9003, 2; 9019, 2; 10299, 7, 14.

sarganē, S 4553; *EDNT* 3.229; MM 569; L&N 6.148; BAGD 742 ‖ *spyris,* S 4711; *EDNT* 3.267; MM 586, 618; L&N 6.149; BDF §34(5); BAGD 764

SB 9176; 9384, 54, 62; *P.Mil.Vogl.* 152, col. II, 52, 59: *eis episkeuēn sarganōn.* There are smaller units, however: *sarganition hena* (*BGU* 236, 11; from AD 57); *sarganion* (*P.Lips.* 21, 18).

A *spyris* is also a woven basket, but more commonly used, although it is unknown in Josephus, and of smaller capacity. The word is used at Matt 15:37 and Mark 8:8, and also at Matt 16:10 and Mark 8:20, in each case referring to the baskets in which the pieces of bread and fish left over from the multiplying of the loaves were placed; the two latter texts place *spyris* parallel with *kophinos.*[6] Some have concluded that a *spyris* is a basket for bread or fish.[7] But, apart from the fact that the *spyris* may be of different sizes (*spyridion, Pap.Lugd.Bat.* II, 8, 13; *P.Tebt.* 414, 19; *P.Oxy.* 1293, 30), it is used for the picnic basket in which each one brings his own food,[8] not only for a basket of good dates (*P.Oxy.* 116, 19), nuts (741, 2), or delicacies (1070, 31) but also dry pitch (*pissēs xēras sphyridas, SB* 1, 9). So the word means a portable container and can be translated "bag" or "parcel." The price of a parcel is figured, as with the baskets of nails in *P.Col.Zen.* 94, 7 (cf. *P.Fay.* 102, 3ff., in AD 105; *timē spyridōn, UPZ* 112, col. V, 18; from 170 BC), and receipt of the parcel is acknowledged in a business letter (*SB* 7572, 3; 9025, 19). There is no specifying the size or shape, since the word refers to an instrument of torture in Philo, who describes a tax agent torturing taxpayers: "He tied a cord with a sliding knot (*brochos*) to a basket full of sand (*ammou spyrida plērē*) which he hung from their necks, a crushing burden" (*Spec. Laws* 3.160).

---

[6] Normally, κοφίνος is used especially for working the earth (Ps 81:6); its measure varies (*PSI* 428, 52: ἐν κοφίνῳ μεγάλῳ), from twenty to forty λίτραι, according to *P.Oxy.* 43 (AD 295).

[7] Cf. Herodotus 5.16—"If you let an empty basket down into the lake with a rope, in a very little while you can pull it out full of fish"; Aristophanes, *Pax* 1005: "eels from Copaïs arrive by the basket"; *P.Ryl.* 127, 34: "a basket containing fifty loaves" (AD 29); *P.Oxy.* 936, 15: a small Kanopic basket with four loaves." The *spyris* was probably part of a fisherman's gear; according to Philip of Thessalonica, "a pair of rush baskets" (δισσὰς σχοινογενεῖς σπυρίδας, *Anth. Pal.* 6.5.4); and Julian, the prefect of Egypt, says, "a pair of well-woven baskets" (ζευγός τ' εὐπλεκέων σπυρίδων, ibid. 28, 5), "two baskets with some cork" (σπυρίδας θ' ἅμα φελλῷ, ibid. 29, 3); but Leonidas of Tarentum specifies, "fish baskets" (τὰς ἰχθυδίκους σπυρίδας, ibid. 4, 2). Cf. "A Note by the Late Dr Hort on the Words κόφινος, σπυρίς, σαργάνη," in *JTS,* 1909, pp. 567–571.

[8] Epictetus 4.10.21: among the advantages of being consul is that of offering to dine from baskets, σπυρίσιν δειπνίσαι; Athenaeus 8.365 *a:* each one brings a meal in a basket, δεῖπνον ἀπὸ σπυρίδος.

σάρξ, σαρκικός, σάρκινος

sarx, flesh; *sarkikos*, of the flesh, carnal; *sarkinos*, fleshy, of the flesh, carnal

E. Schweizer noted that in Homer the word "flesh" was used especially in the plural,[1] a usage that remained common in literary Greek (cf. Hippocrates, *Peri sarkōn;* Quintus of Smyrna, Dio Chrysostom, etc.). It refers to the flesh of the human body (Herondas, *Mimes* 4.6: "flesh that seems to palpitate, hot") but more often, it seems, animal flesh.[2] It is associated with bones,[3] muscles, sinews, veins,[4] viscera,[5] and blood.[6]

---

[1] E. Schweizer, F. Baumgärtel, H. Meyer, "σάρξ," in *TDNT,* vol. 7, pp. 98–151. Cf. E. Schweizer, "Die hellenistische Komponente im neutestamentlichen σάρξ-Begriff," in *ZNW,* 1957, pp. 237–253.

[2] Hesiod, *Th.* 538, Prometheus "had put beneath the skin flesh and entrails heavy with fat"; flesh of fish and small animals (Dioscorides, *Mat. Med.* 2.4; Julius Pollux, *Onom.* 5.51). It can be only an isolated bit of flesh (Euripides, *Bacch.* 1130; 1136: scraps; Nicander, frag. 78, 16), notably sacrificial flesh (Dittenberger, *Syl.* 1047, 7: γλῶσσαν καὶ σάρκας τρεῖς ; 1171, 5; *LSCG,* n. XI, B, 12; XXIX, 4; *Supplément,* n. XIX, 33; *LSAM,* n. XXIV, A, 16: σάρκας καὶ σπλάγχνα: portions of beef); one eats flesh (Aeschylus, *Ag.* 1097; Euripides, *Tro.* 775; Antiphanes, frag. 326 = J. M. Edmonds, *Attic Comedy,* vol. 2, p. 308), but flesh thus consumed is more likely to be called κρέας (Rom 14:21; 1 Cor 8:13; Theocritus, *Id.* 25.224).

[3] Euripides, *Hec.* 1072, Polymestor: "gorge myself on their flesh, their bones"; Plato, *Phd.* 96 *d:* "flesh adds to flesh, bones to bones"; *Tim.* 84 *a:* "what joins the flesh to the bones"; Aristotle, *Part. An.* 2.9.655b23: "bone and flesh"; Aristotle, *Gen. Cor.* 1.5.321b19.

[4] Homer, *Od.* 11.219: "The sinews no longer hold the flesh or the bones"; Plato, *Tim.* 74 *b:* "sinews and flesh"; 82 *c;* Aristotle, *Part. An.* 1.5.645a29: "what humankind is composed of, for example, blood, flesh, bones, vessels, and other such parts"; 2.1.546b15: "the parts that form the organs are composed of bones, sinews, flesh, and other such tissues"; Epictetus 2.9.18: "what is eaten and digested . . . has become sinews, flesh, bones, blooming complexion, healthy respiration"; 4.7.32.

[5] Homer, *Od.* 9.293: "One would have said a lion . . . entrails, flesh (σαρκάς), marrow, bone, he did not leave anything"; Hesiod, *Th.* 538,

[6] Plato, *Symp.* 207 *d:* "Every day a person is new . . . hair, flesh, bones, blood, the

---

sarx, S 4561; *TDNT* 7.98–151; *EDNT* 3.230–233; *NIDNTT* 1.671–672, 674–682; MM 569; L&N 8.4, 8.63, 9.11, 9.12, 9.14, 9.15, 10.1, 22.20, 23.90, 25.29, 26.7, 58.10, 88.279; BDF §§160, 266(2), 258(2), 272, 275(4); BAGD 743–744 ∥ *sarkikos*, S 4559; *TDNT* 7.98–151; *EDNT* 3.229–230; *NIDNTT* 1.671, 764, 677, 682; MM 569; L&N 26.8, 41.42, 79.1, 79.4; BDF §113(2); BAGD 742 ∥ *sarkinos*, S 4560; *TDNT* 7.98–151; *EDNT* 3.229–230; *NIDNTT* 1.671, 674, 682; MM 569; L&N 9.13, 26.8, 41.42, 79.4; BDF §113(2); BAGD 743

232   σάρξ, *sarx*, etc.

Sarx can be pale (Sophocles, *Phil.* 1157) or white (Euripides, *Med.* 1189), old (Aeschylus, *Ag.* 72), vigorous (*Sept.* 622) or torn (Euripides, *Hipp.* 1239, 1343). Being material, flesh finally meets death: "his old flesh was torn from his bones" (Euripides, *Med.* 1217); "the daughter and the father lie dead" (1119); the vital force departs. *Sarx* is contrasted with *nous*,[7] or the immortal *psyche*,[8] or *logos* (Epictetus 1.3.5), or *pneuma* (Euripides, frag. 971: "He who, swelled with flesh, is extinguished like a star fallen from heaven, freeing the spirit for the aether"). It is notably the "miserable flesh" (Epictetus 1.3.5) that distinguishes humans from the gods.[9] What is more, if sensations are detected by means of the sensitivity of the flesh (*paraisthēsis sarkinē*),[10] thinkers from Epicurus on (Epictetus, *Against Epicurus* 2, frag. 6, col. 2) reflect on "pleasure according to the flesh" (*hē kata sarka hēdonē*) as compared to pleasures of the *psyche* (Plutarch, *Quaest. conv.* 5.1) and conclude around the turn of the millennium not only that the latter are greater,[11] but that the *pathē tēs sarkos*

---

whole body." Blood is the most closely related to flesh (Empedocles, frag. 98; cf. H. Diels, *Fragmente der Vorsokratiker*, 8th ed., vol. 1, 346, 23), since the latter is produced from the former. "The mother's blood coagulates, forming the flesh of the embryo, and in the midst of the flesh the navel is separated" (Hippocrates, *Nat. Puer.* 15–17). Cf. flesh and belly (*Loc. Hom.* 1.2), bones (3.1; 4.2; 13.3, 5), veins (3.6), is filled with phlegm (29.1); is tested by cold (10.2), is soft (*Fist.* 1.1), is cut into (*Morb.* 50.4), it swells (48.1); it develops or diminishes according to certain exercises (*Vict.* 2.2; 9.3), long-distance races warm it (63.1), as do certain foods (78.1; 79.3); it is moist (56.7; 57.1; 60.3–4); at maturity a person is well fleshed-out (32.5); it is in the flesh that tumors grow (89.11) and dropsy (Hippocrates, *Acut.*, appendix 52.1); the juice of certain seeds is more laxative than their flesh (pulp; *Vict.* 45.4); rockfish have tender, light flesh (48.1–3; 49.3), etc.

[7] Aeschylus, *Sept.* 622; cf. Euripides, *El.* 387; Empedocles, frag. 126 (= Diels, vol. 1, 362, 5): ἀλλογνῶς χιτὼν σαρκός = strange garment of flesh; used by Plutarch, *De esu carn.* 4 and Porphyry (in Stobaeus, *Ecl.* 1.49, 60; vol. 1, p. 446, 21ff.); Philo, *Heir* 268; *Alleg. Interp.* 2.49.

[8] Plato, *Symp.* 211 c; *Leg.* 12.959 a, "The *psyche* is superior to the *sōma*; it is immortal," and it is contrasted to the "bulk of the flesh (τὸν τῶν σαρκῶν ὄγκον) that is being buried"; Plutarch, *Adv. Col.* 20; *De sera* 17; epitaph of Philoxenos: "Kaunos (a city in Caria) consumed your flesh in a raging fire" (*SB* 4314, 6).

[9] Epictetus 2.8.2: "What then is God really? Flesh? — Never"; Polyaenus, *Strat.* 3.11.1.

[10] Philodemus of Gadara, *Piet.* 116, 13ff.; Philo, *Heir* 71; *Husbandry* 97; *Alleg. Interp.* 2.41; 3.158; *Abraham* 164; *Giants* 35.

[11] Diogenes Laertius 10.137; Ps.-Plutarch, *Cons. ad Apoll.* 13: "To live without being in submission to the slavery of the flesh (ἀδούλωτον τῇ σαρκί) and its passions, which draw the spirit (καὶ τοῖς ταύτης πάθεσι), that is a good and happy fortune"; Plutarch, *De virt. et vit.* 3; *Mor.* 2.1096 c: ταῖς τῆς σαρκὸς ἐπιθυμίαις. The flesh is the seat of the passions: ἐν τῇ σαρκὶ ἡ ἡδονή (Epicurus, *Sent.* 18); "bodily passions, issuing from the flesh, in which they have taken root" (Philo, *Heir* 268); "carnal good is pleasure

(bodily sensations) are a crude sensual pleasure, usually an appeasement of sexual instincts.[12]

The LXX translates the Hebrew *bāśār* especially with *sarx*,[13] referring to the whole living creature, human or animal,[14] the very person (Lev 13:18; Eccl 4:5; 5:5; cf. my *sarx* = me, Ps 119:120), the whole being (Gen 2:23; Ezek 37:6, 8; Job 2:5; Ps 68:2; Eccl 5:5), and especially the body.[15] But since the body's vitality (Hebrew *nepeš*) is in the blood (Gen 9:4–5; Lev 17:1; Deut 12:23), the composite human is referred to by the expression "flesh and blood,"[16] the locution *kol bāśār*; "all flesh," means all human

---

stripped of reason" (*Giants* 40); the way of wisdom is devoted to "attacks and rejections of every companion of the flesh" (*Unchang. God* 143; cf. *Husbandry* 97; *Alleg. Interp.* 2.49–50); 4 Macc 7:18: "Only those who give themselves to piety with vigilance are able to rule the passions of the flesh."

[12] Cf. the Epicurean Metrodorus, in Plutarch, *Adv. Col.* 30; *Suav. viv.* 14. Philo is especially pessimistic: the body and its passions draw people into sin (*Plant.* 43; *Heir* 296); sexual pleasure is the origin of evil (*Alleg. Interp.* 3.143, 159; *Creation* 151–164; *Spec. Laws* 1.192). Since for the soul the flesh is a weight, a servitude, a coffin, a funeral urn, a cadaver to drag about (*Giants* 31; *Heir* 268; *Migr. Abr.* 12; *Husbandry* 25; *Unchang. God* 2), an obstacle to growth in wisdom and to the flight of the soul toward God (*Migr. Abr.* 14; *Dreams* 2.232), one must disengage from it through *askēsis* (*Spec. Laws* 4.114; *Giants* 30; *Change of Names* 32; *Dreams* 2.67; *Unchang. God* 3).

[13] One hundred forty-eight times (always in the singular, except Prov 14:30), but also κρέας (79 times), σῶμα (23 times), and χρώς (14 times, cf. Acts 19:12; literally, the skin, the epidermis); but σάρξ also translates the Hebrew *še'ēr*, "meat" (Lev 18:6; 25:49; Num 27:11—the flesh of his body). Cf. D. Lys, *La Chair dans l'Ancien Testament: Bâśar*, Paris, 1967; J. Scharbert, *Fleisch, Geist und Seele im Pentateuch*, Stuttgart, 1966, P. Dhorme, *Emploi métaphorique*, pp. 7–10, 113; J. Luzzi, "*Basar* en el contexto veterotestamentario," in *Ciencea y fe*, 1958, pp. 3–28.

[14] In the latter case, *sarx* is especially meat used as food (1 Kgs 17:6; 19:21; Num 11:4, 13, 18ff.), which is more often called κρέας (Gen 9:4; Exod 12:8; Deut 12:15, 20; 14:8), notably the flesh of sacrificial victims (Isa 65:4; Jer 11:15; Hag 2:12; Lev 6:20; Num 18:18; Deut 16:4; 1QS 9.4—"the flesh of the whole burnt offerings"); cf. Dittenberger, *Or.* 78, 16.

[15] Gen 2:23; 2 Kgs 5:10, 14; 9:26 (dogs devour Jezebel's body); Job 6:12; 33:21. The corpse (1 Sam 17:44; 2 Kgs 9:36). A part of the body (Lev 6:3; 15:2–3), muscles (Sir 19:12; 38:28; 4 Macc 9:20, 28), tendons (Job 10:11), skin (Exod 4:7; Lev 13:2–4, 11, 38, 39, 43; 13:18, 24; Lam 3:4; Ps 102:6; Job 19:20; Prov 14:30; Josephus, *Ant.* 15.236: the skin of the flesh), bone (Job 2:5; *T. Sim.* 6.2; *Jos. Asen.* 16), heart (Ps 73:26; 84:3; Eccl 2:3; 11:10; Ezek 11:29; 36:26—a heart of flesh = receptive to God's will), the flesh of the foreskin (Gen 17:11, 14, 23–25; Lev 12:3); flesh of uncircumcision (Gen 17:11ff.; Lev 12:3; 13:10ff.), uncircumcision of the flesh (Ezek 44:7, 9; cf. Jdt 14:10; Sir 44:20; *Jub.* 15.13). Cf. stoutness = fat of flesh (Isa 17:4; Dan 1:15).

[16] Sir 14:18; 17:31; Wis 12:5; cf. "all flesh in which is found a breath of life" (Gen 6:17; 7:15).

beings;[17] and kinship is defined as the same biological origin, by blood as well as flesh.[18] God formed the body in the mother's womb (Job 12:10; 34:15—the God of all flesh), beginning with inert earthy matter, which he animated with his breath (Gen 2:7, cf. 6:3, 13); one lives only insofar as one breathes, which means that the body is capable of dying (Ps 104:23; Zech 14:12). Being a creature (Isa 31:3; Jer 17:5; Joel 3:1), it is characterized by weakness and fragility;[19] this is one of the most obvious contrasts with the deity.[20] The Wisdom writers emphasize the devaluation of the flesh. A "body of flesh" is pejorative,[21] as is "eyes of flesh" (Job 10:4), which see poorly: since they discern only appearances, they are deceived. We cannot speak of a dualism of flesh and spirit[22] that would correspond to the opposition between good and evil, but fleshly being, which belongs to the earth, is not only separated from the world of the *pneuma*, which belongs to heaven (4 Ezra 3:1), but is inferior to it.[23]

---

[17] Isa 40:5; Jer 12:12; 25:31; 45:5; Joel 3:1; Zech 2:17; Job 12:10; 34:15; 1QSb 3.28; 1Q34, frag. 3; the population of a land (Ezek 21:4, 9); every living being, beasts included (Gen 6:17; 9:11; Num 18:15; Ps 136:25; Dan 4:9).

[18] Gen 2:23—"flesh of my flesh"; the woman is the very own flesh (ἴδια σάρξ) of the man (Sir 25:26; *Adam and Eve* 3; Gen 29:14; 2 Sam 5:1; 19:13; Judg 9:2; 1 Chr 12:1; Neh 5:5; Lev 18:6; 25:49); between brothers and sisters (Gen 37:27; Lev 18:12–13; 20:19).

[19] Ps 56:5; 78:39; 109:24; Job 6:12; 33:21; Sir 28:5; 31:1; 40:8; Isa 31:3; cf. 2 Chr 32:8—"an arm of *bāśār*" (cf. 1QH 15.12—"a hand of flesh"); the military might of Egypt is only flesh (Ezek 31:3); much study is weariness of *bāśār* (Eccl 12:12); 1QH 4.29; 8.31–32; 15.12, 21.

[20] Isa 31:3; Jer 17:5; Ezek 40:5–6; Joel 3:1; Zech 14:12; Dan 2:11—"gods whose dwelling is not with flesh"; cf. 2:5ff.; CD 2.20—"all flesh that was on the earth succumbed and died" (W. D. Davies, "Paul and the Dead Sea Scrolls: Flesh and Spirit," in K. Stendahl, *The Scrolls and the New Testament*, New York, 1957, pp. 157–182; K. G. Kuhn, "New Light on Temptation, Sin, and Flesh in the New Testament," ibid., pp. 94–113; R. E. Murphy, "BSR in the Qumran Literature and Sarks in the Epistle to the Romans," in *Sacra Pagina*, Paris-Gembloux, 1959, vol. 2, pp. 60–76; J. Pryke, " 'Spirit' and 'Flesh' in the Qumran Documents and Some New Testament Texts," in *RevQ*, 1965, pp. 345–360); *Jub.* 7.4; 21.10; *SB* 2034, 2; 3901, 2; 4949, 2; 6035, 3; 7429, 2; 7430, 1; etc.

[21] Sir 23:17 (Col 1:22; 2:11); *1 Enoch* 102.5; 1QpHab 9.2; Nah 2:6.

[22] Jdt 10:13; Wis 7:1, 7; cf. 4 Macc 7:13; *Pss. Sol.* 16.14; *Jub.* 2.2, 11; 1QH 18.21–24; *T. Abr.* B 13; *T. Job* 27.2, Satan to Job, "you who are flesh, I who am spirit"; 38.2—"Who are we to meddle in heavenly things when we are flesh?"; Josephus, *Ant.* 19.325; *War* 2.154; 6.47: the *psychē* separates from the flesh at the moment of death.

[23] 1QH 15.17. Following Jer 25:31 and Hos 4:1, the Qumran literature represents God putting "all flesh" on trial (CD 1.2)—i.e., sinful humanity—and emphasizes the relationship of flesh to sin: "I stumble because of the sin of the flesh" (1QS 11.12), "flesh of perversity" (9); "flesh of guilt" (1QM 12.11). A "spirit of flesh" (1QH 13.16;

The Synoptic Gospels and the Acts of the Apostles mention flesh only rarely, and always with its OT meanings.[24] Likewise the Fourth Gospel, in which this word always occurs in Jesus' speech.[25] Used six times regarding the Eucharist (John 6:51–56), and made more specific as "the flesh of the Son of Man" or "my flesh and my blood," it refers to the body and soul of Jesus, his person given to communicate eternal life. Twice *sarx* is opposed to *pneuma*.[26] John 8:15 is pejorative: "You judge according to the flesh," that is, according to appearances; this is a superficial, incomplete, and false judgment. These nuances are traditional in Israel, and there is not the slightest theological elaboration.

In the Pauline writings, on the other hand, the "flesh" is constantly mentioned, and with meanings so different that one could almost say that they vary from verse to verse.[27] First, there are a large number of occur-

---

17.25) is a perverse spirit (cf. Rom 8:1–9). Cf. *T. Jud.* 19.4—"I was ignorant, like man and like flesh, corrupted by sin."

[24] Matt 19:56 (Mark 10:8; cf. 1 Cor 6:16; Eph 5:31), regarding monogamous marriage, quotes Gen 2:24—"the two shall be one flesh," a single being. Matt 24:22 (Mark 13:20; Luke 3:6; cf. Isa 40:5): "No flesh (no living being) could be saved"; Matt 26:41 (Mark 14:38; cf. Gal 2:16 = Ps 143:2)—"the flesh is weak" (contrasted with the *pneuma*); Luke 24:39—"a *pneuma* does not have flesh and bone" (no body). The phrase "flesh and blood" refers to humans as incapable of perceiving the divine (Matt 16:17) and inheriting the kingdom of God (1 Cor 15:50; Gal 1:16). Acts 2:17 quotes Joel 2:28; Acts 2:26 quotes Ps 16:9; Acts 2:31—the flesh (the body) of Christ did not see corruption (cf. Ps 16:10).

[25] With the exception of the prologue, where 1:14 should be translated, "The Word became human," i.e., took on a human nature. The depreciative nuance of passible, mortal flesh is an intentional contrast with the divine Logos (1:1), where the filial *doxa* is still evident. This Son of God has sovereignty over "all flesh" (17:2), i.e., over all people. S. de Ausejo, "El concepto de 'carne' aplicado a Cristo en el IV Evangelio," in *Sacra Pagina*, Rome, 1959, vol. 2, pp. 219–234.

[26] John 3:6—"That which is born of the flesh is flesh; that which is born of the spirit is spirit" (cf. Gal 6:8). The flesh begets carnal beings, the spirit begets spiritual beings. St. Augustine emphasizes the contrast between these two types of generation as corresponding to two very different worlds: "Una de terra . . . de mortalitate . . de masculo et femina . . . , alia de caelo . . . de aeternitate . . . de Deo et ecclesia" (on this text). John 6:63—"The spirit makes alive; the flesh (without the spirit) is of no avail" for communicating spiritual life. Cf. the eating of flesh (Rev 17:16; 19:18, 21; Quintus of Smyrna, *Posthomerica* 11.245) and flesh that is eaten away (Jas 5:3).

[27] E. D. Burton, *Spirit, Soul and Flesh*, Chicago, 1918; F. Prat, *La Théologie de saint Paul*, 6th ed., Paris, 1923, vol. 2, pp. 487–489; W. Schauf, Σάρξ: *Der Begriff 'Fleisch' beim Apostel Paulus*, Münster, 1924; H. Mehl-Koehnlein, *L'Homme selon l'Apôtre Paul*, Neuchâtel-Paris, 1951, pp. 12–17; W. D. Stacey, *The Pauline View of Man*, London, 1956; A. Sand, *Der Begriff 'Fleisch' in den paulinischen Hauptbriefen*, Regensburg, 1967; E. Brandenburger, *Fleisch und Geist und die dualistische Weisheit*, Neukirchen, 1968; R. Jewett, *Paul's Anthropological Terms*, Leiden, 1971, pp. 49–166.

rences with the neutral biological meaning, "flesh" as a synonym of "body": "No one ever hated his own flesh" (Eph 5:29); "I am absent in the flesh (physically) but in spirit I am among you."[28] Then there is "human nature" in the noblest sense, since the incarnate Son of God was "born of the race of David, according to the flesh."[29] The "body of his flesh" (Col 1:22) is his humanity. "Flesh" can also mean human existence (1 Pet 4:6) here below (Eph 6:5) and its conditioning: Onesimus is a brother beloved "both according to the flesh and according to the Lord" (Phlm 16), which means humanly and divinely.

There is already a pejorative nuance in 1 Cor 1:26, which observes that at Corinth there were "not many wise according to the flesh," that is,

---

[28] Col 2:5; cf. 2:1—"Those who have not seen my face in the flesh"; 1:24. Circumcision is an operation practiced on the flesh (Rom 2:28; Eph 2:11; Col 2:11, 13). "All flesh is not the same flesh, but there is one of men, another of beasts, another of birds, another of fish" (1 Cor 15:39; in 15:39–41, sun, moon, and stars are referred to as σώματα, celestial bodies. J. Héring describes this meaning as the "chemical sense" of *sarx*). Abraham, "our father according to the flesh" (Rom 4:1; Heb 12:9); the Israelites are "our kinsmen according to the flesh" (Rom 4:1; 11:14; cf. 9:8; 1 Cor 10:18). The OT liturgy could procure only fleshly purity (Heb 9:10, 13). The men of Sodom ran after "other flesh," another kind of body, namely, that of angels (Jude 7). Paul's thorn in the flesh (σκόλοψ τῇ σαρκί), "an angel of Satan to torment me" (2 Cor 12:7), must be an allusion to Num 33:55, where Canaanites who are spared "will become thorns (σκόλοπες) in your eyes." If we recall Gal 4:13–15 ("It was because of an infirmity of the flesh [δι' ἀσθένειαν τῆς σαρκός] that I first preached the gospel to you; even though the infirmity of my flesh was a trial for you, you showed no scorn, no disgust. . . . You would have plucked out your eyes to give them to me"), we will conclude that Paul's missionary activity must have been hindered by an affliction of the eyes, probably by an "eye migraine," described by Dr. Uhle-Wettler ("Der Pfahl im Fleisch und die Fausthiebe Satans bei Paulus," in *Hengstenbergs Evang. Kirchenzeitung*, 1913, pp. 130ff., 145ff.). This illness is distinguished first of all by an agonizing pain (*bohrende*, drilling, boring) in the head, as if the skull had just been smashed with a hammer. In certain cases, the eye was so terrible to look at that even the physician recoiled at the sight. The attacks recur periodically and are of unequal duration. Between attacks—sometimes periods of several years—the patient may have enormous energy. Cf. A. Lechler, *Des Paulus Pfahl im Fleisch*, Giessen, 1947; T. Y. Mullins, "Paul's Thorn in the Flesh," in *JBL*, 1957, pp. 299 (a personal enemy of Paul); P. Andriessen, "L'Impuissance de Paul en face de l'ange de Satan," in *RSR*, 1959, pp. 462–468 (attacks and intrigues of the Jews); P. Menoud, "L'Echarde et l'ange satanique (II Cor. XII, 7)," in *Jésus-Christ et la foi*, Neuchâtel-Paris, 1975, pp. 23–30 (Israel's unbelief); H. Binder, "Die angebliche Krankheit des Paulus," in *TZ*, 1976, pp. 1–13.

[29] Rom 1:3; cf. 9:5; Gal 4:23; Eph 2:14; 1 Tim 3:16; Heb 5:7; 10:20; 1 Pet 3:18; 4:1; John 1:14; 1 John 4:2. Cf. J. A. T. Robinson, *The Body: A Study in Pauline Theology*, London, 1952, pp. 34–48; R. Batey, "The μία σάρξ Union of Christ and the Church, "in *NTS*, vol. 13, 1967, pp. 270–284; P. Bonnard, *Anamnèsis*, Geneva-Lausanne-Neuchâtel, 1980, pp. 187–193; M. Gilbert, " 'Une seule chair' (Gen. II, 24)," in *NRT*, 1978, pp. 66–89; cf. G. Aicher, "Mann und Weib ein Fleisch," in *BZ*, 1907, pp. 159–165.

humanly gifted;[30] and in 1 Cor 7:28, where spouses experience "affliction in the flesh";[31] and also in 2 Cor 5:16—"We no longer know anyone according to the flesh; even if we knew Christ according to the flesh, yet now we no longer know him."[32] This pejorative value of *sarx* is described as a "weakness";[33] the flesh is ephemeral as the grass (1 Pet 1:24; Isa 40:6) and mortal (2 Cor 4:11); it is the seat of sensations and the emotions; it is passible.[34] Its infirmity and poverty are such that "no flesh (creature) may boast before God."[35]

It gets worse. St. Paul, probably inheriting something from the Qumran sect, or in any event depending on contemporary Jewish conceptions, sees the flesh as a source of evil, of dissolute actions,[36] always ready to break free (Gal 5:13), like an insolent slave (cf. Col 2:23, *plēsmonē tēs sarkos*), rebelling and wishing to become an autonomous authority: "When we were in the flesh (under its orders, in a state of sinfulness), the passions . . . acted in our members" (Rom 7:5); "no good dwells in

---

[30] Cf. Gal 6:12—"those who wish to look good in the flesh," make a good impression, εὐπροσωπῆσαι, cf. *P.Tebt.* 19, 12.

[31] This could mean problems of a sexual nature that are difficult to overcome, or family cares, or "the ordinary course of this sad world" (E. B. Allo). Cf. 1 Cor 5:5—the incestuous man is handed over to Satan εἰς ὄλεθρον τῆς σαρκός and so that his spirit may be saved. Cf. J. Cambier, "La Chair et l'esprit en I Cor. V, 5," in *NTS*, vol. 15, 1969, pp. 221, 232.

[32] Κατὰ σάρκα is the norm of judgment: from a human, purely natural point of view; J. Cambier, "Connaissance charnelle et spirituelle du Christ dans II Cor. V, 16," in *Recherches bibliques*, vol. 5, Paris-Tournai, 1960, pp. 72–96; J. W. Fraser, "Paul's Knowledge of Jesus: II Corinthians V, 16 Once More," in *NTS*, vol. 17, 1971, pp. 203–313; J. T. Keegan, "Paul and the Historical Jesus," in *Angelicum*, 1975, pp. 450–484; C. S. Voulgaris, "II Cor. V, 16 and the Problem of St. Paul's Opponents in Corinth," in *Theologica* (Athens), 1975, pp. 3–19 (to know Christ according to the flesh would be to know him as a Jew, a descendant of Abraham, a great teacher in Israel; this would limit salvation to his people and exclude the Gentiles).

[33] Ἀσθένεια, cf. Rom 6:19: "I express myself in human terms because of the (intellectual and moral) weakness of your flesh" means "I take your feebleness and your limitations into account"; 8:3—the resistance of the flesh robbed the law of Moses of its power (ἠσθένει); Gal 3:3—"After beginning with the Spirit, will you now finish with the flesh?" (circumcision, Judaism).

[34] 2 Cor 7:5—"Since our arrival in Macedonia, our flesh has had no relief (ἄνεσις); we have been afflicted in everything." J. Héring translates well, "notre pauvre être."

[35] 1 Cor 1:29; cf. Gal 6:13; 2 Cor 11:18—"Many glory according to the flesh, boasting of human advantages" (birth, fortune, prerogatives); Phil 3:2, 4, place one's confidence in the flesh.

[36] For example, duplicity, inconstancy, fickleness. II Cor 1:17—"Did I act lightly? Or do I want what I want according to the flesh (κατὰ σάρκα), so that with me there is 'Yes, yes' and 'No, no'?"

me, that is, in my flesh" (7:18); "sin dwells in me" (7:21). This is not to say that what we today call the body is corrupt. *Sarx* is almost personified; more precisely, it retains here its basic meaning of "human nature," but human nature as vitiated. It is the "whole person" that is corrupt, a perverse mind and will. Just as the arm and the hand are considered as autonomous and responsible for actions in which they are really just instruments, Paul treats the flesh—the inferior part of a person—as the locus of the passions and covetousness.[37] He attributes to it *epithymia*,[38] which is constantly opposing the *pneuma*: "the flesh lusts against the spirit, and the spirit against the flesh; these are (principles that are) opposed to each other (*tauta gar allēlois antikeitai*) . . . . The works of the flesh are manifest; they are sexual immorality, impurity, debauchery, idolatry, magic, hatred . . ." (Gal 5:17–19). There is a radical opposition between on the one hand *sarx* and *epithymia kakē* (Col 3:5; 1 Cor 10:6) and on the other hand reason, spirit, God's will.[39]

The Pauline parenesis is based on this experience: "With my reason I serve the law of God, but with my flesh the law of sin."[40] The Christian

---

[37] Cf. "inner man" and "outward man." Cf. P. Bonnard, *Anamnèsis*, pp. 66ff.

[38] Rom 13:14; Gal 5:15–16; 1 John 2:16; Eph 2:3—before we were Christians, we lived "according to the desires of the flesh, serving the caprices of the flesh and its (sinful) thoughts (καὶ τῶν διανοιῶν, cf. Col 2:18, ὑπὸ τοῦ νοὸς τῆς σαρκὸς αὐτοῦ), so that we were by nature given over to wrath (God's judgment)." Sensualist false teachers "go after the flesh in impure covetousness" (2 Pet 2:10); "they appeal to the debauched covetousness of the flesh and entice people who have barely left behind those who live in error" (2:18); they soil the flesh (1 Pet 3:21; Jude 8; cf. 1 Pet 2:11); the corruption defiles even the clothing that covers the *sarx* (Jude 23). Cf. H. Räisänen, "Zum Gebrauch von ἐπιθυμία und ἐπιθυμεῖν bei Paulus," in *ST*, vol. 33, 1979, pp. 85–99.

[39] Rom 7:25—"I am the same person, who by reason serve the law of God, but by the flesh, the law of sin"; Gal 6:8—"The one who sows in the flesh will of the flesh reap corruption; the one who sows in the spirit will from the spirit reap eternal life"; Rom 8:3—"Because of sin, God sent his son in a flesh (human nature) like that of sin, and so condemned sin in the flesh." The incarnation of the Son of God in an innocent human nature is, by this very exemption from sin, a defeat for *hamartia* and brings about this defeat in Christians, where it has been acting—"in the flesh"; its tyranny is broken (the sinful condition that issued from the first man, ἐφ' ᾧ πάντες ἥμαρτον, Rom 5:12; cf. Gen 8:21; Philo, *Unchang. God* 55).

[40] Rom 7:24–25. To the references given in C. Spicq, *Théologie morale*, vol. 1, p. 178; vol. 2, p. 636, add J. I. Packer, "The 'Wretched Man' in Romans VII," in F. L. Cross, *SE*, vol. 2, 1964, pp. 621–627; W. G. Kümmel, *Römer VII und das Bild des Menschen im Neuen Testament*, Munich, 1974; R. Schnackenburg, "Römer VII im Zusammenhang des Römerbriefes," in *Festschrift W. G. Kümmel*, Gütersloh, 1975, pp. 283–500; M. Byskov, "Simul Justus et Peccator: A Note on Romans VII, 25 b," in *ST*, 1976, pp. 75–87; Seiichi Yagi, "Weder persönlich noch generell—Zum neutestamentlichen Denken

life is essentially defined as a liberation from *sarx* and a submission to *pneuma:* "We walk not according to the flesh, but according to the spirit. Those who live according to the flesh have their minds set on the things of the flesh; those who live according to the spirit have their minds set on the things of the spirit."[41] Indeed, "the inclinations (*to phronēma*) of the flesh lead to death, but the inclinations of the spirit lead to life and peace (with God). This is why the inclinations of the flesh are enmity toward God, because they are not in submission to the law of God, nor can they be. Now those who are in the flesh cannot please God. But you are not in the flesh, but in the spirit, if it is true that the Spirit of God dwells in you."[42] "Take no thought for the flesh, (to satisfy) its lusts" (Rom 13:14; Gal 5:15); "Let us purify ourselves from every stain in flesh and in spirit, making ourselves perfectly holy, in the fear of God" (2 Cor 7:1; cf. 1 Cor 7:34). The conflict is such that "those who belong to Christ Jesus have crucified the flesh with its passions and lusts" (Gal 5:24). The last denunciation is that given by 1 John 2:16—"All that is in the world— the lust of the flesh, the lust of the eyes, the pride of life—is not of the Father, but of the world."[43]

---

anhand Röm. VII," in *Annual of the Japanese Biblical Institute,* vol. 2, 1976, pp. 159–173; J. M. Cambier et al., *The Law of the Spirit in Rom 7 and 8,* Rome, 1976; A. Feuillet, "Loi de Dieu, loi du Christ et loi de l'Esprit d'après les Epîtres pauliniennes," in *NovT,* 1980, pp. 35–65.

[41] The verb φρονέω (Vulgate *sentire*) is difficult to translate, because it is used for the faculty of thinking and feeling, intentions and will, opinions or evaluations, of a lifestyle, a disposition of the soul, a mentality. Here it has to do with convictions and sentiments, leanings and aspirations, "tastes." Cf. P. N. Lockhart, "φρονεῖν in Homer," in *CP,* 1966, pp. 99–102; *P.Oxy.* 2594, 5: "You thought that I had other sentiments regarding you," i.e., that I would react differently; *P.Ryl.* 624, 18, an allusion "to those in the city who do not think as we do" (τῶν ἀλλῶς φρονούντων); *P.Herm.,* p. 5, n. 33; *Ep. Arist.* 236.

[42] Rom 8:4–9. Let us say again that *sarx* here is not material, as distinct from the soul, nor does it represent sexual desires alone; rather, it is deep-rooted evil which, by means of *epithymia,* leads to sin. Rom 8:12–13—"My brothers, we are not debtors (ὀφειλέται) to the flesh to live according to the flesh, because if you live according to the flesh, you will die. But if by the Spirit you put to death the works of the body, you will live"; 2 Cor 10:2–3: "Some people expect to see us walk according to the flesh; we do indeed walk in the flesh (cf. Gal 2:20; Phil 1:22, 24; 1 Pet 4:2), but we do not do battle according to the flesh."

[43] Ἡ ἐπιθυμία τῆς σαρκός; this subjective genitive makes the flesh the subject of the action; it is the flesh that lusts; hence it is evil and one must not be attached to it. It belongs to this sinful world below. In the last analysis, it is God's enemy. This Johannine dichotomy is less one of flesh and spirit than of earthly and heavenly; cf. N. Lazure, "La Convoitise de la chair in I Jo. II, 16," in *RB,* 1969, pp. 161–205; P. Bonnard, *Anamnèsis,* pp. 187–193.

Sarkikos. — This rare[44] adjective is used by St. Paul with the same nuances as the substantive *sarx*, first of all in the neutral, slightly depreciatory sense of "material goods" (*ta sarkika*), as opposed to spiritual goods (*ta pneumatika*, Rom 15:27, 1 Cor 9:11), then in a pejorative moral sense: "carnal wisdom" (duplicity, hypocrisy, etc.) as opposed to the grace of God (2 Cor 1:12); or "carnal weapons" (*ta hopla . . . sarkika*), which are weak rather than *dynata* (10:4). Finally, there is the most pronounced Pauline theological meaning, describing the human and earthly order: "When there is jealousy and strife among you, are you not carnal (*ouchi sarkikoi este*) and walking according to man (*kata anthrōpon*)?" (1 Cor 3:3). 1 Pet 2:11 emphasizes sinful tones that are discordant with the divine: "I urge you . . . to abstain from these carnal lusts which make war against the soul."

Sarkinos. — Used much more than the preceding verb, this adjective takes on varied meanings in the secular literature; it denotes the carnal nature of the body,[45] sometimes with the nuance "corpulent"[46] or "fleshy": "Look for the fleshy fish (*ton sarkinon ichthyn*) lest you starve to death";[47] sometimes "real."[48] The LXX uses *sarkinos* for weakness and powerless-

---

[44] Unknown in the LXX, Philo, and the papyri. In the years BC, we can cite hardly more than Aristotle, *HA* 10.2.635ª11: the color of the discharge "comes closer to that of flesh" (σαρκικώτερα); and Sotades of Maronea, frag. 19, 3 (in connection with skin, δέρμα), in J. U. Powell, *Collectanea Alexandrina*, Oxford, 1925, p. 244. In the second century AD, *Par. Jer.* 6.6—the body is the "carnal house" of the heart (τῷ σαρκικῷ οἴκῳ σου). *Anth. Pal.* 1.107.3: "to triumph over all carnal defilements" (παντῶν σαρκικῶν μολυσμάτων).

[45] Plato, *Leg.* 10.906 c: illnesses ἐν σαρκίνοις σώμασι; Aristotle, *Eth. Nic.* 3.12.1117ᵇ 3: boxers receive blows, "it is suffering, even if it is fleshly blows"; Hipparchus, ἐντι θνατοὶ καὶ σάρκινοι (in Stobaeus, *Flor.* 4.44.81; vol. 4, p. 980, 15); Philodemus of Gadara, *Sign.*: "living creatures that share our bodily nature" (φύσεως σαρκίνης); Dio Cassius 38.21.3: "the body, since it is carnal (σάρκινον), finds in its substance a thousand pernicious germs." Cf. *TDNT*, vol. 7, pp. 98–151.

[46] Julius Pollux, *Onom.* 2.233, quoting Aristophanes, frag. 711: ἄνδρα σάρκινον, and Eupolis, frag. 387: σαρκίνη γυνή. Cf. Plutarch, *De prof. in virt.* 8 (2.79 c): τὸ σάρκινον τῶν λόγων, fullness or density of discourse.

[47] Ps.-Theocritus 21.66. Cf. Philo, *Sacr. Abel and Cain* 63: "having taken upon ourselves the weight (or bulk) of the flesh" (τὸν σάρκινον ὄγκον); Philo, *Alleg. Interp.* 2.20: "Was the rib that was left not fleshy?"; σαρκίνη seems to imply density.

[48] Artemidorus Daldianus, *Onir.* 2.35: "the gods appear to us in flesh and in bone" or in statues. Philodemus considers the gods to be *sarkinoi* (*Piet.* 59.21ff.; *D.* 3, frag. 6). The papyri offer only one occurrence: σχοινίων σαρκίνων (*P.Lond.* 1177, 169 = vol. 3, p. 186; from the second century AD), noted in the *Wörterbuch* of F. Preisigke, who translates "Stricke aus Darmsaiten gefertigt," and in Moulton-Milligan, "leather ropes."

ness,[49] and St. Paul gives it the same pejorative meaning as *sarx:* "the law is spiritual (*pneumatikos*) but I am carnal (*sarkinos*), sold to sin";[50] "I was not able to speak to you as to spiritual people (*pneumatikois*), but as to carnal people (*sarkinois*), as to nursing infants in Christ" (1 Cor 3:1); babies are only flesh; they are not anti-spiritual, but they are still non-spiritual.

---

[49] 2 Chr 32:8—the arm of Sennacherib is of flesh, whereas the arm of God brings help to Israel. Esth 4:17 *p*, contrasts the carnal king (the idol) with the king of the gods; Prov 29:27. In a positive sense, the heart of flesh (Ezek 11:19; 26:26), contrasted with the heart of stone, is one that is not obstinate, is obedient to God's will. Cf. the heart as a tablet of flesh that is written on (2 Cor 3:3).

[50] Rom 7:14. M. J. Lagrange comments, "σάρκινος, with the ending -ινος, indicates the material of which a thing is made, cf. δερμάτινος (Matt 3:4); ἀκάνθινος (Mark 15:17)." In this sense, the carnal provisions of the old covenant, concerning the priesthood (ἐντολῆς σαρκίνης, Heb 7:16), had bearing only upon physical requirements: carnal descent, privileges of race, bodily wholeness.

σβέννυμι

sbennymi, extinguish, quench

The literal meaning of *sbennymi* is "put out a fire";[1] the fire of Gehenna is not quenched;[2] the OT heroes of the faith "quenched the raging of the fire";[3] but lamps are quenched for want of oil (Matt 25:8; *T. Job* 43.5); the Messiah does not quench the smouldering wick (*linon*);[4] and the shield of faith can put out the flaming darts of the Evil One.[5]

The metaphorical usages are constant, both in the LXX and in the secular literature, meaning "annihilate, cause to disappear." The object can be offspring (2 Sam 14:7; Prov 10:7), prosperity (Job 18:5; Prov 13:9; *Anth. Pal.* 9.178), thought and sound reason (Wis 2:3; Philo, *Dreams* 1.31; *Alleg.*

---

[1] Wis 16:17—"Water, which quenches all, gave the fire even more strength" (cf. Exod 9:22–26); Philo, *Plant.* 10: "fire is not put out with air"; 4 Macc 18:20; 9:20—"the heaped-up coals were extinguished by the dripping blood"; Artemidorus Daldianus, *Onir.* 2.9: "the fire that goes out in the heart is an omen of poverty" (cf. Lang, "σβέννυμι," in *TDNT,* vol. 7, pp. 165–168).

[2] Mark 9:48, following Isa 66:26; cf. Lev 6:2, 5, 6: the fire on the altar of whole burnt offerings is not quenched (Hebrew *kābah*). Inextinguishable fire represents magnitude of punishment (Isa 1:31; 34:10; 66:24; Jer 17:27; Ezek 20:47–48; Amos 5:6); but the sun will disappear at the hour of judgment (*T. Levi* 4.1).

[3] Heb 11:34 (an allusion to the three children in the furnace, Dan 3:49–50; 1 Macc 2:59); cf. Josephus, *War* 7.405: the Romans undertook to extinguish the fire (at Masada); 6.243: Titus ordered his guard to put out the fire.

[4] Matt 12:20—καὶ λίνον τυφόμενον οὐ σβέσει (quoting Isa 42:3); cf. 2 Sam 21:17—"You will not quench the lamp of Israel"; 2 Chr 29:7—"They closed the doors, they put out the lamps (of the sanctuary)"; Isa 43:17—"They are extinguished like a wick, they are consumed"; Job 21:17—"the lamp of the ungodly is extinguished"; Prov 20:20; 24:20; Sir 28:12—"If you spit on a spark, it will go out."

[5] Eph 6:16. *Pila ardentia* are javelins dipped in sulfur, resin, and pitch and set afire before they are thrown, cf. the Numidians at the battle of Zama (Sallust, *Iug.* 57; cf. Caesar, *BCiv.* 2.2.1; Thucydides 2.75.5, πυρφόροις οἰστοῖς).

---

sbennymi, S 4570; *TDNT* 7.165–168; *EDNT* 3.235; *NIDNTT* 3.109–111; MM 570; L&N 14.70, 68.52; BDF §92; BAGD 745

Interp. 1.46), beauty (*Anth. Pal.* 5.62), love (Cant 8:7), wrath,[6] pride (Job 40:12; *Anth. Pal.* 5.300), the power of the passions,[7] tyranny (Plutarch, *Lyc.* 11.13; Josephus, *War* 2.296, the fire of war), the root of lawsuits,[8] etc. But none of these usages clarifies 1 Thess 5:19, "Do not quench the Spirit."[9] The context has to do with spiritual gifts, and the present imperative with *mē* would mean to stop prohibiting those inspired by the Holy Spirit from communicating what they have received (cf. 1 Cor 14:39, *mē kōlyete*). But the singular *to pneuma* points not to the charismatics but to the person of the Holy Spirit, or better the Holy Spirit's inspiration,[10] which is like a shining and burning flame.[11] Just as 2 Tim 1:6 says to revive, rekindle God's gift,[12] 1 Tim 5:19 urges each believer not to suppress or restrain it,[13] according to the principle of 1 Cor 14:32—"the spirits of the prophets are subject to the prophets"—and its application in Rom 12:6–8. A divine communication must not be kept to oneself, since by definition it is intended for the edification of all; and it is even worse to cut oneself off from the source and refuse to hear "what the Spirit says to the churches" (Rev 2:11, 17, 29, etc.).

---

[6] 2 Kgs 22:17 = 2 Chr 34:25; Jer 4:4; 7:20; 21:12; Plato, *Leg.* 10.888 *a*; Aelian, *VH* 5.11.

[7] Philo, *Sacr. Abel and Cain* 15; Plato, *Leg.* 8.835 *d*; 4 Macc 3:17; 16:4; cf. Sir 23:17; *P.Ryl.* 712, 2.

[8] In the fifth-sixth century in the papyri, *C.P.Herm.* 31, 20; *SB* 7033, 34, 67; 9763, 35.

[9] Τὸ πνεῦμα μὴ σβέννυτε. Cf. W. C. Van Unnik, "Den Geist löschet nicht aus," in *NovT*, 1968, pp. 255–269.

[10] H. Almqvist (*Plutarch und das Neue Testament*, p. 123) cites Plutarch, *De Pyth. or.* 17: "If the Pythia no longer prophesies in verse, it is either because she is no longer near the abode of the god or because the inspiring exhalation has completely dried up and its efficacy ended"; on this "exhalation," cf. *De def. or.* 42, 50.

[11] Acts 2:3—"tongues as of fire appeared to them, were distributed, and rested on each of them"; 18:25, Apollos, ζέων τῷ πνεύματι; Rom 12:11, τῷ πνεύματι ζέοντες; cf. John the Baptist, "a lamp that burned and gave light" (John 5:35).

[12] Ἀναζωπυρέω; cf. Plutarch, *Quaest. conv.* 1.2.3; C. Spicq, *Epîtres Pastorales*, vol. 2, pp. 707ff.

[13] The two meanings are equally attested. Sometimes σβέννυμι expresses a complete disappearance, notably with death: "when you are extinguished" (Ezek 32:7); epitaph of Apollos in the second-first century BC: "I was snuffed out at the age of twenty-seven" (*GVI*, n. 1002, 2; E. Bernand, *Inscriptions métriques*, n. 11), sometimes an attenuation, as with Metellus, diminished by age, ἤδη σβεννύμενον ὑπὸ γήρως, as bronze goes soft (Plutarch, *Pomp.* 8.6), springs or liquids dry up little by little (Aristotle, *HA* 3.21.4; *Anth. Pal.* 9.128), the joy of the Romans diminished upon the discovery of a new obstacle (Josephus, *War* 6.31); cf. the calming of sorrow (*Ant.* 11.40).

σεμνός, σεμνότης

semnos, **serious, grave, dignified, majestic, respectable;** *semnotēs*, **seriousness, gravity, dignity, majesty**

These terms, which express seriousness, gravity, dignity, and majesty, and which describe the venerable and august qualities of persons, occur often in classical Greek. They are used seven times by St. Paul; six of these occurrences are in the Pastoral Epistles. Their meaning in no way derives from Stoicism; it corresponds to common Hellenistic usage, as copiously attested in literary texts, honorific inscriptions, and funerary epigrams.

Semnos is a common modifier for divinities[1] and things pertaining to them: the temple (2 Macc 3:12; Philo, *To Gaius* 198), the high priest,[2] the law (2 Macc 6:28; *Ep. Arist.* 5, 171, 313), the Sabbath (2 Macc 6:11), the sacred psalms (Philo, *Contemp. Life* 29), and religious clothing (ibid. 66). Applied to people and things, *semnotēs* suggests grandeur, magnificence, solemnity, a quality that inspires respect, fear, or reverence.[3] It refers

---

[1] Aristophanes, *Av.* 727: Zeus sits in majesty in the clouds; 2 Macc 8:15, the name of God is "august and majestic"; Philo, *Spec. Laws* 2.7, 2.253; Josephus, *Ag. Apion* 2.221; the *semnos theai* = *dii sebastoi* are the venerable gods, especially Isis (*SB* 4094, 8; 8140, 3; 8434 = *SEG* VIII, 550 = E. Bernand, *Philae,* n. 157–158) and Poseidon (Sophocles, *OC* 55; Euripides, *IT* 1415; Aristophanes, *Thesm.* 322; C. Austin, "De nouveaux fragments de l'*Erechthée* d'Euripide," in *RechPap*, vol. 4, Paris, 1967, p. 39, line 93); Aphrodite (Euripides, *Hipp.* 103); Athena (*P.Oxy.* 2619, ed. D. Page, *Supplementum Lyricis Graecis*, Oxford, 1974, p. 26); "Calliope, august among the muses" (E. Bernand, *Inscriptions métriques,* n. 168, 15); the Erinyes are the Fearsome Ones—Σεμναί (Aeschylus, *Eum.* 383, 1041); cf. Foerster, on this word, in *TDNT*, vol. 7, p. 191.

[2] Philo, *To Gaius* 296; Josephus, *War* 4.319. Chairestrate is "august priestess of the Mother of all things" (*GVI,* n. 421, 1).

[3] *Ep. Arist.* 144: "All has been drawn up with this solemnity in order to inspire wholesome reflection and moral reform, through concern for justice"; 258: the king

---

semnos, S 4586; *TDNT* 7.191–196; *EDNT* 3.238; *NIDNTT* 2.91–93; MM 572; L&N 88.47; BAGD 746–747 ‖ *semnotēs,* S 4587; *TDNT* 7.191–196; *EDNT* 3.238; *NIDNTT* 2.91–93; MM 572; L&N 88.46; BAGD 747

especially to honorable conduct, a dignified and level-headed existence, and a high standard of morality: *ho semnos bios* = the religious life.[4] It is in this sense that 1 Tim 2:2 expresses the hope "that we may lead a calm and tranquil life in all godliness and religious dignity" (*en pasē eusebeia kai semnotēti*). The church is the household or family of God (3:5), and its members are a priestly congregation; the *semnotēs* of each one is the dignity of a liturgy, a mode of existence defined by piety and worship, marked by the seriousness, gravity, decency that are fitting in God's presence.[5] The papyri,[6] like the honorific decrees, emphasize the nobility or excellence of *semnotēs*: "for a dignified life" (*epi tē semnotēti tou biou*);[7] a decree of Delphi for an *enkōmiographos*: "exhibited worthi-

---

creates imposing (*semna*) edifices "so that those who see them will spare them because of their beauty"; Philo, *Rewards* 97: "majesty (*semnotēs*), strength, and beneficence protect government from subversion"; *Joseph* 165, 257: impressed by the dignity of Jacob's appearance, the king received him with all the trappings of respect and esteem. Cf. noble thoughts (*Ep. Arist.* 271), a royal task (Philo, *Sacr. Abel and Cain* 49), "noble combat" (Dittenberger, *Syl.* 35 E), a theme that is "lofty and pleasing to the gods" (Ps.-Plutarch, *De mus.* 14). Aristotle defined *semnotēs* as "a mild and becoming form of arrogance" (Aristotle, *Rh.* 2.17.1391ª27); Plutarch, *De vit. pud.* 3: "a serious (*semnos*) man, grand and just." In Strattis (*Lemn.*): σεμνοπρόσωπον (*P.Oxy.* 2743, frag. XVII, 6). Diodorus Siculus 17.34.6: the hieratic majesty of bearing of the Great King of the Persians; 38, 2: the august majesty that must surround the wife of Darius.

[4] Philo, *Contemp. Life* 25: the life of the Therapeutai and Therapeutrides, which is not only a life dedicated to the worship of God, nor even the practice of the leading moral virtues, but a dignified and serious attitude, a sober bearing, even a nobility of appearance that expresses the quality of the soul (cf. a queenly bearing, Dio Chrysostom, *Or.* 1.70: τὸ δὲ πρόσωπον φαιδρὸν ὁμοῦ καὶ σεμνόν); Philo, *Drunkenness* 149: Hannah's sober and austere life; Josephus, *Life* 258: "Ask them how I lived; ask them if I carried out my functions in the land with all the requisite dignity and character" (ἐβίωσα . . . μετὰ πάσης σεμνότητος καὶ πάσης ἀρετῆς).

[5] Cf. Tertullian, *Praescrip.* 43: "ubi metus in Deum, ibi gravitas honesta."

[6] *BGU* 1756, 15: σεμνότατε διοικητά (59/58 BC); 1843, 13: σεμνότατε στρατηγέ (50/49 BC); *P.Bon.* 46, 11; *P.Mil.Vogl.* 24, 5: ἐρρῶσθαι ὡς ἐμὸν σεμνὸν κύριον (second century); *SB* 7530, 8: τῷ σεμνοτάτῳ πολλά τε χαίρειν; E. Bernand, *Inscriptions métriques*, n. 22, col. IV, 3: "a worthy trainer named Hermocrates"; 106, 6: "the prefect's noble and faithful messenger" (= *SEG* VII, 797 = *SB* 7905); 141, 1: "the venerable Memnon"; 168, 7: "I received from the gods the noble gift of eloquent thought." The term is honorific when applied to cities (*Pap.Lugd.Bat.* II, 4, 2; *P.Stras.* 280, 2; *P.Oxy.* 2108, 17; 2476, 17, 34, 41; *SB* 6160, 5; 7375, 8; 7803, 6; cf. I. Biezunska-Malowist, "Acte d'achat d'une esclave," in *P.Coll.Youtie* II, p. 507), to a court (ibid. 8246, 7: τῷ σεμνῷ τούτῳ δικαστηρίῳ; cf. 9825, 5; *P.Oxy.* 2418, 2; *I.Bulg.* 1391, 4: σεμνῷ δεσποσύνῳ), a dinner club (an ἔρανος: σεμνὸς σύνοδος, C. Michel, *Recueil*, 1563, 31); σεμνοτάτᾳ καὶ ἀρχαιοτάτῳ συνεδρίῳ (*MAMA*, vol. 8, 523), to the *gerousia* (*TAM* II, 294, 325), to the *boulē* (*IG* II–III², n. 3962).

[7] Honorific inscription of Iotape, in L. Robert, *Documents*, pp. 78–79.

ness of character" (*ēthōn epedeixato semnotēta*);[8] at Magnesia, a son boasts of his father's dignity: "because of the dignity of his character and the nobility he inherited from his forbears";[9] at Philadelphia in Lydia: "praised for character and for a dignified and stable life" (*epi te ēthei kai biou semnotēti kai eustatheia epainethenta, Ath. Mitt.,* 1900, p. 122, n. 1); at Thyatira, "praised for dignified character and reasonable ways" (*epi te tou ēthous semnotēti kai tropou epieikeia epainoumenon, Hermes,* 1930, p. 109).

Semnotēs has to do not only with bearing and attitude (Philo, *Flacc.* 4), one's comportment in general (*en pasi semnotēti,* Dittenberger, *Syl.* 807, 14; *Or.* 567, 200), or even collective behavior (*to semnon tēs philadelphias hymōn,* BGU, 1024, col. VIII, 7; cf. *1 Clem.* 47.5; 48.1), but with a religious and moral posture that bears the mark of excellence: "Whatsoever things are true, noble (*hosa semna*), just, pure, lovely, honorable . . . think on these things" (Phil 4:8; cf. Dio Chrysostom 31.6). The *episkopos* will raise his children in submission, *meta pasēs semnotētos* (1 Tim 3:4), meaning that the dignity of those in authority inspires fear and respect,[10] or better that the educator imparts flawless moral rectitude to his students.[11] Titus in his teaching is to maintain "purity, dignity (*semnotēta*), speech that is wholesome and unassailable."[12] Deacons must be *semnoi* (1 Tim 3:8), i.e., serious and hon-

---

[8] Ed. L. Robert, *Etudes épigraphiques,* p. 18 (cf. p. 20, an inscription of Aphrodisias, τὴν περὶ τὸν βίον σεμνότητι καὶ σωφροσύνῃ). Idem (in *Opera Minora Selecta,* vol. 1, p. 681) cites an honorific decree from Delphi, διὰ τὴν εὐτονίαν τοῦ ἔργου καὶ τὴν σεμνότητα τοῦ τρόπου; in another, διὰ τὴν τῶν ἠθῶν σεμνότητα καὶ διὰ τὴν τοῦ βίου κοσμιότητα; at Rhodes, τῶν ἠθῶν σεμνότητου ἔνεκεν; *IG,* XII, 1, 84.

[9] Διά τε τὴν τῶν ἠθῶν σεμνότητα καὶ τὴν ἀπὸ τῶν προγόνων εὐγένειαν, *I.Magn.* 163, 1–3 (republished by L. Robert, *Gladiateurs,* n. 152); 113, 12, a physician: ἀνάλογον πεποίηται τὴν ἐπιδημίαν τῇ περὶ ἑαυτὸν σεμνότητι; *MAMA* VIII, 408, 6: ἠθῶν τε σεμνότητε καὶ ἐναρέτου βίου ἀγωγῇ; 409, 2; 410, 4: βίον σεμνὸν καὶ ἐνάρετον; 497, 4: διὰ τὴν τοῦ βίου ἀρετὴν καὶ σεμνότητα; cf. 399, 2: τῷ ἰδίῳ σεμνοτάτῳ μνείας χάριν.

[10] Cf. Philo, *Spec. Laws* 1.142; Diotogenes, in Stobaeus 48.9.62 (vol. 4, p. 268); the king's majesty must be evident in his prudence, and his conduct must have nothing vulgar about it (ibid. 267); cf. Lucian, *Luct.* 5: "all *semnoi* people and trustworthy witnesses." Plutarch, *Ant.* 50.7: "a beautiful and noble sight."

[11] Cf. Sasandros, a sober and dignified (*semnos*) young man, also studious (*MAMA* VIII, 263); *I.Bulg.* 1023, 2: ἤπιος, ἡδὺς ἰδεῖν, σεμνός, ἅπασι φίλος.

[12] Titus 2:7. This "dignity" is above all religious, excluding from preaching profane elements (βεβήλους, 1 Tim 4:7; 6:20), myths, and "sophisticated fables" (2 Pet 1:16), which are so many profanations of the sacred. A "worthy word" is an utterance that is pure and holy (Prov 8:6; 15:26), showing respect for its object (4 Macc 1:17); cf. *Ep. Arist.* 31: "the teaching (of the biblical books) is august and holy"; Philo, *To Gaius* 361; Josephus, *Ag. Apion* 1.225: τὴν σεμνότητα τῆς ἡμετέρας θεολογίας; *1 Clem.* 7.2.

orable, because they carry out a public function that requires respectability in the minister[13] and inspires respect and even praise in those who witness his life, like the high priest Ananus, "a venerable and just man who, despite his noble birth, his dignity, and his honors, loved to treat the humblest as his equals" (Josephus, *War* 4.319), or Caristanius, who is praised in the year 98 for having carried out his command over all Greece "with brilliance and in a praiseworthy manner" (*semnōs kai axiologōs, Fouilles de Delphes*, III, 4; n. 47, 7). There is nothing off-putting about this gravity; seriousness does not rule out kindness.[14]

"Likewise, the women [must be] dignified" (1 Tim 3:11), after the fashion of Aphrodisia, a steady woman, involved in her husband's business: *Aphrodeisia semnotatē kai pistotatē . . . gynaiki.*[15] *Semnotēs* is one of the virtues that is praised in women: Hannah led a calm and austere life;[16] Esther was the same when she appeared before Ahasuerus (Josephus, *Ant.* 11.234); the mother of the Maccabees shared the same virtue (4 Macc 17.5). A woman is adorned not with gold and silver, but *hosa semnotētos, eutaxias, aidous* (Plutarch, *Con. praec.* 26). In the papyri, and especially in the inscriptions, *semnotēs* is sometimes purely honorific,[17] but usually it is an outstanding quality suggestive of reserve and re-

---

[13] Cf. the Latin *gravitas honesta*; O. Hiltbrunner, "Vir gravis," in *Festschrift A. Debrunner,* Berne, 1954, pp. 195–207; J. Gaudemet, " 'Majestas Populi Romani,' " in *Synteleia* (Festschrift for V. Arangio-Ruiz), Naples, 1964, vol. 2, pp. 700ff. J. P. Lévy, "Dignitas, Gravitas, Auctoritas Testium," in *Studi in onore di B. Biondi,* Milan, 1965, vol. 2, pp. 29–94.

[14] Plutarch, *Nic.* 2.4: "the gravity (τὸ σεμνόν) of Nicias was in no way austere or off-putting"; *Per.* 5.3; *Quaest. conv.* 1.1.2: it is in jest that temperance and justice are accused of being too serious; 1.4.2: "one who is by nature serious and grim, not to say sour, relaxes when drinking and becomes more pleasant and friendly"; cf. Philo, *Moses* 1.20.

[15] *MAMA* VIII, 182; with the commentary of L. Robert (*Hellenica,* vol. 13, p. 36), who compares this woman of Cyrene, ἥν πάντες σεμνὴν γεινώσκουσιν . . . πολλῶν πραγματιῶν μέτοχος γενόμαν πιστὴ κατὰ πάντα (1 Tim 3:11 requires *semnas* deaconesses to be πιστὰς ἐν πᾶσιν). Plutarch loves to praise seriousness and respectability as a woman's true adornment (Plutarch, *Con. praec.* 145 E–F), as in the case of Octavia, Cicero's sister, "combining great beauty, seriousness (σεμνότητα) and intelligence" (*Ant.* 31.4; cf. 51.5); of magistrates (*An seni* 793 B–D; 801 D); a virtue that culminates in "royal majesty," as with Demetrius Poliorcetes (Plutarch, *Demetr.* 2.21) but is proper to all who are well-born (εὐγένεια).

[16] Philo, *Drunkenness* 149; same link in *Creation* 164; *Spec. Laws* 4.179; *To Gaius* 167; *SB* 6160, 2, 5.

[17] "The venerable spouse of Emperor Hadrian" (*SB* 8211, 8); "you remembered his august and legitimate spouse" (ibid. 8212, 8); "venerable Persephone, daughter of Demeter" (epitaph at Thermion, first century BC; ibid. n. 8960, 3); "noble offspring" (epitaph of the Cretan Juliana, in E. Bernand, *Inscriptions métriques,* n. 50, 2).

straint, discretion, self-mastery under all circumstances: *gynaika sem-nēn*,[18] whether with respect to young women,[19] or especially married women ("the noble and most dignified wife," *hē kalē kai semnotatē symbios*, *P.Ross.Georg.* V, 6, 27), as at Sinope ("to his wife, Prokope, most reverent, known for her restraint and dignity"—*Prokopē gynaiki heautou eusebestatē kai semnotēti sōphrosynēs memartyrēmenē*, *BCH*, 1920, p. 359), or Aurelia Philotera, who "lived with dignity and distinction" (*semnōs kai epiphanōs zēsasan*, *IG* X, 2, n. 176, 11–13; cf. 194, 6–9: "the dignified and affectionate Pontia Kallistiane," *tēn semnotatēn kai philostorgon Pontian Kallistianēn*). *Semnotēs*, frequently in the superlative,[20] is associated with *philandria* (*MAMA* VIII, 476, 514), *philoteknia* (*SEG* VI, 452), and *sophrosynē* (*MAMA* VIII, 470, 4). An epitaph from the third century AD: "The dignified Berous, daughter of Chrysippus, was a Penelope in deed and not in fiction, chaste in her marriage, prudent despite her youth, a good mistress of her house and her life" (*IGLS* 721, 2–3). Some Jewish women are named Semnous.[21]

Titus 2:2 requires old men to be sober, dignified (*semnous*), level-headed (*sōphronas*); here we could translate *semnos* as "venerable" or "very respectable"; seriousness, which excludes eccentricity and pecularity, is a characteristic of old age,[22] as this epitaph from the high imperial period says: "You were so dignified, while still a child, that you seemed to have the intelligence of an old man."[23]

A Christian cannot have less virtue than the honest pagan whose epitaph reads "in everything you were dignified" (*en panti d' ēstha semnos*, *SEG* VIII, 372, 11; second century; cf. *TAM* II, 422 *a* 17; *b* 15); his name is "revered, admired, worthy to be loved by all."[24]

---

[18] G. E. Bean, T. B. Mitford, *Cilicia*, n. XXXVII, 4; cf. L. and J. Robert, "Bulletin épigraphique," in *REG*, 1964, p. 238, n. 536; p. 252, n. 604; σεμνοτάτη πασῶν; *1 Clem.* 1.3.

[19] Heliodorus, *Aeth.* 10.21.2; τὴν κούρην συνέσει τε καὶ ἤθεσιν ἔργοισι σεμνήν (F. Cumont, *Studia Pontica* III, 80, 1); σεμνὴν θυγατέρα (*SEG* III, 610, 6).

[20] *MAMA* VIII, 37, 116, 182, 370; *GVI*, n. 421, 1.

[21] M. Schwabe and B. Lifshitz, *Beth She'arim*, vol. 2, p. IX, *a*.

[22] 4 Macc 5:36—"You shall not defile the venerable mouth of an old man"; 7:15—"O venerable white hairs"; cf. Philo, *Etern. World* 77: "It is a property not of youth but of old age to discern that which deserves veneration and zeal"; *PSI* 41, 9: a woman declares that she is the offspring ἐκ σεμνῶν γονέων καὶ εὐδοκίμων; *P.Oxy.* 2546, 388: θνητῶν σεμνοτάτων γονέων.

[23] *GVI*, n. 1935, 11 = *SEG* VIII, 372 = E. Bernand, *Inscriptions métriques*, n. 71.

[24] *1 Clem.* 1.1: τὸ σεμνὸν καὶ περιβόητον καὶ πᾶσιν ἀνθρώποις ἀξιαγάπητον ὄνομα.

σημεῖον

sēmeion, **sign**

In secular and biblical Greek, the basic meaning "sign"[1] is applied to very different things: the notice that bears a court's verdict (Plato, *Resp.* 10.614, *c*), a seal or signature,[2] the engraving on a shield,[3] a ship's decoration (Thucydides 6.31.3), a landmark or milestone (Herodian 2.13.18), a flag (Xenophon, *Cyr.* 8.5.13), the ensign of a flagship.[4]

One of the most widespread meanings in the papyri is distinctive "mark" or identifying "sign," whether with respect to things, animals, or people: "this marks the burial place" (*estin de sēmeion tēs taphēs,* P.Paris 18 bis, 10; cf. *SB* 9420, 8); "I sold the female camel whose distinguishing feature is described."[5] Gemellus complains to the *epistratēgos* that he was

---

[1] Hebrew *'ôt,* 79 times in the LXX; cf. C. A. Keller, *Das Wort* אות *als Offenbarungszeichen Gottes,* Basel, 1946.

[2] Plato, *Leg.* 9.856 *a; Tht.* 191 *d;* Xenophon, *Hell.* 5.1.30; P.Rev., col. 26, 5: ἀποδειξάτωσαν τὸ ἐπιβληθὲν σημεῖον ἀσινές.

[3] Herodotus 1.171; Euripides, *Phoen.* 142, 1111, 1114; cf. P.Warr. 15, 11: "during my absence, the weaver made tunics—ἠργάσατο αὐτὰ δίχα σημείου," i.e, of a certain design or model, or without hems or embroidery (Latin *clavus*); cf. J. and L. Robert, "Bulletin épigraphique," in *REG,* 1954, p. 124, n. 88 *a.*

[4] Herodotus 8.92. In the LXX, σημεῖον also translates the Hebrew words *nēs,* "pole, flag, standard" (Num 21:8–9; Isa 11:12; 13:2; 18:3; 28:12, 27; 33:23); *ṣiyûn* "pillar, monument," and *tāw,* "mark" (Ezek 9:4, 6; 39:15); *mô'ēd,* smoke "signal" (Judg 20:38; cf. Josephus, *War* 2.579; 3.88, 105; 6.68; *Ant.* 5.46; 12.404; 18.61); *môpēt,* "prodigy, wonder" (Exod 7:9; 11:9–10); cf. R. Formesyn, "Le Sèmeion johannique et le sèmeion hellénistique," in *ETL,* 1962, pp. 856–894; *'ôt* = "ensign" in 1QM 3.12; 1QpHab 6.4.

[5] Πέπρακα τὸν κάμηλον θήλιαν οὗ τὸ σημεῖον πρόκιται, BGU 427, 30; P.Ross. Georg. II, 18, 226; Pap.Lugd.Bat. XVI, 15, 7: an adult female ass, white, with a mark over the right eye; *SB* 5679, 6: ὄνου λευκῆς οὔσης, ἐχούσης σημεῖον ἐπὶ τοῦ τραχήλου; P.Oxy. 1635, 9 (first century BC). In a Samian law from the second century BC, the *prytaneis* are invited to place the landmarks (σημεῖα ποιήσαντες) and limit the location of each division of the people (χιλιαστύς, Dittenberger, *Syl.* 976, 5).

---

sēmeion, S 4592; *TDNT* 7.200–261; *NIDNTT* 2.626–627, 629; MM 572–573; L&N 33.477; BAGD 747–748

appointed to a *leitourgia* under a false name and without regard to his characteristics.[6] Just as a phylactery is a sign worn around the arm (*Ep. Arist.* 159), circumsion is a mark on the flesh signifying the covenant.[7] These personal "marks" are not necessarily physical; virtues can also be "distinctives": "I considered such things to be the signs of good men" (*hēgoumēn sēmeia agathōn andrōn ta toiauta einai*, Dittenberger, *Syl.* 831, 14; from AD 117). Such are the "signs" or "character traits" (Plutarch, *Cat. Min.* 24.1: *ta tōn ēthōn sēmeia*) by which an apostle may be recognized, according to 2 Cor 12:12 (cf. *b. Sanh.* 98a–b; 1QS 3.14).

So a *sēmeion* is noetic; developed from *sēma*, it is very close to "signal,"[8] "writing,"[9] and "message";[10] literary[11] and papyrological texts often treat

---

[6] Ἢ ἄλλο τι τῶν ἐμῶν σημείων, *P.Mich.* 426, 14; cf. *PSI* 897, 70: σὺν τοῖς ἄλλοις τεκμηρίοις καὶ σημείοις; 1118, 11 (from AD 25 or 37); *SB* 7662, 16: "Maris, the beneficiary, took your name and description" (ἔλαβεν σου τὸ ὄνομα καὶ τὰ σημῖα καὶ λέγι ὅτι . . .); *P.Oxy.* 1463, 29–29: ἀκολούθως τοῖς σημείοις τῷ ὑπομνήματι ἐγγεγραμμένοις (according to *Berichtigungsliste*, vol. 3, p. 137). Cf. J. Hasebroek, *Das Signalement in den Papyrusurkunden*, Berlin-Leipzig, 1921; G. Hübsch, *Die Personalangaben als Identifizierungsvermerk*, Berlin, 1968.

[7] Σημεῖον διαθήκης (Gen 17:11); Rom 4:11—σημεῖον ἔλαβεν περιτομῆς; *b. Šabb.* 137b; cf. *b. B. Qam.* 119; *m. Kil.* 9.10; *b. Menaḥ.* 37b; *BGU* 347, 14; 1064, 18; *SB* 15, 17; 82, 9; 9027, 18: Σηρῆνος ἐπύθετο τῶν παρόντων ἱερογραμματέων εἰ σημῖά τινα ἔχοιεν οἱ παῖδες. The mark of Cain, cf. Gen 4:15; Philo, *Rewards* 72; *Worse Attacks Better* 177; Josephus, *Ant.* 1.59 (there are unfavorable signs; cf. Plutarch, *De vit. pud.* 1.528 c). Cf. "God's mark on the just" and "the mark of perdition" on sinners in *Pss. Sol.* 11.8, 10.

[8] Herodotus 9.59; Josephus, *Ant.* 12.404.

[9] Philo, *Moses* 2.115; *Prelim. Stud.* 146; *P.Mil.Vogl.* 50, 7: ἐὰν οὖν σημεῖόν σοι ἐνέγκῃ ἢ ἐπιστολήν (first century AD); *P.Oxy.* 724, 3; 1QS 10.4; *m. Šabb.* 7.2; 12.3–4; Plutarch, *Cat. Min.* 23.3: Cicero had the scribes instructed in "signs which, in a brief, shortened form, stood for several letters" (a shorthand system). On *sēmeion* as a geometrical point, from Autolycus, cf. C. Mugler, *Terminologie géométrique*, pp. 376–377.

[10] *P.Oxy.* 293, 6: οὔτε διὰ γραπτοῦ οὔτε διὰ σημείου (AD 27); *P.Fay.* 128, 7: ἔδωκεν ἡμῖν σημεῖον; Dittenberger, *Syl.* 685, 70, 75; 2 Macc 15:35—"Judas affixed the head of Nicanor to the citadel as a plain and visible sign to all of God's help." Cf. the sign as portent, Plato, *Phdr.* 244 c; Polybius 3.112.8; Diodorus Siculus 16.27.2ff.; Dan 5:5–9; Philo, *Etern. World* 2; *Creation* 58: σημεῖα μελλόντων; Josephus, *War* 6.285, 296; Sir 43:6; 1QH 12.8; 15.20; 1QS 10.4; 1Q27, frag. 1, 1.5; Dittenberger, *Syl.* 709, 25: προεσάμανε μὲν τὰν μέλλουσαν γίνεσθαι πρᾶξιν διὰ τῶν ἐν τῷ ἱερῷ γενομένων σαμείων (107 BC); *Pap.Graec.Mag.* 1, 65: ἔσται δέ σοι διώκοντι τὸν λόγον σημεῖον τόδε; 74: ἔσται δέ σοι σημεῖον ἐν τάχει τοιοῦτο. This is the meaning of the "signs of the times" (Matt 16:3), signs of the second coming of Jesus (24:3; Mark 13:4; Luke 21:7). These omens are warnings, *Sib. Or.* 3.457; Josephus, *War* 1.28; 3.404; Dio Cassius 66.17.2: there were omens that pointed to the upcoming death of Vespasian.

[11] Sophocles, *El.* 24; *OT* 710; Xenophon, *Ages.* 1.5; *An.* 6.2.2; Theophrastus, *Char.* 28.21; Polybius 4.44.3: "the proof of what I am setting forward"; Philo, *Flight* 204; *Moses* 2.18; *Prelim. Stud.* 92; *Sacr. Abel and Cain* 80. Σημεῖον is synonymous with

"sign" as the equivalent of "proof." This is the authenticating or identifying sign which the Fourth Gospel uses in a theological way and which St. Paul exploits in 2 Thess 3:17—"This greeting is in my hand, Paul's hand, which is the mark (or proof) in every letter; this is how I write." The autographed greeting authenticates the letter.[12] Already in 255 BC, a certain Plato, requesting a service from Zeno, sends him as proof of his goodwill two *artabai* of chick-peas purchased at five drachmas apiece (*sēmeion de hoti soi apesteila para Sōsou erebinthou kriou artabas β′ ēgorasmenas, P.Cair.Zen.* 59192, 8). A century later, Stratonicus, to prove to his wife that it is indeed her husband who is writing to her, mentions as a sign something that he had said to her in private: "Stratonikos to Senchnoubis his wife, greetings. Recognize as a sign: when I said to you to buy the new tunic with the money" (*Stratonikos Senchnoubei tē gynaiki chairein. Sēmeion hote eipa soi lytrōsai ton kainon chitōna apo tōn chalkōn ginōske, SB* 7574, 2: a letter on an ostracon). In the second century AD, the sign to the recipient of a letter that the author is well-informed is that he knows that his wife went out to buy four obols worth of spices (*allo sēmion soi graphō peri autou, hote hē gynē sou exelthousa ēgorake obolōn tessarōn artymata tō nautikō, P.Petaus* 28, 8 and 17). In the same period, Anthestianus, having sent Sarapammon to the potter Psois, who refuses to pay his debts, informs his debtor that he cannot cheat him, because he knows what Psois has said and done.[13] In the fourth century, Probus asks his sister Manatine to pay one and a half talents to his confidential aide Petronius, and as proof that it is he who is writing (*sēmeiou de charin*) says "When I met you at the Caesareion, I said to you, 'Give me a little

σύμβολον in Plato's letter to Dionysius, tyrant of Syracuse (*Ep.* 13.360 *a–b*), where he refers to a conversation between them that only they knew about: "that the beginning of my letter should be at the same time a sign to you of its authenticity" (ἀρχή σοι τῆς ἐπιστολῆς ἔστω καὶ ἅμα σύμβολον παρ' ἐμοῦ ἐστιν; cf. H. C. Youtie, "ΣΗΜΕΙΟΝ in the Papyri and Its Significance for Plato, Epistle 13 [360 a–b]," in *ZPE*, vol. 6, 2, 1970, pp. 105–116; republished in *Scriptiunculae*, vol. 2, pp. 963–975); cf. Appian, *BCiv.* 4.4.14; S. Witkowski, *Epistulae Privatae Graecae* 34, 15: ἀπεδόθη τάδ' αὐτῷ καὶ τὸ σύμβολον τῶν ἐγ. If σύμβολον and σημεῖον are interchangeable in the sense of "conclusive piece of evidence" (cf. Plutarch, *Per.* 6.5), their semantics are quite different (cf. P. Gautier, *Symbola*, p. 72).

[12] Ὁ ἀσπασμὸς τῇ ἐμῇ χειρὶ Παύλου, ὅ ἐστιν σημεῖον ἐν πάσῃ ἐπιστολῇ· οὕτως γράφω. Cf. Gal 6:11—"See what large characters I write to you with my own hand." Cf. the crosses or authors' marks in the papyri: σημεῖον Ἀπολλωνίου (*P.Rein.* 9, line 4 of the summary; 35, 3); σημεῖον Εὐσεβίου (*C.P.Herm.* 34, 32; with the editor's note); *SB* 9759, 4; 9914, 9. The sign is a designation in Philo, *Creation* 49, 98.

[13] *P.Oxy.*, published in *ChrEg*, 1969, pp. 101–105: καὶ λόγον μὲν οὐκ ἔσχες τοῦ Σαραπάμμωνος ἀλλ' ἔφης αὐτῷ ὅτι τὸ νῦν μοι συνχώρησον ἐπεὶ ἀπὸ ξένης ἦλθον μετὰ τῆς πίσσης μου ἵν' εἰδῇς τὸ σημεῖον.

of the money that you have from me, so that I may buy a cauldron,' and you said to me . . ."[14]

Thus *sēmeion* is the sign whereby the recipient may recognize the identity of the sender; the sender mentions circumstances that only the two of them could know about.[15] This meaning is also found in the epigrams: Bacchon sends his slave to borrow money from the perfumer Aischra and tells him that as a sign of his identity he should refer to his amorous exploits.[16] Likewise, Pytias's lover wants to summon her: "As proof that it is I, tell her that he came drunk, passing through thieves, guided by Eros the bold."[17]

In the religious sphere, *sēmeion* has always meant a prodigy that is recognizable and provides proof for everyone.[18] In the NT, it is a category of miracle, together with mighty works (*dynameis*) and wonders (*terata*, Acts 2:22; 2 Thess 2:9; 2 Cor 12:12; Heb 2:4); but it retains its value as a sign or demonstration.[19] With the prophets, a "sign" is proof that a message is truly from God (Exod 3:12; 4:19; Judg 6:17; 1 Sam 10:1, 7; Isa 38:7–8). For Philo, God performs *sēmeia* to indicate his will, to teach people, and to introduce them to the knowledge of heavenly things.[20] More clearly, ac-

---

[14] *P.Oxy.* 1683, 18 (M. Naldini, *Il Cristianesimo in Egitto*, n. 65, 18). Cf. *SB* 8005: πάντως οὖν ἀπαρενόχλητον αὐτὸν ποίησον, ἐμοὶ χαριζόμενος. σημεῖον ὅτι ἡ προθεσμία σου ἐνέστηκεν (with the punctuation of J. R. Rea, "The Use of σημεῖον in SB V 8005," in *ZPE*, vol. 14, 1974, p. 14.)

[15] Cf. the kiss of Judas as a sign of recognition (Matt 26:48), and Tobias' asking his father, "What sign of recognition (σημεῖον) shall I give him that he may know me and give me the money?" (Tob 5:2, LXX).

[16] *Anth. Pal.* 5.181.11: εἰπὲ δὲ σημεῖον· Βάκχων ὅτι πέντ' ἐφίλησεν ἑξῆς; cited by R. Merkelbach, "Σημεῖον im Liebesepigramm," in *ZPE*, vol. 6, 1970, pp. 245–246.

[17] *Anth. Pal.* 5.213: εἰπὲ δὲ σημεῖον, μεθύων ὅτι καὶ διὰ κλωπῶν ἦλθεν.

[18] Polybius 3.112.8: "Every temple, every house was full of signs and wonders"; Strabo 16.2.35; Plutarch, *Alex.* 75.1; *Conv. sept. sap.* 3; Philo, *Spec. Laws* 2.218; *Moses* 1.210; Josephus, *War* 1.28; *Ant.* 10.28; 20.168; *P.Oxy.* 2624, frag. 1, 8, etc. This is very close to τεκμήριον; but according to Aristotle's logic, (Aristotle, *An. Pr.* 70ᵃ11), a τεκμήριον is a demonstrative argument that is certain, whereas a σημεῖον is an argument that is probable; among the Stoics and the Epicureans, it becomes the point of departure for a deductive argument intended to produce certitude concerning the existence of a reality that is not observable, Sextus Empiricus, *Math.* 8.142 e; Zeno, *Sign.* 1.14; Epicurus, *Epist.* 2.43; Philodemus of Gadara, *Sign.* 27.

[19] Hymn to Mandoulis: "I have seen the brilliant signs of your power" (*SB* 4127, 3); cf. *Ep. Arist.* 44: "that is the sign of friendship and affection"; 150, 270; Diogenes Laertius 8.32: τὰ σημεῖα νόσου καὶ ὑγιείας; in the second century, Ptolemaeus writes to his father: "since you do not write to me, this will be the sign that you have forgotten me" (ἐπεὶ τῷ μὴ γράφειν μοι, ἔσται σημῖον τοῦ δηλοῦν μου ἀμνημονεῖν, *P.Mert.* 22, 9).

[20] Philo, *Moses* 1.95: "God indicated his will to them . . . through signs and wonders" (διὰ σημείων καὶ τεράτων τὸ βούλημα δεδηλωκότος); 1.76: "If they no

cording to Josephus, "God uses miracles to convince people" (*Ant.* 2.274, 280); they are designed to inspire faith (2.276). Hence the persistent demand of Jesus' contemporaries: "We want to see a sign from you" (Matt 12:38; 16:1; Mark 8:11; Luke 11:16; John 2:18; 6:30). "The Jews seek signs" (1 Cor 1:22).

This is how St. John sees miracles: they authenticate Jesus as the Messiah announced by the prophets.[21] Since they are wonders and manifestations of power (Matt 9:28–29) as well as of mercy (11:5), they legitimate adherence to his teaching (11:20) and give him personal credibility.[22] They show who he is: "He manifested his glory and his disciples believed in him" (John 2:11; 11:4). They are above all a sign of the Father's favor: "No one can do the signs that you do unless God is with him."[23] By referring to the *mirabilia* done by Jesus as "signs," St. John shows that he understands them as data that allow the discovery of the glory (*doxa*) of the incarnate Word, the revelation that Jesus is with God or comes from God,[24] and finally the recognition of the testimony of the Father on behalf of his Son.[25]

---

longer have confidence, they will change once they have received the teaching of the three signs that no human has yet seen and understood"; 1.82, 90, 91; *Etern. World* 2: "God would not refuse to introduce souls to the knowledge of heavenly things through dreams, oracles, signs, and miracles." Cf. Josephus, *War* 6.285: "God ordered them to ascend to the temple to receive signs of their salvation."

[21] Cf. "Les Miracles, signes messianiques de Jésus et œuvres de Dieu," in *Recueil L. Cerfaux*, vol. 2, pp. 41–50; K. Gatzweiler, "La Conception paulinienne du miracle," in *ETL*, 1961, pp. 813–846; M. E. Boismard, "Foi et miracle dans le quatrième Evangile," in *RB*, 1962, pp. 188ff. C. F. D. Moule, *Miracles*, London, 1966; Rengstorf, "σημεῖον," in *TDNT*, vol. 7, pp. 229ff.

[22] John 6:30; cf. 7:31—"When the Christ comes, will he perform more signs than this man?"; 10:42; J. Kallas, *The Significance of the Synoptic Miracles*, London, 1961.

[23] John 3:2; cf. 5:26; 10:38; 11:42. The most decisive miracle is the resurrection of the crucified, "the sign of Jonah" (Matt 12:39; 16:4; Luke 11:29–30); cf. A. M. Dubarle, "Le Signe du Temple, Jo. II, 19," in *RB*, 1939, pp. 21–44; A. Vögtle, "Der Spruch vom Janaszeichen," in *Synoptische Studien: Festschrift A. Wikenhauser*, Munich, 1954, pp. 230–277; R. Branton, "Resurrection in the Early Church," in A. Wikgren, *Studies in Honor of H. R. Willoughby*, Chicago, 1961, pp. 35–47; J. Sint, "Die Auferstehung Jesu in der Verkündigung der Urgemeinde," in *ZKT*, 1962, pp. 129–151; O. Glombitza, "Das Zeichen des Jona," in *NTS*, 1962, vol. 8, pp. 359–360; R. A. Edwards, *The Sign of Jonas in the Theology of the Evangelists and Q*, London, 1971.

[24] John 9:33; J. P. Michaud, *Le Signe de Cana*, Montreal, 1963; M. Orge, "El σημεῖον de la 'hora' (Jo. XIII, 1–17)," in *Claretianum* (Rome), vol. 5, 1965, pp. 95–140; J. Ramos-Regidor, "Signo y poder: A propósito de la exegesis patrística de Jn. II, 1–11," in *Salesianum*, 1965, pp. 499–562; 1966, pp. 3–64; L. Erdozáin, *La función del signo en la fe según el Quarto Evangelio*, Rome, 1968; A. Geyser, "The Semeion at Cana of the Galilee," in *Studies in John Presented to Pr. J. N. Sevenster*, Leiden, 1970, pp. 12–21; S. S. Smalley, "The Sign in John XXI," in *NTS*, vol. 20, 1974, pp. 275–288.

[25] John 14:10; cf. J. P. Charlier, "La Notion de signe (σημεῖον) dans le IVᵉ Evangile," in *RSPT*, 1959, pp. 434–448; D. Mollat, "Le Semeion johannique," in *Sacra*

This theology enriches and adds subtlety to the concept of *sēmeion*. Should we translate "sign," "indication," or "proof"?[26] What is certain is that the sign itself needs to be verified. If it is a guarantee of the authenticity of the Sent One and of the truth of the teaching, it has demonstrative power only for souls that are well-disposed or believing. It can provoke astonishment or emotion, even admiration (John 2:23; 6:26; Acts 8:9, 13) without adherence: "Even though he had done so many signs in their presence, still they did not believe in him" (John 12:37). It is even possible to slip into superstition at the sight of wonders, like Alexander, according to Plutarch (*Alex.* 75.1ff.). The *semeia* of false prophets appear to confirm error (Deut 13:2–5), and according to 1 Cor 14:22, speaking in tongues is a sign for believers, but not for unbelievers. In other words, the "sign" is intelligible only to the religious intelligence; it is a veiled manifestation that only the eyes of the heart can discover,[27] a propaedeutic to faith, attracting attention and prompting to an initiative, as with Nicodemus (John 3:2). Thus it is necessary to transcend the materiality of the deed in order to get to its meaning, or better, to the signified reality.[28]

Pagina, Paris, 1959, vol. 2, pp. 209–218; W. Nicol, *The Semeia in the Fourth Gospel*, Leiden, 1972.

[26] Σημεῖον can also mean a symbol (Lucian, *Syr. D.* 33; Philo, *Worse Attacks Better* 1), a symptom (ibid. 43); an indication (*Moses* 1.188; Josephus, *Ant.* 18.211).

[27] There are clear signs (Philo, *Rewards* 31; *Abraham* 60; *Spec. Laws* 1.90; *Moses* 1.269); but in any event they must be interpreted (*Dreams* 1.197).

[28] C. P. Grelot, *Sens chrétien de l'Ancien Testament*, Paris-Tournai, 1962, pp. 261ff. H. Baltensweiler, "Wunder und Glaube im N. T.," in *TZ*, 1967, pp. 241–256; M. Whittaker, " 'Signs and Wonders': The Pagan Background," in F. L. Cross, *SE*, vol. 5, Berlin, 1968, pp. 155–158; J. Becker, "Wunder und Christologie," in *NTS*, vol. 16, 1970, pp. 130–148; G. Delling, *Studien zum Neuen Testament*, Göttingen, 1970, pp. 72–129, 146–159.

σηρικός (σιρικός)

sērikos (sirikos), **silk**

Inspired by the lamentation of Ezek 27:9–25 over the ruin of Tyre, the dirge in Rev 18:12 describes the lamentation of the "merchants of the earth" over the ruin of Babylon, the loss of the cargoes from their ships: "cargo of gold and silver, of precious stones and pearls, of fine linen and purple, of silk (*sirikou*) and scarlet cloth." The text is interesting both because it evokes the importation of luxury items from Africa and the Orient[1] and also because of the use of the biblical hapax *sērikon*,[2] which does not appear before the time of Augustus. It derives from *Sēr* (plural *Sēres*), referring to a people of the Far East, probably the Chinese,[3] and also

---

[1] Cf. Pliny, *HN* 12.2: "the man came to ask for material from the Seres"; 12.84—"according to the lowest estimate, India, the Seres, and this peninsula take a hundred million sesterces a year from our empire; that is how dearly our women's love of luxury costs us"; 34.145; cf. 7.21; 14.22; *Peripl. Erythr.* 39: from the city of Thinaï, "cotton, thread and material called *sērikon* are brought by foot (in caravans) across Bactria . . . as far as Limyrica"; Cosmas Indicopleustes, *Top.* 2.45: "There are people who, in order to procure silk for miserable trade, think nothing of traveling to the ends of the earth."

[2] The text has perhaps been altered (twice the case changes from genitive to acccusative). The Jewish tradition (followed by older English translations) identifies the Hebrew *mešî* (fine material) of Ezek 16:10, 13, with which Yahweh wants to clothe Jerusalem, with silk; but silk did not appear before the time of Alexander. Cf. Aristotle: "Through metamorphosis from the larva there comes first a caterpillar, then a cocoon, then from this a nympha. . . . Certain women unwind the cocoons of this insect in order to weave a fabric from it. It is said that the first to practice this weaving was a woman of Cos, Pamphila, daughter of Plates" (*HA* 5.19; text copied almost literally by Pliny, *HN* 11.76). According to the French translator of this text, P. Louis, this has to do not with Chinese silk but with a related species acclimated to Asia Minor.

[3] P. Chantraine, *Dictionnaire étymologique*, on this word. Cf. G. Coedes, *Textes d'auteurs grecs et latins relatifs à l'Extrême Orient*, Paris, 1910 (reprinted as *Testimonia of Greek and Latin Writers on Lands and Peoples of the Far East*, Chicago, 1979); W. R. in *DKP*, vol. 5, p. 78.

---

sērikos, S 4596; *EDNT* 3.242; MM 573, 575; BAGD 751

products originating in China: silk. At Vespasian's triumph, where he was accompanied by Titus, "the emperors were unarmed, clothed in silk (*esthēsin sērikais*) and crowned with laurels" (Josephus, *War* 7.126).

It is a curious fact that the ancients thought that silk came from a plant. According to Strabo 15.1.20, "Nearchus said that (the wool that grew on certain trees) was used to weave fine materials used by the Macedonians for cushions and saddle pads; the serica also are of this kind, Byssus being dried out of certain barks."[4] Pausanias, writing in the time of Marcus Aurelius, is the one who corrects this error: "As for the threads from which the Seres make their clothing, they do not come from a husk but from a different origin, as follows. There exists in their land a small animal, called by the Greeks a *sēr*. . . . Its size is double that of the largest beetle; for the rest, it resembles a spider. . . . The work of these animals is a fine web that is found rolled about their feet."[5]

These silk fabrics, given their quality,[6] enjoyed prodigious success in the first century, especially in the higher classes of society: "The empress's

---

[4] Cf. Virgil, G. 2.121: "From the leaves of trees the Seres unwind fine fleeces"; Horace, *Epod*.8.15–16; Propertius 1.14.22: "What good were his silks (*serica*) of varied texture?"; Ovid, *Am.* 1.14.6; Seneca, *Lucil.* 90.15; *Phdr.* 389: "the threads that the distant Seres gather from their trees"; *Herc.* 667; Pliny, *HN* 6.54: "The Seres, famous for the wool of their forests; they detach the white down from the leaves by watering them; then our women carry out the twofold task of unwinding and weaving it. Thanks to such complicated operations, carried out in countries so distant, our matron can appear in public wearing transparent material"; Silius Italicus, *Pun.* 6.4; 17.595–596: "The Seres who dwell in the East see . . . their wool-laden woods whiten"; Statius, *Silv.* 1.2.122–123; Ammianus Marcellinus 23.6.67.

[5] Pausanias 6.26.6–9; cf. Philostratus, *Imag.* 2.28: "Behold the spider that spins nearby. In the art of weaving it is not surpassed by Penelope or even the Seres whose fabrics are extremely fine and barely visible"; Heliodorus, *Aeth.* 10.25.2: "the ambassadors of the Seres brought fabrics woven with the thread produced by the spider of their country, one robe dyed purple, another brilliant white." Hence Hesychius: "Σῆρες: animals that spin silk; or the the name of the people from which ὁλοσηρικόν comes"; "Σηρῶν: the worms that make *sērika*. Seres are worms."

[6] Plutarch, *De Pyth. or.* 4: "Why should not the same thing be fine and solid? Such is the case with materials of silk and linen" (ὥσπερ τὰ σηρικὰ καὶ τὰ βύσσινα); Dionysius Periegetes 752–757: "The barbarous tribes of the Seres . . . weave multicolored flowers of their desert country and with much art make precious garments with the brilliance of the prairie flowers, which the work of the spiders cannot rival"; Dio Cassius 43.24: Caesar had veils of silk (παραπετάσματα σηρικά) unfurled above the spectators; "Now this fabric is a work of the softness of the barbarians, and from them it has spread to us as a result of the excessive love of luxury of a people that has become completely effeminate." Σηρικόν is attested only once in the papyri, in a list of various articles (*P.Oxy.* 1922, 3; fifth century). Moulton-Milligan cites *IG* XIV, 785, 4 (σιρικοποιός); *IG* III², 3513, 2 (σιρικάριος).

silk robes, brought out from the palace armories" (Martial, *Epigr.* 11.8.5). A slave of Marcella, named Thymele, was her *siricaria*, responsible for the wardrobe of *sericae vestes* (*CIL* VI, 9892). Caligula was not afraid to appear in public dressed in silk (*processit aliquando sericatus*), but he was criticized by Suetonius ("dress unworthy of a Roman and even of a human being," *Calig.* 52). In AD 16, a *senatus consultum* forbade men to wear silk (Tacitus, *Ann.* 2.33; Dio Cassius 57.15). It was only in the sixth century that sericiculture was introduced in the West, at least according to Procopius of Gaza: monks from India, knowing how zealously Emperor Justinian tried to keep the Romans from buying silk from their enemies the Persians, explained to the emperor that it was possible to make silk in Roman territory, "because they said that silk was produced by a worm that nature taught the art and compelled to work. . . . These men brought some eggs to Byzantium; they succeeded in transforming them into worms, which they fed mulberry leaves; and so the Romans began to make silk" (*Goth.* 4.17).

σκληροκαρδία, σκληρός, σκληρότης, σκληροτράχηλος, σκληρύνω

sklērokardia, hard-heartedness; *sklēros*, hard, dry, stiff, inflexible, rigid; *sklērotēs*, hardness; *sklērotrachēlos*, stiff-necked; *sklērynō*, to harden

The substantive *skelos* (cf. *skellō*, in the active, "to parch, dry up"; passive, "to be parched, dry") does not exist,[1] but there is *sklēros*, "hard, dry, stiff," often contrasted with *malakos*, "soft, supple." In its literal sense, it is used for stone,[2] for metals and vegetables,[3] for wood,[4] for wind, air, or climate[5]—as in Jas 3:4, where boats of whatever size are driven by

[1] P. Chantraine, *Dictionnaire étymologique*, on σκέλλομαι. Cf. K. Dieterich, "Bedeutungsgeschichte griechischer Worte," in *RhMus*, 1905, pp. 236–240.

[2] Dittenberger, *Or.* 194, 28 (= *SB* 8334): ἐκ σκληροῦ λίθου; *Syl.* 972, 96; *BGU* 952, 10; Wis 11:4; cf. *SB* 3919: ἐπὶ σκληροῦ βαθμοῦ. Cf. Xenophon, *Oec.* 16.11: "The ground was too hard to turn over with the team and plow"; Philo, *Spec. Laws* 3.34: ground too hard and rocky (contrasted with marshy).

[3] *P.Leid.* X, 1: "To get lead to harden, melt it, sprinkle it with flaked alum and vitriol, ground fine and mixed together; and it will be hard" (καὶ ἔσται σλκηρός); cf. 3: hard silver; 80: tin (R. Halleux, *Les Alchimistes grecs*, Paris, 1981, p. 84), wax (Plato, *Tht.* 191 c), hard and resistant (Philo, *Heir* 181). Cf. "among sponges, there are some that are very hard and rough" (Aristotle, *HA* 5.16); water that is "hard" to the taste, like spring water or rainwater (Athenaeus 33 b = 1.59); "pears are costive" (Hippocrates, *Vict.* 2.55.1).

[4] Hippocrates, *Vict.* 2.65.2: "a body hard as wood"; Diogenes Laertius 6.21; a stick (Pindar, *Ol.* 7.29); Philo, *Flight* 42: "hard as an oak"; cf. κοίτης σκληρᾶς = sleeping on a hard surface (Plato, *Leg.* 12.942 d).

[5] Julius Pollux, *Onom.* 1, segm. 110: ἄνεμος βίαιος, σκληρός; Polybius 4.21.5: the harshest climate in all Achaea; Dittenberger, *Or.* 194, 14.

---

sklērokardia, S 4641; *TDNT* 3.613–614; *EDNT* 3.254; *NIDNTT* 2.152, 156, 180, 184; L&N 88.224; BDF §120(4); BAGD 756 ‖ *sklēros*, S 4642; *TDNT* 5.1022–1024, 1028; *EDNT* 3.254; *NIDNTT* 2.153–156; MM 578; L&N 20.3, 76.15, 88.135, 88.136; BAGD 756 ‖ *sklērotēs*, S 4643; *TDNT* 5.1022–1024, 1028–1029; *EDNT* 3.254; *NIDNTT* 2.153, 155; MM 578; L&N 88.223; BAGD 756 ‖ *sklērotrachēlos*, S 4644; *TDNT* 5.1022–1024, 1029; *EDNT* 3.254; *NIDNTT* 2.153, 155; MM 578; L&N 88.224; BAGD 756 ‖ *sklērynō*, S 4645; *TDNT* 5.1022–1024, 1030–1031; *EDNT* 3.254–255; *NIDNTT* 2.153, 155; MM 578; L&N 88.226; BAGD 756

strong winds (*hypo anemōn sklērōn*)—or for crisp and loud claps of thunder (Hesiod, *Th.* 839; Herodotus 8.12). In Hippocrates and Aristotle, the adjective is often used for bones, skin, and various other parts of the body.[6]

In a figurative sense, the word is used to describe style ("forced" metaphors, Dionysius of Halicarnassus, *Pomp.* 1.2.6), difficult circumstances or a cruel fate,[7] but especially for divine cruelty[8] or inflexibility (Sophocles, *OT* 36), for "kings who are kings' sons, who are harsh and inhumane toward their subjects" (*Ep. Arist.* 289; cf. Matt 25:24—"I knew that you were a hard man"), and for people of rigid, forbidding, uncultured character (Plato, *Tht.* 155 *e*; Plutarch, *Cim.* 1.2), where hardness is rusticity.[9]

The first occurrences in the LXX describe speech: that which is not pleasing to an interlocutor and not acceptable,[10] or which is expressed roughly; Joseph spoke harshly to his brothers.[11] The word is also used for

---

[6] Hippocrates, *Carn.* 3.7: "these bones are harder and more solid"; 15.1: "a hard and dry bone"; 12.1: "the teeth become harder than the bones"; *Acut.* 45.2: the body; *Aph.* 5.20; *Liqu.* 1.1; *Carn.* 5.1; *Acut.* append. 49 = hardened skin; *Aph.* 5.52–53: firm breasts (cf. *Genit.* 2.1); *VM* 18: the nose; *Acut.* append. 26.3: a hard inflammation of the eye; *Liqu.* 6.4: dry part; *P.Mert.* 12.21, letter to a physician: dry plasters (AD 58). A papyrus prescribing the diet for patients suffering from chronic constipation: τοῖς μὲν σκληρὰν ἰσχυρῶς καὶ δυσήκεστον ἔχουσι τὴν κοιλίαν (in L. C. Youtie, H. C. Youtie, "A Medical Papyrus," in *Scritti in onore O. Montevecchi*, Bologne, 1981, p. 432, line 5). Aristotle, *HA* 3.10: "the hair is stiffer"; *Part. An.* 3.3.4: the skin is hard; cf. Plato, *Tht.* 162 *b*: "I am already stiff at my age" (contrasted to young); Plutarch, *Ages.* 13.4: "big and strong athlete"; 59275, 9: bitter dishes.

[7] Antiphon 3.3; Euripides, *Alc.* 500; Sophocles, *OC* 1615; Diodorus Siculus 14.105.2: hard conditions of the decision of Dionysius, tyrant of Syracuse. Cf. Acts 26:14—"It is hard for you to kick against the goad," an effort as useless as it is painful.

[8] Aristophanes, *Nub.* 1264; Plutarch, *De def. or.* 21: σκληροὶ θεοί, Anatolian deities; cf. L. Robert, *Hellenica*, vol. 7, Paris, 1949, pp. 50ff.

[9] Σκληρότης is linked with ἀγριότης, ἀγροικία, Plato, *Resp.* 3.410 *d*; 607 *b*; Aristotle, *Poet.* 15.11; *Eth. Nic.* 4.8.

[10] Gen 21:11–12: σκληρὸν ῥῆμα = Sarah asking Abraham to expel Hagar; 45:5, Joseph to his brothers: "Let it not seem to you to be a hard thing (σκληρὸν φαίνεσθαι) to have sold me"; Deut 1:17—τὸ ῥῆμα σκληρὸν = a matter too difficult for you; 15:8; 2 Sam 19:44—"the word of the men of Judah was harder (ἐσκληρύνθη) than the word of the men of Israel"; 2 Kgs 2:10—"You ask me a difficult thing"; Tob 13:12—λόγον σκληρόν. Demetrius: ὁ λόγος σκληρός (in Stobaeus, *Flor.* 3.8.20; vol. 3, p. 345, 17); BGU 140, 14: τοῦτο οὐκ ἐδόκει σκληρὸν εἶναι. All these texts help us understand John 6:60—after the announcement of the Eucharist, "many of his disciples said σκληρός ἐστιν ὁ λόγος οὗτος." An off-putting utterance, hard to accept (with the will; not "difficult to understand"). Likewise Jude 15: "hard (tough, provocative, insolent) words that godless sinners said against the Lord" (περὶ πάντων τῶν σκληρῶν ὧν ἐλάλησαν); cf. 1 Enoch 5.4; 27.2.

[11] Gen 42:7, 30: ἐλάλησεν σκληρά (Hebrew *qāšeh*); 1 Kgs 12:13—reply harshly; 2 Chr 10:13.

hard work (Exod 1:14; 6:9; Deut 26:6; Isa 14:3; Philo, *Moses* 2.183), for hard battle (2 Sam 2:17), and for heavy servitude;[12] but *sklēros* takes on many more varied meanings in classical Greek, being used especially for persons, sometimes in a positive sense,[13] but more often pejoratively.[14] Finally, "hardening" becomes a religious idea, expressing rebellion, disobedience, or rejection of God's will,[15] to be sure, but with the emphasis especially on obstinacy, inflexibility (Cant 8:6). Sir 3:26–27: "The obstinate heart will fall into misfortune"; Isa 48:4—"I knew that you were obstinate, because your neck is made of iron sinews and your forehead is bronze"; Bar 2:33—"They will repent of their stiff neck . . . because they will remember the way of their fathers"; Deut 31:27.

The metaphor of the neck (Hebrew *'ōrep*), the part of the animal body that connects the head to the backbone, is taken from the draft animal, whose efforts to resist are localized in the neck.[16] When the ass or horse refuses to go on, it tightens and stiffens its neck. So to be "hard- or stiff-necked" means stubborn disobedience, hardening or obstinacy in rebellion. To specify this condition, the Bible uses the compounds *sklēro-trachēlos*, six occurrences (out of nine) of which describe Israel,[17] and

---

[12] 1 Kgs 12:4; 2 Chr 10:4; 2 Macc 6:30—"I endure cruel sufferings"; Isa 8:21—a distressed and hungry land; 19:4—a hard master; 21:2—a painful vision (cf. 1 Kgs 14:6—a hard message); Isa 27:8—a fierce blast.

[13] Job 9:4—"Who has remained strong (solid)?"; 22:21; 28:2—"Someone strong and powerful"; David acknowledged, "the sons of Zeruiah are stronger than I" (2 Sam 3:39).

[14] Korah, Dathan, and Abiram were wicked or perverse (Hebrew *rāšā'*) men, Num 16:26; Hannah declares, "I am a woman whose soul is troubled," literally, "pained in spirit" = in great affliction (1 Sam 1:15; quoted by Philo, *Drunkenness* 149–150); for cruel plans (Jdt 9:13). Nabal was a hard (or uncouth) and mean man (σκληρὸς καὶ πονηρός, 1 Sam 25:3; quoted by Josephus, *Ant.* 6.296); μὴ γίνου σκληρός = do not become wicked (Eccl 7:17); cf. Sir 30:8—"an untamed horse becomes stubborn."

[15] Judg 2:19—"The Israelites corrupted themselves and followed a path of hardening" (= hardened conduct); Prov 28:14—"The one who hardens his heart will fall into misfortune" (hiphil of the Hebrew *qāšāh*). Philo, who contrasts harshness and mildness (*Plant.* 133), the smooth and the coarse (*Migr. Abr.* 50; *Abraham* 239; *Creation* 62), denounces rebellious and hard characters (*Spec. Laws* 2.39), hardened and dried out souls (*Rewards* 114), but thinks that habit can make characters lacking in suppleness malleable and can reeducate them (*Spec. Laws* 4.218).

[16] Cf. the French expressions "coup de collier" (put one's back into it); "franc du collier" (hard-working). P. Dhorme, *Emploi métaphorique*, p. 93.

[17] Exod 33:3, 5; 34:9; Deut 9:6, 13; Bar 2:30. A NT hapax, this adjective is uttered by St. Stephen: "People of stiff necks and uncircumcised hearts and ears, you always resist the Holy Spirit" (Acts 7:51; cf. Prov 9:1; Sir 16:11). Hippocrates noted, "Rigidity of neck (τράχηλος σκληρός) is harmful" (*Coac.* 2.14; ed. Littré, vol. 5, p. 640). Philo does not use this term; cf. the substantive σκληροτραχηλία in *T. Sim.* 6.2.

sklērokardia (Hebrew *'ār^elaṯ lēḇāḇ*). A stiff or hard heart resists divine impulses, refuses to follow that path that God wants it to follow. It is not only closed and insensitive, but disobedient.[18] This substantive is used only twice in the NT, and only by Jesus: "It is because of your hardness of heart that Moses allowed you to put away your wives";[19] "Jesus showed himself to the Eleven. . . . He rebuked their unbelief (*apistia*) and hardness of heart, because they had not believed those who saw him raised (from the dead)" (Mark 16:14). *Sklērokardia* adds to simple unbelief in the resurrection the idea of *refusal* to believe in it.

The verb *sklērynō*, unknown in Philo and rather rare in secular Greek,[20] is common in the LXX, where most of the occurrences have a moral and religious meaning:[21] the Israelites stiffen their neck or their heart[22] rather than return to Yahweh and submit to his will. But it is also said that God himself hardens the heart of the Egyptians (Exod 14:17), that of Sihon, king of Heshbon (Deut 2:30), and even that of Israel when they strayed from God's ways (Isa 63:17). The most typical case is that of Pharaoh, whose heart God hardened (Exod 4:21; 7:3; 9:12; 10:1, 20, 27; 11:10; 14:4, 8); but it is likewise said that "Pharaoh's heart was hardened" (Exod 7:22; 8:15; 9:35; 13:15). This simultaneity poses a theological problem, that of the union of divine action and human freedom, which St. Paul did

---

[18] Deut 10:16 (quoted by *Spec. Laws* 1.305); Jer 4:4; Sir 16:10; cf. the adjective σκληροκάρδιος, Prov 17:20; Sir 16:9; Ezek 3:7.

[19] Matt 19:8. Here "hardness of heart" could mean: (1) an inability to understand the indissolubility of marriage; (2) a failure to obey the law established by God "at the beginning"; (3) recalcitrance of soul, tangible bad will, wickedness; (4) for his disciples, Jesus abrogates Moses' temporary concession and reestablishes a law of perfection, because they have purified hearts.

[20] Hippocrates, *Liqu.* 2.7: "the dried-out body hardens"; 6.3; Aristotle, *HA* 5.16.7: "the wind and bad weather hardened the sponges."

[21] K. L. Schmidt, "Die Verstockung des Menschen durch Gott," in *TZ*, 1945, pp. 1–17; F. W. Danker, "Hardness of Heart," in *CTM*, 1973, pp. 89–100. Several secular occurrences, Ps 90:6—grass "withers in the evening, it is dried up"; Gen 49:7—the rage of Simeon and Levi is violent (Hebrew *qāšâh*); Judg 4:24—"The hand of the sons of Israel became harder (grew heavier and heavier) over Jabin, king of the Canaanites"; 2 Chr 10:4; Sir 30:12—"Beat his sides while he is still a child, lest he become hardened and refuse to obey you."

[22] Deut 10:16; 2 Kgs 17:14; 2 Chr 30:8, 29; 36:13; Neh 9:16; Ps 95:8 (quoted and commented on at Heb 3:8, 15; 4:7; cf. C. Spicq, *Hébreux*, vol. 2, p. 73; and Heb 3:13; cf. W. L. Lorimer, "Hébr. III, 13," in *NTS*, vol. 12, 1966, pp. 390–391); Jer 7:26; 17:23; 19:15. In this last text, it is a refusal to hear the word of God, analogous to that of the Jews in the synagogue at Corinth: "As some of them hardened themselves, refused to believe (unbelief, disobedience), and cursed (spoke ill of) the Way (the Christian religion), Paul broke with them" (Acts 19:9). J. Pathrapankal, "Christianity as a 'Way' according to the Acts of the Apostles," in J. Kremer, *Les Actes des Apôtres*, pp. 533–539.

not clarify by stating that "God shows mercy to whom he will and hardens whom he will";[23] but he suggests the solution in Rom 2:5, where he denounces the hardness of the impenitent heart that scorns the infinite treasures of divine goodness. "By your hardening, by your impenitent heart, you are storing up for yourself a treasury of wrath for the day of wrath." God is free in his justice to penalize one who obstinately refuses his light and his mercy. Pharaoh's *sklērotēs* is voluntary;[24] it has blinded him,[25] keeping him from giving in to the prodigious divine signs wrought by Moses. God uses this obstinacy to free his people, because it is his usual course of action to bring good from evil; just as by giving up his Son to crucifixion he gained the salvation of the world. This salvation, like the crucifixion, was decided from eternity.

---

[23] Rom 9:18. We cannot think that this means mere permission (H. H. Hobbs, *Preaching Values from the Papyri*, Grand Rapids, 1964, pp. 115–117, comparing the physician who is not the cause of a hardening in the patient and who adapts himself to the nature of the patient, recognizing his actual condition); still less does God stir people to evil; but taking the person's refusal into account, he does not give him his grace (which is purely gratuitous), which would convert him, because this voluntary hardening corresponds with his plans to show mercy on his people, cf. M. J. Lagrange, *Epître aux Romains*, Paris, 1931, on this text.

[24] In the literal sense, σκληρότης is hardness, roughness. Aristotle distinguishes among physical characteristics "the soft and the hard, the smooth and the rough" (*HA* 1.4.8; 3.3.4); cf. Plato, *Resp.* 7.523 *e*: "Does the sense of touch adequately feel softness and hardness?" In the LXX, it is used for a sledge (Isa 28:27), for the cruelty of death (2 Sam 22:6), and for Israel's unbelief (Deut 9:27). *Sacr. Abel and Cain* 136: "Those who after working receive no knowledge because they are too hardheaded (διὰ σκληρότητα φύσεως) give up on it"; *Spec. Laws* 1.304 comments on uncircumcision of heart: "rebels because of their hardness of character, rebel stubbornly and shake off the yoke."

[25] Concerning the πώρωσις τῆς καρδίας, cf. " 'L'Aveuglement d'esprit,' dans l'Evangile de saint Marc," in *Recueil L. Cerfaux*, vol. 2, pp. 3–15.

σκύβαλον

skybalon, **scrap, debris, refuse, dung, excrement**

It is not easy to translate this NT hapax at Phil 3:8, where St. Paul, renouncing confidence in the flesh, meaning his privileges as a Jew, says they are worthless, to be discarded (*hēgoumai skybala [einai]*),[1] in order to know Christ, gain him, be in him, share in the power of his resurrection.

I. — *Skybalon* often means "scrap, debris, refuse" (*P.Cair.Zen.* 59494, 16; *CPR* I, 175, 16; *PSI* 184, 7: *en skybalois chortou*), gleanings (*P.Ryl.* 149, 22: "grazed them on the gleaings of my vegetable-seed crop"—*katemenēsan aph' hou eichon lachanospermou skybalou*; in AD 39/40), that which remains (*SB* 9386, 49: *synlegontes skybala ergatai* β′ . . . *oboloi* ιβ′) and is given to the dogs,[2] leftovers (*P.Mich.Zen.* 31, 15). This is the meaning intended by Philo in *Sacr. Abel and Cain* 109: "all the rest should be left as refuse (*hōsper skybala*) to the mortal nature"; by Leonidas of Tarentum: "You shall not taste even the leftovers from my dinner" (*Anth. Pal.* 6.202.6); by Ariston: "the crumbs that fall from the table" (ibid. 6.303.4); by Philip of Thessalonica: the remains of a deceased person (ibid. 7.383.2); by Hegesippus: "the wreckage of a ship" (7.276.2; cf. an anony-

---

[1] The old French versions translated "balayure" (sweepings); Loisy, Crampon, and Bonnard: "ordure" (filth); Goguel and Monnier: "rebut" (scrap); Médebielle: "perte" (waste), with the comment "fumier" (dung); *Bible de Jérusalem*: "déchets" (scraps; cf. *NJB*, "filth"); M. Dibelius, J. Gnilka: "Kehricht" (sweepings); F. W. Beare: "rubbish." C. Lavergne (*Diagnose des suffixes grecs du Nouveau Testament*, Paris, 1977, p. 251, 3): "σκύβαλον, a synthetic word built from the phrase ἐς κύνας βλήμενον = thown to the dogs. σκύβαλα in Phil 3:8 = refuse" (French "immondices").

[2] Cf. the *Suda*, τὸ τοῖς κυσὶ βαλλόμενον, κυσίβαλόν τι ὄν. In this sense σκύβαλον would be comparable to περίψημα-περικαθάρματα (1 Cor 4:13), the residue from the scrubbing and cleaning of an object.

---

skybalon, S 4657; *TDNT* 7.445–447; *EDNT* 3.256; *NIDNTT* 1.480; *MM* 579–580; L&N 6.225; BAGD 758

mous writer: "a half-eaten scrap"—*hēmidaes skybalon*, 9.375); Achilles Tatius: "he reviled the catch and threw it out as refuse of the sea" (*eloidorei tēn agran kai erripsen hōs thalassēs skybalon*, 2.11.5); *Sib. Or.* 7.58: "you will be the miserable refuse of war."[3]

II. — *Skybalon* also has the sense "dung, filth" through popular associatiion with *skōr*, according to Moulton-Milligan, who cite *P.Fay.* 119, 7, where Gemellus informs his son that the donkey-driver has purchased "a little bundle and rotten hay, the whole of it decayed—no better than dung" (*mikran dysmēn kai chorton sapron kai holon lelymenon hōs skybalon*, around AD 100). We may compare CD 4.19 ("the builders attached themselves to filth," Hebrew *ṣô'*, in place of *ṣāw; cf.* the LXX, and the Vulgate of Hos 5:11—*sordes*) and find a correspondence with the Hebrew *tô'ēḇâh*, ordinarily translated *bdelygma* ("abomination"), but also *akatharsia* ("uncleanness"), *ponēriai* ("wickedness"), *makrymmata* (something that is sent away because it is repulsive), and *molynsis* ("defilement, pollution").[4] In any event, "Debris and filth accumulate in the nooks and crannies of houses" (*sesōrentai phorytos kai skybalōn plēthos*, Philo, *Prov.* 2.105), and in ethics the term suggests scorn or disgust: "As when the sieve is shaken the scraps (or impurities, *kopria*) remain, so does a person's filth (or uncleanness, *skybala*) remain in his thoughts" (Sir 27:4; OT hapax). Sir 26:28 uses the verb *skybalizō* with respect to intelligent men who are scornfully rejected.

III. — Again, *skybalon* means "excrement," for example in Artemidorus Daldianus (*Onir.* 2.25) and the medical writers (Aelian, *NA* 5.9; other references in Wettstein). This is how the Vulgate (*stercora*) and Symmachus understood the word in Ezek 4:12, 15. The ritual law of whole burnt offerings, as Philo understood it, was that "nothing should remain of the creature except the excrement and the skin" (*skybalōn kai dermatos*). During the siege of Jerusalem, "many dug through the sewers and old cow dung

---

[3] Σκύβαλον πολέμου λυγρὸν ἔσσῃ. Plutarch, *De Is. et Os.* 352 d: "The residue of foods, *the excess of the secretions*, is vile and impure, and it is the result of a secretion that gives rise to wool, fur, hair, nails"; σκυβαλικός in *Them.* 21.4 is a bad reading in one manuscript for κυβαλικοῖσι. —The proper name Σκύβαλος is attested in the third and fourth centuries, *P.Oxy.* 43, col. III, 25; 2338, 30 (correct to Σκυβάλλου at line 28; cf. R. Coles, in *ZPE*, 1975, p. 202); *P.Harr.* 94, 2; *P.Oslo* 61, 8; *P.Michael.* 26, 9; *PSI* 1358, 1: Κοπρέα καὶ Σκύβαλον; cf. M. Vandoni, "Note di onomastica grecoegizia," in *Hommages à Claire Préaux*, Brussels, 1975, p. 797.

[4] This substantive refers to that which is defective, has a fault or vice, that which is considered impure . . . and for that reason inspires disgust, horror, aversion, is blamed and cursed" (P. Humbert, "L'Etymologie du substantif tô'ébâ," in A. Kuschke, *Verbannung und Heimkehr*, Tübingen, 1961, pp. 157–160).

in order to feed on this ordure; what they would have been unable to loc
at before became food for them."[5]

IV. — In any event, the word means what must be eliminated.[6] J. Hub
comment is exactly right, in spite of the anachronism: "All of that is wo
no more than the contents of a garbage can."[7] To convey the crudit
the Greek, however: "It's all crap."[8]

---

[5] Josephus, *War* 5.571. Hesychius gives this definition: σκύβαλα· κόπρος; the
equation is made in Sir 27:4 and Didymus, *Zech.* 1.390, 394; cf. "lump of excre
(βολβίτῳ κοπρίων), a term for the lazy (Sir 22:2), the euphemism ἀσχημοσύν
23:14; Philo, *Alleg. Interp.* 3.151, 158 = ἀκαθαρσία; 2.27, 29. But κόπρια refers
in Luke 13:8; 14:35; Heraclitus, *All.* 33.6: "Heracles got rid of the large pile of manuⅼᴄ,
the disgusting condition in which humanity was stagnating"; similarly, the alche-
mists used κόπρος and βόλβιτον together (cf. M. Berthelot, *Collection des anciens
alchimistes grecs*, 2d ed., London, 1962, vol. 3, 165, 14; 167, 8; 199, 13; 317, 1 and 142,
19; 146, 15; 221, 22; 222, 13).

[6] Cf. Mark 7:19; Plautus, *Truc.* 556: "amator, qui bona sua pro stercore habet"—"a
lover who treats his goods as dung has them taken out . . . all that he has is swept
outside."

[7] "Tout cela ne vaut pas plus que le contenu d'une poubelle," J. Huby, *Les Epîtres
de la captivité*, Paris, 1934, p. 335.

[8] The translation of E. Osty, "Pour une traduction plus fidèle du N. T.," in *Ecole
de langues orientales anciennes: Mémorial du Cinquantenaire*, Paris, 1964, p. 82: "c'est de
la crotte." Also Lang, in *TDNT*, vol. 7, pp. 446–447 ("Dreck"); M. Dibelius, *An die
Philipper*, 3d ed., Tübingen, 1937, p. 89; E. Lohmeyer, *Der Brief an die Philipper*, 12th
ed., Göttingen, 1961, pp. 135ff. The idea and the word were retained in the patristic
and ascetic tradition (*stercus, lutum*, βόρβορος = mire) to refer to the world, its allure
and its vanity (P. Courcelle, "Les Sources patristiques de Sacy," in *SP*, vol. 4, Berlin,
1961, pp. 401ff.). On the verbs σκυβαλίζω and ἀνασκυβαλίζω in the inscriptions, cf.
J. and L. Robert, "Bulletin épigraphique," in *REG*, 1977, p. 400, n. 423.

σκωληκόβρωτος

skōlēkobrōtos, **worm-eaten**

This compound, which means literally "worm food," i.e., "eaten by worms," belongs to the agricultural vocabulary and is used for plants, trees, fruits, especially grains (Theophrastus, *Hist. Pl.* 3.12.6; 4.11.1; *Caus. Pl.* 5.9.1). It is attested in five or six papyri, all from before Christ. Eudemos asks Zeno to decrease the rent because the harvest has been eaten by worms (*eisig gar hēmin skōlēkobrōtou kai kakou sitou [arourai]* ιε΄, *P.Cair.Zen.* 59433, 14; cf. *Berichtigungsliste* IV, p. 16); ibid. 59728, 5: "worm-eaten corpses" (*tēn skōlēkobrōton sōmata*); *P.Mich.Zen.* 96, 4: "that has become worm-eaten" (*tēs gegenēmenēs skōlēkobrōtou*, referring to sesame seed); *PSI* 490, 4: *tēn genomenēn skōlēkobrōton apokechōrēkasin enkataleipontes tous geōrgountas tēn gēn* (a letter concerning a crop guardian); *P.Grad.* VII, 11: "seed that is not worm-eaten" (*spermatos askōlēkobrōtou*); *P.Tebt.* 701, 74 and 81: "for the worm-eaten ground" (*eis tēn skōlēkobrōton gēn*; cf. the possible restoration in 1008, 18). In 5/4 BC, *P.Oslo* 26, 14 attests the neologism *holoskōlēkobrōtos*.

Since in the Bible "the punishment of the ungodly is the fire and the worm" (Sir 7:17; cf. Isa 66:24 = Mark 9:48), especially worms (Isa 14:11; Sir 19:3; 1 Macc 2:62), which symbolize human emptiness (Job 7:5; 25:6) and the decay and decomposition of corpses (Job 17:14; 21:26; Sir 10:11), Acts 12:23 uses *skōlēkobrōtos* for Herod Agrippa: "he was eaten by worms and died." For all that, this is not a medical term;[1] but in the secular and

---

[1] Against W. K. Hobart, *Medical Language*, p. 42; refuted by Lang, on this word in *TDNT,* vol. 7, pp. 456–457; cf. H. J. Cadbury, *Book of Acts in History,* pp. 38, 54 n. 14. But this could be a case of helminthiasis, cf. Lesêtre, on this word, in *Dictionnaire de la Bible,* vol. 3, pp. 583–585 (helminths are entozoans that take up residence in the intestines, but also in the blood, the muscles, the liver, etc., and can cause fatal illness); *Deutsche medizinische Wochenschrift,* 1963, pp. 287ff. W. Otto, "Herodes," in PWSup, vol. 2, 143.

---

skōlēkobrōtos, S 4662; TDNT 7.456–457; EDNT 3.256; MM 580; L&N 23.166; BAGD 758

religious literature it is used for the death of villains, like Judas (according to Papias)[2] and an uncle (also named Julian) of Julian the Apostate,[3] false prophets like Alexander (Lucian, *Alex.* 59), cruel rulers like Pheretima, queen of the Cyrenians ("still alive, she was crawling with worms," Herodotus 4.205); Sulla, who had a purulent intestinal abscess and an infection that caused his flesh to swarm with vermin (Plutarch, *Sull.* 36.3–4); Pherecydes (Aelian, *VH* 4.28); Herod the Great (Josephus, *Ant.* 17.169); and especially persecutors, from Antiochus IV Epiphanes ("the ungodly man's eyes were crawling with worms," 2 Macc 9:9) and L. Hermianus, the governor of Cappadocia (Tertullian, *Scap.* 3) to Emperor Galerius ("his intestines were crawling with countless worms").[4]

---

[2] Cf. P. Benoit, in *Exégèse et théologie*, vol. 1, p. 345 = ET, vol. 1, pp. 193–194.

[3] Theodoret, *Hist. Eccl.* 3.9.

[4] Eusebius, *Hist. Eccl.* 8.16.4 (most of these examples are cited by E. Jacquier, *Actes*, p. 374); cf. Lactantius, *Mort. Pers.*

σπερμολόγος

spermologos, seed-gatherer, gleaner, prattler, buffoon

At Athens, Paul dialogued (dialegomai, Acts 17:17) with the idlers that he met at the agora (cf. agoraios, 17:5; 19:38), who asked, using Athenian slang, "What does this spermologos mean?" (17:18). It is impossible to give the exact connotations of this biblical hapax, a word unknown in the papyri and, it seems, in the inscriptions as well. It is often translated "prattler, speechifier, driveler." But the etymology is clear: sperma legein means to gather seeds or grains.[1] So as a noun, it refers to sparrows and other birds that peck at seeds scattered on the ground[2] and is in no way pejorative. Used figuratively, however, the word takes on more diverse meanings: the good-for-nothing who wanders about the market and collects the scraps and debris scattered here and there; cf. Demosthenes: "The accuser . . . a miserable gleaner (spermologos), an outcast from the marketplace" (Corona 18.127); or the prattler, chatterer who is always hunting for news and spreading it everywhere, running his mouth carelessly, who pretends to be in the know but actually spouts his gossip without understanding it: an ignoramus. This highly derogatory meaning is the most commonly attested sense of the word in the first-second century. Philo:

---

[1] Cf. Hesychius, Σπερμολόγος· φλύαρος, καὶ ὁ τὸ σπέρματα συλλέγων, καὶ κολοιῶδες ζῶον.

[2] Aristotle (HA 8.3.28.592b) includes among the birds "the wren and the rook (σπερμολόγος)," a variety of crow with a narrow beak, scientifically called Corvus frugilegus; Aristophanes, Av. 232: "Innumerable tribes of barley-eaters (κριθοτράγων), races of seed-peckers (σπερμολόγων)"; 579: "A cloud of sparrows must arise to peck at the seeds"; Artemidorus Daldianus, Onir. 2.20: "the small birds peck at the seeds (σπερμολόγοι) and thus find their food easily." Synonymous with σπερμονόμος in insults εἰς ἀτοραίους καὶ πολυπράγμονας καὶ φιλεγκλήμονας; cf. J Taillardat, Suétone: Περὶ Βλασφημιῶν, Paris, 1967, p. 57.

---

spermologos, S 4691; EDNT 3.264; NIDNTT 3.525; MM 583; L&N 27.19, 33.381; BDF §119(1); BAGD 762

"Helicon, a slave of high lineage, a seed-pecker and outcast from society" (*To Gaius* 203); Plutarch: Alcibiades is accused of abandoning the command of the fleet to "men who owe their influence to their drunkenness and buffoonery (*spermologias*)," (*Alc.* 36.2; cf. Plutarch, *Demetr.* 28.5); "When the soul founders, anger casts aside a jumble of violent, unrestrained words."[3]

Given this definition, which makes the word almost an insult, it is difficult to understand how the Epicurean and Stoic philosophers could immediately afterward lead Paul to the middle of Mars Hill and ask him to expound his teaching before the assembly. M. A. Robinson[4] suggests that Paul must have used the parable of the sower and that this accounts for the use of the word.[5] Hence the play on words, which does not ridicule the preacher but takes aim at his teaching in a humorous way. It is best to translate *spermologos* as "this character."[6]

---

[3] Plutarch, *De cohib. ira* 6. The meaning "gossip" in Lynceus of Samos and Alexander of Myndos, in Athenaeus 8.22 (344 *c*); 9.39 (388 *a*); Dionysius of Halicarnassus 19.5.3. Wettstein cites in addition Maximus of Tyre 30.4 and Strabo 15, p. 1030. —This accounts for the proposed etymology σπείρω + λόγους, sower of words.

[4] M. A. Robinson, "Σπερμολόγος: Did Paul Preach from Jesus' Parables?" in *Bib*, 1975, pp. 231–240.

[5] According to the interpretation given by Jesus and according to a source anterior to Mark 4, which would be Peter (cf. Papias, in Eusebius, *Hist. Eccl.* 3.39.15).

[6] J. Renié, *Actes des Apôtres*, "ce pierrot." The *NJB* translates "this parrot," which overplays lack of intelligence; E. Osty and J. Trinquet translate "ce picoreur" and comment: "a derogatory term for any speechifier whose knowledge is made up of bits and pieces of doctrine gathered here and there and everywhere." Cf. "superfluous refinements due to frivolity" (ταῦτα περίεργα καὶ σπερμολογικά, Plutarch, *Quaest. conv.* 4, q. 1).

σπιλάς

spilas, **gust, squall, (under-sea) rock, boulder**

Jude 12: *houtoi eisin hoi en tais agapais hymōn spilades.*[1] This can be translated "These people are stumbling blocks in your love feasts" or "These people are stains on your love feasts."[2] The biblical hapax *spilas*, unknown in the papyri, can mean "gust, squall,"[3] but the predominant classical meaning is "rock, boulder"; cf. Sophocles, *Trach.* 678: "it dissolved on a rock on the ground"; Theocritus: "an inexhaustible, voiceless stream from the rocks";[4] "Here, beneath this sepulchral rock, O stranger, lies

---

[1] The reading ἀγάπαις (ℵ, B, K, L, 𝔓72, Vulg., Sah., Boh., Arm., Eth.) is preferable to ἀπάταις (A, C, 44, 56, 96), which comes from 2 Pet 2:13 (cf. E. M. Laperrousaz, "Le Testament de Moïse," in *Sem* vol. 19, 1970, p. 65) and εὐωχίαις (miniscules, 6, 66). On *agapai*, cf. P. Batiffol, "Agape," in *Dictionnaire de théologie catholique*, vol. 1, 551–556; idem, *Etudes d'histoire et de théologie positive*, Paris, 1926, pp. 283–325; H. Leclerq, "Agape," in *DACL*, vol. 1, 775–848; L. Thomas, "Agape," in *DBSup*, vol. 1, 134–153 (supplies the bibliography); E. B. Allo, *Première Epître aux Corinthiens*, pp. 285–293; C. Spicq, *Agapè*, vol. 2, pp. 345–351; J. Jeremias, *Eucharistic Words*, pp. 115–122; J. J. von Allmen, *Essai sur le repas du Seigneur*, Neuchâtel, 1966, pp. 65ff.

[2] On the basis of St. Augustine and Erasmus ("in dilectionibus vestris," "inter charitates vestres"), some translate "They are stumbling blocks for your love"; but it is a bit of a stretch to translate ταῖς ἀγάπαις with a singular.

[3] A definition defended by A. D. Knox ("Σπιλάδες," in *JTS*, 1913, pp. 547–549; 1915, p. 78), from Plutarch (*De virt. et vit.* 3; Plutarch, *De tranq. anim.* 17; cf. Heliodorus, *Aeth.* 5.32.1: "the sea whipped up by a cyclone"), confirmed by the usage of the verb κατασπιλάζω (in Philo, *Quest. Gen.* 2.71, ed. R. Marcus, p. 165, n. i, R. Harris, p. 28; pointed out by H. S. Jones, *JTS*, 1922, p. 282); still the meaning in modern Greek: "violent wind, storm-wind, tempest"; cf. M. M. Kokolakis, Πλουταρχεῖα, Athens, 1968.

[4] In *Anth. Pal.* 9.437.6; Simonides: a priest of Rhea took refuge in a cave, literally under an isolated rock, ἐρημαίνην ἤλυθ' ὑπὸ σπιλάδα (ibid. 6.217.2); Philip of Thessalonica: "peace in the shelter of a wild rock" (ibid. 7.382, 4). In the first century,

---

spilas, S 4694; *EDNT* 3.265; MM 583–584; L&N 79.57; BAGD 762

Demas."[5] Usually, *splidades* are rocks that are covered by water and thus dangerous: "the waves smashed their ships on the reefs" (Homer, *Od.* 3.298); "the narrow strait . . . hemmed in by narrow reefs" (Apollonius Rhodius, *Argon.* 2.550; cf. 558); "the vessels, smashed by the waves against the reefs and promontories" (Polybius 1.37.2). In the area around the port of Jaffa, "there is a series of steep cliffs and reefs jutting far out into the water."[6] This meaning is reported by all the lexicographers: "*spilades* are rocks under the sea . . . rocks hidden by the sea" (*spilades hai hyphalos petrai . . . hai hypo thalassan kekrymmenai petrai, Etymol. Mag.*); "Apion says that *spilades* are rocks that form a hollow in the sea, but Heliodoros says they are rocks beside the sea that the waters wash over."[7] J. Pollux sums up precisely: "*spilas*, a reef, a hidden boulder, a stone, a jutting rock, a promontory, a prominence exposed to the wind, a knoll" (*Onom.* 1.9.115). In Jude 12, where a moral portrait of godless folk who slander the way of righteousness is being sketched, the metaphor is excellent; it suggests the pernicious influence of false teachers in promiscuity at banquets. They present a danger of shipwreck, scandal, or ensnarement for believers.[8]

The use of the masculine article *hoi* [*spiloi?*] with the feminine *spilades* suggestes that there might have been a popular confusion of this word with *spilos* ("stain on the skin," and by extension any physical or moral stain).[9] This is how the Vulgate interprets this text ("maculae"). The

a man throws himself from a rock, ὀστέα μὲν καὶ σάρκας ἐμὰς σπιλάδες διέχευαν ἐξεῖαι (G. Kaibel, *Epigrammata* 225, 1).

[5] Jewish epitaph from 117 BC: ῟Ωδ' ὑπὸ τὸ σπιλάδος μέλαθρον, *SEG* VIII, 483, 1 = *SB* 6160 = *CII* 1490 = *C.Pap.Jud.* III, p. 152 = *GVI*, n. 700 = E. Bernand, *Inscriptions métriques*, n. 14.

[6] Josephus, *War* 2.420; Lucillius: "For ships that sail on the sea, submerged rocks are more dangerous than those that are plain to see" (τῶν φανερῶν σπιλάδων, *Anth. Pal.* 11.390, 6); cf. E. Hilgert, *The Ship and Related Symbols in the New Testament*, Assen, 1962, pp. 145ff.

[7] Σπιλάδες, ὁ μὲν Ἀπίων αἱ ἐν ὕδατι κοιλαὶ πέτραι· ὁ δὲ Ἡλιόδωρος αἱ παραθαλάσσιαι πέτραι, καὶ πεπιλημέναι ὑπὸ τῶν ὑδάτων. Apollonius Sophista, *Lex.* (this reference and the one before it given by J. Chaine, *Les Épîtres catholiques*, Paris, 1939, p. 315); cf. Hesychius: Σπιλάδες· αἱ πειερχόμεναι τῇ θαλάσσῃ πέτραι; the *Suda*: Σπιλάδες· αἱ ἐν ὕδατι κοῖλαι πέτραι.

[8] Cf. 1 Tim 1:19. Cf. 1QH 4.10–19: "Teachers of lies and seers of falsehood" address seductive words to the members of the people of God and "to assuage their thirst they give them vinegar (Hebrew *ḥōmeṣ*, a numbing drink) to drink, so that (once they are drunk with this denatured doctrine) they may gaze on their straying and their folly concerning the festivals," i.e., so that they may sin, act insanely.

[9] 2 Pet 2:13—greedy teachers are similarly insulted: "Stains and blemishes (σπίλοι καὶ μῶμοι), reveling in their dissipation, they carouse" (cf. Bo Reicke, *Diakonie, Festfreude und Zelos in Verbindung mit der altchristlichen Agapenfeier*, Uppsala,

272   σπιλάς, spilas

Orphic text *Lithica* 614 is cited: the good woman is "speckled with stains" (*katastiktos spiladessi*). This meaning would make the text less forceful.[10] In any event, the meal of brotherly love in the Christian community requires greater holiness than the *nomos eranistōn* from the imperial period: "Let no one enter into the most venerable meeting of the dinner club before he has been examined for purity, piousness, and goodness."[11]

1951, pp. 354–367); Eph 5:27; cf. σπιλόω, "make a mark" (Wis 15:4), then "a stain" (Jude 23; Jas 3:6).

[10] Cf. in the fourth century the participation of a pagan in a Christian *agapē* under deplorable circumstances: ἐποίησεν δὲ καὶ ἀγάπην ἐν ἐκίνῃ τῇ ἡμέρᾳ, Ἕλλην ὢν, διὰ τὸ ἁμάρτημα ὃ ἐποίησεν (*P.Lond.* 1914, 28; cf. H. I. Bell, *Jews and Christians in Egypt*, p. 59).

[11] Μηδενὶ ἐχέστω ἐπιέναι εἰς τὴν συμνοτάτην σύνοδον τῶν ἐρανιστῶν, πρὶν ἂν δικομασθῇ ἐι ἔστι ἄγνος καὶ εὐσεβὴς καὶ ἀγαθός, published by P. Foucart, *Des Associations religieuses chez les Grecs*, Paris, 1873, p. 202.

σπλάγχνα, σπλαγχνίζομαι

splanchna, entrails, viscera, compassion; *splanchnizomai,* to have compassion, take pity

In the fifth-fourth century, *splanchna* meant the internal parts of a sacrificial victim,[1] mentioned in cultic regulations as part of the compensation of priests and priestesses,[2] so that the verb *splanchnizō* meant "consume the entrails."[3] This means the honorable parts, of course, since the word is also applied to humans,[4] in whom seven viscera are enumerated (Philo, *Alleg. Interp.* 1.12; *Drunkenness* 106; cf. *Spec. Laws* 1.62): "the internal parts are called viscera, these being the stomach, the heart, the lungs, the spleen, the liver, and the two kidneys" (*Creation* 118). The word is also used for the intestines (*Abraham* 241) or the stomach area in general without any anatomical precision.[5]

---

[1] *SEG* XVII, 377 (Chios); 378 (Chios); Dittenberger, *Syl.* 57, 3; 1013, 3, 8; 1015, 12; 1016, 3; 1044, 39; etc.

[2] Cf. *LSCGSup,* n. 76, 3; 77, 6; 78, 5; *LSCG* n. 120, 10; 125, 4; 135, 89; 151 A-33; D 10, 12; Philo, *Spec. Laws* 1.216.

[3] The only attestation of the active voice of the verb in secular Greek: a cultic calendar at Cos, fourth century (*LSCG,* n. 151, *D,* 14); 2 Macc 6:8—take part in a ritual meal.

[4] Koester ("σπλάγχνον," in *TDNT,* vol. 7, p. 548) cites the *Corpus Fabularum Aesopicarum* XLVII, 1 (292, ed. E. Chambry), where a boy who has eaten too much *splanchna* says, " 'Mother, I am vomiting my entrails'; but she said, 'Not your entrails, child, but the ones you ate!' " (ὦ μῆτερ, ἐμῶ τὰ σπλάγχνα· ἡ δὲ εἶπεν, οὐχὶ τὰ σά, τέκνον, ἃ δὲ κατέφαγες).

[5] In the Bible, the entrails stand for whatever is deepest and most intimate (Prov 26:22, Hebrew *beṭen;* cf. Ps 22:15; 40:9; John 7:37); Bar 2:17—the spirit of the deceased has left his entrails; 2 Macc 5:5-6: intestinal pain; Acts 1:18—Judas' entrails spilled out; 4 Macc 5:30; 10:8; 11:19—the entrails are burned or pierced through and drip with blood; Josephus, *Ant.* 15.359 (in the singular); *War* 2.612: "Joseph had them whipped until their entrails showed through"; Menander, *Dysk.* 548: "I cut out the entrails"; *P.Ryl.* 63, 6 (astrological text from the third century), the entrails are the province of Jupiter; *SB* 7452, 23: τῶν τριχῶν καὶ τῶν σπλάγχνων αὐτῆς. In an epitaph

---

splanchna, S 4698; *TDNT* 7.548-559; *EDNT* 3.265-266; *NIDNTT* 2.593, 599-560; MM 584; L&N 8.58, 25.49, 25.50, 25.54, 25.55, 26.11; BAGD 763 ‖ *splanchnizomai,* S 4697; *TDNT* 7.548-559; *EDNT* 3.265; *NIDNTT* 2.599-600; MM 584; L&N 25.49; BDF §§108(3), 176(1), 229(2), 233(2), 235(2); BAGD 762

The emotions are located in the entrails—since they are what is most intimate and hidden (*Post. Cain* 118; cf. Josephus, *War* 4.263)—which are therefore synonymous with what we today call the "heart": "I suffer in my stomach and in my entrails" (*tēn koilian mou kai ta splanchna mou ponō, Pss. Sol.* 2.15); "Abraham, moved to the depths of his entrails, began to weep" (*T. Abr.* A 3, 5); "The consumption reaches to the entrails, causing through its oppression despair and distress."[6] When Aseneth falls in love at the first sight of Joseph, her entrails are smitten (*Jos. Asen.* 6.1), just as the entrails of the father are disturbed with each cry from his son (Sir 30:7), for children are said to be their father's entrails (*hoi paides splanchna legontai*, Artemidorus Daldianus, *Onir.* 1.44; Philo, *Joseph* 25; 4 Macc 14:13). But the entrails of the foolish are also said to be unstable (Sir 33:5), and blows to the entrails cause suffering (Philo, *To Gaius* 368). The nuance of pity is attested in 5 BC (*hyper splanchnou* = through pity, *BGU* 1139, 17).

This last meaning, unusual in secular Greek,[7] is the predominant one in the Bible (cf. Prov 12:10; Wis 10:5), especially in the NT, where the entrails (corresponding to the Hebrew *raḥᵃmîm*) are the seat of compassion (Gen 43:30; 1 Kgs 3:26; Jer 31:20). The feminine singular *reḥem*, moreover, refers to the uterus, the mother's womb; so that the entrails are the locus of the mother's pity for her children (Isa 49:15) and are said to shudder (Isa 16:11; Cant 5:4), to resound and make noise (Isa 43:15), to bubble or seethe (Lam 1:20), or to be in turmoil.[8] It follows that in the Synoptics, where this compassion is twice attributed to God (Matt 18:27; Luke 15:20), once to the Good Samaritan, and nine times to Christ—almost always to

---

[6] Philo, *Rewards* 151; cf. Aeschylus, *Cho.* 413; Sophocles, *Aj.* 995: "the most painful path to my entrails"; Euripides, *Hipp.* 118 (rage); Euripides, *Med.* 220; Aristophanes, *Ran.* 844: "do not overheat your entrails with anger"; 1006: "my entrails are indignant at having to speak to this man"; *Nub.* 1036: "I was suffocating to the depths of my entrails, impatient to overturn these arguments"; Geminus calls love "the god that he carries in his heart" (*Anth. Pal.* 6.260.6); cf. Koester, *TDNT,* vol. 7, p. 549.

[7] It is found late (fifth-sixth century) in *P.Fuad I Univ.* 43, 6 (a theological fragment); *C.P.Herm.* 16, 4: "I beg you to take pity" (cf. the editor's note); *P.Flor.* 296, 23: οὐκ ἐσπλαγχνίσθη ὁ εἰρημένος; *SB* 9402, 6: ὑπὸ τῶν σπλάγχνων μου. But according to biblical language, God says: "Abraham is without pity for the sinner (οὐ σπλαγχνίζεται), whereas I am full of mercy for them (ἐγὼ σπλαγχνίζομαι)" (*T. Abr.* B 12); "Let us be patient until the Lord takes pity and has mercy on us" (σπλαγχνισθεὶς ἐλεήσῃ ἡμᾶς, *T. Job* 26.5).

[8] Job 30:27; cf. P. Dhorme, *Emploi métaphorique*, p. 111ff., 134ff. P. Lacau, *Les Noms des partie du corps en Egyptien et en Sémitique*, Paris, 1970, 219; G. Schmuttermayr, "RHM—Eine lexikalische Studie," in *Bib*, 1970, pp. 499-532.

from the imperial period, Termion suspects that she has been poisoned: "If anyone has ever launched against my entrails or my life the miserable furies of poison" (ibid. 8960, 7 = *GVI,* 1875 = L. Robert, *Hellenica,* vol. 2, pp. 121ff.)

account for a miracle—the word means first of all a physical emotion, true compassion in the face of a neighbor's misery,[9] literally a movement of the entrails at the sight.[10] So translating the passive *esplanchnisthē* as "he took pity" is almost opposite the true sense; "he was taken by (or moved with) pity" would be better. The exact sense is "he had a visceral feeling of compassion."

The affective quality of the entrails is much emphasized by Paul: whereas the entrails of the Corinthians are constricted, those of Titus are open and go out to the believers (2 Cor 6:12; 7:15); Philemon has calmed the entrails of Christians under trial (Phlm 7; cf. verse 20. The apostle loves Onesimus as his own entrails (*tout' estin ta ema splanchna*, verse 12), hence as his own child; and he loves the believers in the entrails of Christ (*epipothō pantas hymas en splanchnois Christou Iēsou*, Phil 1:8). This tender compassion is almost hypostasized;[11] every Christian must be clothed in it,[12] for it is the expression of brotherly love, with strong connotations of mercy.[13]

The compound *eusplanchnos* (Eph 4:32; 1 Pet 3:8) should not be translated "benevolent, good-hearted"; it is intensive. But whereas in secular Greek having good or strong entrails means being courageous,[14] in Christian terms it means to be tenderly merciful, compassionate: "so display your innate love and compassion and tenderness."[15] Jas 5:11 coins a new word for this: having long or abundant entrails (*polysplanchnos estin ho Kyrios kai oiktirmōn*), the equivalent of *polyeleos* (Ps 102:8; *SB* 8726, 9).

---

[9] Luke 10:33 (E. Höhne, "Zum neutestamentlichen Sprachgebrauch," in *ZWKL*, 1882, p. 10); cf. Matt 15:32 (Mark 8:2); 18:27; 20:34; Mark 1:41 (L. Vaganay, "Marc I, 41: Essai de critique textuelle," in *Mélanges E. Podechard*, Lyon, 1945, pp. 237–252); Mark 8:2; 9:22.

[10] Matt 9:36—ἰδὼν . . . ἐσπλαγχνίσθη; 14:14; Luke 7:13; 10:33; 15:20; cf. 1 John 3:17.

[11] God is said to cast his entrails upon the earth: ὁ θεὸς ἀποστελεῖ τὰ σπλάγχνα αὐτοῦ ἐπὶ τῆς γῆς καὶ ὅπου εὕρη σπλάγχνα ἐλέους, ἐν αὐτῷ κατοικεῖ (*T. Zeb.* 8.2); ἄχρις οὗ ἔλθη τὸ σπλάγχνον Κυρίου (*T. Naph.* 4.5; cf. *T. Levi* 4.14).

[12] Col 3:12—σπλάγχνα οἰκτιρμοῦ; cf. Phil 2:1—εἴ τις σπλάγχνα καὶ οἰκτιρμοί (cf. C. Spicq, *Agapè*, vol. 2, pp. 252ff.). The most common Greek equivalent for the Hebrew *raḥᵃmîm* is οἰκτιρμοί; but the Hebrew explains the Greek plural (cf. 2 Cor 1:3).

[13] Cf. Luke 1:78—διὰ σπλάγχνα ἐλέους θεοῦ ἡμῶν; *T. Zeb.* 7.2—σπλαγχνιζόμενοι ἐλεᾶτε; 7.3—συμπάσχετε αὐτῷ ἐν σπλάγχνοις ἐλέους. 1 John 3:17 denounces the rich person who sees the need of the poor person and nevertheless "shuts his entrails" (cf. C. Spicq, *Agapè*, vol. 3, pp. 261ff.).

[14] Euripides, *Rhes.* 192; cf. ἄσπλαγχνος, "cowardly" (Sophocles, *Aj.* 472); Chrysippus, in *SVF*, vol. 2, 249, 12ff.); cf. our expressions "to have guts," "to have no guts."

[15] *P.Lond.* 1916, 31; cf. Pr Man 7: Κύριος ὕψιστος εὔσπλαγχνος, μακρόθυμος καὶ πολυέλεος. A Roman funerary inscription: ἱερός, εὐσπλάγχνος, φιλόξενος (in *IGUR*, II, n. 411). Ὑπὸ τὴν σὴν εὐσπλαγχνίαν (*P.Ryl.* 470: a prayer to the Virgin Mary; cf. J. van Haelst, *Catalogue des papyrus littéraires juifs et chrétiens*, Paris, 1976, p. 314, n. 983).

σπουδάζω, σπουδαῖος, σπουδαίως, σπουδή

spoudazō, to hasten, apply oneself, devote oneself; *spoudaios*, hasty, diligent, virtuous; *spoudaiōs*, hastily, diligently; *spoudē*, haste, urgency, zeal, diligence, gravity, seriousness

---

It is not easy to specify the exact meaning of these terms, which were common in classical and Hellenistic Greek and which translators of the NT almost always take to mean "zeal, urgency." They are absent from Matthew and John.

I. — The idea of "haste, rapidity, alacrity" is in the forefront, with no psychological or moral connotation. "When the sun rose, the angels urged Lot to leave" (Gen 19:15; hiphil of the Hebrew *'ûṣ*); "The servants hurried to leave";[1] the shepherds hastened to Bethlehem (Luke 2:16); "Hasten to come to me, quickly" (*spoudason elthein pros me, techeōs*, 2 Tim 4:9; cf. *BGU* 2349, 5). A meaning well-attested in the papyri: "That has to be sped up" (*P.Panop.Beatty* 2, 78; cf. 218); "Please, sister, hurry to make my tunic" (*P.Fuad I Univ.* VI, 15); "Hurry to go and find my uncle's wife."[2] This is

---

[1] Jdt 13:1. Almost all the other occurrences correspond to the niphal of the Hebrew *bāhal*, "be prompt, arrive suddenly" (Eccl 8:3), with a nuance of suddenness and violence (Isa 21:3); hence "be frightened" (Job 4:5; 21:6; 22:10; 23:15–16).

[2] *P.Fouad* 85, 10: Σπούδασον ἀπελθεῖν πρὸς τὴν γαμετὴν τοῦ κυρίου μου Θίου (note the frequency of the aorist imperative in the epistolary papyri and the construction of σπουδάζω with the infinitive: σπούδασον ποιῆσαι, *SB* 9875, 7; cf. E. Mayser, *Grammatik*, vol. 2, 3, p. 49, n. 1); *P.Corn.* 52, 9: "Hasten to reply to me"; *P.Mich.* 516, 5: "Hurry to set sail"; *P.Mert.* 85, 18: "I want very urgently to hear news from you" (πολὺ σπουδάζω μαθεῖν); *P.Mil.Vogl.* 291, 8 (republished in *SB* 9160); 255, 4 (republished ibid. 9654 *a*); *P.Princ.* 100, 8; 106, 1; *P.Oslo* 88, 26; 162, 13; *P.Oxy.* 2229, 3; Menander, *Dysk.* 148: "Such haste!"; Josephus, *Ant.* 15.119; *War* 2.559; cf. σπουδή,

---

spoudazō, S 4704; *TDNT* 7.559–568; *EDNT* 3.266; *NIDNTT* 3.1168–1169; MM 585; L&N 25.74, 68.63, 68.79; BDF §§77, 392(1*a*); BAGD 763 ‖ *spoudaios*, S 4705; *TDNT* 7.559–568; *EDNT* 3.267; *NIDNTT* 3.1168–1169; MM 585; L&N 25.75, 25.75, 68.65; BDF §§102(1), 244(2); BAGD 763 ‖ *spoudaiōs*, S 4709; *EDNT* 3.267; MM 585; L&N 68.79; BAGD 763 ‖ *spoudē*, S 4710; *TDNT* 7.559–568; *EDNT* 3.267; *NIDNTT* 3.1168–1169; MM 585–586; L&N 25.74, 68.63, 68.79; BAGD 763–764

sometimes the meaning of the adjective *spoudaios* (*P.Brem.* 48, 28) and almost always that of the substantive *spoudē* in the LXX: "You shall eat the lamb in haste."[3] The usage of the Koine is similar, whether in literary texts[4] or (more rarely) in the papyri: "I sailed hastily for Alexandria" (*P.Mich.* 503, 2); "Please carry out the brickyard work as quickly as possible" (*P.Sorb.* 63, 2); "I wrote you quickly."[5] The only NT use of the word in this sense is perhaps Mark 6:45, where Salome, after asking her mother's advice, returned "at once, in haste"; but here there seems to be a psychological nuance,[6] just as the Virgin Mary's departing "with alacrity" (Luke 1:39) means not only "hastily" but "with fervor."

II. — In effect, *spoudazō* with an impersonal object means above all "apply oneself to, actively involve oneself with" and with a personal object "devote oneself to, take the part of."[7] In the papyri, the meaning "deal with, take care of" is predominant,[8] often with connotations of going to some

---

7.190; *Ant.* 7.223; Plutarch, *Ti. Gracch.* 4.3: "Why this haste? Why this rush?"; Diodorus Siculus 17.118.2.

[3] Exod 12:11, μετὰ σπουδῆς (Hebrew *ḥipāzôn*); verse 33 (piel of Hebrew *māhar*); Sus 50; Wis 14:17—"lead back in great haste"; Deut 16:3—"you left Egypt in haste" (ἐν σπουδῇ); 2 Macc 14:43—"because of the liveliness of the combat" (διὰ τὴν σπουδήν); 1 Macc 6:63—"departing in haste, he returned to Antioch" (ἀπῆρεν κατὰ σπουδήν); cf. 1 Sam 21:8; Dan 2:25; Sir 27:3. Whether with ἐν, κατά, μετά, or διά, σπουδή refers to the hasty mode of action; it has adverbial value in the phrase σπουδὴν ἔρχομαι (Sir 20:18; 21:5; 43:22).

[4] Xenophon, *An.* 6.5.14: "speaking brusquely"; 7.6.28: "The Thracians, being compelled to save themselves with great haste"; *Cyr.* 4.5.12: "He only sent his messenger the more hastily"; *Hell.* 6.2.28: "The last ones had to hurry"; Plutarch, *Rom.* 8.1: "He ran hurriedly to Numitor"; *Publ.* 4.2: "seeing them enter hastily"; *Sert.* 4.2: "Sertorius set about the task with zeal and dispatch" (σπουδὴν καὶ τάχος); Thucydides 1.93.2: the hurry to build; 2.90.3: "He gave the order to embark in great haste and against his will"; 5.66.2; Philo, *To Gaius* 338: "He was impatient to arrive as quickly as possible at Alexandria."

[5] *P.Ryl.* 231, 13 (AD 40); *P.Tebt.* 315, 8; *SB* 6745, 5; 9367, n. X, 14.

[6] "The idea of quickness has already been expressed by εὐθύς; μετὰ σπουδῆς, then, is rather 'with gusto' " (M. J. Lagrange, on this text); but "quickly" is not pleonastic and—in reinforcing "immediately"—can suggest the lack of reflection on the part of the daughter of Herodias, who was the mere vehicle of her mother's wishes. Ardor and stubbornness go together (Plutarch, *Ti. Gracch.* 10.5).

[7] Xenophon, *Cyr.* 1.3.11: "I will tell him that Astyages is seeing to it"; *Symp.* 8.17: "He concerned himself more with the honor of the eldest than with his own pleasure"; *Cyr.* 5.4.13; Epictetus 3.4.1: "they came to terms"; Plutarch, *Them.* 5.3: "applying himself to the cithara"; *Per.* 24.5: "Aspasia was the object of Pericles' affection for her learning and her political wisdom"; *Cat. Min.* 14.4; *C. Gracch.* 8.2; Plutarch, *Demetr.* 3.1; *Ant.* 53.8.

[8] *P.Fouad* 85, 13: "take care to safeguard your rights"; *P.Oxy.* 746, 8: "take care of this, as is just" (AD 16); 113, 24: "take care that Onnophoris buys what Irene's mother

trouble[9] and doing one's best.[10] It is in this sense of "trying, applying oneself diligently to" and not "hastening" that the NT occurrences of this verb should be understood.[11]

The adverb spoudaiōs has the same meaning in Titus 3:13, where the apostle's disciple must take care and do his best to provide for the trip of Zenas and Apollos; and in 2 Tim 1:17, where Onesiphorus sought Paul in the Roman prisons with extreme care and without sparing himself any trouble—and succeeded in finding him.[12] Likewise, the substantive spoudē, with this nuance of costly effort,[13] is contrasted with indolence and inertia

told her"; 1842, 4; 2113, 19; P.Lond. 231, 12; 234, 10; 236, 12; 248, 5 (vol. 2, pp. 285, 287, 290, 306); BGU 1677, 10: εὖ οὖν ποιήσεις σπουδάσας ἀπαρτίσασθαι αὐτά (business letter, second century AD); 1764, 22; P.Panop.Beatty 2, 105; P.Bour. 20, 39: "Let Nonna take care to supply Dionysius faithfully with the half-loaf"; P.Ryl. 607, 5: "take care of spending all the Italian money on purchases"; P.NYU 25, 8: "you, above all others, deal with sending the replacement team"; SB 9843, 5 (letter for the preparation of a Jewish festival, in the second century): "take care to send me some wooden bars and some citrons" (ethrog; cf. B. Lifshitz, "Papyrus grecs du Désert de Juda," in Aeg, 1962, p. 241).

[9] A fiancé writes to his future mother-in-law: "you are preoccupied, and you took the trouble to prepare a house for me" (P.Ant. 93, 7); P.Lond. 1912, 34; 1916, 16: ἀναγκαίως οὖν πάνυ σπουδάσατε αὐτῷ ἀόκνως; SB 9156, 9: ἵνα σπουδάσῃς τῷ ἀνδρί; P.Mich. 503, 14; cf. Josephus, Ant. 1.115: ἀπολείποντες σπουδῆς; I.Bulg. 1573, 11: τῆς περὶ παιδείαν καὶ λόγους σπουδῆς.

[10] P.Oxy. 1061, 16 (22 BC). A letter from the second century ends thus: "Do whatever is best, brother" (ἀλλὰ σπούδασον, ἀδελφέ, Pap.Lugd.Bat. I, 15, 29); P.Stras. 154, 5: σπούδασον οὖν, ἄδελφε, ποιῆσαι; SB 8944. Cf. the letter from Heron to Ptollarion in the third century: "You lack diligence (τὸ ἀσπούδαστόν σου); I've known you longer than a day" (P.IFAO II, n. 17, 3). I.Bulg. 41, 9; ISE, n. 103, 15.

[11] Gal 2:10—St. Paul had always taken pains to help the poor (ἐσπούδασα); he tried to see the Thessalonians again (1 Thess 2:17). Christians must make an effort to enter into God's rest: σπουδάσωμεν οὖν εἰσελεῖν (Heb 4:11; cf. Eph 4:3; 2 Tim 2:15; 2 Pet 1:10; 3:14) [2 Pet 1:15 is difficult: "I shall take care that after my departure you will have every occasion to remember these things"; the future σπουδάσω, "I shall do my best," was changed to the present σπουδάζω by א, 𝔓72, Peshitta, Arm., and to the imperative σπουδάσατε]. When the apostle writes to Titus σπούδασον ἐλθεῖν πρός με (Titus 3:12), we cannot translate "hasten" as at 2 Tim 4:9, because on the one hand Titus must await the arrival of Artemas or Tychicus, and on the other hand, the meeting at Nicopolis is set only for the winter. So the sense is "try, endeavor." Cf. Philo, Virtues 218: "trying to be a disciple of God"; 215: "to make harmony reign."

[12] On the difficulty of finding and contacting a prisoner, cf. C. Spicq, Epîtres Pastorales, vol. 1, p. 145; vol. 2, p. 734. Plutarch, Cim. 8.3: "Cimon sought to find his tomb" (ἐσπούδασε τὸν τάφον ἀνευρεῖν, he applied himself diligently to the search, 8.7).

[13] Thucydides 4.30.3: "a greater effort was justified on the part of the Athenians"; Xenophon, Symp. 1.6: "It is truly worth the effort to hear me"; Philo, Virtues 215: Abraham set out to find the One who is one ἀοκνοτάτη σπουδῇ; Josephus, Ant. 2.222,

in Rom 12:11 (*tē spoudē mē oknēroi*) and 2 Pet 1:5 (*spoudēn pasan pareis-enegkantes*); it is not so much a matter of goodwill or zeal, but of making an effort; the formula is classical.[14] Finally, *spoudē* also means "gravity, seriousness."[15] This seems to be the right characteristic for a leader of a Christian community, who must preside *en spoudē* (Rom 12:8)—not with

---

340; 4.214, 261; 8.187; 10.44. A Byzantine gloss contrasts leisure time (σχολή) with business time (σπουδή) in Theophrastus, *Char.* 3.5. After asking for the serious examination of a question (μετὰ σπουδῆς, as in Demosthenes, *Prooem.* 29, 42, 45, 49, 53, 54), Ps.-Plutarch says that it is not the longest life that is best, but the life in which one's time is best spent, the life that is fullest (ὁ σπουδαιότατος), like that of the citharist, orator, or pilot who has practiced his profession perfectly (*Cons. ad Apoll.* 17). The Pythia is as it were "overcome by the relentlessness" of Alexander (*Alex.* 14.7). *I.Ilium*, n. 52, 7; 56, 8; 73, 13. *P.Mich.* 73, 6: τὴν πᾶσαν οὖν σπουδὴν καὶ [ἐπιμέλειαν] ποιήσασθε; *P.Oxy.* 1840, 5: "I do not find that they made much of an effort" (σπουδὴν πολλὴν ἐποίησαι); *P.Tebt.* 703, 90 and 184: τὴν πλείστην σπουδὴν ποιοῦ (third century BC); *P.Panop.Beatty* 2, 222; *I.Bulg.* 314 A 12; cf. τῇ σπουδῇ καὶ ἐπιμελίᾳ (J. and L. Robert, "Bulletin épigraphique," in *REG*, 1953, p. 187, n. 218).

[14] Εἰσφέρειν σπουδήν, Polybius 22.12.12; Diodorus Siculus 1.83, speaking of Italians traveling in Egypt: οἱ ὄχλοι πᾶσαν εἰσεφέροντο σπουδὴν ἐκθεραπεύσαντες τοὺς παρεπιδημοῦντας τῶν ἀπὸ τῆς Ἰταλίας; Josephus, *Ant.* 11.324; 20.204; letter of Seleucus IV to Seleucia: προενηνέγκατο σπουδὴν ἐπὶ τοῦ βασιλέως (*SEG* VII, 62, 13); Dittenberger, *Syl.* 656, 14; 694, 15; inscription from Stratonicea: καλῶς δὲ ἔχι πᾶσαν σπουδὴν ἰσφέρεσθαι (*IGLAM* 519; cf. A. Deissmann, *Bible Studies*, p. 361); *I.Priene* 118, 7: πᾶσαν εἰσφερόμενος σπουδὴν καὶ φιλοτιμίαν (first century BC); 42, 14: καὶ τῶν ἐγδίκων πᾶσαν προσενεγκαμένων σπουδὴν καὶ φιλοτιμίαν; *P.Tebt.* 33, 19: τὴν πᾶσαν προσενέγκαι σπουδήν; other references in M. Holleaux, *Etudes d'épigraphie*, vol. 2, pp. 87ff.

[15] Plato links seriousness and fantasy (σπουδή-παιδία) as complementary ideas (Plato, *Symp.* 197 e; *Leg.* 769 a; 771, e; 803 c; *Ep.* 6.323 d; cf. R. Merkelbach, "ΣΠΟΥΔΗ ΚΑΙ ΠΑΙΔΙΑ," in *ZPE*, vol. 20, 1976, p. 200); likewise Xenophon, *Symp.* 1.1: "serious actions (ἔργα μετὰ σπουδῆς) are the opposite of diversions (ἐν ταῖς παιδιαῖς)"; 1.13: "If the company is entirely serious . . . perhaps they are lacking in gaiety"; 2.17: "Socrates, speaking quite seriously"; Plutarch, *Caes.* 11.4; Plutarch, *Per.* 8.4: "The comedies of the poets of his day took pot-shots at him, sometimes seriously, sometimes playfully"; *Phoc.* 8.3: "wise and serious people" (νήφων καὶ σπουδάζων) (contrasted with amusements); *P.Paris* 63, 131: the penalties were set in seriousness (μετὰ σπουδῆς). Similarly the adjective *spoudaios*: "These are the amusing and the serious things that were said under the tent" (Xenophon, *Cyr.* 2.3.1); "You are wrong to ruin the most serious man in our army by getting him to laugh" (ibid. 2.2.16); "Every time there was nothing more serious to do, they amused themselves with this game" (ibid. 2.3.20); "No Athenian would dare to set about a serious task on that day" (σπουδαίου ἔργου, *Hell.* 1.4.12); Zeno: "All good things are useful, convenient, profitable, advantageous, serious (σπουδαῖα), appropriate, beautiful, suitable" (in Stobaeus, *Ecl.* 2.7.5 d = p. 69, 12). *P.Panop.Beatty* 2, 107: "Your responsibility is to wait for that with as much seriousness as possible"; cf. a serious and dignified bearing, σπουδαίως καὶ εὐσχημόνως (Xenophon, *Cyr.* 1.3.1).

urgency or zeal, but with seriousness, dignity, or solicitude (*Ep. Arist.* 39); or even in such a manner as to win esteem, i.e., honorably (cf. Josephus, *Ant.* 14.186; cf. 2.197; 9.182; Philostratus, *Gym.* 13). It would seem that it was this quality of seriousness that produced in the Corinthians "sorrow according to God," i.e., repentance (2 Cor 7:11).

III. — Whatever the nuance of each particular text, the diligence, care, or effort manifested come from an initial goodwill, the pursuit of something one cares about, a desire to succeed;[16] and *spoudazō*, in the first century AD, expresses the marks of an attentive benevolence, as thoughtful as it is efficient. In 41, Emperor Claudius takes pleasure in the tokens of attachment he has received from the Alexandrians (*P.Lond.* 1912, 25: *spoudasantes kai spoudasthentos;* cf. Severus and Caracalla, in *I.Bulg.* 659, 23), who are for their part impatient to receive tokens of his favor: *ha par' emou labein espoudakate* (line 52; cf. *P.Oxy.* 2558, 3: *Kaisarōn spoudēn;* Dittenberger, *Or.* 723, 1). With regard to the Thasians, he receives "all the tokens of [their] diligence and piety" (*tēs hymeteras spoudēs kai eusebeias apodechomai pantas, I.Thas.* 179, 4), as Octavian wrote to the inhabitants of Rhosos: "Seleucus, my admiral, . . . has shown many tokens of his diligence and eagerness" (*pasan eispheromenos spoudēn kai prothymian, IGLS* 718, 84). This goodwill includes ardor, care, and devotion: "we obtained this thanks to the careful effort of our friends" (*tēs de tōn philōn spoudēs tychontos epetychamen, P.Tebt.* 314, 9); a woman in the second-third century thanks her mother for sending a chair (*charin de soi oida, mētēr, epi tē spoudē tou kathedrariou, P.Oxy.* 963). Someone who is asking a ruler to intervene calls upon the goodwill of the prospective benefactor: "I urge you, sir, to take the initiative in showing your concern for them."[17]

---

[16] *P.Hib.* 77, 4: καθάπερ ὁ βασιλεὺς σπουδάζει, conformably to the king's wishes, to what he seeks; *P.Bour.* 20, 36: τοῦτο γὰρ σπουδάζει, this is the proposed goal; *P.Mich.* 10, 10: περὶ ὧν ἂν σὺ σπουδάζῃς, this matter that you are concerned with (third century BC); edict of Cyrene, second century BC: "We are desirous (σπουδάζομεν) that no subject of our kingdom should be troubled" (*SEG* 9.5.53); ἐνεδείξατο πᾶσιν σπουδὴν ἐξ ἀρχῆς ἐν λυκάβαντι ἐῷ (*I.Bulg.* 657, 5); *P.Oxy.* 2558, 3; *P.Lond.* 1178, 23 (vol. 3, p. 216); 1917, 23: μετὰ σπουδῆς ὅλης καρδίας (fourth century AD); line 22: μαιτὰ (*sic*) σπουδῆς πνεύματος ἁγίου. Cf. Philo, *To Gaius* 242; Josephus, *Ant.* 4.123; 5.120; 13.85; Diodorus Siculus 17.39.4.

[17] Παρακαλῶ οὖν, Κύριέ μου, ὑπάρξαι αὐτοῖς καὶ τὰ τῆς σῆς σπουδῆς, *P.Oxy.* 1068, 13; cf. 2239, 15: "I am prepared to bring all my concern to bear"; 3086, 6: "it is in these things that the active goodwill of friends is seen" (ἐν γὰρ τούτοις αἱ σπουδαὶ τῶν φίλων φαίνονται); *P.Yale* 33, 7: "The *dioikētēs* is acting diligently in this matter" (περὶ τούτων τὴν σπουδὴν ποιεῖται ὁ διοικητής, third century BC = *P.Hib.* 44); *P.Fouad* 86, 18; *P.Oslo* 58, 4; epitaph for a Christian jurist, who offered his diligence to all (σπουδὴν, ἥν εἶχον, πᾶσι χαρίζομενος, *SEG* VI, 210, 20). Cf. the praise for the

Finally, *spoudē* expresses fervor, zeal, and eagerness,[18] as in 2 Cor 7:12—"the zeal that you showed for us"; 8:7—"you excel in all diligence"; 8:8—"to prove by the zeal of others that your own love is sincere"; 8:16–17—Titus is fervent in his care for the Corinthians; Heb 6:11—the Hebrews must be ardent in their efforts to grow the good fruit of their hope. This is exactly the wording of the papyri: "with full eagerness and joy, of one accord" (*meta tēs pleistēs spoudēs kai charas homothymadon*, BGU 1768, 7); "as far as possible, I will show my eagerness";[19] especially the adverb *spoudaiōs:* "Let us use creation with ardor while we are young" (Wis 2:6); the Jewish elders begged Jesus with fervor or insistently.[20] Telling of the effectiveness of a recommendation, the beneficiary writes, "He introduced me to Aemilianus without delay and eagerly" (*anoknōs kai spoudaiōs synestake me*, P.Mich. 498, 14). Philoi shows that he is eager to serve (*hina pempsōmen Philōi spoudaiōs hēmin prosenechthenti*).[21] As for Jude 3, *pasan spoudēn poioumenos graphein hymin*, we could just as easily translate either "I was in a hurry"[22] or "I greatly desired to write to you concerning our common

---

spoudē of Junia Theodora at Corinth in AD 43 (ibid. XVIII, 143, 3, 17, 49, 55), a fancy for dancers (Plutarch, *De frat. amor.* 17).

[18] Xenophon, *An.* 1.8.4: "they set at it with great ardor" (σὺν πολλῇ σπουδῇ); *Cyr.* 4.2.38: "They carried out with great eagerness that which had been commanded them"; *Ep. Arist.* 4: "I performed with eagerness"; Philo, *Husbandry* 166: "the qualities of eagerness to learn (σπουδῆς), of progress (βελτιώσεως), of perfection (τελειώσεως) will never disappear"; Philo, *Spec. Laws* 1.30, 36, 42: "the passion for study"; 79, 144: religious fervor; *Prelim. Stud.* 112: "true goods: instruction, progress, ardor (σπουδήν), desire (πόθον), zeal (ζῆλον) . . . that Moses took along as provision for his journey"; *Dreams* 2.67: in holiness they consecrated their fervent zeal to piety; Josephus, *Ant.* 1.222, 256, 260; 10.25; 13.212; Plutarch, *Caes.* 7.2; *Cat. Min.* 25.11; *Ti. Gracch.* 7.3; cf. *SB* 9156, 4: ὡς πάντως σπουδάσει τῇ ἐντολῇ αὐτοῦ.

[19] P.Lond. 1924, 7; P.Oxy. 2107, 3; 2194, 9; I.Magn. 53, 61: ἀπόδειξιν ποιουμένους τῆς περὶ τὰ μέγιστα σπουδῆς (third century BC); 85, 12: ὅπως . . . σπουδὴ ἔγδηλος γένηται (second century).

[20] Luke 7:4. Cf. Josephus, *Ant.* 8.6: Bersabe promised to intercede zealously (σπουδαίως); cf. 16.85: recommendation made strongly (σπουδαιότερον); perhaps with the nuance "convincingly," cf. διὰ σπουδῆς, 16.214). But St. Paul sends Epaphroditus "as quickly as possible" (Phil 2:28, σπουδαιοτέρως with superlative meaning); the meaning "with care, seriously," in παραφυλάττειν σπουδαίως, παρακολουθεῖν σπουδαίως (G. E. Bean, T. B. Mitford, *Cilicia,* n. 31, *b* 27; *a* 29); *PSI* 742, 6: σπουδαίως μεταδοῦναι μοι διὰ γραμμάτων τὸ τῆς ὑποθέσεως.

[21] P. Giss. Univ. vol. 3, n. 20, 36.

[22] Cf. the letter of the Christian Demetrius to Flavianus: ἕτερά σε γράμματα ἐπικαταλαβεῖν ἐσπούδασα διὰ Εὐφροσύνου, "I was in a hurry for you to receive another letter by way of Euphrosynos" (P.Oxy. 939, 18).

salvation."[23] All the commentators, following Wettstein, emphasize that the formula *pasan spoudēn poioumenos* has classical antecedents going back to Herodotus.[24]

IV. — When St. Paul points out to the Corinthians that Titus has shown himself very eager (*spoudaioteros*) to go to them, of his own accord (2 Cor 8:17), he wants to impress his recipients with the fact that this promptitude comes from the very heart of his envoy; but, nevertheless, he is using the epistolary formula "I know your devotion," which became a cliché: "Knowing your devotion to everyone" (*eidōs sou to spoudeon to pros pantas, P.Oxy.* 929, 3; cf. 1064, 6); "for I know your devotion and fairness."[25] We have every right to think that in choosing the adjective *spoudaios*, he also gave it the connotations "good, excellent, virtuous" that are implied in other NT usages and which were so common in the Koine, that a Roman epitaph uses this word to sum up all the virtues of "Crispina, wife of Procopius, *spoudaia*, loving the law" (*CII* 132). This moral meaning of *spoudaios* comes especially from Aristotle,[26] who probably borrowed it from Antisthenes (Diogenes Laertius 6.104–105). On the one hand, *spoudaios* means "serious, conscientious"; on the other hand, "meticulous, done well, virtuous." There are games that are serious (*tas espoudasmenas paidias*, Aristotle, *Rh.* 1.11.1371ª3–4) in that they require effort, and similarly the work or function (*ergon*) of moral virtue is the virtuous life (*zōē spoudaia*), which requires sustained diligence. Xenophon contrasts honest folk, who deserve respect

---

[23] Cf. H. Windisch, *Die katholischen Briefe*, 3d ed., Tübingen, 1951, p. 38; J. B. Mayor, *The Epistle of St. Jude*, 2d ed., Grand Rapids, 1965, pp. 21ff., 89ff. J. Cantinat, *Les Epîtres de saint Jacques et de saint Jude*, Paris, 1973, p. 294.

[24] Herodotus 5.30: "I will notify with full willingness"; Porphyry, *Abst.* 2.43; *I.Priene* 53, 10: "his goodwill left nothing to be desired; to the contrary, he did all that he could" (to reconcile the adversaries—οὐδὲν ἐλλείπων προθυμίας, ἀλλὰ πᾶσαν σπουδὴν ποιούμενος); 54, 9 and 39; 44, 13: διότι τὴν πᾶσαν σπουδὴν προαιρούμενος ποιεῖσθαι; *PSI* 340, 19: δεόμεθα πᾶσαν σπουδὴν ποιήσασθαι περὶ Πτολεμαίου; 584, 27: περὶ τῆς κυνὸς πᾶσαν σπουδὴν ποίησαι, οὐ γάρ ἐστιν ἐμή (third century BC); *P.Hib.* 71, 9: "From the time you receive this letter, put all your efforts (τὴν πᾶσαν σπουδὴν ποίησαι) into finding the fugitive slave and send him to me under good guard"; *P.Mil.Vogl.* 255, 4.

[25] Οἶδα γάρ σου τὸ σπουδεον καὶ ἐπιεικές, *P.Oxy.* 1218, 4; 2602, 10; *P.Ryl.* 243, 6; *P.Mich.* 211, 7; *P.Abinn.* 6, 5: οἴδαμεν τὸ σπουδεόν σου καὶ τὴν ἀγάπην σου εἰς ἡμᾶς; *C.P.Herm.* 12, 4; *P.Lond.* 1918, 10; *SB* 9607, 2; cf. 9156, 2; 10295, 4. At Philae, in the Byzantine period, the pairing σπουδῇ καὶ ἐπιεικείᾳ recur constantly (ibid. 7439; E. Bernand, *Philae*, vol. 2, n. 194, 6; 219, 1; 220, 8; 221, 7; 224, 4; 225, 1; 228, 1) and already Josephus, *Ant.* 13.245.

[26] Aristotle, *On Nobility* (in Stobaeus, *Flor.* 88, 52; vol. 4, pp. 723ff.; republished with commentary by J. Aubonnet, in P. M. Schuhl, *Aristote*, Paris, 1968, pp. 99–115); *Eth. Nic.* 5.6.1131ª28; *Eth. Eud.* 22.1.1218ᵇ34ff.; cf. Harder, on this word, in *TDNT*, vol. 7, pp. 560ff.

(*hoi spoudaioi*) against rogues (*hoi phauloi*, in *Cyr.* 2.24) and the wicked (*ponēroi*).[27] This vocabulary and doctrine were picked up by the Stoics. According to Zeno, there are two classes of humans (*to men ton spoudaiōn, to de tōn phaulōn*), the former practicing virtue, the others doing evil (Stobaeus, *Ecl.* 2.7.11; vol. 2, p. 99; cf. *SVF*, vol. 1, 216). Chrysippus says that the *spoudaios anēr* is a rare person (Plutarch, *De Stoic. rep.* 31), is perfect and happy and does not fall into error.[28] Philo inherits this tradition and contrasts the good and the wicked (*to phaulon tō spoudaiō, Giants* 56); "The life of the virtuous person consists in deeds (*ho spoudaiou bios en ergois*), that of the wicked (*ho tou phaulou*) in words."[29] As opposed to the slave, the *spoudaios* is not subject to compulsion (*Good Man Free* 60); "He is perfectly virtuous (*pantōs spoudaios*), this man to whom it is said, 'I am your God' " (*Change of Names* 31; cf. Philo, *Sacr. Abel and Cain* 124), "incapable of taking on the burden of any evil whatsoever" (*Creation* 73). As God is the author of all that is worthwhile (*spoudaia*, Philo, *Change of Names* 256), it is possible to specify that "God made all virtuous beings for the sake of their affinity with him" (*Creation* 74).

In everyday Greek, *spoudaios* refers to good quality: "I am sending you some good melon seeds" (*P.Oxy.* 117, 2); "we have no other that is good" (*P.Flor.* 338, 8); the adjective is also used for athletes,[30] good people (*P.Mich.* 213, 11), and true friends,[31] precisely because they are zealous and eager.[32]

---

[27] Xenophon, *Hell.* 2.3.19; cf. Plutarch, *Per.* 1.5: "Ismenias is a worthless fellow (μοχθηρός); otherwise he would not be such a good flute player (σπουδαῖος αὐλητής)"; *Phoc.* 38.3.

[28] Cleanthes, frag. 566 (in Stobaeus, *Ecl.* vol. 2, p. 65, 11), ὅθεν ἀτελεῖς μὲν ὄντας εἶναι φαύλους, τελειωθέντες δὲ σπουδαίους; cf. ibid. vol. 2, p. 112, 8 (= *SVF*, vol. 3, 548), τέλειον ἄνδρα καὶ σπουδαῖον; Sextus Empiricus, *Math.* 7.405; Lucian, *Vit. Auct.* 20; Plotinus, *Enn.* 1.4.14; Gregory of Nazianzus, *Ep.* 32 (*SVF*, vol. 3, 586); Simplicius (ibid., vol. 3, 238), Didymus (ibid., vol. 2, 809). Cf. G. Binder, "Ein neues Epikurfragment bei Didymos dem Blinden," in *ZPE*, vol. 1, 1967, p. 37; D. Tsekourakis, *Studies in the Terminology of Early Stoic Ethics*, Wiesbaden, 1974, pp. 127ff.

[29] *Dreams* 2.302; cf. 34; *Alleg. Interp.* 1.74; 3.67: "Sensation is among the things that are neither bad nor good (οὔτε τῶν φαύλων οὔτε τῶν σπουδαίων) . . . if it arises in a good person, it becomes good (σπουδαία)."

[30] Cf. L. Robert, *Etudes épigraphiques*, p. 26.

[31] Menander, *Dysk.* 824. In Egypt, there are associations of *spoudaioi* (cf. E. Wipszycka, "Les Confréries dans la vie religeuse de l'Egypt chrétienne," in *Proceedings* XII, pp. 511–525) and σπουδαῖος φίλος refers to the zealous friend of an association, cf. J. and L. Robert, "Bulletin épigraphique," in *REG*, 1971, p. 465, n. 441.

[32] It might be said the Philo has a theology of haste: good deeds are done "spontaneously, with no slowness or tardiness" (*Sacr. Abel and Cain* 53); "obedient children do not delay, they do good actions with all the eagerness they are capable of" (μετὰ σπουδῆς πάσης, ibid. 68); Abraham acted "with all the eagerness, all the speed, all the ardor that he was capable of," bidding Sarah act quickly (ibid. 59). "In

V. — We cannot fail to note the connotations of excellence and honor in this term, especially when it is linked with *philotimia*,[33] as is the case in most of the honorific decrees. For example, a decree at Samos in honor of Boulagoras, "showing eagerness and absolute devotion" (*tēm pasan epoiēsato spoudēn kai philotimian antikatastas*, SEG I, 366, 11; second century BC); a decree conferring *proxenia* upon Nicias, who spared no zeal, expense, or devotion;[34] a decree at a city in Cappadocia in behalf of Apollonius;[35] a decree of Apollonia honoring Pamphilos: "With all eagerness and devotion, he set each of these matters in order" (*I.Car.* 167, 8); decree of Smyrna in honor of some Thasian judges: "for the zeal and devotion with which they acted."[36] Heracleans of the Pontus send an embassy to Hadrian to intercede on behalf of their colony "using all zeal and all genuine affection."[37]

This link with *philostorgia* ("affection") exploits the affective connotations of the word *spoudē* during this period[38] and reveals not only the

giving thanks and honor to the Almighty . . . let us tolerate no delay" (ibid. 63). Even the priests hurry, "doing everything with eagerness and promptitude" (*Moses* 2.144), quick in religious service (2.145, 2.170); the tunic that they wear is symbolic of this promptitude (*Spec. Laws* 1.83; cf. 1.98–99; 2.83, 146; *Abraham* 62; according to b. *Šabb.* 20a, "the priests are alert"). Commenting on Gen 24:20, "Rebekah hurried to tip the jar," Philo observes, "In saying that she hurried, Moses shows her promptitude in doing good, the fruit of a disposition of soul from which all jealous feelings are perfectly absent" (*Post. Cain* 140). When Jesus sends the seventy-two disciples on their mission (Luke 10:1ff.), he exhorts them to promptitude (cf. C. F. D. Moule, *The Phenomenon of the New Testament*, London, 1967, pp. 66ff.). Cf. D. Daube, *The Sudden in the Scriptures*, Leiden, 1964, pp. 12ff., 18ff., 74.

[33] Cf. Philo, *Sacr. Abel and Cain* 59; Josephus, *Ant.* 4.105; 6.220.

[34] Εἰς πᾶν σπουδῆς καὶ δαπάνης καὶ φιλοτιμίας οὐθὲν ἐνλείπων, *I.Gonn.* 41, 13 (second century BC); same formulation: σπουδᾶς καὶ φιλοτιμίας οὐθὲν ἐλλείποντες in a decree of the confederation of Ainians (L. Robert, *Opera Minora Selecta*, vol. 1, p. 16); decree at Andros (ibid., p. 56); at Delphi (Dittenberger, *Or.* 305, 4); at Abdera: τὴν πᾶσαν σπουδήν τε καὶ φιλοτιμίαν εἰσήνεγκαν προθυμίας οὐδὲν ἐλλείποντες (*Syl.* 656, 14; cf. P. Hermann, in *ZPE*, vol. 7, 1971, pp. 72–77); at Odessa (*I.Bulg.* 41, 9); Thessalian act of emancipation from the second century BC, σπουδῆς καὶ φιλοτιμίας οὐδὲν ἐνλείπων (L. Vidmann, *Sylloge Inscriptionum Religionis Isiacae et Sarapiacae*, Berlin, 1969, n. 102, 9).

[35] Σπουδὴν καὶ φιλοτιμίαν εἰσενεγκάμενος, C. Michel, *Recueil*, n. 546, 18.

[36] Ἐπὶ τῇ σπουδῇ καὶ φιλοτιμίᾳ ᾗ ἐποήσαντο, cited by L. Robert, *Opera Minora Selecta*, p. 2), like the decrees of Assos (p. 11), of Athens: τὴν πᾶσαν σπουδὴν ποιούμενος (p. 193), of Delphi for a physician from Corone (p. 256).

[37] Πᾶσαι σπουδαῖ καὶ πάσᾳ φιλοστοργίᾳ κεχραμένοι γνασίαι, B. Latyschev, *Inscriptiones Antiquae*, IV, n. 71, 6.

[38] Josephus uses *spoudē* for the violent passion of the wife of Potiphar (*Ant.* 2.53, 225; cf. 14.283; 16.302; 18.292), Herod's devotion to Mariamne (*War* 1.431) or his eunuchs (*Ant.* 16.230). Already Xenophon, *Hell.* 3.1.9: "Those of the Spartans who

elements of affection, spontaneity, and unselfishness in Titus's eagerness to go to Corinth[39] and the cordial aspects of brotherly assistance in the primitive church but also how the believers put their whole heart into bearing fruit.

---

are noble-hearted." In his letter to Rhosos, Augustus writes concerning his envoy: πᾶσαν εἰσφερόμενος σπουδὴν καὶ προθυμίαν ὑπὲρ τῶν ὑμεῖν συμφερόντων (M. Guarducci, *Epigrafia greca*, vol. 2, p. 117); *P.Abinn.* 7, 4: Εὐχαριστοῦμεν τῷ θεῷ περὶ τῆς ὁλοκληρίας καὶ τῆς σπουδήν (*sic*) σου; *P.Lips.* 119, col. II, 5: εἰς χαράν τε ὁμοῦ καὶ σπουδῆς περὶ τὸ ὀρθῶς.

[39] Cf. *P.Flor.* 304, 9, from the sixth century, where Apphous is enjoined to assume the office of *riparius* without remuneration but with this warning: "your zeal (or seriousness) will win you praises (ἐκ σπουδῆς γὰρ ἐπαινεθῆσαι); negligence will bring you serious danger"; contrasted with childishness in Philo, *Spec. Laws* 1.314; cf. 2.2. Τὸ σπουδαῖον σου = your fervor, an expression of friendship, *P.Oxy.* 2602, 10–14; P. J. Parsons, in *P.Coll.Youtie* II, p. 421; cf. pp. 565–566.

στασιαστής, στάσις

stasiastēs, **agitator, troublemaker, fomenter of rebellion;** *stasis*, **standing, controversy, rebellion, uprising**

The biblical hapax *stasiastēs*, used concerning Barabbas, who was in prison "with the seditious" (Mark 15:7), unknown in classical Greek, is attested from the third century BC by two papyri. Païs, a rug-maker, has already brought accusations against Nechtembes to Zeno; today he gives several proofs of his escapades. He has even corrupted other weavers; he is an agitator (*hos estin stasiastes*, PSI 442; republished as *P.Cair.Zen.* 59484, 4). A similar accusation brought by Petosiris against another Païs: "memorandum to Zeno from Petosiris: Païs, the agitator, the farmer" (*hypomnēma Zēnōni para Petosirios: Paeis ho stasiastes ho geōrgos*, *P.Cair.Zen.* 59499, 87). Josephus, *Ant.* 14.8 presents "a friend of Hyrcanus the Idumean, called Antipater . . . ; he was by nature a troublemaker and seditious."[1] The noun is derived from *stasiazō*, "be in dissension, plot an uprising" (Xenophon, *An.* 2.5.28), form parties (Thucydides 4.84.2), revolt.[2]

With the exception of Prov 17:14 (Hebrew *rîḇ*, a private quarrel), all the occurrences of *stasis* in the LXX fit the first meaning of the term: transitively, the act of standing something up; intransitively, the act of standing still,[3] as the moon stood still (Josh 10:13); hence the connotations

---

[1] Δραστήριος δὲ τὴν φύσιν ὤν καὶ στασιαστής, Josephus, *Ant.* 14.8; cf. *War* 6.157: "a large number of agitators, having nothing else to pillage . . . attacked the Roman posts en masse"; Dionysius of Halicarnassus 2.1.3; 6.70; Diodorus Siculus 10.11.1.

[2] Jdt 7:15: "You will inflict severe punishment on them for revolting"; 2 Macc 4:30—"The inhabitants of Tarsus and Mallus revolted"; 14:6—"The Hasideans fomented war and insurrection, not letting the kingdom enjoy peace" (εὐσταθείας); Dio Cassius 10.32: "Violent insurrection led to a revolution against the state"; Zosimus 1.61: Aurelian "quickly subdued the Alexandrians who were agitating and dreaming of revolt" (στασιάσαντας καὶ πρὸς ἀπόστασιν ἰδόντας).

[3] Cf. E. Boisacq, *Dictionnaire étymologique*, on this word. *Stasis* is the place (Deut 28:65; Nah 3:11; Dan 8:17; 10:11; Neh 8:7; Sir 23:12; cf. Polybius 2.68.7: "He held his

---

stasiastēs, *EDNT* 3.267; MM 586; L&N 39.37; BAGD 764 ‖ *stasis*, S 4714; *TDNT* 7.568–571; *EDNT* 3.267; MM 586; L&N 13.72, 33.448, 39.34; BAGD 764

of repose, stability, fixity so emphasized by Philo with moral or religious significance.[4] But the NT uses this meaning—"stand, remain in place"— only once, with respect to the way to the heavenly sanctuary, which was not yet open "so long as the first tent (the tabernacle of the old covenant) remained" (Heb 9:8) or was functional (*echousēs stasin*). This agrees with the usage in 2 Chr 30:16; 35:10, 15; Neh 9:3; 13:11, because holding a place or a position is often synonymous with carrying out a function. Valerius Pius, for example, gives thanks and accepts the position of *secutor* and the assurance that he has been given (*eucharistōn autō kai epidechomenos tēn genētheisan pros auton stasin kai dexian, P.Mich.* 485, 7; cf. Marcus Aurelius 6.41.2).

Standing up can mean standing up in opposition to or disagreement with someone. This sense of *stasis* is attested five times in Acts, with the same connotations as in contemporary Greek. It can be a matter of conflicting ideas, a source of controversy and polemics;[5] these discussions bring out disagreements and stir up commotion and trouble[6] that are hard to smooth over, between either individuals or social groups,[7] like the violent

---

initial position at the summit"; workplace, *BGU* 1122, 18, 21; in 12 BC), especially for the feet (1 Chr 28:2; 1 Macc 10:72); but also the normal state of the house of God (2 Chr 24:13), the stone pillar at Shechem (Judg 9:6, Hebrew *muṣāb*; on this meaning, cf. Xenophon, *Cyn.* 2.8: "stakes"; the erecting of a structure, cf. *P.Petr.* 46, 3, 1; Xenophon, *Cyn.* 9.16: "the setting up of a trap"; A. Deissmann, *Bible Studies,* p. 158ff.); also a "statute," a pact, a royal edict (Dan 6:7; 1 Macc 7:18). In astronomy, στάσις and σύστασις refer to the stability of the weather or the position of the planets in the zodiac, cf. Geminus, *Intro. to Astronomy* 2.8–10; 17.3.47.

[4] *Alleg. Interp.* 2.99: "conduct that upsets the stability of the created and perishable being is what causes misdeeds" (the passions); *Dreams* 2.237: "fixity, stability, and identity made eternal by his immutable, unchanging character" is an attribute of God; cf. 2.222; *Creation* 120; Philo, *Post. Cain* 29: "God orders . . . staying motionless with him"; 23: "the one who approaches God desires immobility"; one prays to obtain it (*Abraham* 58); "stability and unchanging rest are found with God" (*Giants* 49).

[5] Acts 23:7—a controversy between the Pharisees and the Sadducees (ἐγένετο στάσις); cf. Philo, *Heir* 248: "The difficulty of finding and rooting out the truth caused dissensions of the spirit" (στάσεις ἐγέννησε); Josephus, *Life* 143: The Tarichaeans and strangers on the one side and the Galileans and people of Tiberias on the other had differing opinions and conflict arose (γίνεται στάσις); cf. Philo, *Drunkenness* 98: "surges of unreason created internal discord" (στάσιν ἐμφύλιον); *Post. Cain* 183: "having calmed the rebellion in him" (καταπαύσας τὴν αὐτῷ στάσιν); 185; Plutarch, *C. Gracch.* 13.2: seditious talk; *Cic.* 3.3: dissension.

[6] Acts 15:2—the agitation at Antioch arose from a quarrel with the Judaizers. At Seleucia, life is marked by dissension between Greeks and Syrians (ἐν στάσει καὶ διχονοίᾳ, Josephus, *Ant.* 18.374; 16.73).

[7] *P.Col.Zen.* 74, 8, the protest of Paris, drafted against his will into the Egyptian military; *P.Rein.* 18, 16: "unjust quarrel" provoked by a creditor; 19, 12; *P.Stras.* 20, 10 (republished, 280): a contract of renunciation (διάλυσις), persons who have long

dispute in Acts 23:10. Usually, *stasis* refers to social disorders,[8] whether civil war (Dittenberger, *Syl.* 528, 4; third century BC, at Gortyn; Josephus, *Ant.* 14.22), revolution (Thucydides 7.33.5), revolt (Josephus, *Ant.* 20.117), an insurrection,[9] an uprising (*P.Brem.* 11, 30 = *C.Pap.Jud.* 444, 30), a riot. Thus emperor Claudius refers to the *tarachē kai stasis* of the Alexandrians against the Jews,[10] and in a dream Martyrius sees the riots and madness at Lycopolis, followed by attacks and pillage (*P.Oxy.* 1873, 2). All these texts show the gravity and violence implied by Hellenistic *stasis* and help explain the connection between insurrection and murder in Luke 23:19, 25.

---

been in conflict decide to make peace and end their quarrels (στάσεις διαλύσασθαι); Xenophon, *An.* 6.1.29: "There would be less division with a single leader than with several"; Philo, *Spec. Laws* 1.108: "The law attempts to suppress animosities in the lives of the priests"; 3.192: "God destroys the factions in the cities"; Josephus, *War* 2.10; 5.98: "the factions revived the civil war"; *Ant.* 18.8; Plutarch, *Sert.* 4.7: "the faction of Marius." On στάσις as a political party (like μερίς, αἵρεσις, ἑταιρεία), cf. K. D. Stergiopoulos, Τὰ πολιτικὰ κόμματα τῶν ἀρχαίων Ἀθηνῶν, Athens, 1955.

[8] Acts 24:5—the lawyer Tertullus accuses Paul of stirring up disturbances; cf. Josephus, *War* 2.175–176; *Ant.* 20.109; Philo, *Flacc.* 135: "Isidorus, very good at organizing στάσεις and θορύβους." Diodorus Siculus 18, summary 1; 39.4.

[9] Acts 19:40, the clerk of Ephesus: "We run the risk of being accused of insurrection for what has happened today"; Luke 23:25—"Pilate released the one who had been imprisoned for insurrection and murder"; Josephus, *Ant.* 4.59, 76; *War* 1.236; Plutarch, *Cat. Min.* 28.6: "a law that introduced insurrection and civil war to Rome"; 45.7; 47.2; *Ant.* 53.11; *P.Bour.* 10, 18 (= *SB* 6643; 88 BC): "You will do well to watch the region, to be on the defensive, and, if individuals set out to disobey you and start a new insurrection, to arrest them."

[10] *P.Lond.* 1912, 73 = *C.Pap.Jud.* 153, 73. The ταραχή-στάσις link is common in Philo, *Dreams* 2.251; *Post. Cain* 119; *To Gaius* 113; *Prelim. Stud.* 176; Josephus, *Ant.* 20.174; Diodorus Siculus 13.33; cf. θόρυβος, *Flacc.* 135; *P.Brem.* XI, 26, 30; *I.Magn.* 114, 3–4, 11; φιλονεικία (Josephus, *Ag. Apion* 2.243); cf. Delling, "στάσις," in *TDNT*, vol. 7, pp. 568–571. Josephus often emphasizes the damaging effects of *stasis*: troubles that force citizens into exile (*Ag. Apion* 1.194); violation of the laws (*Ant.* 20.117), the ruin of institutions (4.140), assassinations (4.376; 18.8), etc. Cf. the first Roman insurrection that ended in bloodshed, Plutarch, *Ti. Gracch.* 20.1.

στέγω

stegō, **to hide, contain, bear up, endure**

This verb, which is relatively rare in literary Greek, as well as in the papyri and inscriptions, derives from the Indo-European *(s)teg*, "cover, hide" (cf. Kasch, on this word, in *TDNT*, vol. 7, p. 585). It has diverse meanings, as summarized by Hesychius: "*stegei*: hide, contain, bear up, endure" (*kryptei, synechei, bastazei, hypomenei*). The word is used for covering a house with a roof, as in a dedication by a *thiasos* at Olbia ("They covered the synagogue")[1] or for covering a container to keep a liquid from spilling.[2] Hence the connotations of protecting and defending,[3] of enduring and resisting, either literally ("They bore up against the onslaught of the barbarians")[4] or in a moral sense: "Being able to endure the deprivations no longer" (Philo, *Flacc.* 64, *mēketi stegein*); Moses was "unable to contain (*mē stegōn*) a feeling of reciprocal love and affection for his people" (*Virtues* 69); "For my father did me much evil, and I bore up until your arrival" (*ho gar patēr mou polla moi kaka epoiēsen, kai estexa heōs elthēs, P.Oxy.* 1775, 10); "it is necessary to be zealous, to bear up, to speak out" (*zēlotypein*

---

[1] *CII* 682, 9 = B. Lifshitz, *Synagogues juives*, n. 11; cf. Josephus, *Ant.* 5.314: Samson is placed in a room where two columns support the ceiling; Plutarch, *Rom.* 20.6: "the earth covered the wood"; *P.Cair.Zen.* 59251, 7; *P.Ness.* 22, 20, 26. *Enoch* 14.11: αἱ στέγαι = the roofs. Plutarch, *Dem.* 21.2; *I.Perg.* 158.

[2] Plato, *Resp.* 10.621 *a*: "no vase can contain the waters of the River of Forgetfulness"; *Critias* 111 *d*, soil strata made impermeable to rain by clay; Thucydides 2.94.3: "their ships, which were not water-tight (οὐδὲν στέγουσαι) caused them concern"; an epigram of Catilius: "Halting your respectful steps, friend, examine me well" (*SB* 8422, 1); πολλοὶ ἅμα στείχουσι δαήμεναι (ibid. 8356, 5); εἶτ' αὐτοὶ στείχετε σωιζόμενοι (ibid. 8382, 2). The verb στεγάζω in *P.Lond.* 1204, 18; *P.Ryl.* 233, 7: τὸ ἕτερον ὑδροψυγεῖον αὔριον στεγάζεται; cf. G. H. Whitaker, "Love Springs No Leak," in *Expositor*, ser. 8, vol. 21, 1921, pp. 126–128.

[3] Sophocles, *OC* 15: "towers protect the town"; Aeschylus, *Sept.* 797.

[4] Polybius 3.53.2; Aeschylus, *Suppl.* 135: "the vessel halts the assault of the sea"; Antipater of Thessalonica: "his hands no longer had the strength to support so heavy a burden" (*Anth. Pal.* 6.93.4); Dittenberger, *Syl.* 700, 23: ἔστεξεν τὴν ἐπιφερομένην τῶν βαρβάρων ὁρμήν. On the στεγνά of a flock in the countryside, cf. M. Launey, *Armées hellénistiques*, vol. 2, p. 694.

---

stegō, S 4722; *TDNT* 7.585–587; *EDNT* 3.272; MM 587; L&N 25.176; BAGD 765–766

gar dei stegein karterein, P.Grenf. 1.18; second century BC); Palladas: "I cannot hold back this rage" (Anth. Pal. 11.340). It is in this sense that St. Paul, not taking advantage of his right to live off of the gospel, endures all his privations (1 Cor 9:12; panta stegomen) or is unable to endure the impatience or distress caused him by lack of news from the Thessalonians: "no longer being able to bear it" (mēketi stegontes, 1 Thess 3:1, 5).

We may understand 1 Cor 13:7 in the same way: "love bears all things" (hē agapē . . . panta stegei).[5] It seems preferable, however, to give stegō its classical sense, "keep secret, hidden,"[6] which is its meaning in Sir 8:17—"Do not seek advice from a fool; he will not keep the matter confidential" (OT hapax); "remain silent." From Philo: "Not being able to keep quiet the secret of the greatness and beauty of virtue" (Philo, Abraham 261); from Josephus: "Once he was drunk, he could no longer keep secrets" (Life 225; cf. Ant. 19.48); a petition to the king, third century BC: "let him no longer hold out in the district on account of the preceding complaints" (ouketi stēgē en tō nomō dia tas prokeimenas aitias, P.Tebt. 769, 74); or the edict of the prefect Cn. Vergilius Capito, December 7, AD 48: kai toutous de stegē monon dechesthai tous dierchomenous.[7] Thus, in all circumstances, love is characterized by discretion; in particular, it keeps quiet about evils and does not record them on a balance sheet; it covers evil with silence and does not try to exploit it, as mothers excuse their children's faults and as Christ begged pardon for his executioners (Luke 23:34). So St. Paul says, "Persecuted, we show tolerance" (1 Cor 4:12; cf. 1 Pet 4:8 = T. Jos. 17.2). Far from complaining about all of the dishonest and base deeds that may do him harm, the long-suffering charitable person conceals them, in a way, and thus overcomes evil with good (1 Thess 5:15; Rom 12:17, 21; 1 Pet 3:9).

---

[5] St. Cyprian, who translated "omnia diligit" (PL, vol. 4, 632, 733) must have read στέργει. C. K. Barrett (A Commentary on the First Epistle to the Corinthians, London, 1968, p. 304: "supports all things") cites Simeon the Just (third century BC): "By three things the world subsists: by the law, by the service (the temple worship), and by works of love" (Pirqe 'Abot 1.2; cf. C. Spicq, Prolégomènes à une étude de théologie néo-testamentaire, pp. 156ff.).

[6] Sophocles, OT 341: "Well, it will come what will, though I keep mute" (σιγῇ στέγω); Phil. 136: "What must I conceal, what must I say before this man?"; Euripides, El. 273: "They will keep your words secret and mine"; Thucydides 6.72.5: "their secrets would be better kept"; Polybius 4.8.2: "Aratus was skilled both at speaking . . . and at keeping secret what he had decided"; 8.14.5; Lucian, Nav. 11; cf. H. Conzelmann, First Corinthians, pp. 223–224: "draw a veil of silence over"; C. Spicq, Agapè, vol. 2, p. 91. F. Field (Notes on the Translation, pp. 175f.) cites the proverb: Ἀρεοπαγίτου στεγανώτερος.

[7] SEG VIII, 794, 25 = Dittenberger, Or. 665 = SB 8248, 25. Cf. Stobaeus, Flor. 62.19.26 (vol. 4, p. 427): πιστὸν μὲν οὖν εἶναι χρὴ τὸν διάκονον τοιοῦτόν τ' εἶναι, καὶ στέγειν τὰ δεσποτῶν.

στηρίζω

stērizō, to support, sustain, strengthen, fix firmly in place,

---

The basic meaning of this verb is "support, sustain, strengthen," and in the passive voice "lean, settle, be confirmed,"[1] but its nuances vary considerably in various usages. These are first of all cosmic: the "rainbows that the son of Kronos fixed on a cloud";[2] "a wave appeared to us, touching the sky."[3] More common, however, is the meaning "set up, plant, fix." "I did not have the means either to plant my feet or to climb the trunk";[4] the camel's hump "is set on the rest of its body" (perfect passive of *estēriktai*, Aristotle, *HA* 2.1.499ª17). Finally, in medical lan-

---

[1] In the third century BC, Philonides writes to his father: καλῶς ἐπόησας σπουδάσας, ὅπως ἂν παρὰ Τελέστου γραφῆ στηριχθῆς (*SB* 7183, 2).

[2] Homer, *Il.* 11.26; 4.443—"her forehead will lean on heaven"; Aristotle, *Mete.* 376ᵇ23; Ps.-Aristotle, *Mund.* 4.395ᵇ4: τῶν δὲ σελάων (the meteors) ἃ μὲν ἀκοντίζεται, ἃ δὲ στηρίζεται; Plutarch, *Mor.* 75 d, 938 a (of stationary celestial bodies); Aratus, *Phaen.* 10: αὐτὸς γὰρ τά γε σήματ᾽ ἐν οὐρανῷ ἐστήριξεν ἄστρα διακρίνας; cf. the mother of the Maccabees fixed (established) in heaven (4 Macc 17:5).

[3] Euripides, *Hipp.* 1207, οὐρανῷ στηρίζον; cf. *Bacch.* 972, 1083; Hesiod, *Th.* 779: columns of silver πρὸς οὐρανὸν ἐστήρικται; Plutarch, *Sull.* 6.11: "a shining flame rose toward the sky."

[4] Homer, *Od.* 12.434; *Il.* 16.111; Hesiod, *Th.* 498: "Zeus fixed the stone on the earth"; Callimachus, *Hymn. Ap.* 2.23: "the rock set on the Phrygian shore"; 1 Enoch 24.2— "mountains leaning against each other"; *T. Job* 32.7—"set up tables." Leonidas of Tarentum: "I lean now on my staff" (*Anth. Pal.* 7.731; cf. Philo, *Creation* 84); Plutarch, *Eum.* 11.8: "the horses try to lean on their forelimbs." Marcus "set himself up (in effigy, στερηκθέντα) on the field ceded inexpensively by Sperentios" (*IGLS* 2114, 8). Boundaries between towns are referred to by the stereotypical formula λίθον διορίζοντα κώμης Γασιμμέας καὶ Ναμαρρίων στηριχθῆναι (Dittenberger, *Or.* 612, 8; 769, 11; in Gaulanitis, cf. J. and L. Robert, "Bulletin épigraphique," in *REG*, 1956, p. 179, n. 335). Cf. *PSI* 452, 3: κανόνι στηρίξαι ὑπὸ θατέρου μέρους τῶν κοινωνῶν (fourth century).

---

stērizō, S 4741; *TDNT* 7.653–657; *EDNT* 3.276; MM 589; L&N 30.80, 74.19, 85.38; BDF §§71, 74(1), 400(7); BAGD 768

guage, the illness or the pain settles in a certain part of the body.[5] In a number of its late occurrences, stērizō has the nuance of steadfast determination,[6] but apparently it never had a moral significance in classical Greek.

It was the LXX that gave it a religious and moral meaning. It preserves the secular meanings, as with Jacob's ladder "leaning on the earth (estērigmenē, Hebrew nāṣab) and reaching to the heavens" (Gen 28:12; cf. Philo, Dreams 1.3.; 1.133; 2.19), but it emphasizes the meaning "sustain"[7] and "lean" ("If anyone leans on this broken reed that is Egypt, his hand will be pierced").[8] In so doing it gives stērizō a nuance of stability, of lasting fixedness, of solidity,[9] so that the verb has to be translated "strengthen, make firm." According to Exod 17:12, "Aaron and Hur held Moses' hands (Hebrew tāmak), so that his hands were firm (estērigmenai, Hebrew 'emûnâh) until sunset" (cf. Philo, Alleg. Interp. 3.45). On the rare occasion this

---

[5] Hippocrates, Aff. 3.3: ὀδύνη ἐστηριγμένη = the pain has settled (= Acut., append. 25); 4.49.4: "the bilious humor, dispersed in the body or settled"; 4.50.5: "the blood, where it works the most, settles and heats up"; 4.51.8; 4.52.2, 4; 4.53.1–2; 4.54.6: the solitary worm attaches itself also to the back; Aph. 4.33: στηρίζει ἡ νοῦσος = the illness is fixed. With the Athenian plague, "the disease was fixed in the heart" (ἐς τὴν καρδίαν στηρίζειεν, Thucydides 2.49.3).

[6] Sib. Or. 3.27: "He himself fixed the type of appearance of mortals" (ἐστήριξε τύπον μορφῆς μερόπων); Diogenes Laertius 2.136: ἐπὶ δόγματος στηρίζειν = to hold to his opinion.

[7] Gen 27:37—Isaac "sustained Jacob with grain and wine" (Hebrew sāmak); Ps 104:15—"that bread may sustain the heart of man" (Hebrew sāʿad; Cant 2:5—"Sustain me with cakes" (piel of sāmak); Sir 13:21—"the rich person who falters is sustained by his friends"; Prov 15:25—"Yahweh sustains (causes to stand, hiphil of nāṣab) the widow's boundaries"; Sir 3:9; Isa 59:16—"His righteousness sustained him" (sāmak); Ps 51:14—"sustain me with an upright spirit" (sāmak). This latter Hebrew verb is the one usually underlying στηρίζω. At Qumran, it means "give support, strengthen, sustain." 1QH 7.6—"I praise you, Lord, because you have sustained me with your strength"; 2.7—"You sustain my soul and strengthen my heart"; 1QM 8.7, 14—a sustained sound; 1QS 10.25—a solid border; 4.5 and 8.3—strength of character; 1QH 1.35—"a strong inclination"; 2.9—"a firm support for those whose hearts are anxious."

[8] 2 Kgs 18:21 (cf. Philo, Husbandry 75: the horseman "who does not clutch anything that he can depend on falls"); Sir 15:4—the one who relies on wisdom will not be moved; 1 Macc 2:17—"supported by sons and brothers."

[9] Dan 7:38—"The matter was fixed (kept, Aramaic niṭrēt) in my heart"; Ps 111:8—"Your ordinances are fixed forever"; Sir 24:10—"In Zion I was established (settled)"; 38:34—the artisans "keep the fabric of the world stable"; 39:32—"From the beginning I have been convinced"; 40:19—"Children and the founding of a city establish a name"; 42:17—"in [God's] glory the universe stands firm" (Hebrew hithpael of yāṣab, subsist, resist). Cf. join with, share in an inheritance, 1 Sam 26:19 (hithpael of sāpâh).

strengthening is pejorative,[10] but almost always God is the one who does the establishing (Sir 6:37; 1 Macc 14:14; *Pss. Sol.* 16.12), or the heart is what stands firm,[11] that is, what is strong, convinced, persevering. This is a virtue that goes with faithfulness.

Philo inherits this vocabulary: "the plaster must harden and acquire solidity" (*Husbandry* 160); "The feet are the support and the stable base of a man."[12] Not only is the meaning "stability" emphasized, but it becomes a spiritual quality that the hesitant and the divided lack; they are "unable to find a permanent seat" (*Migr. Abr.* 148), "unstable beings, scattered, carried here and there, always moving away without ever establishing (*stērichthēnai*) themselves anywhere" (*Prelim. Stud.* 58). It is precisely in the midst of the worst difficulties that changeless fixedness must be shown: "Do not let yourself be submerged or engulfed, but fix yourself firmly (*stērichtheis*) and energetically turn back the stream of difficulties that are pouring out on you with extreme violence from above to below, from here and there, from all sides at once."[13] This precept is taken up by Christian parenesis. This intensive sense of *stērizō* ("stand firm") is owed to Philo, whose affinities with the vocabulary of the NT are never sufficiently noted.

There is nevertheless a Hebraism that Philo did not exploit, which consists in placing or fixing one's eye or face toward or against someone.[14] In the latter case, hostility is entailed, but "to set one's face" to do some-

---

[10] 1 Macc 2:49—"Now the reign of arrogance and outrage is established."

[11] Judg 19:5, 8: "Strengthen your heart" (Hebrew *sā'ad*); Ps 112:8—"His heart is firm, he does not fear"; Sir 5:10—"Stand firm in your knowledge"; 22:16—"The heart that is fixed on the thought of its plan will not be slack when the time comes"; 1 Macc 14:26—"Simon stood firm" (ἐστήρισε αὐτός, intransitive).

[12] *Drunkenness* 156; *Creation* 67: "the seed deposited in the uterus is fixed there" (στηρίση); *Dreams* 1.144, 157: "the Lord, firmly established at the top of the ladder"; 1.241: "The universe rests solidly on the power of my word."

[13] *Flight* 49 (on Gen 28:2); *Dreams* 2.11; *Spec. Laws* 2.202: "Reason, solidly strengthened (στηριχθείς), as on a path or road that is quite dry, will be able to make its journey without stumbling toward things that deserve to be seen and heard"; *Rewards* 30: "To lean and be established (στηρίσασθαι) only on God, with firm reasoning and unbending and unshakable faith (ἀκλινοῦς καὶ βεβαιοτάτης πίστεως): happy is that one in truth and thrice blessed."

[14] It dates to Amos 9:4—"I will fix my eye on them for misfortune and not for happiness"; στηρίζω translates the Hebrew verb *śûm*, "put, place, establish, turn"; likewise Jer 24:6, but with the opposite meaning: "I will fix my eye on them with kindness." Usually it is the face that is strengthened; Jer 3:12 specifies, "I will not set my face against you (Hebrew hiphil of *nāpal*), for I am merciful." This is an exception, because ordinarily when God set his face against a given city or people, "the young women who prophesy on their own initiative" . . . it is "for evil and not for good" (Jer 21:10; Ezek 6:2; 13:17; 21:2). Moreover, it is the verb *nātan* that is used, "give, give out, produce, establish, make"; cf. Ezek 14:8; 16:7; 21:2, 7; 25:2; 28:21; 29:2; 38:2.

thing expresses an absolutely firm resolve, an unshakable decision or attitude, a definitive intention. This is exactly the meaning in Luke 9:51—at the beginning of the great journey to Jerusalem, during which Jesus crosses Samaria, Judea, the Jordan and even turns his back on the capital, the evangelist notes that "he set his face to go to Jerusalem" (*autos to prosōpon estērisen tou poreuesthai eis Ierousalēm*). Perhaps Luke is thinking of Isa 50:7, "I set my face like a flint"; in any event, he wants to point out Christ's absolutely firm resolve—almost obstinacy—to get to the Holy City, whatever may be the dangers, the suffering, and the diverse circumstances of the pilgrimage.[15]

We must understand the same sense of absoluteness with "the great gulf solidly fixed (perfect passive, *estēriktai*)" that separates poor Lazarus from the wicked rich man (Luke 16:26). It is absolutely uncrossable, cutting off any communication. More important is Jesus' order to Peter: "When you have returned, strengthen your brothers" (*stērison tous adelphous sou*, Luke 22:32). Not only does this verb here find its original technical parenetic meaning, taking on a moral sense, but it envisions a faith thenceforth indefectible: make your brothers unyielding. In his first epistles, St. Paul sees the goal of his apostolic ministry as being "to strengthen and encourage" the faith of the disciples, to establish them solidly, without oscillation, to make them capable of standing fast without discouragement or doubt,[16] notably in the midst of the physical, moral, and doctrinal

---

[15] Cf. J. Starcky, "Obfirmavit faciem suam ut iret Jerusalem: Sens et portée de Luc IX, 51," in *RSR* (Mélanges J. Lebreton), 1951, pp. 197–202 (who translates, "Il durcit son visage et se dirigea vers Jérusalem" ["He hardened his face and set out for Jerusalem"]). E. Delebecque, *Evangile de Luc:* "Il fit sa marche vers Jérusalem sa perspective inflexible." Cajetan emphasizes Christ's force of soul and greatheartedness in facing danger and heading resolutely into it. Cf. H. Conzelmann, *Die Mitte der Zeit*, 1954 = *The Theology of St. Luke*, London, 1960, pp. 60–73; J. H. Davies, "The Purpose of the Central Section of St. Luke's Gospel," in F. L. Cross, *SE*, vol. 2, Berlin, 1964, pp. 164–169; H. H. Farmer, "The Courage of Christ," in *ExpT* 75, 1964, pp. 176ff. C. F. Evans, "The Central Section of St. Luke's Gospel," in D. E. Nineham, *Studies in the Gospels*, Oxford, 1955, pp. 37–53; G. Friedrich, "Lk. IX, 51 und die Entrückungschristologie des Lukas," in *Orientierung an Jesus* (Festschrift J. Schmid), Freiburg-Basel-Vienna, 1973, pp. 48–77.

[16] 1 Thess 3:2, εἰς τὸ στηρίξαι ὑμᾶς καὶ παρακαλέσαι ὑπὲρ τῆς πίστεως ὑμῶν, τὸ μηδένα σαίνεσθαι; 3:13—"May the Lord make you grow and abound in love . . . to strengthen your hearts without reproach toward holiness"; 2 Thess 2:17—"May God encourage and strengthen your hearts in every good deed and word"; 3:3—"The Lord is faithful, who will strengthen you and keep you from evil." The initial goal of Rom 1:11 (εἰς τὸ στηριχθῆναι ὑμᾶς) is repeated in the final doxology (16:25, στηρίξαι). Cf. Acts 18:23—St. Paul, in the course of his third journey, crosses Galatia and Phrygia, στηρίζων πάντας τοὺς μαθητάς.

calamities of the end times. Just as Jesus had entrusted to Peter the responsibility of firmly establishing the apostles, who had been scandalized and disoriented by their Master's passion (Matt 26:31), these in turn strengthen the faithful in the wait for the Parousia. Their resolution must be strong and sustained: "Have patience . . . strengthen your hearts, for the Lord's coming is near" (Jas 5:8); "The God of all grace . . . when you suffer a little (while), he himself will equip you, strengthen you, fortify you, ground you" (*autos katartisei, stērixei, stēnōsei, themeliōsei,* 1 Pet 5:10; the reading with the verb *stērizō* must be kept). Peter addresses persecuted Christians who must remain unshakable in their faith, because their hearts— full of a vigor infused by God—have a sort of immovability in the midst of all the disasters (cf. 5:8, the devil like a roaring lion). The accumulation of the four verbs of stability points out well the importance of "firmness" among the Christian virtues. Once the baptized have committed themselves to the Christian *credo,* they will remain unchangeably fixed in it (*estērigmenous en tē parousē alētheia,* 2 Pet 1:12). No deficiency is to be allowed. The last occurrence of *stērizō* (in the imperative) in the NT is addressed to the church at Sardis: "Be watchful, and strengthen the rest that was close to perishing."[17]

---

[17] Rev 3:2—στήρισον τὰ λοιπὰ ἃ ἔμελλον ἀπαθανεῖν; cf. S. E. Johnson, "Christianity in Sardis," in A. Wikgren, *Early Christian Origins: Studies in Honor of H. R. Willoughby,* Chicago, 1961, pp. 81–90; C. J. Hemer, "The Sardis Letter and the Croesus Tradition," in *NTS,* vol. 19, 1972, pp. 94–97.

στόμαχος

stomachos, **orifice, throat, esophagus, stomach**

Derived from *stoma,* the biblical hapax *stomachos* is almost unknown in the papyri and inscriptions.[1] Its primitive meaning is "opening, orifice." In Homer it refers to the throat, the gullet;[2] in Aristotle, the esophagus;[3] in Hippocrates and the medical writers in general it means the stomach proper: "Suffocation results from the pressing of the liver and the belly against the diaphragm, and from the tightening of the

---

[1] There is almost nothing to add to the two references given by Moulton-Milligan and LSJ: *P.Leid.* W, 18, 36 (second century), ἀμφοτέρας (χεῖρας) ἔχων ἐπὶ τοῦ στομάχου, "with both hands on his stomach" (*Pap.Graec.Mag.* 13, 830, vol. 2, p. 124, 36); *P.Oxy.* 533, 14 (second-third century), in a metaphorical sense, ἵνα μὴ ἔχωμεν στομάχους μηδὲ φθόνον, "so that we may not be caused vexation and annoyance"; *I.Cret.* I, 17, 11 (second century BC), a man miraculously cured of his illness by Asclepius: στομαχικὸν πόνον ἔχοντα. Add *P.Leid.:* "apply the right hand o the mouth and the throat" (ἔστω δὲ ἡ χεὶρ δεξιὰ προσέχουσα τῷ στομάχῳ, *Pap.Graec.Mag.* 12, 128; vol. 2, p. 66, 22).

[2] Homer, *Il.* 3.292: "he cut the lambs' throats"; 17.47: Menelaus spears Euphorbus through the base of the throat; 19.266: "he cut the boar's throat." Cf. Philostratus, *Gym.* 35: "those who have a small, convex chest have illnesses of the throat . . . their breathing is labored"; Epictetus 2.20.33: "They dream only of belching out their little problem and, after exercising their throats, of going to the bath"; Pliny, *Ep.* 9.36.3: "I read in a loud, firm voice, not so much from the larynx as from the chest" ("non tam vocis causa quam stomachi"); Celsus 1.8: "si quis vero stomacho laborat legere clare debet"; Suetonius, *Aug.* 84.2; *Nero* 25, 3; Quintilian, *Inst.* 11.3.19ff.

[3] Aristotle, *HA* 1.16.495b19: "The top end of the esophagus is attached to the mouth, near the tracheal artery . . . at the other end, it crosses the diaphragm and reached the stomach" (εἰς τὴν κοιλίαν; cf. *HA* 3.3.664a20–35); Hippocrates, *Aff.* 4.56.8: "the human esophagus, always wide open, adjoins the stomach"; cf. Nicander, *Alex.* 379: στόμα γαστρός; 20–22, 120.

---

stomachos, S 4751; *EDNT* 3.279; MM 592; L&N 8.66; BAGD 770

orifice of the stomach."[4] Rufus of Ephesus defines this organ thus: "the stomach or esophagus is the conduit through which food and drink descend to the intestines" (*Onom.* 157); "it goes down between the pharynx and the neck vertebrae" (*Anat.* 24; cf. 38). But the *stomachos* is not only the stomach cavity; it is also the neck of the bladder or the cervix.[5]

When 1 Tim 5:23 prescribes, "Stop drinking only water; take a little wine on account of your stomach and your frequent illnesses" (*mēketi hydropotei, alla oinō oligō chrō dia ton stomachon kai tas pyknas sou astheneias*), all exegetes agree that *stomachos* means the stomach proper, even though the Hebrews, alone of all the peoples of antiquity, had practically no knowledge of this organ.[6] It is impossible to diagnose Timothy's trouble, because the lack of vigor (*a-stheneia*) is a very general

---

[4] Καὶ τοῦ στομάχου τῆς γαστρὸς ἀπειλήμμέμου, Hippocrates, *Morb. Sac.* 6.374; cf. Dioscorides, *Mat. Med.* 5.7; Soranus 1.15; Galen, *Comm. Hipp.*, p. 160, 11: "it is the stomach that is in charge of nutrition"; Plutarch, *Conv. sept. sap.* 15: "the organs of nutrition, the teeth, the stomach, the liver"; Marcus Aurelius 10.31.4: "a robust stomach digests all foods"; Athenaeus 3.79 *f*; *T. Naph.* 2.8.

[5] Hippocrates, *Steril.* 217: "When the cervix is hard in its entirety or at the end" (ed. Littré, vol. 8, p. 418; cf. *Mul.* 1.90). Cf. P. Chantraine, "Remarques sur la langue et le vocabulaire du Corpus hippocratique," in *La Collection hippocratique et son rôle dans l'histoire de la médicine* (Colloque de Strasbourg, 1972), Leiden, 1975, p. 40.

[6] P. Dhorme, *Emploi métaphorique*, p. 133. Nevertheless, the observation of gastric symptoms was an established element of Sumerian medicine: "If a person has a distended stomach and rumbling noises"; "if the stomach is full of acid"; "if the patient is nauseous even when fasting . . . has bitter saliva, a bloated face, a distended stomach; if food and drink cause him pain . . . let him vomit . . . if the muscles are sore and weak"; if when he eats "a person has pain accompanied by a burning sensation in the pit of his stomach and vomits bile" (cited by G. Contenau, "Assyriens et Babyloniens," in *Histoire générale de la médicine*, Paris, 1936, vol. 1, p. 84). Likewise in Egypt: "If you find someone who suffers from an obstruction of the orifice of the stomach (stomach = *ro – ib*), if he has a heavy sensation after eating, if his belly is distended, if his heart fails when he walks"; "his belly is ordinarily heavy, his stomach always painful, burning, and fragile, his clothing is always burdensome, he cannot endure many clothes. . . . He has a bad taste in his mouth" (cited by Fournier-Bégniez, "Médicine des Egyptiens," ibid., vol. 1, pp. 102–103). P.Ebers, which is addressed to practitioners, contains eighteen "instructions for (caring for) someone who has a sick stomach" and for making it possible for the patient to take food. It diagnoses gastric troubles (which make the limbs heavy, like the onset of general fatigue), the distension of the stomach, gastric hemorrhages, etc. (cf. G. Lefèbvre, *Essai sur la médicine égyptienne*, Paris, 1956, pp. 124–130). Philo associates nausea of the stomach with intestinal maladies (*Rewards* 143); he notes that the top of the stomach, adjacent to the esophagus (*Spec. Laws* 1.217) is located between the viscera and the heart (*Creation* 118; *Alleg. Interp.* 1.12).

reference to illness.[7] Babylonian, Egyptian, Greek, and Roman physicians are unanimous in pointing out overwhelming fatigue, torpor, general tiredness, chronic bouts of weakness (*BGU* 2065, 10; *Pap.Lugd.Bat.* XVI, 3, 29) as symptoms experienced by *kakostomachoi*,[8] so this could just as well be a case of gastroenteritis as of varices of the esophagus, a gastric ulcer, etc.[9] In any event, without resorting to magic, amulets, or phylacteries,[10] ancient medicine was not without resources to combat stomach illnesses.[11]

In prescribing wine, St. Paul was in agreement with the unanimous opinion of ancient physicians. They prescribed wine as a tonic, a prophylactic, and a remedy to facilitate digestion, combat anorexia, and suppress stomach-rumblings, especially wine sweetened with honey:[12] wine is a

---

[7] Gal 4:13; 2 Cor 12:9; cf. Acts 4:9; 1 Cor 1:11, 30; 2 Tim 4:20; Plutarch, *Mar.* 33.6: Marius 33.6: Marius resigns his command on the pretext that illness has sapped his physical strength (ὡς ἐξαδυνατῶν τῷ σώματι διὰ τὴν ἀσθένειαν); *P.Mich.* 618, 11: ἀσθενὴς τοῖς ὀφθαλμοῖς; 426, 3, 18ff. *P.Flor.* 382, 63.

[8] Epictetus 4.8.34–35. *Stomachikoi* suffer from a burning sensation, lack of appetite, nausea, and spasms, have bad breath (Dioscorides, *Mat. Med.* 4.38), cannot digest all foods (Marcus Aurelius 10.31.6), vomit (Epictetus 3.21.1), lose sleep (Galen, *Comm. Hipp.*, pp. 72ff.; 165, 9), have chronic pain (73, 20; 131, 3), acidity (24, 4), indolence (22, 10, νωθρός), etc.

[9] Cosmas Indicopleustes complains of a "dryness of the stomach" that causes frequent illnesses (*Top. Chr.* 2.1; 72 D). It is very tricky to identify illnesses referred to by the ancients using words that we use today; for example, sciatica (*ischias*) can be either a pain in the hip or a neuralgia of the sciatic nerve; phthisis, apoplexy, pleurisy, erysipelas, and cardiology do not refer to the same things, cf. M. D. Grmek, "La Réalité nosologique au temps d'Hippocrate," in *La Collection hippocratique et son rôle dans l'histoire de la médecine*, pp. 237–255.

[10] A. Delatte, P. Derchain, *Les Intailles magiques gréco-égyptiennes*, Paris, 1964, p. 56; cf. the legend on intaglio number 80: "Keep the stomach of Proclus in good health" (Φίλαξον ὑγειῆ στόμαχον Πρόκλου); on numbers 89, 235, 307, 193: "Stomach, digest!" (στόμαχε πέπτε).

[11] Aristotle "placed a small skin of hot oil on his stomach" (Diogenes Laertius 5.10). Poultices and potions were prescribed by Assyrian and Egyptian physicians (*P.Ebers*). For Marcus Aurelius, whose stomach illness was such that he could "no longer take food without experiencing pain and no longer sleep without having nightmares" (Dio Cassius 71.6 and 24), Galen prescribed "a little pepper in some wine" and "applying to the stomach wool soaked in well heated oil of nard" (cited by P. Seidmann, in *Histoire générale de la médecine*, Paris, 1936, vol. 1, p. 403).

[12] Dioscorides, *Mat. Med.* 5.7.1; Rufus of Ephesus, *Ren. Ves.* 2.26; cf. Strabo 6.1.14. On *vinum conditum* or *piperatum* (seasoned or peppered wine), cf. Apicius 1.1.2; *Anth. Pal.* 9.502; Theophanes Nonnus, *Cur. Morb.*, c. 156, line 12 (vol. 2, p. 12; ed. Bernard). But the various mixtures stabilized the wines and made their transport possible (Pliny, *HN* 14.126), "they work by biting into the stomach; they cause flatulence and help grind up foods" (Athenaeus 1.59 *d*). Applied in a lotion, wine disinfects (Luke 10:34) and stimulates. Hannibal "had his horses washed with old wine . . . it cured their illnesses and scabies" (Polybius 3.88.1).

stimulant for the stomach.[13] The wisdom of this treatment was recognized by secular writers: "For persons who have been weakened by stomach ailments and need a tonic remedy . . . physicians strengthen them with wine."[14]

---

[13] Ἔστω δὲ καὶ οἶνος ἐς ἀνάκλησιν τοῦ στομάχου, Aretaeus of Cappadocia, ed. Hude, Berlin, 1958, p. 146, 15. Other than wines valued for their very good taste (cf. *P.Sorb.* 19, 2: ἀστειότατος = an excellent vintage; 255 BC; Plutarch, *Quaest. conv.* 1.4.2.620 *d*), distinctions were made between wines that were "good for the stomach" like that of Velitrae (Pliny, *HN* 14.27 *a* and *c*; cf. 23.63; Juvenal, *Sat.* 5.32), digestifs like that of Chios (Athenaeus 1.59 *a*, πεπτικός); "the wine called πρότροπος is good for the stomach" (idem 2.24 *e*). Cf. C. Spicq, "I Tim. V, 23," in *L'Evangile hier et aujourd'hui* (Mélanges F. J. Leenhardt), Geneva, 1968, pp. 143–150); P. Boyancé, in *BAGB*, 1951, pp. 3–19.

[14] Plutarch, *Quaest. conv.* 3.5.2; cf. Artemidorus Daldianus, *Onir.* 1.66: "To drink a little wine . . . and not get drunk is good." There is no need to cite all the jokes of drunkards: "a drinker of water (ὕδωρ πίνων) will never do any good" (*Anth. Pal.* 13.20); "Oh, how I pity drinkers of water" (ibid. 9.406), etc. G. Gourevitch, "Stomachus et l'humeur," in *RevPhil*, 1977, pp. 56–74.

στρατολογέω

stratologeō, **to marshall or recruit an army**

"No one who is serving as a soldier lets himself become entangled or involved in the affairs of this life; he seeks only to please the one who enlisted him (*hina tō stratologēsanti aresē*)."[1] The biblical hapax *stratologeō*, "marshall or recruit an army," is unknown in the papyri[2] but attested in several literary texts. When Pharaoh took Sarah, Abraham "enlisted the invincible Ally";[3] "Brasidas had a thousand Helots, and with the allied soldiers who had been enlisted (*ek te symmachōn stratologēthentōn*), a considerable army was put together" (Diodorus Siculus 12.67.5; cf. 14.54). H. J. Mason gives this definition: *stratologeō: dilectum facere, epimelētēs hodōn kai en allois topois s . . .* (*IGRom.* III, 763; Phaselis Lyciae, 144–7 p.; vide St R. II, 1090 adn.). —*stratologia: dilectus, pemphtheis epi s [—] apo Rhōmaiōn* (*IGRom.* III, 824; Thracia, II)."[4]

---

[1] 2 Tim 2:4. The thought is repeated by Ignatius of Antioch (Ign. *Pol.* 6); an analogous idea in Xenophon, *Cyr.* 5.3.48; Xenophon, *Eq. Mag.* 6.1; Aeneas Tacticus 16.5; Dio Chrysostom 3.66–67. On ἀρέσκω, cf. F. W. Danker, "Under Contract," in *Festschrift to Honor F. W. Gingrich*, Leiden, 1972, pp. 198ff.

[2] Only "recuitment" (στρατολογία) is attested; *P.Lips.* 54, 10 and 13 (fourth century AD). To give one's name is to be enrolled: ἔδωκεν τὸ ὄνομα αὐτοῦ ἵνα στρατευθῇ (*P.Abinn.* 19, 14; cf. *P.Oxy.* 1022; *P.Ryl.* 609; J. F. Gilliam, "Enrollment in the Imperial Army," in *Eos* (Symbolae R. Taubenschlag), 1957, vol. 2, pp. 207–216).

[3] Josephus, *War* 5.380: τὸν ἀνίκητον αὐτῷ βοηθόν ἐστρατολόγησεν; cf. Plutarch, *Caes.* 35.1; Dionysius of Halicarnassus 11.24.

[4] H. J. Mason, *Greek Terms*, p. 87. (*Dilectus* [or *delectus*] is a Latin military technical term for a levy, recruiting.) On *dilecti*, cf. Liebemann, in PW, vol. 5, 591ff.

---

stratologeō, S 4753; *TDNT* 7.701–713; *EDNT* 3.280; *NIDNTT* 3.958, 964; MM 592; L&N 55.19, 55.20; BAGD 770

συγγένεια, συγγενής, συγγενίς

syngeneia, **family, kin;** *syngenēs*, **male relative;** *syngenis*, **female relative**

→*see also* συγγενής

These noun forms, which do not appear before Pindar, correspond to the idea of "birth, race"[1] and are formed around *gignomai*, "be born," then "become, occur."[2] So *syngeneia* means "family," "kinship"; *syngenēs* means "belonging to the same *genos*, kin, related"; *syngenis* is a relative; but there are many nuances.

I. — The first meaning, which remains the commonest, is that of blood ties, the racial meaning,[3] which relies on the concept of the family: "the paternal family" (*syngeneia patros*, Euripides, *Tro.* 754); "my father's kinsman" (*Or.* 1233; *Phoen.* 291), "a relative's blood."[4] Aristotle notes,

---

[1] Γένος, "race," or better "lineage, descent," unites all those who trace back to a common ancestor. So it first designated the family group, then in the classical period a group of families by virtue of distant ancestry. Cf. Homer, *Il.* 6.211: "That is the race, the blood, of which I boast to be descended"; Plato, *Euthphr.* 11 *c*; *Chrm.* 155 *a*; *Lysis* 205 *c*.

[2] P. Chantraine, *Dictionnaire étymologique*, pp. 221ff. Idem, "Les noms du mari et de la femme, du père et de la mère en grec," in *REG*, 1946–47, pp. 219–250; J. Wackernagel, "Über einige lateinische und griechische Ableitungen aus den Verwandtschaftswörtern," in *Festgabe A. Kaegi*, Frauenfeld, 1919, pp. 40–65 (reprinted in *Kleine Schriften*, Göttingen, 1956, vol. 1, pp. 468–493). E. des Places, *Syngeneia: La Parenté de l'homme avec Dieu d'Homère à la Patristique*, Paris, 1964.

[3] Cf. συγγένεια associated with the notion of nature (φυά, natural property), Pindar, *Nem.* 1.27; 1.28: "when heredity (συγγενές, the innate, the inborn) makes us able" to make reason prevail; 5.40; 6.8; *Isthm.* 1.40; *Pyth.* 8.44: "his natural disposition (τὸ συγγενές) makes him follow in his father's path"; συγγενής often means "inborn" (Aeschylus, *Ag.* 832).

[4] Euripides, *Supp.* 148: αἷμα συγγενές; *Alc.* 532: "stranger, not related by birth"; *IT* 923; *Andr.* 887: "I want to inquire about a kinswoman"; Sophocles, *El.* 1202: "you are not here as a kinsman"; 1469; *OC* 771, 1157; Plato, *Plt.* 257 *d*, the kinship

---

syngeneia, S 4772; *TDNT* 7.736–742; *EDNT* 3.282; MM 595; L&N 10.5; BDF §110(2); BAGD 772 ‖ *syngenēs*, S 4773; *TDNT* 7.736–742; *EDNT* 3.282; MM 595; L&N 10.6, 11.57; BDF §§47(4), 48, 194(2); BAGD 772 ‖ *syngenis*, *EDNT* 3.282; MM 595; L&N 10.7; BDF §59(3); BAGD 772

"The same person is called son by one, brother by another, by someone else cousin or kinsman by blood, marriage, or affinity."[5] These degrees of kinship are specified as brother (Aeschylus, *Cho.* 199, *adelphos*, from *a*, "one," and *delphys*, "womb"; cf. *Ep. Arist.* 7; *P.Grenf.*II, 78, 13), sister (Aeschylus, *Eum.* 691), cousin (*PV* 855); and relatives and friends are linked with them.[6] Furthermore, *syngeneia* refers to the kinship of the human race with divinity, that is to say, the origin of humanity with and its likeness to divinity.[7] Zeus is "father of gods and men" (Homer, *Il.* 1.544; Hesiod, *Th.* 546, 643; *Op.* 59, 169), "the common author of our two races" (Aeschylus, *Suppl.* 402). From this paternity there derives a resemblance: "Since man shares in the divine lot (*theias metesche moiras*), he attains this state of kinship (*syngeneia*) with the gods."[8] The Stoics

(συγγένεια) of Socrates with Theaetetus; 258 *a*; 298 *b*; *Grg.* 472 *b* (a large family); *Leg.* 1.627 *c*: "house and family"; 5.730 *b*: "friends, relatives"; 11.925 *b.* E. des Places (*Syngeneia*, pp. 86ff.) notes three aspects of Platonic συγγένεια: analogy (especially of modes of being and modes of knowing), exemplarity and similitude (correspondence of a copy to the model), and relation between microcosm and macrocosm (sympathy uniting various realms of the world).

[5] Aristotle, *Pol.* 2.3.7; cf. 2.4.1; 2.4.10; 2.8.20; *Eth. Nic.* 10.1180b6; *Ath. Pol.* 22.4, Hipparchus "was among the relatives (τῶν συγγενῶν) of Pisistratus"; cf. the tomb built ἑαυτοῖς τε καὶ ἐκγόνοις καὶ συγγενέσι of the deceased (*IGUR*, n. 1005); J. Krauss, *Die Inschriften von Sestos*, Bonn, 1980, n. 10, 2: οὔτε δὲ τοῖς τέκνοις οὔτε συγγενεῖσιν.

[6] Plato, *Alc. Maj.* 105 *e*: "neither your tutor (*epitropos*) nor your relatives (*syngenēs*) nor anyone else is in a position to get for you the power that you desire"; Plato, *Leg.* 9.877 *d*: "relatives on both sides"; 11.929 *b*: "his own kin"; *Prt.* 337 *c*: "I consider you all kinsmen (συγγενεῖς), family (οἰκείους), and fellow-citizens by nature, if not by law." Kinsmen and friends or family (*Resp.* 2.378 *c*; 5.470 *b*; 6.485 *c*; Plato, *Leg.* 5.729 *e*: "the stranger without companion or kin"; 6.775 *a*; *Plt.* 306 *c*); Euripides, *Heracl.* 305; *HF* 1154. *P.Mich.* 189, 5: μετὰ κυρίου ἑαυτῆς κατὰ πατέρα συγγενοῦς; *C.P.Herm.* 31, 17: "neither brothers nor sisters, neither nephews nor nieces, neither kin (οὐ συγγενῶν) nor cousins."

[7] Although he contrasts the human race (*genos*) with that of the gods (*Nem.* 6.1ff.), Pindar concludes, "Nevertheless we have some tie with the immortals in sublimity of spirit and also in our physical being" (5.5). Amphitryon "entered into the race of gods" (10.13). After death, the soul "still remains alive, an image of our being; for it alone comes from the gods" (Pindar, *Thren.* 2).

[8] Plato, *Prt.* 322 *a*. Cf. *Leg.* 10.899 *d*: "your belief in the gods is perhaps due to some divine kinship" (συγγένεια θεία); 900 *a*. In the first century BC: "The initiates have a place of honor. . . . How could you not be one of the first to share in this honor, linked as you are to the gods?" (γεννητὴς τῶν θεῶν, Ps.-Plato, *Ax.* 371 *d–e*); Epictetus 2.8.11: "You have in you a part of this god. Why then would you be ignorant of your kinship (συγγένειαν)? Why not know your origin?"; Dio Chrysostom, *Olymp.* 12.27: "The innate (ἔμφυτος) notion of the gods that every reasonable being holds by nature because of his kinship with them."

Cleanthes[9] and Aratus[10] (quoted by St. Paul, *tou gar kai genos esmen*, Acts 17:28) affirm this divine filiation.

II. — From the physical sense we move on to the metaphorical meaning, "affinity, likeness." Thus Plato, *Phd.* 79 *b–c*, which links likeness and kinship (*homoios* and *xyngenēs*); 84 *b*, kinship and similarity (*xyngenēs* and *toioutos*); 86 *b*: "of the same nature and family" (*homophyē te kai xyngenē*); *Resp.* 8.559 *d*. One learns "to know some things by other things if they have some relationship";[11] the lover "does not cease to attach himself to that which is related to him."[12] "Of all human activities, the one that is the most closely related to God's activity (contemplation) is the most blessed" (Aristotle, *Eth. Nic.* 10.9.1178^{b}23; cf. 1179^{a}26). Hence the meanings "of the same type, analogous, having the same properties."[13] From the meaning "natural" we move to "connatural." "Avarice is more natural (innate,

---

[9] Cleanthes, *Hymn to Zeus* 4: ἐκ σοῦ γὰρ γένος ἐσμέν (Stobaeus, *Ecl.* 1.1.12; vol. 1, p. 25). A. J. Festugière, *Dieu cosmique*, p. 211, observing that the line does not scan, corrects γ. ε. to γενόμεσθ' and translates "we come from you." He comments, "Zeus is our father, we are of his race"; and cites *Pap.Graec.Mag.* 4, 961 (ἐκ σοῦ γὰρ), 2836 (ἐκ σέο γὰρ πάντ' ἐστί).

[10] Aratus, *Phaen.* 5: τοῦ γὰρ καὶ γένος εἰμέν, quoted also by the Jewish peripatetic Aristobulus (frag. 4) in Eusebius, *Praep. Evang.* 13.12.6ff. Cf. E. des Places, " 'Ipsius enim et genus sumus' (Act. XVII, 28)," in *Bib*, 1962, pp. 388–395; Musonius 17.

[11] Plato, *Cra.* 438 *e*; cf. *Tht.* 156 *c*; *Soph.* 227 *b*; *Plt.* 280 *b*; *Resp.* 7.531 *d*; Aristotle, *Rh.* 2.23.1398^{a}22.

[12] Plato, *Symp.* 192 *b*; *Phlb.* 11 *b*, *e*; 59 *c*; 66 *c*; cf. *Resp.* 6.486 *d*: "truth is kin to measure"; 487 *a*: "a person is akin to truth." In Philo, who links "brother" and "kin" (*Dreams* 2.166; *Moses* 2.220; *Spec. Laws* 1.253, 297; 3.65; *Virtues* 51; 176; *Prelim. Stud.* 36) or "sister and kin" (*Creation* 12: "eternity is sister and kin to the invisible and the intelligible"; cf. 151; *Contemp. Life* 7; *Post. Cain* 52; *Alleg. Interp.* 2.20; 3.242), *syngeneia* and *syngenēs* have especially the meaning "affinity": "its like and its kin, because of their affinity and their commonality" (*Worse Attacks Better* 164; *Post. Cain* 45); "virtuous beings have an affinity with God" (*Creation* 74, 106, 144, 147; *Migr. Abr.* 178; *Heir* 238; *Moses* 2.8–9; *Spec. Laws* 1.247; 3.192; *Good Man Free* 21) and kinship, relationship: "man has a close kinship with God" (*Spec. Laws* 4.14; *Virtues* 79, 218; *Rewards* 163); "the character that is good and the character that is holy are closely akin to each other" (*Alleg. Interp.* 1.17; 3.33; *Worse Attacks Better* 18, 82, 88, 109; *Giants* 8, 42, 66; *Unchang. God* 69; *Husbandry* 26, 141; *Conf. Tongues* 6; *Change of Names* 98; *Dreams* 1.169; 2.26; *Decalogue* 134; *Spec. Laws* 3.149; 4.69; *Virtues* 134, 196); hence "of the same nature, of the same species": the body fashioned from the earth has "foods of the same nature, those given by the earth" (*Alleg. Interp.* 3.161; *Sacr. Abel and Cain* 39; *Plant.* 15; *Sobr.* 61; *Heir* 146; *Flight* 17; *Spec. Laws* 3.28), "connatural" (*Post. Cain* 136), "sharing the same blood" (*Unchang. God* 4), "inborn" (*Drunkenness* 40, 90; *Moses* 2.243), "innate" (*Joseph* 77), "closely akin" (*Creation* 62, 163; *Alleg. Interp.* 1.4).

[13] Aristotle, *Gen. Cor.* 2.1.329^{b}29; *Mete.* 1.2.339^{a}28; 1.3.339^{b}36; *Ph.* 6.1.231^{a}23; *Cael.* 1.2.268^{b}29; 1.3.270^{a}24; 3.2.301^{a}4; *De An.* 1.4.408^{a}8.

symphyes) to man than prodigality" (ibid. 4.3.1121^{b}14; cf. 3.15.1119^{b}9); "Connaturality (*syngeneia*) disposes children to obey their father."[14]

III. — In usage, and according to their etymology, the terms *syngeneia* and *syngenēs* take on nuances of solidarity, affection, and pride.[15] "His native city, his comrades, his parents—that is what a man cherishes, that is what is sufficient for him" (Pindar, *Paean.* 4.33); "blood ties (*to syngenes*) are terribly strong when friendship is added" (Aeschylus, *PV* 39; cf. 289); "family conversations (*hai syngeneis homiliai*) are a stong potion for hearts";[16] "real kinship produces solid friendship" (Plato, *Menex.* 244 *a*; cf. *Leg.* 5.729 *c*; 11.929 *a*). Aristotle insists on this more than anyone else: "Since whatever is conformable to nature is agreeable, and since things that are akin (*syngenē*) have natural links between them, all things that are akin and all like things are mutually pleasant to each other most of the time" (*Rh.* 1.11.1371^{b}12–13). "The species of friendship (*philia*) are comradeship (*hetaireia*), membership in the same household (*oikeiotēs*), membership in the same family (*syngeneia*), and so on" (*Rh.* 2.4.1381^{b}34); apart from the friendship of association (*en koinōnia*), there is "friendship of kindred (*syngenikē*) and friendship of comrades (*hetairikē*)" (*Eth. Nic.* 8.12.1161^{b}12, 16), friendship based on kinship (9.2.1165^{a}19 and 30).

IV. — Finally, *syngeneia* has a social and political meaning. Plato had already used this term for the "great alliances" of the state (*Resp.* 6.491 *c*), but it becomes common in this meaning from the third century BC in the

---

[14] *Eth. Nic.* 10.9.1180^{b}5–7. Philo, *Migr. Abr.* 178: the natural affinity of earthly and heavenly phenomena spares them from being separated; cf. the connaturality of pleasure, in Epicurus, *Men.* 129, 135; *Pyth.* 93, 116; *Her.* 72, 78. In the properly philosophical sense, the soul has a kinship with the Forms and the Ideas: "the philosopher is in harmony with the words of reason" (τὸ συγγενὲς τῶν λόγων, Plato, *Resp.* 6.494 *d*); *syngeneia* is a link with the intelligible world (6.490 *b* 3–4), a δεσμός (*Epin.* 991 *e*).

[15] Cf. Homer, *Il.* 6.211: "That is the race, the blood, that I boast to be descended from."

[16] Euripides, *Tro.* 51–52; cf. *Med.* 257: "without mother, without brother, without relative (οὐχὶ συγγενῆ), with whom shall I drop anchor?"; *Heracl.* 6, 30, 224, 229, 240; *Or.* 733: "You, the dearest of my companions, my friends, my kinsfolk"; Josephus, *Ant.* 1.165; 12.338; 16.382; *Life* 81; Diodorus Siculus 1.92.1: the relatives of a deceased person "tell friends and family"; *P.Phil.* 2, 1; *P.Mich.* 203, 34. In the epitaph of the scribe Ammonius: "not without plunging kinsfolk into saddest mourning and grief" (E. Bernand, *Inscriptions métriques*, n. 64, 7–8). Philo notes "all the seductions of *syngeneia*" (*Abraham* 170) and distinguishes among family members (*syngeneis*) those whom we call our beloved (*Spec. Laws* 3.155). He constantly links "relative and friend" (*Unchang. God* 79; *Husbandry* 155; *Abraham* 65; *Moses* 1.39, 303, 307; 2.171; *Spec. Laws* 1.68; 2.19; 3.85, 90, 126; 4.141; *Virtues* 103; *Rewards* 17; *Good Man Free* 9, 35; *Contemp. Life* 14; *Flacc.* 60, 64, 72); *syngeneia* must be honored (*Joseph* 172).

vocabulary of the inscriptions: cities unite in bonds of friendship and kinship.[17] Thus Alabanda is "kin to the Greeks";[18] "whereas the Rhodians are a people related to the people of Argos."[19] The formula "kinsmen and friends" (*syngeneis kai philoi*) recurs endlessly: the Acarnanians "celebrate the cult of the gods with piety and conduct toward peoples that are kinsmen and friends a politics that is noble and worthy of their ancestors."[20] The most notable case is that of a subdivision of the tribe (*phylē*) of Sinuri.[21] This *syngeneia* administrates the sanctuary; its members (*syngeneis*) "are pious toward the deity" (n. 9, 7–8) and can be the objects of honorific decrees; thus Nesaios "conducted himself well toward the *syngeneia*" and becomes the brother of the *syngeneis* (n. 73). So this community was a fraternity.

V. — In the inscriptions, and especially in the papyri, *syngenēs*, "king's friend," is a courtly title that usually precedes the person's function (*stratēgos, epistratēgos*). The Alexandrian Chrysermos is "kinsman of king Ptolemy" (*ton syngenē basileōs Ptolemaiou*).[22] King Attalus III calls Athenaeus his kinsman (*hēmōn esti syngenēs, I.Perg.* 248, 28). The papyri notably associate the "kinsman" with the legal guardian: "having as his legal guardian his kinsman Petearmouthos."[23]

---

[17] "In the time of Alexander, in Asia and elsewhere, a number of cities or nations with a more or less superficial patina of Hellenism tried . . . by the expedient of mythical filiations to tighten their bonds with old Greece and to ennoble their origins. . . . This was the golden age of artificial συγγένειαι" (M. Holleaux, *Etudes d'épigraphie*, vol. 3, pp. 154–155). Thus the Hellenists of Jerusalem claimed that the Jewish people had a common origin with the Lacedaemonians and were thus "kin" (2 Macc 5:9).

[18] C. Michel, *Recueil*, n. 252, 11–12. The three tribes of Olymos call themselves *syngeneiai* (*LSAM*, n. 58, 9–10); cf. the *syngeneia* of the Aganiteis (*SEG* II, 537, 2, 6; 538, 8; 546, 8); *IGLAM*, n. 334, 3, 7, 11, 13; 338, 11; 339, 4, 10; 360, 3.

[19] *NCIG*, n. VII, 5 (fourth-third century).

[20] J. Pouilloux, *Choix*, n. XXIX, 58 (third century BC); cf. Iasos and Rhodes (M. Holleaux, *Etudes d'épigraphie*, vol. 4, pp. 147, 149, 315). *I.Magn.* 15, 10 (Cnidos); 38, 29 (Magalopolis); 47, 3 (Magnesians and Macedonians); 52, 17 (Mytilene); 65, 22 (Gortyne); 70, 2 (a city of Crete); 72, 22 (Syracuse); 97, 12 (Teos); 101, 20 (Larbenai); etc. Inscription 53, 5 has been republished by B. Helly, *I.Gonn.* 111: "whereas the peoples of Magnesia-on-the-Maeander enjoy friendly relations with the people of Gonnoi and are their kin . . ."; *I.Lamps.*, n. 4, 25, 31.

[21] *I.Sinur.*, n. 10, 11, 14–20, 30, 46, 50.

[22] Dittenberger, *Or.* 104. Numerous references in A. Bernand, *Philae*; E. Bernand, *Fayoum*. In the papyri, *BGU* 1741, 12 (64–63 BC)–1745, 7; *P.Fouad* 16, 1; *P.Mil.Vogl.* 128, 1; *SB* 8881, 6; *C.Ord.Ptol.* 48, 3; 51, 7; 52, 33; 57, 3; 59, 6; etc. A very rich inventory prepared by W. Peremans, "Sur la titulature aulique in Egypte," in *Symbolae van Owen*, Leiden, 1946, pp. 129–159. Cf. 1 Esdr 3:7; 4:42; 1 Macc 10:89; 11:31; 2 Macc 11:1, 35.

[23] *P.Phil.* 6, 5; *BGU* 975, 13 (AD 45); 1579, 5, 25; *P.Alex.* 10, 5 (AD 69–79); *P.Mich.* 232, 4 (in AD 36); 262, 3; 266, 3 (AD 38); *P.Fam.Tebt.* 1, 31; 9, 9; 27, 6, 21; *P.Oslo* 97, 8; *P.Fouad* 22, col. II, 4, 22; *P.Mert.* 68, 2; *P.Warr.* 9, 6; *P.Mil.Vogl.* 227, 8; *P.Soterichos* 3, 1;

VI. — The OT and the NT conform to current usage without adding any new nuance.[24] The LXX uses *syngeneia* to translate the Hebrew *mišpāḥâh,* "family," in the larger sense of a clan or a tribe;[25] the NT always uses this word for kinship (Luke 1:61; Acts 7:3, 14). *Syngenēs* in the words of Jesus is absolutely conformable to OT usage: "A prophet is not scorned except in his country and among his kinsmen (*en tois syngeneusin autou*) and in his household."[26] St. Luke links it with neighbors (Luke 1:58, *hoi perioikoi*), with acquaintances (2:44, *tois gnōstois*), with brothers (that is, the closest relatives), and with wealthy neighbors (Luke 14:12, *geitonas plousious*), with friends (21:16), and with intimate friends (Acts 10:24, *tous anankaious philous*). For St. Paul, the Israelites are his brothers, his kinsmen according to the flesh (Rom 9:3), that it, they are of the same *genos,* the same race, sharing with the apostle the same Jewish descent, blood relatives;[27] but in the greeting in Rom 16:7, 11, 21, it is not clear why St. Paul would describe Christians in terms of their Jewish origins by calling them his compatriots (*syngeneis*); he must mean instead that they are related by birth in a way that is "oriental-style" (i.e., very broad), but that they are nevertheless related by common origin in the same family.

The biblical hapax *syngenis,*[28] the feminine of *syngenēs,*[29] does not appear in the papyri before the second century AD ("having married my

---

25, 6; *P.Erl.* 22, 4; *PSI* 923, 4; 1031, 12; 1119, 4; 1319. — Συγγενής also means "compatriot" (Josephus, *War* 7.262; 2 Macc 5:6, συγγενεῖς κάτοικοι; *P.Tebt.* 61 *b,* 79; 62, 58; *UPZ* 14, 8, p. 158), and συγγένεια means "family" (*P.Oxy.* 487, 9; *P.Bour.* 25, 15; *SB* 8542, 8); cf. *Ep. Arist.* 241; Josephus, *War* 7.204; Diodorus Siculus 16.52.3: "Mentor was eager to have Artabazus and Memnon come to him with his whole family."

[24] Lev 18:14; 20:20 uses συγγενής to translate the Hebrew *dôḏâh,* "aunt." Elsewhere, it is just a "relative" (2 Macc 8:1; 12:39; 15:18; Tob 6:11), "member of the family" (Lev 25:45), linked with a husband (Sus 63), children, and household members (Sus 50).

[25] Exod 6:14; 12:21; Lev 20:5; Judg 9:1; 13:2; etc.; cf. Gen 12:1 (Hebrew *môleḏeṯ*) and Num 1:20ff. (Hebrew *tôlēḏôṯ*).

[26] Mark 6:4. On this declension, cf. F. M. Abel, *Grammaire,* 9 *f.* M. J. Lagrange comments, "τοῖς συγγενεῦσιν by metaplasm for συγγενέσιν, since the singular is συγγενής; but there has been influence from the resemblance to γονεύς; συγγενεῦσι is already in Hippocrates 7.456 C, in Strabo, in Josephus . . . no man is great for his own people; Pliny, *HN* 35.36. . . . This feeling arises from jealousy, so common in small places, and from familiarity." We may cite also Epictetus 3.16.11; Philostratus, *VA* 1.354.12; Dio Chrysostom (cf. G. Mussies, *Dio Chrysostom,* p. 64); and the rabbis (Str-B, vol. 1, p. 678). Cf. the logion, οὐκ ἔστιν δεκτὸς προφήτης ἐν τῇ πατρίδι αὐτοῦ, οὐδὲ ἰατρὸς ποιεῖ θεραπείας εἰς τοὺς γινώσκοντες αὐτόν (*P.Oxy.* I, recto 8–14).

[27] Cf. *Recueil* L. Cerfaux, vol. 2, pp. 339–364.

carry off," notably with violence.[5] But the meaning "plunder, despoil," well attested in the classical period, is confirmed in the Koine: "In time of war and in time of peace, they pillage (sylōsin), they despoil, enslave, ravage, sack, insult, mistreat, destroy, dishonor, assassinate."[6] In the papyri, the word means especially theft with breaking and entering (P.Stras. 296, verso 10) and violence ("they robbed me and carried me off," esylēsan me bastazontes, P.Erl. 27, 9) or objects stolen, for example, tools in a tower (P.Ryl. 138, 19; from AD 34; etc; cf. SB 9534, 10), and most often a house that has been plundered.[7] There is a softened expression in a letter of Serapias to his son Herminis asking him to bring his daughter to him as a favor: "Do not deprive me for the cost of renting a donkey, so that I may show you affection" (mē syla mou peri tou naulou tou ōnou, hina philiazō sou, P.Oxf. 19, 7; third century AD). None of these meanings shed any light on the Pauline text.

To the contrary, if we refer to the technical legal meaning of sylaō ("retaliate by seizing"), the right of seizure being at the root of the exercise of retaliation.[8] This was an official institution,[9] cited by Demos-

---

[5] Ps.-Hesiod, Sc. 480: "Kykmos despoiled by violence" (βίῃ σύλασκεν); Plato, Leg. 9.869 b; cf. Aeschylus, PV 761: "Who will snatch the almighty scepter away from him?"; Euripides, Hel. 669: "what god snatched you away from your country?"; Pindar, Pyth. 12.16: "the head of Medusa, carried off by him"; Euripides, Ion 917: "a child carried off by birds of prey."

[6] Philo, Conf. Tongues 47; Decalogue 136: thieves "despoil entire cities, caring nothing for punishment"; Spec. Laws 3.203: "What good are foods in abundance when one has been despoiled (σεσυλῆσθαι) and deprived of the implements necessary for eating them" (the teeth); Alleg. Interp. 3.20: "you have despoiled me of the power to think well" (ἐσύλησάς μου καὶ τὸ φρονεῖν); T. Job 11.10—debtors who have been "robbed" beg Job to show patience toward them.

[7] P.Tebt. 330, 5: εὗρον τὴν οἰκίαν μου σεσυλημένην = I found my house pillaged; P.Gen. 47, 9; P.Lond. 412, 8 (vol. 2, 280); BGU 2242 b 1 (?); P.Mil.Vogl. 229, 5: ἐσυλήθην τῶν ἐν τῇ οἰκίᾳ μου ὑπὸ λῃστηρίου ἐκπεφορημένων.

[8] Herodotus 6.101: the Persians pillage and burn temples "in retaliation (συλήσαντες) for the burning of the sanctuaries of Sardis"; Demosthenes, Cor. Trier. 51.13: "When an undertaker of trierarchy sets out on an expedition, he carries out pillage everywhere; the profit is for him, but the first one of you who happens along suffers the loss: you are the only ones who cannot go anywhere without a safe-conduct, because of the seizures of persons and reprisals on property (διὰ τὰς ὑπὸ τούτων ἀνδροληψίας καὶ σύλας) that they have provoked." Cf. R. Dareste, "Du droit des représailles principalement chez les anciens Grecs," in REG, 1889, pp. 305–320; again in Nouvelles Etudes d'histoire du droit, Paris, 1902, pp. 38–47; K. Latte, "συλᾶν," in PW, vol. 4 A 1, col. 1035–1040; Julie Vélissaropoulos, Les Nauclères grecs, Geneva-Paris, 1980, pp. 146ff.

[9] Cf. in the fifth century BC, the convention established between Cnossos and Tylissos forbidding the pillaging of Cnossian territories and regulating the sharing of

thenes, *C. Lacr.* 35.26: "Without our having done them any wrong, without having any judgment against us, they carried out a seizure of our
property (*sesylēmetha*)—they, Phaselites, as if a right of seizure (*sylōn*),
had been granted the Phaselites against the Athenians. What are we to
call the refusal to give back what one has received? Is this not the removal
by force of another's property?"[10] Likewise Ps.-Aristotle, *Oec.* 2.2.10:
since the Chalcedonians could not pay the foreign mercenaries, they
"proclaimed that if anyone, citizen or resident alien, held right of reprisal
(*sylon echei*) against a city or a private person, and if he wanted to
exercise it, he had only to sign up. When a great number had signed up,
the Chalcedonians—on the pretext of their legal right—seized (*esylōn*)
the ships that were leaving for the Pontus. . . . Thus they gathered a great
deal of money . . . and they set up a tribunal to decide the claims" (*hyper
de tōn sylōn diedikasanto*).[11]

---

spoils (Dittenberger, *Syl.* 56), the seizures carried out on the Rhodians (Polybius 4.53),
on the Boeotians (Polybius 22.4); Lysias, *C. Nicom.* 30.22: "The Boeotians carry out
seizures (σύλας ποιουμένους) because we cannot pay them two talents"; the decree
of the Acarnanians (*IG* VII, 1, 573, 5, 6, 9, 10), the convention between Oianthesia
and Chaleion (*IG* IX, 1², 717), the right of seizure (περὶ τῷ σύλῳ) in the treaty between
Miletus and Magnesia (Dittenberger, *Syl.* 588, 47), between Delphi and Pellana (B.
Haussoullier, *Traité entre Delphes et Pellana: Etude de droit grec*, Paris, 1917, pp. 20–25,
107), at Eresus (*IG* XII, 2; 527, 3–4); J. and L. Robert, "Bulletin épigraphique," in *REG*,
1964, p. 245, n. 565.

[10] Cf. *Lacr.* 13: "a place where there are no rights of reprisal" (ὅπου ἂν μὴ σύλαι
ὦσιν). The editor, L. Gernet, notes: "Σῦλαι are seizures carried out by the individual
who has not been able to obtain justice from a foreigner against this foreigner's
compatriots."

[11] P. Gauthier (*Symbola*, pp. 210–219), who distinguishes between three meanings
of *sylaō*: (1) the act of pillage: piracy, an act of vengeance or sacrilege; (2) a legal and
justified act of reprisal, because of a harm for which the victim seeks compensation;
the victim himself can seize the person or property of his adversary (even his slaves);
(3) associated with a judicial decision, *sylon* is executory seizure, the *praxis* (*exagōgē*),
an act of self-defense, whereby restitution for harm is carried out by dispossessing
the adversary. — Συλάω can also mean "retake a person by force," a freedman wrongly
reduced to servitude. A decree of Gortyne stipulates: "No one will be able to reduce
emancipated persons to servitude. If any such thing happens, and the guarantors of
the emancipated person retake him by force (ὑπὸ τιτᾶν συλοῖτο), the *kosmos* for
foreigners shall not return him. If the guarantors do not retake him (αἱ δὲ μὴ
συλοῖεν), each of them shall pay the freedman one hundred staters. . ." (*RIJG*, p. 103
E, 4). In acts of emancipation at Delphi, it is constantly stipulated: If anyone tries to
reduce Manes to slavery, "Manes shall have the right to defend himself by force, as a
free man" (κύριος ἔστω Μάνης αὐσωτὸν συλέων ὡς ἐλεύθερος ὤν); "Dorcis shall
have the right to defend herself by force" (κύρια ἔστω αὐσαυτὰν συλέουσα). M. P.
Foucart, who quotes these texts (*Mémoire sur l'affranchissement des esclaves*, Paris, 1867,
p. 11), comments: "The word συλέειν, which refers to the rights of the emancipated

is getting bigger, and in which the life of the trunk conveys life and fruit-bearing strength to the branches. Through baptism, Christians share in the "virtue" of the crucified Christ.[13] The members and the head make up a unity; the two organisms are in a vital union, suggesting the "incorporating personality" of the Lord,[14] "una persona mystica" (St. Thomas Aquinas, on this verse).

---

[13] Cf. P. Gaechter, "Zur Exegese von Röm. VI, 5," in *ZKT,* 1930, pp. 88–92; F. Mussner, "Zusammengewachsen durch die Ähnlichkeit mit seinem Tode," in *TTZ,* 1954, pp. 257–265; V. Warnach, "Taufe und Christusgeschehen nach Röm. VI," in *Archiv für Liturgiewissenschaft,* vol. 3, 1954, pp. 284–366; E. Stommel, "Das Abbild seines Todes (Röm. VI, 5) und der Taufritus," in *RQ,* 1955, pp. 1–21; J. Gewiess, "Das Abbild des Todes Christi (Röm VI, 5)," in *Historisches Jahrbuch* (Festschrift B. Altaner), vol. 77, 1958, pp. 330–346.

[14] Cf. J. de Fraine, *Adam et son lignage,* Bruges, 1959.

συμφωνέω, συμφώνησις, συμφωνία, σύμφωνος

symphōneō, to agree, consent, be of the same feeling; symphōnēsis, accord, agreement; symphōnia, the sound of musical or instruments or instruments and voices together; agreement; symphōnos, agreeing, harmonious

---

When the older son returns from the field, he hears "music and choirs" in his father's house (Luke 15:25). Symphōnia can mean the sound produced by a certain musical instrument[1] or of voices and instruments "in concert," more specifically what we call a band or an orchestra.[2] This is the meaning here, given the subsequent detail "of choirs." From Plato on (Plato, Leg. 3.689 d), the word is used for agreement or harmony of feelings and the union that results therefrom among humans,[3] and the

---

[1] Dan 3:5, 7, 10, 15 (Theodotion) = Nebuchadnezzar's orchestra (cf. E. Gerson-Kiwi, "Musique," in DBSup, vol. 5, col. 1432). Ordinarily P.Flor. 74, 5 is cited: συμφωνίας πάσης μουσικῶν τε καὶ ἄλλων (181 BC); P.Oxy. 1275, 9: ὁ προεστὼς συμφωνίας αὐλητῶν καὶ μουσικῶν; P.Lond. 968, (vol. 3, p. XLIX): ὑπὲρ συμφωνίας τυμπάνων. Cf. Str-B, "Excurs XV," vol. 4, 1, pp. 396, 400; O. Montevecchi, La papirologia, Turin, 1973, p. 222.

[2] Aristotle, Cael. 2.9.3.290^b. "Certain exegetes who think that symphōnia is a sort of instrument are wrong; this word actually refers to collective singing, praising God in harmony; for the Greek word symphōnia is translated by the Latin consonantia" (St. Jerome, Epist. 21.29). Cf. the dispute on this meaning between P. Barry and G. F. Moore, in JBL 1904, pp. 180ff.; 1905, pp. 116ff.; 1908, pp. 99ff. On a Roman epitaph: Ὀστᾶ Ἀγαθοῦτος συμφωνιακῆς Ὀκταουίας (IGUR, II, n. 272). L. Moretti comments, "Fuit Agathus symphoniaca, id est dominae suae Octaviae musicos concentus comparabat," and cites CIL VI, 23369, 37765.

[3] Ep. Arist. 302: "The translators set to the task, coming to agreement (σύμφωνα ποιοῦντες) on each point of confrontation. From the rest that resulted from this

---

symphōneō, S 4856; TDNT 9.304–309; EDNT 3.290; MM 598–599; L&N 31.15, 64.10; BDF §§179(1), 202, 227(2), 409(3); BAGD 780–781 ‖ symphōnēsis, S 4857; TDNT 9.304–309; EDNT 3.290; MM 599; L&N 31.15; BAGD 781 ‖ symphōnia, S 4858; TDNT 9.304–309; EDNT 3.290; MM 599; L&N 14.83; BAGD 781 ‖ symphōnos, S 4859; TDNT 9.304–309; EDNT 3.290; MM 599; L&N 31.15; BAGD 781